Lecture Notes in Artificial Intelligence   6793

Edited by R. Goebel, J. Siekmann, and W. Wahlster

Subseries of Lecture Notes in Computer Science

W0193331

Kai Brünnler   George Metcalfe (Eds.)

Automated Reasoning with Analytic Tableaux and Related Methods

20th International Conference, TABLEAUX 2011
Bern, Switzerland, July 4-8, 2011
Proceedings

 Springer

Series Editors

Randy Goebel, University of Alberta, Edmonton, Canada
Jörg Siekmann, University of Saarland, Saarbrücken, Germany
Wolfgang Wahlster, DFKI and University of Saarland, Saarbrücken, Germany

Volume Editors

Kai Brünnler
Universität Bern
Institut für Informatik und Angewandte Mathematik
Neubrückstr. 10, 3012 Bern, Switzerland
E-mail: kai@iam.unibe.ch

George Metcalfe
Universität Bern
Mathematisches Institut
Sidlerstr. 5, 3012 Bern, Switzerland
E-mail: george.metcalfe@math.unibe.ch

ISSN 0302-9743   e-ISSN 1611-3349
ISBN 978-3-642-22118-7   e-ISBN 978-3-642-22119-4
DOI 10.1007/978-3-642-22119-4
Springer Heidelberg Dordrecht London New York

Library of Congress Control Number: 2011930102

CR Subject Classification (1998): I.2.3, F.4.1-2, I.2, D.1.6, D.2.4

LNCS Sublibrary: SL 7 – Artificial Intelligence

Typesetting: Camera-ready by author, data conversion by Scientific Publishing Services, Chennai, India

Printed on acid-free paper

Springer is part of Springer Science+Business Media (www.springer.com)

Preface

This volume contains the research papers presented at the 20th International Conference on Automated Reasoning with Analytic Tableaux and Related Methods (TABLEAUX 2011) held July 4-8, 2011 in Bern, Switzerland.

The Program Committee of TABLEAUX 2011 received 34 submissions. Each paper was reviewed by at least three referees and, following a thorough and lively online discussion phase, 16 research papers and 2 system descriptions were accepted based on their originality, technical soundness, presentation, and relevance to the conference. We would like to sincerely thank both the authors for their contributions and the members of the Program Committee and additional referees for their much appreciated time, energy, and professionalism in the review and selection process.

In addition to the contributed papers, the program of TABLEAUX 2011 included three keynote talks by distinguished researchers in the field of automated reasoning and proof theory: Maria Paola Bonacina (Università degli Studi di Verona, Italy), Ulrich Furbach (University of Koblenz-Landau, Germany), and Kazushige Terui (Kyoto University, Japan). There were also two tutorials: "Tableaux(-like) Methods for the Satisfiability Problems of Temporal Logics" by Martin Lange (University of Kassel, Germany), and "Introduction to Proof Nets" by Lutz Strassburger (INRIA Saclay, France).

Two workshops are held in conjunction with TABLEAUX 2011: "FTP 2011, the 8th International Workshop on First-Order Theorem Proving" chaired by Martin Giese (University of Oslo, Norway), and the second edition of "Gentzen Systems and Beyond" organized by Roman Kuznets and Richard McKinley (University of Bern, Switzerland).

We would like to thank the members of the Organizing Committee for their much appreciated support and expertise: Samuel Bucheli, Roman Kuznets, Richard McKinley, and Nia Stephens-Metcalfe.

Finally, we would like to thank our sponsors for their generous and very welcome support: the Bürgergemeinde Bern, the Kurt Gödel Society, the Swiss Academy of Sciences, the Swiss Mathematical Society, the Swiss National Science Foundation, the Hasler Foundation, and the University of Bern. We would also like to acknowledge the Easychair conference management system which greatly facilitated the smooth running of the review process and compilation of these proceedings.

May 1, 2011

George Metcalfe
Kai Brünnler

Organization

Program Committee

Arnon Avron	Tel Aviv University, Israel
Peter Baumgartner	National ICT, Australia
Bernhard Beckert	Karlsruhe Institute of Technology, Germany
Torben Braüner	Roskilde University, Denmark
Kai Brünnler	University of Bern, Switzerland
Agata Ciabattoni	TU Vienna, Austria
Marta Cialdea Mayer	University of Rome 3, Italy
Roy Dyckhoff	University of St. Andrews, UK
Martin Giese	University of Oslo, Norway
Valentin Goranko	Technical University of Denmark
Rajeev Gore	The Australian National University
Ullrich Hustadt	University of Liverpool, UK
Reiner Hähnle	Chalmers University of Technology, Sweden
Martin Lange	University of Kassel, Germany
George Metcalfe	University of Bern, Switzerland
Dale Miller	INRIA Saclay, France
Neil Murray	University at Albany SUNY, USA
Nicola Olivetti	Paul Cézanne University, France
Jens Otten	Potsdam University, Germany
Dirk Pattinson	Imperial College London, UK
Andre Platzer	Carnegie Mellon University, USA
Renate Schmidt	University of Manchester, UK
Viorica Sofronie-Stokkermans	MPI, Saarbrücken, Germany
Ulrich Ultes-Nitsche	University of Fribourg, Switzerland
Luca Viganò	University of Verona, Italy
Arild Waaler	University of Oslo, Norway

Additional Reviewers

Antonsen, Roger	Egly, Uwe
Bílková, Marta	Facchini, Alessandro
Cerrito, Serenella	Fermüller, Christian
Chapman, Peter	Garg, Deepak
Dawson, Jeremy	Giese, Martin
Deyoung, Henry	Gladisch, Christoph

Gliozzi, Valentina
Hetzl, Stefan
Hodkinson, Ian
Jia, Limin
Khodadadi, Mohammad
Klebanov, Vladimir
Kontchakov, Roman
Kuznets, Roman
Lian, Espen H.
Martins, Joao
Matusiewicz, Andrew
Pozzato, Gian Luca
Qi, Guilin
Ramanayake, Revantha
Renshaw, David

Roschger, Christoph
Sauro, Luigi
Schneider, Thomas
Serre, Olivier
Shapirovsky, Ilya
Son, Tran Cao
Stolpe, Audun
Straccia, Umberto
Strassburger, Lutz
Terui, Kazushige
Tishkovsky, Dmitry
Tiu, Alwen
Wischnewski, Patrick
Zeilberger, Noam

Previous Meetings

1992 Lautenbach, Germany
1993 Marseille, France
1994 Abingdon, UK
1995 St. Goar, Germany
1996 Terrasini, Italy
1997 Pont-à-Mousson, France
1998 Oisterwijk, The Netherlands
1999 Saratoga Springs, USA
2000 St. Andrews, UK
2001 Siena, Italy (part of IJCAR)
2002 Copenhagen, Denmark
2003 Rome, Italy
2004 Cork, Ireland (part of IJCAR)
2005 Koblenz, Germany
2006 Seattle, USA (part of IJCAR)
2007 Aix-en-Provence, France
2008 Sydney, Australia (part of IJCAR)
2009 Oslo, Norway
2010 Edinburgh, UK (part of IJCAR)

TABLEAUX Steering Committee

Rajeev Goré (President)   Australian National University, Australia
Kai Brünnler   University of Bern, Switzerland
Martin Giese   University of Oslo, Norway
Valentin Goranko   Technical University of Denmark

Reiner Hähnle   Chalmers University of Technology, Sweden
George Metcalfe   University of Bern, Switzerland
Angelo Montanari   University of Udine, Italy
Neil Murray   University at Albany - SUNY, USA

Sponsors

Bürgergemeinde Bern
Haslerstiftung
Kurt Gödel Society
Swiss Academy of Sciences
Swiss Mathematical Society
Swiss National Science Foundation
University of Bern

Table of Contents

On Interpolation in Decision Procedures*

Maria Paola Bonacina and Moa Johansson

Dipartimento di Informatica, Università degli Studi di Verona
Strada Le Grazie 15, I-37134 Verona, Italy
mariapaola.bonacina@univr.it, moakristin.johansson@univr.it

Abstract. Interpolation means finding intermediate formulae between given formulae. When formulae decorate program locations, and describe sets of program states, interpolation may enable a program analyzer to discover information about intermediate locations and states. This mechanism has an increasing number of applications, that are relevant to program analysis and synthesis. We study interpolation in theorem proving decision procedures based on the DPLL($\mathcal{T}$) paradigm. We survey interpolation systems for DPLL, equality sharing and DPLL($\mathcal{T}$), reconstructing from the literature their completeness proofs, and clarifying the requirements for interpolation in the presence of equality.

1 Introduction

Automated deduction and program verification have always been connected, as described, for instance, in [34] and [1]. A theorem proving technique that has recently found application in verification is *interpolation*. Informally, interpolants are formula 'in between' other formulæ in a proof, containing only their shared symbols. Interpolation was proposed for *abstraction refinement* in software model checking, first for propositional logic and propositional satisfiability [25], and then for quantifier-free fragments of first-order theories, their combinations, and satisfiability modulo theories [18,26,35,21,11,12,17,6,7,9]. Considered theories include equality [26,16], linear rational arithmetic [26,21], Presburger or linear integer arithmetic [21,6], or fragments thereof [12], and arrays without extensionality [21,7,8]. In these papers the theory reasoning is done either by specialized sequent-style inference systems [18,26,6,7] or by satisfiability procedures, such as congruence closure for equality [16], integrated in a DPLL($\mathcal{T}$) framework [35,11,12,17]. Subsequently, interpolation was suggested for *invariant generation*, and in the context of inference systems for first-order logic with equality, based on resolution and superposition [27,23,19]. An early lead towards this application can be traced back to [10]. More recently, interpolation was related to *abstract interpretation* [14] and applied to improve the quality of annotations [28].

The aim of this paper is to present the core of the state of the art in interpolation for the proofs generated by theorem provers for satisfiability modulo

* Research supported in part by MIUR grant no. 2007-9E5KM8 and EU COST Action IC0901.

K. Brünnler and G. Metcalfe (Eds.): TABLEAUX 2011, LNAI 6793, pp. 1–16, 2011.

theories, also known as SMT-solvers, based on the DPLL($\mathcal{T}$) paradigm (e.g., [31,33]), where DPLL refers to the Davis-Putnam-Logemann-Loveland procedure for propositional satisfiability, and $\mathcal{T} = \bigcup_{i=1}^{n} \mathcal{T}_i$ is a union of theories.

In this paper we present:

- A framework of definitions for interpolation, including that of *completeness* of an interpolation system;
- Two interpolation systems for propositional logic, HKPYM [20,24,32] and MM [25,26], already surveyed in [15], with a reconstruction of the proof of completeness of HKPYM in [35];
- An analysis of interpolation in the presence of equality, which explains the relation between the notion of *equality-interpolating theory* of [35] and that of *separating ordering* of [27,23,19] and provides a proof of the result that the quantifier-free fragment of the theory of equality is equality-interpolating, which was sketched in [35];
- The interpolation system of [35] for equality sharing [29], which we name EQSH, with a reconstruction of its proof of completeness in [35] and the observation that it applies also to *model-based theory combination* [13];
- The interpolation system for DPLL($\mathcal{T}$) obtained in [35] by uniting HKPYM and EQSH, which we name HKPYM–T.

We emphasize the contributions of [35], because it is where the crucial notion of equality-interpolating theory appeared, and because all subsequent papers that we are aware of refer to [35] for the proofs of completeness of HKPYM and EQSH, whence HKPYM–T. However, those proofs appeared only in the technical report companion to [35], and with discrepancies in definitions and notations between [35] and the technical report. Thus, we choose to present them here.

2   A Framework of Definitions for Interpolation

We assume the basic definitions commonly used in theorem proving. Let A and B be two formulæ with respective signatures Σ_A and Σ_B:

Definition 1. *A non-variable symbol is* A-colored, *if it is in* $\Sigma_A \backslash \Sigma_B$; B-colored, *if it is in* $\Sigma_B \setminus \Sigma_A$; *and* transparent, *if it is in* $\Sigma_T = \Sigma_A \cap \Sigma_B$.

Let $\mathcal{L}_X$ denote, ambiguously, the language of Σ_X-terms, Σ_X-literals or Σ_X-formulæ, where X stands for either A, B or T.

Definition 2. *A formula I is an* interpolant *of formulæ A and B such that* $A \vdash B$, *or an interpolant of (A, B), if (i) $A \vdash I$, (ii) $I \vdash B$ and (iii) $I \in \mathcal{L}_T$.*

The following classical result is known as Craig's Interpolation Lemma:

Lemma 1. *Let A and B be closed formulæ such that $A \vdash B$. If Σ_T contains at least one predicate symbol, an interpolant I of (A, B) exists and it is a closed formula; otherwise, either B is valid and I is $\top$, or A is unsatisfiable and I is $\bot$.*

From now on we consider only closed formulæ. Since most theorem provers work refutationally, it is useful to adopt the following:

Definition 3. *A formula I is a* reverse interpolant *of formulæ A and B such that $A, B \vdash \perp$, if (i) $A \vdash I$, (ii) $B, I \vdash \perp$ and (iii) $I \in \mathcal{L}_T$.*

A reverse interpolant of (A, B) is an interpolant of $(A, \neg B)$. A theory is presented by a set T of sentences, meaning that the theory is the set of all logical consequences of T. If Σ_T is the signature of T, $\mathcal{L}_T$ is redefined to be the language built from $\Sigma_T \cup \Sigma_T$, so that theory symbols are transparent:

Definition 4. *A formula I is a* theory interpolant *of formulæ A and B such that $A \vdash_T B$, if (i) $A \vdash_T I$, (ii) $I \vdash_T B$ and (iii) $I \in \mathcal{L}_T$. A formula I is a* reverse theory interpolant *of formulæ A and B such that $A, B \vdash_T \perp$, if (i) $A \vdash_T I$, (ii) $B, I \vdash_T \perp$ and (iii) $I \in \mathcal{L}_T$.*

The distinction between interpolant and reverse interpolant appeared in [23]. Since we consider refutational systems, and in keeping with most of the literature, we write "interpolant" for "reverse interpolant" and omit "theory," unless relevant. Because most systems work with clauses, that are disjunctions of literals, from now on A and B are sets of clauses.

Definition 5. *A ground term, literal, or clause is* transparent, *if all its symbols are;* A-colored, *if it contains at least one A-colored symbol, and the others are transparent;* B-colored, *if it contains at least one B-colored symbol, and the others are transparent; and* AB-mixed, *otherwise. A clause is* colorable *if it contains no AB-mixed literals.*

Some authors use *A-local* in place of *A*-colored, *B-local* in place of *B*-colored, and *AB-common*, or *global*, in place of transparent. In the following "colored" may mean non-transparent.

Definition 6. *Let C be a disjunction (conjunction) of literals. The* projection *$C|_X$ of C on $\mathcal{L}_X$ is the disjunction (conjunction) obtained by removing from C any literal whose atom is not in $\mathcal{L}_X$. If C is a disjunction and $C|_X$ is empty, then $C|_X = \perp$; if C is a conjunction and $C|_X$ is empty, then $C|_X = \top$.*

Projection commutes with negation $(\neg(C|_X) = (\neg C)|_X)$ and distributes over conjunction and disjunction: $(C \lor D)|_X = C|_X \lor D|_X$ and $(C \land D)|_X = C|_X \land D|_X$. Since transparent literals of C belong to both $C|_A$ and $C|_B$, if C is a conjunction, $C|_A \Rightarrow C|_T$ and $C|_B \Rightarrow C|_T$; if C is a disjunction, $C|_T \Rightarrow C|_A$ and $C|_T \Rightarrow C|_B$. Alternatively, transparent literals may be put only in the projection on $\mathcal{L}_B$:

Definition 7. *Let C be a disjunction (conjunction) of literals. The* asymmetric projections *of C are $C \setminus_B = C|_A \setminus C|_T$ and $C \downarrow_B = C|_B$.*

Since [25], approaches to interpolation work by annotating each clause C in a refutation of A and B with auxiliary formulæ, unnamed in [25,26], named *C-interpolants* in [23], and *partial interpolants* in [35,15,6]:

Definition 8. *A partial interpolant $PI(C)$ of a clause C occurring in a refutation of $A \cup B$ is an interpolant of $g_A(C) = A \wedge \neg(C|_A)$ and $g_B(C) = B \wedge \neg(C|_B)$.*

If C is the empty clause, which is written $\square$ and represents a contradiction, $PI(C)$ is an interpolant of (A, B). Since $A \wedge B \vdash C$, $g_A(C) \wedge g_B(C) = A \wedge B \wedge \neg C \vdash \perp$, and it makes sense to seek an interpolant of $g_A(C)$ and $g_B(C)$, which may be seen as an interpolant of (A, B) in a proof of C. We also write $c|_X$, $PI(c)$, $g_A(c)$ and $g_B(c)$ if c is the label of clause C, written $c\colon C$. By Definition 3 applied to Definition 8, a partial interpolant needs to satisfy the following requirements:

1. $g_A(C) \vdash PI(C)$ or $A \wedge \neg(C|_A) \vdash PI(C)$ or $A \vdash C|_A \vee PI(C)$
2. $g_B(C) \wedge PI(C) \vdash \perp$ or $B \wedge \neg(C|_B) \wedge PI(C) \vdash \perp$ or $B \wedge PI(C) \vdash C|_B$, and
3. $PI(C)$ is transparent.

Indeed, since the signatures of $g_A(C)$ and $g_B(C)$ are Σ_A and Σ_B, transparency is always with respect to A and B.

3   Transition Systems, Proofs and Interpolation Systems

DPLL and DPLL($\mathcal{T}$) are presented as *transition systems* (e.g., [31,4]) that operate in two modes, *search mode* and *conflict resolution mode*. In search mode, the state has the form $M \parallel F$, where F is a set of clauses and M is a sequence of *assigned literals*, that represents a partial assignment to ground literals, possibly with a justification, and therefore a partial model, or a set of candidate models. An assigned literal can be either a *decided literal* or an *implied literal*. A decided literal represents a guess, and has no justification (*decision* or *splitting*). An implied literal l_C is a literal l justified by a clause C: all other literals of C are false in M so that l needs to be true (*unit propagation*). If there is a clause C whose literals are all false in M, C is *in conflict*, it is called *conflict clause*, and the system switches to conflict resolution mode, where the state has the form $M \parallel F \parallel C$. In conflict resolution mode, a conflict clause $C \vee \neg l$ may be resolved with the justification $D \vee l$ of l in M to yield a new conflict clause $C \vee D$ (*explanation*). Any clause thus derived can be added to F (*learning*). Backjumping unassigns at least one decided literal and drives the system back from conflict resolution mode to search mode. In state $M \parallel F \parallel \square$, unsatisfiability is detected.

Definition 9. *Let $\mathcal{U}_1$ stand for DPLL and $\mathcal{U}_2$ for DPLL($\mathcal{T}$), and S be the input set of clauses. A transition system derivation, or $\mathcal{U}_j$-derivation, where $j \in \{1, 2\}$, is a sequence of state transitions $\Delta_0 \Longrightarrow_{\mathcal{U}_j} \Delta_1 \Longrightarrow_{\mathcal{U}_j} \ldots \Delta_i \Longrightarrow_{\mathcal{U}_j} \Delta_{i+1} \Longrightarrow_{\mathcal{U}_j} \ldots,$ where $\forall i \geq 0$, Δ_i is of the form $M_i \parallel F_i$ or $M_i \parallel F_i \parallel C_i$, each transition is determined by a transition rule in $\mathcal{U}_j$, $\Delta_0 = \parallel F_0$ and $F_0 = S$.*

As noticed first in [36], according to [34], a proof produced by DPLL is made of propositional resolution steps between conflict clauses (*explanations*). Let $C^* = \{C_i | i > 0\}$ be the set of all conflict clauses in a derivation:

Definition 10. *For DPLL-derivation $\Delta_0 \Longrightarrow_{\mathcal{U}_1} \ldots \Delta_i \Longrightarrow_{\mathcal{U}_1} \Delta_{i+1} \Longrightarrow_{\mathcal{U}_1} \ldots,$ for all $C \in C^*$ the DPLL-proof tree $\Pi_{\mathcal{U}_1}(C)$ of C is defined as follows:*

- *If $C \in F_0$, $\Pi_{\mathcal{U}_1}(C)$ consists of a node labelled by C;*
- *If C is generated by resolving conflict clause C_1 with justification C_2, $\Pi_{\mathcal{U}_1}(C)$ consists of a node labelled by C with subtrees $\Pi_{\mathcal{U}_1}(C_1)$ and $\Pi_{\mathcal{U}_1}(C_2)$.*

If the derivation halts reporting unsatisfiable, $\Pi_{\mathcal{U}_1}(\square)$ is a DPLL-refutation.

Since a justification C_2 is either an input clause or a learnt clause, which was once a conflict clause, $\Pi_{\mathcal{U}_1}(C_2)$ is defined.

DPLL($\mathcal{T}$) builds into DPLL a $\mathcal{T}$-*satisfiability procedure*, that decides whether a set of ground $\mathcal{T}$-literals has a $\mathcal{T}$-model. In most cases, $\mathcal{T}$ is a union of theories $\bigcup_{i=1}^{n} \mathcal{T}_i$, and a $\mathcal{T}$-satisfiability procedure is obtained by combining n $\mathcal{T}_i$-satisfiability procedures, that we name $\mathcal{Q}_i$, for $1 \le i \le n$, according to *equality sharing* [29] (see Chapter 10 of [5] for a modern presentation). The $\mathcal{T}_i$'s are quantifier-free fragments of first-order theories such as the theory of equality, linear arithmetic or theories of common data structures. For the theory of equality, also known as equality with uninterpreted, or free, symbols (EUF), the satisfiability procedure is based on *congruence closure* (e.g., [30], and Chapter 9 of [5] for a modern presentation).

Equality sharing requires that the $\mathcal{T}_i$'s are pairwise *disjoint*, which means the only shared symbol, beside constants, is equality, and *stably infinite*, which means that any quantifier-free $\mathcal{T}_i$-formula has a $\mathcal{T}_i$-model if and only if it has an infinite one. Equality sharing separates occurrences of function symbols from different signatures to ensure that each $\mathcal{Q}_i$'s deals with $\mathcal{T}_i$-literals: for example, $f(g(a)) \simeq b$, where f and g belong to different signatures, becomes $f(c) \simeq b \wedge g(a) \simeq c$, where c is a new constant. Each $\mathcal{Q}_i$ propagates all disjunctions of equalities between shared constants that are $\mathcal{T}_i$-entailed by the problem. If a theory is *convex*, whenever a disjunction is entailed, a disjunct is also entailed, and therefore it is sufficient to exchange equalities. *Model-based theory combination* [13] is a version of equality sharing that assumes that each $\mathcal{Q}_i$ maintains a candidate $\mathcal{T}_i$-model, and replaces propagation of entailments by addition to M of equalities that are true in the current candidate $\mathcal{T}_i$-model. These equalities are *guesses*, because it is not known whether they are true in all $\mathcal{T}_i$-models consistent with M. If one of them turns out to be inconsistent, backjumping will withdraw it and update the $\mathcal{T}_i$-model.

In DPLL($\mathcal{T}$), the $\mathcal{T}$-satisfiability procedure propagates $\mathcal{T}$-consequences of M to the DPLL engine: if whenever literals $l_1, \dots, l_n$ are true, some literal l must also be true in $\mathcal{T}$, l is added to M with the $\mathcal{T}$-lemma $\neg l_1 \vee \dots \vee \neg l_n \vee l$ as justification (*theory propagation*); if a subset $l_1, \dots, l_n$ of M is $\mathcal{T}$-inconsistent, the system switches to conflict resolution mode with $\mathcal{T}$-*conflict clause* $\neg l_1 \vee \dots \vee \neg l_n$. Proofs produced by DPLL($\mathcal{T}$) are ground, but not propositional, and include also $\mathcal{T}$-conflict clauses. Thus, we need to assume that the $\mathcal{Q}_i$'s and their combination produce proofs, that we denote by $\Pi_{\mathcal{T}}(C)$:

Definition 11. *For DPLL($\mathcal{T}$)-derivation $\Delta_0 \Longrightarrow_{\mathcal{U}_2} \dots \Delta_i \Longrightarrow_{\mathcal{U}_2} \Delta_{i+1} \Longrightarrow_{\mathcal{U}_2} \dots$, for all $C \in C^*$ the DPLL($\mathcal{T}$)-proof tree $\Pi_{\mathcal{U}_2}(C)$ of C is defined as follows:*

- *If $C \in F_0$, $\Pi_{\mathcal{U}_2}(C)$ consists of a node labelled by C;*

- If C is generated by resolving conflict clause C_1 with justification C_2, $\Pi_{\mathcal{U}_2}(C)$ consists of a node labelled by C with subtrees $\Pi_{\mathcal{U}_2}(C_1)$ and $\Pi_{\mathcal{U}_2}(C_2)$;
- If C is a $\mathcal{T}$-conflict clause, $\Pi_{\mathcal{U}_2}(C) = \Pi_{\mathcal{T}}(C)$.

If the derivation halts reporting unsatisfiable, $\Pi_{\mathcal{U}_2}(\Box)$ is a DPLL(T)-refutation.

An *interpolation system* is a mechanism to annotate clauses in a proof with partial interpolants; its most important property is completeness:

Definition 12. *An interpolation system is* complete *for transition system* $\mathcal{U}$, *if for all sets of clauses A and B, such that $A \cup B$ is unsatisfiable, and for all $\mathcal{U}$-refutations of $A \cup B$, it generates an interpolant of (A, B).*

Since $PI(\Box)$ is an interpolant of (A, B), in order to prove that an interpolation system is complete, it is sufficient to show that it annotates the clauses in any refutation with clauses that are partial interpolants.

We conclude recalling that stable infiniteness is connected to interpolation: the set of disjunctions of equalities exchanged by $\mathcal{T}_1$ and $\mathcal{T}_2$ in equality sharing is a reverse interpolant of (F_1, F_2), where F_i, for $i \in \{1, 2\}$, is the conjunction of input $\mathcal{T}_i$-literals after separation. Stable-infiniteness ensures that quantifier-free interpolants suffice (cf. Chapter 10 of [5] for details). This is obviously not sufficient to make a combination of interpolating satisfiability procedures interpolating, because (F_1, F_2) is a partition of the input based on the signatures of $\mathcal{T}_1$ and $\mathcal{T}_2$, whereas we need to generate interpolants of an arbitrary partition (A, B) of the input where both A and B may mix $\mathcal{T}_1$-symbols and $\mathcal{T}_2$-symbols.

4   Propositional Interpolation Systems

If the input $S = A \cup B$ is a set of propositional clauses, the set of literals that may appear in a refutation is determined once and for all by the set of literals that occur in S. Since input literals are either A-colored or B-colored or transparent, *there are no AB-mixed literals in proofs*. Interpolation systems attach a partial interpolant to every resolution step, distinguishing whether the literal resolved upon is A-colored or B-colored or transparent. The first interpolation system for propositional resolution, called HKP in [15] from the initials of three independent authors, appeared in [20,24,32]. We call it HKPYM, because Yorsh and Musuvathi reformulated it and reproved it complete in the context of DPLL(T):

Definition 13 (HKPYM interpolation system). *Let $c\colon C$ be a clause that appears in a refutation of $A \cup B$ by propositional resolution:*

- *If $c\colon C \in A$, then $PI(c) = \bot$,*
- *If $c\colon C \in B$, then $PI(c) = \top$,*
- *If $c\colon C \vee D$ is a propositional resolvent of $p_1\colon C \vee l$ and $p_2\colon D \vee \neg l$ then:*
  - *If l is A-colored, then $PI(c) = PI(p_1) \vee PI(p_2)$,*
  - *If l is B-colored, then $PI(c) = PI(p_1) \wedge PI(p_2)$ and*
  - *If l is transparent, then $PI(c) = (l \vee PI(p_1)) \wedge (\neg l \vee PI(p_2))$.*

The system of [25,26], that we call MM, allows a more informative interpolant for clauses in A and treats transparent literals resolved upon like B-colored ones:

Definition 14 (MM interpolation system). *Let* $c: C$ *be a clause that appears in a refutation of* $A \cup B$ *by propositional resolution:*

- *If* $c: C \in A$, *then* $PI(c) = C|_T$,
- *If* $c: C \in B$, *then* $PI(c) = \top$,
- *If* $c: C \vee D$ *is a propositional resolvent of* $p_1: C \vee l$ *and* $p_2: D \vee \neg l$ *then:*
  - *If* l *is A-colored, then* $PI(c) = PI(p_1) \vee PI(p_2)$,
  - *If* l *is B-colored or transparent, then* $PI(c) = PI(p_1) \wedge PI(p_2)$.

Intuitively, HKPYM is symmetric with respect to A and B, and assumes the symmetric notion of projection (cf. Definition 6), while MM is slanted towards B, and assumes the asymmetric notion of projection (cf. Definition 7). In [35], projection is defined to be asymmetric; however, the proof of completeness of HKPYM in the companion technical report, requires projection to be symmetric. The following proof fixes this discrepancy:

Theorem 1 (Yorsh and Musuvathi, 2005). *HKPYM is a complete interpolation system for propositional resolution.*

Proof: We need to prove that for all clauses $c: C$ in the refutation, $PI(c)$ satifies Requirements (1), (2) and (3) listed at the end of Section 2. The proof is by induction on the structure of the refutation.
Base case:

- If $c: C \in A$, then $\neg(C|_A) = \neg C$; and $g_A(c) = A \wedge \neg C = \bot$, since $C \in A$. Since $PI(c) = \bot$, both (1) and (2) reduce to $\bot \vdash \bot$, which is trivially true, and $PI(c)$ is trivially transparent.
- If $c: C \in B$, then $\neg(C|_B) = \neg C$; and $g_B(c) = B \wedge \neg C = \bot$, since $C \in B$. Since $PI(c) = \top$, (1) is trivial, (2) reduces to $\bot \vdash \bot$, which is trivially true, and $PI(c)$ is trivially transparent.

Induction hypothesis: for $k \in \{1,2\}$ $PI(p_k)$ *satifies Requirements (1), (2) and (3).*
Induction case:

(a) l is A-colored: $PI(c) = PI(p_1) \vee PI(p_2)$.
First we observe that $p_1|_A \wedge p_2|_A \Rightarrow C|_A \vee D|_A$ (*). Indeed, since l is A-colored, $p_1|_A = (l \vee C)|_A = l \vee C|_A$ and $p_2|_A = (\neg l \vee D)|_A = \neg l \vee D|_A$. Then, $p_1|_A \wedge p_2|_A = (l \vee C|_A) \wedge (\neg l \vee D|_A) \Rightarrow C|_A \vee D|_A$ by resolution.
We show (1) $g_A(c) \Rightarrow PI(c)$:
$g_A(c) = A \wedge \neg((C \vee D)|_A) = A \wedge \neg(C|_A \vee D|_A)$
$A \wedge \neg(C|_A \vee D|_A) \Rightarrow A \wedge \neg(p_1|_A \wedge p_2|_A)$ by (*)
$A \wedge \neg(p_1|_A \wedge p_2|_A) = A \wedge (\neg p_1|_A \vee \neg p_2|_A) = (A \wedge \neg p_1|_A) \vee (A \wedge \neg p_2|_A) = g_A(p_1) \vee g_A(p_2)$ and $g_A(p_1) \vee g_A(p_2) \Rightarrow PI(p_1) \vee PI(p_2)$ by induction hypothesis.
We show (2) $g_B(c) \wedge PI(c) \Rightarrow \bot$:
$g_B(c) \wedge PI(c) = B \wedge \neg((C \vee D)|_B) \wedge PI(c) = B \wedge \neg(C|_B \vee D|_B) \wedge PI(c) =$

$B \wedge \neg(C|_B) \wedge \neg(D|_B) \wedge (PI(p_1) \vee PI(p_2)) \Rightarrow$
$(B \wedge \neg(C|_B) \wedge PI(p_1)) \vee (B \wedge \neg(D|_B) \wedge PI(p_2)) =$
$(B \wedge \neg((l \vee C)|_B) \wedge PI(p_1)) \vee (B \wedge \neg((\neg l \vee D)|_B) \wedge PI(p_2)) =$
(because $l \notin \mathcal{L}_B$ and, therefore, $C|_B = (l \vee C)|_B$ and $D|_B = (\neg l \vee D)|_B$)
$= (B \wedge \neg(p_1|_B) \wedge PI(p_1)) \vee (B \wedge \neg(p_2|_B) \wedge PI(p_2)) =$
$(g_B(p_1) \wedge PI(p_1)) \vee (g_B(p_2) \wedge PI(p_2)) \Rightarrow \bot \vee \bot = \bot$ by induction hypothesis.
Requirement (3) follows by induction hypothesis.

(b) l is B-colored: $PI(c) = PI(p_1) \wedge PI(p_2)$.
Similar to Case (a), we have that $p_1|_B \wedge p_2|_B \Rightarrow C|_B \vee D|_B$ (**).
We show (1) $g_A(c) \Rightarrow PI(c)$:
$g_A(c) = A \wedge \neg((C \vee D)|_A) = A \wedge \neg(C|_A \vee D|_A) = A \wedge \neg(C|_A) \wedge \neg(D|_A) =$
$A \wedge \neg((l \vee C)|_A) \wedge \neg((\neg l \vee D)|_A) =$
(because $l \notin \mathcal{L}_A$ and, therefore, $C|_A = (l \vee C)|_A$ and $D|_A = (\neg l \vee D)|_A$)
$= A \wedge \neg(p_1|_A) \wedge \neg(p_2|_A) = (A \wedge \neg(p_1|_A)) \wedge (A \wedge \neg(p_2|_A)) = g_A(p_1) \wedge g_A(p_2)$
and $g_A(p_1) \wedge g_A(p_2) \Rightarrow PI(p_1) \wedge PI(p_2)$ by induction hypothesis.
We show (2) $g_B(c) \wedge PI(c) \Rightarrow \bot$:
$g_B(c) \wedge PI(c) = B \wedge (\neg((C \vee D)|_B)) \wedge PI(p_1) \wedge PI(p_2) =$
$B \wedge (\neg(C|_B \vee D|_B)) \wedge PI(p_1) \wedge PI(p_2) \Rightarrow$ by (**)
$B \wedge (\neg(p_1|_B \wedge p_2|_B)) \wedge PI(p_1) \wedge PI(p_2) = B \wedge (\neg(p_1|_B) \vee \neg(p_2|_B)) \wedge PI(p_1) \wedge$
$PI(p_2) = [(B \wedge \neg(p_1|_B)) \vee (B \wedge \neg(p_2|_B))] \wedge PI(p_1) \wedge PI(p_2) =$
$(g_B(p_1) \wedge PI(p_1) \wedge PI(p_2)) \vee (g_B(p_2) \wedge PI(p_1) \wedge PI(p_2)) \Rightarrow$
$(g_B(p_1) \wedge PI(p_1)) \vee (g_B(p_2) \wedge PI(p_2)) \Rightarrow \bot \vee \bot = \bot$ by induction hypothesis.
Requirement (3) follows by induction hypothesis.

(c) l is transparent: $PI(c) = (l \vee PI(p_1)) \wedge (\neg l \vee PI(p_2))$.
We show (1) $g_A(c) \Rightarrow PI(c)$, or, equivalently, $g_A(c) \wedge \neg PI(c) \Rightarrow \bot$:
$g_A(c) \wedge \neg PI(c) = A \wedge (\neg(C|_A \vee D|_A)) \wedge \neg[(l \vee PI(p_1)) \wedge (\neg l \vee PI(p_2))] =$
$A \wedge \neg(C|_A) \wedge \neg(D|_A) \wedge [\neg(l \vee PI(p_1)) \vee \neg(\neg l \vee PI(p_2))] =$
$[A \wedge \neg(C|_A) \wedge \neg(D|_A) \wedge \neg(l \vee PI(p_1))] \vee [A \wedge \neg(C|_A) \wedge \neg(D|_A) \wedge \neg(\neg l \vee PI(p_2))] \Rightarrow$
$[A \wedge \neg(C|_A) \wedge \neg(l \vee PI(p_1))] \vee [A \wedge \neg(D|_A) \wedge \neg(\neg l \vee PI(p_2))] =$
$[A \wedge \neg(C|_A) \wedge \neg l \wedge \neg PI(p_1)] \vee [A \wedge \neg(D|_A) \wedge l \wedge \neg PI(p_2)] = (l$ is transparent$)$
$= [A \wedge \neg((l \vee C)|_A) \wedge \neg PI(p_1)] \vee [A \wedge \neg((\neg l \vee D)|_A) \wedge \neg PI(p_2)] =$
$(g_A(p_1) \wedge \neg PI(p_1)) \vee (g_A(p_2) \wedge \neg PI(p_2)) \Rightarrow \bot \vee \bot = \bot$ by induction hypothesis.
We show (2) $g_B(c) \wedge PI(c) \Rightarrow \bot$:
$g_B(c) \wedge PI(c) = B \wedge \neg(C|_B \vee D|_B) \wedge [(l \vee PI(p_1)) \wedge (\neg l \vee PI(p_2))] =$
$B \wedge \neg(C|_B) \wedge \neg(D|_B) \wedge [(l \vee PI(p_1)) \wedge (\neg l \vee PI(p_2))]$ (***)
at this point we reason that l is either true or false; if l is true, l holds, l
subsumes $l \vee PI(p_1)$ and simplifies $\neg l \vee PI(p_2)$ to $PI(p_2)$; if l is false, $\neg l$
holds, $\neg l$ subsumes $\neg l \vee PI(p_2)$ and simplifies $l \vee PI(p_1)$ to $PI(p_1)$; thus, (***)
implies $[B \wedge \neg(C|_B) \wedge \neg(D|_B) \wedge l \wedge PI(p_2)] \vee [B \wedge \neg(C|_B) \wedge \neg(D|_B) \wedge \neg l \wedge PI(p_1)]$
which implies $[B \wedge \neg(D|_B) \wedge l \wedge PI(p_2)] \vee [B \wedge \neg(C|_B) \wedge \neg l \wedge PI(p_1)] =$
$[B \wedge \neg(D|_B \vee \neg l) \wedge PI(p_2)] \vee [B \wedge \neg(C|_B \vee l) \wedge PI(p_1)] = (l$ is transparent$)$
$= (B \wedge \neg(p_2|_B) \wedge PI(p_2)) \vee (B \wedge \neg(p_1|_B) \wedge PI(p_1)) =$
$(g_B(p_2) \wedge PI(p_2)) \vee (g_B(p_1) \wedge PI(p_1)) \Rightarrow \bot \vee \bot = \bot$ by induction hypothesis.
Requirement (3) holds by induction hypothesis and l being transparent. □

5   Interpolation and Equality

In propositional logic the notion of being A-colored, B-colored and transparent is stable: if a literal is transparent in the initial state of a derivation, it will be transparent in all. Once equality is added, even in the ground case, this is no longer obvious. Assume that t_a is an A-colored ground term, t_b is a B-colored ground term, and the AB-mixed equation $t_a \simeq t_b$ is derived. The congruence classes of t_a and t_b have to be merged. Assume that the congruence class of t_a only contains A-colored terms, that of t_b only contains B-colored terms, and t_a and t_b are the representatives of their congruence classes. If t_b were chosen as the representative of the new class, it should become transparent. If either one of the two classes already contains a transparent term t, the AB-mixed equation $t_a \simeq t_b$ is not problematic, because t can be the representative of the new class. The issue is the same if we reason about equality by rewriting: if an AB-mixed equation $t_a \simeq t_b$ is generated, where both t_a and t_b are in normal form with respect to the current set of equations, and $t_a \succ t_b$ in the ordering, all occurrences of t_a, including those in A, should be replaced by t_b, which should become transparent. In order to prevent such instability of transparency, one needs to require that all theories are *equality-interpolating*, a property that appeared first in [35]:

Definition 15. *A theory $\mathcal{T}$ is* equality-interpolating *if for all $\mathcal{T}$-formulæ A and B, whenever $A \wedge B \models_{\mathcal{T}} t_a \simeq t_b$, where t_a is an A-colored ground term and t_b is a B-colored ground term, then $A \wedge B \models_{\mathcal{T}} t_a \simeq t \wedge t_b \simeq t$ for some transparent ground term t.*

Then, in congruence closure, it is sufficient to adopt t as the representative of the new congruence class. Operationally, as suggested in [35], if $t_a \simeq t_b$ is generated before $t_a \simeq t$ and $t_b \simeq t$, one may add a new transparent constant c and the equations $t_a \simeq c$ and $t_b \simeq c$: if the theory is equality-interpolating, $c \simeq t$ will be generated eventually, so that c is only a name for t. In a rewrite-based setting, one needs to assume the following:

Definition 16. *An ordering $\succ$ is* separating *if $t \succ s$ whenever s is transparent and t is not, for all terms, or literals, s and t.*

Thus, both t_a and t_b will be rewritten to t. This requirement on the ordering appeared in [27], under the name AB-*oriented ordering*, and then in [22], where it was justified intuitively in terms of symbol elimination: since interpolants have to be transparent, the ordering should orient equations in such a way that rewriting eliminates colored symbols. However, it was not related to the notion of equality-interpolating theory.

Ground proofs made only of equalities and containing no AB-mixed equality were termed *colorable* in [17]. We adopt the name and apply it to any proof made of clauses:

Definition 17. *A proof is* colorable *if all its clauses are.*

If A-local, B-local and AB-common, or global, are used in place of A-colored, B-colored and transparent, respectively, acceptable proofs are called *local*.

It was proved in [35] that the quantifier-free fragments of the theories of *equality, linear arithmetic* and *non-empty, possibly cyclic lists* are equality-interpolating. The proof that the theory of lists is equality-interpolating relies on that for the theory of equality. However, the proof for the latter was only sketched in [35] (cf. Lemma 2 in [35]), and therefore we reconstruct it here using the notion of separating ordering:

Lemma 2. *If the ordering is separating, all ground proofs by resolution and rewriting are colorable.*

Proof: By induction on the structure of the proof:
Base Case: By definition, there are no AB-mixed literals in the input.
Induction Hypothesis: The premises do not contain AB-mixed literals.
Induction Case:

- *Resolution:* Since a ground resolvent is made of literals inherited from its parents, it does not contain AB-mixed literals by induction hypothesis.
- *Rewriting:* let $s \simeq r$ be a ground equation such that $s \succ r$, and $l[s]$ be the literal it applies to. By induction hypothesis, neither $s \simeq r$ nor $l[s]$ are AB-mixed. Thus, since the ordering is separating and $s \succ r$, either r has the same color as s or it is transparent. If s and r have the same color, also $l[s]$ and $l[r]$ have the same color. If s is colored and r is transparent, then $l[r]$ either has the same color as $l[s]$ or it is transparent, the latter if s was its only colored term. In either case, $l[r]$ is not AB-mixed. □

To show the following we only need to consider purely equational proofs, that are represented as equational *chains*. *Unfailing*, or *ordered*, *completion* reduces any ground equational proof $s \overset{*}{\leftrightarrow} t$ to a *rewrite proof*, or *valley proof* in the form $s \overset{*}{\rightarrow} \circ \overset{*}{\leftarrow} t$ (see [2] for a recent treatment with ample references):

Theorem 2. *The quantifier-free fragment of the theory of equality is equality-interpolating.*

Proof: Assume ground completion employs a separating ordering. If $A \wedge B \models t_a \simeq t_b$, where t_a is an A-colored ground term and t_b is a B-colored ground term, then, since unfailing completion is refutationally complete, it generates a contradiction from $A \cup B \cup \{t_a \not\simeq t_b\}$. The only rôle of $t_a \not\simeq t_b$ in the derivation is to be rewritten, until a contradiction is generated in the form $t \not\simeq t$. The resulting proof is made only of rewriting steps and therefore it is a rewrite proof $t_a \overset{*}{\rightarrow} t \overset{*}{\leftarrow} t_b$. Since the ordering is separating, this proof contains no AB-mixed equations by Lemma 2, which means that it must contain at least a transparent term. Since the ordering is separating, the smallest term t is transparent. It follows that $A \wedge B \models t_a \simeq t \wedge t_b \simeq t$, because the inferences are sound. □

From now on, we assume that *the built-in theories $\mathcal{T}_i$, $1 \leq i \leq n$, are equality-interpolating*, so that there are no AB-mixed literals, and all proofs are colorable.

6   Interpolation for Equality Sharing and DPLL($\mathcal{T}$)

The treatment of interpolation for equality sharing in [35] temporarily assumes that the theories in $\mathcal{T} = \bigcup_{i=1}^{n} \mathcal{T}_i$ are convex, so that it is sufficient to propagate equalities. We do not need to assume convexity, not even as a temporary assumption, neither we need to deal with propagation of disjunctions, because we adopt model-based theory combination, where only equalities are propagated. For equality sharing, the input $A \cup B$ is a set of ground $\mathcal{T}$-literals, or unit $\mathcal{T}$-clauses. Separation applies in such a way to respect colors: for example, if $f(g(a)) \simeq b$, where f and g belong to the signatures of different theories, becomes $f(c) \simeq b \wedge g(a) \simeq c$, the new constant c is stipulated to be A-colored, B-colored or transparent, depending on whether $g(a)$ is A-colored, B-colored or transparent, respectively.

Every $\mathcal{Q}_i$ deals with a set $A_i \cup B_i \cup K$, where A_i contains the $\mathcal{T}_i$-literals in A, B_i contains the $\mathcal{T}_i$-literals in B, and K is the set of propagated equalities. Although for equality sharing it suffices to propagate equalities between shared constants, in DPLL($\mathcal{T}$) the propagation is done by adding the literal to M, and model-based theory combination may propagate equalities between ground terms. Thus, we assume that K is a set of equalities between ground terms.

We assume that each $\mathcal{Q}_i$ is capable of generating $\mathcal{T}_i$-interpolants for its proofs. A crucial observation in [35] is that these $\mathcal{T}_i$-interpolants cannot be $\mathcal{T}_i$-interpolants of (A, B), since the input to $\mathcal{Q}_i$ is $A_i \cup B_i \cup K$. They are $\mathcal{T}_i$-interpolants of some partition (A', B') of $A_i \cup B_i \cup K$. This is where the assumption that theories are equality-interpolating plays a rôle: K contains no AB-mixed literals. Therefore, it is possible to define A' and B' based on colors as defined by the original (A, B) partition, using projections with respect to A and B: let A' be $(A_i \cup B_i \cup K)|_A = A_i \cup K|_A$ and B' be $(A_i \cup B_i \cup K)|_B = B_i \cup K|_B$. It follows that $\mathcal{L}_{A'} = \mathcal{L}_A$, $\mathcal{L}_{B'} = \mathcal{L}_B$, and what is transparent with respect to (A', B') is transparent with respect to (A, B), so that $\mathcal{T}_i$-interpolants of (A', B') can be used to build the $\mathcal{T}$-interpolant of (A, B):

Definition 18. *For all ground literals l, such that $A_i \cup B_i \cup K \vdash_{\mathcal{T}_i} l$, where A_i is the set of $\mathcal{T}_i$-literals in A, B_i is the set of $\mathcal{T}_i$-literals in B, and K is a set of propagated equalities between ground terms, the* theory-specific partial interpolant *of l, denoted by $PI^i_{(A', B')}(l)$, is the $\mathcal{T}_i$-interpolant of $(A' \wedge \neg(l|_A), B' \wedge \neg(l|_B))$ generated by $\mathcal{Q}_i$, where $A' = A_i \cup K|_A$ and $B' = B_i \cup K|_B$.*

Note how there is no need to require that only equalities between shared constants are propagated.

In equality sharing the refutation is found by one of the theories, and therefore has the form $A_i \cup B_i \cup K \vdash_{\mathcal{T}_i} \bot$ for some i. The method of [35] shows how to extract a $\mathcal{T}$-interpolant of (A, B) from such a refutation, by combining the theory-specific partial interpolants computed by the $\mathcal{Q}_i$'s for the propagated equalities in K. We state it as an *interpolation system for equality sharing*:

Definition 19 (EQSH interpolation system). *Let C be a literal, or unit clause, that appears in a refutation of $A \cup B$ by equality sharing:*

- If $C \in A$, then $PI(C) = \bot$,
- If $C \in B$, then $PI(C) = \top$,
- If $A_i \cup B_i \cup K \vdash_{\mathcal{T}_i} C$ for some i, $1 \leq i \leq n$, then

$$PI(C) = (PI^i_{(A',B')}(C) \vee \bigvee_{l \in A'} PI(l)) \wedge \bigwedge_{l \in B'} PI(l),$$

where $A' = A_i \cup K|_A$ and $B' = B_i \cup K|_B$.

If there were only one theory, K would be empty, and the partial interpolant in the inductive case of Definition 19 would be equal to the theory-specific partial interpolant in that theory.

Theorem 3 (Yorsh and Musuvathi, 2005). *EQSH is a complete interpolation system for equality sharing.*

Proof: We need to prove that for all unit clauses C in the refutation, $PI(C)$ satifies Requirements (1), (2) and (3), listed at the end of Section 2, in theory $\mathcal{T}$. The base case is the same as for Theorem 1. The inductive case, for a C such that $A_i \cup B_i \cup K \vdash_{\mathcal{T}_i} C$ for some i, $1 \leq i \leq n$, requires another induction on K:
Base case: if $K = \emptyset$, then $A' = A_i$, $B' = B_i$, and $PI(C) = PI^i_{(A',B')}(C)$.
By Definition 18, $PI(C)$ is a $\mathcal{T}_i$-interpolant of $(A_i \wedge \neg(C|_A), B_i \wedge \neg(C|_B))$; since $A_i \subseteq A$ and $B_i \subseteq B$, $PI(C)$ is also a $\mathcal{T}$-interpolant of $A \wedge \neg(C|_A)$ and $B \wedge \neg(C|_B)$.
Induction case: if $K \neq \emptyset$, then $A' = A_i \cup K|_A$, $B' = B_i \cup K|_B$ and $PI(C) = (PI^i_{(A',B')}(C) \vee \bigvee_{l \in K|_A} PI(l)) \wedge \bigwedge_{l \in K|_B} PI(l)$, because $PI(l) = \bot$ for all $l \in A_i$ and $PI(l) = \top$ for all $l \in B_i$.
We continue with the main claim:
Induction hypothesis: for all $l \in K|_A$, $PI(l)$ is a $\mathcal{T}$-interpolant of $(A \wedge \neg(l|_A), B \wedge \neg(l|_B))$, that is, a $\mathcal{T}$-interpolant of $(A \wedge \neg l, B)$, because $l|_A = l$ and $l|_B = \bot$, since $l \in K|_A$; for all $l \in K|_B$, $PI(l)$ is a $\mathcal{T}$-interpolant of $(A \wedge \neg(l|_A), B \wedge \neg(l|_B))$, that is, a $\mathcal{T}$-interpolant of $(A, B \wedge \neg l)$, because $l|_A = \bot$ and $l|_B = l$, since $l \in K|_B$; so that the inductive hypothesis is:

- For all $l \in K|_A$,
  (1A) $A \wedge \neg l \vdash_{\mathcal{T}} PI(l)$ or, equivalently, $A \vdash_{\mathcal{T}} l \vee PI(l)$,
  (2A) $B \wedge PI(l) \vdash_{\mathcal{T}} \bot$,
  (3A) $PI(l)$ is transparent; and
- For all $l \in K|_B$,
  (1B) $A \vdash_{\mathcal{T}} PI(l)$,
  (2B) $B \wedge \neg l \wedge PI(l) \vdash_{\mathcal{T}} \bot$, or, equivalently, $B \wedge PI(l) \vdash_{\mathcal{T}} l$,
  (3B) $PI(l)$ is transparent.

Induction case:

1. $A \wedge \neg(C|_A) \vdash_{\mathcal{T}} PI(C)$:
   By Definition 18, $A_i \wedge K|_A \wedge \neg(C|_A) \vdash_{\mathcal{T}_i} PI^i_{(A',B')}(C)$, or, equivalently, $A_i \wedge \neg(C|_A) \vdash_{\mathcal{T}_i} \neg K|_A \vee PI^i_{(A',B')}(C)$ (*), where $\neg K|_A$ is the disjunction $\neg l_1 \vee \ldots \vee \neg l_q$, if $K|_A$ is the conjunction $l_1 \wedge \ldots \wedge l_q$. By induction hypothesis

(1A), we have $A \vdash_T l_j \vee PI(l_j)$ for $1 \leq j \leq q$ (**). By q resolution steps between (*) and (**), and since $A \Rightarrow A_i$, it follows that $A \wedge \neg(C|_A) \vdash_T PI^i_{(A',B')}(C) \vee \bigvee_{l \in K|_A} PI(l)$. By induction hypothesis (1B), $A \vdash_T PI(l)$ for all $l \in K|_B$. Therefore, we conclude that $A \wedge \neg(C|_A) \vdash_T (PI^i_{(A',B')}(C) \vee \bigvee_{l \in K|_A} PI(l)) \wedge \bigwedge_{l \in K|_B} PI(l)$.

2. $B \wedge \neg(C|_B) \wedge PI(C) \vdash_T \bot$:

   By Definition 18, $B_i \wedge K|_B \wedge \neg(C|_B) \wedge PI^i_{(A',B')}(C) \vdash_{T_i} \bot$. Since $B \Rightarrow B_i$, we have $B \wedge K|_B \wedge \neg(C|_B) \wedge PI^i_{(A',B')}(C) \vdash_{T_i} \bot$ (*). By induction hypothesis (2A), $B \wedge PI(l) \vdash_T \bot$ for all $l \in K|_A$, and thus $B \wedge \bigvee_{l \in K|_A} PI(l) \vdash_T \bot$, and $B \wedge K|_B \wedge \neg(C|_B) \wedge \bigvee_{l \in K|_A} PI(l) \vdash_T \bot$ (**). Combining (*) and (**) gives $B \wedge K|_B \wedge \neg(C|_B) \wedge (PI^i_{(A',B')}(C) \vee \bigvee_{l \in K|_A} PI(l)) \vdash_T \bot$, or, equivalently, $B \wedge \neg(C|_B) \wedge (PI^i_{(A',B')}(C) \vee \bigvee_{l \in K|_A} PI(l)) \vdash_T \neg K|_B$ (†), where $\neg K|_B$ is the disjunction $\neg l_1 \vee \ldots \vee \neg l_q$, if $K|_B$ is the conjunction $l_1 \wedge \ldots \wedge l_q$. By induction hypothesis (2B), $B \wedge PI(l_j) \vdash_T l_j$ for $1 \leq j \leq q$ (‡). By q resolution steps between (†) and (‡), we get $B \wedge \neg(C|_B) \wedge (PI^i_{(A',B')}(C) \vee \bigvee_{l \in K|_A} PI(l)) \wedge \bigwedge_{l \in K|_B} PI(l) \vdash_T \bot$, that is, $B \wedge \neg(C|_B) \wedge PI(C) \vdash_T \bot$.

3. $PI(C)$ is transparent, because $PI^i_{(A',B')}(C)$ is transparent by Definition 18, and the $PI(l)$'s are transparent by induction hypotheses (3A) and (3B). $\square$

This proof does not depend on assuming that K contains only equalities between shared constants, neither does it depend on assuming that K contains all such equalities entailed by the theories. Thus, EQSH is a complete interpolation system for equality sharing, *regardless of whether equality sharing is implemented in its original form, or by model-based theory combination.*

Having an interpolation system for DPLL and an interpolation system for equality sharing, we have all the ingredients for an interpolation system for DPLL(T). Let A and B be two sets of ground T-clauses, for which we need to find a T-interpolant. Let CP_T be the set of the T-conflict clauses that appear in the DPLL(T)-refutation of $A \cup B$ (cf. Definition 11). Such a refutation shows that $A \cup B$ is T-unsatisfiable, by showing that $A \cup B \cup CP_T$ is propositionally unsatisfiable. An interpolation system for DPLL(T) will be given by an interpolation system for propositional resolution plus partial interpolants for the T-conflict clauses. A clause C is a T-conflict clause, because its negation $\neg C$, which is a set, or conjunction, of literals, was found T-unsatisfiable. Then, $(\neg C)|_A \wedge (\neg C)|_B$ is T-unsatisfiable, and we can compute a T-interpolant of $((\neg C)|_A, (\neg C)|_B)$ by EQSH. This T-interpolant provides the partial interpolant for C.

We call the resulting interpolation system HKPYM–T, because it is obtained by adding to HKPYM (cf. Definition 13) another case for T-conflict clauses. The case for T-conflict clauses is a third base case, because they are sort of input clauses from the point of view of the propositional engine:

Definition 20 (HKPYM–T interpolation system). *Let $c: C$ be a clause that appears in a DPLL(T)-refutation of $A \cup B$:*

- *If $c: C \in A$, then $PI(c) = \bot$,*

– If c: $C \in B$, then $PI(c) = \top$,
– If c: C is generated by T-Conflict, $PI(c)$ is the $\mathcal{T}$-interpolant of $((\neg C)|_A, (\neg C)|_B)$ produced by EQSH from the refutation $\neg C \vdash_{\mathcal{T}} \bot$;
– If c: $C \vee D$ is a propositional resolvent of p_1: $C \vee l$ and p_2: $D \vee \neg l$ then:
  • If l is A-colored, then $PI(c) = PI(p_1) \vee PI(p_2)$,
  • If l is B-colored, then $PI(c) = PI(p_1) \wedge PI(p_2)$ and
  • If l is transparent, then $PI(c) = (l \vee PI(p_1)) \wedge (\neg l \vee PI(p_2))$.

The case analysis on literals resolved upon remains unchanged, because the requirement that all theories in $\mathcal{T}$ are equality-interpolating guarantees that the $\mathcal{T}$-conflict clauses do not introduce in the proof AB-mixed literals. The completeness of HKPYM–T follows from the completeness of HKPYM and EQSH.

7   Future Work

We are working on interpolation for superposition [3] in order to obtain an interpolation system for the theorem proving method DPLL($\Gamma + \mathcal{T}$) [4], which integrates a superposition-based inference system Γ into DPLL($\mathcal{T}$). Interpolation for ground superposition proofs was approached in [27] and then explored further in [23], using a notion of *colored proof*, which is stronger than colorable, since it excludes AB-mixed clauses. The observation that a separating ordering makes proofs colorable (cf. Lemma 2) generalizes easily to ground proofs in a full-fledged superposition-based inference system [3]. The analysis of interpolation and equality reported here means that for DPLL($\Gamma + \mathcal{T}$) we need to assume that the built-in theories in $\mathcal{T}$ are equality-interpolating and the ordering used by Γ is separating. The remark that the interpolation system of [35] for equality sharing works also for model-based theory combination is another step towards interpolation in DPLL($\Gamma + \mathcal{T}$), since DPLL($\Gamma + \mathcal{T}$) uses model-based theory combination.

References

1. Bonacina, M.P.: On theorem proving for program checking – Historical perspective and recent developments. In: Fernandez, M. (ed.) Proc. of the 12th Int. Symp. on Principles and Practice of Declarative Programming, pp. 1–11. ACM Press, New York (2010)
2. Bonacina, M.P., Dershowitz, N.: Abstract canonical inference. ACM Trans. on Computational Logic 8(1), 180–208 (2007)
3. Bonacina, M.P., Johansson, M.: On theorem proving with interpolation for program checking. In: Technical report, Dipartimento di Informatica. Università degli Studi di Verona (April 2011)
4. Bonacina, M.P., Lynch, C.A., de Moura, L.: On deciding satisfiability by theorem proving with speculative inferences. Journal of Automated Reasoning, 1–29 (in press); (Published online December 22, 2010) doi:10.1007/s10817-010-9213-y
5. Bradley, A.R., Manna, Z. (eds.): The Calculus of Computation – Decision Procedures with Applications to Verification. Springer, Heidelberg (2007)

6. Brillout, A., Kroening, D., Rümmer, P., Wahl, T.: An Interpolating Sequent Calculus for Quantifier-Free Presburger Arithmetic. In: Giesl, J., Hähnle, R. (eds.) IJCAR 2010. LNCS, vol. 6173, pp. 384–399. Springer, Heidelberg (2010)
7. Brillout, A., Kroening, D., Rümmer, P., Wahl, T.: Program verification via Craig interpolation for Presburger arithmetic with arrays. Notes of the 6th Int. Verification Workshop (2010), http://www.philipp.ruemmer.org/
8. Bruttomesso, R., Ghilardi, S., Ranise, S.: Rewriting-based quantifier-free interpolation for a theory of arrays. In: Proc. of the 22nd Int. Conf. on Rewriting Techniques and Applications, LIPICS. Leibniz-Zentrum für Informatik, Dagsthul Publishing (2011)
9. Bruttomesso, R., Rollini, S., Sharygina, N., Tsitovich, A.: Flexible interpolation generation in satisfiability modulo theories. In: Proc. of the 14th Int. Conf. on Computer-Aided Design, pp. 770–777. IEEE Computer Society Press, Los Alamitos (2010)
10. Chadha, R., Plaisted, D.A.: On the mechanical derivation of loop invariants. Journal of Symbolic Computation 15(5-6), 705–744 (1993)
11. Cimatti, A., Griggio, A., Sebastiani, R.: Efficient Interpolant Generation in Satisfiability Modulo Theories. In: Ramakrishnan, C.R., Rehof, J. (eds.) TACAS 2008. LNCS, vol. 4963, pp. 397–412. Springer, Heidelberg (2008)
12. Cimatti, A., Griggio, A., Sebastiani, R.: Interpolant Generation for UTVPI. In: Schmidt, R. (ed.) CADE-22. LNCS (LNAI), vol. 5663, pp. 167–182. Springer, Heidelberg (2009)
13. de Moura, L., Bjørner, N.: Model-based theory combination. In: Krstić, S., Oliveras, A. (eds.) CAV 2007. ENTCS, vol. 198(2), pp. 37–49. Elsevier, Amsterdam (2008)
14. D'Silva, V.: Propositional Interpolation and Abstract Interpretation. In: Gordon, A.D. (ed.) ESOP 2010. LNCS, vol. 6012, pp. 185–204. Springer, Heidelberg (2010)
15. D'Silva, V., Kroening, D., Purandare, M., Weissenbacher, G.: Interpolant Strength. In: Barthe, G., Hermenegildo, M. (eds.) VMCAI 2010. LNCS, vol. 5944, pp. 129–145. Springer, Heidelberg (2010)
16. Fuchs, A., Goel, A., Grundy, J., Krstić, S., Tinelli, C.: Ground Interpolation for the Theory of Equality. In: Kowalewski, S., Philippou, A. (eds.) TACAS 2009. LNCS, vol. 5505, pp. 413–427. Springer, Heidelberg (2009)
17. Goel, A., Krstić, S., Tinelli, C.: Ground Interpolation for Combined Theories. In: Schmidt, R. (ed.) CADE-22. LNCS, vol. 5663, pp. 183–198. Springer, Heidelberg (2009)
18. Henzinger, T.A., Jhala, R., Majumdar, R., McMillan, K.L.: Abstractions from proofs. In: Leroy, X. (ed.) Proc. of the 31st ACM SIGACT-SIGPLAN Symp. on Principles of Programming Languages, pp. 232–244. ACM Press, New York (2004)
19. Hoder, K., Kovács, L., Voronkov, A.: Interpolation and Symbol Elimination in Vampire. In: Giesl, J., Hähnle, R. (eds.) IJCAR 2010. LNCS (LNAI), vol. 6173, pp. 188–195. Springer, Heidelberg (2010)
20. Huang, G.: Constructing Craig interpolation formulas. In: Proc. of the 1st Annual Int. Conf. on Computing and Combinatorics, pp. 181–190. Springer, Heidelberg (1995)
21. Kapur, D., Majumdar, R., Zarba, C.G.: Interpolation for data structures. In: Devambu, P. (ed.) Proc. of the 14th ACM SIGSOFT Symp. on the Foundations of Software Engineering, ACM Press, New York (2006)
22. Kovács, L., Voronkov, A.: Finding loop invariants for programs over arrays using a theorem prover. In: Chechik, M., Wirsing, M. (eds.) FASE 2009. LNCS, vol. 5503, pp. 470–485. Springer, Heidelberg (2009)

23. Kovács, L., Voronkov, A.: Interpolation and Symbol Elimination. In: Schmidt, R. (ed.) CADE-22. LNCS (LNAI), vol. 5663, pp. 199–213. Springer, Heidelberg (2009)
24. Krajíček, J.: Interpolation theorems, lower bounds for proof systems, and independence results for bounded arithmetic. Journal of Symbolic Logic 62(2), 457–486 (1997)
25. McMillan, K.L.: Interpolation and SAT-Based Model Checking. In: Hunt, W.J., Somenzi, F. (eds.) CAV 2003. LNCS, vol. 2725, pp. 1–13. Springer, Heidelberg (2003)
26. McMillan, K.L.: An interpolating theorem prover. Theoretical Computer Science 345(1), 101–121 (2005)
27. McMillan, K.L.: Quantified Invariant Generation Using an Interpolating Saturation Prover. In: Ramakrishnan, C.R., Rehof, J. (eds.) TACAS 2008. LNCS, vol. 4963, pp. 413–427. Springer, Heidelberg (2008)
28. McMillan, K.L.: Lazy Annotation for Program Testing and Verification. In: Cook, B., Jackson, P., Touili, T. (eds.) CAV 2010. LNCS, vol. 6174, pp. 104–118. Springer, Heidelberg (2010)
29. Nelson, G., Oppen, D.C.: Simplification by cooperating decision procedures. ACM Trans. on Programming Languages and Systems 1(2), 245–257 (1979)
30. Nelson, G., Oppen, D.C.: Fast decision procedures based on congruence closure. Journal of the ACM 27(2), 356–364 (1980)
31. Nieuwenhuis, R., Oliveras, A., Tinelli, C.: Solving SAT and SAT modulo theories: From an abstract Davis–Putnam–Logemann–Loveland procedure to DPLL(T). Journal of the ACM 53(6), 937–977 (2006)
32. Pudlàk, P.: Lower bounds for resolution and cutting plane proofs and monotone computations. Journal of Symbolic Logic 62(3), 981–998 (1997)
33. Sebastiani, R.: Lazy satisfiability modulo theory. Journal on Satisfiability, Boolean Modelling and Computation 3, 141–224 (2006)
34. Shankar, N.: Automated deduction for verification. ACM Computing Surveys 41(4), 40–96 (2009)
35. Yorsh, G., Musuvathi, M.: A Combination Method for Generating Interpolants. In: Nieuwenhuis, R. (ed.) CADE 2005. LNCS (LNAI), vol. 3632, pp. 353–368. Springer, Heidelberg (2005); Early version in MSR-TR-2004-108 (October 2004)
36. Zhang, L., Malik, S.: Validating SAT solvers using an independent resolution-based checker: practical implementations and other applications. In: Proc. of the Conf. on Design Automation and Test in Europe, pp. 10880–10885. IEEE Computer Society Press, Los Alamitos (2003)

First-Order Tableaux in Applications (Extended Abstract)

Ulrich Furbach

Department of Computer Science
University of Koblenz-Landau
uli@uni-koblenz.de

High performance first-order theorem proving is dominated by saturation-based proof procedures. This is true, at least when one looks at competitions like the yearly CASC, the CADE ATP System Competition, where the winners in the CNF division (conjunctive normal form, non-propositional problems) usually use superposition-based calculi. This was different in the early days of CASC, when a tableau prover (SETHEO) even won the MIX category.

Since many years the Koblenz AI Group has been focusing its research on tableau-based automated reasoning. As an attempt to bring together the best of two worlds, namely a 'single proof object' from tableau proving and free variables from resolution, we came up with the hyper tableau calculus [2] in the 1990s. This is a clause normal form tableau calculus which implements the main idea from hyperresolution, which is a kind of simultaneous resolution of all negative literals in a clause. When the calculus extends a branch of the tableau, the unifier, which is constructed for this inference rule, is applied only to the variables of the newly generated leaves – there are no rigid variables anymore.

In [3] we managed to incorporate efficient equality handling into hyper tableaux. We used an adapted version of the superposition inference rule, where equations used for paramodulation are drawn (only) from a set of positive unit clauses, which forms the current candidate model. The calculus also features a generic, semantically justified simplification rule which covers many redundancy elimination techniques known from superposition theorem proving. This is implemented in the theorem prover E-KRHyper, which is the main tool for the applications described in the following.

Applications. In applications it turned out to be very helpful to use the proof object which is manipulated by the calculus, i. e. the computation, as a result of the proof. In the projects *Slicing Book* and *in2math* we used the hyper tableau proof to 'calculate' a LaTex document (see [1]). For this an entire book is represented as a knowledge base of small pieces of LaTex code together with meta-data. If a user wants to read such a book, his personalized invocation of the book is formulated as a query, for which a proof attempt is made by the prover. If this results in an open branch, the nodes of the branch contain the identifiers of those LaTex pieces which together form the document which meets the users requirements.

Another application of E-KRHyper is within the *LogAnswer*-project ([5]). LogAnswer is an open domain question answering system; it receives a natural-language question regarding any topic, and it returns a natural-language answer

K. Brünnler and G. Metcalfe (Eds.): TABLEAUX 2011, LNAI 6793, pp. 17–19, 2011.

found in a knowledge base. The knowledge base consists of several parts: A formal logical representation of a snapshot of the entire German Wikipedia. These are 12 millions sentences which are transformed semi-automatically into a logical representation. A second part consists of background knowledge, e. g . knowledge about spatial and temporal relations, which is necessary to answer arbitrary natural language questions. Such a question is transformed into a logical representation; let us consider the question 'Rudy Giuliani war Bürgermeister welcher US-Stadt?'[1] as a running example. The system generates from the Wikipedia text 200 answer candidates, which are text passages which might contain material to answer the question. For each of the 200 candidates the system takes the logical representation and tries to prove the given query. For the entire processing, the linguistic analysis of the query, the search for the 200 candidates and the 200 proof tasks the system has a time limit of 5 seconds (this is the maximum time we can keep the user waiting for an answer). While adapting the E-KRHyper prover for this application we found several interesting problems which might be of interest for other applications as well:

Time Restrictions. As mentioned above, the system has to perform over 200 proof tasks within short time; hence there is no chance to allow the prover a very deep analysis within every proof. For each of the subgoals we give a time limit which forces the prover to abort the current subgoal and to proceed with the next one. In other words, completeness is no issue for this application. In most cases we get a time-out for some of the proof attempts for a subgoal, even if there exists a proof.

Relaxations. If LogAnswer gets a time-out for a subgoal, it deletes this subgoal and tries the entire proof again. In our example query, which contains the nickname 'Rudy', it may happen that the knowledge base contains a passage about the mayor Rudolph Giuliani and hence the system cannot prove that Rudy is the mayor. Deleting the subgoal, which asked for the given name Rudy, results in a proof with one relaxation. However we have to rate the generated answer a bit lower in confidence, because of the relaxation. Currently we are working towards using abductive reasoning for relaxations. Instead of deleting a subgoal we are substituting it by a more general one, which can be deduced from a background knowledge base.

Background Knowledge Base. Currently LogAnswer uses background knowledge which consists of approx. 12,000 axioms. We are planning to extend this by using the general ontology OpenCyc, which contains 3.3 million formulae. This mere number of the formulae challenges a prover. State of the art is to partition this huge set of clauses according to a given query and to use only those partitions which are necessary for the proof. In our case the partitioning via pre-processing is not possible, because relaxation results in several, previously not known queries. As a way out we are working towards clustering methods, which can be used without knowing the query in advance.

---

[1] Rudy Giuliani was mayor of which US city?

Webservices. Another possibility to extend the knowledge base is to use external webservices. We modified and extended the inference rules of the hyper tableau calculus, such that calls of external services can be managed. Currently E-KRHyper is connected to Yahoo GeoPlanet, a weather service and a currency converter.

Over the years we learned from various applications that theorem provers for applications cannot be used off the peg. They have to be modified and extended and indeed, it turned out that this offers a lot of interesting and challenging theoretical problems.

Currently we are working towards an application where LogAnswer is a participant in a question answering forum. For such an application it is of particular importance to avoid wrong answers, which can occur although the calculus is correct (see [4]).

References

1. Baumgartner, P., Furbach, U., Gross-Hardt, M., Sinner, A.: Living Book – Deduction, Slicing, and Interaction. Journal of Automated Reasoning 32(3), 259–286 (2004)
2. Baumgartner, P., Furbach, U., Niemelä, I.: Hyper tableaux. In: Alferes, J.J., Pereira, L.M., Orlowska, E. (eds.) JELIA 1996. LNCS, vol. 1126, pp. 1–17. Springer, Heidelberg (1996)
3. Baumgartner, P., Furbach, U., Pelzer, B.: Hyper tableaux with equality. In: Pfenning, F. (ed.) CADE 2007. LNCS (LNAI), vol. 4603, pp. 492–507. Springer, Heidelberg (2007)
4. Dong, T., Furbach, U., Glöckner, I., Pelzer, B.: A natural language question answering system as a participant in human Q&A portals. To appear in IJCAI (2011)
5. Furbach, U., Glöckner, I., Pelzer, B.: An application of automated reasoning in natural language question answering. AI Commun. 23(2-3), 241–265 (2010)

Proof Theory and Algebra
in Substructural Logics

Kazushige Terui

RIMS, Kyoto University,
Kitashirakawa Oiwakecho, Sakyo-ku, Kyoto 606-8502, Japan

It is quite well understood that propositional logics are tightly connected to ordered algebras via algebraic completeness, and because of this connection proof theory is often useful in the algebraic context too. A prominent example is that one *deductively* proves the interpolation theorem for a given logic in order to derive the *algebraic* amalgamation property for the corresponding variety as a corollary. Other examples include uniform interpolation, disjunction property, local deduction theorem, and termination of complete proof search with their corresponding algebraic properties.

Proof theory is, however, not merely an external device for deriving algebraic consequences as corollaries. The connection is even tighter, and it also works *inside* algebra as a source of various algebraic constructions. For instance, Maehara's sequent-based method for proving the interpolation theorem gives rise to a direct construction of an algebra required for the amalgamation property. Finding a new variant of sequent calculus (such as hypersequent calculus) amounts to finding a new variant of MacNeille completions (generalizations of Dedekind's completion $\mathbb{Q} \hookrightarrow \mathbb{R}$). Proving cut elimination for such a generalized sequent calculus is closely related to proving that a variety is closed under the corresponding generalized completions. Finally, transforming Hilbert axioms into Gentzen rules is not only important for proving cut elimination and related conservativity results, but also crucial for ensuring that the above proof theoretic constructions do work in algebra properly.

In this talk, we will discuss such internal contributions of proof theory in algebra. Our basic framework is substructural logics, which comprise linear, relevance, fuzzy and superintuitionistic logics. Algebraically, they correspond to varieties of residuated lattices, that include Heyting algebras and many others. We will exemplify several proof theoretic methods that directly work for residuated lattices, then develop a general theory for such internal constructions in terms of residuated frames, and see their possibilities and limitations in terms of the substructural hierarchy — a hierarchy that classifies nonclassical axioms according to how difficult they are to deal with in proof theory.

K. Brünnler and G. Metcalfe (Eds.): TABLEAUX 2011, LNAI 6793, p. 20, 2011.

CSymLean: A Theorem Prover for the Logic CSL over Symmetric Minspaces

Régis Alenda and Nicola Olivetti

LSIS - UMR CNRS 6168, Université de Provence – St-Jérôme, Marseille (France)
regis.alenda@lsis.org, nicola.olivetti@univ-cezanne.fr

Abstract. The logic CSL of comparative concept similarity has been introduced by Sheremet, et al. to capture a form of qualitative similarity comparison. We present here $\mathcal{CSym\mathcal{L}}$ean, the first theorem-prover for CSL interpreted on symmetric minspaces. It is a Prolog implementation of a labelled tableau calculus recently proposed for this logic, and it is inspired by the Lean methodology.

1 The Logic $\mathcal{CSL}$

$\mathcal{CSL}$ is a propositional modal logic introduced by Sheremet, Tishkovsky, Wolter and Zakharyaschev for reasoning about the comparative similarity between concepts and/or objects [4]. In $\mathcal{CSL}$ one can formulate assertions of the form "objects A are more similar to B than to C". This type of assertions may be added to an ontology to express qualitative comparisons between concepts. Moreover, $\mathcal{CSL}$ can also be interpreted as a formalism for spatial reasoning where "similarity" is replaced by "spatial closeness". *Formulas* of $\mathcal{CSL}$ are defined as follows:
$C, D \overset{\text{def}}{=} \perp \mid P_i \mid \neg C \mid C \sqcup D \mid C \sqcap D \mid C \Leftarrow D$.

The semantics of $\mathcal{CSL}$ is defined in terms of *distance spaces* [4], that is to say Kripke models equipped by a distance function. Different properties of the distance function (namely, symmetry, triangular inequality and existence of the minimum of a set of distances) give rise to variants of $\mathcal{CSL}$. Its relations with topological modal logics, axiomatisation, decidability and other properties are extensively investigated in [5]. In this paper, we consider the case of $\mathcal{CSL}$ defined by symmetric distances spaces where the minimum of a set of distances always exists, the so-called symmetric minspace models. Briefly, a symmetric minspace model has the form $\mathcal{I} = (\Delta, d, \cdot^{\mathcal{I}})$ where Δ is a non-empty set and d is a *metric* from Δ to $\mathbb{R}^{\geq 0}$ satisfying the additional *minspace* property [1]; the interpretation of $\Leftarrow$ is given by $(A \Leftarrow B)^{\mathcal{I}} = \{x | d(x, A^{\mathcal{I}}) < d(x, B^{\mathcal{I}})\}$.

It has been shown in [3] that the semantics of $\mathcal{CSL}$ can be equivalently formulated in terms of *preferental models* that abstract away any reference to numeric distances. The preferential semantics is closer to the standard semantics of modal logic and it is more suitable for studying proof systems and automated deduction

---

[1] The property is the following: $d(C, D) \overset{\text{def}}{=} \inf\{d(x, y) \mid x \in C, y \in D\} = \min\{d(x, y) \mid x \in C, y \in D\}$ for all non-empty subsets C, D of Δ.

K. Brünnler and G. Metcalfe (Eds.): TABLEAUX 2011, LNAI 6793, pp. 21–26, 2011.

$(T1\Leftarrow)$: $\dfrac{\Gamma[x : A \Leftarrow B,\ y : C]}{\Gamma,\ y : \neg B \mid \Gamma,\ y : B}$

$(F1\Leftarrow)$: $\dfrac{\Gamma[x : \neg(A \Leftarrow B),\ y : C]}{\Gamma,\ y : A \mid \Gamma,\ y : \neg A}$

$(T2\Leftarrow)$: $\dfrac{\Gamma[x : A \Leftarrow B]}{\Gamma,\ z : f(x, A),\ z : A}\ (*)$

$(F2\Leftarrow)$: $\dfrac{\Gamma[x : \neg(A \Leftarrow B),\ y : A]}{\Gamma,\ z : f(x, B),\ z : B}\ (*)$

$(T3\Leftarrow)$: $\dfrac{\Gamma[x : A \Leftarrow B,\ z : f(x, A),\ y : B]}{\Gamma,\ \{x, z\} < \{x, y\}}$

$(F3\Leftarrow)$: $\dfrac{\Gamma[x : \neg(A \Leftarrow B),\ z : f(x, B),\ y : A]}{\Gamma,\ \{x, y\} \leq \{x, z\}}$

(cnt): $\dfrac{\Gamma[x : A,\ y : B]}{\Gamma(y/x) \mid \Gamma,\ \{x, x\} < \{x, y\},\ \{y, y\} < \{y, x\}}$

(asm): $\dfrac{\Gamma[\{x, y\} < \{z, u\}]}{\Gamma,\ \{z, u\} \leq \{x, y\}}$

(mod): $\dfrac{\Gamma[\{x, y\} \leq \{v, w\},\ \{v, w\} \leq \{z, u\}]}{\Gamma,\ \{x, y\} \leq \{z, u\}}$

(tr): $\dfrac{\Gamma[\{x, y\} < \{v, w\},\ \{v, w\} < \{z, u\}]}{\Gamma,\ \{x, y\} < \{z, u\}}$

$(r\bot)$: $\dfrac{\Gamma[\{x, y\} < \{z, u\},\ \{x, y\} \leq \{z, u\}]}{\bot}$

$(\bot)$: $\dfrac{\Gamma[x : A,\ x : \neg A]}{\bot}$

(*) z is a new label not occurring in the current branch.

Fig. 1. Tableau calculus $\mathbf{T}\text{CSL}_s$ for $\mathcal{CSL}$ [3]

for this logic. In particular the tableau calculus implemented by $\mathcal{CSymLean}$ is based on the preferential semantics of $\mathcal{CSL}$. In a preferential model $\mathcal{I} = (\Delta, <, \cdot^{\mathcal{I}})$ the distance function is replaced by a total preorder $<$ between two-element multisets of elements of the domain: $\{x, y\} \leq \{z, u\}$ stands for $d(x, y) \leq d(z, u)$. The relation $<$ satisfies some additional conditions, namely, pair-centering ($\{x, x\} < \{x, y\}$ or $x = y$), modularity, asymmetry, and limit assumption (for all nonempty subsets C, D of Δ, $\min_<\{\{x, y\} | x \in C, y \in D\} \neq \varnothing$). The interpretation of $\Leftarrow$ is given by:

$$(A \Leftarrow B)^{\mathcal{I}} = \{x \in \Delta | \exists y \in A^{\mathcal{I}}, \forall z \in B^{\mathcal{I}}, \{x, y\} < \{x, z\}\}.$$

A labelled tableau calculus $\mathbf{T}\text{CSL}_s$ is presented in Figure 1 (obvious boolean rules are omitted). Tableau formulas are either of the form $x : A$, or $\{x, y\} < \{z, u\}$ or $z : f(x, A)$, the latter meaning intuitively that z is an A-element whose distance from x is minimal. A *tableau set* Γ is a set of tableau formulas and a tableau derivation is a tree whose nodes are tableau sets. The notation $\Gamma[A]$ means that A occurs in Γ. In the (cnt) rule $\Gamma(y/x)$ denotes the result of substituting y by x in every tableau formulas of Γ. Finally, a rule is *dynamic* if it introduces a new label (the rules $(T2\Leftarrow)$ and $(F2\Leftarrow)$), and *static* if it does not.

In order to make the calculus terminating, some restrictions (blocking) on the application of the rules are needed. Given a derivation branch $\mathbf{B}$ we assume a chronological (hence strict) order in the introduction of the labels and we define $\Pi_\Gamma(x) = \{A | A \in \mathcal{L}_{\mathcal{CSL}} \text{ and } x : A \in \Gamma\}$. There are three restrictions: the first one **(irredundancy)** prevents unnecessary applications of the rules to a tableau set if the corresponding saturation condition is already fulfilled by the tableau set, the others two are: **(Subset blocking)** Do not apply $(T2\Leftarrow)$ to $x : A \Leftarrow B \in \Gamma$, or $(F2\Leftarrow)$ to $x : \neg(A \Leftarrow B), y : A$ in Γ if there exists a label z older than x and such that $\Pi_\Gamma(x) \subseteq \Pi_\Gamma(z)$. **(Centering)** Apply (cnt) to $x : A, y : B$ in Γ only if x is older than y.

We say that a tableau set is *finished* if it is closed (ie: it contains $\bot$) or no rule is applicable to it and that a tableau derivation is *finished* if every leaf tableau set is finished. Moreover, we say that a tableau set Γ in a derivation is *bad* if (i) it is open (ie: not closed), (ii) it is finished (iii) there exist some label x and y such that x is *older* than y and $\Pi_\Gamma(y) \subseteq \Pi_\Gamma(x)$. Finally, a tableau derivation is *closed* if all its leaf nodes are either closed or *bad*. A tableau derivation for a formula C is a derivation whose root node is the tableau set $\{x : C\}$ (for an arbitrary label x). The formula C is satisfiable iff there exists an open tableau derivation for C. Observe that the tableau calculus contains a non-standard closure condition: *bad* tableau sets, although open, are disregarded; the intuitve reason is that they may potentially provide an infinite model which would violate the limit assumption.

As shown in [3], the calculus is sound and complete for $\mathcal{CSL}$ over symmetric minspaces; moreover, it always terminates under the above restricions, without assuming any futher constraint on rule application strategy.

2   The Theorem Prover $\mathcal{CSym\mathcal{L}}$ean

In this section we describe $\mathcal{CSym\mathcal{L}}$ean, a Prolog implementation[2] of the calculus $\mathbf{TCSL_s}$. The theorem prover is implemented using SWI-Prolog. The main predicate, implementing the tableau calculus, is:

```
csl_lean_aux(Gamma, Labels, OldCCS, PrefRel, NPrefRel)
```

which succeeds if and only if Γ is unsatisifable, where the tableau set Γ is partitioned into the Prolog lists Gamma, PrefRel and NPrefRel. Gamma is a list containing, for each label x occurring in a tableau set, a pair [X,Formulas] where Formulas is the list of *all* formulas F such that $x : F \in \Gamma$. In other words, formulas of each node are grouped by the labels. Labels are represented by Prolog's constants. The argument Labels is the list of labels introduced in the current tableau set. It has to be noted that this list is sorted (by construction) in anti-chronological order. The predicate NewLabel is called by the dynamic rules to create a new label, which will be added to the head of the list. OldCCS is a list of pairs [X,A], where X is a label and A is a formula, used by dynamic rules to check wether a label with $f(x, A)$ already exists in the tableau set. The lists PrefRel and NPrefRel contain lists [x,y,z,u], representing formulas of the form $\{x, y\} < \{z, u\}$ and $\{x, y\} \leq \{z, u\}$ respectively. To add a preferential relation, we call the predicate addPrefRel(X,Y,Z,U,Prel,NewPrel) which is defined as follows:

```
addPrefRel(X,Y,Z,U,PRel,NPrel) :-
        ordLabel(X,Y,X1,Y1),
        ordLabel(Z,U,Z1,U1),
        union([[X1,Y1,Z1,U1]],PRel,NPrel).
ordLabel(X,Y,Y,X) :- Y @< X, !.
ordLabel(X,Y,X,Y) :-.
```

Each pair of label is sorted according to the Prolog ordering of terms to encode the fact that $\{x, y\} = \{y, x\}$. Thus, addPrefRel(X,Y,Z,U,Prel,NewPrel) is equivalent to addPrefRel(Y,X,U,Z,Prel,NewPrel). As described in [3], we can

---

[2] The source files can be found at: http://www.lsis.org/alendar/csymlean/

adapt $\mathcal{CS}ym\mathcal{L}ean$ to the non symmetric case by deleting the first clause of the definition of `ordLabel`, so that the pairs will not be treated as symmetric.

As an example, to check whether $(A \Leftarrow B) \sqcap (B \Leftarrow A)$ is unsatisfiable, one queries $\mathcal{CS}ym\mathcal{L}ean$ with the goal:

```
csl_lean_aux([[x,(a<<-b) and (b<<-a)], [x], [], [], []).
```

Each clause of the predicate `csl_clean_aux` encodes a rule. Their structure is the same; each clause looks for a formula to which the corresponding rule could be applied, then it checks if one of the termination restrictions prevent applicability, and finally, the rule is applied. For instance, the clause which implements the $(F3 \Leftarrow)$ rules is:

```
csl_lean_aux(Gamma, Labels, OldCCS, PrefRel, NPrefRel) :-
        member([Z,ZFormulas],Gamma),
        member(f(X,B),ZFormulas),
        memberchk([X,XFormulas],Gamma),
        member(neg(A <<- B), XFormulas),
        member([Y,YFormulas],Gamma),
        memberchk(A,YFormulas),
        \+inPrel(X,Y,X,Z,NPrefRel),!,
        addPrefRel(X,Y,X,Z,NPrefRel,NewNPrefRel),
        csl_lean_aux(Gamma, Labels, OldCCS, PrefRel, NewNPrefRel).
```

The centering rule is not implemented by a `csl_lean_aux` clause and is handled differently: when a dynamic rule needs to introduce a new label, it calls the predicate `csl_lean_cent`. Intuitively, this predicate corresponds to an eager application of the centering rule, just after the introduction of a new label.

Before applying a dynamic rule, we have to check whether its application is blocked by subset blocking. This is implemented by the predicate `subsetBlocked(X,Gamma,LabelList)`, where X is a label, which succeeds if there exists a label Y older than X such that $\Pi_\Gamma(X) \subseteq \Pi_\Gamma(Y)$. For instance, here is the clause implementing the $(T2 \Leftarrow)$ rule:

```
csl_lean_aux(Gamma, Labels, OldCCS, PrefRel, NPrefRel):-
        member([X,XFormulas],Gamma),
        member(A <<- _, XFormulas),
        \+memberchk([X,A], OldCCS),
        \+subsetBlocked(X,Gamma,Labels),!,
        csl_lean_cent([A, f(X,A)],Labels,Gamma, Labels,
                      [[X,A]|OldCCS], PrefRel, NPrefRel).
```

If no rule is applicable (i.e: the tableau set is finished), we have to check whether we have found a bad set. This is implemented by the last clause of `csl_lean_aux`, which suceeds (and thus closes the branch) if there is a label in the tableau set which is blocked by subset blocking.

```
csl_lean_aux(Gamma, Labels, _, _, _) :- isBadSet(Gamma,Labels).
isBadSet(Gamma,[X|Lab]) :- subsetBlocked(X,Gamma,[X|Lab]), !.
isBadSet(Gamma,[_|Lab]) :- isBadSet(Gamma,Lab).
```

Statistics and Performance

We have tested $\mathcal{CS}$ym$\mathcal{L}$ean over randomly generated formulas (valid, unsatisfiable and satisfiable) on an Intel Core 2 Quad @ 2.0Ghz machine (4GB RAM) with SWI Prolog 5.8.0 (32-bits version). The test samples have been generated by fixing two parameters:

- the number of propositional variables involved in the generated formulas;
- the *depth* of connectives, i.e. the maximum level of nesting of connectives in the generated formulas. This corresponds to the depth of the formula tree.

We consider two other theorem provers: $\mathcal{CS}$ym$\mathcal{L}$ean-NoSym is the non-symmetric version of $\mathcal{CS}$ym$\mathcal{L}$ean, and CslLean 1.0 is an implementation of another tableau calculus for the non symmetric case [2,1]. The table below shows the number of proofs successfully completed (with either a positive or a negative answer) with respect to a 1s time limit. The first column shows the two parameters taken into account in generating test formulas mentioned above, namely the number of propositional variables and the depth of the formulas. For each row, we have considered 1000 test samples.

Prop. vars - Depth	$\mathcal{CS}$ym$\mathcal{L}$ean	$\mathcal{CS}$ym$\mathcal{L}$ean-NoSym	CslLean 1.0
2 - 2	1000	1000	998
2 - 4	965	969	937
3 - 4	966	967	941
5 - 7	568	573	652

We also tested it on a set of significant formulas including various instances of $\mathcal{CSL}$ axioms (the list is available on the web page), axioms from modal and conditional logics that can be translated in $\mathcal{CSL}$, and finally the following formula, which is unsatisfiable in symmetric minspaces whereas it is satisfiable in non-symmetric ones [4], which seems particularly hard[3]:

$$p \sqcap \Box(p \rightarrow (q \Leftarrow r)) \sqcap \Box(q \rightarrow (r \Leftarrow p)) \sqcap \Box(r \rightarrow (p \Leftarrow q)).$$

3   Conclusion and Further Work

We have presented $\mathcal{CS}$ym$\mathcal{L}$ean, the first theorem prover for $\mathcal{CSL}$ over symmetric minspaces, based on a recently proposed tableau calculus for this logic. Although it does not comprise any optimization, its performances are encouraging. Of course many optimizations are possible, either based on refinements of the calculus itself (logical restrictions on the rules), or on a more efficient handling of data structures and rule application. We intend to experiment both.

References

1. Alenda, R., Olivetti, N., Pozzato, G.L.: Csl-lean: A theorem-prover for the logic of comparative concept similarity. In: Proc. M4M-6. ENTCS, vol. 262, pp. 3–16 (2010)
2. Alenda, R., Olivetti, N., Schwind, C.: Comparative concept similarity over minspaces: Axiomatisation and tableaux calculus. In: Giese, M., Waaler, A. (eds.) TABLEAUX 2009. LNCS, vol. 5607, pp. 17–31. Springer, Heidelberg (2009)

---

[3] It took 3.8 seconds for $\mathcal{CS}$ym$\mathcal{L}$ean to prove its unsatisfiability.

3. Alenda, R., Olivetti, N., Schwind, C., Tishkovsky, D.: Tableau calculi for CSL over minspaces. In: Dawar, A., Veith, H. (eds.) CSL 2010. LNCS, vol. 6247, pp. 52–66. Springer, Heidelberg (2010)
4. Sheremet, M., Tishkovsky, D., Wolter, F., Zakharyaschev, M.: Comparative similarity, tree automata, and diophantine equations. In: Sutcliffe, G., Voronkov, A. (eds.) LPAR 2005. LNCS (LNAI), vol. 3835, pp. 651–665. Springer, Heidelberg (2005)
5. Sheremet, M., Wolter, F., Zakharyaschev, M.: A modal logic framework for reasoning about comparative distances and topology. Annals of Pure and Applied Logic 161(4), 534–559 (2010)

Schemata of SMT-Problems[*]

Vincent Aravantinos and Nicolas Peltier

Laboratoire d'Informatique de Grenoble/CNRS
{Vincent.Aravantinos,Nicolas.Peltier}@imag.fr

Abstract. A logic is devised for reasoning about iterated schemata of SMT problems. The satisfiability problem is shown to be undecidable for this logic, but we present a proof procedure that is sound, complete w.r.t. satisfiability and terminating for a precisely characterized class of problems. It is parameterized by an external procedure (used as a black box) for testing the satisfiability of ground instances of the schema in the considered theory (e.g. integers, reals etc.).

1 Introduction

In [1] a logic is defined for reasoning on schemata of propositional formulae. It extends standard propositional logic by using *indexed symbols* (e.g. p_0, p_i, p_{i+1}, etc.), *arithmetic parameters* (i.e. constant symbols interpreted as natural numbers) and *iterated connectives* such as $\bigvee_{i=0}^{n} p_i$ or $\bigwedge_{i=0}^{n} p_i$ (where n denotes a *parameter*, not a fixed number) that can be viewed as formulae with bounded quantifiers $\exists i \in [0, n], p_i$ and $\forall i \in [0, n], p_i$. It is shown that the validity problem is undecidable when arbitrary indices and (linear) arithmetic expressions are considered. The problem is co-semi-decidable and decision procedures of "reasonable" complexity can be defined for some interesting classes (see [2] for details). A simple example is the following schema: $p_0 \wedge p_{n+1} \wedge \bigwedge_{i=0}^{n}(p_i \Leftrightarrow \neg p_{i+1})$, that is satisfiable if and only if n is odd. This formula can be reduced into a propositional one by fixing the value of n, e.g. for $n \leftarrow 0$: $p_0 \wedge p_1 \wedge (p_0 \Leftrightarrow \neg p_1)$, or for $n \leftarrow 1$: $p_0 \wedge p_2 \wedge (p_0 \Leftrightarrow \neg p_1) \wedge (p_1 \Leftrightarrow \neg p_2)$. A SAT-solver can determine whether the formula is satisfiable or unsatisfiable for a given value of n and a model can be found (if it exists) by enumerating all possible values ($n \leftarrow 0, 1, 2, \dots$). However, proving that such a formula is unsatisfiable *for all values of* n (which is the case for instance if one adds the constraint $n = 2 \times m$) is much more difficult, and usually requires to use some particular form of mathematical induction. The proof procedure described in [1] combines usual tableaux-based decomposition rules with lazy instantiation of the parameter and a loop detection mechanism that captures a restricted form of "descente infinie" induction reasoning ensuring completeness in some cases.

Our aim in this paper is to extend these results to schemata of (quantifier-free) SMT-problems (standing for **S**atisfiability **M**odulo **T**heory). Proving the unsatisfiability (or satisfiability) of a ground formula modulo some background theory

[*] This work has been partly funded by the project ASAP of the French *Agence Nationale de la Recherche* (ANR-09-BLAN-0407-01).

K. Brünnler and G. Metcalfe (Eds.): TABLEAUX 2011, LNAI 6793, pp. 27–42, 2011.

is an essential problem in computer science, in particular for the automatic verification of complex systems. In software verification for example, the background theory can define data structures such as integers, arrays or lists. These problems are known as $\mathcal{T}$-*decision problems* or more commonly, *SMT problems*, and the tools capable of solving these problems are known as $\mathcal{T}$-*decision procedures*, or *SMT solvers*. A lot of research has been devoted to the design of SMT solvers that are both efficient and scalable. A survey can be found in [3].

The schemata we consider in this paper may be seen as (countably infinite) families of SMT-problems, parameterized by a natural number n. Both the signature of problems and the set of axioms may depend on n. Consider for instance the following formula, representative of those arising in, e.g, verifying programs handling arrays: $\bigwedge_{i=0}^{n} a_{i+1} \succeq a_i \wedge \bigwedge_{i=0}^{n} b_{i+1} \preceq b_i \wedge a_0 \succeq b_0 \wedge a_{n+1} \preceq c \wedge b_{n+1} \succ c$. It is not hard to see that this example is unsatisfiable. Again, by instantiating n, say to 1, we get a ground formula: $a_1 \succeq a_0 \wedge a_2 \succeq a_1 \wedge b_1 \preceq b_0 \wedge b_2 \preceq b_1 \wedge a_0 \succeq b_0 \wedge a_2 \preceq c \wedge b_2 \succ c$. The satisfiability of this formula modulo, e.g., arithmetic can be tested by any SMT-solver. However proving that the original schema is unsatisfiable *for every* $n \in \mathbb{N}$ is out of the scope of these tools. One can of course encode such a schema as a *non-ground* (i.e. with universal quantifier) SMT-problem, simply by considering n as a constant symbol of sort integer, by writing indices as arguments, and by replacing iterated connectives by quantifiers:

$$\forall i, 0 \preceq i \wedge i \preceq n \Rightarrow a(i+1) \succeq a(i)$$
$$\wedge \quad \forall i, 0 \preceq i \wedge i \preceq n \Rightarrow b(i+1) \preceq b(i)$$
$$\wedge \, a(0) \succeq b(0) \wedge a(n+1) \preceq c \wedge b(n+1) \succ c$$

However, this is of no practical use since of course there is no complete and terminating procedure for solving non-ground SMT-problem. The heuristics that are used by SMT-solvers to handle quantifiers, although rather efficient and powerful in some cases, cannot handle such formulae. For instance the well-known SMT-solver Yices [6] that uses E-matching [5] for instantiating universally quantified variables fails to establish the unsatisfiability of this schema. Some complete techniques have been proposed for instantiating universal quantifiers [7] but they do not terminate in our case. Alternatively, indexed constant symbols can be modeled by arrays (with quantifiers on the indices), however the obtained formulae are again outside the known decidable classes [4]. The reason is that the formulae obtained by encoding schemata of SMT-problems cannot, in general, be reduced to unsatisfiable ground formulae by *finitely* grounding the universally quantified variables: the logic is not compact and using mathematical induction is required. Our approach extends SMT-solvers with a limited form of mathematical induction.

2   Preliminaries

We define the logic of $\mathcal{T}$-*schemata*, where $\mathcal{T}$ is a theory (more precisely a class of interpretations) for which the satisfiability problem is assumed to be decidable.

2.1   Syntax

We consider terms built on a signature containing indexed constants and function symbols, where the indices are arithmetic expressions. We assume that the symbols are indexed by at most one index (e.g. $a_{i,j}$ is forbidden) and that the expressions contain at most one occurrence of an arithmetic variable (e.g. a_{i+j} and even a_{i+i} are not allowed, but $f_{i+1}(a_i)$ and $f_0(a_i)$ are)[1]. We also assume that the considered formulae contain a unique parameter, which is interpreted by a natural number. More formally:

Let n and i be two distinct symbols. n is the *parameter* and i is the *index variable*. The set of *index expressions* is $\{i, i+1\} \cup \{succ^k(0) \mid k \in \mathbb{N}\} \cup \{succ^k(n) \mid k \in \mathbb{N}\}$. As usual, the expressions $succ^k(0)$ and $succ^k(n)$ (where $k \in \mathbb{N}$) are written k and $n + k$ respectively.

Let Sorts denote a set of *sort symbols* (containing in particular a symbol bool) and let $\mathcal{F}$ denote a set of *function symbols*, partitioned into two disjoint sets $\mathcal{F} = \mathcal{F}_I \uplus \mathcal{F}_{NI}$: the *indexed symbols* $\mathcal{F}_I$ and the *non-indexed symbols* $\mathcal{F}_{NI}$. Each symbol $f \in \mathcal{F}$ is mapped to a unique *profile* of the form $s_1, \ldots, s_k \to s$, where $k \in \mathbb{N}$ and $s_1, \ldots, s_k, s \in$ Sorts. This is written $f : s_1, \ldots, s_k \to s$ or simply $f : s$ if $k = 0$ (in this case f is a *constant*). If $s =$ bool then f is a *predicate symbol*. We call k the *arity* of f. We assume that $\mathcal{F}_{NI}$ contains in particular a symbol true : bool.

The set $T(s)$ of *terms of sort* s is the smallest set of expressions satisfying the following conditions:

- If $f : s_1, \ldots, s_k \to s$ is a non-indexed function symbol and if $u_1, \ldots, u_k$ are terms of sort $s_1, \ldots, s_k$ respectively, then $f(u_1, \ldots, u_k)$ is a term of sort s.
- If $f : s_1, \ldots, s_k \to s$ is an indexed function symbol, if α is an index expression and if $u_1, \ldots, u_k$ are terms of sort $s_1, \ldots, s_k$ respectively, then $f_\alpha(u_1, \ldots, u_k)$ is a term of sort s.

Note that, by construction, the only variable occurring in a term is i (there are no non-arithmetic variables).

For instance, if $\mathcal{F}_I = \{a : \text{elem}, f : \text{elem}, \text{elem} \to \text{elem}\}$ and $\mathcal{F}_{NI} = \{b : \text{elem}, p : \text{elem} \to \text{bool}\}$ then $a_0, a_n, a_{i+1}, f_{n+2}(a_0, b), f_0(a_{i+1}, a_3)$ are terms of sort elem and $p(a_{i+1})$ is a term of sort bool. Terms such as a_{i+2}, a_{i+n} are not allowed (indeed, $i + 2$ and $i + n$ are not index expressions).

Now we define the syntax of formulae. For technical convenience, we assume that all formulae are in negative normal form. An *atom* is of the form $u \approx v$, where u and v are two terms of the same sort. An atom of the form $u \approx$ true is *non-equational*. A *literal* is of the form $u \approx v$ or $u \not\approx v$. For readability a literal $u \approx$ true or $u \not\approx$ true is simply written u or $\neg u$; false is a shorthand for $\neg$true.

An *iteration body* is inductively defined as either a literal *not containing* n or a formula of the form $\phi \vee \psi$ or $\phi \wedge \psi$ where ϕ and ψ are iteration bodies. Finally, a *schema* is inductively defined as follows:

---

[1] Removing these conditions yields undecidable logics, even in the purely propositional case [1,2], thus we prefer to add them immediately rather than defining a very general formalism that will have to be strongly restricted at a later stage (as done in [1]).

- A literal *not containing* i is a schema.
- If ϕ and ψ are schemata then $\phi \vee \psi$ and $\phi \wedge \psi$ are schemata.
- If ϕ is an iteration body containing i and α is an index expression of the form k or $\mathbf{n} + k$ (where $k \in \mathbb{N}$) then $\bigvee_{i=0}^{\alpha} \phi$ and $\bigwedge_{i=0}^{\alpha} \phi$ are schemata.

For readability, we will sometimes use the abbreviation $u \approx v \Rightarrow \psi$ (resp. $u \not\approx v \Rightarrow \psi$) for $u \not\approx v \vee \psi$ (resp. $u \approx v \vee \psi$).

$\mathfrak{S}$ denotes the set of all schemata. A schema is *iteration-free* iff it contains no iterated connective $\bigvee$ or $\bigwedge$ and *parameter-free* if it contains no occurrence of n. A *sentence* is a schema that is both iteration-free and parameter-free. Such a schema may be viewed as a standard (quantifier-free) formula in the usual sense (with function symbols indexed by natural numbers), but we prefer not to use the word "formula" to avoid confusions.

For instance $\phi_1 : \bigvee_{i=0}^{n} (a_{i+1} \approx f(b_i) \wedge b_{i+1} \approx g(a_i))$, $\phi_2 : a_{n+1} \approx f(b_n) \wedge b_{n+1} \approx g(a_n)$, $\phi_3 : \bigvee_{i=0}^{3} (a_{i+1} \approx f(b_i) \wedge b_{i+1} \approx g(a_i))$ and $\phi_4 : a_1 \approx f(b_0) \wedge b_1 \approx g(a_0)$ are schemata. ϕ_2 and ϕ_4 are iteration-free, ϕ_3 and ϕ_4 are parameter-free and ϕ_4 is a sentence.

An *expression* may be a term, a vector of terms, an iteration body or a schema. It is *ground* if it contains no occurrence of i (notice that it *may contain* the parameter n) and *non-indexed* if it contains no indexed symbols (by definition all non-indexed expressions are ground).

Let α be a ground index expression. If ϕ is an iteration body then $\phi\{i \leftarrow \alpha\}$ denotes the iteration-free schema obtained from ϕ by replacing all occurrences of i by α. If ϕ is a schema or an index expression, then $\phi\{n \leftarrow \alpha\}$ is the schema or index expression obtained from ϕ by replacing all occurrences of n by α.

If ϕ is an iteration-free schema or an iteration body, we denote by $Ind(\phi)$ the set of index expressions occurring in ϕ: $Ind(u_\alpha) \stackrel{\text{def}}{=} \{\alpha\}$, $Ind(u \approx v) = Ind(u \not\approx v) = Ind(u) \cup Ind(v)$, $Ind(\phi \star \psi) \stackrel{\text{def}}{=} Ind(\phi) \cup Ind(\psi)$ if $\star \in \{\vee, \wedge\}$.

2.2 Semantics

The semantics is straightforwardly defined. The only difference with first-order logic is that the parameter must be interpreted by a natural number and that the index variable ranges over $\mathbb{N}$. More precisely, a *schema interpretation* (or *interpretation* for short) I is a function mapping n to a natural number $\langle n \rangle^I$, mapping each sort $s \in \mathsf{Sorts}$ to a non-empty set $\langle s \rangle^I$, mapping each non-indexed function symbol $f : s_1, \ldots, s_k \to s$ to a function $\langle f \rangle^I : \langle s_1 \rangle^I, \ldots, \langle s_k \rangle^I \to \langle s \rangle^I$ and mapping each indexed function symbol $f : s_1, \ldots, s_k \to s$ to a family of functions $\langle f \rangle_l^I : \langle s_1 \rangle^I, \ldots, \langle s_k \rangle^I \to \langle s \rangle^I$ (where $l \in \mathbb{N}$). The function $x \mapsto \langle x \rangle^I$ is then extended to any *ground* term or atom and to any schema as follows:

- If α is an index expression, then $\langle \alpha \rangle^I \stackrel{\text{def}}{=} \alpha\{n \leftarrow \langle n \rangle^I\}$. Notice that $\langle \alpha \rangle^I$ is then equivalent to a natural number.
- $\langle f(v_1, \ldots, v_k) \rangle^I \stackrel{\text{def}}{=} \langle f \rangle^I (\langle v_1 \rangle^I, \ldots, \langle v_k \rangle^I)$.
- $\langle f_\alpha(v_1, \ldots, v_k) \rangle^I \stackrel{\text{def}}{=} \langle f \rangle_{\langle \alpha \rangle^I}^I (\langle v_1 \rangle^I, \ldots, \langle v_k \rangle^I)$.
- $\langle \bigvee_{i=0}^{\alpha} \phi \rangle^I \stackrel{\text{def}}{=} \mathbf{true}$ if there exists $l \in [0, \langle \alpha \rangle^I]$ such that $\langle \phi\{i \leftarrow l\} \rangle^I = \mathbf{true}$.

- $\langle \bigwedge_{i=0}^{\alpha} \phi \rangle^I \overset{\text{def}}{=} \textbf{true}$ if for all $l \in [0, \langle \alpha \rangle^I]$ we have $\langle \phi\{i \leftarrow l\} \rangle^I = \textbf{true}$.

We omit the definitions for the symbols $\approx, \not\approx, \vee, \wedge$, which are standard. If ϕ is a schema, we write $I \models \phi$ iff $\langle \phi \rangle^I = \textbf{true}$. In this case, I is a *model* of ϕ and ϕ is *satisfiable*.

Usually, satisfiability is tested w.r.t. a particular class of interpretations, in which the semantics of some of the symbols is fixed (for instance the sort symbol `int` is interpreted as $\mathbb{Z}$ and $+$ is interpreted as the addition). Let $\mathcal{T}$ be a class of interpretations. ϕ is $\mathcal{T}$-*satisfiable* iff there exists $I \in \mathcal{T}$ such that $I \models \phi$. Two schemata ϕ and ψ are $\mathcal{T}$-*equivalent* iff we have $I \models \phi \Leftrightarrow I \models \psi$ for every interpretation $I \in \mathcal{T}$ and $\mathcal{T}$-*sat-equivalent* iff ϕ and ψ are both $\mathcal{T}$-satisfiable or both $\mathcal{T}$-unsatisfiable. We assume that there exists an algorithm for checking whether a given sentence (i.e. a schema without iterated connective and without parameter) is $\mathcal{T}$-satisfiable or not.

A function f is *non-built-in* if its interpretation is arbitrary, i.e. for every interpretation $I \in \mathcal{T}$, the interpretation obtained from I by changing only the interpretation of f is also in $\mathcal{T}$. We assume that every indexed symbol is non-built-in (i.e. the only symbols whose interpretation is fixed are non-indexed).

Note that if I is an interpretation and α is a ground expression, then by definition $I \circ \{n \mapsto \alpha\}$ is also an interpretation. $I \circ \{n \mapsto \alpha\}$ and I coincide on every symbol, except on n. If $\alpha \in \mathbb{N}$ then $\langle n \rangle^{I \circ \{n \mapsto \alpha\}} = \alpha$ and otherwise $\langle n \rangle^{I \circ \{n \mapsto \alpha\}} = \langle \alpha \rangle^I$.

There exists an algorithm transforming every parameter-free schema ϕ into a sentence that is $\mathcal{T}$-equivalent to ϕ. Thus the $\mathcal{T}$-satisfiability problem is decidable for parameter-free schemata.

As usual in SMT problems, we shall assume that the schemata are *flattened*, i.e. for every term of the form $f(u_1, \ldots, u_k)$ occurring in the schema (where f is possibly indexed) $u_1, \ldots, u_k$ are (possibly indexed) constant symbols (this ensures that the set of terms is finite). This is not restrictive, for instance a term of the form $f(g(a_i), g_{i+1}(a_0))$ can be replaced by $f(b_i, c_i)$, where the axioms $\bigwedge_{i=0}^{n} b_i \approx g(a_i)$ and $\bigwedge_{i=0}^{n} c_i \approx g_{i+1}(a_0)$ are added to the schema.

2.3   Extensions of the Language

Several extensions of this basic language can be considered. We did not include them in the previous definitions because they do not increase the expressive power, but for readability we shall sometimes use them in the following.

- **Inequality tests.** Atoms of the form $i \leq k$ (where $k \in \mathbb{N}$) can be added in iteration bodies. This does not increase the expressive power since such atoms can be equivalently replaced by atoms of the form $p_i^{\leq k}$, where $p^{\leq k}$ is a fresh constant symbol of sort `bool` (depending on k), defined by the following axioms: $p_0^{\leq k} \wedge \cdots \wedge p_k^{\leq k} \wedge \neg p_{k+1}^{\leq k} \wedge \bigwedge_{i=0}^{n}(p_{i+1}^{\leq k} \Rightarrow p_i^{\leq k})$.
- **Arbitrary lower bounds.** Iterations whose lower bound is distinct from 0 can easily be expressed using the previous atoms: $\bigwedge_{i=k}^{n} \phi$ is written $\bigwedge_{i=0}^{n}(i \leq k - 1 \vee \phi)$ (if $k > 0$).

- **Arbitrary translations.** Terms of the form a_{i+k} can also be considered, where $k > 1$. Indeed, such a term can be replaced by a fresh constant symbol a_i^{+k}, where a^{+k} is defined by the following axioms: $\bigwedge_{i=0}^{n+k} \left(a_i^{+0} \approx a_i \wedge a_i^{+1} \approx a_{i+1}^{+0} \wedge \cdots \wedge a_i^{+k} \approx a_{i+1}^{+k-1} \right)$.
- **Additional parameters.** Inequalities of the form $i \leq m$ where m is an additional parameter interpreted as an element of $[0, n]$ can be encoded by atoms $p_i^{\leq m}$ defined by the following axioms: $\neg p_{n+1}^{\leq m} \wedge p_0^{\leq m} \wedge \bigwedge_{i=0}^{n} (p_{i+1}^{\leq m} \Rightarrow p_i^{\leq m})$. Then $i \approx m$ can be defined using $\bigwedge_{i=0}^{n} (p_i^{=m} \Leftrightarrow p_i^{\leq m} \wedge \neg p_{i+1}^{\leq m})$ and a disequality $m \not\approx k$ can be tested by the schema: $\bigwedge_{i=0}^{n} (\neg p_i^{=m} \vee \neg p_i^{=k})$.
- **Using the parameter in iteration bodies.** A term of the form a_n can be replaced by a fresh non-indexed constant b, with the axiom: $b \approx a_n$.

In all the previous definitions, we assumed that the defined indexed symbols are used only in the range $[0, n]$. If it is not the case (for instance if an equality test $i \leq k$ appears in the scope of an iteration $\bigvee_{i=1}^{n+2}$) then the definitions should be extended accordingly (we omit the details for conciseness).

2.4   Undecidability

The next theorem states that the considered logic is undecidable in general.

Theorem 1. *The satisfiability problem is undecidable for $\mathfrak{S}$.*

This result does *not* follow from the undecidability results in [1] or [2] (for propositional schemata) because the schemata considered here are much more restricted. The satisfiability problem is actually decidable if we restrict to propositional formulae (see Section 4.1). Intuitively, even though the language is sufficiently restricted to obtain decidability in the non-equational case, the equational part of the language adds enough power to "retrieve" the undecidability. This shows that the extension of schemata to SMT-problems is a difficult task.

3   Proof Procedure

We define a proof procedure for testing the satisfiability of schemata that is sound and complete w.r.t. satisfiability. We show that, under some particular *semantic* conditions (depending both on the theory $\mathcal{T}$ and on the considered class of schemata), this procedure can be turned into a decision procedure.

3.1   Enumerating Interpretations

We first define a semi-decision procedure for schemata. It is parameterized by a *simplification function* which is a function replacing a schema by a set of schemata (interpreted as a disjunction) in such a way that satisfiability is preserved.

Definition 1. *Let ϕ be a schema and let Ψ be a set of schemata. We write $\phi \leadsto \Psi$ iff the following conditions hold:*

1. *For every $I \in \mathcal{T}$, if $I \models \phi$ then there exists $\psi \in \Psi$ such that $I \models \psi$.*
2. *For every $I \in \mathcal{T}$, if there exists $\psi \in \Psi$ such that $I \models \psi$ then there exists an interpretation $J \in \mathcal{T}$ such that $J \models \phi$ and $\langle \mathbf{n} \rangle^J = \langle \mathbf{n} \rangle^I$.*

For instance, we have $\phi \vee \psi \rightsquigarrow \{\phi, \psi\}$, $(\phi \vee \phi') \wedge \psi \rightsquigarrow \{\phi \wedge \psi, \phi' \wedge \psi\}$, or $p_0 \wedge \phi \rightsquigarrow \{\phi\}$ if the indexed predicate symbol p does not occur in ϕ. We also have $\bigvee_{i=0}^{n+1} \phi \rightsquigarrow \{\bigvee_{i=0}^{n} \phi, \phi\{i \leftarrow n+1\}\}$. However we have $\neg p_0 \wedge p_n \not\rightsquigarrow \{\text{true}\}$ or $\neg p_0 \wedge \bigvee_{i=0}^{n} p_i \not\rightsquigarrow \{\text{true}\}$ (although $\neg p_0 \wedge p_n$, $\neg p_0 \wedge \bigvee_{i=0}^{n} p_i$ and true are $\mathcal{T}$-sat-equivalent). Notice that if $\phi \rightsquigarrow \Psi$ then ϕ is $\mathcal{T}$-sat-equivalent to the disjunction of the schemata in Ψ. Furthermore, if ϕ and the disjunction of the schemata in Ψ are equivalent then obviously $\phi \rightsquigarrow \Psi$.

Definition 2. *A simplification function is a total function $\Gamma : \mathfrak{S} \to 2^{\mathfrak{S}}$ such that for every $\phi \in \mathfrak{S}$, $\phi \rightsquigarrow \Gamma(\phi)$.*

As explained in the Introduction, a trivial way to construct a model of a schema ϕ (if it exists) is to enumerate all the possible values for $\mathbf{n}$ and then test the $\mathcal{T}$-satisfiability of the obtained sentences. Definition 3 formalizes this idea in a way that will be convenient for our purpose. We enumerate all possible instances of ϕ by instantiating recursively $\mathbf{n}$ by $\mathbf{n}+1$. A given simplification function Γ is systematically applied to the instantiated schemata:

Definition 3. *Let Γ be a simplification function. The Γ-expansion of a schema $\phi \in \mathfrak{S}$ is the set of schemata $\mathcal{E}_{\Gamma}(\phi)$ inductively built as follows:*

1. *$\phi \in \mathcal{E}_{\Gamma}(\phi)$.*
2. *If $\psi \in \mathcal{E}_{\Gamma}(\phi)$ then $\Gamma(\psi\{\mathbf{n} \leftarrow \mathbf{n}+1\}) \subseteq \mathcal{E}_{\Gamma}(\phi)$.*

Theorem 2. *Let Γ be a simplification function. A schema ϕ is $\mathcal{T}$-satisfiable iff $\mathcal{E}_{\Gamma}(\phi)$ contains a schema ψ such that $\psi\{\mathbf{n} \leftarrow 0\}$ is $\mathcal{T}$-satisfiable.*

Theorem 2 implies that $\mathcal{T}$-satisfiability is semi-decidable for schemata in $\mathfrak{S}$. Indeed, to test whether $\phi \in \mathfrak{S}$ is $\mathcal{T}$-satisfiable, it suffices to construct the Γ-expansion $\mathcal{E}_{\Gamma}(\phi)$ of ϕ (using a straightforward simplification function, e.g. $\Gamma(\phi) = \{\phi\}$). By Definition 3, $\mathcal{E}_{\Gamma}(\phi)$ is recursively enumerable. By Theorem 2, ϕ is $\mathcal{T}$-satisfiable iff a schema ψ such that $\psi\{\mathbf{n} \leftarrow 0\}$ is $\mathcal{T}$-satisfiable is eventually obtained. The satisfiability of $\psi\{\mathbf{n} \leftarrow 0\}$ is obviously decidable. Of course, as such, this algorithm is very inefficient and seldom terminates (when the schema at hand is unsatisfiable): its efficiency and termination essentially depend on the choice of the simplification function.

The next definition states a condition on Γ ensuring that all the schemata in $\mathcal{E}_{\Gamma}(\phi)$ remain in a given class.

Definition 4. *Let $\mathcal{C}$ be a class of schemata. A simplification function Γ is $\mathcal{C}$-preserving iff $\phi \in \mathcal{C} \Rightarrow \Gamma(\phi\{\mathbf{n} \leftarrow \mathbf{n}+1\}) \subseteq \mathcal{C}$.*

Obviously, if $\mathcal{C}$ be a class of schemata and Γ is a $\mathcal{C}$-preserving simplification function, then $\phi \in \mathcal{C} \Rightarrow \mathcal{E}_{\Gamma}(\phi) \subseteq \mathcal{C}$.

Many distinct semi-decision procedures can be obtained, simply by replacing the simplification function Γ by concrete procedures. In the next section, we define a simplification function that ensures termination.

3.2   Termination

The intuitive idea is the following: the Γ-expansion of a given schema ϕ is infinite in general, since the recursive replacement of n by $n+1$ creates schemata with increasingly deep index expressions. For instance from $\bigwedge_{i=0}^{n}(p_i \Rightarrow p_{i+1})$ one gets $\bigwedge_{i=0}^{n+1}(p_i \Rightarrow p_{i+1})$, $\bigwedge_{i=0}^{n+2}(p_i \Rightarrow p_{i+1})$, ... A first step towards termination would be to have the iteration $\bigwedge_{i=0}^{n}(p_i \Rightarrow p_{i+1})$ instead of this infinite set of iterations. This is easily obtained by *unfolding* the previous iterations (i.e. taking out the ranks $n+1$, $n+2$, etc.). However we are of course left with the new formulae introduced by those unfoldings. For instance, in the same example, one would get $p_{n+1} \Rightarrow p_{n+2}$, $p_{n+2} \Rightarrow p_{n+3}$, etc. One way to obtain termination is if we are able to somehow simplify those new formulae (of course this simplification depends on the considered theory $\mathcal{T}$) so that they belong to a finite set. This goal can be reached, in particular, if the indices of the involved atoms are restricted to be lower than $n+k$ for some fixed $k \in \mathbb{N}$. It is actually sufficient to consider $k=1$, which leads to the following notion:

Definition 5. *A schema is* n-elementary *if it contains no index of the form* $n+k$ *where* $k>1$.

The major problem is, of course, to transform the schemata into n-elementary ones (preserving $\mathcal{T}$-sat-equivalence). This may be done, *in some particular cases*, by using decomposition and simplification rules. In the previous example, the unfolding yields: $\bigwedge_{i=0}^{n}(p_i \Rightarrow p_{i+1}) \wedge (p_{n+1} \Rightarrow p_{n+2})$. Then, in order to eliminate all the indices greater than $n+1$, we only have to eliminate p_{n+2}, which can be done in this simple case by considering all the possible values for p_{n+2} (**true** or **false**). This yields the disjunction of the following schemata: $\bigwedge_{i=0}^{n}(p_i \Rightarrow p_{i+1}) \wedge \neg p_{n+1}$ (if p_{n+2} is false) and $\bigwedge_{i=0}^{n}(p_i \Rightarrow p_{i+1})$ (if p_{n+2} is true).

Of course this case is an easy one, since the domain of the constant symbols is finite (thus every constant can be eliminated, if needed, by instantiation). But consider the case: $\bigwedge_{i=0}^{n+1}(a_i \approx f(a_{i+1}))$. Here the unfolding yields the literal $a_{n+1} \approx f(a_{n+2})$. Since the domain is, a priori, not finite, the same technique cannot apply. Thus the ability to eliminate a_{n+2} depends on the theory $\mathcal{T}$: if, for instance, f is the successor function on $\mathbb{N}$ then it suffices to state that $a_{n+1} \succ 0$.

To ensure that non-n-elementary literals can always be eliminated, we will have to impose additional conditions on the class of interpretations $\mathcal{T}$ and on the considered schemata. To restrict the class of schemata we shall actually impose conditions on the literals occurring in it:

Definition 6. *A frame* $\mathfrak{L}$ *is a finite set of literals such that for every* $\lambda \in \mathfrak{L}$, *the two following conditions hold:*

1. $\lambda\{i \leftarrow n+1\} \in \mathfrak{L}$.
2. *If* λ *is* n-elementary *then* $\lambda\{n \leftarrow n+1\} \in \mathfrak{L}$.

A schema ϕ *is* $\mathfrak{L}$-dominated *if every literal occurring in* ϕ *(both in iteration bodies and outside iterations) is in* $\mathfrak{L}$.

Those conditions are useful to ensure that a class of n-elementary schemata is closed under replacement of n by $n + 1$ and unfolding of the iterations.

Example 1. The following set $\mathfrak{L}$ is a frame: $\{f(a_i) \approx b_i, f(a_i) \not\approx g(b_{i+1}), f(a_n) \approx b_n, f(a_n) \not\approx g(b_{n+1}), f(a_{n+1}) \approx b_{n+1}, f(a_{n+1}) \not\approx g(b_{n+2}), f(a_{n+2}) \approx b_{n+2}\}$. The literals $f(a_i) \approx b_i$, $f(a_i) \not\approx g(b_{i+1})$, $f(a_n) \approx b_n$, $f(a_n) \not\approx g(b_{n+1})$ and $f(a_{n+1}) \approx b_{n+1}$, are n-elementary, $f(a_{n+1}) \not\approx g(b_{n+2})$ and $f(a_{n+2}) \approx b_{n+2}$ are not.

$\phi : (\bigvee_{i=0}^{n} f(a_i) \approx b_i) \wedge f(a_n) \not\approx g(b_{n+1})$ and $\psi : (\bigwedge_{i=0}^{n} f(a_i) \not\approx g(b_{i+1})) \vee f(a_{n+2}) \approx b_{n+2}$ are $\mathfrak{L}$-dominated. ϕ is n-elementary, ψ is not.

The definition of the simplification function is divided into two steps: *unfolding* and *decomposition*.

Unfolding. The first step simply aims at unfolding iterations, for instance by replacing $\bigvee_{i=0}^{n+1} \phi$ by $\bigvee_{i=0}^{n} \phi \vee \phi\{i \leftarrow n + 1\}$. Obviously this is possible only if the lower bound of the iteration is strictly lower than the upper bound.

Definition 7. *If ϕ is a schema, we denote by $\mathrm{unfold}(\phi)$ the schema obtained from ϕ by replacing every subschema of the form $\bigwedge_{i=0}^{n+k} \psi$ or $\bigvee_{i=0}^{n+k} \psi$ occurring in ϕ such that $k > 0$ by (respectively): $(\bigwedge_{i=0}^{n} \psi) \wedge \psi\{i \leftarrow n+1\} \wedge \cdots \wedge \psi\{i \leftarrow n+k\}$ and $(\bigvee_{i=0}^{n} \psi) \vee \psi\{i \leftarrow n + 1\} \vee \cdots \vee \psi\{i \leftarrow n+k\}$.*

The unfolding transformation does not affect the semantics of the considered schema. It is useful only to extract (when possible) the last operands of the iterations in order to pave the way for the elimination of the terms with greatest indices, which is done in the next subsection.

Decomposing Schemata. The second step is more complex. It aims at eliminating, in a schema ϕ, all the symbols whose index is greater than $n + 1$. This is the crucial part of our procedure, since the elimination of those symbols will ensure that only finitely many distinct schemata can be generated, hence that $\mathcal{E}_\Gamma(\phi)$ is finite. We now introduce the conditions on $\mathfrak{L}$ and $\mathcal{T}$ that ensure that the elimination of literals whose indices are strictly greater than $n+1$ is feasible.

If I, J are two interpretations, we write $I \sim^{\mathfrak{L}} J$ iff I and J coincide on every literal obtained from a literal in $\mathfrak{L}$ by replacing i by a natural number lower or equal to n. More precisely, $I \sim^{\mathfrak{L}} J$ if I and J coincide on n and on every sort symbol in Sorts, and if for every literal $\lambda \in \mathfrak{L}$ containing i and for every $k \in [0, \langle n \rangle^I]$ we have $\langle \lambda\{i \leftarrow k\} \rangle^I = \langle \lambda\{i \leftarrow k\} \rangle^J$.

Definition 8. *A frame $\mathfrak{L}$ is stably decomposable, relatively to a function $\Delta : \mathfrak{S} \to \mathfrak{S}$, iff for all ground non-n-elementary literals $\lambda_1, \ldots, \lambda_k \in \mathfrak{L}$ the following conditions hold:*

- *$\Delta(\lambda_1 \wedge \cdots \wedge \lambda_k)$ is a boolean combination of ground n-elementary literals in $\mathfrak{L}$.*
- *For every interpretation I, $I \models \Delta(\lambda_1 \wedge \cdots \wedge \lambda_k)$ iff there exists an interpretation J such that $J \sim^{\mathfrak{L}} I$ and $J \models \lambda_1 \wedge \cdots \wedge \lambda_k$.*

In what follows, we assume the existence of a frame $\mathfrak{L}$ and of a function Δ s.t. $\mathfrak{L}$ is stably decomposable w.r.t. Δ. Both depend on the theory $\mathcal{T}$. Thus, applying our method to a theory $\mathcal{T}$ requires that $\mathcal{T}$ be accompanied with a frame $\mathfrak{L}$ and a function Δ (examples are provided in Section 4).

We now define the simplification function. It is defined by means of a tableaux calculus, using the usual propositional decomposition rules. These rules are restricted to apply only on non-n-elementary schemata. The goal is to decompose the schema in order to get rid of all non-n-elementary literals occurring at non-root level. Then a new rule is defined, the so-called *Elimination rule*, in order to eliminate non-n-elementary literals at root level, by taking advantage of the existence of a function Δ satisfying the conditions of Definition 8.

A *branch* is a conjunction of schemata and a *tableau* is a set of branches. As usual, tableaux are constructed using a set of *expansion rules* that are written in the form: $\dfrac{\mathcal{S}}{\mathcal{S}_1 \mid \ \cdots \ \mid \mathcal{S}_k}$ meaning that a branch that is of the form $\mathcal{S} \wedge \mathcal{S}'$ (up to the AC-properties of the connective $\wedge$) is deleted from the tableau and replaced by the k branches $\mathcal{S}_1 \wedge \mathcal{S}'$, ..., $\mathcal{S}_k \wedge \mathcal{S}'$. If $k = 0$ the rule simply deletes (or *closes*) the branch. This is written $\dfrac{\mathcal{S}}{\bot}$. Initially, the tableau contains only one branch, defined by the schema at hand. We denote by ρ the following set of expansion rules:

$\vee$-Elimination: $\dfrac{\phi \vee \psi}{\phi \mid \psi}$ If $\phi \vee \psi$ is not n-elementary.

Closure: $\dfrac{\phi \wedge \neg\phi}{\bot}$

Elimination: $\dfrac{\lambda_1 \wedge \cdots \wedge \lambda_k}{\Delta(\lambda_1 \wedge \cdots \wedge \lambda_k)}$ If $\{\lambda_1, \ldots, \lambda_k\} \subseteq \mathfrak{L}$ is the set of *all* the non-n-elementary literals occurring in the branch.

We do not need a specific rule for the connective $\wedge$ since branches are considered as conjunctions (thus the $\wedge$-rule is implicitly replaced by the associativity of $\wedge$). Note that there are no rules for the connectives $\bigvee_{i=0}^{n}$ and $\bigwedge_{i=0}^{n}$. The reason is that our goal is *only* to get rid of non-n-elementary literals, so that termination can be ensured (satisfiability will be tested afterward, using usual decision procedures, as explained in Section 3.1). Moreover, due to the restrictions on the syntax, the body of these connectives cannot contain non-n-elementary literals, neither explicitly (as it would be the case in, e.g., $\bigvee_{i=0}^{n} p_{n+2}$) nor implicitly (as in $\bigvee_{i=0}^{n} p_{i+2}$). Indeed, n cannot occur in iterations bodies and the indices containing i must be of the form i or i + 1, thus their value is bounded by n + 1. This explains why we do not have to decompose such schemata.

Proposition 1. *The non-deterministic application of the rules in ρ terminates on any schema.*

For every schema ϕ, we denote by $\rho^*(\phi)$ an arbitrarily chosen normal form of the tableau $\{\phi\}$ by the rules in ρ. Since tableaux are defined as sets of schemata (conjunctions), $\rho^*(\phi)$ is a set of (irreducible) schemata (i.e. the leaves).

Example 2. Let $\phi = \{(a_{n+2} \succeq 0 \wedge a_{n+2} \approx b_{n+1} \vee p_{n+1} \vee p_n) \wedge \neg p_{n+1} \wedge (p_n \vee q_{n+1})\}$. The application of the rules $\vee$-Elimination and Closure yields the two following branches:

$$a_{n+2} \succeq 0 \wedge a_{n+2} \approx b_{n+1} \wedge \neg p_{n+1} \wedge (p_n \vee q_{n+1})$$

and

$$p_n \wedge \neg p_{n+1} \wedge (p_n \vee q_{n+1})$$

Notice that the schema $(p_n \vee q_{n+1})$ is not decomposed, because it is n-elementary. The second branch contains no non-n-elementary schema hence is irreducible. The non-n-elementary conjuncts in the first branch are $a_{n+2} \succeq 0$ and $a_{n+2} \approx b_{n+1}$. The rule Elimination applies, and the function Δ replaces these conjuncts by some $\mathcal{T}$-sat-equivalent conjunction of n-elementary literals. In this case, it is intuitively obvious that we should take: $\Delta(a_{n+2} \succeq 0 \wedge a_{n+2} \approx b_{n+1}) = b_{n+1} \succeq 0$ (see Section 4 for the formal definition). Thus $\rho^*(\phi) = \{b_{n+1} \succeq 0 \wedge \neg p_{n+1} \wedge (p_n \vee q_{n+1}), p_n \wedge \neg p_{n+1} \wedge (p_n \vee q_{n+1})\}$.

Let $\mathfrak{S}(\mathfrak{L})$ be the class of schemata ϕ such that $unfold(\phi\{n \leftarrow n+1\})$ is $\mathfrak{L}$-dominated and such that the upper bound of all iterations in ϕ is n.

Lemma 1. *$\rho^* \circ unfold$ is an $\mathfrak{S}(\mathfrak{L})$-preserving simplification function[2].*

Note that Proposition 1 and Lemma 1 still hold if the Closure rule is simply removed. This rule is useful only to prune the search space by removing some (unsatisfiable) branches. From a purely theoretical point of view, it would be possible to postpone all satisfiability tests to the second phase of the procedure, when n is instantiated by 0 and when the obtained formula is fed to the SMT-solver (according to Theorem 2). One could also use a more powerful Closure rule which tests for $\mathcal{T}$-satisfiability instead of simply detecting trivial contradictions (then a branch containing, e.g., $1 = 0$ would be closed immediately).

To ensure termination, we introduce a contraction operation: $\phi \wedge \phi \rightarrow \phi$ which is applied modulo the usual AC properties of the connective $\wedge$. Obviously this rule preserves equivalence. A set of schemata is *finite up to contraction* if its normal form by the previous rule is finite.

Theorem 3. *Let $\mathfrak{L}$ be a stably decomposable frame. If $\phi \in \mathfrak{S}(\mathfrak{L})$ then $\mathcal{E}_{\rho^* \circ unfold}(\phi)$ is finite up to contraction[3]. Thus the satisfiability problem is decidable for $\mathfrak{S}(\mathfrak{L})$.*

4 Examples of Stably Decomposable Frames

Theorems 2 and 3 define a procedure for deciding the satisfiability of schemata in $\mathfrak{S}(\mathfrak{L})$. However, it relies on the fact that $\mathfrak{L}$ is stably decomposable, and on the

---

[2] See Definition 4 for the notion of $\mathfrak{S}(\mathfrak{L})$-preserving function.

[3] See Definition 3 for the notation $\mathcal{E}_\Gamma(\phi)$.

existence of a function Δ satisfying the conditions of Definition 8. Thus, it would be of no use if no concrete example of (reasonably expressive) stably decomposable frame could be exhibited. The purpose of the present section is precisely to turn this abstract and generic result into concrete decision procedures.

4.1   Literals Containing at Most One Index

The first example is independent of the theory $\mathcal{T}$. Intuitively, it corresponds to the case in which each literal contains at most one index. We assume in this section that all non-indexed symbols have a fixed interpretation in $\mathcal{T}$ (hence they are built-in).

Let $\mathfrak{L}_\diamond$ be the set of flattened literals λ such that $Ind(\lambda) \in \{\{n\}, \{n+1\}, \{n+2\}, \{i\}, \{i+1\}, \{0\}\}$. It is easy to check that $\mathfrak{L}_\diamond$ is a frame (it is finite if the signature is finite). Let $\Delta_\diamond$ be the function defined as follows:

$$\Delta_\diamond(\lambda_1 \wedge \cdots \wedge \lambda_k) \stackrel{\text{def}}{=} \begin{cases} \text{true} & \text{if } (\lambda_1 \wedge \cdots \wedge \lambda_k)\{n \leftarrow 0\} \text{ is } \mathcal{T}\text{-satisfiable} \\ \text{false} & \text{otherwise.} \end{cases}$$

Theorem 4. *$\mathfrak{L}_\diamond$ is stably decomposable w.r.t. $\Delta_\diamond$.*

For instance, any purely propositional schema (i.e. any schema in which all atoms are non-equational) is in $\mathfrak{S}(\mathfrak{L}_\diamond)^4$. Such schemata are essentially equivalent to the ones considered in [1]. The function $\Delta_\diamond$ should be compared with the pure literal rule in [1] that serves a similar purpose. The intuition is that the interpretation of the non-n-elementary literals does not interfere with the one of n-elementary literals. Notice that the analysis is much simpler in the present paper due to the strong syntactic restrictions.

4.2   Ordered Theories

The second example is more specific and also more complex. We assume that the signature contains a predicate symbol $\preceq$ interpreted as a non-strict ordering (in $\mathcal{T}$). Let $\mathcal{C}_\approx$, $\mathcal{C}_\preceq$ be two disjoint sets of indexed constant symbols. Intuitively, the constants in $\mathcal{C}_\preceq$ will only occur *at the root level* in non-strict inequations or equations, whereas the ones in $\mathcal{C}_\approx$ only occur in equations of some particular form. More precisely, we assume that every constant symbol $a \in \mathcal{C}_\approx$ is mapped to a finite set of terms $\theta(a)$, intended to denote the set of terms u such that $a_{n+2} \approx u$ is allowed to occur in the considered schema. Furthermore, we assume that for all $u, v \in \theta(a)$, there exists an iteration-free n-elementary schema $\tau(u \approx v)$ such that $\tau(u \approx v) \equiv_{\mathcal{T}} u \approx v$. The intuition is as follows. If u and v occur in $\theta(a)$, then the considered schema will possibly contain a conjunction of the form $a_{n+2} \approx u \wedge a_{n+2} \approx v$. As explained in Section 3.2, the symbol a_{n+2} will have to be eliminated (since it is non-n-elementary) by applying an appropriate function Δ. But to this purpose, one necessarily has to ensure that the equation $u \approx v$ holds. The existence of the function τ guarantees that this property can be expressed as an n-*elementary* schema.

---

[4] Provided indices greater than $n + 2$ or 0 are eliminated as explained in Section 2.3.

Definition 9. *Let $\mathfrak{L}_{\preceq}$ be the set of literals λ satisfying one of the following conditions:*

- *λ is of the form $u \preceq v$[5], where each of the u, v is either a non-indexed term or of the form a_α where $a \in \mathcal{C}_{\prec}$ and $\alpha \in \{n, n+1, n+2, i, i+1\}$.*
- *λ is of the form $a_{n+2} \approx u$ where $a \in \mathcal{C}_{\approx}$ and $u \in \theta(a)$.*
- *λ is of the form $a_{i+1} \approx v$ (resp. $a_{n+1} \approx v$) where $a \in \mathcal{C}_{\approx}$ and $v\{i \leftarrow n+1\} \in \theta(a)$ (resp. $v\{n \leftarrow n+1\} \in \theta(a)$).*

It is easy to check that $\mathfrak{L}_{\preceq}$ is a frame. We assume furthermore that for every $a \in \mathcal{C}_{\approx}$ and for all terms $u, v \in \theta(a)$, $\tau(u \approx v)$ is $\mathfrak{L}_{\preceq}$-dominated.

Before proceeding, we give a concrete example of a theory $\mathcal{T}$ for which $\theta(a)$ and τ can be defined (it will be used in forthcoming examples).

Example 3. Assume that `Sorts` contains in particular the sort symbols `nat`, `int` and `real` with their usual meanings. We assume that the signature contains the usual functions $+$ and $\preceq$[6] and built-in constant symbols $0, \ldots, k$ of sort `nat`. If $a : s \in \mathcal{C}_{\approx}$, we define $\theta(a)$ as the set containing all terms in $0, \ldots, k$ (if s is `nat`) and all terms of the form $a_{n+1} + u$ where u is either a non-indexed term or of the form b_{n+1} where $b \in \mathcal{C}_{\prec}$. Then the function τ can be defined as follows:

- $\tau(a_{n+1} + u \approx a_{n+1} + v) \stackrel{\text{def}}{=} u \approx v$.
- $\tau(l \approx l') \stackrel{\text{def}}{=} l \approx l'$ if $Ind(l \approx l') = \emptyset$.
- $\tau(a_{n+1} + u \approx l) \stackrel{\text{def}}{=} \bigvee_{l_1+l_2=l}(a_{n+1} \approx l_1 \wedge u \approx l_2)$ if $l \in \{0, \ldots, k\}$. Note that the number of pairs (l_1, l_2) such that $l_1 + l_2 = l$ must be finite since by definition of $\theta(a)$, a (and thus l, l_1 and l_2) must be of sort `nat`. Hence this iteration is *not* a formal one but belongs to the meta-language. This would not be the case if a was of sort `int` or `real`.

It is easy to check that this function τ satisfies the desired properties.

Definition 10. *Let $\Delta_{\preceq}$ be the function defined as follows. For every conjunction of literals ϕ, we denote by $E(\phi)$ the smallest set of schemata such that:*
- *If ϕ contains two literals of the form $a_{n+2} \approx u$ and $a_{n+2} \approx v$ then $\tau(u \approx v) \in E(\phi)$.*
- *If $\phi \models u \preceq v$, $u \preceq v$ is an n-elementary literal in $\mathfrak{L}_{\preceq}$ and $u \neq v$ then $u \preceq v \in E(\phi)$.*
We define: $\Delta_{\preceq}(\phi) \stackrel{\text{def}}{=} \bigwedge_{\psi \in E(\phi)} \psi$. Notice that $E(\phi)$ is necessarily finite.

Example 4. Let $a : \mathtt{nat}, b : \mathtt{int} \in \mathcal{C}_{\approx}$, $c : \mathtt{int}, d : \mathtt{int} \in \mathcal{C}_{\prec}$, $e : \mathtt{int}$ and $f : \mathtt{int}$. Let $\theta(a) = \{a_{n+1} + 1, 0, 1, 2\}$ and $\theta(b) = \{b_{n+1} + c_{n+1}, b_{n+1} + e\}$.

Let ϕ be the conjunction of the following literals:

$$a_{n+2} \approx a_{n+1} + 1 \qquad a_{n+2} \approx 2 \qquad b_{n+2} \approx b_{n+1} + c_{n+1}$$
$$b_{n+2} \approx b_{n+1} + e \qquad c_{n+1} \preceq d_{n+2} \qquad d_{n+2} \preceq d_{n+1} \qquad d_{n+2} \preceq f + 1$$

---

[5] Of course, equations $u \approx v$ can also be considered, as abbreviations for $u \preceq v \wedge v \preceq u$.
[6] For readability, we use the same notation for the symbols $+$ and $\preceq$ whatever may be the type of their arguments.

Then $\Delta_\preceq(\phi)$ is the conjunction of the following schemata:

$$a_{n+1} \approx 1 \qquad c_{n+1} \approx e \qquad c_{n+1} \preceq d_{n+1} \qquad c_{n+1} \preceq f + 1$$

Theorem 5. $\mathfrak{L}_\preceq$ *is stably decomposable w.r.t.* $\Delta_\preceq$.

Another trivial example of stably decomposable sets of literals that we do not develop here, is the one in which every constant symbol indexed by an expression $n + l$ where $l > 1$, is of a finite sort. Indeed, in this case all such constants can be straightforwardly eliminated by replacing them by each possible value (yielding a disjunction of n-elementary schemata).

5   Examples

We provide in this section some examples of application of our technique.

Example 5. Let ϕ be the schema considered in the Introduction:

$$\bigwedge_{i=0}^{n} (a_{i+1} \succeq a_i) \wedge \bigwedge_{i=0}^{n} (b_{i+1} \preceq b_i) \wedge a_0 \succeq b_0 \wedge a_{n+1} \preceq c \wedge b_{n+1} \succeq c + 1.$$

We compute the set of schemata $\mathcal{E}_{\rho^* \circ unfold}(\phi)$. According to the definition, n must be instantiated by $n + 1$ and the iterations are unfolded, yielding: $\bigwedge_{i=0}^{n} (a_{i+1} \succeq a_i) \wedge a_{n+2} \succeq a_{n+1} \wedge \bigwedge_{i=0}^{n} (b_{i+1} \preceq b_i) \wedge b_{n+2} \preceq b_{n+1} \wedge a_0 \succeq b_0 \wedge a_{n+2} \preceq c \wedge b_{n+2} \succeq c + 1$. In order to get rid of the symbols indexed by $n + 2$, we apply the rules in ρ. Since the schema is already a conjunction of iterations and literals, no rule applies, except Elimination. The conjunction of literals that are not n-elementary is $a_{n+2} \succeq a_{n+1} \wedge b_{n+2} \preceq b_{n+1} \wedge a_{n+2} \preceq c \wedge b_{n+2} \succeq c + 1$. Applying the function $\Delta_\preceq$ (see Definition 10), we obtain: $c \succeq a_{n+1} \wedge c + 1 \preceq b_{n+1}$. Replacing the previous conjunction by its image by $\Delta_\preceq$ yields a schema that is actually identical to the first one. Hence the procedure stops (no further schema is generated) and we get $\mathcal{E}_{\rho^* \circ unfold}(\phi) = \{\phi\}$. By Theorem 2, the $\mathcal{T}$-satisfiability of ϕ is thus equivalent to the one of $\phi\{n \leftarrow 0\}$ which can be easily tested by any SMT-solver.

Example 6. Consider the algorithm below, counting the number of occurrences o of an element e in an array t. We want to check that if the final value of o is 1 then the formula $\forall i, j, a_i \approx e \wedge a_j \approx e \Rightarrow i \approx j$ holds. This is modeled by a schema ϕ defined as follows (o_i : nat denotes the value of o at step i and t_i : int is $t[i]$, notice that we cannot use the theory of arrays, since no stably decomposable frame has been defined for this theory – this is left to future work).

$$\phi:$$

```
i ← 0
o ← 0
while i ⪯ n do
    if t[i] = e then
        o ← o + 1
    end if
    i ← i + 1
end while
```

$$o_0 \approx 0$$
$$\bigwedge_{i=0}^{n} (t_i \approx e \Rightarrow o_{i+1} \approx o_i + 1)$$
$$\bigwedge_{i=0}^{n} (t_i \not\approx e \Rightarrow o_{i+1} \approx o_i)$$
$$o_{n+1} \approx 1$$
$$\bigvee_{i=0}^{n} (i \approx m \wedge t_i \approx e)$$
$$\bigvee_{i=0}^{n} (i \approx k \wedge t_i \approx e)$$
$$m \not\approx k$$

m, k are additional parameters interpreted as elements of $[0, n]$. These parameters and the literals $i \approx m$, $i \approx k$ and $m \not\approx k$ can be encoded in our language as explained in Section 2.3 (we omit the translation for readability). The schema is in $\mathfrak{S}(\mathfrak{L}_{\preceq})$ (with $t \in \mathcal{C}_{\preceq}$ and $o \in \mathcal{C}_{\approx}$). The reader can check that $\mathcal{E}_{\rho^* \circ unfold}(\phi) = \{\phi, \psi_1, \psi_2, \psi_3\}$, where ψ_1, ψ_2 and ψ_3 are defined respectively by:

$$
\begin{array}{c|c|c}
\begin{aligned}
&\psi_1 : \\
&o_0 \approx 0 \\
&\bigwedge\nolimits_{i=0}^{n} t_i \approx e \Rightarrow o_{i+1} \approx o_i + 1 \\
&\bigwedge\nolimits_{i=0}^{n} t_i \not\approx e \Rightarrow o_{i+1} \approx o_i \\
&o_{n+1} \approx 0 \\
&t_{n+1} \approx e \\
&n + 1 \approx m \\
&\bigvee\nolimits_{i=0}^{n} i \approx k \wedge t_i \approx e \\
&m \not\approx k
\end{aligned}
&
\begin{aligned}
&\psi_2 : \\
&o_0 \approx 0 \\
&\bigwedge\nolimits_{i=0}^{n} t_i \approx e \Rightarrow o_{i+1} \approx o_i + 1 \\
&\bigwedge\nolimits_{i=0}^{n} t_i \not\approx e \Rightarrow o_{i+1} \approx o_i \\
&o_{n+1} \approx 0 \\
&t_{n+1} \approx e \\
&n + 1 \approx k \\
&\bigvee\nolimits_{i=0}^{n} i \approx m \wedge t_i \approx e \\
&m \not\approx k
\end{aligned}
&
\begin{aligned}
&\psi_3 : \\
&o_0 \approx 0 \\
&\bigwedge\nolimits_{i=0}^{n} t_i \approx e \Rightarrow o_{i+1} \approx o_i + 1 \\
&\bigwedge\nolimits_{i=0}^{n} t_i \not\approx e \Rightarrow o_{i+1} \approx o_i \\
&o_{n+1} \approx 0 \\
&t_{n+1} \approx e \\
&\bigvee\nolimits_{i=0}^{n} i \approx m \wedge t_i \approx e \\
&\bigvee\nolimits_{i=0}^{n} i \approx k \wedge t_i \approx e \\
&m \not\approx k
\end{aligned}
\end{array}
$$

In order to check that ϕ is $\mathcal{T}$-unsatisfiable, one only has to test the $\mathcal{T}$-satisfiability of the sentences $\phi\{n \leftarrow 0\}$, $\psi_1\{n \leftarrow 0\}$, $\psi_2\{n \leftarrow 0\}$ and $\psi_3\{n \leftarrow 0\}$.

6 Conclusion

A logic has been defined for reasoning on parameterized families of SMT-problems and a sound and complete (w.r.t. satisfiability) proof procedure has been designed. It does not terminate in general (the logic is proven to be undecidable) but we have devised semantic conditions on the underlying theory and on the considered class of formulae that ensure that this proof procedure can be turned into a decision procedure by adding appropriate simplification rules. Then, concrete examples of theories and classes of schemata satisfying these conditions have been provided. Some simple examples of application have also been proposed. Our method relies on the use of an external decision procedure for the underlying theory. It applies to a wide range of theories (provided they are decidable). In the present work, we mainly focus on examples in verification, but one could also handle for instance schemata of formulae in (decidable) modal or description logics.

The implementation of this technique is part of future work. Another obvious line of research is to identify other classes of stably decomposable frames (see Section 3.2) in order to extend the scope of our results (in particular, the important theory of arrays should be considered). Concerning potential applications in verification, automatic procedures for extracting schemata modeling the algorithms as the ones in Section 5 ought to be devised and comparison with the numerous existing techniques should be provided. A longer term goal would be to consider quantification, either as standard quantification such as $\forall x, \forall y, p(x, y)$ or of *schemata of quantifications* such as $\forall x_1, \ldots, x_n, p(x_1, \ldots, x_n)$ (where the indexed variables and dots are *part of the language*).

References

1. Aravantinos, V., Caferra, R., Peltier, N.: A schemata calculus for propositional logic. In: Giese, M., Waaler, A. (eds.) TABLEAUX 2009. LNCS, vol. 5607, pp. 32–46. Springer, Heidelberg (2009)
2. Aravantinos, V., Caferra, R., Peltier, N.: Decidability and undecidability results for propositional schemata. Journal of Artificial Intelligence Research 40, 599–656 (2011)
3. Barrett, C., Sebastiani, R., Seshia, S., Tinelli, C.: Satisfiability modulo theories. In: Biere, A., Heule, M.J.H., van Maaren, H., Walsh, T. (eds.) Handbook of Satisfiability. Frontiers in Artificial Intelligence and Applications, ch. 26, vol. 185, pp. 825–885. IOS Press, Amsterdam (2009)
4. Bradley, A.R., Manna, Z., Sipma, H.B.: What's decidable about arrays? In: Emerson, E.A., Namjoshi, K.S. (eds.) VMCAI 2006. LNCS, vol. 3855, pp. 427–442. Springer, Heidelberg (2005)
5. de Moura, L.M., Bjørner, N.: Efficient E-Matching for SMT Solvers. In: Pfenning, F. (ed.) CADE 2007. LNCS (LNAI), vol. 4603, pp. 183–198. Springer, Heidelberg (2007)
6. Dutertre, D., de Moura, L.M.: The YICES SMT-solver. In: SMT-COMP: Satisfiability Modulo Theories Competition, http://yices.csl.sri.com
7. Ge, Y., de Moura, L.M.: Complete instantiation for quantified formulas in satisfiabiliby modulo theories. In: Bouajjani, A., Maler, O. (eds.) CAV 2009. LNCS, vol. 5643, pp. 306–320. Springer, Heidelberg (2009)

Kripke Semantics for Basic Sequent Systems

Arnon Avron and Ori Lahav*

School of Computer Science, Tel Aviv University, Israel
{aa,orilahav}@post.tau.ac.il

Abstract. We present a general method for providing Kripke semantics for the family of fully-structural multiple-conclusion propositional sequent systems. In particular, many well-known Kripke semantics for a variety of logics are easily obtained as special cases. This semantics is then used to obtain semantic characterizations of analytic sequent systems of this type, as well as of those admitting cut-admissibility. These characterizations serve as a uniform basis for semantic proofs of analyticity and cut-admissibility in such systems.

1 Introduction

This paper is a continuation of an on-going project aiming to get a unified semantic theory and understanding of analytic Gentzen-type systems and the phenomenon of strong cut-admissibility in them. In particular: we seek for general effective criteria that can tell in advance whether a given system is analytic, and whether the cut rule is (strongly) admissible in it (instead of proving these properties from scratch for every new system). The key idea of this project is to use semantic tools which are constructed in a *modular* way. For this it is essential to use *non-deterministic* semantics. This was first done in [6], where the family of propositional multiple-conclusion canonical systems was defined, and it was shown that the semantics of such systems is provided by two-valued non-deterministic matrices – a natural generalization of the classical truth-tables. The sequent systems of this family are fully-structural (i.e. include all standard structural rules), and their logical derivation rules are all of a certain "ideal" type. Then single-conclusion canonical systems were semantically characterized in [5], using non-deterministic intuitionistic Kripke frames. In both works the semantics was effectively used for the goals described above.

The goal of the present paper is to extend the framework, methods, and results of [6] and [5] to a much broader family of sequent systems: the family of what we call *basic systems*, which includes every multiple-conclusion propositional sequent system we know that has all of Gentzen's original structural rules. Thus this family includes the various standard sequent systems for modal logics, as well as the usual *multiple*-conclusion systems for intuitionistic logic, its dual, and bi-intuitionistic logic — none of which is canonical in the sense of [6,5].

The structure of the paper is as follows. We begin by precisely defining the family of basic systems. We then generalize Kripke semantics, and present a

---

* This research was supported by The Israel Science Foundation (grant no. 280-10).

K. Brünnler and G. Metcalfe (Eds.): TABLEAUX 2011, LNAI 6793, pp. 43–57, 2011.

general method for providing such semantics for any given basic system. This method is modular, as we separately investigate the semantic effect of every logical rule of a basic system (and in fact even of the main ingredients of such rules), and combine these effects to obtain the full semantics of the system. In a variety of important cases, this leads to the known semantics of the corresponding logic. In addition, this method can be applied to new basic systems, including basic systems with non-deterministic connectives. Based on this method, in sections 5 and 6 we present semantic characterizations of analyticity and cut-admissibility in basic systems. These characterizations pave the way to uniform semantic proofs of these properties[1].

Two important notes before we start: first, we consider here derivations from a set of assumptions (or "non-logical axioms"), and so we deal with *strong* soundness and completeness, and *strong* cut-admissibility ([2]). Second, we only investigate here propositional systems and logics, leaving the more complicated first-order case to a future work.

Most of the proofs are omitted due to lack of space, and will appear in the full version of the paper.

2   Preliminaries

In what follows $\mathcal{L}$ is a propositional language, and $Frm_{\mathcal{L}}$ is its set of wffs. We assume that $p_1, p_2, \ldots$ are the atomic formulas of $\mathcal{L}$. Since we only deal with fully-structural systems, it is most convenient to define sequents using *sets*:

Definition 1. A *signed formula* is an expression of the form $f{:}\psi$ or $t{:}\psi$, where ψ is a formula. A *sequent* is a finite set of signed formulas.

We shall usually employ the usual sequent notation $\Gamma \Rightarrow \Delta$, where Γ and Δ are finite sets of formulas. $\Gamma \Rightarrow \Delta$ is interpreted as $\{f{:}\psi \mid \psi \in \Gamma\} \cup \{t{:}\psi \mid \psi \in \Delta\}$. We also employ the standard abbreviations, e.g. Γ, φ instead of $\Gamma \cup \{\varphi\}$, and $\Gamma \Rightarrow$ instead of $\Gamma \Rightarrow \emptyset$.

Definition 2. An $\mathcal{L}$-*substitution* is a function $\sigma : Frm_{\mathcal{L}} \to Frm_{\mathcal{L}}$, such that $\sigma(\diamond(\psi_1, \ldots, \psi_n)) = \diamond(\sigma(\psi_1), \ldots, \sigma(\psi_n))$ for every n-ary connective $\diamond$ of $\mathcal{L}$. An $\mathcal{L}$-substitution is extended to signed formulas, sequents, etc. in the obvious way.

Given a set μ of signed formulas, we denote by $frm[\mu]$ the set of (ordinary) formulas appearing in μ, and by $sub[\mu]$ the set of subformulas of the formulas of $frm[\mu]$. frm and sub are extended to sets of sets of signed formulas in the obvious way. Given a set $\mathcal{E}$ of formulas, a formula ψ (resp. sequent s) is called an $\mathcal{E}$-*formula* ($\mathcal{E}$-*sequent*) if $\psi \in \mathcal{E}$ ($frm[s] \subseteq \mathcal{E}$).

---

[1]   Many efforts have been devoted to characterize cut-free sequent systems. For example, a semantic characterization of cut-admissibility was the subject of [7]. There, however, the authors consider substructural single-conclusion systems, and use phase semantics, which is significantly more abstract and complex than Kripke semantics.

3   Basic Systems

In this section we precisely define the family of *basic systems*, and present some examples of them. For doing so, we define the general structure of derivation rules allowed to appear in basic systems. Rules of this structure will be called *basic rules*. A key idea here is to explicitly differentiate between a rule and its application. Roughly speaking, the rule itself is a schema that is used in proofs by applying some substitution and (optionally) adding context-formulas.

To explain the intuition behind the following definition of a basic rule, we begin with specific examples. Consider the following schemas for introducing a unary connective $\Box$ (used in usual systems for modal logics, see e.g. [17]):

$$(1)\ \frac{\Gamma, \psi \Rightarrow \Delta}{\Gamma, \Box\psi \Rightarrow \Delta} \qquad (2)\ \frac{\Box\Gamma \Rightarrow \psi}{\Box\Gamma \Rightarrow \Box\psi} \qquad (3)\ \frac{\Gamma_1, \Box\Gamma_2 \Rightarrow \psi}{\Box\Gamma_1, \Box\Gamma_2 \Rightarrow \Box\psi}$$

$\Box\Gamma$ here is an abbreviation for $\{\Box\varphi \mid \varphi \in \Gamma\}$. An obvious distinction in these schemas is the distinction between *context* formulas and *non-context* formulas (see e.g. [15]). Here Γ, Γ_1 and Γ_2 are sets of context formulas, and ψ and $\Box\psi$ are non-context formulas. While the exact number of non-context formulas is explicitly specified in the scheme, any number of context formulas is possible. These three schemas demonstrate three possibilities regarding context-formulas:

1. No constraint on context-formulas on either side of the sequent (as in (1)).
2. Limiting the allowed set of context-formulas (as in (2), where only $\Box$-formulas may appear on the left, and no context-formulas are allowed on the right).
3. Modifying some context-formulas in the rule application (as in (3), where Γ_1 in the premise becomes $\Box\Gamma_1$ in the conclusion).

To deal with the different options concerning the treatment of context formulas, we associate with each rule a set of *context-relations*. The context-relations determine the required relation between the context formulas of the premises of the rule and those of the corresponding conclusion.

Definition 3

1. A *context-relation* is a finite binary relation between signed formulas. Given a context-relation π, we denote by $\bar{\pi}$ the binary relation between signed formulas $\bar{\pi} = \{\langle\sigma(x), \sigma(y)\rangle \mid \sigma \text{ is an } \mathcal{L}\text{-substitution, and } \langle x, y\rangle \in \pi\}$. A pair of sequents $\langle s_1, s_2\rangle$ is called a π-*instance* if there exist (not necessarily distinct) signed formulas $x_1, \ldots, x_n$ and $y_1, \ldots, y_n$ such that $s_1 = \{x_1, \ldots, x_n\}$, $s_2 = \{y_1, \ldots, y_n\}$, and $x_i \bar{\pi} y_i$ for every $1 \le i \le n$.
2. A *basic premise* is an ordered pair of the form $\langle s, \pi\rangle$, where s is a sequent and π is a context-relation.
3. A *basic rule* is an expression of the form S/C, where S is a finite set of basic premises, and C is a sequent.
4. An *application* of the basic rule $\{\langle s_1, \pi_1\rangle, \ldots, \langle s_n, \pi_n\rangle\}/C$ is any inference step of the following form:

$$\frac{\sigma(s_1) \cup c_1 \quad \ldots \quad \sigma(s_n) \cup c_n}{\sigma(C) \cup c_1' \cup \ldots \cup c_n'}$$

where σ is an $\mathcal{L}$-substitution, and $\langle c_i, c_i' \rangle$ is a π_i-instance for every $1 \leq i \leq n$.

Example 1. Below we present well-known examples of basic rules and context relations used in them (note that the names given here to these context-relations will be used in the sequel):

Implication. The usual rules for classical implication are the two basic rules $\{\langle \Rightarrow p_1, \pi_0 \rangle, \langle p_2 \Rightarrow, \pi_0 \rangle\}/p_1 \supset p_2 \Rightarrow$ and $\{\langle p_1 \Rightarrow p_2, \pi_0 \rangle\}/ \Rightarrow p_1 \supset p_2$, where $\pi_0 = \{\langle f{:}p_1, f{:}p_1 \rangle, \langle t{:}p_1, t{:}p_1 \rangle\}$. π_0 is the most simple context-relation, and it is used in all sequent systems. By definition, π_0-instances are the pairs of the form $\langle s, s \rangle$. Thus, applications of these rules have the form (respectively):

$$\frac{\Gamma_1 \Rightarrow \Delta_1, \psi \quad \Gamma_2, \varphi \Rightarrow \Delta_2}{\Gamma_1, \Gamma_2, \psi \supset \varphi \Rightarrow \Delta_1, \Delta_2} \qquad \frac{\Gamma, \psi \Rightarrow \Delta, \varphi}{\Gamma \Rightarrow \Delta, \psi \supset \varphi}$$

For intuitionistic implication, one replaces the second rule with the rule $\{\langle p_1 \Rightarrow p_2, \pi_{int} \rangle\}/ \Rightarrow p_1 \supset p_2$, where $\pi_{int} = \{\langle f{:}p_1, f{:}p_1 \rangle\}$. π_{int}-instances are all pairs of the form $\langle \Gamma \Rightarrow, \Gamma \Rightarrow \rangle$. Thus, applications of this rule allow to infer $\Gamma \Rightarrow \psi \supset \varphi$ from $\Gamma, \psi \Rightarrow \varphi$.

Exclusion. The rules for dual-intuitionistic exclusion (in a multiple-conclusion sequent system) are the basic rules $\{\langle p_1 \Rightarrow p_2, \{\langle t{:}p_1, t{:}p_1 \rangle\} \rangle\}/p_1 \prec p_2 \Rightarrow$ and $\{\langle \Rightarrow p_1, \pi_0 \rangle, \langle p_2 \Rightarrow, \pi_0 \rangle\}/ \Rightarrow p_1 \prec p_2$ (see [8]). Applications of these rule have the form:

$$\frac{\psi \Rightarrow \Delta, \varphi}{\psi \prec \varphi \Rightarrow \Delta} \qquad \frac{\Gamma_1 \Rightarrow \Delta_1, \psi \quad \Gamma_2, \varphi \Rightarrow \Delta_2}{\Gamma_1, \Gamma_2 \Rightarrow \Delta_1, \Delta_2, \psi \prec \varphi}$$

Modal Necessity. Different basic rules for introducing $\Box$ are used in different modal logics (see [17] for a survey; for GL see e.g. [13,1]). For example, the systems **K**, **K4**, **GL**, **S4** and **S5** are obtained by adding the following rules to the standard sequent system for classical logic:

(K) $\{\langle \Rightarrow p_1, \pi_K \rangle\}/ \Rightarrow \Box p_1$. where $\pi_K = \{\langle f{:}p_1, f{:}\Box p_1 \rangle\}$ (π_K-instances are all pairs of the form $\langle \Gamma \Rightarrow, \Box \Gamma \Rightarrow \rangle$).

($K4$) $\{\langle \Rightarrow p_1, \pi_{K4} \rangle\}/ \Rightarrow \Box p_1$, where $\pi_{K4} = \{\langle f{:}p_1, f{:}\Box p_1 \rangle, \langle f{:}\Box p_1, f{:}\Box p_1 \rangle\}$.

(GL) $\{\langle \Box p_1 \Rightarrow p_1, \pi_{K4} \rangle\}/ \Rightarrow \Box p_1$.

($S4$) $\{\langle \Rightarrow p_1, \pi_{S4} \rangle\}/ \Rightarrow \Box p_1$ where $\pi_{S4} = \{\langle f{:}\Box p_1, f{:}\Box p_1 \rangle\}$.

($S5$) $\{\langle \Rightarrow p_1, \pi_{S5} \rangle\}/ \Rightarrow \Box p_1$ where $\pi_{S5} = \{\langle f{:}\Box p_1, f{:}\Box p_1 \rangle, \langle t{:}\Box p_1, t{:}\Box p_1 \rangle\}$.

($\Box \Rightarrow$) In **S4** and **S5**, the following rule is also added: $\{\langle p_1 \Rightarrow, \pi_0 \rangle\}/\Box p_1 \Rightarrow$.

Applications of these rules have the form:

$$(K)\ \frac{\Gamma \Rightarrow \psi}{\Box \Gamma \Rightarrow \Box \psi} \qquad (K4)\ \frac{\Gamma_1, \Box \Gamma_2 \Rightarrow \psi}{\Box \Gamma_1, \Box \Gamma_2 \Rightarrow \Box \psi} \qquad (GL)\ \frac{\Gamma_1, \Box \Gamma_2, \Box \psi \Rightarrow \psi}{\Box \Gamma_1, \Box \Gamma_2 \Rightarrow \Box \psi}$$

$$(S4)\ \frac{\Box \Gamma \Rightarrow \psi}{\Box \Gamma \Rightarrow \Box \psi} \qquad (S5)\ \frac{\Box \Gamma \Rightarrow \Box \Delta, \psi}{\Box \Gamma \Rightarrow \Box \Delta, \Box \psi} \qquad (\Box \Rightarrow)\ \frac{\Gamma, \psi \Rightarrow \Delta}{\Gamma, \Box \psi \Rightarrow \Delta}$$

Finally, we define *basic systems*, and the consequence relations induced by them.

Definition 4

- A *basic system* **G** consists of a finite set of basic rules, such that:
  1. The *identity axiom* is in **G**. The identity axiom is the basic rule $\emptyset/p_1 \Rightarrow p_1$. Applications of this rule provide all axioms of the form $\psi \Rightarrow \psi$.
  2. The *cut rule* is in **G**. Cut is the basic rule $\{\langle p_1 \Rightarrow, \pi_0\rangle, \langle \Rightarrow p_1, \pi_0\rangle\}/ \Rightarrow$. Applications of this rule allow one to infer $\Gamma_1, \Gamma_2 \Rightarrow \Delta_1, \Delta_2$ from $\Gamma_1, \psi \Rightarrow \Delta_1$ and $\Gamma_2 \Rightarrow \Delta_2, \psi$.
  3. The *weakening rules* are in **G**. These are the basic rules $\{\langle \Rightarrow, \pi_0\rangle\}/p_1 \Rightarrow$ and $\{\langle \Rightarrow, \pi_0\rangle\}/ \Rightarrow p_1$. Applications of them allow one to infer $\Gamma, \psi \Rightarrow \Delta$ and $\Gamma \Rightarrow \Delta, \psi$ from $\Gamma \Rightarrow \Delta$.
  We denote by $\Pi_{\mathbf{G}}$ the set of context-relations appearing in the rules of **G**.
- A sequent s *follows* in basic system **G** from a set of sequents $\mathcal{S}$ ($\mathcal{S} \vdash_{\mathbf{G}} s$) if there exists a proof in **G** of s from $\mathcal{S}$.

Example 2. We list some known sequent systems, each of which is either a basic system, or it can easily be shown to be equivalent to a basic system:

- The family of canonical systems studied in [6] (which includes the propositional part of Gentzen's **LK** for classical logic).
- The propositional part of **LJ'** from [14] (the multiple-conclusion version of Gentzen's **LJ** for intuitionistic logic).
- The propositional part of **SLK**[1] from [8] for bi-intuitionistic logic.
- All modal ordinary sequent systems described in [17], as well as that for **GL** described in Example 1.
- The (fully-structural) sequent systems for finite-valued logics in [3].
- All paraconsistent sequent systems investigated in [4].

4   Kripke Semantics

In this section we introduce a method for providing Kripke semantics for any given basic system. We provide a general definition of a (Kripke-) frame, and show that every basic system **G** induces a class of frames for which it is strongly sound and complete. Various fundamental soundness and completeness theorems for known logics are easily obtained as special cases.

Definition 5. A *frame* is a tuple $\langle W, \mathcal{R}, v\rangle$, where W is a set (of *worlds*), $\mathcal{R}$ is a finite set of binary relations on W (called *accessibility relations*), and $v : W \times Frm_{\mathcal{L}} \to \{\mathrm{T}, \mathrm{F}\}$ is a valuation function. Given a frame $\langle W, \mathcal{R}, v\rangle$, we say that a signed formula of the form $f{:}\psi$ (resp. $t{:}\psi$) is *true* in a world $a \in W$ if $v(a, \psi) = \mathrm{F}$ ($v(a, \psi) = \mathrm{T}$).

Three notions of truth of *sequents* are defined as follows:

Definition 6. Let $\mathcal{W} = \langle W, \mathcal{R}, v\rangle$ be a frame, and s be a sequent.

1. s is *true* in some $a \in W$ if there exists $x \in s$ such that x is true in a.
2. Let $R \in \mathcal{R}$. s is *R-true* in $a \in W$ if s is true in every $b \in W$ such that aRb.

3. $\mathcal{W}$ is a *model* of s if s is true in every $a \in W$. $\mathcal{W}$ is a model of a set of sequents $\mathcal{S}$ if it is a model of every $s \in \mathcal{S}$.

Since we deal with arbitrary basic systems, no constraints on the set of relations and on the valuation function were imposed in the definition of a frame. These constraints are directly related to the context-relations and the basic rules of a specific basic system. The idea is that each context-relation and each basic rule imposes constraints on the set of frames. Next we describe these constraints.

Definition 7. Let **G** be a basic system. A frame $\mathcal{W} = \langle W, \mathcal{R}, v \rangle$ is **G**-*legal* if the following conditions are met:

(1) $\mathcal{R}$ consists of a relation R_π for every context-relation $\pi \in \Pi_{\mathbf{G}}$, where R_{π_0} is the identity relation.
(2) For every $a, b \in W$, and $\pi \in \Pi_{\mathbf{G}}$, if $aR_\pi b$ then for every two signed formulas x, y such that $x\bar{\pi}y$, either x is not true in b or y is true in a.
(3) For every $a \in W$, $\mathcal{L}$-substitution σ, and $S/C \in \mathbf{G}$, if $\sigma(s)$ is R_π-true in a for every $\langle s, \pi \rangle \in S$, then $\sigma(C)$ is true in a.

Example 3. The constraints imposed by the context-relations π_{int} and π_K according to condition (2) of the previous definition are:

(1) Assume that $\pi_{int} \in \Pi_{\mathbf{G}}$. In **G**-legal frames, if $aR_{\pi_{int}}b$, then for every formula ψ, either $f{:}\psi$ is not true in b or $f{:}\psi$ is true in a. Or equivalently, if $aR_{\pi_{int}}b$ and $v(a, \psi) = \mathrm{T}$, then $v(b, \psi) = \mathrm{T}$. Thus π_{int} imposes the usual persistence condition of intuitionistic logic (with respect to $R_{\pi_{int}}$).
(2) Assume that $\pi_K \in \Pi_{\mathbf{G}}$. In **G**-legal frames, if $aR_{\pi_K}b$, then either $f{:}\psi$ is not true in b or $f{:}\Box\psi$ is true in a. Equivalently, if $aR_{\pi_K}b$ and $v(a, \Box\psi) = \mathrm{T}$, then $v(b, \psi) = \mathrm{T}$. Thus π_K imposes "one half" of the usual semantics of $\Box$.

Example 4. We present the constraints imposed by some basic rules according to condition (3) of the previous definition:

(1) Assume that **G** contains a rule of the form $\{\langle \Rightarrow p_1, \pi \rangle\}/ \Rightarrow \Box p_1$. In **G**-legal frames, $v(a, \Box\psi) = \mathrm{T}$ whenever $v(b, \psi) = \mathrm{T}$ for every world b such that $aR_\pi b$. Thus this rule imposes the "other half" of the usual semantics of $\Box$.
(2) Assume that **G** contains a rule of the form $\{\langle \Rightarrow p_1, \pi \rangle, \langle p_2 \Rightarrow, \pi \rangle\}/p_1 \supset p_2 \Rightarrow$. In **G**-legal frames, $v(a, \psi \supset \varphi) = \mathrm{F}$ if $v(b, \psi) = \mathrm{T}$ and $v(b, \varphi) = \mathrm{F}$ for every world b such that $aR_\pi b$.
(3) Assume that **G** contains a rule of the form $\{\langle p_1 \Rightarrow p_2, \pi \rangle\}/ \Rightarrow p_1 \supset p_2$. In **G**-legal frames, $v(a, \psi \supset \varphi) = \mathrm{T}$ whenever for every world b such that $aR_\pi b$, either $v(b, \psi) = \mathrm{F}$ or $v(b, \varphi) = \mathrm{T}$.
(4) Assume that **G** contains a rule of the form $\{\langle \Rightarrow, \pi \rangle\}/ \Rightarrow$ (application of this rule allow to infer s' from s where $\langle s, s' \rangle$ is a π-instance). In **G**-legal frames, $(\Rightarrow)$ (the empty sequent) should be true in every world, in which it is R_π-true. Since $(\Rightarrow)$ is not true in any world, this condition would hold iff for every world a there exists a world b such that $aR_\pi b$. In other words, if $\{\langle \Rightarrow, \pi \rangle\}/ \Rightarrow$ is in **G**, then R_π should be a serial relation.

Example 5. Let **LK** be the usual basic system for classical logic. Here $\Pi_{\mathbf{LK}} = \{\pi_0\}$. In **LK**-legal frames, $\mathcal{R}$ consists of one relation R_{π_0} which is the identity relation. π_0 imposes a trivial condition, $v(a, \psi) = v(b, \psi)$ whenever $a = b$. The basic rules of **LK** impose the usual truth-tables in each world, e.g. $v(a, \psi \supset \varphi) = \text{T}$ iff either $v(a, \psi) = \text{F}$ or $v(a, \varphi) = \text{T}$.

Example 6. Assume that **G** contains the two standard rules for intuitionistic implication. Example 4 (3) and the combination of Example 3 (1) and Example 4 (2) together imply that in **G**-legal frames $v(a, \psi \supset \varphi) = \text{T}$ iff for every world b such that $aR_{\pi_{int}}b$, either $v(b, \psi) = \text{F}$ or $v(b, \varphi) = \text{T}$. Thus the two rules and π_{int} impose the usual Kripke semantics of intuitionistic implication.

We define the *semantic* consequence relation induced by a basic system **G**.

Definition 8. Let **G** be a basic system, and $\mathcal{S} \cup \{s\}$ be a set of sequents. $\mathcal{S} \vDash_{\mathbf{G}} s$ if every **G**-legal frame which is a model of $\mathcal{S}$ is also a model of s.

Remark 1. It can easily be seen that in any basic system **G** like **LK**, in which $\Pi_{\mathbf{G}} = \{\pi_0\}$, it suffices to consider only trivial Kripke frames which have a single world, and the corresponding accessibility relation is the identity relation.

Theorem 1 (Strong Soundness and Completeness). $\vdash_{\mathbf{G}} = \vDash_{\mathbf{G}}$ *for every basic system* **G**.

Theorem 1 generalizes several well-known completeness theorems for specific basic systems. For example:

Example 7 (KD). Let **KD** be the basic system for the modal logic KD (see [17]) obtained adding the rules $\{\langle \Rightarrow p_1, \pi_K \rangle\}/ \Rightarrow \Box p_1$ and $\{\langle \Rightarrow, \pi_K \rangle\}/ \Rightarrow$ to the usual system for classical logic. Applications of the latter allow to infer $\Box \Gamma \Rightarrow$ from $\Gamma \Rightarrow$. As $\Pi_{\mathbf{KD}} = \{\pi_0, \pi_K\}$, **KD**-legal frames include two relations, R_{π_0} (the identity relation) and R_{π_K}. Following Examples 3, 4 and 5, all connectives of **KD** have their usual semantics. By Example 4, in the presence of the second rule, R_{π_K} is a serial relation. Thus, we obtain the usual semantics of KD.

Theorem 1 is sometimes difficult to use directly. However, there is a subclass of **G**-legal frames that is still sufficient for completeness, and in many cases leads to simpler conditions on the accessibility relations.

Definition 9. Given a basic system **G**, a **G**-legal frame $\mathcal{W} = \langle W, \mathcal{R}, v \rangle$ is called *maximal* if for every $a, b \in W$, and $\pi \in \Pi_{\mathbf{G}}$, $aR_\pi b$ iff (*if and only if*) for every two signed formulas x, y such that $x\bar{\pi}y$, either x is not true in b or y is true in a.

Proposition 1. *Let* **G** *be a basic system, and* $\mathcal{W} = \langle W, \mathcal{R}, v \rangle$ *be a maximal* **G**-legal frame. The following hold for every $\pi_1, \pi_2, \pi_3 \in \Pi_{\mathbf{G}}$:

(1) If $\pi_1 = \emptyset$, *then* R_{π_1} *is the full relation.*
(2) If $\bar{\pi}_3 = \bar{\pi}_1 \cup \bar{\pi}_2$, *then* $R_{\pi_3} = R_{\pi_2} \cap R_{\pi_1}$. *In particular:*
    (a) If $\bar{\pi}_1 \subseteq \bar{\pi}_2$, *then* $R_{\pi_2} \subseteq R_{\pi_1}$.

(b) If $\bar{\pi}_1 \subseteq \bar{\pi}_0$, then R_{π_1} is a reflexive relation.

(3) If $\bar{\pi}_3 \subseteq \bar{\pi}_1 \circ \bar{\pi}_2$, then $R_{\pi_2} \circ R_{\pi_1} \subseteq R_{\pi_3}$. In particular, if $\bar{\pi}_1 \subseteq \bar{\pi}_1 \circ \bar{\pi}_1$, then R_{π_1} is a transitive relation.

(4) If $x\bar{\pi}_2 y$ implies $\bar{y}\bar{\pi}_1\bar{x}$ (where $\overline{f{:}\psi} \doteq t{:}\psi$ and $\overline{t{:}\psi} \doteq f{:}\psi$), then $R_{\pi_1} \subseteq R_{\pi_2}^{-1}$. In particular, if $x\bar{\pi}_1 y$ implies $\bar{y}\bar{\pi}_1\bar{x}$, then R_{π_1} is a symmetric relation.

Example 8. Assume that $\pi_0, \pi_{int} \in \Pi_{\mathbf{G}}$ (as in the system for intuitionistic logic). Since $\pi_{int}^- \circ \pi_{int}^- = \pi_{int}^-$, $R_{\pi_{int}}$ is a transitive relation in maximal **G**-legal frames. Since $\pi_{int}^- \subseteq \pi_0^-$, $R_{\pi_{int}}$ is reflexive. We obtain that in maximal **G**-legal frames $R_{\pi_{int}}$ is a preorder, as Kripke semantics for intuitionistic logic is usually defined.

Theorem 2. *Let* **G** *be a basic system, and* $\mathcal{S}\cup\{s\}$ *be a set of sequents. If* $\mathcal{S} \not\vdash_{\mathbf{G}} s$ *then there exists a* maximal **G***-legal frame which is a model of* $\mathcal{S}$, *but not of* s.

Taken together, Theorems 1 and 2 imply various well-known completeness theorems for specific basic systems. Indeed, with the exception of GL (which we discuss later), for every system in Example 2 our semantics is equivalent to the usual Kripke semantics of the corresponding logic. Here are some other examples:

Example 9 (KB). Let **KB** be the basic system for the modal logic KB ([17]), obtained from the system for classical logic by adding the rule $\{\langle \Rightarrow p_1, \pi\rangle\}/ \Rightarrow \Box p_1$, where $\pi = \{\langle f{:}p_1, f{:}\Box p_1\rangle, \langle t{:}\Box p_1, t{:}p_1\rangle\}$. Applications of this rule allow to infer $\Box\Gamma \Rightarrow \Delta, \Box\psi$ from $\Gamma \Rightarrow \Box\Delta, \psi$. **KB**-legal frames include two relations, R_{π_0} (the identity relation) and R_{π}. The rules of **KB** dictate the usual semantics of modal logic for every connective. By Proposition 1, in maximal **KB**-legal frames R_{π} is a symmetric relation. It follows that **KB** is sound and complete with respect to usual symmetric Kripke frames.

Example 10 (Intuitionistic S5). Consider the basic system $\mathbf{G}_3$ from [11] (obtained from the propositional part of **LJ**′ by adding the usual $S5$ rules for $\Box$). Here $\Pi_{\mathbf{G}_3} = \{\pi_0, \pi_{int}, \pi_{S5}\}$. Maximal $\mathbf{G}_3$-legal frames include three relations, R_{π_0} (the identity relation), a preorder $R_{\pi_{int}}$, and an equivalence relation $R_{\pi_{S5}}$. π_{S5} and the rules for $\Box$ enforce the usual Kripke semantics of $\Box$ with respect to $R_{\pi_{S5}}$. π_{int} and the rules for the intuitionistic connective dictate the usual Kripke intuitionistic semantics with respect to $R_{\pi_{int}}$. Note that π_{int} also enforces persistence of $\Box$-formulas, i.e. if $aR_{\pi_{int}}b$ and $v(a, \Box\psi) = \mathrm{T}$ then $v(b, \Box\psi) = \mathrm{T}$. This condition is equivalent to the following one: if $aR_{\pi_{int}}b$ and $v(c, \psi) = \mathrm{T}$ for every world c such that $aR_{\pi_{S5}}c$, then $v(d, \psi) = \mathrm{T}$ for every world d such that $bR_{\pi_{S5}}d$. The Kripke semantics presented in [11] is not identical to the one obtained by our method. In particular, in our semantics $R_{\pi_{S5}}$ should be an equivalence relation, and no direct conditions bind $R_{\pi_{int}}$ and $R_{\pi_{S5}}$.

Example 11. Consider the basic system **G** obtained from the propositional part of **LJ**′ by adding the rules: $\{\langle \Rightarrow \neg p_1, \pi_{S4}\rangle\}/ \Rightarrow \Box\neg p_1$ and $\{\langle p_1 \Rightarrow, \pi_0\rangle\}/\Box p_1 \Rightarrow$. Applications of the first rule allow to infer $\Box\Gamma \Rightarrow \Box\neg\psi$ from $\Box\Gamma \Rightarrow \neg\psi$. Maximal **G**-legal frames include the identity relation R_{π_0}, and two preorders $R_{\pi_{int}}$ and $R_{\pi_{S4}}$, such that $R_{\pi_{int}} \subseteq R_{\pi_{S4}}$. The rules of **LJ**′ dictate the usual semantics of the intuitionistic connectives, The two other rules and π_{S4} impose the following three conditions: (1) if $v(b, \neg\psi) = $ T for every world b such that $aR_{\pi_{S4}}b$ then $v(a, \square\neg\psi) = $ T; (2) if $v(a, \psi) = $ F then $v(a, \square\psi) = $ F; (3) if $v(a, \square\psi) = $ T then $v(b, \square\psi) = $ T for every world b such that $aR_{\pi_{S4}}b$. As in Example 10, π_{int} also enforces persistence of $\square$-formulas. But, since $R_{\pi_{int}} \subseteq R_{\pi_{S4}}$, this condition must hold if (3) holds. In this case we get non-deterministic semantics. To see this, note that if ψ is not of the form $\neg\varphi$ and $v(b, \psi) = $ T whenever $aR_{\pi_{S4}}b$, then $v(a, \square\psi)$ can be freely chosen between T and F.

Remark 2. The last example provides a case in which the various constraints imposed by the rules (and context-relations) of a system do not uniquely determine the truth-value of a compound formula. Another, more natural, example is given by the system for *primal* intuitionistic logic from [10] (see also [5]). These examples demonstrate the need in general of *non-deterministic* semantics.

Example 12 (GL). Let **GL** be the basic system for the modal logic of provability GL (see Example 1). It is well-known that **GL** is sound and complete with respect to the set of modal Kripke frames whose accessibility relation is transitive and conversely well-founded. However, **GL** is not *strongly* complete with respect to this set of frames ([16]), and the compactness theorem fails for the logic induced by this semantics. Using our method, one obtains a different Kripke semantics for GL with an unusual interpretation of $\square$. Indeed, maximal **GL**-legal frames include one (non-trivial) transitive relation, $R_{\pi_{K4}}$. The rules and context-relations of **GL** impose the usual truth-tables in every world for the classical connectives. Concerning $\square$, a maximal **GL**-legal frame admits the usual semantics of $\square$, and it should also satisfy the following condition: if $v(b, \psi) = $ F for some b such that $aR_{\pi_{K4}}b$, then there is some c such that $aR_{\pi_{K4}}c$, $v(c, \psi) = $ F and $v(c, \square\psi) = $ T. By Theorems 1 and 2, GL is *strongly* sound and complete with respect to this semantics (and so the compactness theorem does hold for this semantic consequence relation). It can easily be verified that every usual GL-frame is **GL**-legal. However, the converse is not true.

5   Semantic Characterization of Analyticity

In this section we investigate the crucial property of *analyticity* in the framework of basic systems. Roughly speaking, a sequent system is (strongly) *analytic* if whenever some sequent is provable in it (from a set of assumptions), then this sequent can be proven using only the syntactic material available within (the assumptions and) the proven sequent. For the formal definition, we use the following relation:

Definition 10. Let **G** be a basic system, $\mathcal{S} \cup \{s\}$ be a set of sequents, and $\mathcal{E}$ be a set of formulas. $\mathcal{S} \vdash^{\mathcal{E}}_{\mathbf{G}} s$ if there exists a proof in **G** of s from $\mathcal{S}$, containing only formulas from $\mathcal{E}$.

Definition 11. A basic system **G** is *analytic* if $\mathcal{S} \vdash_{\mathbf{G}} s$ implies $\mathcal{S} \vdash^{sub[\mathcal{S} \cup \{s\}]}_{\mathbf{G}} s$.

The following are two major consequences of analyticity.

Proposition 2 (Consistency). *Let* **G** *be an analytic basic system. Assume that the basic rule* $\emptyset / \Rightarrow$ *is not in* **G**. *Then,* $\nvdash_{\mathbf{G}} \Rightarrow$.

Proof. Assume that $\vdash_{\mathbf{G}} \Rightarrow$. Since **G** is analytic, $\vdash_{\mathbf{G}}^{\emptyset} \Rightarrow$. The only way one can prove $\Rightarrow$ without using any formulas, is using a rule of the form $\emptyset / \Rightarrow$. □

Proposition 3 (Decidability). *Let* **G** *be an analytic basic system. Given a finite set* $\mathcal{S}$ *of sequents and a sequent* s, *it is decidable whether* $\mathcal{S} \vdash_{\mathbf{G}} s$ *or not.*

Proof. Let $\mathcal{S}'$ be the set of sequents consisting of formulas from $sub[\mathcal{S} \cup \{s\}]$, and let $n = |\mathcal{S}'|$. Since **G** is analytic, if $\mathcal{S} \vdash_{\mathbf{G}} s$ then there exists a proof of s from $\mathcal{S}$ in **G** having length $\leq n$ (viewing a proof as a sequence), and consisting only of sequents from $\mathcal{S}'$. Thus an exhaustive proof-search is possible. □

We shall obtain a characterization of analyticity by identifying a *semantic* consequence relation that corresponds to $\vdash_{\mathbf{G}}^{\mathcal{E}}$. For this purpose, we define *semiframes*.

Definition 12. Let $\mathcal{E}$ be a set of formulas.

1. An $\mathcal{E}$-*semiframe* is a tuple $\langle W, \mathcal{R}, v \rangle$, where W and $\mathcal{R}$ are as in Definition 5, and $v : W \times \mathcal{E} \to \{\text{T}, \text{F}\}$ is a valuation function.
2. Given an $\mathcal{E}$-semiframe $\langle W, \mathcal{R}, v \rangle$, a signed formula of the form $f{:}\psi$ (resp. $t{:}\psi$) is *true* in some world $a \in W$ if $\psi \in \mathcal{E}$ and $v(a, \psi) = \text{F}$ ($v(a, \psi) = \text{T}$).
3. A frame $\langle W, \mathcal{R}, v' \rangle$ (see Definition 5) *extends* an $\mathcal{E}$-semiframe $\langle W, \mathcal{R}, v \rangle$ if $v'(a, \psi) = v(a, \psi)$ whenever $\psi \in \mathcal{E}$.

Note that a frame (Definition 5) is obtained as a special case, when $\mathcal{E} = Frm_{\mathcal{L}}$.

Definition 13. Given an $\mathcal{E}$-semiframe $\mathcal{W} = \langle W, \mathcal{R}, v \rangle$ and a sequent s:

1. s is *true* in some $a \in W$ if s is an $\mathcal{E}$-sequent and there exists $x \in s$ such that x is true in a.
2. Let $R \in \mathcal{R}$. s is R-*true* in $a \in W$ if s is an $\mathcal{E}$-sequent and s is true in every $b \in W$ such that aRb.
3. $\mathcal{W}$ is a *model* of a sequent s if s is true in every $a \in W$. $\mathcal{W}$ is a model of a set of sequents $\mathcal{S}$ if it is a model of every $s \in \mathcal{S}$.

(Maximal) **G**-legal semiframes are defined as follows:

Definition 14. Let **G** be a basic system, and $\mathcal{E}$ be a set of formulas.

- An $\mathcal{E}$-semiframe $\mathcal{W} = \langle W, \mathcal{R}, v \rangle$ is **G**-*legal* if the following hold:
  (1) $\mathcal{R}$ consists of a relation R_π for every context-relation $\pi \in \Pi_{\mathbf{G}}$, where R_{π_0} is the identity relation.
  (2) For every $a, b \in W$, and $\pi \in \Pi_{\mathbf{G}}$, if $aR_\pi b$ then for every two signed $\mathcal{E}$-formulas x, y such that $x\bar{\pi}y$, either x is not true in b, or y is true in a.
  (3) For every $a \in W$, $\mathcal{L}$-substitution σ, and $S/C \in \mathbf{G}$, if $frm[\sigma(C)] \subseteq \mathcal{E}$, and $\sigma(s)$ is R_π-true in a for every $\langle s, \pi \rangle \in S$, then $\sigma(C)$ is true in a.
- A **G**-legal $\mathcal{E}$-semiframe $\mathcal{W} = \langle W, \mathcal{R}, v \rangle$ is called *maximal* if for every $a, b \in W$ and $\pi \in \Pi_{\mathbf{G}}$, the converse of the condition in (2) holds as well.

Proposition 4. *Let* **G** *be a basic system, and* $\mathcal{W} = \langle W, \mathcal{R}, v \rangle$ *be a maximal* **G**-*legal* $\mathcal{E}$-*semiframe.*

1. (1), (2) *and* (4) *from Proposition 1 hold without any changes.*
2. *If for every two signed* $\mathcal{E}$-*formulas* x, y, $x\bar{\pi}_3 y$ *implies that there exists a signed* $\mathcal{E}$-*formula* z *such that* $x\bar{\pi}_1 z$ *and* $z\bar{\pi}_2 y$, *then* $R_{\pi_2} \circ R_{\pi_1} \subseteq R_{\pi_3}$.
3. $|W| \leq 2^{|\mathcal{E}|}$.

We now define the semantic consequence relation $\vDash_{\mathbf{G}}^{\mathcal{E}}$, and prove a stronger soundness and completeness theorem.

Definition 15. *Let* **G** *be a basic system,* $\mathcal{S} \cup \{s\}$ *be a set of sequents, and* $\mathcal{E}$ *be a set of formulas.* $\mathcal{S} \vDash_{\mathbf{G}}^{\mathcal{E}} s$ *if every* **G**-*legal* $\mathcal{E}$-*semiframe which is a model of every* $\mathcal{E}$-*sequent* $s' \in \mathcal{S}$, *is also a model of* s.

Theorem 3. *Let* **G** *be a basic system, and* $\mathcal{E}$ *be a set of formulas.*

1. $\vdash_{\mathbf{G}}^{\mathcal{E}} = \vDash_{\mathbf{G}}^{\mathcal{E}}$.
2. *If* $\mathcal{S} \nvdash_{\mathbf{G}}^{\mathcal{E}} s$ *then there exists a* maximal **G**-*legal* $\mathcal{E}$-*semiframe which is a model of every* $\mathcal{E}$-*sequent* $s' \in \mathcal{S}$, *but not a model of* s.

Theorems 1 and 2 are derived now as corollaries, by choosing $\mathcal{E} = Frm_{\mathcal{L}}$. Together with Proposition 4, Theorem 3 makes it possible to have a semantic decision procedure for $\vdash_{\mathbf{G}}$ in case **G** is analytic (compare with the syntactic one in Proposition 3). Indeed, let $\mathcal{E} = sub[\mathcal{S} \cup \{s\}]$. To decide whether $\mathcal{S} \vdash_{\mathbf{G}} s$, it suffices to check triples of the form $\langle W, \mathcal{R}, v \rangle$ where $|W| \leq 2^{|\mathcal{E}|}$, $|\mathcal{R}| = |\Pi_{\mathbf{G}}|$, and $v \in W \times \mathcal{E} \to \{\text{T}, \text{F}\}$. $\mathcal{S} \nvdash_{\mathbf{G}}^{\mathcal{E}} s$ iff one of these semiframes is a **G**-legal model of $\mathcal{S}$, which is not a model of s. If **G** is analytic, then $\mathcal{S} \vdash_{\mathbf{G}}^{\mathcal{E}} s$ iff $\mathcal{S} \vdash_{\mathbf{G}} s$. In this case the semantics is effective, leading to a counter-model search procedure. Another corollary is the following characterization of analyticity.

Corollary 1 (Semantic Characterization of Analyticity). *A basic system* **G** *is analytic iff for every* $\mathcal{S}$ *and* s, $\mathcal{S} \vDash_{\mathbf{G}} s$ *implies* $\mathcal{S} \vDash_{\mathbf{G}}^{sub[\mathcal{S} \cup \{s\}]} s$.

The above characterization might be quite complicated to be used in practice. We present a simpler *sufficient* criterion:

Corollary 2. *Let* **G** *be a basic system. If every maximal* **G**-*legal* $\mathcal{E}$-*semiframe can be extended to a* **G**-*legal frame for every finite set* $\mathcal{E}$ *of formulas closed under subformulas, then* **G** *is analytic.*

The last corollary provides a uniform and simple method of proving that a specific basic system is analytic. Indeed, the required "extension property" can very easily be proved for the Kripke semantics of various basic systems mentioned above. This includes (the propositional parts of): **LK**, **LJ**′, **SLK**[1] from [8], various systems for modal logics from [17] (including those presented in Examples 7 and 9), the family of coherent canonical systems from [6], and many more. Hence all of them are analytic.[2]

---

[2] Concerning **SLK**[1], it was shown in [9] and [12] that it does not enjoy cut-admissibility. From our results it follows that it is nevertheless analytic. This answers a question raised in [12].

Remark 3. The criterion given in Corollary 2 is *not necessary for analyticity.* For example, the system **GL** (see Example 12) is analytic (and even enjoys strong cut-admissibility, as can be shown by a straightforward generalization of the proof of cut-admissibility for it given in [1]), yet it does not meet the semantic condition of Corollary 2. To see this, let $\mathcal{E} = \{p_1, \Box p_1\}$, and let $\mathcal{W} = \langle W, \{R_{\pi_{K4}}\}, v\rangle$ be an $\mathcal{E}$-semiframe, where $W = \{a, b\}$, $R_{\pi_{K4}} = \{\langle a, a\rangle, \langle a, b\rangle\}$, $v(a, p_1) = v(b, p_1) = v(a, \Box p_1) = \text{F}$ and $v(b, \Box p_1) = \text{T}$. W is a maximal **GL**-legal $\mathcal{E}$-semiframe, but it cannot be extended to a **GL**-legal frame: there is no way to assign a truth-value to $\Box\Box p_1$. This phenomenon might be connected with the fact that the natural first-order extension of **GL** does *not* enjoy cut-admissibility ([1]). Further research is needed to clarify this issue (and hopefully to find an effective semantic criterion which is both sufficient and necessary).

Remark 4. While analyticity is defined using the *subformula* relation, it is also possible to study more general notions of analyticity. Indeed, let $\preceq$ be any partial order on $Frm_{\mathcal{L}}$, such that $\{\psi \mid \psi \preceq \varphi\}$ is finite and computable for every φ. For every set $\mathcal{S}$ of sequents, let $\preceq[\mathcal{S}] = \{\psi \mid \exists\varphi \in frm[\mathcal{S}].\psi \preceq \varphi\}$. It is now possible to define $\preceq$-analyticity as in Definition 11 with $\preceq$ instead of *sub*. Consistency and decidability of a basic system follow from its $\preceq$-analyticity. By a straightforward generalization of Corollary 1, we obtain that a basic system **G** is $\preceq$-analytic iff $\mathcal{S} \models_{\mathbf{G}} s$ implies $\mathcal{S} \models_{\mathbf{G}}^{\preceq[\mathcal{S}\cup\{s\}]} s$. This can be used for basic systems which are not strictly analytic, but are nevertheless $\preceq$-analytic for some well-founded partial order on $Frm_{\mathcal{L}}$. For example, this is the case with some systems of the family **LJ(S)** in [4], which extend **LJ**$'$ with different rules for negation. For these systems, it can be proven that whenever $\mathcal{S} \vdash s$, then there also exists a proof involving only subformulas of $S \cup \{s\}$ and their negations.

6 Semantic Characterization of Strong Cut-Admissibility

While analyticity of a proof system suffices for many desirable properties, cut-admissibility is traditionally preferred (especially if all other rules enjoy the subformula property, in which case cut-admissibility implies analyticity). Since in this work we deal with proofs from arbitrary sets of assumptions (not necessarily the empty one), we again consider a stronger property: the one which was called *strong* cut-admissibility in [2]. In this section we provide a semantic characterization of the basic sequent systems which enjoy this property. This characterization can serve as a uniform basis for semantic proofs of many (strong) cut-admissibility theorems in various basic systems.

Definition 16. Let **G** be a basic system, $\mathcal{S} \cup \{s\}$ be a set of sequents, and $\mathcal{E}$ be a set of formulas. $\mathcal{S} \vdash_{\mathbf{G}}^{\mathcal{E}_{cuts}} s$ if there exists a proof in **G** of s from $\mathcal{S}$, in which the cut formula of every application of the cut rule is in $\mathcal{E}$.

Definition 17. A basic system **G** enjoys *strong cut-admissibility* if $\mathcal{S} \vdash_{\mathbf{G}} s$ implies $\mathcal{S} \vdash_{\mathbf{G}}^{frm[\mathcal{S}]_{cuts}} s$.

As for analyticity, the semantic characterization of cut-admissibility is obtained by identifying a semantic consequence relation that corresponds to $\vdash_{\mathbf{G}}^{\mathcal{E}_{cuts}}$. For that purpose, we define another generalization of frames, called *quasiframes*.

Definition 18. Let $\mathcal{E}$ be a set of formulas.

1. An $\mathcal{E}$-*quasiframe* is a tuple $\langle W, \mathcal{R}, v \rangle$, where W and $\mathcal{R}$ are as in Definition 5, and $v : W \times Frm_{\mathcal{L}} \rightarrow \{\text{T}, \text{F}, \text{I}\}$ is a valuation function, such that $v(w, \psi) \in \{\text{T}, \text{F}\}$ for every $\psi \in \mathcal{E}$.
2. Given an $\mathcal{E}$-quasiframe $\langle W, \mathcal{R}, v \rangle$, a signed formula of the form $f{:}\psi$ (resp. $t{:}\psi$) is *true* in some world $a \in W$ if $v(a, \psi) \in \{\text{F}, \text{I}\}$ ($v(a, \psi) = \{\text{T}, \text{I}\}$).
3. A frame $\langle W, \mathcal{R}, v' \rangle$ (see Definition 5) *refines* an $\mathcal{E}$-quasiframe $\langle W, \mathcal{R}, v \rangle$ if $v'(a, \psi) \geq_k v(a, \psi)$ for every $a \in W$ and $\psi \in Frm_{\mathcal{L}}$, where the partial order $\geq_k$ on $\{\text{T}, \text{F}, \text{I}\}$ is defined by: $x \geq_k x, \text{T} \geq_k \text{I}$, and $\text{F} \geq_k \text{I}$.

The third truth-value I is used in quasiframes to distinguish the formulas that belong to $\mathcal{E}$ (on which cut is allowed) from those that do not. Note that if $\psi \notin \mathcal{E}$ then $v(a, \psi)$ can be I, making both $f{:}\psi$ and $t{:}\psi$ true in a. Note also that a frame (Definition 5) is again obtained as a special case: it is an $Frm_{\mathcal{L}}$-quasiframe. Definition 6 is extended to quasiframes without any changes. (Maximal) **G**-legal quasiframes are defined as follows:

Definition 19. Let **G** be a basic system, and $\mathcal{E}$ be a set of formulas.

1. An $\mathcal{E}$-quasiframe $\mathcal{W} = \langle W, \mathcal{R}, v \rangle$ is **G**-*legal* if the conditions formulated in Definition 7 hold for $\mathcal{W}$, except for the third condition, which should apply to all basic rules *except for the cut-rule*.
2. A **G**-legal $\mathcal{E}$-quasiframe $\mathcal{W}$ is called *maximal* if the condition in Definition 9 holds for $\mathcal{W}$.

Proposition 5. *Properties* $(1) - (3)$ *from Proposition 1 hold for maximal **G**-legal quasiframes.*

We now define the relation $\models_{\mathbf{G}}^{\mathcal{E}_{cuts}}$, and strengthen Theorems 1 and 2.

Definition 20. Let **G** be a basic system, $\mathcal{S} \cup \{s\}$ be a set of sequents, and $\mathcal{E}$ be a set of formulas. $\mathcal{S} \models_{\mathbf{G}}^{\mathcal{E}_{cuts}} s$ if every **G**-legal $\mathcal{E}$-quasiframe which is a model of $\mathcal{S}$, is also a model of s.

Theorem 4. *Let **G** be a basic system, and $\mathcal{E}$ be a set of formulas.*

1. $\vdash_{\mathbf{G}}^{\mathcal{E}_{cuts}} = \models_{\mathbf{G}}^{\mathcal{E}_{cuts}}$.
2. *If $\mathcal{S} \nvdash_{\mathbf{G}}^{\mathcal{E}_{cuts}} s$ then there exists a maximal **G**-legal $\mathcal{E}$-quasiframe which is a model of $\mathcal{S}$, but not a model of s.*

The following characterization of strong cut-admissibility is a simple corollary.

Corollary 3 (Semantic Characterization of Strong Cut-Admissibility).
*A basic system **G** enjoys strong cut-admissibility iff $\mathcal{S} \models_{\mathbf{G}} s$ implies $\mathcal{S} \models_{\mathbf{G}}^{\mathcal{E}_{cuts}} s$ where $\mathcal{E} = frm[\mathcal{S}]$.*

Example 13. It is well-known that the system **S5** (see Example 1) does not admit strong cut-admissibility. We demonstrate this fact using our semantic characterization. Let s be the sequent $\Rightarrow p_1, \Box\neg\Box p_1$. It is easy to see that s is provable in **S5** (using a cut on $\Box p_1$), and so (by soundness) $\vDash_{\mathbf{S5}} s$. Let $\mathcal{E} = \{p_1, \Box\neg\Box p_1\}$. We show that $\nvdash_{\mathbf{S5}}^{\mathcal{E}_{cuts}} s$ by constructing a **S5**-legal $\mathcal{E}$-quasiframe $\mathcal{W} = \langle W, \mathcal{R}, v \rangle$ which is not a model of s. Let $W = \{a_0, b_0\}$, and $\mathcal{R} = \{R_{\pi_0}, R_{\pi_{S5}}\}$, where R_{π_0} is the identity relation, and $R_{\pi_{S5}} = \{\langle a_0, a_0 \rangle, \langle b_0, b_0 \rangle, \langle a_0, b_0 \rangle\}$. Define $v(a_0, p_1) = v(a_0, \Box\neg\Box p_1) = $ F and $v(a_0, \psi) = $ I for other formulas, $v(b_0, p_1) = v(b_0, \Box p_1) = $ T, $v(b_0, \neg\Box p_1) = v(b_0, \Box\neg\Box p_1) = $ F, and $v(b_0, \psi) = $ I for other formulas. One can now verify that $\mathcal{W}$ is not a model of s and that it a **S5**-legal $\mathcal{E}$-quasiframe. Indeed, all conditions from Definition 7 are met. For example:[3]

- The conditions imposed by π_{S5} are: (1) if $aR_{\pi_{S5}}b$ and $v(a, \Box\psi) = $ T then $v(b, \Box\psi) = $ T; (2) if $aR_{\pi_{S5}}b$ and $v(a, \Box\psi) = $ F then $v(b, \Box\psi) = $ F. Both (1) and (2) hold for $\mathcal{W}$.
- The rules for $\Box$ impose the following conditions: (1) if $v(b, \psi) \in \{$T, I$\}$ for every b such that $aR_{\pi_{S5}}b$, then $v(a, \Box\psi) \in \{$T, I$\}$; (2) if $v(a, \psi) \in \{$F, I$\}$ then $v(a, \Box\psi) \in \{$F, I$\}$. Again, both (1) and (2) hold for $\mathcal{W}$.

Corollary 3 implies that **S5** does not admit strong cut-admissibility.

We present a simpler *sufficient* criterion for strong cut-admissibility.[4]

Corollary 4. *Let* **G** *be a basic system. If every maximal* **G***-legal $\mathcal{E}$-quasiframe can be refined to a* **G***-legal frame, then* **G** *enjoys (strong) cut-admissibility.*

Example 14. It is easy to verify that the criterion given in Corollary 4 holds for the systems **LK**, **LJ$'$**, **K**,**K4**, and **S4** from Example 1, and for **KD** from Example 7. Hence all these systems enjoy strong cut-admissibility.

Example 15 (Intuitionistic S4). Consider the basic system **G$_0$** from [11], obtained from the propositional part of **LJ$'$** by adding the usual $S4$ rules for $\Box$ (see Example 1). Maximal **G$_0$**-legal quasiframes include R_{π_0} (the identity relation), and two preorders $R_{\pi_{int}}$ and $R_{\pi_{S4}}$, such that $R_{\pi_{int}} \subseteq R_{\pi_{S4}}$. The context-relations and the rules of this system dictate the usual Kripke semantics of $\Box$ with respect to $R_{\pi_{S4}}$, and of the intuitionistic connectives with respect to $R_{\pi_{int}}$. It is straightforward to verify that every maximal **G$_0$**-legal quasiframe can be refined to a **G$_0$**-legal frame. It follows that **G$_0$** enjoys (strong) cut-admissibility.

7   Further Research Topics

The examples we have given are somewhat limited in comparison to the generality of the framework we have presented. For example, the conclusions of the

---

[3] The condition of Definition 9 also holds for $\mathcal{W}$, and so $\mathcal{W}$ is a *maximal* **S5**-legal quasiframe. Recall that property (4) from Proposition 1 does not necessarily hold for quasiframes, and so $R_{\pi_{S5}}$ can be non-symmetric.

[4] Here too the example of **GL** shows that this is not a necessary criterion.

basic rules were all either singletons or empty, and only one context-relation was involved in every basic rule. We leave it as a further research to exploit the full power of this framework. In addition, the following extensions of the framework will be investigated in the future: single-conclusion systems, hypersequential systems, systems employing more than two signs, substructural systems, first order logics and beyond.

References

1. Avron, A.: On Modal Systems having arithmetical interpretations. Journal of Symbolic Logic 49, 935–942 (1984)
2. Avron, A.: Gentzen-Type Systems, Resolution and Tableaux. Journal of Automated Reasoning 10, 265–281 (1993)
3. Avron, A.: Classical Gentzen-type Methods in Propositional Many-Valued Logics. In: Fitting, M., Orlowska, E. (eds.) Beyond Two: Theory and Applications of Multiple-Valued Logic, Studies in Fuzziness and Soft Computing, vol. 114, pp. 117–155. Physica Verlag, Heidelberg (2003)
4. Avron, A.: A Non-Deterministic View on Non-Classical Negations. Studia Logica 80, 159–194 (2005)
5. Avron, A., Lahav, O.: On Constructive Connectives and Systems. Journal of Logical Methods in Computer Science 6 (2010)
6. Avron, A., Lev, I.: Non-deterministic Multiple-valued Structures. IJCAR 2001 15 (2005); Avron, A., Lev, I.: Canonical Propositional Gentzen-Type Systems. In: Goré, R.P., Leitsch, A., Nipkow, T. (eds.) IJCAR 2001. LNCS (LNAI), vol. 2083, p. 529. Springer, Heidelberg (2001)
7. Ciabattoni, A., Terui, K.: Towards a Semantic Characterization of Cut-Elimination. Studia Logica 82, 95–119 (2006)
8. Crolard, T.: Subtractive Logic. Theoretical Computer Science 254, 151–185 (2001)
9. Goré, R., Postniece, L.: Combining Derivations and Refutations for Cut-free Completeness in Bi-intuitionistic Logic. Journal of Logic and Computation 20(1), 233–260 (2010)
10. Gurevich, Y., Neeman, I.: The Infon Logic: the Propositional Case. To appear in ACM Transactions on Computation Logic 12 (2011)
11. Ono, H.: On some intuitionistic modal logic, pp. 687–722. Publications of Research Institute for Mathematical Sciences, Kyoto University (1977)
12. Pinto, L., Uustalu, T.: Proof Search and Counter-Model Construction for Bi-intuitionistic Propositional Logic with Labelled Sequents. In: Giese, M., Waaler, A. (eds.) TABLEAUX 2009. LNCS, vol. 5607, pp. 295–309. Springer, Heidelberg (2009)
13. Sambin, G., Valentini, S.: The modal logic of provability. The sequential approach. Journal of Philosophical Logic 11, 311–342 (1982)
14. Takeuti, G.: Proof Theory. North-Holland, Amsterdam (1975)
15. Troelstra, A.S., Schwichtenberg, H.: Basic Proof Theory. Cambridge University Press, Cambridge (1996)
16. Rineke, V.: Provability Logic. In: Zalta, E.N. (ed.) The Stanford Encyclopedia of Philosophy (2010), http://plato.stanford.edu/entries/logic-provability/ (revision November 2010)
17. Wansing, H.: Sequent Systems for Modal Logics. In: Gabbay, D.M., Guenthner, F. (eds.) Handbook of Philosophical Logic, 2nd edn. vol. 8, pp. 61–145 (2002)

Hybrid and First-Order Complete Extensions of CaRet

Laura Bozzelli[1] and Ruggero Lanotte[2]

[1] DLSIIS, Technical University of Madrid (UPM), Madrid, Spain
[2] Università dell'Insubria, Via Valleggio 11, 22100 - Como, Italy

Abstract. We investigate the hybrid extension of CaRet, denoted HyCaRet, obtained by adding the standard existential binder operator $\exists$. We show that the one variable fragment 1-HyCaRet of HyCaRet is expressively complete for the first-order logic FO_μ which extends FO over words with a binary matching predicate. While all the known FO_μ-complete and elementary extensions of CaRet can be linearly translated in 1-HyCaRet, 1-HyCaRet can be exponentially more succinct than them. Moreover, the complexity of its satisfiability and pushdown model-checking problems are 2EXPTIME-complete, which is the same complexity as that of two known FO_μ-complete extensions of CaRet suitable for compositional and modular reasoning, namely CaRet + 'within' and CaRet + 'forgettable past'. Finally, we show that for each $h \geq 1$, satisfiability and pushdown model-checking of the fragment HyCaRet^h of HyCaRet consisting of formulas with nesting depth of $\exists$ at most h is exactly $(h+1)$-EXPTIME-complete.

1 Introduction

The linear temporal logic CaRet and its extensions. CaRet [AEM04] is a well-known context–free extension of LTL + Past, obtained by adding non-regular versions of the standard LTL + Past temporal modalities. Even though verifying context-free properties of pushdown systems is in general undecidable, model checking pushdown systems against CaRet is decidable with the same complexity as standard LTL model-checking for pushdown systems, i.e. EXPTIME-complete [BEM97]. In [AM04], the class of *non-deterministic visibly pushdown automata* (NVPA) is proposed as an automata-theoretic generalization of CaRet. NVPA are pushdown automata where the input symbol determines when the automaton can push or pop, and thus the stack depth at every position. The resulting class of languages (*visibly pushdown languages* or VPL) is closed under all boolean operations, and problems such as universality and inclusion that are undecidable for context–free languages are EXPTIME–complete for VPL. Moreover, NVPA have the same expressiveness as MSO_μ [AM04], which extends the classical monadic second-order logic (MSO) over words with a binary matching predicate. The logic CaRet is less expressive than NVPA and is easily expressible in the first-order fragment FO_μ of MSO_μ. However, it is an open question whether CaRet is FO_μ-complete [AAB08].

More recently, some elementary and FO_μ-complete extensions of CaRet have been introduced. In particular, Alur et al. [AAB08] propose two extensions of CaRet. One, the logic NWTL$^+$, is obtained by adding since and until modalities interpreted on *summary paths*. The other one, more suitable for modular and compositional reasoning, extends CaRet with the non-regular unary modality "within" W. Satisfiability and pushdown model-checking of NWTL$^+$ (resp., CaRet + W) are EXPTIME-complete (resp.,

K. Brünnler and G. Metcalfe (Eds.): TABLEAUX 2011, LNAI 6793, pp. 58–72, 2011.

2EXPTIME-complete). An other extension of CaRet has been studied in [Boz08], where the extension is obtained by adding the well-known unary regular modality "from now on" N [LS95,LMS02]. Satisfiability and pushdown model checking for the resulting logic are shown to be 2EXPTIME-complete.

As illustrated in [AM06], besides software model checking, the theory of CaRet and VPL has applications also in the processing of semistructured data, such as XML documents, where each open-tag is matched with a closing-tag in a well-nested manner.

Hybrid logics. Hybrid logics extend temporal logics by first-order concepts which provide very natural modeling facilities. The main ingredients that set hybrid logics apart from temporal logics are operators for accessing states by names and for dynamically creating new names for states. Applications of hybrid logics range from verification tasks to reasoning about semistructured data [FR06]. Full regular linear-time hybrid logic has been investigated in [FRS03]. Like LTL, it is FO-complete, but its satisfiability problem is non-elementary, and this already holds for the fragment with only two variables [SW07]. However, for its one-variable fragment, which is still FO-complete, satisfiability is elementary and precisely EXPSPACE-complete [SW07,BL08].

Our contribution. In this paper we introduce and investigate a non-regular linear-time hybrid logic, denoted by HyCaRet, which extends CaRet by (position) variables and the binder modality $\exists x$, which binds variable x to some position of the given word.

First, we show that the one-variable fragment 1-HyCaRet of HyCaRet is FO_μ-complete, and this, surprisingly, already holds for *weak* 1-HyCaRet, obtained by disallowing all *non-regular until* modalities. Moreover, 1-HyCaRet represents a unifying and convenient framework for specifying FO_μ-properties. Indeed, we demonstrate that all the known FO_μ-complete and *elementary* extensions of CaRet, namely CaRet + W, CaRet + N, and NWTL$^+$, can be linearly translated into 1-HyCaRet, but (weak) 1-HyCaRet can be 'simultaneously' more succinct than them (w.r.t. the same family of FO_μ-properties). Moreover, for this new logic, the complexity of its satisfiability and pushdown model-checking problems is the same as that of CaRet + N and CaRet + W, i.e., 2EXPTIME-complete. Compared with NWTL$^+$, we pay for conciseness with added complexity. However, we think that the semantics of 1-HyCaRet-modalities is more suitable for reasoning and verification tasks than that of NWTL$^+$-modalities. Furthermore, we conjecture that there is no elementary translation from (weak) 1-HyCaRet to NWTL$^+$ (resp., CaRet + W, CaRet + N).

Second, we show that for each $h \geq 1$, satisfiability and pushdown model-checking of the fragment HyCaRet^h of HyCaRet consisting of formulas with nesting depth of $\exists$ at most h is exactly $(h+1)$-EXPTIME-complete (and this already holds for the two-variable fragment of HyCaRet^h). For the upper bounds, we exploit an automata-theoretic approach based on a translation of HyCaRet formulas into a subclass of generalized Büchi (one-way) *alternating jump automata* (AJA) [Boz07]. The construction, which generalizes the standard tableau-based construction for LTL, is *direct* and *compositional*, and is based on a non-trivial characterization of the satisfaction relation, for a given formula φ, in terms of sequences of pairs of sets associated with φ satisfying determined requirements which can be checked by AJA. Moreover, the AJA $\mathcal{A}_\varphi$ associated with a HyCaRet formula φ has a special structure, and we show that it can be translated into an equivalent Büchi NVPA $\mathcal{P}_\varphi$ which has the same size as $\mathcal{A}_\varphi$ w.r.t. $|\varphi|$. This translation is direct and is a non-trivial readaptation of the standard construction used to convert a

Büchi one-way alternating finite-state word automaton into an equivalent nondeterministic one [MH84]. Finally, for the logic 1-HyCaRet, we show that nested occurrences of $\exists$ can be avoided at no cost, hence membership in 2EXPTIME for its satisfiability and pushdown model-checking problems follows from the above results.

Due to lack of space, many proofs are omitted and can be found in [BL11].

2   Preliminaries

2.1   The Linear Hybrid Logic HyCaRet and Known Extensions of CaRet

A *pushdown alphabet* Σ is a finite alphabet which is partitioned in three disjoint sets Σ_{int}, Σ_c, and Σ_r, where Σ_{int} is a set of *internal actions*, Σ_c is a set of *calls*, and Σ_r is a set of *returns*. For a word w over Σ, $|w|$ is the length of w (we set $|w| = \infty$ if w is infinite). For all $i \leq j < |w|$, $w(i)$ is the ith symbol of w, $w[i, j]$ is the finite word $w(i)w(i+1)$ $\ldots w(j)$, and w^i and $w[i, |w|]$ denote the suffix of w from position i. A finite word w is *well-matched* if inductively or (1) w is empty, or (2) $w = \sigma w'$, $\sigma \in \Sigma_{int}$ and w' is well-matched, or (3) $w = \sigma_c w' \sigma_r w''$, $\sigma_c \in \Sigma_c$, $\sigma_r \in \Sigma_r$, and w' and w'' are well-matched. Let i be a call position of a word w (i.e. $w(i) \in \Sigma_c$). If there is $j > i$ such that j is a return position of w (i.e. $w(j) \in \Sigma_r$) and $w[i+1, j-1]$ is well-matched (note that j is uniquely determined), we say that j is the matching return of i, and i is the matching call of j. We consider five different notions of successor for a position i along a word w [AEM04]:

- The *forward local successor of i along w*, written $\mathrm{succ}(+, w, i)$, is $i+1$ if $i+1 < |w|$, and it is $\perp$ otherwise (the symbol $\perp$ is for 'undefined').
- The *backward local successor*, $\mathrm{succ}(-, w, i)$, is $i-1$ if $i > 0$, and it is $\perp$ otherwise.
- The *forward abstract successor of i along w*, $\mathrm{succ}(a^+, w, i)$. If $w(i) \in \Sigma_c$, then $\mathrm{succ}(a^+, w, i)$ is the matching return of i if any, otherwise $\mathrm{succ}(a^+, w, i) = \perp$. If instead $w(i) \notin \Sigma_c$, then $\mathrm{succ}(a^+, w, i) = i+1$ if $i+1 < |w|$ and $i+1$ is not a matched return position, and $\mathrm{succ}(a^+, w, i) = \perp$ otherwise.
- The *backward abstract successor of i along w*, $\mathrm{succ}(a^-, w, i)$. If there is a position j of w such that $\mathrm{succ}(a^+, w, j) = i$ (note that $j < i$ and j is uniquely determined), then $\mathrm{succ}(a^-, w, i) = j$; otherwise, $\mathrm{succ}(a^-, w, i) = \perp$.
- The *caller of i along w*, $\mathrm{succ}(c, w, i)$, points to the greatest call position $i_c < i$ such that either $\mathrm{succ}(a^+, w, i_c) = \perp$ or $\mathrm{succ}(a^+, w, i_c) > i$ if such a call position exists; otherwise, $\mathrm{succ}(c, w, i) = \perp$.

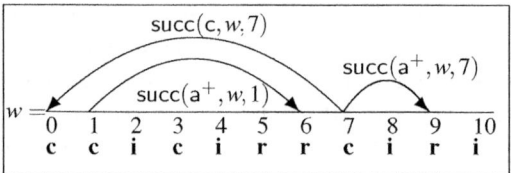

For $i < |w|$ and $dir \in \{+, -, a^+, a^-, c\}$, the *dir-path of w from i*, is the maximal sequence of positions $v = j_0, j_1, \ldots$ such that $j_0 = i$ and $j_h = \mathrm{succ}(dir, w, j_{h-1})$ for each $0 < h < |v|$. Intuitively, the forward and backward abstract paths (i.e., the a^+-paths and a^--paths) capture the local computation within a procedure removing computation fragments corresponding to nested calls, while a caller path (i.e., a c-path) captures the content of the call-stack of a procedure. For example, in the figure above, the sequence $4, 3, 1, 0$ is a caller path, while the sequence $1, 6, 7, 9, 10$ is a forward abstract path.

The hybrid logic HyCaRet: Fix a finite set AP of atomic propositions and let $call, ret,$ int be three special symbols not in AP. The pushdown alphabet induced by AP is $\Sigma = \{call, ret, int\} \times 2^{AP}$, where $\Sigma_{int} = \{int\} \times 2^{AP}$, $\Sigma_c = \{call\} \times 2^{AP}$, and $\Sigma_r = \{ret\} \times 2^{AP}$. Fix a countable set $\{x_1, x_2, \ldots\}$ of variables. The syntax of HyCaRet on AP is as follows:

$$\varphi ::= \text{true} \mid p \mid x_h \mid \neg\varphi \mid \varphi \wedge \varphi \mid X^{dir}\varphi \mid \varphi U^{dir}\varphi \mid \varphi \widetilde{U}^c\varphi \mid \exists x_h.\varphi$$

where $p \in AP \cup \{call, ret, int\}$, and $dir \in \{+, -, a^+, a^-, c\}$. For each type of successor, HyCaRet provides the corresponding versions of the usual 'next' operator and 'until' operator. Moreover, the logic provides the forward version of the caller until operator U^c, denoted $\widetilde{U}^c$, and the standard *existential binder* operator $\exists$. As in standard LTL, for each $dir \in \{+, -, a^+, a^-, c\}$, we will use $F^{dir}\varphi$ as an abbreviation for $\text{true} U^{dir}\varphi$, and $G^{dir}\varphi$ for $\neg F^{dir}\neg\varphi$. A formula φ is *open* if there is some variable x_h which occurs *free* in φ (i.e., the occurrence is not in the scope of $\exists x_h$). A non-open formula is called *sentence*. The size $|\varphi|$ of a formula φ is the number of distinct subformulas of φ.

HyCaRet is interpreted on words w over $\Sigma = \{call, ret, int\} \times 2^{AP}$. A *valuation* for w is a mapping g assigning to each variable a position $j < |w|$. The satisfaction relation $(w, i, g) \models \varphi$, meaning that φ holds at position i along w w.r.t. the valuation g, is defined by induction as follows (we omit the rules for boolean connectives which are standard):

$(w, i, g) \models p$ iff $w(i) = (d, Y)$ and either $p \in Y$ or $p = d$

$(w, i, g) \models x_h$ iff $g(x_h) = i$

$(w, i, g) \models X^{dir}\varphi$ iff $\text{succ}(dir, w, i) \neq \bot$ and $(w, \text{succ}(dir, w, i), g) \models \varphi$

$(w, i, g) \models \varphi_1 U^{dir}\varphi_2$ iff for the dir-path $\nu = j_0, j_1, \ldots$ of w from i, there is $n < |\nu|$ such that $(w, j_n, g) \models \varphi_2$ and for all $0 \leq h < n, (w, j_h, g) \models \varphi_1$

$(w, i, g) \models \varphi_1 \widetilde{U}^c\varphi_2$ iff there is a prefix of a caller-path $j_0, j_1, \ldots, j_n$ of w leading to $j_n = i$ s.t. $(w, j_0, g) \models \varphi_2$, and for all $0 < h \leq n, (w, j_h, g) \models \varphi_1$

$(w, i, g) \models \exists x_h.\varphi$ iff $(w, i, g[x_h \leftarrow m]) \models \varphi$ for some $m < |w|$

where $g[x_h \leftarrow m](x_h) = m$ and $g[x_h \leftarrow m](x_i) = g(x_i)$ for $i \neq h$. Note that the satisfaction relation depends only on the values assigned to the variables occurring free in the formula. We write $(w, i) \models \varphi$ to mean that $(w, i, g_0) \models \varphi$, where $g_0(x_h) = 0$ for each h.

As example, let us consider the requirement: "*before any occurrence* of condition *cond* within a procedure A, every request p is followed by a response q", which can be expressed in the one-variable fragment of HyCaRet as follows, where t_A holds iff the control is within procedure A:

$$G^+[(t_A \wedge cond) \longrightarrow \exists x. (x \wedge G^{a^-}(p \rightarrow F^{a^+}(q \wedge F^+x)))]$$

In the following, unless stated otherwise, a given HyCaRet formula is assumed to be a sentence. Note that the fragment of HyCaRet obtained by disallowing variables and $\exists$ corresponds to full CaRet [AEM04], while the fragment of HyCaRet obtained by disallowing the non-regular modalities, i.e. X^{dir}, U^{dir}, $\widetilde{U}^c$ with $dir \in \{a^+, a^-, c\}$, corresponds to standard linear hybrid logic [FRS03]. W.l.o.g. we assume that if a formula φ uses at most n-variables, these variables are $x_1, \ldots, x_n$, and we write $(w, i, j_1, \ldots, j_n) \models \varphi$ to mean that $(w, i, g) \models \varphi$ for any valuation g for w such that $g(x_h) = j_h$ for $1 \leq h \leq n$.

We denote by *weak* HyCaRet, the set of HyCaRet formulas obtained by disallowing the *non-regular* modalities, with the exception of the non-regular next-modalities X^{a^+}

and X^c. For each $k \geq 0$, k-HyCaRet denotes the fragment of HyCaRet using at most k variables. For all $h, k \geq 0$, HyCaRet^h and k-HyCaRet^h denote the fragments of HyCaRet and k-HyCaRet, respectively, where the nesting depth of the binder $\exists$-operator is at most h. The *weak* versions of the considered fragments are defined in the obvious way. In the rest of this Section, we recall known extensions of the logic CaRet.

CaRet with forgettable past [Boz08]: this logic is obtained from CaRet by adding the regular unary modality "from Now on" N [LS95,LMS02], which intuitively chops away the past. Formally, the semantics of N is as follows: $(w,i) \models N\varphi$ iff $(w^i, 0) \models \varphi$.

CaRet plus "within" [AEM04,AAB08]: this logic is obtained from CaRet by adding the non-regular unary modality 'within' W, whose semantics is given by

$$(w,i) \models W\varphi \quad \text{iff} \quad w(i) \text{ is a } call \text{ and} (w[i, r_w(i)], 0) \models \varphi$$

where $r_w(i) = \text{succ}(a^+, w, i)$ if i is a matched-call position, and $r_w(i) = |w|$ otherwise. In other words, $W\varphi$ evaluates φ on a subword restricted to a single procedure.

The logics NWTL and NWTL$^+$[AAB08]: these logics are based on the notion of *summary path*. Formally, for a word w, $i \leq j < |w|$, a *summary path of w from i to j* is a sequence $i = j_0 < j_1 \ldots < j_n = j$ such that for each $0 \leq h < n$: if j_h is a matched-call and $\text{succ}(a^+, w, j_h) \leq j$, then $j_{h+1} = \text{succ}(a^+, w, j_h)$; otherwise $j_{h+1} = j_h + 1$. Note that there is exactly one summary path from i to j. The logic NWTL$^+$ extends CaRet with the binary modalities U^σ and S^σ, which correspond to the standard until and since modalities of LTL interpreted on summary paths. Thus, for example, $(w,i) \models \varphi_1 U^\sigma \varphi_2$ iff there is $j \geq i$ such that for the summary path $i = j_0 < j_1 \ldots < j_n = j$ from i to j, $(w,j) \models \varphi_2$ and $(w,j_p) \models \varphi_1$ for each $0 \leq p < n$. NWTL is obtained from NWTL$^+$ by disallowing modalities $U^{dir}, \widetilde{U}^c, X^c$, where $dir \in \{+, -, a^+, a^-, c\}$. [1]

The *satisfiability problem* for any of the considered logics $\mathfrak{F}$ is to decide given a formula φ of $\mathfrak{F}$, whether $\mathcal{L}(\varphi) \neq \emptyset$, where $\mathcal{L}(\varphi)$ denotes the set of *infinite* words w such that $(w,0) \models \varphi$. Given two formulas φ_1 and φ_2, we say that φ_1 and φ_2 are *(globally) equivalent* iff for each word w and $0 \leq i < |w|$, $(w,i) \models \varphi_1 \Leftrightarrow (w,i) \models \varphi_2$.

We will use the following notion. For a word w over a pushdown alphabet Σ and $i < |w|$, the *next unmatched return of i in w*, $\text{UM}(w,i)$, is defined as: if the caller of i is defined and has matching return i_r, then $\text{UM}(w,i) = i_r$; otherwise, $\text{UM}(w,i) = \bot$.

2.2 Automata for Visibly Pushdown Languages

A Büchi *Nondeterministic Visibly Pushdown Automaton* (NVPA) [AEM04] is a tuple $\mathcal{P} = \langle \Sigma, Q, Q_0, \Gamma, \Delta, F \rangle$, where $\Sigma = \Sigma_c \cup \Sigma_r \cup \Sigma_{int}$ is a pushdown alphabet, Q is a finite set of states, $Q_0 \subseteq Q$ is the set of initial states, Γ is the finite stack alphabet, $\Delta \subseteq (Q \times \Sigma_c \times Q \times \Gamma) \cup (Q \times \Sigma_r \times (\Gamma \cup \{\gamma_0\}) \times Q) \cup (Q \times \Sigma_{int} \times Q)$ is the transition relation (where $\gamma_0 \notin \Gamma$ is the *stack bottom symbol*), and $F \subseteq Q$ is a Büchi condition on Q. On reading a call σ_c, $\mathcal{P}$ chooses a push transition of the form (q, σ_c, q', B), pushes the symbol $B \neq \gamma_0$ onto the stack, and the control changes from q to q'. On reading a return σ_r, $\mathcal{P}$ chooses a pop transition of the form (q, σ_r, B, q'), where B is popped from the stack. Finally, on

---

[1] The caller until modalities in [AAB08] have semantics slightly different from that considered here and in [AEM04]. They can be trivially expressed in terms of the caller until modalities $U^c, \widetilde{U}^c$ considered here and the next modalities X^{a^+} and X^c.

reading an internal action σ_{int}, $\mathcal{P}$ can choose only transitions of the form (q, σ_{int}, q') which do not use the stack. The notion of ω-language $L(\mathcal{P})$ accepted by $\mathcal{P}$ is defined as for standard Büchi pushdown automata (for details, see [BL11]). An ω-language L over Σ is a *visibly pushdown language* (VPL) if $L = L(\mathcal{P})$ for some Büchi NVPA $\mathcal{P}$.

We also recall the class of generalized Büchi *Alternating Jump Automata* (AJA) [Boz07], which capture exactly the class of VPL. AJA extend standard alternating finite–state automata by also allowing non-local moves: on reading a matched-call σ_c, a copy of the automaton can move (jump) in a single step to the matching-return of σ_c.

For a set X, $\mathcal{B}_p(X)$ denotes the set of positive boolean formulas over X built from elements in X using $\lor$ and $\land$. A subset Y of X *satisfies* $\theta \in \mathcal{B}_p(X)$ iff the truth assignment assigning `true` to the elements in Y and `false` to the elements of $X \setminus Y$ satisfies θ. A generalized Büchi AJA is a tuple $\mathcal{A} = \langle \Sigma, Q, Q_0, \delta, \mathcal{F} \rangle$, where Σ is a pushdown alphabet, Q is a finite set of states, $Q_0 \subseteq Q$ is the set of initial states, $\delta : Q \times \Sigma \to \mathcal{B}_p(\{+, \mathsf{a}^+\} \times Q \times Q)$ is the transition function, and $\mathcal{F} = \{F_1, \ldots, F_k\}$ is a set of sets of accepting states. A run of $\mathcal{A}$ over an infinite word $w \in \Sigma^\omega$ is a $\mathbb{N} \times Q$-labeled tree r such that the root is labeled by $(0, q_0)$ with $q_0 \in Q_0$ and for each node x with label (i, q) (describing a copy of $\mathcal{A}$ in state q which reads $w(i)$), there is a *minimal* set $H = \{(dir_1, q'_1, q''_1), \ldots, (dir_m, q'_m, q''_m)\} \subseteq \{+, \mathsf{a}^+\} \times Q \times Q$ satisfying $\delta(q, w(i))$ such that x has m children $x_1, \ldots, x_m$, and for each $1 \le h \le m$: x_h has label $(i+1, q''_h)$ if $\mathrm{succ}(dir_h, w, i) = \bot$, and label $(\mathrm{succ}(dir_h, w, i), q'_h)$ otherwise. The run r is *accepting* if for each infinite path $x_0 x_1 \ldots$ in the tree and each accepting component $F \in \mathcal{F}$, there are infinitely many $i \ge 0$ such that x_i is labeled by some state in F. The ω-language of $\mathcal{A}$, $L(\mathcal{A})$, is the set of $w \in \Sigma^\omega$ such that there is an accepting run r of $\mathcal{A}$ over w.

Pushdown model-checking: In order to model verification problems of pushdown systems M using specifications (such as NVPA) denoting VPL languages, we choose a suitable pushdown alphabet $\Sigma = \Sigma_c \cup \Sigma_r \cup \Sigma_{int}$, and associate a symbol in Σ with each transition of M with the restriction that push transitions are mapped to Σ_c, pop transitions are mapped to Σ_r, and transitions that do not use the stack are mapped to Σ_{int}. Note that M equipped with such a labeling is a Büchi NVPA where all the states are accepting. The specification S describes another VPL $L(S)$ over Σ, and M is correct iff $L(M) \subseteq L(S)$.

Given a class C of finite specifications S describing VPL over a pushdown alphabet Σ, the *pushdown model checking problem against C-specifications* is to decide, given a pushdown system M over Σ and a specification S in the class C, whether $L(M) \subseteq L(S)$. Note that all the considered linear logics capture a subclass of the class of VPL.

3   Expressiveness and Succinctness of 1-HyCaRet

In this section, we show that the (weak) one-variable fragment of HyCaRet is expressively complete for the first-order logic FO_μ [AM04], which extends standard FO over words with a binary matching predicate $\mu(x, y)$ that holds iff y is the matching return for the call position x. Moreover, while the FO_μ-complete logics NWTL$^+$, CaRet + N, and CaRet + W can be *linearly* translated into 1-HyCaRet, 1-HyCaRet is exponentially more succinct than them. Note that FO_μ can be trivially and linearly translated into HyCaRet, and vice-versa [AAB08].

FO_μ-completeness of weak 1-HyCaRet: We show that NWTL, which is FO_μ-complete [AAB08], can be *linearly* translated into weak 1-HyCaRet. Hence, the result follows.

We need preliminary results (Claims 1–4 below) whose proofs are in [BL11]. Fix a word w (over a pushdown alphabet Σ) and two positions $i \leq j < |w|$. We say that the summary path of w from i to j is of *type I* if *either* $j = i$, *or* $j > i$ and j is a matched return position whose matching call $\mathrm{succ}(a^-, w, j)$ satisfies $\mathrm{succ}(a^-, w, j) < i$. Moreover, we say that the summary path of w from i to j is of *type II* if *either* $j = i$, *or* $j > i$ and i is a call position such that either $\mathrm{succ}(a^+, w, i) = \bot$ or $\mathrm{succ}(a^+, w, i) > j$.

Claim 1: let π be a summary path of w from i to $j \geq i$ of type I. Then, for all $h \in [i, j[$, π visits position h *if and only if* $\mathrm{succ}(c, w, h) \neq \bot$ and $\mathrm{succ}(c, w, h) < i$.

Claim 2: let π be a summary path of w from i to $j \geq i$ of type II. Then, for all $h \in [i, j]$, π visits position h *if and only if* $\mathrm{UM}(w, h) \neq \bot$ implies $\mathrm{UM}(w, h) > j$.

Claim 3: A sequence $\pi = i_0 < i_1 < \ldots < i_p$ of positions in w is a summary path of w *iff* there are two positions N_I and N_{II} such that $i_0 \leq N_I \leq N_{II} \leq i_p$ and π is the concatenation of three summary paths:

- the first one is a summary path of w from i_0 to N_I of type I;
- the second one is a prefix leading to position N_{II} of the forward abstract path of w from position N_I;
- the third one is a summary path of w from N_{II} to i_p of type II.

Claim 4: let φ_1 and φ_2 be two weak 1-HyCaRet formulas. Then, one can construct in linear time two weak 1-HyCaRet formulas $\mathsf{U}^{a^+}(\varphi_1, \varphi_2)$ and $\mathsf{U}^{a^-}(\varphi_1, \varphi_2)$ such that $\mathsf{U}^{a^+}(\varphi_1, \varphi_2) \equiv \varphi_1 \mathsf{U}^{a^+} \varphi_2$ and $\mathsf{U}^{a^-}(\varphi_1, \varphi_2) \equiv \varphi_1 \mathsf{U}^{a^-} \varphi_2$.

Theorem 1. *Weak 1-HyCaRet is FO_μ-complete. Moreover, NWTL$^+$ can be linearly translated into 1-HyCaRet, and NWTL can be linearly translated into weak 1-HyCaRet.*

Proof. Since NWTL is known to be FO_μ-complete [AAB08], it suffices to show that NWTL can be linearly translated into weak 1-HyCaRet. The next modality X^{a^-} can be easily translated into weak 1-HyCaRet. It remains to show that given two weak 1-HyCaRet formulas φ_1 and φ_2, one can construct in linear time two weak 1-HyCaRet formulas, denoted by $\mathsf{U}^\sigma(\varphi_1, \varphi_2)$ and $\mathsf{S}^\sigma(\varphi_1, \varphi_2)$, such that $\mathsf{U}^\sigma(\varphi_1, \varphi_2) \equiv \varphi_1 \mathsf{U}^\sigma \varphi_2$ and $\mathsf{S}^\sigma(\varphi_1, \varphi_2) \equiv \varphi_1 \mathsf{S}^\sigma \varphi_2$. Here, we illustrate the construction of $\mathsf{U}^\sigma(\varphi_1, \varphi_2)$ (the construction of $\mathsf{S}^\sigma(\varphi_1, \varphi_2)$ is given in [BL11]). First, by using Claims 1 and 2, we construct in linear time two weak 1-HyCaRet formulas $\mathsf{U}_I^\sigma(\varphi_1, \varphi_2)$ and $\mathsf{U}_{II}^\sigma(\varphi_1, \varphi_2)$ such that: $(w, i) \models \mathsf{U}_I^\sigma(\varphi_1, \varphi_2)$ (resp., $(w, i) \models \mathsf{U}_{II}^\sigma(\varphi_1, \varphi_2)$) *iff* there is $j > i$ so that the summary path π of w from i to j is of type I (resp., type II), and φ_1 "until" φ_2 holds along π.

$$\mathsf{U}_I^\sigma(\varphi_1, \varphi_2) := \exists x. \Big[x \wedge \mathsf{X}^+ \mathsf{F}^+ \Big(ret \wedge \varphi_2 \wedge \big(\mathsf{X}^-(\neg call \wedge \mathsf{X}^c \mathsf{X}^+ \mathsf{F}^+ x) \big) \wedge$$
$$\mathsf{X}^- \mathsf{G}^- \big(\mathsf{F}^- x \to \mathsf{X}^c \mathsf{X}^+ \mathsf{F}^+ x \to \varphi_1 \big) \Big) \Big]$$

$$\mathsf{U}_{II}^\sigma(\varphi_1, \varphi_2) := \exists x. \Big((\mathsf{X}^+ \mathsf{F}^+ x) \wedge call \wedge (\mathsf{X}^{a^+} \mathrm{true} \to \mathsf{X}^{a^+} \mathsf{X}^- \mathsf{F}^- x) \wedge \mathsf{F}^+ (x \wedge \varphi_2) \wedge$$
$$\mathsf{G}^+ \big(\mathsf{X}^+ \mathsf{F}^+ x \to \big(\mathsf{X}^c \mathsf{X}^{a^+} \mathrm{true} \to \mathsf{X}^c \mathsf{X}^{a^+} \mathsf{X}^- \mathsf{F}^- x \big) \to \varphi_1 \big) \Big)$$

By Claim 4, we can construct in linear time a weak 1-HyCaRet formula $\mathsf{U}^{a^+}(\varphi_1, \varphi_2)$ such that $\mathsf{U}^{a^+}(\varphi_1, \varphi_2) \equiv \varphi_1 \mathsf{U}^{a^+} \varphi_2$. Then, the formula $\mathsf{U}^\sigma(\varphi_1, \varphi_2)$ is given by

$$\mathsf{U}^\sigma(\varphi_1, \varphi_2) := \mathsf{U}^{a^+}(\varphi_1, \varphi_2) \vee \mathsf{U}_I^\sigma(\varphi_1, \mathsf{U}^{a^+}(\varphi_1, \varphi_2)) \vee \mathsf{U}^{a^+}(\varphi_1, \mathsf{U}_{II}^\sigma(\varphi_1, \varphi_2)) \vee$$
$$\mathsf{U}_I^\sigma(\varphi_1, \mathsf{U}^{a^+}(\varphi_1, \mathsf{U}_{II}^\sigma(\varphi_1, \varphi_2)))$$

By Claim 3 it follows that $U^\sigma(\varphi_1, \varphi_2) \equiv \varphi_1 U^\sigma \varphi_2$.   □

Moreover, we show the following (a proof is given in [BL11]).

Theorem 2. *CaRet* + N *and CaRet* + W *can be linearly translated into* 1-*HyCaRet.*

Succinctness issues: We show that weak 1-HyCaRet can be *simultaneously* exponentially more succinct than CaRet + N, CaRet + W, and NWTL$^+$, i.e. for some set of propositions AP, there is a family $(\varphi_n)_{n\in\mathbb{N}}$ of weak 1-HyCaRet formulas over AP such that for each n, φ_n has size polynomial in n and each equivalent formula of any of the logics CaRet + N, CaRet + W, and NWTL$^+$ has size at least $2^{\Omega(n)}$.

Let $AP = \{a, b, c, 0, 1, \$, \#\}$. An *n-configuration* is a finite word C over 2^{AP} of the form $\{d_1\} \cdot w_1 \ldots \{d_{2^n}\} \cdot w_{2^n}$ s.t. for each $1 \leq i \leq 2^n$, $d_i \in \{a, b\}$ and $w_i \in \{\{0\}, \{1\}\}^n$ is the binary code of $i - 1$. A finite word w over the pushdown alphabet $\Sigma = \{call, ret, int\} \times 2^{AP}$ is *n-good* iff $w = w_1 \cdot w_2$, where w_1 is a *well-matched* word over Σ whose projection over 2^{AP} is of the form $\{c\}^k$ for some $k \geq 0$, and w_2 satisfies the following: w_2 consists of internal actions, and the projection of w_2 over 2^{AP} has the form $\{\$\} \cdot C_1 \cdot \{\$\} \ldots \{\$\} \cdot C_p \cdot \{\$\}$ such that $p > 1$, for each $1 \leq h \leq p$, C_h is a n-configuration, and there is $k > 1$ such that $C_k = C_1$. An infinite n-good word is of the form $w \cdot (int, \{\#\})^\omega$ such that w is a finite n-good word. Note that the set of infinite n-good words is *not* ω-regular.

Lemma 1. *For each* $n \geq 1$, *there is a weak* 1-*HyCaRet formula* φ_n *over AP of size* $O(n^2)$ *such that* $\mathcal{L}(\varphi_n)$ *is the set of infinite n-good words.*

Lemma 2. *For each* $n \geq 1$, *any generalized Büchi AJA accepting the set of infinite n-good words needs at least* $2^{2^{\Omega(n)}}$ *states.*

The proof of Lemmata 1 and 2 are given in [BL11]. In particular, the proof of Lemma 2 is based on the following additional result of independent interest: for an AJA over *finite* words with k states accepting the language L, one can build a *dual deterministic* NVPA over finite words of size $2^{O(k)}$ accepting the reverse of L, where a dual NVPA is defined as a NVPA with the difference that the automaton pushes onto the stack on reading returns, pops the stack on reading calls, and does not use the stack on internal actions.

For each n, let φ_n be the weak 1-HyCaRet formula of Lemma 1 of size $O(n^2)$, and let ψ_n (resp., θ_n) be an equivalent CaRet + N (resp., NWTL$^+$) formula. Since ψ_n can be translated into a generalized Büchi AJA of size $2^{O(|\psi_n|)}$ accepting $\mathcal{L}(\psi_n) = \mathcal{L}(\varphi_n)$ [Boz08], by Lemma 2 it follows that $|\psi_n|$ is at least $2^{\Omega(n)}$. Moreover, since the NWTL$^+$ formula θ_n can be translated into a Büchi NVPA of size $2^{O(|\theta_n|)}$ accepting $\mathcal{L}(\theta_n) = \mathcal{L}(\varphi_n)$ [AAB08], and Büchi NVPA can be translated in quadratic time into equivalent Büchi AJA [Boz07], by Lemma 2 it follows that $|\theta_n|$ is at least $2^{\Omega(n)}$. Since CaRet + W can be linearly translated into CaRet + N [Boz08], by Theorem 2 we obtain the following.

Theorem 3. 1-*HyCaRet (resp., weak* 1-*HyCaRet) is (resp., can be) simultaneously exponentially more succinct than CaRet* + W, *CaRet* + N, *and NWTL$^+$.*

4   Decision Procedures for HyCaRet

In this section we describe an optimal automata-theoretic algorithm to solve satisfiability and pushdown model-checking of HyCaRet and 1-HyCaRet, which is based on a direct translation of HyCaRet formulas into a subclass of generalized Büchi AJA, we call *AJA with main states* (MAJA). Formally, a generalized Büchi MAJA is a generalized Büchi AJA whose set of states is partitioned into a set Q_m of *main states* and into a set Q_s of *secondary* states. Moreover, the following *semantic requirement* holds: in each run of the MAJA and for each input position i, there is at most one copy of the automaton which is in a main state and reads position i (i.e., for each $i \geq 0$, there is at most one node in the run-tree whose label has the form (i, q), where q is a main state).

Theorem 4. *Given a generalized Büchi MAJA $\mathcal{A}$ with set of states $Q = Q_m \cup Q_s$ and acceptance condition $\mathcal{F} = \{F_1, \ldots, F_k\}$, one can construct a Büchi NVPA $\mathcal{P}_{\mathcal{A}}$ with size polynomial in $|Q_m|$ and singly exponential in k and $|Q_s|$ such that $L(\mathcal{P}_A) = L(\mathcal{A})$.*

Sketched proof. In order to obtain an equivalent Büchi NVPA of the desired size, we cannot use the construction in [Boz07] to convert a parity *two-way* AJA into an equivalent Büchi NVPA with a single exponential-time blow-up. Instead the construction proposed here is a non-trivial readaptation of the standard construction used to convert a Büchi one-way alternating finite-state word automaton into an equivalent nondeterministic one with a single exponential-time blow-up [MH84].

Fix a generalized Büchi MAJA $\mathcal{A} = \langle \Sigma, Q = Q_m \cup Q_s, Q_0, \delta, \mathcal{F} \rangle$. By using the standard construction to convert a generalized Büchi nondeterministic finite-state word automaton (NWA) into an equivalent Büchi NWA (see, for example, [Wol00]), we can easily convert $\mathcal{A}$ into an equivalent Büchi MAJA whose set of states $Q' = Q'_m \cup Q'_s$ satisfy $|Q'_m| = k \cdot |Q_m|$ and $|Q'_s| = k \cdot |Q_s|$. Thus, in the following, we can assume that $\mathcal{A}$ is a Büchi MAJA, i.e., $\mathcal{F} = \{F\}$ is a singleton.

We construct a Büchi NVPA $\mathcal{P}_N$ with number of states $O(|Q_m| \cdot 2^{O(|Q_s|)})$ accepting $L(\mathcal{A})$. Essentially, for the given input word w, $\mathcal{P}_N$ guesses a run r of $\mathcal{A}$ over w and checks that it is accepting. At a given position $i > 0$ of a run of $\mathcal{P}_N$, $\mathcal{P}_N$ keeps track by its finite control of the set U_i of states of $\mathcal{A}$ associated with the nodes of r whose input position is i and which have been obtained from the parent node by an ordinary move (obviously, if i is not a matched return position, then all the nodes of r whose input position is i have been obtained in this way). If i is a matched return position with matching call i_c, then the NVPA on reading $w(i_c)$ pushes onto the stack the guessed set R_i of states of $\mathcal{A}$ associated with the copies of $\mathcal{A}$ which read i and have been obtained by a jump-move (starting from position i_c). This ensures that R_i is on the top of the stack when the input position i is read. Moreover, in order to check that r is accepting, the set $\overline{U}_i$, where $\overline{U}_i = U_i$ if i is not a matched return position, and $\overline{U}_i = U_i \cup R_i$ otherwise, is split into two sets, say $\overline{U}_i^1$ and $\overline{U}_i^2$, in order to distinguish between paths of the run tree r that hit F recently and paths that did not hit F recently. The crucial observation is that each infinite path of r from the root visits all the positions i such that $\mathsf{UM}(w, i) = \bot$, and the set of these positions is always infinite (also if we remove from this set those positions j such that j is a matched return). Thus, by König's Lemma, if r is accepting, then the set of input positions can be partitioned into infinitely many nonempty segments such that: (1) for each segment, its starting position i satisfies $\mathsf{UM}(w, i) = \bot$ and i is not a matched return, and (2) each suffix of an infinite path of r that starts at the beginning of a segment will visit an accepting state in F before reaching the end of the segment. Then, the set $\overline{U}_i^1$ (resp., $\overline{U}_i^2$) represents the set of states associated with the copies of the automaton $\mathcal{A}$ (reading i) in r that have not visited so far (have already visited) a state in

F in the current segment. Furthermore, in the construction we use the fact that for each input position i, there is at most one node of r whose label is of the form (i, q), where q is a main state. Details of the construction of $\mathcal{P}_N$ are given in [BL11]. $\square$

In the following, first we give a characterization of the satisfaction relation $(w, 0) \models \varphi$, for a given formula HyCaRet φ, in terms of sequences of pairs of sets associated with φ satisfying determined requirements which can be checked by generalized Büchi MAJA. Then, we describe the translation into MAJA based on this characterization. For all $n, k \geq 0$, let $\text{Tower}(n, 0) = n$ and $\text{Tower}(n, k+1) = 2^{\text{Tower}(n,k)}$.

Characterization of the satisfaction relation. Fix $n \geq 1$ and a (*possibly open*) formula φ in n-HyCaRet over a finite set AP of atomic propositions. Let $[n] = \{1, \dots, n\}$ and $\Sigma = \{call, ret, int\} \times 2^{AP}$. For clarity of presentation, we assume that φ does not contain occurrences of modality $\widetilde{U}^c$. It is easy to extend the construction to allow also $\widetilde{U}^c$ without changing the time complexity of the translation (for details see [BL11]). We denote by $d_\exists(\varphi)$ the nesting depth of modality $\exists$ in φ. A formula ψ is a *first-level subformula of* φ if there is an occurrence of ψ in φ which is *not* in the scope of modality $\exists$. The *closure* $\text{cl}(\varphi)$ of φ is the smallest set containing true, each proposition in $AP \cup \{call, ret, int\}$, variable x_h for each $h \in [n]$, $X^{dir}\text{true}$ for each $dir \in \{+, -, a^+, a^-, c\}$, all the *first-level* subformulas of φ, $X^{dir}(\psi_1 U^{dir} \psi_2)$ for any *first-level* subformula $\psi_1 U^{dir} \psi_2$ of φ, and the negations of all these formulas (we identify $\neg\neg\psi$ with ψ). For each forward local until formula $\psi_1 U^+ \psi_2 \in \text{cl}(\varphi)$, we introduce a new symbol τ_{ψ_2} associated with the liveness requirement ψ_2, and denote by $P(\varphi)$ the set of these symbols. The intended meaning of proposition τ_{ψ_2} is as follows: fix a word w and a matched-call position i_c with matching return i_r such that $\text{UM}(w, i_c) = \bot$. Then, τ_{ψ_2} 'holds' at position i_c iff ψ_2 holds at some position in $[i_c, i_r]$ (w.r.t. a fixed valuation of variables $x_1, \dots, x_n$).

Essentially, for each infinite word w over Σ and valuation $j_1, \dots, j_n$ of variables $x_1, \dots, x_n$, we associate to w infinite sequences $\pi = (A_0^r, A_0), (A_1^r, A_1) \dots$ of pairs of sets, where for each $i \geq 0$, A_i is an *atom* and intuitively describes a maximal set of subformulas of φ which can hold at position i along w w.r.t. the valuation $j_1, \dots, j_n$ of variables $x_1, \dots, x_n$, while $A_i^r = \emptyset$ if $\text{UM}(w, i) = \bot$, and $A_i^r = A_{\text{UM}(w,i)}$ otherwise. The set $\text{Atoms}(\varphi)$ of *atoms of* φ is defined by induction on $d_\exists(\varphi)$. In particular, we require that each atom $A \in \text{Atoms}(\varphi)$ contains some arbitrary elements of $P(\varphi)$ and the following objects:

- some formulas in $\text{cl}(\varphi)$. As for LTL, the set S of these formulas has to satisfy additional requirements, which syntactically capture the semantic of boolean connectives, the fixpoint characterization of the until modalities in terms of the next modalities of the same type, and some consistency constraints between different next modalities. Thus, for example, we require that for each $\psi_1 U^{dir} \psi_2 \in \text{cl}(\varphi)$ (where $dir \in \{+, -, a^+, a^-, c\}$), $\psi_1 U^{dir} \psi_2 \in S$ iff *either* $\psi_2 \in S$ *or* $\psi_1, X^{dir}(\psi_1 U^{dir} \psi_2) \in S$.
- for each $k \in [n]$, A contains exactly one pair of the form (x_k, dir) for some $dir \in \{+, -, 0\}$ (with $x_k \in A$ iff $(x_k, 0) \in A$). Intuitively, if A is associated with position i of the word w, then for each $k \in [n]$, the unique pair $(x_k, dir) \in A$ keeps track whether the position j_k referenced by variable x_h strictly precedes ($dir = -$), strictly follows ($dir = +$), or coincides ($dir = 0$ and $x_h \in A$) with the current position i.
- for each $\exists x_h . \psi \in \text{cl}(\varphi)$, A contains tuples of the form (B_r, B, ψ, h), where $B \in \text{Atoms}(\psi)$ and $B_r \in \{\emptyset\} \cup \text{Atoms}(\psi)$. Intuitively, if A is associated with position i of the word w w.r.t. the valuation $j_1, \dots, j_n$ of variables $x_1, \dots, x_n$, then B describes the set of subformulas of ψ which hold at position i of w w.r.t. a valuation of

variables $x_1, \ldots, x_n$ of the form $j_1, \ldots, j_{h-1}, m, j_{h+1}, \ldots, j_n$ for some position $m \geq 0$ (in particular, we syntactically require that for each $k \in [n] \setminus \{h\}$, $(x_k, dir) \in B$ iff $(x_k, dir) \in A$). Thus, the semantics of the binder modality $\exists$ is syntactically captured by requiring that: $\exists x_h . \psi \in A$ if and only if there is $(B_r, B, \psi, h) \in A$ such that $\psi \in B$.

Formally, the set $\mathsf{Atoms}(\varphi)$ is inductively defined as: $A \in \mathsf{Atoms}(\varphi) \Leftrightarrow A \subseteq \mathsf{cl}(\varphi) \cup P(\varphi) \cup \bigcup_{h \in [n]} (\{x_h\} \times \{-, 0, +\}) \cup \bigcup_{\exists x_h . \psi \in \mathsf{cl}(\varphi)} (\mathsf{Atoms}(\psi) \cup \{\emptyset\}) \times \mathsf{Atoms}(\psi) \times \{\psi\} \times \{h\}$

and the following additional conditions hold:

1. $\mathrm{true} \in A$ and A contains exactly one proposition in $\{call, ret, int\}$;
2. if $\psi \in \mathsf{cl}(\varphi)$, then $\psi \in A$ iff $\neg\psi \notin A$;
3. if $\psi_1 \wedge \psi_2 \in \mathsf{cl}(\varphi)$, then $\psi_1 \wedge \psi_2 \in A$ iff $\psi_1, \psi_2 \in A$;
4. if $\psi_1 \, \mathsf{U}^{dir} \psi_2 \in \mathsf{cl}(\varphi)$ for $dir \in \{+, -, \mathsf{a}^+, \mathsf{a}^-, \mathsf{c}\}$, then $\psi_1 \, \mathsf{U}^{dir} \psi_2 \in A$ iff *either* $\psi_2 \in A$ *or* $\psi_1, \mathsf{X}^{dir}(\psi_1 \, \mathsf{U}^{dir} \psi_2) \in A$;
5. if $\mathsf{X}^{dir} \psi \in A$ (where $dir \in \{-, \mathsf{a}^+, \mathsf{a}^-, \mathsf{c}\}$), then $\mathsf{X}^{dir} \mathrm{true} \in A$;
6. if $\neg\mathsf{X}^- \mathrm{true} \in A$, then $\neg\mathsf{X}^{\mathsf{a}^-} \mathrm{true}, \neg\mathsf{X}^{\mathsf{c}} \mathrm{true} \in A$, and $(x_h, -) \notin A$ for each $h \in [n]$;
7. for each $h \in [n]$, $x_h \in A$ iff $(x_h, 0) \in A$;
8. for each $h \in [n]$, A contains exactly one pair of the form (x_h, dir) for some $dir \in \{-, 0, +\}$;
9. if $(B_r, B, \psi, h) \in A$, then (i) $\neg\mathsf{X}^- \mathrm{true} \in B$ iff $\neg\mathsf{X}^- \mathrm{true} \in A$, (ii) for each $p \in AP \cup \{call, ret, int\}$, $p \in A$ iff $p \in B$, and (iii) for each $k \in [n]$ with $k \neq h$ and $dir \in \{-, 0, +\}$, $(x_k, dir) \in B$ iff $(x_k, dir) \in A$;
10. for each $\exists x_h . \psi \in \mathsf{cl}(\varphi)$, there is $(B_r, B, \psi, h) \in A$ such that $x_h \in B$;
11. for each $\exists x_h . \psi \in \mathsf{cl}(\varphi)$, $\exists x_h . \psi \in A$ iff there is $(B_r, B, \psi, h) \in A$ with $\psi \in B$.

Assuming w.l.o.g. that each proposition $p \in AP$ occurs in φ, and $x_1, \ldots, x_n$ occur in φ, by construction it follows that $|\mathsf{Atoms}(\varphi)| = \mathsf{Tower}(O(|\varphi|), d_\exists(\varphi) + 1)$. For $A \in \mathsf{Atoms}(\varphi)$, let $\sigma(A) = (d, A \cap AP)$, where d is the unique element in $A \cap \{call, ret, int\}$. Let $\pi = (A_0^r, A_0), (A_1^r, A_1) \ldots$ be an infinite sequence of pairs in $(\mathsf{Atoms}(\varphi) \cup \{\emptyset\}) \times \mathsf{Atoms}(\varphi)$ and $w \in \Sigma^\omega$. We say that π is a φ-*sequence over* w iff for each $i \geq 0$: (1) $A_i^r = \emptyset$ if $\mathsf{UM}(w, i) = \bot$, and $A_i^r = A_{\mathsf{UM}(w,i)}$ otherwise, (2) $w(i) = \sigma(A_i)$, and (3) $(A_{i+1}^r, A_{i+1}) \in \mathsf{Jump\_Succ}_\varphi(A_i^r, A_i)$. The function $\mathsf{Jump\_Succ}_\varphi$ (which is formally defined in [BL11]) syntactically, *locally*, and recursively captures the semantics of the regular and non-regular next modalities. For example, if $w(i)$ is a call, $w(i+1)$ is not a return, and $\mathsf{UM}(w, i+1) \neq \bot$, then $\mathsf{UM}(w, i+1)$ represents the matching return position of i along w. Thus, in particular, we have to require that the forward-abstract-next requirements in A_i are exactly the ones that hold in A_{i+1}^r, i.e. for each $\mathsf{X}^{\mathsf{a}^+} \psi \in \mathsf{cl}(\varphi)$, $\mathsf{X}^{\mathsf{a}^+} \psi \in A_i$ iff $\psi \in A_{i+1}^r$. Moreover, the definition of $\mathsf{Jump\_Succ}_\varphi$ ensures that for each $k \in [n]$, there is at most a position j_k such that $x_k \in A_{j_k}$. We say that the φ-sequence π is *good* if such a j_k exists (intuitively, in this case, π is associated with the valuation $j_1, \ldots, j_n$ of variables $x_1, \ldots, x_n$). Furthermore, there are some subtleties in the definition of $\mathsf{Jump\_Succ}_\varphi$ ensuring that for each $i \geq 0$ and $(B_r, B, \psi, h) \in A_i$:

Condition A: there is a ψ-sequence $\rho = (B_0^r, B_0), (B_1^r, B_1), \ldots$ over w s.t. $(B_i^r, B_i) = (B_r, B)$ and $(B_j^r, B_j, \psi, h) \in A_j$ for each $j \geq 0$ (hence, for $k \in [n] \setminus \{h\}$, $x_k \in B_j$ iff $x_k \in A_j$).

Finally, we have to require that the φ-sequence $\pi = (A_0^r, A_0), (A_1^r, A_1) \ldots$ on w satisfies additional *non-local* fairness requirements in order to ensure that it is good, and to capture the liveness requirements ψ_2 in forward until subformulas $\psi_1 \, U^{dir} \psi_2$ of φ with $dir \in \{+, a^+\}$. Formally, we say that π is *fair* iff the following is *inductively* satisfied:

1. there is $K \geq 0$ s.t. for each $h \in [n]$, $(x_h, -) \in A_K$ and for all $i \geq K$ if $(B_r, B, \psi, h) \in A_i$ and $A_i^r = \emptyset$, then there is a *fair* ψ-sequence over the *suffix* w^i of w from (B_r, B);
2. if $\psi_1 \, U^{a^+} \psi_2 \in cl(\varphi)$, then for infinitely many $h \geq 0$, $\{\psi_2, \neg(\psi_1 \, U^{a^+} \psi_2)\} \cap A_h \neq \emptyset$ and $A_h^r = \emptyset$;
3. if $\psi_1 \, U^+ \psi_2 \in cl(\varphi)$, then for infinitely many $h \geq 0$, $A_h^r = \emptyset$, and or $\psi_2 \in A_h$, or $\neg(\psi_1 \, U^+ \psi_2) \in A_h$, or $(\tau_{\psi_2}, X^{a^+} \, true \in A_h$ and $\sigma(A_h) \in \Sigma_c)$.

As we will see, the MAJA associated with φ guesses a φ-sequence π over the input word and checks that it is fair. The automaton keeps tracks by its finite control of the current pair of π, and in particular, its 'main' copy tracks an infinite path in the run which visits all and only the nodes associated with the pairs (A_r, A) of π such that $A_r = \emptyset$ (i.e., the next unmatched return of the current position is undefined). Thus, the acceptance condition of the MAJA (when interpreted on the main path) reflects Properties 2 and 3 above. In particular, the propositions τ_{ψ_2} are used to guarantee that in case $\psi_1 \, U^+ \psi_2$ is asserted at a node x of the main path and the liveness requirement ψ_2 does not hold along the suffix of the main path from x, then ψ_2 holds at some other position $j \geq i$ (i.e., there is a pair (A_r, A) with $A_r \neq \emptyset$ of the guessed φ-sequence associated with position j for some $j \geq i$ such that $\psi_2 \in A$). Moreover, Property 1 and Condition **A** above ensure that the semantics of HyCaRet is recursively fully captured. In particular, we obtain the following two results, whose proofs are given in [BL11].

Lemma 3. *Each fair φ-sequence $(A_0^r, A_0), (A_1^r, A_1), \ldots$ on a word w s.t. $\neg X^- true \in A_0$ is good (i.e., for each $k \in [n]$, there is exactly one position j_k such that $x_k \in A_{j_k}$).*

Lemma 4. *Let $\pi = (A_0^r, A_0), (A_1^r, A_1), \ldots$ be a fair φ-sequence over w with $\neg X^- true \in A_0$. Then, for all $i \geq 0$, $m \geq i$, and $(B_r, B, \psi, h) \in A_i$, there exists a fair ψ-sequence $(B_0^r, B_0), (B_1^r, B_1), \ldots$ over w such that $(B_i^r, B_i) = (B_r, B)$, $\neg X^- true \in B_0$, for each $j \leq m$, $(B_j^r, B_j, \psi, h) \in A_j$, and for each $k \in [n] \setminus \{h\}$ and $l \geq 0$, $x_k \in B_l$ iff $x_k \in A_l$.*

Now, we show that the notion of good fair φ-sequence over w provides a characterization of the satisfaction relation $(w, 0) \models \varphi$.

Theorem 5 (Correctness). *Let $\pi = (A_0^r, A_0), (A_1^r, A_1), \ldots$ be a fair φ-sequence over $w \in \Sigma^\omega$ such that $\neg X^- true \in A_0$, and for each $h \in [n]$, let j_h be the unique index such that $x_h \in A_{j_h}$.[2] Then, for each $i \geq 0$ and $\psi \in cl(\varphi)$, $(w, i, j_1, \ldots, j_h) \models \psi \Leftrightarrow \psi \in A_i$.*

Proof. By induction on $d_\exists(\varphi)$. The base step ($d_\exists(\varphi) = 0$) and the induction step ($d_\exists(\varphi) > 0$) are similar, and we focus on the induction step. Thus, we can assume that the theorem holds for each formula θ and fair θ-sequence such that $\exists x_h. \theta \in cl(\varphi)$ for some $h \in [n]$ (note that if $d_\exists(\varphi) = 0$, there is no such formula). Fix a fair φ-sequence $\pi = (A_0^r, A_0), (A_1^r, A_1), \ldots$ over $w \in \Sigma^\omega$ such that $\neg X^- true \in A_0$, and for each $h \in [n]$, let j_h be the unique index such that $x_h \in A_{j_h}$. Let $i \geq 0$ and $\psi \in cl(\varphi)$. By a nested induction on the structure of ψ, we show that $(w, i, j_1, \ldots, j_n) \models \psi \Leftrightarrow \psi \in A_i$. Here, we consider the case where $\psi = \exists x_h. \psi_1$ for some $h \in [n]$ (for the other cases, see [BL11]):

---

[2] whose existence is guaranteed by Lemma 3

$(w,i,j_1,\ldots,j_n) \models \psi \Rightarrow \psi \in A_i$: assume that $(w,i,j_1,\ldots,j_n) \models \psi$. Then, for some $l \geq 0$, $(w,i,j_1,\ldots,j_{h-1},l,j_{h+1},\ldots,j_n) \models \psi_1$. By Property 10 in definition of atom, there is $(B_r,B,\psi_1,h) \in A_l$ such that $x_h \in B$. Since $\neg X^- \texttt{true} \in A_0$, by Lemma 4 there is a fair ψ_1-sequence $\rho = (B_0^r,B_0),(B_1^r,B_1),\ldots$ over w such that $(B_i^r,B_l) = (B_r,B)$ (hence, $x_h \in B_l$), $\neg X^- \texttt{true} \in B_0$, $(B_i^r,B_i,\psi_1,h) \in A_i$, and for each $k \in [n] \setminus \{h\}, x_k \in B_{j_k}$. Since the theorem holds for ψ_1 (and the fair ψ_1-sequence $\rho = (B_0^r,B_0),(B_1^r,B_1),\ldots$) and $(w,i,j_1,\ldots,j_{h-1},l,j_{h+1},\ldots,j_n) \models \psi_1$, it follows that $\psi_1 \in B_i$. Since $(B_i^r,B_i,\psi_1,h) \in A_i$, by Property 11 in definition of atom we obtain that $\psi \in A_i$.

$\psi \in A_i \Rightarrow (w,i,j_1,\ldots,j_n) \models \psi$: let $\psi \in A_i$. By Property 11 in def. of atom there is $(B_r,B,\psi_1,h) \in A_i$ with $\psi_1 \in B$. Since $\neg X^- \texttt{true} \in A_0$, by Lemma 4 there is a fair ψ_1-sequence $\rho = (B_0^r,B_0),(B_1^r,B_1),\ldots$ over w such that $(B_1^r,B_i) = (B_r,B)$, $\neg X^- \texttt{true} \in B_0$, and for each $k \in [n] \setminus \{h\}, x_k \in B_{j_k}$. Let $l \geq 0$ be the unique index such that $x_h \in B_l$. Since the theorem holds for ψ_1 and $\psi_1 \in B_i$, we obtain that $(w,i,j_1,\ldots,j_{h-1},l,j_{h+1},\ldots,j_n) \models \psi_1$, hence $(w,i,j_1,\ldots,j_n) \models \psi$.   □

Theorem 6 (Completeness). *For each infinite word w over Σ and $j_1,\ldots,j_n \in \mathbb{N}$, there exists a fair φ-sequence $\pi = (A_0^r,A_0),(A^r,A_1),\ldots$ over w such that $\neg X^- \texttt{true} \in A_0$ and for each $k \in [n], x_k \in A_{j_k}$.*

Theorem 6 is proved in [BL11]. By Theorems 5–6, we obtain the desired result.

Corollary 1. *For each word $w \in \Sigma^\omega$, $(w,0) \models \varphi$ iff there is a fair φ-sequence $\pi = (A_0^r,A_0),(A_1^r,A_1),\ldots$ on w s.t. $\varphi, \neg X^- \texttt{true}, x_h \in A_0$ for each $h \in [n]$ (note that $A_0^r = \emptyset$).*

Translation into MAJA Now, we illustrate the translation of HyCaRet formulas into generalized Büchi MAJA based on the result of Corollary 1.

Theorem 7. *Let φ be a n-HyCaRet formula for some $n \geq 1$. Then, one can construct a generalized Büchi MAJA $\mathcal{A}_\varphi$ with $O(|\varphi|)$ accepting components and states $Q_m \cup Q_s$ s.t. $L(\mathcal{A}_\varphi) = L(\varphi)$, $|Q_m| = \mathsf{Tower}(O(|\varphi|),\mathsf{d}_\exists(\varphi)+1)$, and $|Q_s| = \mathsf{Tower}(O(|\varphi|),\mathsf{d}_\exists(\varphi))$.*

Proof. We construct a generalized Büchi MAJA $\mathcal{A}_\varphi$ of the desired size with set of main states containing $(\mathsf{Atoms}(\varphi) \cup \{\emptyset\}) \times \mathsf{Atoms}(\varphi)$ and initial states of the form $(\emptyset,A) \in \{\emptyset\} \times \mathsf{Atoms}(\varphi)$ with $\varphi, \neg X^- \texttt{true}, x_h \in A$ for each $h \in [n]$ such that for all main states of the form $(\emptyset,A)$ and infinite words w, $\mathcal{A}_\varphi$ has an accepting run over w starting from $(\emptyset,A)$ if and only if there is a fair φ-sequence over w from $(\emptyset,A)$. Hence, the result follows from Corollary 1. The construction is given by induction on $\mathsf{d}_\exists(\varphi)$. Thus, we can assume that for each $\exists x_h. \psi \in \mathsf{cl}(\varphi)$, one can construct the MAJA $\mathcal{A}_\psi$ associated with ψ. We informally describe the construction (the formal definition is given in [BL11]).

Essentially, starting from a main state of the form $(0,A)$, $\mathcal{A}_\varphi$ guesses a φ-sequence over the input w and checks that it is fair. The *first-level* copy of $\mathcal{A}_\varphi$, which reads all and only the positions i such that $\mathsf{UM}(w,i) = \bot$, behaves as follows. Assume that i is a matched-call position and $w(i+1) \notin \Sigma_r$ (the other cases being simpler). Note that $\mathcal{A}_\varphi$ can check whether this condition is satisfied or not. Let $(0,A)$ be the current main state. Then, $\mathcal{A}_\varphi$ guesses a pair $(A_r',A') \in \mathsf{Jump\_Succ}_\varphi(0,A)$ with $A_r' \neq \emptyset$, where A_r' represents the guessed atom associated with the matching return position i_r of i. Thus, a copy (the first-level copy) jumps to the matching-return i_r of i in state $(0,A_r')$ (note that $\mathsf{UM}(w,i) = \mathsf{UM}(w,i_r) = \bot$), and another copy moves to position $i+1$ in state (A_r',A'). The goal of this last copy is also to check that the guess A_r' is correct. The behavior of these auxiliary copies, which are in main states of the form (A_r, A) with $A_r \neq \emptyset$ is as follows. If the input symbol $w(i)$ is a call (note that i is a matched call-position) or ($w(i) \notin \Sigma_c$ and $w(i+1) \notin \Sigma_r$), the behavior is similar to that of the first-level copy. If instead $w(i) = \sigma(A)$ is not a call and $w(i+1)$ is a return, then $A_r \neq \emptyset$ is the guessed atom associated with $w(i+1)$. Thus, the considered copy terminates with success its computation iff $\sigma(A_r) = w(i+1)$ and $(A'_r, A_r) \in \mathsf{Jump\_Succ}_\varphi(A_r, A)$ for some A'_r (note that since $\sigma(A) \notin \Sigma_c$, $\sigma(A_r) \in \Sigma_r$, and $A_r \neq \emptyset$, the definition of $\mathsf{Jump\_Succ}_\varphi$ ensures that the fulfilment of this condition is independent on the value of A'_r). Moreover, in order to check that Property 1 in definition of fair φ-sequence is satisfied, the first-level copy guesses a point along the input word (the constant K in Property 1), checks that $(x_h, -)$ is in the current atom for each $h \in [n]$, and from this instant forward, whenever the first-level copy reads a position j (where $\mathsf{UM}(w, j) = \perp$) with associated guessed pair $(\emptyset, A)$, it starts an additional copy of the MAJA $\mathcal{A}_\psi$ in the secondary state (B_r, B) for each $(B_r, B, \psi, h) \in A$ (the definition of $\mathsf{Jump\_Succ}_\varphi$ ensures that $B_r = \emptyset$). The construction guarantee that in each run and for each input position i, there is exactly one node of the run whose label has the form (i, q), where q is a main state. Thus, the semantic requirement in def. of MAJA is satisfied.

Finally, the acceptance condition of $\mathcal{A}_\varphi$ extends the acceptance conditions of the MAJAs $\mathcal{A}_\psi$, where $\exists x_h. \psi \in \mathsf{cl}(\varphi)$ for some $h \in [n]$, with additional sets used to check that the infinite sequence of states visited by the first-level copy of $\mathcal{A}_\varphi$ (note that these states correspond to the pairs (A_r, A) visited by the guessed φ-sequence over w such that $A_r = \emptyset$) satisfies Properties 2 and 3 in definition of fair φ-sequence. □

For the one-variable fragment of HyCaRet, we can do better.

Theorem 8. *Given a 1-HyCaRet formula φ over AP, one can construct a Büchi NVPA $\mathcal{P}_\varphi$ on $\{call, ret, int\} \times 2^{AP}$ of size doubly exponential in the size of φ s.t. $L(\mathcal{P}_\varphi) = L(\varphi)$.*

Proof. Note that for $\widehat{AP} \supset AP$ and a Büchi NVPA $\mathcal{P}$ on $\{call, ret, int\} \times 2^{\widehat{AP}}$, $L(\mathcal{P})$ can be seen as a language on $(\{call, ret, int\} \times 2^{AP}) \times 2^{\widehat{AP} \setminus AP}$. Since we can easily build a Büchi NVPA of the same size as $\mathcal{P}$ accepting the projection of $L(\mathcal{P})$ on $\{call, ret, int\} \times 2^{AP}$, the result follows from Theorems 7 and 4, and the following claim, essentially establishing that nested occurrences of $\exists$ in 1-HyCaRet can be avoided at no cost.

Claim. For a 1-HyCaRet formula φ over AP, one can construct a 1-HyCaRet[1] formula ψ ($\mathsf{d}_\exists(\psi) \leq 1$) on a set of propositions $\widehat{AP} \supseteq AP$ s.t. $|\psi| = O(|\varphi|)$ and for each infinite word w over $\{call, ret, int\} \times 2^{AP}$, $(w, 0) \models \varphi$ iff there is an $\widehat{AP}$-extension $\widehat{w}$ of w (i.e., for each $i \geq 0$, $\widehat{w}(i) = (d, X_1 \cup X_2)$, where $(d, X_1) = w(i)$ and $X_2 \subseteq \widehat{AP} \setminus AP$) s.t. $(\widehat{w}, 0) \models \psi$.

The claim above is a generalization of a similar result given in [SW07] for the one-variable fragment of regular linear hybrid logic (a proof is given in [BL11]). □

Now, we can prove the main result of this Section. For $h \geq 1$, let h-EXPTIME be the class of languages which can be decided in deterministic time of exponential height h.

Theorem 9. *For each $h \geq 1$ and $n \geq 2$, satisfiability and pushdown model-checking of (weak) HyCaRet[h] and (weak) n-HyCaRet[h] are $(h+1)$-EXPTIME-complete. Moreover, for (weak) 1-HyCaRet, the same problems are 2EXPTIME-complete.*

Proof. By Theorems 7 and 4 (resp., Theorem 8) for a HyCaRet[h] (resp., 1-HyCaRet) formula φ, one can build an equivalent Büchi NVPA $\mathcal{P}_\varphi$ of size $\mathsf{Tower}(O(|\varphi|), h+1)$

(resp., $\text{Tower}(O(|\varphi|), 2)$). Moreover, for a pushdown system M and a HyCaRet formula φ, checking whether $L(M) \subseteq L(\varphi)$ reduces to checking emptiness of $L(M) \cap L(\mathcal{P}_{\neg\varphi})$, where $\mathcal{P}_{\neg\varphi}$ is the Büchi NVPA associated with $\neg\varphi$. By [AM04] this can be done in time polynomial in the size of M and $\mathcal{P}_{\neg\varphi}$. Since nonemptiness of Büchi NVPA is in PTIME, the upper bounds follows. The proof for the lower bounds is given in [BL11]. □

References

AAB08. Alur, R., Arenas, M., Barcelo, P., Etessami, K., Immerman, N., Libkin, L.: First-order and temporal logics for nested words. Logical Methods in Computer Science 4(4) (2008)

AEM04. Alur, R., Etessami, K., Madhusudan, P.: A temporal logic of nested calls and returns. In: Jensen, K., Podelski, A. (eds.) TACAS 2004. LNCS, vol. 2988, pp. 467–481. Springer, Heidelberg (2004)

AM04. Alur, R., Madhusudan, P.: Visibly pushdown languages. In: Proc. 36th STOC, pp. 202–211. ACM, New York (2004)

AM06. Alur, R., Madhusudan, P.: Adding nesting structure to words. In: Ibarra, O.H., Dang, Z. (eds.) DLT 2006. LNCS, vol. 4036, pp. 1–13. Springer, Heidelberg (2006)

BEM97. Bouajjani, A., Esparza, J., Maler, O.: Reachability Analysis of Pushdown Automata: Application to Model-Checking. In: Mazurkiewicz, A., Winkowski, J. (eds.) CONCUR 1997. LNCS, vol. 1243, pp. 135–150. Springer, Heidelberg (1997)

BL08. Bozzelli, L., Lanotte, R.: Complexity and succinctness issues for linear-time hybrid logics. In: Hölldobler, S., Lutz, C., Wansing, H. (eds.) JELIA 2008. LNCS (LNAI), vol. 5293, pp. 48–61. Springer, Heidelberg (2008)

BL11. Bozzelli, L., Lanotte, R.: Hybrid and first-order complete extensions of CARET. Technical report - (2011), http://dscpi.uninsubria.it/staff/Lanotte

Boz07. Bozzelli, L.: Alternating automata and a temporal fixpoint calculus for visibly pushdown languages. In: Caires, L., Vasconcelos, V.T. (eds.) CONCUR 2007. LNCS, vol. 4703, pp. 476–491. Springer, Heidelberg (2007)

Boz08. Bozzelli, L.: Caret with forgettable past. In: Proc. 5th Workshop on Methods for Modalities. ENTCS. Elsevier, Amsterdam (2008)

FR06. Franceschet, M., de Rijke, M.: Model checking hybrid logics (with an application to semistructured data). J. Applied Logic 4(3), 279–304 (2006)

FRS03. Franceschet, M., de Rijke, M., Schlingloff, B.H.: Hybrid logics on linear structures: Expressivity and complexity. In: Proc. 10th TIME, pp. 166–173. IEEE Computer Society, Los Alamitos (2003)

LMS02. Laroussinie, F., Markey, N., Schnoebelen, P.: Temporal logic with forgettable past. In: Proc. 17th LICS, pp. 383–392. IEEE Comp. Soc. Press, Los Alamitos (2002)

LS95. Laroussinie, F., Schnoebelen, P.: A hierarchy of temporal logics with past. Theoretical Computer Science 148(2), 303–324 (1995)

MH84. Miyano, S., Hayashi, T.: Alternating finite automata on ω-words. Theoretical Computer Science 32, 321–330 (1984)

SW07. Schwentick, T., Weber, V.: Bounded-variable fragments of hybrid logics. In: Thomas, W., Weil, P. (eds.) STACS 2007. LNCS, vol. 4393, pp. 561–572. Springer, Heidelberg (2007)

Wol00. Wolper, P.: Constructing automata from temporal logic formulas: A tutorial. In: Brinksma, E., Hermanns, H., Katoen, J.-P. (eds.) EEF School 2000 and FMPA 2000. LNCS, vol. 2090, pp. 261–277. Springer, Heidelberg (2001)

Optimal Tableau Systems for Propositional Neighborhood Logic over All, Dense, and Discrete Linear Orders

Davide Bresolin[1], Angelo Montanari[2],
Pietro Sala[1], and Guido Sciavicco[3,4]

[1] Department of Computer Science, University of Verona, Verona, Italy
{davide.bresolin,pietro.sala}@univr.it
[2] Department of Mathematics and Computer Science,
University of Udine, Udine, Italy
angelo.montanari@dimi.uniud.it
[3] Department of Information, Engineering and Communications,
University of Murcia, Murcia, Spain
guido@um.es
[4] University of Information Science and Technology, Ohrid, Macedonia
guido.sciavicco@uist.edu.mk

Abstract. In this paper, we focus our attention on tableau systems for the propositional interval logic of temporal neighborhood (Propositional Neighborhood Logic, PNL for short). PNL is the proper subset of Halpern and Shoham's modal logic of intervals whose modalities correspond to Allen's relations meets and met by. We first prove by a model-theoretic argument that the satisfiability problem for PNL over the class of all (resp., dense, discrete) linear orders is decidable (and NEXPTIME-complete). Then, we develop sound and complete tableau-based decision procedures for all the considered classes of orders, and we prove their optimality. (As a matter of fact, decidability with respect to the class of all linear orders had been already proved via a reduction to the decidable satisfiability problem for the two-variable fragment of first-order logic of binary relational structures over ordered domains).

1 Introduction

Propositional interval temporal logics play a significant role in computer science, as they provide a natural framework for representing and reasoning about temporal properties [10]. This is the case, for instance, of natural language semantics, where significant interval-based logical formalisms have been developed to represent and reason about tenses and temporal prepositions, e.g., [17]. As another example, the possibility of encoding and reasoning about various constructs of imperative programming in interval temporal logic has been systematically explored by Moszkowski in [15]. Unfortunately, for a long time the computational complexity of most interval temporal logics has limited their systematic investigation and extensive use for practical applications: the two prominent ones,

K. Brünnler and G. Metcalfe (Eds.): TABLEAUX 2011, LNAI 6793, pp. 73–87, 2011.
© Springer-Verlag Berlin Heidelberg 2011

namely, Halpern and Shoham's HS [12] and Venema's CDT [18], are highly undecidable. A renewed interest in interval temporal logics has been stimulated by a number of recent positive results [13].

A general, non-terminating, tableau system for CDT, interpreted over partially ordered temporal domains, has been devised in [11]. It combines features of the classical tableau method for first-order logic with those of explicit tableau methods for modal logics with constraint label management, and it can be easily tailored to most propositional interval temporal logics proposed in the literature, including propositional temporal neighborhood logic. A tableau-based decision procedure for Moszkowski's ITL [15], interpreted over finite linearly ordered domains, has been devised by Bowman and Thompson [2]. As a matter of fact, decidability is achieved by making a simplifying assumption, called *locality* principle, that constrains the relation between the truth value of a formula over an interval and its truth values over the initial subintervals of that interval. Tableau-based decision procedures have been recently developed for some meaningful fragments of HS, interpreted over relevant classes of temporal structures, without resorting to any simplifying assumption. The most significant ones are the logics of temporal neighborhood and those of the subinterval relation.

In the following, we focus our attention on the propositional fragment of Neighborhood Logic [8], called Propositional Neighborhood Logic (PNL). PNL can be viewed as the fragment of HS that features the two modal operators $\langle A \rangle$ and $\langle \overline{A} \rangle$, that respectively correspond to Allen's relations *meets* and *met-by*. Basic logical properties of PNL have been investigated by Goranko et al. in [9]. The authors first introduce interval neighborhood frames and provide representation theorems for them; then, they develop complete axiomatic systems for PNL with respect to various classes of interval neighborhood frames. The satisfiability problem for PNL has been addressed by Bresolin et al. in [3]. Decidability over the classes of all linearly ordered domains, well-ordered domains, finite linearly ordered domains, and natural numbers has been proved via a reduction to the satisfiability problem for the two-variable fragment of first-order logic of binary relational structures over ordered domains [16].

Despite these significant achievements, the problem of devising decision procedures of practical interest for PNL has been only partially solved. A tableau system for its future fragment RPNL, interpreted over the natural numbers, has been developed in [7], and later extended to full PNL over the integers [4], while a tableau system for RPNL over the class of all linear orders can be found in [5]. In this paper, we develop a NEXPTIME tableau-based decision procedure for PNL interpreted over the class of all linear orders and then we show how to tailor it to the subclasses of dense linear orders and of (weakly) discrete linear orders. NEXPTIME-hardness can be proved exactly as in [7], and thus the proposed procedures turn out to be optimal. From a technical point of view, the proposed tableau systems are quite different from that for RPNL. Besides additional rules for the past-time existential and universal modalities, a revision of the definition of blocked points is needed, to distinguish between right-blocked (points that do not require the addition of new points to their future) and left-blocked (points that do not require the addition of new points to their past) points. These changes have a relevant impact on the way in which soundness, completeness, and termination of the tableau systems can be proved.

The paper is organized as follows. In Section 2, we introduce syntax and semantics of PNL. Then, in Section 3 we introduce the notion of labeled interval structure (LIS) and we show that PNL satisfiability can be reduced to the existence of a fulfilling LIS. In Section 4 we prove the decidability of PNL over different classes of linear orders by a model-theoretic argument. Next, in Section 5, by taking advantage of the results given in the previous section, we develop optimal tableau-based decision procedures for PNL over the considered classes of linear orders. Conclusions provide an assessment of the work and outline future research directions.

2   Propositional Neighborhood Logic

In this section, we give syntax and semantics of PNL interpreted over different classes of linear orders. Let D be a set of points and $\mathbb{D} = \langle D, < \rangle$ be a linear order on it. We say that $\mathbb{D}$ is (weakly) *discrete* if any point having a successor (resp., predecessor) has an immediate one and that $\mathbb{D}$ is *dense* if for every pair of points $d_i < d_j$ there exists a point d_k such that $d_i < d_k < d_j$. In the following, we will focus our attention on the representative classes of all linear orders, dense linear orders, and (weakly) discrete linear orders. In fact, similar results can be obtained for other classes of linear orders [3].

An *interval* on $\mathbb{D}$ is an ordered pair $[d_i, d_j]$ such that $d_i, d_j \in D$ and $d_i < d_j$ (strict semantics)[1]. The set of all intervals over $\mathbb{D}$ will be denoted by $\mathbb{I}(\mathbb{D})$. For every pair of intervals $[d_i, d_j], [d'_i, d'_j] \in \mathbb{I}(\mathbb{D})$, we say that $[d'_i, d'_j]$ is a *right* (resp., *left*) *neighbor* of $[d_i, d_j]$ if and only if $d_j = d'_i$ (resp., $d'_j = d_i$).

The language of PNL consists of a set AP of propositional letters, the connectives $\neg$ and $\lor$, and the modal operators $\langle A \rangle$ and $\langle \overline{A} \rangle$. The other connectives, as well as the logical constants $\top$ (true) and $\bot$ (false), can be defined as usual. *Formulae* of PNL, denoted by $\varphi, \psi, \ldots$, are recursively defined by the following grammar:

$$\varphi ::= p \mid \neg\varphi \mid \varphi \lor \varphi \mid \langle A \rangle \varphi \mid \langle \overline{A} \rangle \varphi.$$

We denote by $|\varphi|$ the length of φ, that is, the number of symbols in φ (in the following, we shall use $|\,|$ to denote the cardinality of a set as well). A formula of the form $\langle A \rangle \psi$, $\neg \langle A \rangle \psi$, $\langle \overline{A} \rangle \psi$, or $\neg \langle \overline{A} \rangle \psi$ is called a *temporal formula* (from now on, we identify $\neg \langle A \rangle \neg \psi$ with $[A]\psi$ and $\neg \langle \overline{A} \rangle \neg \psi$ with $[\overline{A}]\psi$).

An interval *model* for a PNL formula is a pair $\mathbf{M} = \langle \mathbb{D}, \mathcal{V} \rangle$, where $\mathbb{D} = \langle D, < \rangle$ and $\mathcal{V} : \mathbb{I}(\mathbb{D}) \mapsto 2^{AP}$ is a *valuation function* assigning to every interval the set of propositional letters true over it. Given a model $\mathbf{M} = \langle \mathbb{D}, \mathcal{V} \rangle$ and an interval $[d_i, d_j] \in \mathbb{I}(\mathbb{D})$, the semantics of PNL is defined recursively by the *satisfiability relation* $\Vdash$ as follows:

---

[1] As an alternative, one may assume a non-strict semantics which admits point intervals, that is, intervals of the form $[d_i, d_i]$. It is not difficult to show that all results in the paper can be adapted to the case in which non-strict semantics is assumed.

- for every propositional letter $p \in AP$, $\mathbf{M}, [d_i, d_j] \Vdash p$ iff $p \in \mathcal{V}([d_i, d_j])$;
- $\mathbf{M}, [d_i, d_j] \Vdash \neg \psi$ iff $\mathbf{M}, [d_i, d_j] \not\Vdash \psi$;
- $\mathbf{M}, [d_i, d_j] \Vdash \psi_1 \vee \psi_2$ iff $\mathbf{M}, [d_i, d_j] \Vdash \psi_1$ or $\mathbf{M}, [d_i, d_j] \Vdash \psi_2$;
- $\mathbf{M}, [d_i, d_j] \Vdash \langle A \rangle \psi$ iff $\exists d_k \in D$ such that $d_k > d_j$ and $\mathbf{M}, [d_j, d_k] \Vdash \psi$;
- $\mathbf{M}, [d_i, d_j] \Vdash \langle \overline{A} \rangle \psi$ iff $\exists d_k \in D$ such that $d_k < d_i$ and $\mathbf{M}, [d_k, d_i] \Vdash \psi$.

We do not impose any constraint on the valuation function, thus placing ourselves in the most general (and difficult) setting. As an example, given an interval $[d_i, d_j]$, it may happen that $p \in \mathcal{V}([d_i, d_j])$ and $p \notin \mathcal{V}([d_i', d_j'])$ for all intervals $[d_i', d_j']$ (strictly) contained in $[d_i, d_j]$.

It can be shown that PNL is expressive enough to distinguish between satisfiability over the class of all linear orders and the class of discrete (resp., dense) linear orders. As a matter of fact, PNL also allows one to distinguish between satisfiability over the class of all (resp., dense, discrete) linear orders and over the integers. To this end, it suffices to exhibit a formula that is satisfiable over the former and unsatisfiable over the latter. The formulae are the following:

- Let $ImmediateSucc$ be the PNL formula $\langle A \rangle \langle A \rangle p \wedge [A][A][A] \neg p$. It is possible to show that $ImmediateSucc$ is satisfiable over the class of all (resp., discrete) linear orders, but it is not satisfiable over dense linear orders.
- Let $NoImmediateSucc$ be the PNL formula $(\langle \overline{A} \rangle \top \wedge [\overline{A}](p \wedge [A] \neg p \wedge [\overline{A}]p)) \wedge \langle A \rangle \langle A \rangle [\overline{A}]([\overline{A}]p \vee \langle \overline{A} \rangle \langle \overline{A} \rangle \neg p)$. It is possible to show that $NoImmediateSucc$ is satisfiable over the class of all (resp., dense) linear orders, but it is not satisfiable over discrete linear orders.
- Let $[G]$ be the *universally-in-the-future* operator defined as follows: $[G]\psi = \psi \wedge [A]\psi \wedge [A][A]\psi$ and let seq_p be a shorthand for $p \rightarrow \langle A \rangle p$. Consider the formula $AccPoints = \langle A \rangle p \wedge [G]seq_p \wedge \langle A \rangle [G] \neg p$. It is possible to show that $AccPoints$ is unsatisfiable over $\mathbb{Z}$, while it is satisfiable whenever the temporal structure in which it is interpreted has at least one *accumulation point*, that is, a point which is the right bound of an infinite (ascending) chain of points, thus including all, dense, and discrete linear orders.

Detailed proofs of these statements are given in [6]. A precise characterization of PNL expressiveness with respect to that of the other HS fragments can be found in [14].

3   Labeled Interval Structures and Satisfiability

In this section, we introduce preliminary notions and we state basic results on which our tableau method for PNL relies. Let φ be a PNL formula to be checked for satisfiability and let AP be the set of its propositional letters. The *closure* $\mathrm{CL}(\varphi)$ of φ is the set of all subformulae of φ and of their negations (we identify $\neg \neg \psi$ with ψ). Moreover, the set of *temporal formulae* of φ is the set $\mathrm{TF}(\varphi) = \{\langle A \rangle \psi \mid \langle A \rangle \psi \in \mathrm{CL}(\varphi)\} \cup \{[A]\psi \mid [A]\psi \in \mathrm{CL}(\varphi)\} \cup \{\langle \overline{A} \rangle \psi \mid \langle \overline{A} \rangle \psi \in \mathrm{CL}(\varphi)\} \cup \{[\overline{A}]\psi \mid [\overline{A}]\psi \in \mathrm{CL}(\varphi)\}$. Finally, a *maximal set of requests* for φ is a set $S \subseteq$

$\mathrm{TF}(\varphi)$ that satisfies the following conditions: (i) for every $\langle A \rangle \psi \in \mathrm{TF}(\varphi)$, $\langle A \rangle \psi \in S$ iff $\neg \langle A \rangle \psi \notin S$; (ii) for every $\langle \overline{A} \rangle \psi \in \mathrm{TF}(\varphi)$, $\langle \overline{A} \rangle \psi \in S$ iff $\neg \langle \overline{A} \rangle \psi \notin S$. By induction on the structural complexity of φ, we can easily prove that, for every formula φ, $|\mathrm{CL}(\varphi)|$ is less than or equal to $2 \cdot (|\varphi| + 1)$, while $|\mathrm{TF}(\varphi)|$ is less than or equal to $2 \cdot |\varphi|$. We are now ready to introduce the notion of φ-atom.

Definition 1. *A φ-atom is a set $A \subseteq \mathrm{CL}(\varphi)$ such that (i) for every $\psi \in \mathrm{CL}(\varphi)$, $\psi \in A$ iff $\neg \psi \notin A$, and (ii) for every $\psi_1 \vee \psi_2 \in \mathrm{CL}(\varphi)$, $\psi_1 \vee \psi_2 \in A$ iff $\psi_1 \in A$ or $\psi_2 \in A$.*

We denote the set of all φ-atoms by A_φ. It can be easily checked that $|A_\varphi| \leq 2^{|\varphi|+1}$. We now define a suitable labeling of intervals based on φ-atoms.

Definition 2. *A φ-labeled interval structure (φ-LIS for short) is a pair $\mathbf{L} = \langle \mathbb{D}, \mathcal{L} \rangle$, where $\mathbb{D} = \langle D, < \rangle$ and $\mathcal{L} : \mathbb{I}(\mathbb{D}) \mapsto A_\varphi$ is a labeling function such that, for every pair of neighboring intervals $[d_i, d_j], [d_j, d_k] \in \mathbb{I}(\mathbb{D})$, it holds that (i) for every $[A]\psi \in \mathrm{CL}(\varphi)$, if $[A]\psi \in \mathcal{L}([d_i, d_j])$, then $\psi \in \mathcal{L}([d_j, d_k])$, and (ii) for every $[\overline{A}]\psi \in \mathrm{CL}(\varphi)$, if $[\overline{A}]\psi \in \mathcal{L}([d_j, d_k])$, then $\psi \in \mathcal{L}([d_i, d_j])$.*

For the sake of simplicity, hereafter we will write LIS for φ-LIS. We say that a LIS $\mathbf{L} = \langle \mathbb{D}, \mathcal{L} \rangle$ is *discrete* (resp., *dense*) if $\mathbb{D}$ is discrete (resp., dense). If we interpret the labeling function as a valuation function, LISs represent *candidate models* for φ: the truth of formulae devoid of temporal operators follows from the definition of φ-atom, and universal temporal conditions, imposed by $[A]/[\overline{A}]$ operators, are forced by conditions *(i)* and *(ii)*. To actually get a model for φ, we must also guarantee the satisfaction of existential temporal conditions, imposed by $\langle A \rangle / \langle \overline{A} \rangle$ operators. To this end, we introduce the notion of fulfilling LIS.

Definition 3. *A LIS $\mathbf{L} = \langle \mathbb{D}, \mathcal{L} \rangle$ is fulfilling iff (i) for every temporal formula $\langle A \rangle \psi \in \mathrm{TF}(\varphi)$ and every interval $[d_i, d_j] \in \mathbb{I}(\mathbb{D})$, if $\langle A \rangle \psi \in \mathcal{L}([d_i, d_j])$, then there exists a right neighbor interval $[d_j, d_k] \in \mathbb{I}(\mathbb{D})$ such that $\psi \in \mathcal{L}([d_j, d_k])$ and (ii) for every temporal formula $\langle \overline{A} \rangle \psi \in \mathrm{TF}(\varphi)$ and every interval $[d_i, d_j] \in \mathbb{I}(\mathbb{D})$, if $\langle \overline{A} \rangle \psi \in \mathcal{L}([d_i, d_j])$, then there exists a left neighbor interval $[d_k, d_i] \in \mathbb{I}(\mathbb{D})$ such that $\psi \in \mathcal{L}([d_k, d_i])$.*

The next theorem proves that for any given formula φ, the satisfiability of φ is equivalent to the existence of a fulfilling LIS with an interval labeled by φ.

Theorem 1. *A PNL formula φ is satisfiable iff there exists a fulfilling LIS $\mathbf{L} = \langle \mathbb{D}, \mathcal{L} \rangle$ with $\varphi \in \mathcal{L}([d_i, d_j])$ for some $[d_i, d_j] \in \mathbb{I}(\mathbb{D})$.*

The implication from left to right is straightforward; the opposite implication is proved by induction on the structural complexity of the formula [6]. From now on, we say that a fulfilling LIS $\mathbf{L} = \langle \mathbb{D}, \mathcal{L} \rangle$ *satisfies* φ if and only if there exists an interval $[d_i, d_j] \in \mathbb{I}(\mathbb{D})$ such that $\varphi \in \mathcal{L}([d_i, d_j])$.

Definition 4. *Given a LIS $\mathbf{L} = \langle \mathbb{D}, \mathcal{L} \rangle$ and $d \in D$, the set of future temporal requests of d is the set $\mathrm{REQ}_f^{\mathbf{L}}(d) = \{(A)\xi \in \mathrm{TF}(\varphi) : \exists d' \in D \ (A)\xi \in \mathcal{L}([d', d])\}$, where $(A) \in \{\langle A \rangle, [A]\}$, and the set of past temporal requests of d is the set $\mathrm{REQ}_p^{\mathbf{L}}(d) = \{(\overline{A})\xi \in \mathrm{TF}(\varphi) : \exists d' \in D \ (\overline{A})\xi \in \mathcal{L}([d, d'])\}$, where $(\overline{A}) \in \{\langle \overline{A} \rangle, [\overline{A}]\}$. The set of temporal requests of d is the set $\mathrm{REQ}^{\mathbf{L}}(d) = \mathrm{REQ}_p^{\mathbf{L}}(d) \cup \mathrm{REQ}_f^{\mathbf{L}}(d)$.*

Definition 5. *Given a LIS $\mathbf{L} = \langle \mathbb{D}, \mathcal{L} \rangle$, $d \in D$, and $\langle A \rangle \psi \in \mathrm{REQ}^{\mathbf{L}}(d)$ (resp., $\langle \overline{A} \rangle \psi \in \mathrm{REQ}^{\mathbf{L}}(d)$), we say that $\langle A \rangle \psi$ (resp., $\langle \overline{A} \rangle \psi$) is fulfilled for d in $\mathbf{L}$ if there exists $d' \in D$, with $d' > d$ (resp., $d' < d$), such that $\psi \in \mathcal{L}([d, d'])$ (resp., $\psi \in \mathcal{L}([d', d])$). We say that d is fulfilled in $\mathbf{L}$ if for every $\langle A \rangle \psi \in \mathrm{REQ}^{\mathbf{L}}(d)$ (resp., $\langle \overline{A} \rangle \psi \in \mathrm{REQ}^{\mathbf{L}}(d)$) $\langle A \rangle \psi$ (resp., $\langle \overline{A} \rangle \psi \in \mathrm{REQ}^{\mathbf{L}}(d)$) is fulfilled for d in $\mathbf{L}$.*

Definition 6. *Given a LIS $\mathbf{L} = \langle \mathbb{D}, \mathcal{L} \rangle$ for a PNL formula φ and $d \in D$, we say that d (resp., $\mathrm{REQ}(d)$) is unique in $\mathbf{L}$ if for every $\tilde{d} \in D$, with $\tilde{d} \neq d$, $\mathrm{REQ}(\tilde{d}) \neq \mathrm{REQ}(d)$.*

Given a formula φ, let REQ_{φ} be the set of all possible sets of requests. It is not difficult to show that $|\mathrm{REQ}_{\varphi}|$ is equal to $2^{\frac{|\mathrm{TF}(\varphi)|}{2}}$.

Definition 7. *Given a LIS $\mathbf{L} = \langle \mathbb{D}, \mathcal{L} \rangle$, with $\mathbb{D} = \langle D, < \rangle$, $D' \subseteq D$, and $\mathcal{R} \in \mathrm{REQ}_{\varphi}$, we say that $\mathcal{R}$ occurs n times in D' iff there exist exactly n distinct points $d_{i_1}, \ldots, d_{i_n} \in D'$ such that $\mathrm{REQ}^{\mathbf{L}}(d_{i_j}) = \mathcal{R}$, for all $1 \leq j \leq n$.*

4   Decidability of PNL

In this section, we prove that the satisfiability problem for PNL over the classes of all linear orders is decidable. Moreover, we explain how to tailor the proof to the cases of dense and discrete linear orders.

Definition 8. *Let φ be a PNL formula, A be a φ-atom, and $S_1, S_2 \subseteq \mathrm{TF}(\varphi)$ be two maximal sets of requests. The triplet $\langle S_1, A, S_2 \rangle$ is an interval-tuple iff*

(i) for every $[A]\psi \in S_1$, $\psi \in A$;
(ii) for every $[\overline{A}]\psi \in S_2$, $\psi \in A$;
(iii) for every $\langle A \rangle \psi \in \mathrm{TF}(\varphi)$, $\langle A \rangle \psi \in A$ iff $\langle A \rangle \psi \in S_2$;
(iv) for every $\langle \overline{A} \rangle \psi \in \mathrm{TF}(\varphi)$, $\langle \overline{A} \rangle \psi \in A$ iff $\langle \overline{A} \rangle \psi \in S_1$;
(v) for every $\psi \in A$ such that $\langle A \rangle \psi \in \mathrm{TF}(\varphi)$, $\langle A \rangle \psi \in S_1$;
(vi) for every $\psi \in A$ such that $\langle \overline{A} \rangle \psi \in \mathrm{TF}(\varphi)$, $\langle \overline{A} \rangle \psi \in S_2$.

Let $\mathbf{L} = \langle \mathbb{D}, \mathcal{L} \rangle$ be a LIS for a PNL formula φ. By Definition 2 and Definition 4, it easily follows that, for every $d, d' \in D$, the triplet $\langle \mathrm{REQ}^{\mathbf{L}}(d), \mathcal{L}([d, d']), \mathrm{REQ}^{\mathbf{L}}(d') \rangle$ is an interval-tuple.

Definition 9. *Let $\mathbf{L} = \langle \mathbb{D}, \mathcal{L} \rangle$ be a LIS and $\langle R, A, R' \rangle$ be an interval-tuple. If there exists $[d, d'] \in \mathbb{I}(\mathbb{D})$ such that $\mathcal{L}([d, d']) = A$, $\mathrm{REQ}^{\mathbf{L}}(d) = R$, and $\mathrm{REQ}^{\mathbf{L}}(d') = R'$, we say that $\langle R, A, R' \rangle$ occurs in $\mathbf{L}$ (at $[d, d']$). Moreover, if $\langle R, A, R' \rangle$ occurs in $\mathbf{L}$ at $[d, d']$ and both d and d' are fulfilled in $\mathbf{L}$, we say that $\langle R, A, R' \rangle$ is fulfilled in $\mathbf{L}$ (via $[d, d']$).*

Definition 10. *Given a finite LIS $\mathbf{L} = \langle \mathbb{D}, \mathcal{L} \rangle$ for a PNL formula φ, we say that $\mathbf{L}$ is a pseudo-model for φ if every interval-tuple $\langle R, A, R' \rangle$ that occurs in $\mathbf{L}$ is fulfilled.*

From the fact that all interval-tuples are fulfilled in $\mathbf{L}$, that is, $\mathbf{L}$ is a pseudo-model for φ, it does not follow that $\mathbf{L}$ is fulfilling, since in $\mathbf{L}$ there can be multiple occurrences of the same interval-tuple, associated with different intervals. Thus, to turn a pseudo-model into a fulfilling LIS (for φ) some additional effort is needed. The next definition introduces an important ingredient of such a process.

Definition 11. *Let φ be a PNL formula and $\mathbf{L} = \langle \mathbb{D}, \mathcal{L} \rangle$ be a fulfilling LIS that satisfies it. For any $d \in D$, we say that:*

(future) a set $ES_f^d \subseteq D$ is a future essential set *for d if (i) for every $\langle A \rangle \psi \in$ $\mathrm{REQ}^\mathbf{L}(d)$, there exists $d' \in ES_f^d$ such that $\psi \in \mathcal{L}([d, d'])$ (fulfilling condition) and (ii) for every $d' \in ES_f^d$ there exists a formula $\langle A \rangle \psi \in \mathrm{REQ}^\mathbf{L}(d)$ such that, for every $d'' \in (ES_f^d \setminus \{d'\})$, $\neg\psi \in \mathcal{L}([d, d''])$ (minimality);*

(past) a set $ES_p^d \subseteq D$ is a past essential set *for d if (i) for every $\langle \overline{A} \rangle \psi \in$ $\mathrm{REQ}^\mathbf{L}(d)$, there exists $d' \in ES_p^d$ such that $\psi \in \mathcal{L}([d', d])$ (fulfilling condition) and (ii) for every $d' \in ES_p^d$ there exists a formula $\langle \overline{A} \rangle \psi \in \mathrm{REQ}^\mathbf{L}(d)$ such that, for every $d'' \in (ES_p^d \setminus \{d'\})$, $\neg\psi \in \mathcal{L}([d'', d])$ (minimality).*

Let $d \in D$. By Definition 11, for all $d' \in ES_f^d$ (resp., $d' \in ES_p^d$), there exists at least one formula ψ belonging to $\mathcal{L}([d, d'])$ (resp., $\mathcal{L}([d', d])$) only. On the contrary, we cannot exclude the existence of formulas ψ that belong to the labeling of more than one interval $[d, d']$ (resp., $[d', d]$), with $d' \in ES_f^d$ (resp., $d' \in ES_p^d$).

The decidability of the satisfiability problem for PNL over the class of all linear orders rests on the following lemma.

Lemma 1. *Given a pseudo-model $\mathbf{L} = \langle \mathbb{D}, \mathcal{L} \rangle$ for a PNL formula φ, there exists a fulfilling LIS $\mathbf{L}'$ that satisfies φ.*

Proof. We show how to obtain a fulfilling LIS $\mathbf{L}'$ starting from the pseudo-model $\mathbf{L}$ as the limit of a possibly infinite sequence of pseudo-models $\mathbf{L}_0(= \mathbf{L}), \mathbf{L}_1, \mathbf{L}_2, \dots$. In the following, we describe how to obtain the pseudo-model $\mathbf{L}_{i+1} = \langle \mathbb{D}_{i+1}, \mathcal{L}_{i+1} \rangle$, with $\mathbb{D}_{i+1} = \langle D_{i+1}, < \rangle$, from the pseudo-model $\mathbf{L}_i = \langle \mathbb{D}_i, \mathcal{L}_i \rangle$, with $\mathbb{D}_i = \langle D_i, < \rangle$, for any $i \geq 0$. Let Q_i be the queue of all points $d \in D_i$ that must be checked for fulfillment (Q_0 consists of all and only the points $d \in D$ such that d is not fulfilled in $\mathbf{L}$). If Q_i is empty, then we stop the procedure by putting $\mathbf{L}' = \mathbf{L}_i$. Otherwise, $\mathbf{L}_{i+1}$ is built as follows. Let d be the first element of the queue Q_i. If d is fulfilled, we remove it from the queue and put $\mathbf{L}_{i+1} = \mathbf{L}_i$ (every point in the queue is not fulfilled at insertion time; however, it may happen that subsequent expansions of the domain make it fulfilled before the time at which it is taken into consideration). Otherwise, either there exists $\langle A \rangle \psi \in \mathrm{REQ}^{\mathbf{L}_i}(d)$ which is not fulfilled, or there exists $\langle \overline{A} \rangle \psi \in \mathrm{REQ}^{\mathbf{L}_i}(d)$ which is not fulfilled, or both.

Suppose that there exists (at least) one $\langle A \rangle$-formula in $\mathrm{REQ}^{\mathbf{L}_i}(d)$ which is not fulfilled. Two cases may arise:

1) There exists $d' > d$ such that $\mathrm{REQ}^{\mathbf{L}_i}(d') = \mathrm{REQ}^{\mathbf{L}_i}(d)$ and d' is fulfilled. Let $ES_f^{d'} = \{d_1, \dots, d_k\}$. For $j = 1, \dots, k$, we proceed as follows:

a) If d_j is unique, we put $\mathcal{L}_{i+1}([d,d_j]) = \mathcal{L}_i([d',d_j])$. We prove that such a replacement does not introduce new defects for d_j. Suppose by contradiction that it is not the case. Then there must exist a formula $\langle \overline{A} \rangle \theta \in \mathrm{REQ}^{\mathbf{L}_i}(d_j)$ that is fulfilled only by the interval $[d,d_j]$ (in $\mathbf{L}_i$). Since the interval-tuple $\langle \mathrm{REQ}^{\mathbf{L}_i}(d), \mathcal{L}_i([d,d_j]), \mathrm{REQ}^{\mathbf{L}_i}(d_j) \rangle$ is fulfilled in $\mathbf{L}_i$, there exists an interval $[d'',d''']$ such that $\langle \mathrm{REQ}^{\mathbf{L}_i}(d), \mathcal{L}_i([d,d_j]), \mathrm{REQ}^{\mathbf{L}_i}(d_j) \rangle$ is fulfilled in $\mathbf{L}_i$ via $[d'',d''']$. Since d_j is unique, $d''' = d_j$. However, since d in not fulfilled in $\mathbf{L}_i$, $d'' \neq d$, and thus the interval $[d'',d_j]$ fulfills $\langle \overline{A} \rangle \theta$, in contradiction with the hypothesis that $\langle \overline{A} \rangle \theta$ causes a defect for d_j. This case is depicted in Figure 1.

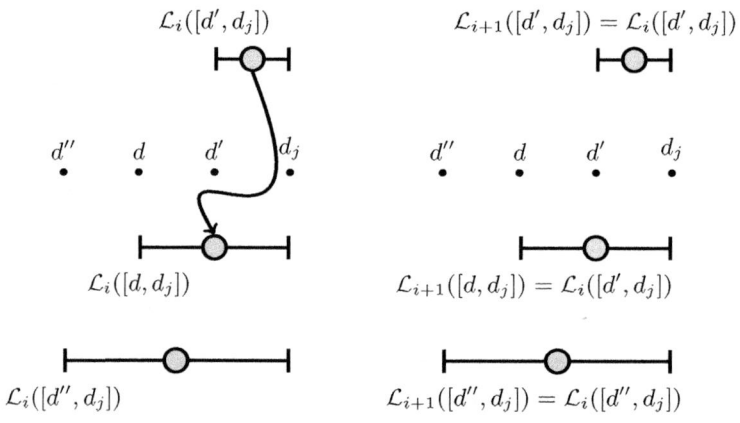

Fig. 1. Relabeling of the interval $[d,d_j]$ in Case 1a

b) If d_j is not unique, there exists $\overline{d} \neq d_j$, with $\mathrm{REQ}^{\mathbf{L}_i}(\overline{d}) = \mathrm{REQ}^{\mathbf{L}_i}(d_j)$. In such a case, we introduce a new point $\widehat{d}$ immediately after d_j with the same requests as d_j, that is, we put $D_{i+1} = D_i \cup \{\widehat{d}\}$, with $d_j < \widehat{d}$ and for all $\tilde{d}$, if $\tilde{d} > d_j$, then $\tilde{d} > \widehat{d}$, and we force $\mathrm{REQ}^{\mathbf{L}_{i+1}}(\widehat{d})$ to be equal to $\mathrm{REQ}^{\mathbf{L}_i}(d_j)$. To this end, for every $d'' \notin \{d,d_j,d'\}$, we put $\mathcal{L}_{i+1}([d'',\widehat{d}]) = \mathcal{L}_i([d'',d_j])$ (when $d'' < \widehat{d}$) and $\mathcal{L}_{i+1}([\widehat{d},d'']) = \mathcal{L}_i([d_j,d''])$ (when $d'' > \widehat{d}$). Moreover, we put $\mathcal{L}_{i+1}([d,\widehat{d}]) = \mathcal{L}_i([d',d_j])$ and $\mathcal{L}_{i+1}([d',\widehat{d}]) = \mathcal{L}_i([d,d_j])$, as depicted in Figure 2. In such a way, d satisfies over $[d,\widehat{d}]$ the request that d' satisfies over $[d',d_j]$. At the same time, we guarantee that $\widehat{d}$ satisfies the same past requests that d_j satisfies: $\widehat{d}$ satisfies over $[d,\widehat{d}]$ (resp., $[d',\widehat{d}]$) the request that d_j satisfies over $[d',d_j]$ (resp., $[d,d_j]$) and it satisfies the remaining past requests over intervals that start at the same point where the intervals over which d_j satisfies them start. Finally, if $\overline{d} > d_j$, we put $\mathcal{L}_{i+1}([d_j,\widehat{d}]) = \mathcal{L}_i([d_j,\overline{d}])$, and $\mathcal{L}_{i+1}([d_j,\widehat{d}]) = \mathcal{L}_i([\overline{d},d_j])$ otherwise. For all the remaining pairs d_r, d_s the labeling remains unchanged, that is, $\mathcal{L}_{i+1}([d_r,d_s]) = \mathcal{L}_i([d_r,d_s])$. Now, we observe that, by definition of $\mathcal{L}_{i+1}$, if d_j is fulfilled (in $\mathbf{L}_i$), then $\widehat{d}$ is fulfilled (in $\mathbf{L}_{i+1}$), while if d_j is not fulfilled (in $\mathbf{L}_i$), being $\widehat{d}$ fulfilled or not (in $\mathbf{L}_{i+1}$) depends on the labeling of the interval $[d_j, \widehat{d}]$. If $\widehat{d}$ is not fulfilled (in $\mathbf{L}_{i+1}$), we insert it into the queue Q_{i+1}.

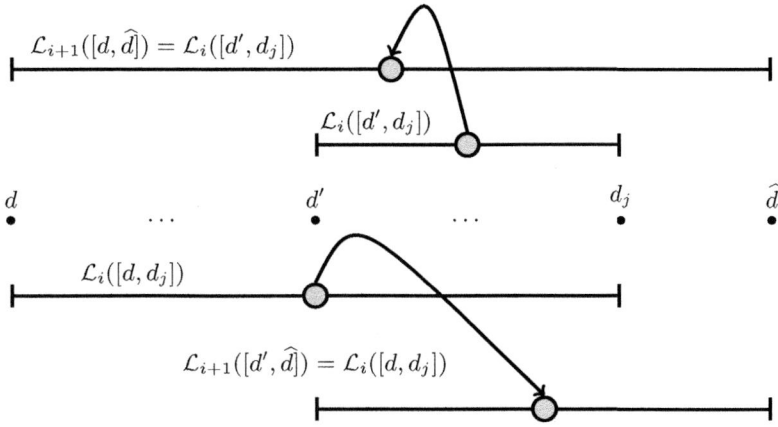

Fig. 2. Labeling of the intervals $[d, \widehat{d}]$ and $[d', \widehat{d}]$ in Case 1b

2) For every $d' > d$, with $\text{REQ}^{\mathbf{L}_i}(d') = \text{REQ}^{\mathbf{L}_i}(d)$, d' is not fulfilled. Let $d' < d$ such that $\text{REQ}^{\mathbf{L}_i}(d') = \text{REQ}^{\mathbf{L}_i}(d)$, d' is fulfilled, and, for every $d' < d'' < d$, if $\text{REQ}^{\mathbf{L}_i}(d'') = \text{REQ}^{\mathbf{L}_i}(d)$, then d'' is not fulfilled. For every point $\tilde{d} \in D$, we define the set $\text{Past}^{\mathbf{L}_i}(\tilde{d}) = \{\text{REQ}^{\mathbf{L}_i}(\hat{d}) \mid \hat{d} < \tilde{d}\}$. As a preliminary step, we prove that $\text{Past}^{\mathbf{L}_i}(d') = \text{Past}^{\mathbf{L}_i}(d)$. Suppose, by contradiction, that there exists $d' < d'' < d$ such that $\text{REQ}^{\mathbf{L}_i}(d'') \notin \text{Past}^{\mathbf{L}_i}(d')$. Since $\mathbf{L}_i$ is a pseudo-model, there exist $\overline{d}, \overline{d}' \in D_i$ such that the interval-tuple $\langle \text{REQ}^{\mathbf{L}_i}(d''),$ $\mathcal{L}_i([d'', d]), \text{REQ}^{\mathbf{L}_i}(d)\rangle$ is fulfilled in $\mathbf{L}_i$ via $[\overline{d}, \overline{d}']$. By definition, both $\overline{d}$ and $\overline{d}'$ are fulfilled; moreover, $\text{REQ}^{\mathbf{L}_i}(\overline{d}) = \text{REQ}^{\mathbf{L}_i}(d'')$, $\text{REQ}^{\mathbf{L}_i}(\overline{d}') = \text{REQ}^{\mathbf{L}_i}(d)$, and $\mathcal{L}_i([\overline{d}, \overline{d}']) = \mathcal{L}_i([d'', d])$. Since $\text{REQ}^{\mathbf{L}_i}(d'') \notin \text{Past}^{\mathbf{L}_i}(d')$, $d' < \overline{d}$ and thus $d' < \overline{d}'$. However, since d' is the largest fulfilled element in D_i with $\text{REQ}^{\mathbf{L}_i}(d') = \text{REQ}^{\mathbf{L}_i}(d)$, $\overline{d}'$ cannot be greater than d' (contradiction). Hence, $\text{Past}^{\mathbf{L}_i}(d') = \text{Past}^{\mathbf{L}_i}(d)$.

Let $ES_f^{d'} = \{d_1, ..., d_k\}$. For every $j = 1, ..., k$, we proceed as follows:

a) If d_j is unique, then $d_j > d$, since $\text{Past}^{\mathbf{L}_i}(d') = \text{Past}^{\mathbf{L}_i}(d)$. We proceed as in Case 1a.

b) If d_j is not unique and $d_j > d$, then we proceed as in Case 1b.

c) If d_j is not unique and $d' < d_j < d$, then we introduce a new point $\widehat{d}$ immediately after d with the same requests as d_j, that is, we put $D_{i+1} = D_i \cup \{\widehat{d}\}$, with $d < \widehat{d}$ and for all $\tilde{d}$, if $\tilde{d} > d$, then $\tilde{d} > \widehat{d}$, and we force $\text{REQ}^{\mathbf{L}_{i+1}}(\widehat{d})$ to be equal to $\text{REQ}^{\mathbf{L}_i}(d_j)$. To this end, for every $\overleftarrow{d}$ with $\overleftarrow{d} < d_j$ (resp., for every $\overrightarrow{d}$ with $\overrightarrow{d} > \widehat{d}$), we put $\mathcal{L}_{i+1}([\overleftarrow{d}, \widehat{d}]) = \mathcal{L}_i([\overleftarrow{d}, d_j])$ (resp., $\mathcal{L}_{i+1}([\widehat{d}, \overrightarrow{d}]) = \mathcal{L}_i([d_j, \overrightarrow{d}])$). Then, for all $d_j \leq \overleftrightarrow{d} < d$, there exists $d'' < d'$ such that $\text{REQ}^{\mathbf{L}_i}(d'') = \text{REQ}^{\mathbf{L}_i}(\overleftrightarrow{d})$, since $\text{Past}^{\mathbf{L}_i}(d') = \text{Past}^{\mathbf{L}_i}(d)$. Hence, we put $\mathcal{L}_{i+1}([\overleftrightarrow{d}, \widehat{d}]) = \mathcal{L}_i([d'', d_j])$. Moreover, we put $\mathcal{L}_{i+1}([d, \widehat{d}]) = \mathcal{L}_i([d', d_j])$. Finally, if $\widehat{d}$ is not fulfilled, we insert it into the queue Q_{i+1}. This case is depicted in Figure 3.

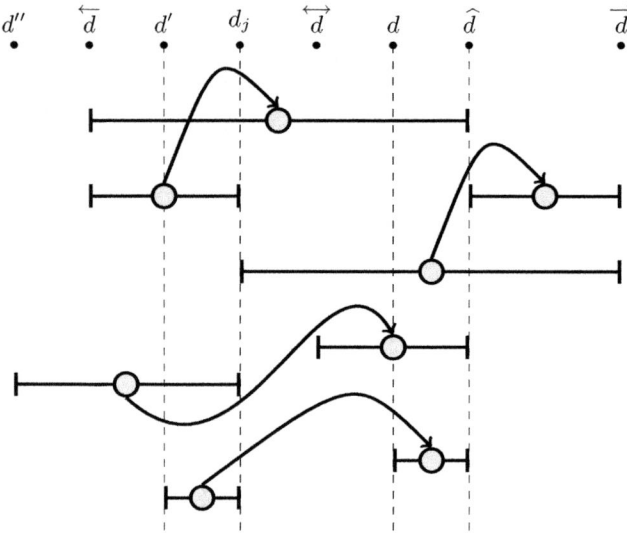

$$d'' \quad \overleftarrow{d} \quad d' \quad d_j \quad \overleftrightarrow{d} \quad d \quad \widehat{d} \quad \overrightarrow{d}$$

Fig. 3. Labeling of intervals starting/ending in $\widehat{d}$ in Case 2c

The case in which there exists (at least) one $\langle \overline{A} \rangle$-formula in $\text{REQ}^{\mathbf{L}_i}(d)$ which is not fulfilled is completely symmetric, and thus its description is omitted. This concludes the construction of $\mathbf{L}_{i+1}$. Since all points which are fulfilled in $\mathbf{L}_i$ remain fulfilled in $\mathbf{L}_{i+1}$, it is immediate to conclude that $\mathbf{L}_{i+1}$ is a pseudo-model. Moreover, as d is fulfilled in $\mathbf{L}_{i+1}$, it can be safely removed from the queue. As it can be easily checked, the proposed construction does not remove any point, but it can introduce new ones, possibly infinitely many. However, the use of a queue to manage points which are (possibly) not fulfilled guarantees that the defects of each of them sooner or later will be fixed.

   To complete the proof, it suffices to show that the fulfilling LIS $\mathbf{L}'$ for φ we were looking for is the limit of this (possibly infinite) construction. Let $\mathbf{L}_i^-$ be equal to $\mathbf{L}_i$ devoid of the labeling of all intervals consisting of a (non-unique) point in Q_i and a unique point (in $D_i \setminus Q_i$). We define $\mathbf{L}'$ as the (possibly infinite) union $\cup_{i \geq 0} \mathbf{L}_i^-$ (if Q_i turns out to be empty for some i, then $\mathbf{L}'$ is simply equal to $\mathbf{L}_i$). It is trivial to check that for every pair $D_i, D_{i+1}, D_i \subseteq D_{i+1}$. To prove that for every pair $\mathcal{L}_i^-, \mathcal{L}_{i+1}^-$, it holds that $\mathcal{L}_i^- \subseteq \mathcal{L}_{i+1}^-$, we observe that: (i) the labeling of intervals whose endpoints are both non-unique points (resp., unique points) never changes, that is, it is fixed once and for all, and (ii) for every pair of point $d, d' \in D_i \setminus Q_i$ such that d is a non-unique point and d' is a unique one, if $d < d'$ (resp., $d' < d$), then $\mathcal{L}_j([d, d']) = \mathcal{L}_i([d, d'])$ (resp., $\mathcal{L}_j([d', d]) = \mathcal{L}_i([d', d])$) for all $j \geq i$, that is, the labeling of an interval consisting of a non-unique point and a unique one may possibly change when the non-unique point is removed from the queue and then it remains unchanged forever (notice that non-unique points which are fulfilled from the beginning never change "their labeling"). Finally, to prove that all points are fulfilled in $\cup_{i \geq 0} \mathbf{L}_i^-$, it is sufficient to observe that: (i) all unique points belong to D_0 and are fulfilled in the restriction of $\mathbf{L}_0$ to $D_0 \setminus Q_0$ (and thus in $\mathbf{L}_0^-$), and (ii) for every $i \geq 0$, all points in $D_i \setminus Q_i$ are fulfilled in $\mathbf{L}_i^-$ and the first element of Q_i may be not fulfilled in $\mathbf{L}_i$ (and thus in $\mathbf{L}_i^-$), but it is fulfilled in $\mathbf{L}_{i+1}^-$. Every point is indeed either directly inserted into $D_i \setminus Q_i$ or added to Q_i (and thus it becomes the first element of Q_j for some $j > i$) for some $i \geq 0$.   □

Lemma 2. *Given a PNL formula φ and a fulfilling LIS $\mathbf{L} = \langle \mathbb{D}, \mathcal{L} \rangle$ that satisfies it, there exists a pseudo-model $\mathbf{L}'$ for φ, with $|D'| \leq 2 \cdot |\varphi| \cdot 2^{3 \cdot |\varphi|+1}$.*

Decidability of PNL over the class of all linear orders immediately follows.

Theorem 2. *The satisfiability problem for PNL over the class of all linear orders is decidable.*

We conclude the section by explaining how to tailor the above proofs to the cases of dense and discrete linear orders (details can be found in [6]).

To cope with dense linear orders, we introduce the notion of covering.

Definition 12. *Let $\mathbf{L} = \langle \mathbb{D}, \mathcal{L} \rangle$ be a pseudo-model for a PNL formula φ and $d \in D$. We say that d is covered if either d is not unique or (d is unique and) both its immediate predecessor (if any) and successor (if any) are not unique. We say that $\mathbf{L}$ is covered if every $d \in D$ is covered.*

The construction of Lemma 1 is then revised to force each point in a pseudo-model for φ to be *covered* so that we can always insert a point in between any pair of consecutive points, thus producing a dense model for φ.

To deal with discrete orders, we make us of the notion of *safe pseudo-model*.

Definition 13. *Let $\mathbf{L} = \langle \mathbb{D}, \mathcal{L} \rangle$ be a pseudo-model for a PNL formula φ and $d \in D$. We say that d is safe if either d is not unique or (d is unique and) both its immediate predecessor (if any) and successor (if any) are fulfilled. We say that $\mathbf{L}$ is safe if every $d \in D$ is safe.*

Such a safety condition guarantees that the building procedure of Lemma 1 can be done in such a way that all points added during the construction get their (definitive) immediate successor and immediate predecessor in at most one step.

As for complexity, it is possible to show that forcing covering (resp., safety) does not cause any exponential blow-up in the maximum size of a pseudo-model. More formally, by suitably adapting Lemma 2, we can prove that if φ is satisfiable over dense (resp., discrete) linear orders, then there exists a covered (resp., safe) pseudo-model $\mathbf{L} = \langle \mathbb{D}, \mathcal{L} \rangle$ for it with $|D| \leq 4 \cdot |\varphi| \cdot 2^{3 \cdot |\varphi|+1}$ (resp., $|D| \leq 2 \cdot |\varphi| \cdot 2^{4 \cdot |\varphi|+1}$). It easily follows that the satisfiability problem for PNL over all (resp., dense, discrete) linear orders belongs to the NEXPTIME complexity class.

NEXPTIME-hardness immediately follows from [7], where a reduction of the exponential tiling problem, which is known to be NEXPTIME-complete [1], to the satisfiability problem for the future fragment of PNL is provided (as it can be easily verified, the reduction is completely independent from the considered linear order). This allows us to conclude that the satisfiability problem for PNL over all (resp., dense, discrete) linear orders is NEXPTIME-complete.

5   Tableau Systems for PNL

In this section, we develop tableau-based decision procedures for PNL over all, dense, and discrete linear orders. We describe in detail the tableau system for the general case (all linear orders), and then we briefly explain how to specialize it to deal with the dense and discrete cases. The presentation is organized as follows. First, we give the rules of the tableau system; then, we describe expansion strategies and blocking conditions; finally, we state termination, soundness, and completeness of the method. We conclude the section by proving the optimality of all the proposed tableau-based decision procedures.

We preliminarily introduce basic concepts and notation. A tableau for a PNL formula φ is a special *decorated tree* $\mathcal{T}$. We associate a finite linear order $\mathbb{D}_B = \langle D_B, < \rangle$ and a *request function* $\mathrm{REQ}_B : D_B \mapsto \mathrm{REQ}_\varphi$ with every branch B of $\mathcal{T}$. Every node n in B is labeled with a pair $\langle [d_i, d_j], A_n \rangle$ such that the triple $\langle \mathrm{REQ}_B(d_i), A_n, \mathrm{REQ}_B(d_j) \rangle$ is an interval-tuple. The *initial tableau* for φ consists of a single node (and thus of a single branch B) labeled with the pair $\langle [d_0, d_1], A_\varphi \rangle$, where $\mathbb{D}_B = \{d_0 < d_1\}$ and $\varphi \in A_\varphi$.

Given a point $d \in D_B$ and a formula $\langle A \rangle \psi \in \mathrm{REQ}_B(d)$, we say that $\langle A \rangle \psi$ is *fulfilled in B for d* if there exists a node $n' \in B$ such that n' is labeled with $\langle [d, d'], A_{n'} \rangle$ and $\psi \in A_{n'}$. Similarly, given a point $d \in D_B$ and a formula $\langle \overline{A} \rangle \psi \in \mathrm{REQ}_B(d)$, we say that $\langle \overline{A} \rangle \psi$ is *fulfilled in B for d* if there exists a node $n' \in B$ such that n' is labeled with $\langle [d', d], A_{n'} \rangle$ and $\psi \in A_{n'}$. Given a point $d \in D_B$, we say that d *is fulfilled in B* if every $\langle A \rangle \psi$ (resp., $\langle \overline{A} \rangle \psi$) in $\mathrm{REQ}_B(d)$ is fulfilled in B for d.

Let $\mathcal{T}$ be a tableau and B be a branch of $\mathcal{T}$, with $\mathbb{D}_B = \{d_0 < \ldots < d_k\}$. We denote by $B \cdot n$ the expansion of B with an immediate successor node n and by $B \cdot n_1 | \ldots | n_h$ the expansion of B with h immediate successor nodes $n_1, \ldots, n_h$. To possibly expand B, we apply one of the following *expansion rules*:

1. $\langle A \rangle$*-rule.* If there exist $d_j \in D_B$ and $\langle A \rangle \psi \in \mathrm{REQ}_B(d_j)$ such that $\langle A \rangle \psi$ is not fulfilled in B for d_j, we proceed as follows. If there is not an interval-tuple $\langle \mathrm{REQ}_B(d_j), A_\psi, S \rangle$, with $\psi \in A_\psi$, we *close* the branch B. Otherwise, let $\langle \mathrm{REQ}_B(d_j), A_\psi, S \rangle$ be such an interval-tuple. We take a new point d and we expand B with $h = k - j + 1$ immediate successor nodes $n_1, \ldots, n_h$ such that, for every $1 \le l \le h$, $\mathbb{D}_{B \cdot n_l} = \mathbb{D}_B \cup \{d_{j+l-1} < d < d_{j+l}\}$ (for $l = h$, we simply add a new point d, with $d > d_k$, to the linear order), $n_l = \langle [d_j, d], A_\psi \rangle$, with $\psi \in A_\psi$, $\mathrm{REQ}_{B \cdot n_l}(d) = S$, and $\mathrm{REQ}_{B \cdot n_l}(d') = \mathrm{REQ}_B(d')$ for every $d' \in D_B$.

2. $\langle \overline{A} \rangle$*-rule.* It is symmetric to the $\langle A \rangle$-rule and thus its description is omitted.

3. *Fill-in rule.* If there exist two points d_i, d_j, with $d_i < d_j$, such that there is not a node in B decorated with the interval $[d_i, d_j]$, but there exists an interval-tuple $\langle \text{REQ}_B(d_i), A, \text{REQ}_B(d_j) \rangle$, we expand B with a node $n = \langle [d_i, d_j], A \rangle$. If such an interval-tuple does not exist, then we *close B*.

The application of any of the above rules may result in the replacement of the branch B with one or more new branches, each one featuring one new node n. However, while the *Fill-in rule* decorates such a node with a new interval whose endpoints already belong to D_B, the $\langle A \rangle$-rule (resp., $\langle \overline{A} \rangle$-rule) adds a new point d to D_B which becomes the ending (resp., beginning) point of the interval associated with the new node.

We say that a node $n = \langle [d_i, d_j], A \rangle$ in a branch B is *active* if for every predecessor $n' = \langle [d, d'], A' \rangle$ of n in B, the interval-tuples $\langle \text{REQ}_B(d_i), A, \text{REQ}_B(d_j) \rangle$ and $\langle \text{REQ}_B(d), A', \text{REQ}_B(d') \rangle$ are different. Moreover, we say that a point $d \in D_B$ is *active* if and only if there exists an active node n in B such that $n = \langle [d, d'], A \rangle$ or $n = \langle [d', d], A \rangle$, for some $d' \in D_B$ and some atom A. Given a non-closed branch B, we say that B is *complete* if for every $d_i, d_j \in D_B$, with $d_i < d_j$, there exists a node n in B labeled with $n = \langle [d_i, d_j], A \rangle$, for some atom A. It can be easily seen that if B is complete, then the tuple $\langle \mathbb{D}_B, \mathbb{I}(\mathbb{D}_B), \mathcal{L}_B \rangle$ such that, for every $[d_i, d_j] \in \mathbb{I}(\mathbb{D}_B)$, $\mathcal{L}_B([d_i, d_j]) = A$ if and only if there exists a node n in B labeled with $\langle [d_i, d_j], A \rangle$, is a LIS. Given a non-closed branch B, we say that B is *blocked* if B is complete and for every active point $d \in B$ we have that d is fulfilled in B.

We start from an initial tableau for φ and we apply the expansion rules to all the non-blocked and non-closed branches B. The expansion strategy is the following one:

1. Apply the *Fill-in rule* until it generates no new nodes in B.
2. If there exist an active point $d \in D_B$ and a formula $\langle A \rangle \psi \in \text{REQ}_B(d)$ such that $\langle A \rangle \psi$ is not fulfilled in B for d, then apply the $\langle A \rangle$-rule on d. Go back to step 1.
3. If there exist an active point $d \in D_B$ and a formula $\langle \overline{A} \rangle \psi \in \text{REQ}_B(d)$ such that $\langle \overline{A} \rangle \psi$ is not fulfilled in B for d, then apply the $\langle \overline{A} \rangle$-rule on d. Go back to step 1.

A tableau $\mathcal{T}$ for φ is *final* if and only if every branch B of $\mathcal{T}$ is closed or blocked.

Theorem 3 (Termination). *Let $\mathcal{T}$ be a final tableau for a PNL formula φ and B be a branch of $\mathcal{T}$. We have that $|B| \leq (2 \cdot |\varphi| \cdot 2^{3 \cdot |\varphi| + 1}) \cdot (2 \cdot |\varphi| \cdot 2^{3 \cdot |\varphi| + 1} - 1)/2$.*

Theorem 4 (Soundness). *Let $\mathcal{T}$ be a final tableau for a PNL formula φ. If $\mathcal{T}$ features one blocked branch, then φ is satisfiable over all linear orders.*

Theorem 5 (Completeness). *Let φ be a PNL formula which is satisfiable over the class of all linear orders. Then there exists a final tableau for φ with at least one blocked branch.*

The above tableau system can be tailored to the dense and discrete cases.

As for the dense case, it suffices to apply the following rule immediately after the $\langle \overline{A} \rangle / \langle A \rangle$-*rules*:

Dense rule. If there exist two consecutive non-covered points d_i, d_{i+1}, we proceed as follows. If there is not an interval-tuple $\langle \text{REQ}_B(d_i), A, S \rangle$ for some $S \in \text{REQ}_\varphi$ and $A \in A_\varphi$, we *close* the branch B. Otherwise, let $\langle \text{REQ}_B(d_i), A, S \rangle$ be such an interval-tuple. We expand B with a node n, labeled with $\langle [d_i, d], A \rangle$, such that $\text{REQ}_{B \cdot n}(d) = S$ and $\mathbb{D}_{B \cdot n} = \mathbb{D}_B \cup \{d_i < d < d_{i+1}\}$.

The discrete case is more complex. First, we partition nodes (intervals) in two classes, namely, *free* and *unit* nodes. Free nodes are labeled with triples of the form $\langle [d, d'], A, free \rangle$, meaning that a point can be added in between d and d'; unit nodes, labeled with triples of the form $\langle [d, d'], A, unit \rangle$, denote unit intervals (insertions are forbidden). The set of expansion rules is then updated as follows. The *Fill-in* rule remains unchanged. The $\langle A \rangle / \langle \overline{A} \rangle$-rules are revised to prevent the insertion of points inside *unit*-intervals. The introduction of unit intervals is managed by two additional rules (*Predecessor* and *Successor* rules) to be applied immediately after the $\langle \overline{A} \rangle / \langle A \rangle$-*rules*.

Successor rule. If there exists $d_j \in D_B$ such that d_j is unique in D_B, its immediate successor d_{j+1} in D_B is not fulfilled, there exists a node n labeled by $\langle [d_j, d_{j+1}], A_n, free \rangle$, for some atom A_n, in B, and there exists no node n' labeled by $\langle [d_j, d_{j+1}], A_{n'}, unit \rangle$, for some atom $A_{n'}$, in B, then we proceed as follows. We expand B with 2 immediate successor nodes n_1, n_2 such that $n_1 = \langle [d_j, d_{j+1}], A_n, unit \rangle$ and $n_2 = \langle [d_j, d], A', unit \rangle$, with $d_j < d < d_{j+1}$ and there exists an interval-tuple $\langle \text{REQ}_B(d_j), A', S \rangle$, for some A' and S (the existence of such an interval tuple is guaranteed by the existence of a node n with label $\langle [d_j, d_{j+1}], A_n, free \rangle$). We have that $\mathbb{D}_{B \cdot n_1} = \mathbb{D}_B$ and $\mathbb{D}_{B \cdot n_2} = \mathbb{D}_B \cup \{d_j < d < d_{j+1}\}$. Moreover, $\text{REQ}_{B \cdot n_2}(d) = S$ and $\text{REQ}_{B \cdot n_2}(d') = \text{REQ}_B(d')$ for every $d' \in D_B$.

Predecessor rule. Symmetric to the successor rule and thus omitted.

As for the complexity, in both cases (dense and discrete), no exponential blow-up in the maximum length of a branch B (with respect to the general case) occurs. More formally, following the reasoning path of Theorem 3, we can prove that the maximum length of a branch B in the dense (resp., discrete) case is $|B| \leq (4 \cdot |\varphi| \cdot 2^{3 \cdot |\varphi| + 1} - 1) \cdot (4 \cdot |\varphi| \cdot 2^{3 \cdot |\varphi| + 1} - 2)/2$ (resp., $|B| \leq (2 \cdot (3 \cdot |\varphi| + 1) \cdot 2^{3 \cdot |\varphi| + 1}) \cdot (2 \cdot (3 \cdot |\varphi| + 1) \cdot 2^{3 \cdot |\varphi| + 1} - 1)/2)$. Optimality easily follows.

6   Conclusions and Future Work

In this paper, we have developed an optimal tableau system for PNL interpreted over the class of all linear orders, and we have shown how to adapt it to deal with the subclasses of dense and (weakly) discrete linear orders. We are currently working at the implementation of the three tableau systems.

References

1. Börger, E., Grädel, E., Gurevich, Y.: The Classical Decision Problem. Perspectives of Mathematical Logic. Springer, Heidelberg (1997)
2. Bowman, H., Thompson, S.: A decision procedure and complete axiomatization of finite interval temporal logic with projection. Journal of Logic and Computation 13(2), 195–239 (2003)
3. Bresolin, D., Goranko, V., Montanari, A., Sciavicco, G.: Propositional interval neighborhood logics: Expressiveness, decidability, and undecidable extensions. Annals of Pure and Applied Logic 161(3), 289–304 (2009)
4. Bresolin, D., Montanari, A., Sala, P.: An optimal tableau-based decision algorithm for propositional neighborhood logic. In: Thomas, W., Weil, P. (eds.) STACS 2007. LNCS, vol. 4393, pp. 549–560. Springer, Heidelberg (2007)
5. Bresolin, D., Montanari, A., Sala, P., Sciavicco, G.: Optimal tableaux for right propositional neighborhood logic over linear orders. In: Hölldobler, S., Lutz, C., Wansing, H. (eds.) JELIA 2008. LNCS (LNAI), vol. 5293, pp. 62–75. Springer, Heidelberg (2008)
6. Bresolin, D., Montanari, A., Sala, P., Sciavicco, G.: Tableau-based decision procedures for Propositional Neighborhood Logic. Technical Report 01, Dipartimento di Matematica e Informatica, Università di Udine, Italy (2010)
7. Bresolin, D., Montanari, A., Sciavicco, G.: An optimal decision procedure for Right Propositional Neighborhood Logic. Journal of Automated Reasoning 38(1-3), 173–199 (2007)
8. Chaochen, Z., Hansen, M.R.: An adequate first order interval logic. In: de Roever, W.-P., Langmaack, H., Pnueli, A. (eds.) COMPOS 1997. LNCS, vol. 1536, pp. 584–608. Springer, Heidelberg (1998)
9. Goranko, V., Montanari, A., Sciavicco, G.: Propositional interval neighborhood temporal logics. Journal of Universal Computer Science 9(9), 1137–1167 (2003)
10. Goranko, V., Montanari, A., Sciavicco, G.: A road map of interval temporal logics and duration calculi. Journal of Applied Non-Classical Logics 14(1-2), 9–54 (2004)
11. Goranko, V., Montanari, A., Sciavicco, G., Sala, P.: A general tableau method for propositional interval temporal logics: theory and implementation. Journal of Applied Logic 4(3), 305–330 (2006)
12. Halpern, J., Shoham, Y.: A propositional modal logic of time intervals. Journal of the ACM 38(4), 935–962 (1991)
13. Montanari, A.: Back to interval temporal logics. In: Garcia de la Banda, M., Pontelli, E. (eds.) ICLP 2008. LNCS, vol. 5366, pp. 11–13. Springer, Heidelberg (2008)
14. Montanari, A., Puppis, G., Sala, P.: Maximal decidable fragments of halpern and shoham's modal logic of intervals. In: Abramsky, S., Gavoille, C., Kirchner, C., Meyer auf der Heide, F., Spirakis, P.G. (eds.) ICALP 2010. LNCS, vol. 6199, pp. 345–356. Springer, Heidelberg (2010)
15. Moszkowski, B.: Reasoning about digital circuits. Tech. rep. stan-cs-83-970, Dept. of Computer Science, Stanford University, Stanford, CA (1983)
16. Otto, M.: Two variable first-order logic over ordered domains. Journal of Symbolic Logic 66(2), 685–702 (2001)
17. Pratt-Hartmann, I.: Temporal prepositions and their logic. Artificial Intelligence 166(1-2), 1–36 (2005)
18. Venema, Y.: A modal logic for chopping intervals. Journal of Logic and Computation 1(4), 453–476 (1991)

Craig Interpolation in Displayable Logics

James Brotherston[1] and Rajeev Goré[2]

[1] Dept. of Computing, Imperial College London
J.Brotherston@imperial.ac.uk
[2] School of Computer Science, ANU Canberra
Rajeev.Gore@anu.edu.au

Abstract. We give a general proof-theoretic method for proving Craig interpolation for displayable logics, based on an analysis of the individual proof rules of their display calculi. Using this uniform method, we prove interpolation for a spectrum of display calculi differing in their structural rules, including those for multiplicative linear logic, multiplicative additive linear logic and ordinary classical logic. Our analysis of proof rules also provides new insights into why interpolation fails, or seems likely to fail, in many substructural logics. Specifically, contraction appears particularly problematic for interpolation except in special circumstances.

1 Introduction

> I believe or hope that Display logic can be used as a basis for establishing an interpolation theorem; but that remains to be seen.

Nuel D. Belnap, *Display Logic* [1], 1982

Craig's original *interpolation* theorem for first-order logic [6] states that for any provable entailment $F \vdash G$ between formulas, an "intermediate formula" or *interpolant* I can be found such that both $F \vdash I$ and $I \vdash G$ are provable and every nonlogical symbol occurring in I occurs in both F and G. This seemingly innocuous property turns out to have considerable mathematical significance because Craig interpolation is intimately connected with consistency, compactness and definability (see [8] for a survey). In computer science, it plays an important rôle in settings where modular decomposition of complex theories is a concern, and has been applied to such problems as invariant generation [16], type inference [12], model checking [5,15] and the decomposition of complex ontologies [13]. Whether a given logic satisfies interpolation is thus of practical importance in computer science as well as theoretical importance in logic.

In this paper, we give a proof-theoretic method for establishing Craig interpolation in the setting of Belnap's *display logic*. Display logic is a general consecution framework which allows us to combine multiple families of logical connectives into a single *display calculus* [1]. Display calculi are characterised by the availability of a "display-equivalence" relation on consecutions which allows us to rearrange a consecution so that a selected substructure appears alone on one side of the proof turnstile. Various authors have shown how to capture large

K. Brünnler and G. Metcalfe (Eds.): TABLEAUX 2011, LNAI 6793, pp. 88–103, 2011.
© Springer-Verlag Berlin Heidelberg 2011

classes of modal and substructural logics within this framework [2,11,14,20], and how to characterise the class of Kripke frame conditions that can be captured by displayed logics [10]. A major advantage of display calculi is that they enjoy an extremely general cut-elimination theorem which relies on checking eight simple conditions on the rules of the calculus. Restall has also shown how decidability results can be obtained from cut-free display calculi [17].

In the case that a cut-free sequent calculus à la Gentzen is available, interpolation for the logic in question can typically be established by induction over cut-free derivations (see e.g. [4]). Besides its theoretical elegance, this method has the advantage of being fully constructive. One of the main criticisms levelled against display calculi is that they do not enjoy a true sub-formula property and hence, in contrast to the situation for sequent calculi, Belnap's general cut-elimination theorem cannot be used to prove results like interpolation for display calculi. Indeed, to our knowledge there are no interpolation theorems for display calculi in the literature. Here we (partially) rebut the aforementioned criticism by giving a general Craig interpolation result for a large class of displayed logics.

The main idea of our approach is to construct a *set* of interpolants at each step of a given proof, one for every possible "rearrangement" of the consecution using both display-equivalence and any native associativity principles. Our aim is then to show that, given interpolants for all rearrangements of the premises of a rule, one can find interpolants for all rearrangements of its conclusion. This very general interpolation method applies to a wide range of logics with a display calculus presentation and is potentially extensible to even larger classes of such logics. However, some proof rules enjoy the aforementioned property only under strong restrictions, with contraction being the most problematic among the rules we study in this paper. This gives a significant new insight into the reasons why interpolation fails, or appears likely to fail, in many substructural logics.

Section 2 introduces the display calculi that we work with throughout the paper. We develop our interpolation methodology incrementally in Sections 3, 4 and 5. Section 6 concludes. The proofs in this paper have been abbreviated for space reasons; detailed proofs can be found in an associated technical report [3].

2 Display Calculus Fundamentals

We now give a basic display calculus which can be customised to various logics by adding structural rules. In general, one may formulate display calculi for logics involving arbitrarily many families of formula and structure connectives. To limit the bureaucracy and technical overhead due to such generality, we limit ourselves in this paper to display calculi employing only a single family of connectives. For similar reasons, we also restrict to commutative logics.

Definition 2.1 (Formula, Structure, Consecution). *Formulas* and *structures* are given by the following grammars, where P ranges over a fixed infinite set of propositional variables, F ranges over formulas, and X over structures:

$$F ::= P \mid \top \mid \bot \mid \neg F \mid F \mathbin{\&} F \mid F \vee F \mid F \to F \mid \top_a \mid \bot_a \mid F \mathbin{\&}_a F \mid F \vee_a F$$
$$X ::= F \mid \emptyset \mid \sharp X \mid X \mathbin{;} X$$

(The subscript "a" is for "additive".) A structure is called *atomic* if it is either a formula or $\emptyset$. When we reason by induction on a structure X, we typically conflate the cases $X = F$ and $X = \emptyset$ into the case where X is atomic. We use F, G, I etc. to range over formulas, W, X, Y, Z etc. to range over structures, and A, B etc. to range over atomic structures. We write $\mathcal{V}(X)$ for the set of propositional variables occurring in the structure X. If X and Y are structures then $X \vdash Y$ is a *consecution*. We use $\mathcal{C}, \mathcal{C}'$ etc. to range over consecutions.

Definition 2.2 (Interpretation of structures). For any structure X we define the formulas Ψ_X and Υ_X by mutual structural induction on X as:

$$\Psi_F = F \qquad \Psi_\emptyset = \top \qquad \Upsilon_F = F \qquad \Upsilon_\emptyset = \bot$$
$$\Psi_{\sharp X} = \neg \Upsilon_X \qquad \Psi_{X_1;X_2} = \Psi_{X_1} \,\&\, \Psi_{X_2} \qquad \Upsilon_{\sharp X} = \neg \Psi_X \qquad \Upsilon_{X_1;X_2} = \Upsilon_{X_1} \vee \Upsilon_{X_2}$$

For any consecution $X \vdash Y$ we define its *formula interpretation* to be $\Psi_X \vdash \Upsilon_Y$.

Definition 2.3 (Antecedent and consequent parts). A *part* of a structure X is an occurrence of one of its substructures. We classify the parts of X as either *positive* or *negative* in X as follows:

– X is a positive part of itself;
– a negative / positive part of X is a positive / negative part of $\sharp X$;
– a positive / negative part of X_1 or X_2 is a positive / negative part of $X_1 \,;\, X_2$.

Z is said to be an *antecedent / consequent part* of a consecution $X \vdash Y$ if it is a positive / negative part of X or a negative / positive part of Y.

Definition 2.4 (Display-equivalence). We define *display-equivalence* $\equiv_D$ to be the least equivalence on consecutions containing the (symmetric) relation $\rightleftarrows_D$ given by the following *display postulates*:

$$X;Y \vdash Z \quad \rightleftarrows_D \quad X \vdash \sharp Y; Z \quad \rightleftarrows_D \quad Y;X \vdash Z$$
$$X \vdash Y; Z \quad \rightleftarrows_D \quad X; \sharp Y \vdash Z \quad \rightleftarrows_D \quad X \vdash Z;Y$$
$$X \vdash Y \quad \rightleftarrows_D \quad \sharp Y \vdash \sharp X \quad \rightleftarrows_D \quad \sharp\sharp X \vdash Y$$

Note that Defn. 2.4 builds in the commutativity of ; on the left and right of consecutions, i.e., we are assuming both $\&$ and $\vee$ commutative.

Proposition 2.5 (Display property). *For any antecedent / consequent part Z of a consecution $X \vdash Y$, one can construct a structure W such that $X \vdash Y \equiv_D Z \vdash W$ / $X \vdash Y \equiv_D W \vdash Z$, respectively.*

Proof. (Sketch) For any $X \vdash Y$, the display postulates of Defn. 2.4 allow us to display each of the immediate substructures of X and Y (as the antecedent or consequent as appropriate). The proposition follows by iterating. $\square$

Rearranging $X \vdash Y$ into $Z \vdash W$ or $W \vdash Z$ in Prop. 2.5 is called *displaying Z*.

Figure 1 gives the proof rules of a basic display calculus $\mathcal{D}_0$ which only uses the logical connectives $\top, \bot, \neg, \&, \vee$, and $\rightarrow$. Figure 2 presents "structure-free" rules

Identity rules:

$$\frac{}{P \vdash P}\ (\mathrm{Id}) \qquad\qquad \frac{X' \vdash Y'}{X \vdash Y}\ \ X \vdash Y \equiv_D X' \vdash Y'\ (\equiv_D)$$

Logical rules:

$$\frac{\emptyset \vdash X}{\top \vdash X}\ (\top\mathrm{L}) \qquad \frac{}{\emptyset \vdash \top}\ (\top\mathrm{R}) \qquad \frac{F\,;G \vdash X}{F \& G \vdash X}\ (\&\mathrm{L}) \qquad \frac{X \vdash F \quad Y \vdash G}{X\,;Y \vdash F \& G}\ (\&\mathrm{R})$$

$$\frac{}{\bot \vdash \emptyset}\ (\bot\mathrm{L}) \qquad \frac{X \vdash \emptyset}{X \vdash \bot}\ (\bot\mathrm{R}) \qquad \frac{F \vdash X \quad G \vdash Y}{F \vee G \vdash X\,;Y}\ (\vee\mathrm{L}) \qquad \frac{X \vdash F\,;G}{X \vdash F \vee G}\ (\vee\mathrm{R})$$

$$\frac{\sharp F \vdash X}{\neg F \vdash X}\ (\neg\mathrm{L}) \qquad \frac{X \vdash \sharp F}{X \vdash \neg F}\ (\neg\mathrm{R}) \qquad \frac{X \vdash F \quad G \vdash Y}{F \to G \vdash \sharp X\,;Y}\ (\to\mathrm{L}) \qquad \frac{X\,;F \vdash G}{X \vdash F \to G}\ (\to\mathrm{R})$$

Fig. 1. Proof rules for the basic display calculus $\mathcal{D}_0$

$$\frac{}{\bot_a \vdash X}\ (\bot_a\mathrm{L}) \qquad \frac{F_i \vdash X}{F_1 \&_a F_2 \vdash X}\ i \in \{1,2\}\,(\&_a\mathrm{L}) \qquad \frac{F \vdash X \quad G \vdash X}{F \vee_a G \vdash X}\ (\vee_a\mathrm{L})$$

$$\frac{}{X \vdash \top_a}\ (\top_a\mathrm{R}) \qquad \frac{X \vdash F \quad X \vdash G}{X \vdash F \&_a G}\ (\&_a\mathrm{R}) \qquad \frac{X \vdash F_i}{X \vdash F_1 \vee_a F_2}\ i \in \{1,2\}\,(\vee_a\mathrm{R})$$

Fig. 2. Structure-free proof rules for the "additive" logical connectives

for the *additive* logical connectives $\top_a$, $\bot_a$, $\&_a$ and $\vee_a$, and Figure 3 presents some *structural rules* governing the behaviour of the structural connectives $\emptyset$, ';' and $\sharp$. The rules in Figures 2 and 3 should be regarded as optional: if $\mathcal{D}$ is a display calculus and $\mathcal{R}$ is a list of rules from Figures 2 and 3 then the *extension* $\mathcal{D} + \mathcal{R}$ of $\mathcal{D}$ is the display calculus obtained from $\mathcal{D}$ by adding all rules in $\mathcal{R}$. We write $\mathcal{D}_0^+$ to abbreviate the extension of $\mathcal{D}_0$ with all of the structure-free rules in Figure 2.

We prove interpolation by induction over cut-free derivations, so we omit the cut rule from $\mathcal{D}_0$. The following theorem says that this omission is harmless.

Theorem 2.6. *The following cut rule is admissible in any extension of $\mathcal{D}_0$:*

$$\frac{X \vdash F \quad F \vdash Y}{X \vdash Y}\ (Cut)$$

Proof. (Sketch) Given the display property (Prop. 2.5), we verify that the proof rules in Figures 1–3 meet Belnap's conditions C1–C8 for cut-elimination [1]. □

$$\frac{\emptyset; X \vdash Y}{X \vdash Y}\,(\emptyset C_L) \qquad \frac{X \vdash Y; \emptyset}{X \vdash Y}\,(\emptyset C_R) \qquad \frac{X \vdash Y}{\emptyset; X \vdash Y}\,(\emptyset W_L) \qquad \frac{X \vdash Y}{X \vdash Y; \emptyset}\,(\emptyset W_R)$$

$$\frac{(W; X); Y \vdash Z}{W; (X; Y) \vdash Z}\,(\alpha) \qquad \frac{X \vdash Z}{X; Y \vdash Z}\,(W) \qquad \frac{X; X \vdash Y}{X \vdash Y}\,(C)$$

Fig. 3. Some structural rules

Comment 2.7. *Under the formula interpretation of consecutions given by Definition 2.2, certain of our display calculi can be understood as follows:*

$\mathcal{D}_{\mathrm{MLL}} = \mathcal{D}_0 + (\alpha), (\emptyset C_L), (\emptyset C_R), (\emptyset W_L), (\emptyset W_R)$ *is multiplicative linear logic (LL);*
$\mathcal{D}_{\mathrm{MALL}} = \mathcal{D}_0^+ + (\alpha), (\emptyset C_L), (\emptyset C_R), (\emptyset W_L), (\emptyset W_R)$ *is multiplicative additive LL;*
$\mathcal{D}_{\mathrm{CL}} = \mathcal{D}_0 + (\alpha), (\emptyset C_L), (\emptyset C_R), (W), (C)$ *is standard classical propositional logic.*

3 Interpolation: Nullary, Unary and Structure-Free Rules

We now turn to our main topic: whether *interpolation* holds in our display calculi.

Definition 3.1 (Interpolation). A display calculus $\mathcal{D}$ has the *interpolation* property if for any $\mathcal{D}$-provable consecution $X \vdash Y$ there is an *interpolant* formula I such that $X \vdash I$ and $I \vdash Y$ are both $\mathcal{D}$-provable with $\mathcal{V}(I) \subseteq \mathcal{V}(X) \cap \mathcal{V}(Y)$.

We note that, by cut-admissibility (Theorem 2.6), the existence of an interpolant for a consecution $\mathcal{C}$ implies the provability of $\mathcal{C}$.

We aim to emulate the spirit of the classical proof-theoretic approach to interpolation for cut-free sequent calculi such as Gentzen's LK (see e.g. [4]). That is, given a cut-free display calculus proof of a consecution, we aim to construct its interpolant by induction over the structure of the proof. However, the display postulates introduce a difficulty: for example, given an interpolant I for $X ; Y \vdash Z$, it is not clear how to use I to obtain an interpolant for $X \vdash \sharp Y ; Z$. In fact, similar problems arise for sequent calculi as well (e.g., in the classical negation rules of LK), and the usual solution is to simultaneously construct interpolants for *all possible decompositions* of each sequent. We employ an analogue of this strategy for the setting of display calculi: we simultaneously construct interpolants for *all possible rearrangements* of each consecution, where the notion of "rearrangement" is provided by the combination of display-equivalence and, if it is present in the calculus, the associativity rule (α). The latter inclusion is necessary for similar reasons to those for the inclusion of the display postulates.

Definition 3.2. Let $\mathcal{D}$ be a display calculus and $\mathcal{C}, \mathcal{C}'$ be consecutions. We define $\mathcal{C} \to_A \mathcal{C}'$ to hold iff $\mathcal{D}$ includes (α) and $\mathcal{C}$ is the premise of an instance of (α) with conclusion $\mathcal{C}'$. Then the relation $\to_{AD}$ is defined to be $\to_A \cup \rightleftarrows_D$ and the relation $\equiv_{AD}$ is defined to be the reflexive-transitive closure of $\to_{AD}$.

Clearly $\equiv_D \subseteq \equiv_{AD}$, and $\equiv_{AD}$ is exactly $\equiv_D$ in any display calculus without (α).

Comment 3.3. *The relation $\equiv_{AD}$ is indeed an equivalence relation. Furthermore, the following proof rule is derivable in any extension of $\mathcal{D}_0$:*

$$\frac{X' \vdash Y'}{X \vdash Y} \quad X \vdash Y \equiv_{AD} X' \vdash Y' \;\; (\equiv_{AD})$$

Our definition of $\equiv_{AD}$ gives rise to the following "local AD-interpolation" property for display calculus proof rules.

Definition 3.4 (LADI property). A proof rule of a display calculus $\mathcal{D}$ with conclusion $\mathcal{C}$ is said to have the *local AD-interpolation* (LADI) property if, given that for each premise of the rule $\mathcal{C}_i$ we have interpolants for all $\mathcal{C}'_i \equiv_{AD} \mathcal{C}_i$, we can construct interpolants for all $\mathcal{C}' \equiv_{AD} \mathcal{C}$.

Lemma 3.5. *If the proof rules of a display calculus $\mathcal{D}$ each have the LADI property, then $\mathcal{D}$ has the interpolation property.*

Proof. (Sketch) We require an interpolant for each $\mathcal{D}$-provable consecution $\mathcal{C}$. We construct interpolants for all $\mathcal{C}' \equiv_{AD} \mathcal{C}$ by induction on the proof of $\mathcal{C}$, using LADI for the proof rules at each induction step, giving an interpolant for $\mathcal{C}$. □

Thus the LADI property gives a sufficient condition, in terms of individual proof rules, for interpolation to hold in display calculi. In proving this property for a given rule, we will require to track the atomic parts of a consecution being rearranged using $\equiv_{AD}$, and possibly substitute other structures for these parts. It is intuitively obvious how to do this: the next definitions formalise the concept.

Definition 3.6 (Substitution). Let Z be a part of the structure X. We write the substitution notation $X[Y/Z]$, where Y is a structure, to denote the replacement of Z (which we emphasise is a substructure *occurrence*) by the structure Y. We extend substitution to consecutions in the obvious way.

Definition 3.7 (Congruence). Let $\mathcal{C} \rightarrow_{AD} \mathcal{C}'$, whence $\mathcal{C}$ and $\mathcal{C}'$ are obtained by assigning structures to the structure variables occurring in our statement of some display postulate (see Defn. 2.4) or the rule (α) (see Figure 3). Two atomic parts A and A' of $\mathcal{C}$ and $\mathcal{C}'$ respectively are said to be *congruent* if they occupy the same position in the structure assigned to some structure variable.

(E.g., the two indicated occurrences of F are congruent in $X; (F; \emptyset) \vdash Z \rightarrow_{AD} X \vdash \sharp(F; \emptyset); Z$, as are the two indicated occurrences of $\emptyset$, because they occupy the same position in the structure $(F; \emptyset)$ assigned to the structure variable Y in our statement of the display postulate $X; Y \vdash Z \rightleftarrows_D X \vdash \sharp Y; Z$.)

We extend congruence to atomic parts A and A' of consecutions $\mathcal{C}$ and $\mathcal{C}'$ such that $\mathcal{C} \equiv_{AD} \mathcal{C}'$ by reflexive-transitive induction on $\equiv_{AD}$ in the obvious way. That is, any atomic part of $\mathcal{C}$ is congruent to itself, and if $\mathcal{C} \rightarrow_{AD} \mathcal{C}'' \equiv_{AD} \mathcal{C}'$ then A and A' are congruent if there is an atomic part A'' of $\mathcal{C}''$ such that A is congruent to A'' and A'' is congruent to A'.

Finally, we extend congruence to non-atomic parts of consecutions as follows. If $\mathcal{C} \equiv_{AD} \mathcal{C}'$ and Z, Z' are parts of $\mathcal{C}, \mathcal{C}'$ respectively then Z and Z' are congruent if every atomic part A of Z is congruent to an atomic part A' of Z', such that the position of A in Z is identical to the position of A' in Z'.

Comment 3.8. *If $C \equiv_{AD} C'$ then, for any atomic part of C, there is a unique congruent atomic part of C'. Moreover, congruent parts of C and C' are occurrences of the same structure. We use identical names for parts of $\equiv_{AD}$-related consecutions to mean that those parts are congruent. E.g., we write $C[Z/A] \equiv_{AD} C'[Z/A]$ to mean that the two indicated parts A are congruent.*

Lemma 3.9 (Substitution lemma). *If $C \equiv_{AD} C'$ and A is an atomic part of C then, for any structure Z, we have $C[Z/A] \equiv_{AD} C'[Z/A]$.*

Proof. (Sketch) Since the display postulates and the associativity rule (α) are each closed under substitution of an arbitrary structure for congruent atomic parts, this follows by an easy reflexive-transitive induction on $C \equiv_{AD} C'$. □

Proposition 3.10. *The proof rules $(\equiv_D)$, (Id), $(\top L)$, $(\top R)$, $(\bot L)$, $(\bot R)$, $(\neg L)$, $(\neg R)$, $(\&L)$, $(\vee R)$, and $(\rightarrow R)$ each have the LADI property in any extension of $\mathcal{D}_0$. Furthermore, the associativity rule (α) has the LADI property in any extension of $\mathcal{D}_0 + (\alpha)$, and the structure-free rules $(\top_a R)$, $(\bot_a L)$, $(\&_a L)$, $(\&_a R)$, $(\vee_a L)$, and $(\vee_a R)$ each have the LADI property in any extension of $\mathcal{D}_0^+$.*

Proof. (Sketch) We treat each rule separately, noting that $(\equiv_D)$ and (α) are more or less immediate by assumption. We just show one case here, the structure-free rule $(\vee_a L)$. In that case, we must produce interpolants for all $W \vdash Z \equiv_{AD} F \vee_a G \vdash X$. We distinguish two subcases: either the indicated $F \vee_a G$ occurs in W or in Z. We suppose it occurs in Z, so that by Lemma 3.9 we have $F \vdash X \equiv_{AD} W \vdash Z[F/F \vee_a G]$ and $G \vdash X \equiv_{AD} W \vdash Z[G/F \vee_a G]$. Let I_1 and I_2 be the interpolants given by assumption for $W \vdash Z[F/F \vee_a G]$ and $W \vdash Z[G/F \vee_a G]$ respectively. We claim that $I_1 \&_a I_2$ is an interpolant[1] for $W \vdash Z$. The variable condition is easily seen to hold, so it remains to check the provability conditions. Given that $W \vdash I_1$ and $W \vdash I_2$ are provable by assumption, we can derive $W \vdash I_1 \&_a I_2$ by a single application of $(\&_a R)$. Finally, given that $I_1 \vdash Z[F/F \vee_a G]$ and $I_2 \vdash Z[G/F \vee_a G]$ are provable by assumption, we must show that $I_1 \&_a I_2 \vdash Z$ is provable. First, since the indicated $F \vee_a G$ occurs in Z by assumption, we have $I_1 \&_a I_2 \vdash Z \equiv_D F \vee_a G \vdash U$ for some U by the display property (Prop. 2.5). Thus by Lemma 3.9 we have $I_1 \&_a I_2 \vdash Z[F/F \vee_a G] \equiv_D F \vdash U$ and $I_1 \&_a I_2 \vdash Z[G/F \vee_a G] \equiv_D G \vdash U$. So we can derive $I_1 \&_a I_2 \vdash Z$ as follows:

$$
\cfrac{\cfrac{\cfrac{\vdots}{I_1 \vdash Z[F/F \vee_a G]}}{\cfrac{I_1 \&_a I_2 \vdash Z[F/F \vee_a G]}{F \vdash U} (\equiv_D)} (\&_a L) \qquad \cfrac{\cfrac{\vdots}{I_2 \vdash Z[G/F \vee_a G]}}{\cfrac{I_1 \&_a I_2 \vdash Z[G/F \vee_a G]}{G \vdash U} (\equiv_D)} (\&_a L)}{\cfrac{F \vee_a G \vdash U}{I_1 \&_a I_2 \vdash Z} (\equiv_D)} (\vee_a L)
$$

If the indicated $F \vee_a G$ instead occurs in W, then the argument is similar but we pick the interpolant to be $I_1 \vee_a I_2$. This completes the case, and the proof. □

---

[1] Equivalently, $\neg(\neg I_1 \vee_a \neg I_2)$ also works. Note that, because of the display postulate $X \vdash Y \rightleftarrows_D \sharp Y \vdash \sharp X$, it is not possible to construct $\neg$-free interpolants in general.

4   Interpolation: Binary Logical Rules

We now extend our basic method for proving LADI of display calculus proof rules to the binary logical rules of $\mathcal{D}_0$. These cases are considerably harder than the simple rules considered in the previous section because they combine arbitrary structures from the two premises, leading to many new $\equiv_{AD}$-rearrangements of the conclusion compared to the premises. To deal with this complexity, we will require several technical substitutivity lemmas for $\equiv_{AD}$.

The following notion of *deletion* of a part of a structure is similar to that used by Restall [17]. We write $\natural^n$ for a string of n occurrences of $\natural$. Recall that identical names are used to denote congruent parts of $\equiv_{AD}$-equivalent consecutions.

Definition 4.1 (Deletion). A part Z of a structure X is *delible from* X if X is not of the form $\natural^n Z$ for some $n \geq 0$, i.e., X contains a substructure occurrence of the form $\natural^n Z; W$ (up to commutativity of ";"). If Z is delible from X, we write $X \setminus Z$ for the structure $X[W/(\natural^n Z; W)]$, the result of deleting Z from X.

A part Z of a consecution $\mathcal{C}$ is delible from $\mathcal{C}$ if it can be deleted from the side of $\mathcal{C}$ of which it is a part, and we write $\mathcal{C} \setminus Z$ for the consecution obtained by deleting Z from the appropriate side of $\mathcal{C}$.

The following lemma says that $\equiv_{AD}$-rearrangement is (essentially) preserved under deletion of congruent parts. This is crucial to the subsequent substitutivity Lemmas 4.3 and 4.5, which say that $\equiv_{AD}$-rearrangement does not depend on the presence of "contextual" structure not directly affected by the rearrangement.

Lemma 4.2 (Deletion lemma). *Let $\mathcal{C}$ be a consecution and let A be an atomic part of $\mathcal{C}$. If $\mathcal{C} \equiv_{AD} \mathcal{C}'$ and A is delible from $\mathcal{C}$ then the following hold:*

1. *if A is delible from $\mathcal{C}'$ then $\mathcal{C} \setminus A \equiv_{AD} \mathcal{C}' \setminus A$;*
2. *if A is not delible from $\mathcal{C}'$ then one side of $\mathcal{C}'$ is of the form $\natural^m(Z_1; Z_2)$ and we have $\mathcal{C} \setminus A \equiv_{AD} Z_1 \vdash \natural Z_2$ if $(Z_1; Z_2)$ is an antecedent part of $\mathcal{C}'$, and $\mathcal{C} \setminus A \equiv_{AD} \natural Z_1 \vdash Z_2$ if $(Z_1; Z_2)$ is a consequent part of $\mathcal{C}'$.*

Proof. (Sketch) By reflexive-transitive induction on $\mathcal{C} \equiv_{AD} \mathcal{C}'$. In the reflexive case we have $\mathcal{C}' = \mathcal{C}$ and are trivially done. In the transitive case we have $\mathcal{C} \equiv_{AD} \mathcal{C}'' \to_{AD} \mathcal{C}'$, and we distinguish subcases on $\mathcal{C}'' \to_{AD} \mathcal{C}'$. The nonstraightforward subcases are those where A is delible from $\mathcal{C}''$ but not from $\mathcal{C}'$ or vice versa. For example, consider the case $S; T \vdash U \to_{AD} S \vdash \natural T; U$, and suppose (for 1) that A is delible from $S \vdash \natural T; U$ but not from $S; T \vdash U$. Then we must have $U = \natural^n A$, whence we have by part 2 of the induction hypothesis that $(S; T \vdash U) \setminus A \equiv_{AD} S \vdash \natural T$ (because $S; T$ is an antecedent part of $S; T \vdash U$). Then 1 holds as required because, given $U = \natural^n A$, we have $S \vdash \natural T = (S \vdash \natural T; U) \setminus A$. $\qquad\square$

Lemma 4.3 (Substitutivity I). *For all W, X, Y, Z, if $W \vdash X \equiv_{AD} W \vdash Y$ then $Z \vdash X \equiv_{AD} Z \vdash Y$, and if $X \vdash W \equiv_{AD} Y \vdash W$ then $X \vdash Z \equiv_{AD} Y \vdash Z$.*

Proof. (Sketch) By Lemma 3.9 it suffices to consider the case in which Z is a formula F. We prove both implications simultaneously by structural induction on W. The atomic case follows by Lemma 3.9. The case $W = \sharp W'$ is straightforward by induction hypothesis. In the case $W = W_1; W_2$ we obtain, for the first implication, $F; G \vdash X \equiv_{AD} F; G \vdash Y$ using the induction hypothesis. Thus we obtain, by Lemma 4.2, $(F; G \vdash X) \setminus G \equiv_{AD} (F; G \vdash Y) \setminus G$, i.e. $F \vdash X = F \vdash Y$ as required. The second implication is similar. □

Definition 4.4. *Let $C \equiv_{AD} C'$ and let Z, Z' be parts of C and C' respectively. We write $Z' \lhd Z$ if every atomic part of Z' is congruent to an atomic part of Z.*

Lemma 4.5 (Substitutivity II). *For all structures W, W', X, Y and for any atomic structure A, all of the following hold:*

1. *if $W \vdash X \equiv_{AD} W' \vdash Y$ and $W' \lhd W$ then $\exists U. \, W \vdash A \equiv_{AD} W' \vdash U$;*
2. *if $X \vdash W \equiv_{AD} W' \vdash Y$ and $W' \lhd W$ then $\exists U. \, A \vdash W \equiv_{AD} W' \vdash U$;*
3. *if $W \vdash X \equiv_{AD} Y \vdash W'$ and $W' \lhd W$ then $\exists U. \, W \vdash A \equiv_{AD} U \vdash W'$;*
4. *if $X \vdash W \equiv_{AD} Y \vdash W'$ and $W' \lhd W$ then $\exists U. \, A \vdash W \equiv_{AD} U \vdash W'$.*

(Also, in each case we still have $W' \lhd W$ under the replacement of X by A.)

Proof. (Sketch) We show all four implications simultaneously by structural induction on X. The atomic case follows from Lemma 3.9. The case $X = \sharp X'$ is straightforward by induction hypothesis. In the case $X = X_1; X_2$ we obtain, for the first implication, $W \vdash A; A \equiv_{AD} W' \vdash V$ for some V using the induction hypothesis (twice). Since $W' \lhd W$, both indicated occurrences of A must occur in, and be delible from V. Thus by Lemma 4.2, we have $W \vdash A \equiv_{AD} W' \vdash (V \setminus A)$ and are done by taking $U = V \setminus A$. The other implications are similar. □

Our final lemma says that if two separate structures have been "mixed up" by $\equiv_{AD}$, then the resulting structure can be "filtered" into its component parts.

Lemma 4.6 (Filtration). *Let $X; Y \vdash U \equiv_{AD} W \vdash Z$, where $W \lhd X; Y$ but $W \not\lhd X$ and $W \not\lhd Y$. Then there exist W_1 and W_2 such that $W \vdash Z \equiv_{AD} W_1; W_2 \vdash Z$ with $W_1 \lhd X$ and $W_2 \lhd Y$. Similarly, if $X; Y \vdash U \equiv_{AD} Z \vdash W$ with $W \lhd X; Y$ but $W \not\lhd X$ and $W \not\lhd Y$, then there exist W_1 and W_2 such that $Z \vdash W \equiv_{AD} Z \vdash W_1; W_2$ with $W_1 \lhd X$ and $W_2 \lhd Y$.*

Proof. (Sketch) We prove both implications simultaneously by structural induction on W. The difficult case is when $W = W_1; W_2$. If $W_1 \lhd X$ and $W_2 \lhd Y$ or vice versa then we are done. If not, in the case of the first implication we have $X; Y \vdash U \equiv_{AD} W_1; W_2 \vdash Z$ where $W_1; W_2 \lhd X; Y$ and either $W_1 \not\lhd X$ and $W_1 \not\lhd Y$, or $W_2 \not\lhd X$ and $W_2 \not\lhd Y$ (we assume both here). It is clear by inspection of the display postulates that this situation can only arise when the rule (α) is present. Using the induction hypotheses, we obtain $W_1' \lhd X$, $W_1'' \lhd Y$, $W_2' \lhd X$ and $W_2'' \lhd Y$ such that $W_1; W_2 \vdash Z \equiv_{AD} (W_1'; W_1''); (W_2'; W_2'') \vdash Z$. Thus, given that $\equiv_{AD}$ incorporates (α), we obtain $W_1; W_2 \vdash Z \equiv_{AD} (W_1'; W_2'); (W_1''; W_2'') \vdash Z$ where $(W_1'; W_2') \lhd X$ and $(W_1''; W_2'') \lhd Y$ as required. □

Theorem 4.7 (Binary rules). *The rules $(\& R)$, $(\vee L)$ and $(\rightarrow L)$ all have the local AD-interpolation property in any extension of $\mathcal{D}_0$.*

Proof. (Sketch) We consider the case (&R), in which case we must produce interpolants for all $W \vdash Z \equiv_{AD} X; Y \vdash F\&G$. We suppose the indicated $F\&G$ occurs in Z, in which case $W \lhd X; Y$, and distinguish three subcases: $W \lhd X$; $W \lhd Y$; and $W \ntriangleleft X$, $W \ntriangleleft Y$. We just show the last case, the hardest. By the first part of Lemma 4.6 there exist W_1 and W_2 such that $W \vdash Z \equiv_{AD} W_1; W_2 \vdash Z$ with $W_1 \lhd X$ and $W_2 \lhd Y$. Thus we have $X \vdash \sharp Y; F \& G \equiv_{AD} W_1 \vdash \sharp W_2; Z$ with $W_1 \lhd X$, and $Y \vdash \sharp X; F \& G \equiv_{AD} W_2 \vdash \sharp W_1; Z$ with $W_2 \lhd Y$. Hence by part 1 of Lemma 4.5 we have $X \vdash F \equiv_{AD} W_1 \vdash U_1$ for some U_1 and $Y \vdash G \equiv_{AD} W_2 \vdash U_2$ for some U_2. Let I_1, I_2 be the interpolants given by assumption for $W_1 \vdash U_1$ and $W_2 \vdash U_2$ respectively. We claim that $I_1 \& I_2$ is an interpolant for $W \vdash Z$.

First, we show that $W \vdash I_1 \& I_2$ is provable. We have $W_1 \vdash I_1$ and $W_2 \vdash I_2$ provable by assumption, so $W_1; W_2 \vdash I_1 \& I_2$ is provable by applying (&R). Since $W_1; W_2 \vdash Z \equiv_{AD} W \vdash Z$, we have $W_1; W_2 \vdash I_1 \& I_2 \equiv_{AD} W \vdash I_1 \& I_2$ by Lemma 4.3, and so $W \vdash I_1 \& I_2$ is provable by applying the rule $(\equiv_{AD})$.

Next, we must show that $I_1 \& I_2 \vdash Z$ is derivable, given that $I_1 \vdash U_1$ and $I_2 \vdash U_2$ are derivable. First, note that because $X \vdash F \equiv_{AD} W_1 \vdash U_1$ and $W_1 \lhd X$, the indicated F is a part of U_1, and thus $I_1 \vdash U_1 \equiv_D V_1 \vdash F$ for some V_1 by Prop. 2.5. Similarly, $I_2 \vdash U_2 \equiv_D V_2 \vdash G$ for some V_2. Next, using Lemma 3.9, we have $W_1 \vdash \sharp W_2; Z \equiv_{AD} W_1 \vdash U_1[(\sharp Y; F \& G)/F]$. Thus by Lemma 4.3 we have $I_1 \vdash \sharp W_2; Z \equiv_{AD} I_1 \vdash U_1[(\sharp Y; F \& G)/F]$. Since $I_1 \vdash U_1 \equiv_D V_1 \vdash F$ we have, using Lemma 3.9, $I_1 \vdash \sharp W_2; Z \equiv_{AD} V_1; Y \vdash F \& G$. Now, since $Y \vdash G \equiv_{AD} W_2 \vdash U_2$ we obtain using Lemma 3.9 $W_2 \vdash \sharp I_1; Z \equiv_{AD} W_2 \vdash U_2[(\sharp V_1; F \& G)/G]$. So by applying Lemma 4.3 we have $I_2 \vdash \sharp I_1; Z \equiv_{AD} I_2 \vdash U_2[\sharp V_1; F \& G/G]$. Since $I_2 \vdash U_2 \equiv_D V_2 \vdash G$ we obtain $I_1; I_2 \vdash Z \equiv_{AD} V_1; V_2 \vdash F \& G$ (again using Lemma 3.9). This enables us to derive $I_1 \& I_2 \vdash Z$ as follows:

$$
\dfrac{\dfrac{\vdots}{\dfrac{I_1 \vdash U_1}{V_1 \vdash F}\,(\equiv_D) \quad \dfrac{\dfrac{\vdots}{I_2 \vdash U_2}}{V_2 \vdash G}\,(\equiv_D)}{\dfrac{\dfrac{V_1; V_2 \vdash F \& G}{I_1; I_2 \vdash Z}\,(\equiv_{AD})}{I_1 \& I_2 \vdash Z}\,(\&L)}}{}\,(\&R)
$$

Finally, we check the variable condition. We have $\mathcal{V}(I_1) \subseteq \mathcal{V}(W_1) \cap \mathcal{V}(U_1)$ and $\mathcal{V}(I_2) \subseteq \mathcal{V}(W_2) \cap \mathcal{V}(U_2)$. It is clear that $\mathcal{V}(W_1) \subseteq \mathcal{V}(W)$ and $\mathcal{V}(W_2) \subseteq \mathcal{V}(W)$ because $W \vdash Z \equiv_{AD} W_1; W_2 \vdash Z$. Moreover, $\mathcal{V}(U_1) \subseteq \mathcal{V}(Z)$ because we have $X \vdash F \equiv_{AD} W_1 \vdash U_1$ and $X \vdash \sharp Y; F \& G \equiv_{AD} W_1 \vdash \sharp W_2; Z$ while $W_1 \lhd X$ and $W_2 \lhd Y$ (or, alternatively, it is clear by inspection of the derivation above). Similarly $\mathcal{V}(U_2) \subseteq \mathcal{V}(Z)$ and thus $\mathcal{V}(I_1 \& I_2) \subseteq \mathcal{V}(W) \cap \mathcal{V}(Z)$ as required.

The subcases $W \lhd X$ and $W \lhd Y$ are similar except that we directly use the interpolant given by just one of the premises. If the indicated $F\&G$ occurs in W rather than Z we again distinguish three subcases and take the interpolant $I_1 \vee I_2$ in the analogue of the subcase above. This completes the proof. $\square$

Corollary 4.8. *For any* $\mathcal{D} \in \{\mathcal{D}_0, \mathcal{D}_0^+, \mathcal{D}_0 + (\alpha), \mathcal{D}_0^+ + (\alpha)\}$, *the proof rules of* $\mathcal{D}$ *all have the LADI property in (any extension of)* $\mathcal{D}$, *and thus* $\mathcal{D}$ *has the interpolation property.*

Proof. LADI for the proof rules of $\mathcal{D}$ in any extension of $\mathcal{D}$ is given by Prop. 3.10 and Theorem 4.7. Interpolation for $\mathcal{D}$ then follows by Lemma 3.5. □

5 Interpolation: Structural Rules

We now examine the LADI property for the structural rules given in Figure 3.

Proposition 5.1 (Unit contraction rules). *The unit left-contraction rule* $(\emptyset C_L)$ *has the LADI property in any extension of* $\mathcal{D}_0 + (\emptyset C_L)$. *Similarly, the rule* $(\emptyset C_R)$ *has the LADI property in any extension of* $\mathcal{D}_0 + (\emptyset C_R)$.

Proof. (Sketch) We consider $(\emptyset C_L)$ here; $(\emptyset C_R)$ is similar. We require to construct interpolants for all $W \vdash Z \equiv_{AD} X \vdash Y$. First, by reflexive-transitive induction on $W \vdash Z \equiv_{AD} X \vdash Y$, we show that $\emptyset; X \vdash Y \equiv_{AD} (W \vdash Z)[(\emptyset; U)/U]$ or $\emptyset; X \vdash Y \equiv_{AD} (W \vdash Z)[(\sharp\emptyset; U)/U]$ for some U. We claim that the assumed interpolant I for $W' \vdash Z'$ is an interpolant for $W \vdash Z$. The variable condition is easily seen to be satisfied, so it remains to check the provability conditions. We assume without loss of generality that U is a part of Z, so that $W \vdash I$ is provable by assumption. To prove $I \vdash Z$, we start with the assumed derivation of $I \vdash Z'$ and use Prop. 2.5 to display the structure $\emptyset; U$ or $\sharp\emptyset; U$. We then remove the $\emptyset$ using $(\emptyset C_L)$ and obtain $I \vdash Z$ by inverting the previous display moves. □

Proposition 5.2 (Unit weakening rules). *The unit weakening rule* $(\emptyset W_L)$ *has the LADI property in any extension of* $\mathcal{D}_0 + (\emptyset W_L)$. *Similarly, the rule* $(\emptyset W_R)$ *has the LADI property in any extension of* $\mathcal{D}_0 + (\emptyset W_R)$.

Proof. (Sketch) We just consider $(\emptyset W_L)$, as $(\emptyset W_R)$ is similar. We require to find interpolants for all $W \vdash Z \equiv_{AD} \emptyset; X \vdash Y$. We distinguish two cases. First of all, if the indicated $\emptyset$ is not delible from $W \vdash Z$, then W or Z is of the form $\sharp^n\emptyset$. We suppose $Z = \sharp^n\emptyset$ in which case n must be odd (because the indicated $\emptyset$ is an antecedent part of $\emptyset; X \vdash Y$ and thus of $W \vdash Z$) and we pick the interpolant for $W \vdash Z$ to be $\neg\top$. The variable condition is trivially satisfied, and $\neg\top \vdash Z = \neg\top \vdash \sharp^n\emptyset$ is easily provable. $W \vdash \neg\top$ is provable from the premise $X \vdash Y$ using the rule $(\emptyset W_L)$ and the derived rule $(\equiv_{AD})$ by observing that $\emptyset; X \vdash Y \equiv_{AD} \emptyset \vdash \sharp W$. The case where $W = \sharp^n\emptyset$ is symmetric.

If the indicated $\emptyset$ *is* delible from $W \vdash Z$ then, by Lemma 4.2, we have $X \vdash Y = (\emptyset; X \vdash Y) \setminus \emptyset \equiv_{AD} (W \vdash Z) \setminus \emptyset$. We claim that the interpolant I given for $(W \vdash Z) \setminus \emptyset$ by assumption is also an interpolant for $W \vdash Z$. Without loss of generality, we assume that the indicated $\emptyset$ occurs in Z, so that $(W \vdash Z) \setminus \emptyset = W \vdash (Z \setminus \emptyset)$. It is easy to see that the required variable condition holds. It remains to check the provability conditions. We have $W \vdash I$ provable by assumption, so it just remains to show that $I \vdash Z$ is provable, given that $I \vdash (Z \setminus \emptyset)$ is provable. By the definition of deletion (Defn. 4.1), $Z \setminus \emptyset = Z[U/(\sharp^n\emptyset; U)]$ for some U. Thus, by Prop. 2.5, and assuming $(\sharp^n \emptyset; U)$ an antecedent part of Z, we have $I \vdash Z \equiv_D \emptyset; U \vdash V$ and $I \vdash (Z \setminus \emptyset) \equiv_D U \vdash V$ for some V (note that the *same* V is obtained in both cases). Thus we can derive $I \vdash Z$ from $I \vdash (Z \setminus \emptyset)$ by applications of $(\equiv_D)$ and $(\emptyset W_L)$. □

Theorem 5.3 (Weakening). *The weakening rule* (W) *has the LADI property in any extension of* $\mathcal{D}_0 + (W), (\emptyset C_L)$ *or* $\mathcal{D}_0 + (W), (\emptyset C_R)$.

Proof. (Sketch) We require to find interpolants for all $W \vdash Z \equiv_{AD} X; X' \vdash Y$. We distinguish three cases: $W \lhd X'$; $Z \lhd X'$; and $W \not\lhd X'$, $Z \not\lhd X'$. In the case $W \lhd X'$, we choose the interpolant I to be $\top$ if $(\emptyset C_L)$ is available (which guarantees $W \vdash \top$ is provable), or $\neg \bot$ if $(\emptyset C_R)$ is available (which guarantees $W \vdash \neg \bot$ is provable). To see that $I \vdash Z$ is provable, note that $W \vdash Z \equiv_{AD} X' \vdash \sharp X; Y$ with $(\sharp X; Y) \lhd Z$. Thus, using part 4 of Lemma 4.5, we have $I \vdash Z \equiv_{AD} X; U \vdash Y$ for some U, whence we can derive $I \vdash Z$ from the premise $X \vdash Y$ by applying (W) and the derived rule $(\equiv_{AD})$. The case $Z \lhd X'$ is symmetric. In the case $W \not\lhd X'$ and $Z \not\lhd X'$, we first show that there are atomic parts $A_1, \ldots, A_n$ of X' with

$$X \vdash Y \equiv_{AD} (\ldots (((W \vdash Z) \setminus A_1) \setminus A_2) \ldots) \setminus A_n = W' \vdash Z'$$

(This can be proven by structural induction on X', using Lemma 4.2 in the atomic case.) We claim that the interpolant I for $W' \vdash Z'$ given by assumption is also an interpolant for $W \vdash Z$. First we check the variable condition. We have $\mathcal{V}(I) \subseteq \mathcal{V}(W') \cap \mathcal{V}(Z')$ by assumption. It is clear that $\mathcal{V}(W') \subseteq \mathcal{V}(W)$ and $\mathcal{V}(Z') \subseteq \mathcal{V}(Z)$ since W' and Z' are obtained by deleting some parts of W and Z respectively. Thus $\mathcal{V}(I) \subseteq \mathcal{V}(W) \cap \mathcal{V}(Z)$ as required.

It remains to check the provability conditions. We have $W' \vdash I$ provable by assumption. By the definition of deletion (Defn. 4.1), W' is obtained from W by replacing a number of substructure occurrences of the form $\sharp^n A; S$ by S. We obtain the required derivation of $W \vdash I$ by, working backwards, using the display property (Prop. 2.5) to display each such $\sharp^n A; S$ and then removing $\sharp^n A$ using (W). (Formally, we proceed by induction on the number of substructure occurrences deleted from W to obtain W'.) Deriving $I \vdash Z$ is similar. □

Proposition 5.4 (Contraction). *The contraction rule* (C) *has the LADI property in any extension of* $\mathcal{D}_0 + (\alpha)$.

Proof. (Sketch) We require to find interpolants for all $W \vdash Z \equiv_{AD} X \vdash Y$. First, using the fact that $\equiv_{AD}$ contains (α) by assumption, we show that there exist atomic parts $A_1, \ldots, A_n$ of X such that

$$X; X \vdash Y \equiv_{AD} (W \vdash Z)[(A_1; A_1)/A_1, \ldots, (A_n; A_n)/A_n] = W' \vdash Z'$$

(This is proven by structural induction on X, using Lemma 3.9 in the atomic case.) We claim that the interpolant I for $W' \vdash Z'$ given by assumption is also an interpolant for $W \vdash Z$. We have $\mathcal{V}(I) \subseteq \mathcal{V}(W') \cap \mathcal{V}(Z')$ by assumption and, clearly, $\mathcal{V}(W) = \mathcal{V}(W')$ and $\mathcal{V}(Z) = \mathcal{V}(Z')$, so we easily have the required variable condition $\mathcal{V}(I) \subseteq \mathcal{V}(W) \cap \mathcal{V}(Z)$.

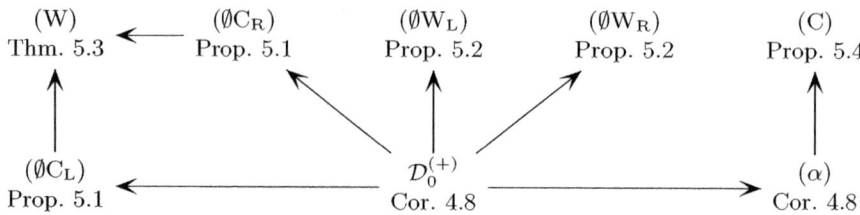

Fig. 4. Diagrammatic summary of our results. Local AD-interpolation of the proof rule(s) at a node holds in a calculus with all of the proof rules at its ancestor nodes.

Next we check the provability conditions. We have $W' \vdash I$ provable by assumption, and W' is obtained from W by replacing a number of its atomic parts A by the structure $A; A$. We obtain the required derivation of $W \vdash I$ by, working backwards, using the display property (Prop. 2.5) to display each such A and then duplicating it using (C). (Formally, we proceed by induction on the number of atomic parts of W duplicated to obtain W'.) Deriving $I \vdash Z$ is similar.   □

Our reliance on the presence of the associativity rule (α) in Prop. 5.4 can be motivated by considering the following instance of contraction:

$$\frac{(X_1; X_2); (X_1; X_2) \vdash Y}{X_1; X_2 \vdash Y}$$

For the LADI property, we need in particular an interpolant for $X_1 \vdash \sharp X_2; Y \equiv_D X_1; X_2 \vdash Y$. However, without associativity, we cannot rearrange the premise into $X_1; X_1 \vdash (\sharp X_2; \sharp X_2); Y$ as would otherwise be provided by Prop. 5.4. The best we can do without associativity is $X_1 \vdash \sharp X_2; (\sharp(X_1; X_2); Y)$, whose interpolant I is too weak to serve as an interpolant for $X_1 \vdash \sharp X_2; Y$ both in terms of provability and in terms of the variable condition. A similar problem occurs if there is more than one binary structural connective, even if both are associative.

The various conditions for the LADI property to hold of each proof rule are set out in Figure 4. In consequence, we have the following interpolation results.

Theorem 5.5 (Interpolation). *Let D be an extension of D_0 where: if D contains* (C) *it must also contain* (α), *and if D contains* (W) *then it must also contain either* $(\emptyset C_L)$ *or* $(\emptyset C_R)$. *Then D has the interpolation property.*

Proof. By Lemma 3.5 it suffices to prove the LADI property in D for each proof rule of D. The rules of D_0, and (α) if applicable, satisfy the LADI property in D by Corollary 4.8. The other structural rules of D, if applicable, satisfy LADI in D by Theorem 5.3 and Propositions 5.1, 5.2 and 5.4.

Drawing on the observations in Comment 2.7, Thm 5.5 yields the following:

Corollary 5.6. D_{MLL}, D_{MALL} *and* D_{CL} *all have the interpolation property.*

6   Related and Future Work

Our central contribution is a general, fully constructive proof-theoretic method for proving Craig interpolation in a large class of displayable logics, based upon an analysis of the individual rules of the display calculi. This analysis is "as local as possible" in that the LADI property required for each proof rule typically depends only on the presence of certain other rules in the calculus, and the syntax of the rule itself. The practicality and generality of our method is demonstrated by its application to a fairly large family of display calculi differing in their structural rules (and the presence or otherwise of additive logical connectives). We obtain by this uniform method the interpolation property for MLL, MALL and ordinary classical logic, as well as numerous variants of these logics. To our knowledge, ours are the first interpolation results based on display calculi, thereby answering positively Belnap's long-standing open question (see p1) about this possibility.

While interpolation based on display calculi appears to be new, interpolation for substructural logics is of course not new. The closest work to ours is probably Roorda's on interpolation for various fragments of classical linear logic [18], using induction over cut-free sequent calculus proofs. Roorda also identifies fragments where interpolation fails (usually because certain logical connectives are unavailable). Many of Roorda's positive interpolation results overlap with our own but we cover some additional logics (e.g., nonassociative, strict or affine variants, plus full classical logic) and offer an analysis of the roles played by individual structural rules. An entirely different approach to interpolation for substructural logics is offered by Galatos and Ono [9], who establish very general interpolation theorems for certain substructural logics extending the Lambek calculus, based on their algebraisations.

Our methodology transfers easily to calculi for intuitionistic logics in which our "classical" display postulates (Defn. 2.4) are replaced by "residuated" ones of the form $X, Y \vdash Z \rightleftarrows_D X \vdash Y, Z \rightleftarrows_D Y, X \vdash Z$ (where the comma is interpreted as conjunction in antecedent position and as implication in consequent position). A more challenging technical extension is to the case where we have such a family of structural connectives *alongside* the first, as is typically needed to display relevant logics [17] or bunched logics [2]. Here, the main technical obstacle is in extending the substitutivity principles in Section 4 to the more complex notion of display-equivalence induced by this extension. Other possible extensions to our calculi include the addition of modalities, quantifiers or linear exponentials. In the main, these extensions appear more straightforward than adding new connective families, since they necessitate little or no modification to display-equivalence. We also note that our notion of interpolant in this paper is relatively blunt since it does not distinguish between positive and negative occurrences of variables. It should be possible to read off a sharpened version of interpolation, that does make this distinction, more or less directly from our proof.

As well as showing interpolation for a variety of substructural logics, our proof gives insights into the reasons why interpolation fails in some logics. Specifically, we identify contraction as being just as problematic for interpolation as it typically is for decidability (and even weakening causes an issue for interpolation when the logic lacks strong units). Our interpolation method is bound to fail for any multiple-family display calculus including a contraction rule, due to our observation that contraction generally has the required LADI property only in circumstances which are precluded by the presence of multiple binary structural connectives. This observation is in keeping with the fact that interpolation fails for the relevant logic **R**, as shown by Urquhart [19], since its display calculus employs two families of connectives and a contraction rule. We conjecture that interpolation might fail in bunched logics such as BI for similar reasons.

The technical overhead of our method is fairly substantial, but the techniques themselves are elementary: we mainly appeal to structural and reflexive-transitive inductions. This means that our proofs are good candidates for mechanisation in a theorem proving assistant. Dawson is currently working on an Isabelle formalisation of our proofs, based upon earlier work on mechanising display calculus with Goré [7]. As well as providing the greatest possible degree of confidence in our proofs, such a mechanisation might eventually provide the basis for an automated interpolation tool.

References

1. Belnap Jr., N.D.: Display logic. Journal of Philosophical Logic 11, 375–417 (1982)
2. Brotherston, J.: A unified display proof theory for bunched logic. In: Proceedings of MFPS-26. ENTCS, pp. 197–211. Elsevier, Amsterdam (2010)
3. Brotherston, J., Goré, R.: Craig interpolation in displayable logics. Tech. Rep. DTR11-1, Imperial College London (2011)
4. Buss, S.R.: Introduction to Proof Theory. In: Handbook of Proof Theory, ch. I. Elsevier Science, Amsterdam (1998)
5. Caniart, N.: MERIT: An interpolating model-checker. In: Touili, T., Cook, B., Jackson, P. (eds.) CAV 2010. LNCS, vol. 6174, pp. 162–166. Springer, Heidelberg (2010)
6. Craig, W.: Three uses of the Herbrand-Gentzen theorem in relating model theory and proof theory. Journal of Symbolic Logic 22(3), 269–285 (1957)
7. Dawson, J.E., Goré, R.: Formalised cut admissibility for display logic. In: Carreño, V.A., Muñoz, C.A., Tahar, S. (eds.) TPHOLs 2002. LNCS, vol. 2410, pp. 131–147. Springer, Heidelberg (2002)
8. Feferman, S.: Harmonious logic: Craig's interpolation theorem and its descendants. Synthese 164, 341–357 (2008)
9. Galatos, N., Ono, H.: Algebraization, parametrized local deduction theorem and interpolation for substructural logics over FL. Studia Logica 83, 279–308 (2006)
10. Goré, R.: Gaggles, Gentzen and Galois: How to display your favourite substructural logic. Logic Journal of the IGPL 6(5), 669–694 (1998)
11. Goré, R.: Substructural logics on display. Logic J of the IGPL 6(3), 451–504 (1998)
12. Jhala, R., Majumdar, R., Xu, R.-G.: State of the union: Type inference via craig interpolation. In: Grumberg, O., Huth, M. (eds.) TACAS 2007. LNCS, vol. 4424, pp. 553–567. Springer, Heidelberg (2007)
13. Konev, B., Lutz, C., Ponomaryov, D., Wolter, F.: Decomposing description logic ontologies. In: 12th Knowledge Representation and Reasoning Conf. AAAI, Menlo Park (2010)

14. Kracht, M.: Power and weakness of the modal display calculus. In: Wansing, H. (ed.) Proof Theory of Modal Logic, pp. 93–121. Kluwer Academic Publishers, Boston (1996)
15. McMillan, K.L.: Applications of craig interpolants in model checking. In: Halbwachs, N., Zuck, L.D. (eds.) TACAS 2005. LNCS, vol. 3440, pp. 1–12. Springer, Heidelberg (2005)
16. McMillan, K.L.: Quantified invariant generation using an interpolating saturation prover. In: Ramakrishnan, C.R., Rehof, J. (eds.) TACAS 2008. LNCS, vol. 4963, pp. 413–427. Springer, Heidelberg (2008)
17. Restall, G.: Displaying and deciding substructural logics 1: Logics with contraposition. Journal of Philosophical Logic 27, 179–216 (1998)
18. Roorda, D.: Interpolation in fragments of classical linear logic. Journal of Symbolic Logic 59(2), 419–444 (1994)
19. Urquhart, A.: Failure of interpolation in relevant logics. Journal of Philosophical Logic 22, 449–479 (1993)
20. Wansing, H.: Displaying Modal Logics. Kluwer, Boston (1998)

A Tableaux Based Decision Procedure for a Broad Class of Hybrid Formulae with Binders

Serenella Cerrito[1] and Marta Cialdea Mayer[2]

[1] Lab. Ibisc, Université d'Evry Val d'Essonne, France
[2] Università di Roma Tre, Italy

Abstract. In this paper we provide the first (as far as we know) direct calculus deciding satisfiability of formulae in negation normal form in the fragment of hybrid logic with the satisfaction operator and the binder, where no occurrence of the $\Box$ operator is in the scope of a binder. A preprocessing step, rewriting formulae into equisatisfiable ones, turns the calculus into a satisfiability decision procedure for the fragment $\mathsf{HL}(@, \downarrow)$ $\backslash \Box \downarrow \Box$, *i.e.* formulae in negation normal form where no occurrence of the binder is both in the scope of and contains in its scope a $\Box$ operator.

The calculus is based on tableaux, where nominal equalities are treated by means of substitution, and termination is achieved by means of a form of anywhere blocking with indirect blocking. Direct blocking is a relation between nodes in a tableau branch, holding whenever the respective labels (formulae) are equal up to (a proper form of) nominal renaming. Indirect blocking is based on a partial order on the nodes of a tableau branch, which arranges them into a tree-like structure.

1 Introduction

The Hybrid Logic $\mathsf{HL}(@, \downarrow)$ is an extension of modal (propositional, possibly multi-modal) logic K by means of three constructs: *nominals* (propositions which hold in exactly one state of the model), the *satisfaction operator* @ (allowing one to state that a given formula holds at the state named by a given nominal), and the *binder* $\downarrow$, accompanied by *state variables*, which allows one to give a name to the current state (see [2] for an overview of the subject).

The satisfiability problem for formulae of basic Hybrid Logic $\mathsf{HL}(@)$ (without the binder)[1] is decidable, and it stays decidable even with the addition of other operators, such as the global and converse modalities. On the contrary, an unrestricted addition of the binder causes a loss of decidability [1,3].

However, similarly to what happens for first order logic, one can obtain decidable fragments of hybrid logic with the binder by imposing syntactic restrictions on the way formulae are built. Some decidability results are proved in [13], which

---

[1] The notation $\mathsf{HL}(Op_1, ..., Op_n)$ is commonly used to denote the extension of modal logic K by means of the operators $Op_1...Op_n$. In particular, $\mathsf{HL}(@, \downarrow, \mathsf{E}, \Diamond^-)$ and $\mathsf{HL}(@, \mathsf{E}, \Diamond^-)$ include the existential global modality E (and its dual A) and the converse operator $\Diamond^-$ (and its dual $\Box^-$).

K. Brünnler and G. Metcalfe (Eds.): TABLEAUX 2011, LNAI 6793, pp. 104–118, 2011.

considers full Hybrid Logic $\mathsf{HL}(@, \downarrow, \mathsf{E}, \Diamond^-)$, that will henceforth be abbreviated as FHL. In that work it is proved that the source of undecidability is the occurrence of a specific *modal pattern* in formulae in negation normal form (NNF). A pattern π is a sequence of operators, and a formula is a π-formula, where $\pi = Op_1...Op_n$, if it is in NNF and contains some occurrence of Op_1 that contains in its scope an occurrence of Op_2, that in turn has in its scope an occurrence of Op_3, *etc.* For simplicity, moreover, when the $\Box$ operator is used in a pattern, it actually stands for any *universal operator, i.e.* one of the modalities $\Box, \Box^-$ or A. In particular, a $\Box\downarrow$-formula is a hybrid formula in NNF where some occurrence of the binder is in the scope of a universal operator; a $\downarrow\Box$-formula is a hybrid formula in NNF where some occurrence of a universal operator is in the scope of a binder; and a $\Box\downarrow\Box$-formula is a hybrid formula in NNF containing a universal operator in the scope of a binder, which in turn occurs in the scope of a universal operator. Finally, if π is a pattern, the fragment $\mathsf{HL}(Op_1, ..., Op_k) \setminus \pi$ is constituted by the class of NNF hybrid formulae in $\mathsf{HL}(Op_1, ..., Op_k)$ excluding π-formulae.

The main decidability result on syntactic restrictions proved in [13] is the following:

1. The satisfiability problem for $\mathsf{FHL} \setminus \Box\downarrow\Box$ is decidable.

This result is tight, in the sense that there is no pattern π that contains $\Box\downarrow\Box$ as a subsequence and such that the satisfiability problem for $\mathsf{FHL} \setminus \pi$ is still decidable. Therefore, the fragment $\mathsf{FHL} \setminus \Box\downarrow\Box$ is particularly interesting.

For the aim of the present work, it is important to recall the intermediate results allowing [13] to prove 1:

2. The satisfiability problem for $\mathsf{FHL} \setminus \Box\downarrow$ is decidable. This is proved by showing that there exists a satisfiability preserving translation from $\mathsf{FHL} \setminus \Box\downarrow$ to $\mathsf{HL}(@, \mathsf{E}, \Diamond^-)$. The translation is obtained by first replacing any occurrence of the binder by a full existential quantification over states (*i.e.* $\downarrow x.F$ is replaced by $\exists x(x \wedge F)$); in the resulting formula, no existential quantifier is in the scope of a universal operator, so that the existential quantifiers can be moved in front of the formula, and, finally, they are skolemized away by use of fresh nominals.
3. The satisfiability problem for $\mathsf{FHL} \setminus \downarrow\Box$ is decidable. This holds because the standard translation ST of FHL into first order classical logic [1,13] maps formulae in the considered fragment into *universally guarded formulae* [13], that have a decidable satisfiability problem [8].

Result 1 easily follows from 2 and 3. Let in fact F be any formula in $\mathsf{FHL} \setminus \Box\downarrow\Box$. Any occurrence of the binder that contains in its scope a universal operator is not, in its turn, in the scope of a universal operator. Therefore it can be skolemized away like in the proof of 2. Repeating this transformation for every $\downarrow\Box$-subformula of F, an equisatisfiable formula F' is obtained, where no occurrence of a universal operator is in the scope of a binder. Satisfiability of F' can be decided because of result 3.

The above sketched approach to proving result 1 shows also that any decision procedure for formulae in FHL $\setminus \downarrow \Box$ can easily be turned into a decision procedure for formulae in the largest fragment FHL $\setminus \Box \downarrow \Box$, by preprocessing formulae.

Satisfiability of formulae in the fragment FHL $\setminus \downarrow \Box$ can be tested by translation, by use of any calculus for the guarded fragment, such as the tableau calculi defined in [9,10], or the decision procedure based on resolution given in [7]. The translation can be obtained in polynomial time [13], hence the theoretical complexity does not increase. However, in practice, the overhead coming from the translation cannot be completely ignored. In fact, the standard translation of F is a *universally guarded* formula, which has to be rewritten into an equisatisfiable *guarded* one [8]. Moreover, decision procedures for guarded logic such as the above mentioned ones apply to constant-free formulae. Since formulae obtained from the translation may in general contain constants (deriving from nominals), a further rewriting would be necessary to eliminate them [8,12].

Beyond the generally recognized interest of having direct calculi for modal logics, we therefore consider that the problem of defining direct decision procedures for decidable fragments of hybrid logics deserves a specific attention.

In this paper we provide the first (as far as we know) direct calculus deciding satisfiability of formulae in $HL(@, \downarrow) \setminus \downarrow \Box$. A preprocessing step, rewriting a formula into an equisatisfiable one, like explained above, turns the calculus into a satisfiability decision procedure for $HL(@, \downarrow) \setminus \Box \downarrow \Box$.

The work is organized as follows. In the rest of this section we recall the syntax and semantics of $HL(@, \downarrow)$. In Section 2 we define the tableau system, and section 3 contains a brief outline of the termination and completeness proofs, whose details can be found in [6]. Section 4 concludes this work, and includes a comparison of some aspects of our work with techniques already present in the literature.

Hybrid Logic. Let PROP (the set of propositional letters) and NOM (the set of nominals) be disjoint sets of symbols. Let VAR be a set of *state variables*. Hybrid formulae F in $HL(@, \downarrow)$ are defined by the following grammar:

$$F := p \mid a \mid x \mid \neg F \mid F \wedge F \mid F \vee F \mid \Diamond F \mid \Box F \mid t : F \mid \downarrow x.F$$

where $p \in$ PROP, $a \in$ NOM, $x \in$ VAR and $t \in$ VAR $\cup$ NOM. In this work, the notation $t : F$ is used rather than the more usual one $@_t F$. We use metavariables a, b, c, possibly with subscripts, for nominals, while x, y, z are used for variables.

A formula of the form $a : F$ is called a *satisfaction statement*, whose *outermost nominal* is a and F is its *body*. The operator $\downarrow$ is a *binder* for state variables. A variable x is *free* in a formula if it does not occur in the scope of a $\downarrow x$. A formula is *ground* if it contains no free variables.

A *subformula* of a formula F is a substring of F (possibly F itself) that is itself a formula. An *instance* of a formula F is an expression obtained by replacing every free variable of F with some nominal.

An *interpretation* $\mathcal{M}$ is a tuple $\langle W, R, N, I \rangle$ where W is a non-empty set (whose elements are the *states* of the interpretation), $R \subseteq W \times W$ is a binary relation on W (the *accessibility relation*), N is a function NOM $\to W$ and I a function $W \to 2^{\mathsf{PROP}}$. We shall write wRw' as a shorthand for $\langle w, w' \rangle \in R$.

A *variable assignment* σ for $\mathcal{M}$ is a function VAR $\to W$. If $x \in$ VAR and $w \in W$, the notation σ_x^w stands for the variable assignment σ' such that: $\sigma'(y) = \sigma(y)$ if $y \neq x$ and $\sigma'(x) = w$.

If $\mathcal{M} = \langle W, R, N, I \rangle$ is an interpretation, $w \in W$, σ is a variable assignment for $\mathcal{M}$ and F is a formula, the relation $\mathcal{M}_w, \sigma \models F$ is inductively defined as follows:

1. $\mathcal{M}_w, \sigma \models p$ if $p \in I(w)$, for $p \in$ PROP.
2. $\mathcal{M}_w, \sigma \models a$ if $N(a) = w$, for $a \in$ NOM.
3. $\mathcal{M}_w, \sigma \models x$ if $\sigma(x) = w$, for $x \in$ VAR.
4. $\mathcal{M}_w, \sigma \models \neg F$ if $\mathcal{M}_w, \sigma \not\models F$.
5. $\mathcal{M}_w, \sigma \models F \wedge G$ if $\mathcal{M}_w, \sigma \models F$ and $\mathcal{M}_w, \sigma \models G$.
6. $\mathcal{M}_w, \sigma \models F \vee G$ if either $\mathcal{M}_w, \sigma \models F$ or $\mathcal{M}_w, \sigma \models G$.
7. $\mathcal{M}_w, \sigma \models a : F$ if $\mathcal{M}_{N(a)}, \sigma \models F$, for $a \in$ NOM.
8. $\mathcal{M}_w, \sigma \models x : F$ if $\mathcal{M}_{\sigma(x)}, \sigma \models F$, for $x \in$ VAR.
9. $\mathcal{M}_w, \sigma \models \Box F$ if for each w' such that wRw', $\mathcal{M}_{w'}, \sigma \models F$.
10. $\mathcal{M}_w, \sigma \models \Diamond F$ if there exists w' such that wRw' and $\mathcal{M}_{w'}, \sigma \models F$.
11. $\mathcal{M}_w, \sigma \models \downarrow x.F$ if $\mathcal{M}_w, \sigma_x^w \models F$.

A formula F is *satisfiable* if there exist an interpretation $\mathcal{M}$, a variable assignment σ for $\mathcal{M}$ and a state w of $\mathcal{M}$, such that $\mathcal{M}_w, \sigma \models F$. Two formulae F and G are logically equivalent ($F \equiv G$) when, for every interpretation $\mathcal{M}$, assignment σ and state w of $\mathcal{M}$, $\mathcal{M}_w, \sigma \models F$ if and only if $\mathcal{M}_w, \sigma \models G$.

It is worth pointing out that, if $t \in$ VAR $\cup$ NOM and F is a formula:

$$\neg(t : F) \equiv t : \neg F \qquad \neg\downarrow x.F \equiv \downarrow x.\neg F \qquad \neg\Diamond F \equiv \Box\neg F \qquad \neg\Box F \equiv \Diamond\neg F$$

This allows one to restrict attention to formulae in negation normal form (NNF).

2   The Tableau Calculus

A *tableau branch* is a sequence of *nodes* $n_0, n_1, ...$, where each node is labelled by a ground satisfaction statement in NNF, and a tableau is a set of branches. If n occurs before m in the branch $\mathcal{B}$, we shall write $n < m$. The label of the node n will be denoted by $label(n)$. The notation $(n)\, a : F$ will be used to denote the node n, and simultaneously say that its label is $a : F$.

A tableau for a formula F is initialized with a single branch, constituted by the single node $(n_0)\, a_0 : F$, where a_0 is a new nominal. The formula $a_0 : F$ is the *initial formula* of the tableau, which is assumed to be ground and in NNF.

A tableau is expanded by application of the rules in Table 1, which are applied to a given branch. Their reading is standard: a rule is applicable if the branch contains a node (two nodes) labelled by the formula(e) shown as premiss(es) of the rules. The rules $\wedge, @, \downarrow, \Box$ and $\Diamond$ add one or two nodes to the branch, labelled by the conclusion(s); the rule $\vee$ replaces the current branch $\mathcal{B}$ with two branches,

Table 1. Expansion rules

$$\frac{a : (F \wedge G)}{\begin{array}{l} a : F \\ a : G \end{array}} \ (\wedge) \qquad\qquad \frac{a : (F \vee G)}{a : F \quad | \quad a : G} \ (\vee)$$

$$\frac{a : b : F}{b : F} \ (@) \qquad \frac{a : {\downarrow}x.F}{a : F[a/x]} \ (\downarrow) \qquad \begin{array}{c} [\mathcal{B}] \\ a : b \\ \hline \mathcal{B}[b/a] \end{array} \ (=)$$
$$\text{(not applicable if } a = b\text{)}$$

$$\frac{a : \Box F \quad a : \Diamond b}{b : F} \ (\Box) \qquad \frac{a : \Diamond F}{\begin{array}{l} a : \Diamond b \\ b : F \end{array}} \ (\Diamond)$$
$$\text{where } b \text{ is a new nominal}$$
$$\text{(not applicable if } F \text{ is a nominal)}$$

each of which is obtained by adding $\mathcal{B}$ a new node, labelled, respectively, by the formula shown on the left and right below the inference line.

The $\Box$ rule has two premisses, which must both occur in the branch, in any order. The leftmost premiss of the $\Box$ rule is called its *major premiss*, the rightmost one its *minor premiss*. The minor premiss is a *relational formula*, *i.e.* a satisfaction statement of the form $a : \Diamond b$ (where b is a nominal). A formula of the form $\Box F$ is called a *universal formula*. The $\Diamond$ rule is called *blockable rule*, a formula of the form $a : \Diamond F$, where F is not a nominal, is a *blockable formula* and a node labelled by a blockable formula is a *blockable node*.

If F is a formula, the notation $F[a/x]$ is used to denote the formula that is obtained from F replacing a for every free occurrence of the variable x. Analogously, if a and b are nominals, $F[b/a]$ is the formula obtained from F replacing b for every occurrence of a. The *equality rule* $(=)$ does not add any node to the branch, but modifies the labels of its nodes. The schematic formulation of this rule in Table 1 indicates that it can be fired whenever a branch $\mathcal{B}$ contains a *nominal equality* of the form $a : b$ (with $a \neq b$); as a result of the application of the rule, every node label F in $\mathcal{B}$ is replaced by $F[b/a]$.

The first node of a branch $\mathcal{B}$ is called the *top node* and its label the *top formula* of $\mathcal{B}$. The nominals occurring in the top formula are called *top nominals*. Note that the notion of top nominal is relative to a tableau branch. In fact, applications of the equality rule may change the top formula, hence the set of top nominals.

In the following definition, the current branch is left implicit, so as to lighten the notation.

Definition 1. *If a node n is added to a branch by application of the rule $\mathcal{R}$ to the node m then we write $m \leadsto^{\mathcal{R}} n$. In the case of rules with two conclusions,* *we write $m \leadsto^{\mathcal{R}} (n, k)$, or, sometimes, $m \leadsto^{\mathcal{R}} n$ and $m \leadsto^{\mathcal{R}} k$. In the case of the two premisses rule $\square$ we write $(m, k) \leadsto^{\square} n$.*

Note that the application of the equality rule does not change nodes, but only their labels, therefore it does not change the relation $\leadsto^{\mathcal{R}}$ between *nodes*, for any rule $\mathcal{R}$.

We say that a formula $a : F$ occurs in a tableau branch $\mathcal{B}$ (or $a : F \in \mathcal{B}$) if for some node n of the branch, $label(n) = a : F$. Similarly, a nominal occurs in a branch $\mathcal{B}$ if it occurs in the label of some node of $\mathcal{B}$. Finally, a nominal a *labels* a formula F in $\mathcal{B}$ if $a : F \in \mathcal{B}$.

Termination is achieved by means of a loop-checking mechanism using nominal renaming. In fact, in the presence of the binder, non-top nominals may occur in the body of any node label. In order to define this mechanism, some preliminary definitions are necessary.

Definition 2 (Nominal compatibility and mappings). *If $\mathcal{B}$ is a tableau branch and a is a nominal occurring in $\mathcal{B}$, then*

$$\Phi_{\mathcal{B}}(a) = \{p \mid p \in \mathsf{PROP} \ and \ a : p \in \mathcal{B}\} \cup \{\square F \mid a : \square F \in \mathcal{B}\}$$

If a and b are nominals occurring in a tableau branch $\mathcal{B}$, then a and b are compatible *in $\mathcal{B}$ if $\Phi_{\mathcal{B}}(a) = \Phi_{\mathcal{B}}(b)$, i.e. if they label the same propositions in* PROP *and the same universal formulae.*

A mapping π for a branch $\mathcal{B}$ is an injective function from non-top *nominals to* non-top *nominals such that for all a, a and $\pi(a)$ are compatible in $\mathcal{B}$.*

A mapping π for $\mathcal{B}$ maps a formula F to a formula G if:

1. *$\pi(F) = G$;*
2. *π is the identity for all nominals which do not occur in F.*

A formula F can be mapped to a formula G in $\mathcal{B}$ if there exists a mapping π for $\mathcal{B}$ mapping F to G.

Since a mapping π is the identity almost everywhere, it can be represented by a finite set of pairs of the form $\{b_1/a_1, ..., b_n/a_n\}$ where $a_i \neq b_i$, whenever $\pi(a_i) = b_i$ and $\pi(c) = c$ for all $c \notin \{a_1, ..., a_n\}$.

The application of the blockable rule is restricted by blocking conditions: a direct blocking condition, which forbids the application of the blockable rule to a node n, whenever the label of a previous node can be mapped to $label(n)$; and also an indirect blocking condition. In fact, since a node may be (directly) blocked in a branch after that it has already been expanded, all the nodes which, in some sense, depend from that expansion must be blocked too. So, a notion of indirect blocking is needed, which in turn requires a new partial order on nodes. The following definition introduces a binary relation on nodes, which organizes them into a family of trees.

Definition 3. *Let $\mathcal{B}$ be a tableau branch. The relation $n \prec_{\mathcal{B}} m$ between nodes of $\mathcal{B}$ is inductively defined as follows:*

Base case. *If $n \leadsto^{\Diamond} (m, k)$, then $n \prec_{\mathcal{B}} m$ and $n \prec_{\mathcal{B}} k$;*
Inductive cases. *If $m \prec_{\mathcal{B}} n$, then:*

1. *if $n \leadsto^{\mathcal{R}} k$, where $\mathcal{R} \in \{\vee, @, \downarrow, \wedge\}$, then $m \prec_{\mathcal{B}} k$;*
2. *if $label(n)$ is a relational formula and for some n', $(n', n) \leadsto^{\Box} k$, then $m \prec_{\mathcal{B}} k$.*

If $m \prec_{\mathcal{B}} n$ then n is said to be a child *of m w.r.t. $\prec_{\mathcal{B}}$, and m the* parent *of n. A node n in $\mathcal{B}$ is called a* root node *if it has no parent. Two nodes n and k are called* siblings *if either both of them are root nodes, or for some m, $m \prec_{\mathcal{B}} n$ and $m \prec_{\mathcal{B}} k$.*

The relation $\prec_{\mathcal{B}}^{+}$ is the transitive closure of $\prec_{\mathcal{B}}$. If $n \prec_{\mathcal{B}}^{+} m$, then n is an ancestor *of m and m a* descendant *of n w.r.t. $\prec_{\mathcal{B}}$.*

In other terms, when the blockable rule is applied to a node n, a first pair of children of n w.r.t. $\prec_{\mathcal{B}}$ is generated. The application of rules other than $\Diamond$ generates siblings, where, in the case of the two premisses rule $\Box$, it is the minor premiss which is added a sibling. Intuitively, when $n \prec_{\mathcal{B}} m$, n is the node which is taken to be the main "responsible" of the presence of m in the branch. In fact, the first "children" of a node n are nodes obtained from n by application of the blockable rule. And, if a node m is obtained from m' (as the minor premiss, in the case of the $\Box$ rule) by means of applications of non-blockable rules, then they are "siblings" *w.r.t.* $\prec_{\mathcal{B}}$.

Example 1. As an example, consider the tableau branch for

$$F = a : (\Diamond p \wedge \Box \downarrow x. \Diamond (p \wedge \neg x \wedge \downarrow y.a : \Diamond y))$$

represented in Figure 1. Node numbering reflects the order in which nodes are added to the branch. The right column reports the $\leadsto^{\mathcal{R}}$ relation justifying the addition of the corresponding node to the branch. *W.r.t.* the relation $\prec_{\mathcal{B}}$, $0, 1$ and 3 are root nodes with no children; 2 is also a root node, with children $4, 5, 6$ and 7; nodes 8–17 are all children of 7.

The relation $\prec_{\mathcal{B}}$ enjoys the following important properties:

1. For each node n in a tableau branch $\mathcal{B}$, there exists at most one node m such that $m \prec_{\mathcal{B}} n$. Therefore, there is exactly one maximal chain

$$n_1 \prec_{\mathcal{B}} n_2 \prec_{\mathcal{B}} \ldots \prec_{\mathcal{B}} n_k = n$$

   where n_1 is any root node.
2. If for some n, $m \prec_{\mathcal{B}} n$, then m is a blockable node. Therefore, for any chain

$$n_1 \prec_{\mathcal{B}} n_2 \prec_{\mathcal{B}} \ldots \prec_{\mathcal{B}} n_k \prec_{\mathcal{B}} n_{k+1}$$

$n_1, \ldots, n_k$ are all blockable nodes.

Consequently, $\prec_{\mathcal{B}}$ arranges the nodes of a branch into a forest of trees, where non-terminal nodes are blockable nodes.

We can now define the notions of direct and indirect blocking.

$(0)\ a_0 : a : (\Diamond p \wedge \Box \downarrow x.\Diamond(p \wedge \neg x \wedge \downarrow y.a : \Diamond y))$

$(1)\ a : (\Diamond p \wedge \Box \downarrow x.\Diamond(p \wedge \neg x \wedge \downarrow y.a : \Diamond y))$ $0 \rightsquigarrow^{@} 1$

$(2)\ a : \Diamond p$ $1 \rightsquigarrow^{\wedge} 2$

$(3)\ a : \Box \downarrow x.\Diamond(p \wedge \neg x \wedge \downarrow y.a : \Diamond y)$ $1 \rightsquigarrow^{\wedge} 3$

$(4)\ a : \Diamond b$ $2 \rightsquigarrow^{\Diamond} 4$

$(5)\ b : p$ $2 \rightsquigarrow^{\Diamond} 5$

$(6)\ b : \downarrow x.\Diamond(p \wedge \neg x \wedge \downarrow y.a : \Diamond y)$ $(3,4) \rightsquigarrow^{\Box} 6$

$(7)\ b : \Diamond(p \wedge \neg b \wedge \downarrow y.a : \Diamond y)$ $6 \rightsquigarrow^{\downarrow} 7$

$(8)\ b : \Diamond c$ $7 \rightsquigarrow^{\Diamond} 8$

$(9)\ c : p \wedge \neg b \wedge \downarrow y.a : \Diamond y$ $7 \rightsquigarrow^{\Diamond} 9$

$(10)\ c : p \wedge \neg b$ $9 \rightsquigarrow^{\wedge} 10$

$(11)\ c : \downarrow y.a : \Diamond y$ $9 \rightsquigarrow^{\wedge} 11$

$(12)\ c : p$ $10 \rightsquigarrow^{\wedge} 12$

$(13)\ c : \neg b$ $10 \rightsquigarrow^{\wedge} 13$

$(14)\ c : a : \Diamond c$ $11 \rightsquigarrow^{\downarrow} 14$

$(15)\ a : \Diamond c$ $14 \rightsquigarrow^{@} 15$

$(16)\ c : \downarrow x.\Diamond(p \wedge \neg x \wedge \downarrow y.a : \Diamond y)$ $(3,15) \rightsquigarrow^{\Box} 16$

$(17)\ c : \Diamond(p \wedge \neg c \wedge \downarrow y.a : \Diamond y)$ $16 \rightsquigarrow^{\downarrow} 17$

Fig. 1. A tableau branch for $a : (\Diamond p \wedge \Box \downarrow x.\Diamond(p \wedge \neg x \wedge \downarrow y.a : \Diamond y))$

Definition 4 (Direct and indirect blocking). *A node* $(n)\ a : \Diamond F$ *is directly blocked by* $(m)\ b : \Diamond G$ *in* $\mathcal{B}$ *if*

- $m < n$, *m is neither directly blocked in* $\mathcal{B}$ *nor it has any ancestor w.r.t.* $\prec_{\mathcal{B}}$ *which is directly blocked in* $\mathcal{B}$;
- $b : G$ *can be mapped to* $a : F$ *in* $\mathcal{B}$.

A node n *is directly blocked in* $\mathcal{B}$ *if it is blocked by some* m *in* $\mathcal{B}$, *and it is indirectly blocked in* $\mathcal{B}$ *if it has an ancestor w.r.t.* $\prec_{\mathcal{B}}$ *which is directly blocked in* $\mathcal{B}$. *An indirectly blocked node is called a* phantom node *(or, simply, a phantom).*

The tableau branch $\mathcal{B}$ represented in Figure 1 represents a blocking case: node 17 is blocked by 7, because b e c are compatible ($\Phi_{\mathcal{B}}(b) = \Phi_{\mathcal{B}}(c) = \{p\}$).

It must be remarked that the blocking relation is dynamic, *i.e.* blockings are not established forever, since they are relative to a tableau branch, and can be undone when expanding the branch. In fact, a node may be blocked in a branch $\mathcal{B}$ and then unblocked after expanding $\mathcal{B}$, because the addition of new nodes or changes in node labels may destroy nominal compatibility. Possibly, a new blocking can be introduced (but compatibilities must be checked again), by means of a different mapping.

The application of the expansion rules is restricted by the following conditions:

Definition 5 (Restrictions on the expansion rules). *The expansion of a tableau branch* $\mathcal{B}$ *is subject to the following restrictions:*

R1. *no node labelled by a formula already occurring in* $\mathcal{B}$ *as the label of a* non-phantom *node is ever added to* $\mathcal{B}$;

R2. *a blockable node n cannot be expanded if there are $k_0, k_1 \in \mathcal{B}$ such that $n \leadsto^{\Diamond} (k_0, k_1)$;*

R3. *a phantom node cannot be expanded by means of a single-premiss rule, nor can it be used as the minor premiss of the $\Box$ rule;*

R4. *a blockable node cannot be expanded if it is directly blocked in $\mathcal{B}$.*

It is worth pointing out that termination would not be guaranteed if restriction **R1** were replaced by the condition that a node (or pair of nodes) is never expanded more than once on the branch.

A branch is *closed* whenever it contains, for some nominal a, either a pair of nodes $(n)\,a : p$, $(m)\,a : \neg p$ for some $p \in \mathsf{PROP}$, or a node $(n)\,a : \neg a$. As usual, we assume that a closed branch is never expanded further on. A branch which is not closed is *open*. A branch is *complete* when it cannot be further expanded. For instance, the tableau branch represented in Figure 1 is complete and open.

This section concludes with some further examples. In each of them, $\mathcal{B}$ denotes the considered branch, and the notation $\mathcal{B}_n$ is used to denote the branch segment up to node n, while Φ_n abbreviates $\Phi_{\mathcal{B}_n}$.

Example 2. Figure 2 represents a closed one-branch tableau for

$$F = (\Diamond{\downarrow}x.\Diamond(x : p)) \wedge (\Diamond{\downarrow}y.\Diamond(y : \neg p)) \wedge (\Diamond{\downarrow}z.(\Diamond(z : p) \wedge \Diamond(z : \neg p)))$$

where the first applications of the $\wedge$-rule are collapsed into one.

(0) $a_0 : F$			(14) $b_1 : b : \neg p$	$12 \leadsto^{\Diamond} 14$
(1) $a_0 : \Diamond{\downarrow}x.\Diamond x : p$	$0 \leadsto^{\wedge} 1$		(15) $b : \neg p$	$14 \leadsto^{@} 15$
(2) $a_0 : \Diamond{\downarrow}y.\Diamond y : \neg p$	$0 \leadsto^{\wedge} 2$		(16) $a_0 : \Diamond c$	$3 \leadsto^{\Diamond} 16$
(3) $a_0 : \Diamond{\downarrow}z.(\Diamond(z : p)$			(17) $c : {\downarrow}z.(\Diamond(z : p)$	
$\quad \wedge \Diamond(z : \neg p))$	$0 \leadsto^{\wedge} 3$		$\quad \wedge \Diamond(z : \neg p))$	$3 \leadsto^{\Diamond} 17$
(4) $a_0 : \Diamond a$	$1 \leadsto^{\Diamond} 4$		(18) $c : \Diamond c : p \wedge \Diamond c : \neg p$	$17 \leadsto^{\downarrow} 18$
(5) $a : {\downarrow}x.\Diamond x : p$	$1 \leadsto^{\Diamond} 5$		(19) $c : \Diamond c : p$	$18 \leadsto^{\wedge} 19$
(6) $a : \Diamond a : p$	$5 \leadsto^{\downarrow} 6$		(20) $c : \Diamond c : \neg p$	$18 \leadsto^{\wedge} 20$
(7) $a : \Diamond a_1$	$6 \leadsto^{\Diamond} 7$		(21) $c : \Diamond c_1$	$19 \leadsto^{\Diamond} 21$
(8) $a_1 : a : p$	$6 \leadsto^{\Diamond} 8$		(22) $c_1 : c : p$	$19 \leadsto^{\Diamond} 22$
(9) $a : p$	$8 \leadsto^{@} 9$		(23) $c : p$	$22 \leadsto^{@} 23$
(10) $a_0 : \Diamond b$	$2 \leadsto^{\Diamond} 10$		(24) $c : \Diamond c_2$	$20 \leadsto^{\Diamond} 24$
(11) $b : {\downarrow}y.\Diamond y : \neg p$	$2 \leadsto^{\Diamond} 11$		(25) $c_2 : c : \neg p$	$20 \leadsto^{\Diamond} 25$
(12) $b : \Diamond b : \neg p$	$11 \leadsto^{\downarrow} 12$		(26) $c : \neg p$	$25 \leadsto^{@} 26$
(13) $b : \Diamond b_1$	$12 \leadsto^{\Diamond} 13$			

Fig. 2. Example 2

The relation $\prec_{\mathcal{B}}$ in this branch can be described as follows: 0–3 are root nodes, $1 \prec_{\mathcal{B}} \{4, 5, 6\}$, $6 \prec_{\mathcal{B}} \{7, 8, 9\}$, $2 \prec_{\mathcal{B}} \{10, 11, 12\}$, $12 \prec_{\mathcal{B}} \{13, 14, 15\}$, $3 \prec_{\mathcal{B}} \{16, 17, 18, 19, 20\}$, $19 \prec_{\mathcal{B}} \{21, 22, 23\}$, $20 \prec_{\mathcal{B}} \{24, 25, 26\}$.[2]

---

[2] $n \prec_{\mathcal{B}} \{m_1, ..., m_k\}$ abbreviates $n \prec_{\mathcal{B}} m_1$ and ... $n \prec_{\mathcal{B}} m_k$.

The branch is closed because of nodes 23 and 26. In $\mathcal{B}_{20}$, node 19 is not blocked by 6, since $a : \Diamond a : p$ cannot be mapped to $c : \Diamond c : p$ because c and a are not compatible in $\mathcal{B}_{20}$ ($\Phi_{20}(c) = \varnothing \neq \{p\} = \Phi_{20}(a)$); therefore, node 19 can be expanded. In the same branch segment, on the contrary, node 20 is blocked by 12, because $\Phi_{20}(c) = \varnothing = \Phi_{20}(b)$.

When the construction proceeds, expanding the non-blocked node 19, and nodes 21–23 are added to the branch, c and b are no more compatible ($\Phi_{23}(c) = \{p\}$ while $\Phi_{23}(b)$ is still empty), so node 20 is unblocked and it is expanded, producing 24–26 and the branch closes.

Note moreover that, after the addition of node 23, a and c become compatible, so that in $\mathcal{B}_{23}$ node 19 is blocked by 6, and 21–23 are phantom nodes. Since 20 is not a descendant of 19 $w.r.t. \prec_{\mathcal{B}}$, it is not a phantom, thus it can be expanded.

Example 3. This example shows the need of indirect blocking (restriction **R3**) to ensure termination. Let

$$F = a : ((\Box{\downarrow}x.\Diamond{\downarrow}y.(x : p \wedge a : \Diamond y)) \wedge \Diamond q)$$

Figure 3 shows a complete branch in a tableau for F.

(1) $a_0 : F$		(17) $b_1 : \Diamond{\downarrow}y.(b_1 : p \wedge a : \Diamond y)$	$16 \rightsquigarrow^{\downarrow} 17$
(2) $a : ((\Box{\downarrow}x.\Diamond{\downarrow}y.$		(18) $b_1 : \Diamond b_2$	$17 \rightsquigarrow^{\Diamond} 18$
$\quad (x : p \wedge a : \Diamond y)) \wedge \Diamond q)$	$1 \rightsquigarrow^{@} 2$	(19) $b_2 : {\downarrow}y.(b_1 : p \wedge a : \Diamond y)$	$17 \rightsquigarrow^{\Diamond} 19$
(3) $a : \Box{\downarrow}x.\Diamond{\downarrow}y.$		(20) $b_2 : (b_1 : p \wedge a : \Diamond b_2)$	$19 \rightsquigarrow^{\downarrow} 20$
$\quad (x : p \wedge a : \Diamond y)$	$2 \rightsquigarrow^{\wedge} 3$	(21) $b_2 : b_1 : p$	$20 \rightsquigarrow^{\wedge} 21$
(4) $a : \Diamond q$	$2 \rightsquigarrow^{\wedge} 4$	(22) $b_2 : a : \Diamond b_2$	$20 \rightsquigarrow^{\wedge} 22$
(5) $a : \Diamond b$	$4 \rightsquigarrow^{\Diamond} 5$	(23) $b_1 : p$	$21 \rightsquigarrow^{@} 23$
(6) $b : q$	$4 \rightsquigarrow^{\Diamond} 6$	(24) $a : \Diamond b_2$	$22 \rightsquigarrow^{@} 24$
(7) $b : {\downarrow}x.\Diamond{\downarrow}y.$		(25) $b_2 : {\downarrow}x.\Diamond{\downarrow}y.$	
$\quad x : p \wedge a : \Diamond y)$	$(3,5) \rightsquigarrow^{\Box} 7$	$\quad (x : p \wedge a : \Diamond y)$	$(3,24) \rightsquigarrow^{\Box} 25$
(8) $b : \Diamond{\downarrow}y.(b : p \wedge a : \Diamond y)$	$7 \rightsquigarrow^{\downarrow} 8$	(26) $b_2 : \Diamond{\downarrow}y.(b_2 : p \wedge a : \Diamond y)$	$25 \rightsquigarrow^{\downarrow} 26$
(9) $b : \Diamond b_1$	$8 \rightsquigarrow^{\Diamond} 9$	(27) $b_2 : \Diamond b_3$	$26 \rightsquigarrow^{\Diamond} 27$
(10) $b_1 : {\downarrow}y.(b : p \wedge a : \Diamond y)$	$8 \rightsquigarrow^{\Diamond} 10$	(28) $b_3 : {\downarrow}y.(b_2 : p \wedge a : \Diamond y)$	$26 \rightsquigarrow^{\Diamond} 28$
(11) $b_1 : (b : p \wedge a : \Diamond b_1)$	$10 \rightsquigarrow^{\downarrow} 11$	(29) $b_3 : (b_2 : p \wedge a : \Diamond b_3)$	$28 \rightsquigarrow^{\downarrow} 29$
(12) $b_1 : b : p$	$11 \rightsquigarrow^{\wedge} 12$	(30) $b_3 : b_2 : p$	$29 \rightsquigarrow^{\wedge} 30$
(13) $b_1 : a : \Diamond b_1$	$11 \rightsquigarrow^{\wedge} 13$	(31) $b_3 : a : \Diamond b_3$	$29 \rightsquigarrow^{\wedge} 31$
(14) $b : p$	$12 \rightsquigarrow^{@} 14$	(32) $b_2 : p$	$30 \rightsquigarrow^{@} 32$
(15) $a : \Diamond b_1$	$13 \rightsquigarrow^{@} 15$	(33) $a : \Diamond b_3$	$31 \rightsquigarrow^{@} 33$
(16) $b_1 : {\downarrow}x.\Diamond{\downarrow}y.$			
$\quad (x : p \wedge a : \Diamond y)$	$(3,15) \rightsquigarrow^{\Box} 16$		

Fig. 3. Example 3

The relation $\prec_{\mathcal{B}}$ in this branch can be described as follows: the root nodes are 1–4, $4 \prec_{\mathcal{B}} \{5, ..., 8\}$, $8 \prec_{\mathcal{B}} \{9, ..., 17\}$, $17 \prec_{\mathcal{B}} \{18, ..., 26\}$ and $26 \prec_{\mathcal{B}} \{27, ..., 33\}$.

In $\mathcal{B}_{17}$ node 17 is not blocked by 8 because $\Phi_{17}(b) = \{q, p\} \neq \varnothing = \Phi_{17}(b_1)$. And it is not blocked by 8 in $\mathcal{B}_n$ for any $n \geq 23$ either, where $\Phi_n(b) = \{q, p\} \neq$

$\{p\} = \Phi_n(b_1)$. Moreover in $\mathcal{B}_{26}$ node 26 is blocked neither by 8 nor by 17, because $\Phi_{26}(b) = \{q, p\}$, $\Phi_{26}(b_1) = \{p\}$, and $\Phi_{26}(b_2) = \emptyset$.

But in $\mathcal{B}_{33}$ node 26 is blocked by 17, because $\Phi_{33}(b_1) = \{p\} = \Phi_{33}(b_2)$. Therefore, its children $w.r.t.$ $\prec_{\mathcal{B}_{33}}$, $i.e.$ 27–33 are all phantom nodes, and, in particular, node 33 cannot participate, with node 3, to an expansion via the $\Box$ rule.

Without restriction **R3**, the construction of the branch would go on forever. In fact, the following nodes could be added:

$$(34)\ b_3 : \downarrow x. \Diamond \downarrow y. (x : p \wedge a : \Diamond y)\ (3, 33) \leadsto^{\Box} 34$$
$$(35)\ b_3 : \Diamond \downarrow y. (b_3 : p \wedge a : \Diamond y)\quad 34 \leadsto^{\downarrow} 35$$

In $\mathcal{B}_{35}$ node 35 would not be blocked, because $\Phi_{35}(b_3) = \emptyset$, while $\Phi_{35}(b_1) = \Phi_{35}(b_2) = \{p\}$. So a sequence of new nodes could be added, with labels obtained from the labels of 27–34, by renaming b_2 with b_3 and b_3 with a new nominal b_4. A neverending story ...

3   Properties of the Calculus

The tableau calculus defined in Section 2 is trivially sound. Moreover it terminates and can be proved complete, *provided that the initial formula is in the $HL(@, \downarrow) \setminus \downarrow \Box$ fragment*. Since space restrictions do not allow for a full account of the termination and completeness proofs, which are in some points quite subtle, this section gives only a brief and simplified outline of these proofs. Their details can be found in [6].

For the purposes of proving termination and completeness, the main property of the considered fragment is that, if $\Box G$ is a subformula of the initial formula, it contains no free variable. As a consequence, for any node label of the form $a : \Box G$, G does not contain any non-top nominal. In other terms, $\Box G$ is a subformula of the top formula of the branch (*strong subformula property*).

A looser subformula property holds for node labels in general: if $a : F$ is the label of some node in a tableau branch $\mathcal{B}$, then F is an *instance* of some subformula F' of the top formula of $\mathcal{B}$, i.e. F is obtained from F' by replacing the free variables occurring in F' with nominals (*loose subformula property*).

Termination is proved by showing that the nodes of a branch $\mathcal{B}$ are arranged by $\prec_{\mathcal{B}}$ into a bounded sized set of trees, each of which has bounded width and bounded depth. Hence any tableau branch $\mathcal{B}$ has a number of nodes that is bounded by a function of the size N of the initial formula.

The above statement is proved by use of the following intermediate results:

1. The number of siblings $w.r.t.$ $\prec_{\mathcal{B}}$ of any node n is bounded by a function of N. This is not as trivial a task as it may appear at first sight. In fact, it is not sufficient to show that the number of formulae that can label the siblings of a given node is bounded, because, in principle, a given formula might be the label of an infinite number of nodes. In fact, notwithstanding restriction **R1**, distinct node labels can become equal by effect of substitution.

However, it can be shown that the label of any sibling of n has a *matrix* taken from a bounded stock of formulae, that can be built in the language of the branch *at the time n is added to it*. Node labels with a same matrix are always equal, at any construction stage of the branch, since they are obtained from the same formula (matrix) by application of the same nominal renaming. Since siblings always have the same phantom/non-phantom state, restrictions **R1** and **R3** ensure that any node can only produce a bounded number of siblings.

Note that the above sketched reasoning would not work if it were the major premiss of the $\square$ rule to be added a sibling *w.r.t.* $\prec_\mathcal{B}$. In fact, a node labelled by a universal formula can in principle produce an infinite number of expansions.

2. The length of any chain of nodes $n_1 \prec_\mathcal{B} n_2 \prec_\mathcal{B} ... \prec_\mathcal{B} n_k$ is bounded by a function of N. This is due to the "loose" subformula property and the fact that the set of elements in $\mathsf{PROP} \cup \{\square G \mid \square G$ occurs in some node label$\}$ is bounded by N (by the "strong" subformula property). Therefore, restrictions **R2** and **R4** ensure that the blockable rule cannot be applied to extend any chain of nodes beyond a given depth.

It is worth pointing out that the considerations underlying the termination argument in [6] establish a doubly exponential upper bound on the number of nodes in a tableau branch. Therefore, the decision procedure defined in this paper is not worst-case optimal, since the satisfiability problem for $\mathsf{HL}(@, \downarrow) \setminus \downarrow\square$ is in 2-ExpTime [13].

Completeness is proved in the standard way, by showing how to define a model of the initial formula from a complete and open tableau branch. However, for the calculus defined in this work, the fact that the labels of blocked and blocking nodes are not identical must be taken into account. A model cannot be simply built from a set of states consisting of equivalence classes of nominals, and establishing that two nominals are in the same class whenever some blocking mapping maps one to the other. In fact, it might be the case that a nominal a is mapped to a nominal b to block a given node, although the branch contains a node labelled by $a : \neg b$ (like in Example 1).

Thus, a different approach is followed, showing that a (possibly infinite) model can be built out of a complete and open branch $\mathcal{B}$ by means of a preliminary infinitary extension $\mathcal{N}_\mathcal{B}^\infty$ of a subset $\mathcal{N}_0$ of $\mathcal{B}$. More precisely, $\mathcal{N}_0$ is the union of the non-phantom nodes in $\mathcal{B}$ and the nodes $(n)\, a : F$ where either $F \in \mathsf{PROP}$ or F has the form $\square G$.

$\mathcal{N}_\mathcal{B}^\infty$ is built by stages, as the union of a (possibly infinite) series of extensions $\mathcal{N}_0 \subseteq \mathcal{N}_1 \subseteq \mathcal{N}_2....$ of $\mathcal{N}_0$. The purpose of each stage is the creation of a *witness* for a given blockable node, where a nominal b is called a witness for a node labelled by a blockable formula of the form $a : \Diamond F$ if there exist nodes labelled, respectively, by $a : \Diamond b$ and $b : F$. Each sequence of (labelled) nodes $\mathcal{N}_i$ is associated a *blocking relation* $\mathbf{B}_i$, containing triples of the form (n, m, π), where n and m are nodes, $m < n$ and π is an injective mapping such that $\pi(label(m)) = label(n)$. The construction ensures that:

1. for any $(n, m, \pi) \in \mathbf{B}_i$:
   (a) n and m are labelled by blockable formulae;
   (b) $m \in \mathcal{N}_0$ and it has a witness in $\mathcal{N}_0$.
2. For any blockable node $n \in \mathcal{N}_i$, if n has no witness in $\mathcal{N}_i$, then $(n, m, \pi) \in \mathbf{B}_i$, for some m and π.

Each extension $\mathcal{N}_i$ is built so as to add a *witness* to the first "blocked" node $n \in \mathcal{N}_{i-1}$, *i.e.* such that for some m and π, $(n, m, \pi) \in \mathbf{B}_{i-1}$. The label of each new node added to $\mathcal{N}_i$ is obtained from a node in $\mathcal{N}_0$ by suitably renaming non-top nominals. Specifically, an injective mapping θ_i is defined, that will guide the construction of the new nodes of $\mathcal{N}_i$. The mapping θ_i is the identity except for the following cases:

- if a occurs in $label(m)$, then $\theta_i(a) = \pi(a)$;
- if b is the witness of m and b does not occur in $label(m)$, then $\theta_i(b) = b^i$, where b^i is a fresh nominal. Note that, at the time the witness of m was added to the branch by an application of the $\diamond$ rule, it was obviously fresh *w.r.t.* to the current branch, but it may subsequently have been replaced by the equality rule.

The sequence $\mathcal{N}_i$ is then obtained from $\mathcal{N}_{i-1}$ by adding new nodes, labelled by $\theta_i(label(k))$ for each $k \in \mathcal{N}_0$ such that $\theta_i(label(k))$ does not already occur in $\mathcal{N}_{i-1}$. Hence, in particular, a pair of nodes is added, representing the fact that b^i is the witness of n in $\mathcal{N}_i$.

Consistently, the triple (n, m, π) is removed from the blocking relation. Possibly, new nodes with no witness are created; for each of them, a blocking node and blocking mapping are defined, and the corresponding triple is added to $\mathbf{B}_i$.

Each of the sets of nodes $\mathcal{N}_i$ enjoys a form of *saturation property*: it is consistent (there are no labels of the form $a : \neg a$, or both $a : p$ and $a : \neg p$), it does not contain non-trivial equalities ($a : b$ with $a \neq b$, so that the equality rule does not need to be taken into account), and, for any node or pair of nodes in $\mathcal{N}_i$ that could be the premiss(es) of some expansion rule other than $\diamond$, its expansion(s) are also in $\mathcal{N}_i$.

The proof of such a saturation property exploits the following (non trivial) properties of the construction:

- If $i > 0$ and θ_i is the mapping used to extend $\mathcal{N}_{i-1}$ to $\mathcal{N}_i$, then for any nominal a, a and $\theta_i(a)$ are compatible in $\mathcal{N}_i$;
- for every triple $(n, m, \pi) \in \mathbf{B}_i$ and for any nominal a, a and $\pi(a)$ are compatible in $\mathcal{N}_i$.

In the union $\mathcal{N}_B^\infty = \bigcup_{i \in \mathbb{N}} \mathcal{N}_i$ every blockable node has a witness, and a model can be defined from it, made up of a state for each nominal occurring in $\mathcal{N}_B^\infty$. Such a model can easily be extended to a model of the initial formula.

4   Concluding Remarks

In this work a tableau calculus for $\mathsf{HL}(@, \downarrow)$ is defined, which is provably terminating (independently of the rule application strategy) and complete for formulae belonging to the fragment $\mathsf{HL}(@, \downarrow) \setminus \downarrow\square$. A preprocessing step transforming formulae into equisatisfiable ones turns the calculus into a satisfiability decision procedure for $\mathsf{HL}(@, \downarrow) \setminus \square\downarrow\square$.

The main features of the calculus can be summarized as follows. A tableau branch is a sequence of nodes, each of which is labelled by a satisfaction statement. Since nominal equalities are dealt with by means of substitution, different occurrences of the same formula may occur as labels of different nodes in a branch. The fact that when two formulae become equal by the effect of substitution the corresponding nodes do not collapse, allows for the definition of a binary relation $\prec_B$ on nodes which organizes them into a family of trees. Each tree of the family has a bounded width, and this is due to the fact that, when applying the two premisses $\square$ rule, it is the minor premiss, labelled by a relational formula, which is taken to be the "main responsible" of the expansion.

The fact that each tree has a bounded depth is guaranteed by a blocking mechanism which forbids the application of the $\diamond$ rule to a node n whenever it has already been applied to another node whose label is equal to the label of n, *modulo non-top nominal renaming* (accompanied by suitable restrictions). Renaming is essential, because, in the presence of the binder, non-top nominals may occur in the body of any node label. The blocking mechanism is *anywhere* blocking, paired with indirect blocking, relying on the relation $\prec_B$.

This mechanism differs from [4,5], where calculi for hybrid logic with the global and converse modalities (and no binders) are defined. In fact, such calculi adopt ancestor blocking, where *nominals* (and not nodes) are blocked, and indirect blocking relies on a partial order on nominals (instead of nodes). Differently from [5], moreover, the calculus defined in this work does not require nominal deletion to ensure termination. This is due, again, to the fact that a branch is not a set of formulae, but a sequence of nodes.

Also the tableau system defined in [11] for hybrid logic with the difference and converse modalities makes use of ancestor blocking, relying on an ancestor relation among nominals. The blocking mechanism used for converse free formulae in the same work is different and more similar to ours. In fact, an existential formula, such as, for instance, $a : \diamond F$, is blocked (independently of its outermost nominal a) whenever there exists a nominal b labelling both F and every formula G such that $a : \square G$ is in the branch. However, the sub-calculus does not terminate unless applications of the $\square$ rule are prioritized.

A tableau calculus testing satisfiability of formulae in the *constant-free clique guarded fragment* has been proposed in [9]. A restriction of the algorithm to the guarded fragment has been defined and implemented [10]. A tableau branch, in these calculi, is a tree of nodes, and the label of each node is a set of formulae. A node is directly blocked by a previously created node if, essentially, their labels are the same modulo constant renaming. Our comparison modulo renaming method was in fact originally inspired by [9,10] (although there are some differences). A further contact point between these calculi and ours is anywhere blocking coupled with indirect blocking (which, in [9,10] relies on the ancestor relation in the tree).

We are presently working at the next natural step, *i.e.* the extension of the calculus to the global and converse modalities, so as to obtain a tableau based decision procedure for the fragment $\mathsf{HL}(@, \downarrow, \mathsf{E}, \Diamond^-) \setminus \Box \downarrow \Box$.

References

1. Areces, C., Blackburn, P., Marx, M.: A road-map on complexity for hybrid logics. In: Flum, J., Rodríguez-Artalejo, M. (eds.) CSL 1999. LNCS, vol. 1683, pp. 307–321. Springer, Heidelberg (1999)
2. Areces, C., ten Cate, B.: Hybrid logics. In: Blackburn, P., Wolter, F., van Benthem, J. (eds.) Handbook of Modal Logics, pp. 821–868. Elsevier, Amsterdam (2007)
3. Blackburn, P., Seligman, J.: Hybrid languages. Journal of Logic, Language and Information 4, 251–272 (1995)
4. Bolander, T., Blackburn, P.: Termination for hybrid tableaus. Journal of Logic and Computation 17(3), 517–554 (2007)
5. Cerrito, S., Cialdea Mayer, M.: Nominal substitution at work with the global and converse modalities. In: Beklemishev, L., Goranko, V., Shehtman, V. (eds.) Advances in Modal Logic, vol. 8, pp. 57–74. College Publications (2010)
6. Cerrito, S., Cialdea Mayer, M.: A calculus for a decidable fragment of hybrid logic with binders. Technical Report RT-DIA-181-2011, Dipartimento di Informatica e Automazione, Università di Roma Tre (2011),
   http://www.dia.uniroma3.it/Plone/ricerca/technical-reports/2011
7. Ganzinger, H., De Nivelle, H.: A superposition decision procedure for the guarded fragment with equality. In: Proc. 14th Symposium on Logic in Computer Science, pp. 295–305. IEEE Computer Society Press, Los Alamitos (1999)
8. Grädel, E.: On the restraining power of guards. Journal of Symbolic Logic 64, 1719–1742 (1998)
9. Hirsch, C., Tobies, S.: A tableau algorithm for the clique guarded fragment. In: Wolter, F., Wansing, H., de Rijke, M., Zakharyaschev, M. (eds.) Advances in Modal Logic, vol. 3, pp. 257–277. CSLI Publications, Stanford (2001)
10. Hladik, J.: Implementation and optimisation of a tableau algorithm for the guarded fragment. In: Egly, U., Fermüller, C.G. (eds.) TABLEAUX 2002. LNCS (LNAI), vol. 2381, pp. 145–159. Springer, Heidelberg (2002)
11. Kaminski, M., Smolka, G.: Terminating tableau systems for hybrid logic with difference and converse. Journal of Logic, Language and Information 18(4), 437–464 (2009)
12. ten Cate, B., Franceschet, M.: Guarded fragments with constants. Journal of Logic, Language and Information 14, 281–288 (2005)
13. ten Cate, B.D., Franceschet, M.: On the complexity of hybrid logics with binders. In: Ong, L. (ed.) CSL 2005. LNCS, vol. 3634, pp. 339–354. Springer, Heidelberg (2005)

Basic Constructive Connectives, Determinism and Matrix-Based Semantics

Agata Ciabattoni[1], Ori Lahav[2,*], and Anna Zamansky[1]

[1] Vienna University of Technology
[2] Tel Aviv University
{agata,annaz}@logic.at, orilahav@post.tau.ac.il

Abstract. (Non-)deterministic Kripke-style semantics is used to characterize two syntactic properties of single-conclusion canonical sequent calculi: invertibility of rules and axiom-expansion. An alternative matrix-based formulation of such semantics is introduced, which provides an algorithm for checking these properties, and also new insights into basic constructive connectives.

1 Introduction

Single-conclusion canonical systems were introduced in [3] to provide a general characterization of basic constructive connectives.[1] These systems are single-conclusion sequent calculi, which in addition to the axioms and structural rules of Gentzen's LJ calculus have only logical rules, in which exactly one occurrence of a connective is introduced and no other connective is mentioned. It was shown in [3] that every single-conclusion canonical system induces a class of Kripke frames, for which it is strongly sound and complete. The key idea behind this semantics is to relax the principle of truth-functionality, and to use *non-deterministic* semantics, in which the truth-values of the subformulas of some compound formula ψ do not always uniquely determine the truth-value of ψ. The non-deterministic Kripke-style semantics was also applied in [3] to characterize the single-conclusion canonical systems that enjoy cut-admissibility.

As shown in [3], basic constructive connectives include the standard intuitionistic connectives together with many others. Some of these connectives induce a deterministic Kripke-style semantics, while others only have a non-deterministic one. The first goal of this paper is to investigate the relationship between determinism of basic constructive connectives and two syntactic properties of their rules: invertibility and completeness of atomic axioms (axiom-expansion). Invertibility of rules is important for guiding proof search in sequent calculi and simplifies automated proofs of cut-admissibility. Axiom expansion is sometimes considered crucial when designing "well-behaved" sequent systems. Here we prove that the determinism of the underlying Kripke-style semantics is a necessary and sufficient condition for a basic constructive connective to admit axiom expansion. The same connection

---

* Supported by The Israel Science Foundation (grant no. 280-10).
[1] See e.g. [9,5] for alternative proposals.

also holds with the invertibility of the right introduction rule for the connective, provided that the calculus contains exactly one such rule.

A similar investigation was carried out in [2] for *multiple-conclusion* canonical calculi. This was based on their (much simpler) semantics, defined in terms of non-deterministic two-valued matrices ([1]) – a natural generalization of the standard two-valued truth-tables.

Despite the important properties discussed above, the formulation of the non-deterministic Kripke-style semantics in [3] does not provide an algorithmic approach for checking determinism of basic constructive connectives. Accordingly, the second goal of this paper is to overcome this problem by providing an alternative formulation of this semantics based on a generalization of non-deterministic two-valued matrices. These generalized matrices, used to characterize the set of frames induced by a single-conclusion canonical system, have two main advantages. First, *decidability*: there is a simple algorithm for checking whether the induced semantics is deterministic, which in turn can be used for deciding invertibility and axiom-expansion in single-conclusion canonical systems. Second, *modularity*: the semantic effect of each syntactic rule can be directly read off the corresponding matrix, therefore providing new insights into the semantic meaning of basic constructive connectives.

2   Preliminaries

In what follows $\mathcal{L}$ is a propositional language, and $Frm_{\mathcal{L}}$ is its set of wffs. We assume that the atomic formulas of $\mathcal{L}$ are $p_1, p_2, \ldots$. We use Γ, Σ, Π, E to denote finite subsets of $Frm_{\mathcal{L}}$, where E is used for sets which are either singletons or empty. A *(single-conclusion) sequent* is an expression of the form $\Gamma \Rightarrow E$. We denote sequents of the form $\Gamma \Rightarrow \{\varphi\}$ (resp. $\Gamma \Rightarrow \emptyset$) by $\Gamma \Rightarrow \varphi$ (resp. $\Gamma \Rightarrow$).

Below we shortly reproduce definitions and results from [3].

Definition 1. *A substitution is a function* $\sigma : Frm_{\mathcal{L}} \to Frm_{\mathcal{L}}$, *such that for every n-ary connective* $\diamond$ *of* $\mathcal{L}$ *we have:* $\sigma(\diamond(\psi_1, \ldots, \psi_n)) = \diamond(\sigma(\psi_1), \ldots, \sigma(\psi_n))$. *A substitution is extended to sets of formulas in the obvious way.*

Henceforth we denote by σ_{id} the substitution σ, such that $\sigma(p) = p$ for every atomic formula p. Moreover, given formulas $\psi_1, \ldots, \psi_n$, $\sigma_{\psi_1, \ldots, \psi_n}$ denotes the substitution σ such that $\sigma(p_i) = \psi_i$ for $1 \leq i \leq n$ and $\sigma(p_i) = p_i$ for $i > n$.

2.1   Single-Conclusion Canonical Systems

Definition 2. *A single-conclusion sequent calculus is called a (single-conclusion) canonical system iff its axioms are sequents of the form* $\psi \Rightarrow \psi$ *(identity axioms), cut and weakening are among its rules, and each of its other rules is either a single-conclusion canonical right rule or a single-conclusion canonical left rule, where:*

1. *A (single-conclusion canonical) left rule for a connective* $\diamond$ *of arity n is an expression of the form:* $\langle \{\Pi_i \Rightarrow E_i\}_{1 \leq i \leq m}, \{\Sigma_i \Rightarrow\}_{1 \leq i \leq k}\rangle / \diamond(p_1, \ldots, p_n) \Rightarrow,$

where $m, k \geq 0$, $\Pi_i \cup E_i \subseteq \{p_1, \ldots, p_n\}$ *for* $1 \leq i \leq m$, *and* $\Sigma_i \subseteq \{p_1, \ldots, p_n\}$
for $1 \leq i \leq k$. *The sequents* $\Pi_i \Rightarrow E_i$ $(1 \leq i \leq m)$ *are called the* hard premises
of the rule, while $\Sigma_i \Rightarrow$ $(1 \leq i \leq k)$ *are its* soft premises, *and* $\diamond(p_1, \ldots, p_n) \Rightarrow$
is its conclusion.
An application *of such rule is any inference step of the form:*

$$\frac{\{\Gamma, \sigma(\Pi_i) \Rightarrow \sigma(E_i)\}_{1 \leq i \leq m} \quad \{\Gamma, \sigma(\Sigma_i) \Rightarrow E\}_{1 \leq i \leq k}}{\Gamma, \sigma(\diamond(p_1, \ldots, p_n)) \Rightarrow E}$$

where $\Gamma \Rightarrow E$ *is an arbitrary sequent, and* σ *is a substitution.*

2. *A* (single-conclusion canonical) right rule *for a connective* $\diamond$ *of arity* n *is an expression of the form:* $\{\Pi_i \Rightarrow E_i\}_{1 \leq i \leq m} / \Rightarrow \diamond(p_1, \ldots, p_n)$, *where* m, *and* $\Pi_i \Rightarrow$
   E_i *are as above.* $\Pi_i \Rightarrow E_i$ $(1 \leq i \leq m)$ *are called the* premises *of the rule, and*
   $\Rightarrow \diamond(p_1, \ldots, p_n)$ *is its* conclusion.
   An application *of such rule is any inference step of the form:*

$$\frac{\{\Gamma, \sigma(\Pi_i) \Rightarrow \sigma(E_i)\}_{1 \leq i \leq m}}{\Gamma \Rightarrow \sigma(\diamond(p_1, \ldots, p_n))}$$

where Γ *is a finite set of formulas and* σ *is a substitution.*

Given a canonical system $\mathbf{G}$, *and a set of sequents* $\mathcal{S} \cup \{s\}$, *we write* $\mathcal{S} \vdash_{\mathbf{G}} s$ *iff there exists a derivation in* $\mathbf{G}$ *of* s *from* $\mathcal{S}$.

The following condition of coherence,[2] characterizing (a stronger form of) cut-admissibility in canonical systems, is an extension of the analogous condition for multiple-conclusion canonical systems (see [1]).

Definition 3. *A set* $\mathcal{R}$ *of canonical rules for an* n-*ary connective* $\diamond$ *is* coherent *if* $S_1 \cup S_2 \cup S_3$ *is classically inconsistent whenever* $\mathcal{R}$ *contains both* $\langle S_1, S_2 \rangle / \diamond$
$(p_1, \ldots, p_n) \Rightarrow$ *and* $S_3 / \Rightarrow \diamond(p_1, \ldots, p_n)$. *A canonical system* $\mathbf{G}$ *is called* coherent *if for each connective* $\diamond$, *the set of rules for* $\diamond$ *in* $\mathbf{G}$ *is coherent.*

2.2   Non-deterministic Kripke-Style Semantics

Definition 4. *Let* $\mathcal{F}$ *be a set of formulas closed under subformulas. An* $\mathcal{F}$-*semiframe is a triple* $\mathcal{W} = \langle W, \leq, v \rangle$ *such that:*

1. $\langle W, \leq \rangle$ *is a nonempty partially ordered set, whose elements are called* worlds.
2. v *is a function from* $W \times \mathcal{F}$ *to* $\{t, f\}$ *obeying the persistence condition, i.e.*
   $v(a, \varphi) = t$ *implies* $v(b, \varphi) = t$ *for every* $b \geq a$.

When $\mathcal{F} = Frm_{\mathcal{L}}$ *then the* $\mathcal{F}$-*semiframe is called a* frame.

Definition 5. *Let* $\mathcal{W} = \langle W, \leq, v \rangle$ *be an* $\mathcal{F}$-*semiframe, and let* $a \in W$.

---

[2] Coherence is also equivalent to the reductivity condition of [6], which applies in presence of arbitrary structural rules.

1. *A sequent* $\Gamma \Rightarrow E$ *is* locally true *in a iff* $\Gamma \cup E \subseteq \mathcal{F}$ *and either* $v(a, \psi) = f$ *for some* $\psi \in \Gamma$, *or* $E = \{\varphi\}$ *and* $v(a, \varphi) = t$.
2. *A sequent* s *is* true *in a iff* s *is locally true in every* $b \geq a$.
3. $\mathcal{W}$ *is a* model *of a sequent* s *if* s *is locally true in every* $b \in W$. $\mathcal{W}$ *is a model of a set of sequents* $\mathcal{S}$ *if it is a model of every* $s \in \mathcal{S}$.

Definition 6. *Let* $\mathcal{W} = \langle W, \leq, v \rangle$ *be an* $\mathcal{F}$*-semiframe.*

1. *Let* σ *be a substitution, and let* $a \in W$.
   (a) σ *(locally)* satisfies *a sequent* $\Gamma \Rightarrow E$ *in* a *if* $\sigma(\Gamma) \Rightarrow \sigma(E)$ *is (locally) true in* a.
   (b) σ fulfils *a* left rule r *in* a *if it satisfies in* a *every hard premise of* r, *and locally satisfies in* a *every soft premise of* r.
   (c) σ fulfils *a* right rule r *in* a *if it satisfies in* a *every premise of* r.
2. *Let* r *be a canonical rule for an* n-*ary connective* $\diamond$. $\mathcal{W}$ respects r *if for every* $a \in W$ *and every substitution* σ: *if* σ *fulfils* r *in* a *and* $\sigma(\diamond(p_1, \ldots, p_n)) \in \mathcal{F}$ *then* σ *locally satisfies* r's *conclusion in* a.
3. *Given a coherent canonical system* **G**, $\mathcal{W}$ *is called* **G**-legal *if it respects all the rules of* **G**.

Henceforth, when speaking of (local) trueness of sequents and fulfilment of rules by substitutions, we add "with respect to $\mathcal{W}$", whenever the (semi)frame $\mathcal{W}$ is not clear from context.

Note that a certain substitution σ may not fulfil any right rule for an n-ary connective $\diamond$ in a world a of a **G**-legal frame, and at the same time σ may not fulfil any left rule for $\diamond$ in all worlds $b \geq a$. In this case there are no restrictions on the truth-value assigned to $\sigma(\diamond(p_1, \ldots, p_n))$ in a, and the semantics of **G** is non-deterministic.

Definition 7. *Let* **G** *be a coherent canonical system, and* $\mathcal{S} \cup \{s\}$ *be a set of sequents.* $\mathcal{S} \vDash_{\mathbf{G}} s$ *iff every* **G**-*legal frame which is a model of* $\mathcal{S}$ *is a model of* s.

Theorem 1 (7.1 in [3]). *Let* **G** *be a coherent canonical system, and* $\mathcal{F}$ *be a set of formulas closed under subformulas. If* $\mathcal{W} = \langle W, \leq, v \rangle$ *is a* **G**-*legal* $\mathcal{F}$-*semiframe, then* v *can be extended to a function* v' *so that* $\mathcal{W}' = \langle W, \leq, v' \rangle$ *is a* **G**-*legal frame.*

The above theorem ensures that the semantics of **G**-legal semiframes is analytic, in the sense that every **G**-legal semiframe can be extended to a **G**-legal (full) frame. This means that in order to determine whether $\mathcal{S} \vDash_{\mathbf{G}} s$, it suffices to consider semiframes, defined only on the set of all subformulas of $\mathcal{S} \cup \{s\}$.

The following theorems establish an exact correspondence between coherent canonical systems, Kripke semantics and (strong) cut-admissibility. In what follows, **G** is a coherent canonical system.

Theorem 2 (6.1 in [3]). *If* $\mathcal{S} \vdash_{\mathbf{G}} s$ *then* $\mathcal{S} \vDash_{\mathbf{G}} s$.

Theorem 3 (6.3 in [3]). *If* $\mathcal{S} \vDash_{\mathbf{G}} s$ *then* $\mathcal{S} \vdash_{\mathbf{G}} s$, *and moreover, there exists a proof in* **G** *of* s *from* $\mathcal{S}$ *in which all cut-formulas appear in* $\mathcal{S}$.

Theorem 3 will be strengthened in the proof of Theorem 4 below. In order to make this paper self-contained, we include here an outline of the original proof.

Proof (Outline). Assume that s does not have a proof in **G** from $\mathcal{S}$ in which all cut-formulas appear in $\mathcal{S}$ (call such a proof a *legal* proof). We construct a **G**-legal frame $\mathcal{W}$ which is a model of $\mathcal{S}$ but not of s. Let $\mathcal{F}$ be the set of subformulas of $\mathcal{S} \cup \{s\}$. Given a set $E \subseteq \mathcal{F}$, which is either a singleton or empty, call a theory $\mathcal{T} \subseteq \mathcal{F}$ *E-maximal* if there is no finite subset $\Gamma \subseteq \mathcal{T}$ such that $\Gamma \Rightarrow E$ has a legal proof, but every proper extension $\mathcal{T}' \subseteq \mathcal{F}$ of $\mathcal{T}$ contains such a finite subset Γ. Now let $\mathcal{W} = \langle W, \subseteq, v \rangle$, where W is the set of all E-maximal theories for some $E \subseteq \mathcal{F}$, and v is defined inductively as follows:
For atomic formulas, $v(\mathcal{T}, p) = t$ iff $p \in \mathcal{T}$. Suppose $v(\mathcal{T}, \psi_i)$ has been defined for every $\mathcal{T} \in W$ and $1 \leq i \leq n$. We let $v(\mathcal{T}, \diamond(\psi_1, \ldots, \psi_n)) = t$ iff at least one of the following holds with respect to the semiframe at this stage:

1. There exists a right rule for $\diamond$ which is fulfilled in $\mathcal{T}$ by $\sigma_{\psi_1, \ldots, \psi_n}$.
2. $\diamond(\psi_1, \ldots, \psi_n) \in \mathcal{T}$ and there do not exist $\mathcal{T}' \in W$, $\mathcal{T} \subseteq \mathcal{T}'$, and a left rule for $\diamond$ which is fulfilled in $\mathcal{T}'$ by $\sigma_{\psi_1, \ldots, \psi_n}$.

One can now prove that $\mathcal{W}$ is a **G**-legal frame. The fact that $\mathcal{W}$ is a model of $\mathcal{S}$ but not of s follows from the following properties:
For every $\mathcal{T} \in W$ and every formula $\psi \in \mathcal{F}$:

(a) If $\psi \in \mathcal{T}$ then $v(\mathcal{T}, \psi) = t$.
(b) If $\mathcal{T}$ is $\{\psi\}$-maximal then $v(\mathcal{T}, \psi) = f$.

(a) and **(b)** are proven together by a simultaneous induction on the complexity of ψ. For atomic formulas they easily follow from v's definition, and the fact that $p \Rightarrow p$ is an axiom. For the induction step, assume that **(a)** and **(b)** hold for $\psi_1, \ldots, \psi_n \in \mathcal{F}$. We prove **(b)** for $\diamond(\psi_1, \ldots, \psi_n) \in \mathcal{F}$ (**(a)** is proved analogously). Assume that $\mathcal{T}$ is $\{\diamond(\psi_1, \ldots, \psi_n)\}$-maximal, but $v(\mathcal{T}, \diamond(\psi_1, \ldots, \psi_n)) = t$. Thus $\diamond(\psi_1, \ldots, \psi_n) \notin \mathcal{T}$ (because $\diamond(\psi_1, \ldots, \psi_n) \Rightarrow \diamond(\psi_1, \ldots, \psi_n)$ is an axiom). Hence there exists a right rule, $\{\Pi_i \Rightarrow E_i\}_{1 \leq i \leq m}/ \Rightarrow \diamond(p_1, \ldots, p_n)$, which is fulfilled in $\mathcal{T}$ by the substitution $\sigma = \sigma_{\psi_1, \ldots, \psi_n}$. It follows that there exists $1 \leq i_0 \leq m$ such that $\Gamma, \sigma(\Pi_{i_0}) \Rightarrow \sigma(E_{i_0})$ has no legal proof for any finite $\Gamma \subseteq \mathcal{T}$. Extend $\mathcal{T} \cup \sigma(\Pi_{i_0})$ to a $\sigma(E_{i_0})$-maximal theory $\mathcal{T}'$. The induction hypothesis implies that σ does not locally satisfy $\Pi_{i_0} \Rightarrow E_{i_0}$ in $\mathcal{T}'$. Thus contradicts our assumption. $\qquad\square$

We now present some examples of canonical rules and their induced semantics (see [3] for more examples).

Example 1 (Implication). All the rules of Gentzen's LJ calculus for intuitionistic logic are canonical. For instance, the rules for implication are:

$$\langle \{\Rightarrow p_1\}, \{p_2 \Rightarrow\} \rangle \ / \ p_1 \supset p_2 \Rightarrow \quad \text{and} \quad \{p_1 \Rightarrow p_2\} \ / \ \Rightarrow p_1 \supset p_2$$

A frame $\mathcal{W} = \langle W, \leq, v \rangle$ respects the rule $(\supset\Rightarrow)$ iff for every $a \in W$, $v(a, \varphi \supset \psi) = f$ whenever $v(b, \varphi) = t$ for every $b \geq a$ and $v(a, \psi) = f$. $\mathcal{W}$ respects $(\Rightarrow\supset)$ iff for every $a \in W$, $v(a, \varphi \supset \psi) = t$ whenever for every $b \geq a$, either $v(b, \varphi) = f$ or $v(b, \psi) = t$. Using the persistence condition, it is easy to see that the two rules impose the well-known Kripke semantics for intuitionistic implication ([8]).

Example 2 (Affirmation). The unary connective $\rhd$ is defined by the rules:

$$\langle \emptyset, \{p_1 \Rightarrow\}\rangle \; / \; \rhd \, p_1 \Rightarrow \quad \text{and} \quad \{\Rightarrow p_1\} \; / \; \Rightarrow\rhd \, p_1$$

A frame $\mathcal{W} = \langle W, \leq, v \rangle$ respects the rule $(\rhd\Rightarrow)$ if $v(a, \rhd \, \psi) = f$ whenever $v(a, \psi) = f$. It respects $(\Rightarrow\rhd)$ if $v(a, \rhd \, \psi) = t$ whenever $v(b, \psi) = t$ for every $b \geq a$. By the persistence condition, this means that for every $a \in W$, $v(a, \rhd \, \psi)$ simply equals $v(a, \psi)$.

Example 3 (Weak Affirmation). The unary connective $\blacktriangleright$ is defined by the rules:

$$\langle \{p_1 \Rightarrow\}, \emptyset \rangle \; / \; \blacktriangleright \, p_1 \Rightarrow \quad \text{and} \quad \{\Rightarrow p_1\} \; / \; \Rightarrow\blacktriangleright \, p_1$$

A frame $\mathcal{W} = \langle W, \leq, v \rangle$ respects the rule $(\blacktriangleright\Rightarrow)$ if $v(a, \blacktriangleright \, \psi) = f$ whenever $v(b, \psi) = f$ for every $b \geq a$. It respects $(\Rightarrow\blacktriangleright)$ if $v(a, \blacktriangleright \, \psi) = t$ whenever $v(b, \psi) = t$ for every $b \geq a$. This implies that $v(a, \blacktriangleright \, \psi)$ is free to be t or f when $v(a, \psi) = f$ and $v(b, \psi) = t$ for some $b > a$ (hence this semantics is "non-deterministic"). In particular it follows that this connective cannot be expressed by the usual intuitionistic connectives.

Applications of the rules for $\supset$ are the standard ones, while those for $\rhd$ and $\blacktriangleright$ have the following forms:

$$\frac{\Gamma, \varphi \Rightarrow E}{\Gamma, \rhd \, \varphi \Rightarrow E} \qquad \frac{\Gamma \Rightarrow \varphi}{\Gamma \Rightarrow\rhd \, \varphi} \qquad \frac{\Gamma, \varphi \Rightarrow}{\Gamma, \blacktriangleright \, \varphi \Rightarrow E} \qquad \frac{\Gamma \Rightarrow \varphi}{\Gamma \Rightarrow\blacktriangleright \, \varphi}$$

3   Deterministic Connectives

In general, an n-ary connective $\diamond$ is called deterministic (see e.g. [2]), if the truth-functionality principle holds for it. In other words, the truth-values assigned to $\psi_1, \ldots, \psi_n$ uniquely determine the truth-value assigned to $\diamond(\psi_1, \ldots, \psi_n)$. Adapting this property for Kripke-style semantics, one can require that the truth-values assigned to $\psi_1, \ldots, \psi_n$ *in every world of the frame* would uniquely determine whether or not the frame is a model of $\Rightarrow \diamond(\psi_1, \ldots, \psi_n)$ (i.e. $\diamond(\psi_1, \ldots, \psi_n)$ is true in all worlds). This can be formalized as follows.

Definition 8. *Two $\mathcal{F}$-semiframes $\mathcal{W}_1$ and $\mathcal{W}_2$ agree on some $\psi \in \mathcal{F}$, if either both are models of $\Rightarrow \psi$, or both are not models of $\Rightarrow \psi$.*

Henceforth we denote by $SF[\psi]$ and $PSF[\psi]$ the sets of subformulas of a formula ψ and proper subformulas of ψ, respectively.

Definition 9. *Let $\mathbf{G}$ be a coherent canonical system.*

1. *Given a formula ψ, a $\mathbf{G}$-legal $PSF[\psi]$-semiframe $\mathcal{W}$ is called ψ-determined in $\mathbf{G}$ if all $\mathbf{G}$-legal $SF[\psi]$-semiframes extending $\mathcal{W}$ agree on ψ.*
2. *$\diamond$ admits* unique analycity *in $\mathbf{G}$ if for every $\psi_1, \ldots, \psi_n \in Frm_{\mathcal{L}}$, every $\mathbf{G}$-legal $PSF[\diamond(\psi_1, \ldots, \psi_n)]$-semiframe is $\diamond(\psi_1, \ldots, \psi_n)$-determined in $\mathbf{G}$.*

Example 4. Consider the coherent canonical system $\mathbf{G}$ consisting of the two rules for $\blacktriangleright$ from Example 3. Let $W = \{a, b\}$ and $\leq = \{\langle a, a \rangle, \langle b, b \rangle, \langle a, b \rangle\}$. Consider a $\{p_1\}$-semiframe $\mathcal{W} = \langle W, \leq, v \rangle$, where $v(a, p_1) = f$ and $v(b, p_1) = t$. Let $\mathcal{W}_1 = \langle W, \leq, v_1 \rangle$ and $\mathcal{W}_2 = \langle W, \leq, v_2 \rangle$ be two $\{p_1, \blacktriangleright p_1\}$-semiframes which extend $\mathcal{W}$, where $v_1(a, \blacktriangleright p_1) = f$ and $v_1(b, \blacktriangleright p_1) = v_2(a, \blacktriangleright p_1) = v_2(b, \blacktriangleright p_1) = t$. Following Example 3, both semiframes are $\mathbf{G}$-legal. Clearly, $\mathcal{W}_1$ and $\mathcal{W}_2$ do not agree on $\blacktriangleright p_1$. It follows that $\blacktriangleright$ does not admit *unique analycity* in $\mathbf{G}$.

We introduce below an alternative definition of determinism of connectives and show its equivalence with unique analycity.

Definition 10. *A $\{p_1, \ldots, p_n\}$-semiframe $\mathcal{W} = \langle W, \leq, v \rangle$, such that $\langle W, \leq \rangle$ has a minimum is called an n-atomic frame. We denote by $\min(\mathcal{W})$ the minimum of $\langle W, \leq \rangle$.*

Definition 11. *An n-ary connective $\diamond$ is called* deterministic *in a coherent canonical system $\mathbf{G}$, if for every n-atomic frame $\mathcal{W} = \langle W, \leq, v \rangle$, either σ_{id} fulfils a right rule for $\diamond$ in $\min(\mathcal{W})$, or σ_{id} fulfils a left rule for $\diamond$ in some $b \in W$.*

Proposition 1. *If an n-ary connective $\diamond$ is deterministic in a coherent canonical system $\mathbf{G}$, then for every $\mathbf{G}$-legal frame $\mathcal{W} = \langle W, \leq, v \rangle$, $a \in W$ and a substitution σ, either σ fulfils a right rule for $\diamond$ in a, or σ fulfils a left rule for $\diamond$ in some $b \in W$ such that $b \geq a$.*

Proof. Let $\mathcal{W} = \langle W, \leq, v \rangle$ be a $\mathbf{G}$-legal frame, let $a \in W$, and let σ be a substitution. Define an n-atomic frame $\mathcal{W}' = \langle W', \leq', v' \rangle$, where $W' = \{b \in W \mid b \geq a\}$, $\leq'$ is the restriction of $\leq$ to W', and $v'(b, p_i) = v(b, \sigma(p_i))$ for $1 \leq i \leq n$ and $b \in W'$. Note that $a = \min(\mathcal{W}')$. Since $\diamond$ is deterministic in $\mathbf{G}$, either σ_{id} fulfils a right rule r for $\diamond$ in $\min(\mathcal{W}')$ with respect to $\mathcal{W}'$, or σ_{id} fulfils a left rule r for $\diamond$ in some $b \in W'$ such that $b \geq' a$ with respect to $\mathcal{W}'$. In the first case, it easily follows that σ fulfils r in a with respect to $\mathcal{W}$. Similarly, in the second case, it follows that since $b \geq' a$, also $b \geq a$, and so σ fulfils r in b with respect to $\mathcal{W}$. $\quad\square$

Proposition 2. *Let $\mathbf{G}$ be a coherent canonical system. A connective $\diamond$ is deterministic in $\mathbf{G}$ iff it admits unique analycity in $\mathbf{G}$.*

Proof. $(\Rightarrow)$: Assume that $\diamond$ is deterministic in $\mathbf{G}$. Let $\psi_1, \ldots, \psi_n \in Frm_{\mathcal{L}}$ and let $\mathcal{W} = \langle W, \leq, v \rangle$ be a $\mathbf{G}$-legal $PSF[\diamond(\psi_1, \ldots, \psi_n)]$-semiframe. We show that $\mathcal{W}$ is $\diamond(\psi_1, \ldots, \psi_n)$-determined in $\mathbf{G}$. Indeed, let $\mathcal{W}_1 = \langle W, \leq, v_1 \rangle$ and $\mathcal{W}_2 = \langle W, \leq, v_2 \rangle$ be $\mathbf{G}$-legal $SF[\diamond(\psi_1, \ldots, \psi_n)]$-semiframes which extend $\mathcal{W}$. We show that $v_1(a, \diamond(\psi_1, \ldots, \psi_n)) = v_2(a, \diamond(\psi_1, \ldots, \psi_n))$ for every $a \in W$, and so $\mathcal{W}_1$ and $\mathcal{W}_2$ agree on ψ. Let $a \in W$. By Proposition 1, and since v_1 and v_2 are defined identically on $\psi_1, \ldots, \psi_n$ one of the following holds:

- $\sigma_{\psi_1,\ldots,\psi_n}$ fulfils a right rule for $\diamond$ in a with respect to $\mathcal{W}_1$ and to $\mathcal{W}_2$. Since they are both **G**-legal, $v_1(a, \diamond(\psi_1, \ldots, \psi_n)) = v_2(a, \diamond(\psi_1, \ldots, \psi_n)) = t$.
- $\sigma_{\psi_1,\ldots,\psi_n}$ fulfils a left rule for $\diamond$ in some $b \geq a$ with respect to $\mathcal{W}_1$ and to $\mathcal{W}_2$. Since they are both **G**-legal, $v_1(b, \diamond(\psi_1, \ldots, \psi_n)) = v_2(b, \diamond(\psi_1, \ldots, \psi_n)) = f$. By the persistence condition $v_1(a, \diamond(\psi_1, \ldots, \psi_n)) = v_2(a, \diamond(\psi_1, \ldots, \psi_n)) = f$.

($\Leftarrow$) : Assume that $\diamond$ is not deterministic in **G**. By definition, there exists an n-atomic frame, $\mathcal{W} = \langle W, \leq, v \rangle$, such that σ_{id} does not fulfil any right rule for $\diamond$ in $\min(\mathcal{W})$, and it does not fulfil any left rule for $\diamond$ in any $b \in W$. Since $\mathcal{W}$ is n-atomic frame, it is vacuously **G**-legal. Define $\mathcal{W}_1 = \langle W, \leq, v_1 \rangle$ and $\mathcal{W}_2 = \langle W, \leq, v_2 \rangle$ to be $SF[\diamond(p_1, \ldots, p_n)]$-semiframes which extend $\mathcal{W}$ such that: (1) $v_1(\min(\mathcal{W}), \diamond(p_1, \ldots, p_n)) = f$ and $v_1(b, \diamond(p_1, \ldots, p_n)) = t$ for every $b > \min(\mathcal{W})$; and (2) $v_2(b, \diamond(p_1, \ldots, p_n)) = t$ for every $b \in W$. It is easy to see that $\mathcal{W}_1$ and $\mathcal{W}_2$ are **G**-legal extensions of $\mathcal{W}$. Clearly $\mathcal{W}_1$ and $\mathcal{W}_2$ do not agree on $\diamond(p_1, \ldots, p_n)$. $\square$

4   Axiom-Expansion

Below we show that in a coherent canonical system determinism of its connectives is equivalent to axiom expansion. We use the terms *atomic axioms* for axioms of the form $p \Rightarrow p$ (where p is an atomic formula), and *non-atomic axioms* for axioms of the form $\diamond(\psi_1, \ldots, \psi_n) \Rightarrow \diamond(\psi_1, \ldots, \psi_n)$.

Definition 12. *An n-ary connective $\diamond$ admits* axiom-expansion *in a coherent canonical system* **G***, if $\diamond(p_1, \ldots, p_n) \Rightarrow \diamond(p_1, \ldots, p_n)$ has a cut-free proof in* **G** *that does not contain non-atomic axioms.*

Let **G** be a coherent canonical system in the language $\mathcal{L}$. Henceforth we denote by $\mathbf{G}^{\triangleright}$ the system **G** augmented with the rules for $\triangleright$ in Example 2 ($\mathbf{G} = \mathbf{G}^{\triangleright}$ if $\triangleright \in \mathcal{L}$). It is easy to see that $\mathbf{G}^{\triangleright}$ is coherent.

Lemma 1. *Let $\diamond$ be an n-ary connective ($n \geq 1$), and* **G** *be a coherent canonical system. If $\vdash_{\mathbf{G}^{\triangleright}} \diamond(p_1, \ldots, p_n) \Rightarrow \diamond(\triangleright\, p_1, \ldots, p_n)$ then $\diamond$ is deterministic in* **G***.*

Proof. Assume that $\diamond$ is not deterministic in **G**. Thus, there exists an n-atomic frame, $\mathcal{W} = \langle W, \leq, v \rangle$, such that σ_{id} does not fulfil any right rule for $\diamond$ in $\min(\mathcal{W})$, and it does not fulfil any left rule for $\diamond$ in any $b \in W$. Let $\mathcal{F} = \{p_1, \ldots, p_n, \triangleright\, p_1, \diamond(\triangleright\, p_1, \ldots, p_n), \diamond(p_1, \ldots, p_n)\}$. Define an $\mathcal{F}$-semiframe $\mathcal{W}_1 = \langle W, \leq, v_1 \rangle$ which extends $\mathcal{W}$: (a) For every $b \in W$, $v_1(b, \diamond(p_1, \ldots, p_n)) = t$ and $v_1(b, \triangleright\, p_1) = v(b, p_1)$; (b) $v_1(\min(\mathcal{W}), \diamond(\triangleright\, p_1, \ldots, p_n)) = f$, and $v_1(b, \diamond(\triangleright\, p_1, \ldots, p_n)) = t$ for every $b > \min(\mathcal{W})$. It is easy to see that $\mathcal{W}_1$ is a $\mathbf{G}^{\triangleright}$-legal $\mathcal{F}$-semiframe. Hence by Theorem 1, it can be extended to a $\mathbf{G}^{\triangleright}$-legal frame $\mathcal{W}_1'$. $\mathcal{W}_1'$ is not a model of $\diamond(p_1, \ldots, p_n) \Rightarrow \diamond(\triangleright\, p_1, \ldots, p_n)$ (since it is not locally true in $\min(\mathcal{W})$). Therefore, $\nvdash_{\mathbf{G}^{\triangleright}} \diamond(p_1, \ldots, p_n) \Rightarrow \diamond(\triangleright\, p_1, \ldots, p_n)$. $\square$

Theorem 4. *Let* **G** *be a coherent canonical system. An n-ary connective $\diamond$ admits axiom-expansion in* **G** *iff $\diamond$ is deterministic in* **G***.*

Proof. $(\Rightarrow)$: Assume we have a cut-free proof δ of $\diamond(p_1, \ldots, p_n) \Rightarrow \diamond(p_1, \ldots, p_n)$ in $\mathbf{G}$ that uses only atomic axioms. By suitably modifying δ we can obtain a proof $\delta^{\triangleright}$ of $\diamond(p_1, \ldots, p_n) \Rightarrow \diamond(\triangleright\ p_1, \ldots, p_n)$ in the extended system $\mathbf{G}^{\triangleright}$. The claim therefore follows by Lemma 1. $\delta^{\triangleright}$ is obtained from δ as follows: as δ contains only atomic axioms, the formula $\diamond(p_1, \ldots, p_n)$ is inferred in succedents of sequents in (possibly) various nodes of δ by applications of weakening or of right rules for $\diamond$.[3] In the first case, we simply replace each application of weakening with formula $\diamond(p_1, \ldots, p_n)$, with an application of weakening with formula $\diamond(\triangleright\ p_1, \ldots, p_n)$. When $\diamond(p_1, \ldots, p_n)$ is inferred in a sequent $\Gamma \Rightarrow \diamond(p_1, \ldots, p_n)$ by a right rule r for $\diamond$, we consider the premise of this application. These have the form $\Gamma, \Pi, p_1 \Rightarrow E$; $\Gamma, \Pi \Rightarrow p_1$; and/or $\Gamma, \Pi \Rightarrow E$. Therefore we first apply the left and/or right rules for $\triangleright$ to infer $\Gamma, \Pi, \triangleright\ p_1 \Rightarrow E$ and/or $\Gamma, \Pi \Rightarrow \triangleright\ p_1$, and then we apply r to derive the sequent $\Gamma \Rightarrow \diamond(\triangleright\ p_1, \ldots, p_n)$. The rest of the proof is changed accordingly.

$(\Leftarrow)$: We first prove the following strengthening of Theorem 3: $(*)$ If $\mathcal{S} \vDash_{\mathbf{G}} s$ then there exists a proof in $\mathbf{G}$ of s from $\mathcal{S}$ in which all cut-formulas appear in $\mathcal{S}$, and identity axioms of the form $\diamond(\psi_1, \ldots, \psi_n) \Rightarrow \diamond(\psi_1, \ldots, \psi_n)$ are not used when $\diamond$ is deterministic in $\mathbf{G}$. Since every frame is a model of $\diamond(p_1, \ldots, p_n) \Rightarrow \diamond(p_1, \ldots, p_n)$ for every n-ary connective $\diamond$, it follows that when $\diamond$ is deterministic in $\mathbf{G}$, $\diamond(p_1, \ldots, p_n) \Rightarrow \diamond(p_1, \ldots, p_n)$ has a cut-free proof in $\mathbf{G}$ that uses only atomic axioms.

To prove $(*)$, note that the only place in which non-atomic axioms are used in the proof of Theorem 3 (see a proof outline in Section 2) is for proving property **(b)**, namely that if $\mathcal{T}$ is $\{\psi\}$-maximal then $v(\mathcal{T}, \psi) = f$.[4] More specifically, non-atomic axioms are only used to dismiss the possibility that $\diamond(\psi_1, \ldots, \psi_n) \in \mathcal{T}$ when $\mathcal{T}$ is $\{\diamond(\psi_1, \ldots, \psi_n)\}$-maximal and $v(\mathcal{T}, \diamond(\psi_1, \ldots, \psi_n)) = t$. If $\diamond$ is deterministic in $\mathbf{G}$, we can handle this possibility as follows:

> Since $\mathcal{W}$ is $\mathbf{G}$-legal and $v(\mathcal{T}, \diamond(\psi_1, \ldots, \psi_n)) = t$, there cannot exist $\mathcal{T}' \in W$, $\mathcal{T} \subseteq \mathcal{T}'$, and a left rule for $\diamond$ which is fulfilled in $\mathcal{T}'$ by $\sigma_{\psi_1, \ldots, \psi_n}$. When $\diamond$ is deterministic in $\mathbf{G}$, by Proposition 1, there exists a right rule for $\diamond$, which is fulfilled in $\mathcal{T}$ by $\sigma_{\psi_1, \ldots, \psi_n}$. The rest of the proof proceeds as in the original proof.

$\square$

Remark 1. [6] investigates single-conclusion systems with non-standard sets of structural rules. An algebraic semantics using phase spaces is provided for left and right introduction rules for connectives; a result similar to Theorem 4 is shown, namely a connective $\diamond$ has a "deterministic semantics" (i.e., the interpretations for the left and right rules coincide) iff $\diamond$ admits axiom expansion.

5   Invertibility of Rules

We investigate the connection between rules invertibility and determinism in coherent canonical systems.

---

[3] Weakening can also be done by applying a left rule which does not have soft premises.

[4] Identity axioms are not needed to prove property **(a)** (see Theorem 6.3 in [3]).

Definition 13. *A canonical rule r is* canonically invertible *in a coherent canonical system* **G** *iff each premise of r has a proof in* **G** *from r's conclusion.*

In contrast with the multiple-conclusion case (see [2]) determinism does not guarantee invertibility of *left rules* and the latter does not imply determinism. One direction can be easily seen by considering the usual left rule for implication (Example 1): $\supset$ is deterministic but $(\supset\!\Rightarrow)$ is not canonically invertible. The other direction follows by the next example:

Example 5. ▶ is non-deterministic in a canonical system including the two rules for ▶ (see Example 4). However, the left rule for ▶ is canonically invertible ($p_1 \Rightarrow$ can be easily derived from ▶ $p_1 \Rightarrow$ using an identity axiom, the rule $(\Rightarrow\!▶)$ and a cut on ▶ p_1).

For right rules the following theorem holds (notice that the $(\Rightarrow)$ direction needs the existence in **G** of *exactly one* right rule for $\diamond$):

Theorem 5. *If a coherent canonical system* **G** *includes exactly one right rule for an n-ary connective $\diamond$, then $\diamond$ is deterministic in* **G** *if and only if this rule is canonically invertible in* **G**.

Proof. $(\Rightarrow)$: Let r be the right rule for $\diamond$, and let s be one of its premises. We show that $\Rightarrow \diamond(p_1, \ldots, p_n) \vDash_{\mathbf{G}} s$. Canonical invertibility of r then follows by Theorem 3. For this we show that every **G**-legal frame that is not a model of s is also not a model of $\Rightarrow \diamond(p_1, \ldots, p_n)$. Let $\mathcal{W} = \langle W, \leq, v \rangle$ be a **G**-legal frame, which is not a model of s. By definition, σ_{id} does not locally satisfy s in some $a \in W$. Hence, σ_{id} does not fulfil r in a. Since $\diamond$ is deterministic in **G** and $\diamond$ has no other right rules, Proposition 1 implies that there exists a left rule for $\diamond$, which is fulfilled by σ_{id} in some $b \geq a$. But, since $\mathcal{W}$ is **G**-legal, $\mathcal{W}$ respects this rule, and hence $v(b, \diamond(p_1, \ldots, p_n)) = f$. Hence, $\mathcal{W}$ is not a model of $\Rightarrow \diamond(p_1, \ldots, p_n)$.

$(\Leftarrow)$: Let r be a right rule for $\diamond$. Assume that $\diamond$ is not deterministic in **G**. Thus, there exists an *n*-atomic frame, $\mathcal{W} = \langle W, \leq, v \rangle$, such that σ_{id} does not fulfil r in $\min(\mathcal{W})$, and it does not fulfil any left rule for $\diamond$ in any $b \in W$. In particular, there exists a premise s of r, which is not satisfied in $\min(\mathcal{W})$ by σ_{id}. Define an extension of $\mathcal{W}$, $\mathcal{W}_1 = \langle W, \leq, v_1 \rangle$, which is an $SF[\diamond(p_1, \ldots, p_n)]$-semiframe, such that for every $a \in W$, $v_1(a, \diamond(p_1, \ldots, p_n)) = t$. It is easy to see that $\mathcal{W}_1$ is a **G**-legal $SF[\diamond(p_1, \ldots, p_n)]$-semiframe. Thus, by Theorem 1, it can be extended to a **G**-legal frame, $\mathcal{W}_1' = \langle W, \leq, v_1' \rangle$. $\mathcal{W}_1'$ is a model of $\Rightarrow \diamond(p_1, \ldots, p_n)$, but it is not a model of s. By Theorem 3, $\Rightarrow \diamond(p_1, \ldots, p_n) \not\vDash_{\mathbf{G}} s$.   □

6   Matrix-Based (Kripke) Semantics

The formulation of the Kripke-style semantics presented in Section 2.2 is too abstract to provide a constructive method for checking determinism of connectives in canonical systems. In this section we introduce an alternative formulation of this semantics, which is a generalization of the two-valued non-deterministic matrices used in [1,2] to characterize multiple-conclusion canonical systems. The new formulation can be constructively extracted from the rules of a canonical calculus, and it provides an *algorithmic* and natural way of checking determinism of logical connectives.

For an intuitive motivation of this approach, recall that in a (standard or non-deterministic) two-valued matrix, the interpretation of an n-ary connective $\diamond$ is a function applied to n-ary vectors of truth-values. Thus, the truth-value of $\diamond(\psi_1, \ldots, \psi_n)$ depends on (although is not necessarily uniquely determined by) the truth-values assigned to $\psi_1, \ldots, \psi_n$. In the context of Kripke-style frames, however, the interpretation is more complex: the truth-value assigned to $\diamond(\psi_1, \ldots, \psi_n)$ in a world a depends, in addition to the truth-values assigned to $\psi_1, \ldots, \psi_n$ in a, also on the truth-values assigned to these formulas in all worlds $b \geq a$. However, which truth-values are assigned to $\psi_1, \ldots, \psi_n$ in which world is immaterial, what matters is their distribution[5] $D = \{\langle v_1^b, \ldots, v_n^b \rangle |\ b \geq a\}$, where v_i^b is the truth-value assigned to ψ_i in the world b. This information can be captured by an n-ary distribution vector of the form $\langle \langle v_1^a, \ldots, v_n^a \rangle, D \rangle$. Note that since $\geq$ is reflexive, $\langle v_1^a, \ldots, v_n^a \rangle \in D$ for all frames. Moreover, a formula assigned t in some world a remains true also in all accessible worlds $b \geq a$. This can be formalized as follows:

Definition 14. *For $n \geq 1$, an n-ary distribution vector V is a pair of the form $\langle \langle x_1, \ldots, x_n \rangle, D \rangle$ where $x_1, \ldots, x_n \in \{t, f\}$, $D \subseteq \{t, f\}^n$, and which satisfies: (i) $\langle x_1, \ldots, x_n \rangle \in D$, and (ii) if $x_i = t$ then $y_i = t$ for all $\langle y_1, \ldots, y_n \rangle \in D$. We denote the set of n-ary distribution vectors by $\mathbf{V}_n$.*

Definition 15. *A two-valued distribution Nmatrix (2Nmatrix) $\mathcal{M}$ for $\mathcal{L}$ is a set of (two-valued) interpretations, such that for every n-ary connective $\diamond$ of $\mathcal{L}$, $\mathcal{M}$ includes an interpretation function $\tilde{\diamond}_{\mathcal{M}} : \mathbf{V}_n \to P^+(\{t, f\})$.*

Definition 16. *Let $\langle x_1, \ldots, x_n \rangle \in \{t, f\}^n$. A sequent $\Pi \Rightarrow E$ over $\{p_1, \ldots, p_n\}$ is compatible with $\langle x_1, \ldots, x_n \rangle$ if any two-valued valuation v, such that $v(p_i) = x_i$ satisfies $\Pi \Rightarrow E$ (i.e., there is some $1 \leq i \leq n$, such that either $p_i \in \Pi$ and $v(p_i) = f$, or $p_i \in E$ and $v(p_i) = t$).*

Definition 17. *Let $V = \langle \overline{x}, D \rangle$ be any n-ary distribution vector.*

1. *A right rule r is V-valid if every premise of r is compatible with every $\overline{y} \in D$.*
2. *A left rule of r is V-valid if every hard premise of r is compatible with every $\overline{y} \in D$, and every soft premise of r is compatible with $\overline{x}$.*

Definition 18. *Let $\mathbf{G}$ be a coherent canonical system. The 2Nmatrix $\mathcal{M}_G$ induced by $\mathbf{G}$ is defined as follows. For every n-ary connective $\diamond$ and every $V \in \mathbf{V}_n$:*

$$\tilde{\diamond}_{\mathcal{M}_G}(V) = \begin{cases} \{t\} & \mathbf{G} \text{ has a } V\text{-valid right rule for } \diamond \\ \{f\} & \mathbf{G} \text{ has a } V\text{-valid left rule for } \diamond \\ \{t, f\} & \text{otherwise} \end{cases}$$

---

[5] A "distribution-based approach" is usually used to interpret quantifiers in many-valued matrices (see, e.g. [11]). For instance, the classical interpretation of $\forall$ is a function $\tilde{\forall} : P^+(\{t, f\}) \to \{t, f\}$. Given a structure with a set of elements D, we compute $\tilde{\forall}(\{v(\psi\{\overline{a}/x\}) |\ a \in D\})$, where $\overline{a}$ is an individual constant denoting a for every $a \in D$.

It is easy to see that checking V-validity of rules is constructive. The following proposition guarantees that $\tilde{\diamond}_{\mathcal{M}_G}$ is well-defined:

Proposition 3. *A coherent canonical system $\mathbf{G}$ has no pair of a left and a right rules for the same n-ary connective $\diamond$, which are both V-valid for some $V \in \mathbf{V}_n$.*

Proof. Suppose by contradiction that there are a right rule r_r and a left rule r_l for $\diamond$ in $\mathbf{G}$, which are both V-valid for some $V = \langle \overline{x}, D \rangle \in \mathbf{V}_n$. Since $\overline{x} \in D$, all the premises of r_r and r_l are compatible with $\overline{x}$. Thus these premises are all satisfiable by a classical two-valued valuation, and so are classically consistent, in contradiction to the coherence of $\mathbf{G}$. □

It is important to note that given a coherent canonical system $\mathbf{G}$, its associated 2Nmatrix $\mathcal{M}_G$ does not yet faithfully represent the meaning of the connectives of $\mathbf{G}$, as $\mathcal{M}_G$ might contain some options forbidden by the persistence condition.

Example 6. Let $\mathbf{G}$ be the canonical system consisting only of the right rule for implication and $\mathbf{G}'$ be the system obtained by adding to $\mathbf{G}$ the left rule for implication (see Example 1). The induced 2Nmatrices $\mathcal{M}_G$ and $\mathcal{M}_{G'}$ are displayed in the table below (columns $\tilde{\supset}_{\mathcal{M}_G}$ and $\tilde{\supset}_{\mathcal{M}_{G'}}$, respectively). Note that $\tilde{\supset}_{\mathcal{M}_{G'}}$ contains some non-deterministic choices, although the semantics for implication given in Example 1 is completely deterministic.

	D	$\tilde{\supset}_{\mathcal{M}_G}$	$\tilde{\supset}_{\mathcal{M}_{G'}}$	$\mathsf{R}(\tilde{\supset}_{\mathcal{M}_{G'}})$
$\langle t,t \rangle$	$\{\langle t,t \rangle\}$	$\{t\}$	$\{t\}$	$\{t\}$
$\langle t,f \rangle$	$\{\langle t,f \rangle\}$	$\{t,f\}$	$\{f\}$	$\{f\}$
$\langle t,f \rangle$	$\{\langle t,f \rangle, \langle t,t \rangle\}$	$\{t,f\}$	$\{f\}$	$\{f\}$
$\langle f,t \rangle$	$\{\langle f,t \rangle\}$	$\{t\}$	$\{t\}$	$\{t\}$
$\langle f,t \rangle$	$\{\langle f,t \rangle, \langle t,t \rangle\}$	$\{t\}$	$\{t\}$	$\{t\}$
$\langle f,f \rangle$	$\{\langle f,f \rangle\}$	$\{t\}$	$\{t\}$	$\{t\}$
$\langle f,f \rangle$	$\{\langle f,f \rangle, \langle t,t \rangle\}$	$\{t\}$	$\{t\}$	$\{t\}$
$\langle f,f \rangle$	$\{\langle f,f \rangle, \langle f,t \rangle\}$	$\{t\}$	$\{t\}$	$\{t\}$
$\langle f,f \rangle$	$\{\langle f,f \rangle, \langle t,f \rangle\}$	$\{t,f\}$	$\{t,f\}$	$\{f\}$
$\langle f,f \rangle$	$\{\langle f,f \rangle, \langle t,t \rangle, \langle f,t \rangle\}$	$\{t\}$	$\{t\}$	$\{t\}$
$\langle f,f \rangle$	$\{\langle f,f \rangle, \langle t,f \rangle, \langle f,f \rangle\}$	$\{t,f\}$	$\{t,f\}$	$\{f\}$
$\langle f,f \rangle$	$\{\langle f,f \rangle, \langle t,f \rangle, \langle f,t \rangle\}$	$\{t,f\}$	$\{t,f\}$	$\{f\}$
$\langle f,f \rangle$	$\{\langle f,f \rangle, \langle t,f \rangle, \langle f,t \rangle, \langle t,t \rangle\}$	$\{t,f\}$	$\{t,f\}$	$\{f\}$

We now formulate a procedure for removing the illegal options. As shown below, its application to any 2Nmatrix $\mathcal{M}_G$ leads to a matrix-based representation which faithfully reflects the semantics from Section 2.2.

Definition 19. *Let $\tilde{\diamond} : \mathbf{V}_n \rightarrow P^+(\{t,f\})$ be an interpretation of an n-ary connective $\diamond$. The reduced interpretation $\mathsf{R}(\tilde{\diamond})$ is obtained by the following algorithm:*

- $L_0 \leftarrow \tilde{\diamond}$ *and* $i \leftarrow 0$.
Repeat
    − $i \leftarrow i+1$ *and* $L_i \leftarrow L_{i-1}$.

- Let $V = \langle \overline{x}, D \rangle$, such that $L_{i-1}(V) = \{t, f\}$. If there is some $\overline{y} \in D$, such that for every $D' \subseteq D$, such that $\langle \overline{y}, D' \rangle \in \mathbf{V}_n$: $L_{i-1}(\langle \overline{y}, D' \rangle) = \{f\}$, then $L_i(V) \leftarrow \{f\}$.

Until $L_i = L_{i-1}$

Example 7. By applying the algorithm to the 2Nmatrix $\mathcal{M}_{G'}$ in Example 6, we obtain the reduced 2Nmatrix displayed in the last column of the table above (denoted by $\mathsf{R}(\tilde{\supset}_{\mathcal{M}_{G'}})$). Note that $\mathsf{R}(\tilde{\supset}_{\mathcal{M}_{G'}})$ does not codify a particular Kripke frame, as in the matrix-based semantics for intuitionistic logic described in [10]; $\mathsf{R}(\tilde{\supset}_{\mathcal{M}_{G'}})$ represents instead the "semantic meaning" of intuitionistic implication.

Below we show that for any coherent canonical system $\mathbf{G}$, the determinism of $\mathsf{R}(\tilde{\diamond}_{\mathcal{M}_G})$ is equivalent to the determinism of $\diamond$ in $\mathbf{G}$ (in the sense of Definition 11), thus obtaining an algorithm for checking the latter.

Definition 20. *Given an n-atomic frame $\mathcal{W} = \langle W, \leq, v \rangle$, the distribution vector $\mathsf{V}_{\mathcal{W}}$ induced by $\mathcal{W}$ is defined as follows: $\mathsf{V}_{\mathcal{W}} = \langle \langle v(a, p_1), \ldots, v(a, p_n) \rangle, \mathsf{D}_{\mathcal{W}} \rangle$, where $a = \min(\mathcal{W})$ and $\mathsf{D}_{\mathcal{W}} = \{ \langle v(b, p_1), \ldots, v(b, p_n) \rangle | \ b \in W \}$.*

Lemma 2. *Let $\mathcal{W}$ be an n-atomic frame. σ_{id} fulfils a canonical rule r in $\min(\mathcal{W})$ with respect to $\mathcal{W}$ iff r is $\mathsf{V}_{\mathcal{W}}$-valid.*

Lemma 3. *Let $\mathbf{G}$ be a coherent canonical system for $\mathcal{L}$ and $\diamond$ an n-ary connective of $\mathcal{L}$. If $\mathsf{R}(\tilde{\diamond}_{\mathcal{M}_G})(V) = \{f\}$, then for every n-atomic frame $\mathcal{W}$ inducing V, σ_{id} fulfils a left rule for $\diamond$ of $\mathbf{G}$ in some world $b \geq \min(\mathcal{W})$ with respect to $\mathcal{W}$.*

Proof. We prove by induction on i that the claim holds for every L_i as defined in Definition 19. It follows that the claim holds for $\mathsf{R}(\tilde{\diamond}_{\mathcal{M}_G})$. For $i = 0$, $L_i = \tilde{\diamond}_{\mathcal{M}_G}$, and hence the claim follows from Lemma 2 by the definition of $\mathcal{M}_G$. Suppose that the claim holds for all $i < k$ and let $i = k$. Let $\mathcal{W}$ be an n-atomic frame inducing $V \in \mathbf{V}_n$. If $L_{k-1}(V) = \{f\}$, the claim holds by the induction hypothesis. Otherwise $L_{k-1}(V) = \{t, f\}$, and there is some $\overline{y} \in D$, such that for every $D' \subseteq D$ for which $\langle \overline{y}, D' \rangle \in \mathbf{V}_n$: $L_{k-1}(\langle \overline{y}, D' \rangle) = \{f\}$. Let $b \geq \min(\mathcal{W})$ be a world such that $v(b, p_i) = y_i$ (it exists since $\overline{y} \in D$). Let $D_0 = \{ \langle v(c, p_1), \ldots, v(c, p_n) \rangle | \ c \geq b \}$. Since $D_0 \subseteq D$, $L_{k-1}(V_0) = \{f\}$, where $V_0 = \langle \overline{y}, D_0 \rangle$. Let $\mathcal{W}_0$ be the subframe of $\mathcal{W}$, such that $\min(\mathcal{W}_0) = b$. Since $\mathcal{W}_0$ induces V_0, by the induction hypothesis, there is some $c \geq b$, in which σ_{id} fulfils a left rule r in $\mathbf{G}$ for $\diamond$ with respect to $\mathcal{W}_0$. It easily follows that σ_{id} fulfils r in $c \geq b \geq \min(\mathcal{W})$ with respect to $\mathcal{W}$. $\square$

Theorem 6. *Let $\mathbf{G}$ be a coherent canonical system. An n-ary connective $\diamond$ is deterministic in $\mathbf{G}$ if and only if $\mathsf{R}(\tilde{\diamond}_{\mathcal{M}_G})$ is deterministic (i.e. $\mathsf{R}(\tilde{\diamond}_{\mathcal{M}_G})(V)$ is either $\{t\}$ or $\{f\}$ for every $V \in \mathbf{V}_n$).*

Proof. ($\Leftarrow$): Denote by R_r and R_l the sets of right and left rules for $\diamond$ in $\mathbf{G}$ (respectively). Suppose that $\diamond$ is deterministic in $\mathbf{G}$, and assume by contradiction that $\mathsf{R}(\tilde{\diamond}_{\mathcal{M}_G})(V)$ is not deterministic. Define a partial order on n-ary vectors over $\{t, f\}$ as follows: $\overline{x} <_n \overline{y}$ if for every $1 \leq i \leq n$: either $x_i = y_i$ or $x_i = f$ and

$y_i = t$. Choose $V = \langle \overline{x}, D \rangle \in \mathbf{V}_n$ to be such that $\mathsf{R}(\tilde{\diamond}_{\mathcal{M}_G})(V) = \{t, f\}$ and $\overline{x}$ is maximal with respect to $<_n$. We construct an n-atomic frame $\mathcal{W}$, such that σ_{id} does not fulfil any $r \in R_r$ in $\min(\mathcal{W})$, and any $r \in R_l$ in any $b \geq \min(\mathcal{W})$ (with respect to $\mathcal{W}$). If $D = \{\overline{x}\}$, then let $\mathcal{W}$ be the n-atomic frame with one world a, such that $v(a, p_i) = x_i$. Since $\mathsf{R}(\tilde{\diamond}_{\mathcal{M}_G})(V) = \{t, f\}$, it must be the case that $\tilde{\diamond}_{\mathcal{M}_G}(V) = \{t, f\}$. Then by definition of $\mathcal{M}_G$, there is no V-valid rule in $R_r \cup R_l$. By Lemma 2, σ_{id} does not fulfil any $r \in R_r \cup R_l$ in a with respect to $\mathcal{W}$. Otherwise, $D = \{\overline{x}, \overline{y}^1, \ldots, \overline{y}^m\}$. Let $\mathcal{W}$ be the n-atomic frame $\mathcal{W} = \langle W, \leq, v \rangle$, such that $W = \{a, a_1, \ldots, a_m\}$, where $a < a_j$ for all $1 \leq j \leq m$, $v(a, p_i) = x_i$, and $v(a_j, p_i) = y_i^j$. Like in the above case, it can be shown that σ_{id} does not fulfil any $r \in R_r \cup R_l$ in $a = \min(\mathcal{W})$. It remains to show that no $r \in R_l$ is fulfilled in a_j. Suppose by contradiction that this is the case for some $r \in R_l$ and a_j. Let $\mathcal{W}'$ be the subframe of $\mathcal{W}$ such that $\min(\mathcal{W}') = a_j$. The distribution vector induced by $\mathcal{W}'$ is $V_j = \langle \overline{y}^j, \{\overline{y}^j\} \rangle$. By Lemma 2, r is V_j-valid, and so $\tilde{\diamond}_{\mathcal{M}}(V_j) = \{f\}$. Hence also $\mathsf{R}(\tilde{\diamond}_{\mathcal{M}_G})(V_j) = \{f\}$. One of the following cases holds:

- For all $D_0 \subseteq D$, such that $V' = \langle \overline{y}^j, D_0 \rangle \in \mathbf{V}_n$, $\mathsf{R}(\tilde{\diamond}_{\mathcal{M}_G})(V') = \{f\}$. But then $\mathsf{R}(\tilde{\diamond}_{\mathcal{M}_G})(V) = \{f\}$, contradicting our assumption.
- There is some $D_0 \subseteq D$, such that $V' = \langle \overline{y}^j, D_0 \rangle \in \mathbf{V}_n$ and $\mathsf{R}(\tilde{\diamond}_{\mathcal{M}_G})(V') = \{t\}$, and so also $\tilde{\diamond}_{\mathcal{M}}(V') = \{t\}$. This means that there exists some V'-valid $r \in R_r$. By definition, r is $\langle \overline{y}^j, D' \rangle$-valid for every $D' \subseteq D_0$. It follows that $\tilde{\diamond}_{\mathcal{M}}(\langle \overline{y}^j, \{\overline{y}^j\} \rangle) = \{t\}$, in contradiction to our assumption.
- There is some $D_0 \subseteq D$, such that $V' = \langle \overline{y}^j, D_0 \rangle \in \mathbf{V}_n$ and $\mathsf{R}(\tilde{\diamond}_{\mathcal{M}_G})(V') = \{t, f\}$. But since $\overline{x} <_n \overline{y}^j$, this is in contradiction to the maximality of $\overline{x}$.

Thus it cannot be the case that σ_{id} fulfils a rule from R_l in some $a_j \geq \min(\mathcal{W})$, hence $\diamond$ is not deterministic in $\mathbf{G}$, in contradiction to our assumption.

($\Rightarrow$): Suppose that $\mathsf{R}(\tilde{\diamond}_{\mathcal{M}_G})$ is deterministic and assume by contradiction that there is some n-atomic frame $\mathcal{W}$, such that σ_{id} does not fulfil any right rule of $\mathbf{G}$ for $\diamond$ in $\min(\mathcal{W})$, and any left rule of $\mathbf{G}$ for $\diamond$ in any $b \geq \mathcal{W}$. Let V be the distribution vector induced by $\mathcal{W}$. By Lemma 2, there is no V-valid right rule for $\diamond$ in $\mathbf{G}$, and so by definition of $\mathcal{M}_G$, $\tilde{\diamond}_{\mathcal{M}}(V_{\mathcal{W}}) \neq \{t\}$, and so also $\mathsf{R}(\tilde{\diamond}_{\mathcal{M}_G})(V_{\mathcal{W}}) \neq \{t\}$. Since $\mathsf{R}(\tilde{\diamond}_{\mathcal{M}_G})$ is deterministic, it must be the case that $\mathsf{R}(\tilde{\diamond}_{\mathcal{M}_G})(V_{\mathcal{W}}) = \{f\}$. But then by Lemma 3, for every n-atomic frame $\mathcal{W}'$ inducing V, σ_{id} fulfils a left rule for $\diamond$ in $\mathbf{G}$ in some $b \geq \min(\mathcal{W}')$. In particular, this holds for $\mathcal{W}$, in contradiction to our assumption. □

Corollary 1. *For a coherent canonical system $\mathbf{G}$, the following questions are decidable: (i) Is $\diamond$ deterministic in $\mathbf{G}$? (ii) Does $\mathbf{G}$ admit axiom-expansion? (iii) (If $\mathbf{G}$ has exactly one right rule r for $\diamond$) is r invertible?.*

Finally, we establish the equivalence between the new matrix-based semantics and the non-deterministic Kripke-style semantics of [3].

Theorem 7. *Let $\mathbf{G}$ be a coherent canonical system. A frame $\mathcal{W} = \langle W, \leq, v \rangle$ is $\mathbf{G}$-legal (see Definition 6) iff for every $a \in W$ and every formula $\diamond(\psi_1, \ldots, \psi_n)$,*

$v(a, \diamond(\psi_1, \ldots, \psi_n)) \in \tilde{\diamond}_{\mathcal{M}_G}(\langle \overline{x}, D \rangle)$, where $\overline{x} = \langle v(a, \psi_1), \ldots, v(a, \psi_n) \rangle$ and D is the set $\{\langle v(b, \psi_1), \ldots, v(b, \psi_n) \rangle | \ b \geq a\}$.

Proof. ($\Rightarrow$): Suppose that $\mathcal{W}$ is **G**-legal. Let $a \in W$ and $\diamond(\psi_1, \ldots, \psi_n) \in Frm_{\mathcal{L}}$. Suppose that $\tilde{\diamond}_{\mathcal{M}_G}(\langle \overline{x}, D \rangle) = \{t\}$. By definition of $\mathcal{M}_G$, there is some right rule r for $\diamond$ in **G**, such that every premise of r is compatible with every $\overline{y} \in D$. It is easy to see that this implies that $\sigma_{\psi_1, \ldots, \psi_n}$ fulfils r in a. Since $\mathcal{W}$ is **G**-legal, it respects r, and so $\Rightarrow \diamond(\psi_1, \ldots, \psi_n)$ is locally true in a. It follows that $v(a, \diamond(\psi_1, \ldots, \psi_n)) = t$. The case when $\tilde{\diamond}_{\mathcal{M}_G}(\langle \overline{x}, D \rangle) = \{f\}$ is handled similarly.

($\Leftarrow$): Suppose that for every $a \in W$ and every formula $\varphi = \diamond(\psi_1, \ldots, \psi_n)$, $v(a, \varphi) \in \tilde{\diamond}_{\mathcal{M}_G}(\langle \langle v(a, \psi_1), \ldots, v(a, \psi_n) \rangle, \{\langle v(b, \psi_1), \ldots, v(b, \psi_n) \rangle | \ b \geq a\} \rangle)$. Let r be a right rule in **G** for an n-ary connective $\diamond$ (left rules are handled similarly). We prove that $\mathcal{W}$ respects r. Suppose that a substitution σ fulfils r in some $a \in W$. Hence, it locally satisfies every premise of r in every $b \geq a$. Let $x_i^b = v(b, \sigma(p_i))$ for every $b \geq a$. It is easy to see that every premise of r is compatible with $\langle x_1^b, \ldots, x_n^b \rangle$ for every $b \geq a$. By definition of $\mathcal{M}_G$, $\tilde{\diamond}(\langle \overline{x}, D \rangle) = \{t\}$, where $\overline{x} = \langle x_1^a, \ldots, x_n^a \rangle$ and $D = \{\langle x_1^b, \ldots, x_n^b \rangle | \ b \geq a\}$. Therefore, $v(a, \sigma(\diamond(p_1, \ldots, p_n))) \in \{t\}$. Hence σ locally satisfies r's conclusion in a. □

References

1. Avron, A., Lev, I.: Non-deterministic Multi-valued Structures. Journal of Logic and Computation 15, 241–261 (2005)
2. Avron, A., Ciabattoni, A., Zamansky, A.: Canonical calculi: Invertibility, axiom expansion and (Non)-determinism. In: Frid, A., Morozov, A., Rybalchenko, A., Wagner, K.W. (eds.) CSR 2009. LNCS, vol. 5675, pp. 26–37. Springer, Heidelberg (2009)
3. Avron, A., Lahav, O.: On Constructive Connectives and Systems. Logical Methods in Computer Science 6(4:12) (2010)
4. Avron, A., Zamansky, A.: Non-deterministic Semantics for Logical Systems - A Survey. In: Gabbay, D., Guenther, F. (eds.) Handbook of Philosophical Logic. Kluwer, Dordrecht (to appear, 2011)
5. Bowen, K.A.: An extension of the intuitionistic propositional calculus. Indagationes Mathematicae 33, 287–294 (1971)
6. Ciabattoni, A., Terui, K.: Towards a semantic characterization of cut-elimination. Studia Logica 82(1), 95–119 (2006)
7. Gurevich, Y., Neeman, I.: The logic of Infons. Bulletin of European Association for Theoretical Computer Science 98 (June 2009)
8. Kripke, S.: Semantical analysis of intuitionistic logic I. In: Crossly, J., Dummett, M. (eds.) Formal Systems and Recursive Functions, pp. 92–129 (1965)
9. McCullough, D.P.: Logical connectives for intuitionistic propositional logic. Journal of Symbolic Logic 36(1), 15–20 (1971)
10. Mints, G.: A Short Introduction to Intuitionistic Logic. Plenum Publishers, New York (2000)
11. Urquhart, A.: Many-valued Logic. In: Gabbay, D., Guenthner, F. (eds.) Handbook of Philosophical Logic, vol. 2, pp. 249–295. Kluwer Academic Publishers, Boston (2001)

On the Proof Complexity of Cut-Free Bounded Deep Inference

Anupam Das

University of Bath

Abstract. It has recently been shown that cut-free deep inference systems exhibit an exponential speed-up over cut-free sequent systems, in terms of proof size. While this is good for proof complexity, there remains the problem of typically high proof search non-determinism induced by the deep inference methodology: the higher the depth of inference, the higher the non-determinism. In this work we improve on the proof search side by demonstrating that, for propositional logic, the same exponential speed-up in proof size can be obtained in bounded-depth cut-free systems. These systems retain the top-down symmetry of deep inference, but can otherwise be designed at the same depth level of sequent systems. As a result the non-determinism arising from the choice of rules at each stage of a proof is smaller than that of unbounded deep inference, while still giving access to the short proofs of deep inference.

1   Introduction

Deep inference is a proof methodology whose proof systems allow the application of inference rules on any connective appearing in a formula, in contrast to traditional proof systems whose inference rules only operate on the main connective of a formula. Within deep inference several formalisms have been defined, the most developed being the *Calculus of Structures* (CoS), and more recently an extension of it, *Open Deduction* [8]. Throughout this work we use the latter, but present complexity results for CoS so that they are more directly comparable to existing results. The two systems are polynomially equivalent and, for the reader familiar with CoS, the use of open deduction can be considered as just a convenient notation to present CoS proofs more clearly and with less syntax.

In this paper we consider "cut-free" or "analytic" deep inference systems as defined in [3]. For deep inference systems the "cut" rule is $\dfrac{A \wedge \bar{A}}{\mathsf{f}}$, which can be considered a generalized version of the cut from sequent calculi since it can be applied in any context. There are cut-elimination procedures for deep inference systems and they yield the results we would expect from such procedures, e.g. consistency of the system and Herbrand's Theorem. There is also a generalized version of the subformula property for cut-free deep inference systems: atoms appearing in a proof are just those that appear in its conclusion. This specializes to the traditional subformula property when restricted to the sequent calculus. A

K. Brünnler and G. Metcalfe (Eds.): TABLEAUX 2011, LNAI 6793, pp. 134–148, 2011.

more detailed account of the cut rule in deep inference systems and the corollaries of cut-elimination can be found in [2].

Recently, in [3], Bruscoli and Guglielmi have shown that cut-free deep inference systems exhibit an exponential speedup over cut-free sequent systems in size of proofs. The Statman tautologies are shown to have polynomial-size proofs in the cut-free calculus of structures, while their proofs in cut-free sequent calculi have long been known to grow exponentially [6]. The first three Statman tautologies are shown below, from which the basic pattern should be apparent:

$$S_1 \equiv (c_1 \wedge d_1) \vee \left[\bar{c}_1 \vee \bar{d}_1\right] \quad,$$
$$S_2 \equiv (c_2 \wedge d_2) \vee \left[\left(\left(\left[\bar{c}_2 \vee \bar{d}_2\right] \wedge c_1\right) \wedge \left(\left[\bar{c}_2 \vee \bar{d}_2\right] \wedge d_1\right)\right) \vee \left[\bar{c}_1 \vee \bar{d}_1\right]\right] \quad,$$
$$S_3 \equiv (c_3 \wedge d_3) \vee \left(\left(\left[\bar{c}_3 \vee \bar{d}_3\right] \wedge c_2\right) \wedge \left(\left[\bar{c}_3 \vee \bar{d}_3\right] \wedge d_2\right)\right) \vee$$
$$\left(\left(\left(\left[\bar{c}_3 \vee \bar{d}_3\right] \wedge \left[\bar{c}_2 \vee \bar{d}_2\right]\right) \wedge c_1\right) \wedge \left(\left(\left[\bar{c}_3 \vee \bar{d}_3\right] \wedge \left[\bar{c}_2 \vee \bar{d}_2\right]\right) \wedge d_1\right)\right) \vee$$
$$\left[\bar{c}_1 \vee \bar{d}_1\right] \quad.$$

It is not difficult to see that cut-free sequent calculus proofs of these tautologies are forced to create $O(2^n)$ branches, as demonstrated in [5]. However with deep inference systems it is possible to prove these formulae 'from the inside out' by copying the first disjunct into each following disjunct, reducing the formula to the previous tautology and repeating the process, yielding polynomial-size proofs.

It can be argued that the use of deep inference in this case is trivial as inference rules operate just beneath the surface of the formula; in particular the number of $\wedge$-$\vee$ alternations, or *depth*, of the Statman tautologies is constant. In this paper we introduce systems where the depth at which inference rules may apply is bounded. We refer to these as *bounded-depth* systems, although this should not be confused with bounded-depth Frege systems in which the depth of formulae appearing in a proof, rather than inference steps, is bounded.

In [3] it was conjectured that bounded-depth deep inference systems, while still giving polynomial-size proofs of the Statman tautologies, would result in an exponential blowup in the size of proofs for some other classes of tautologies. In Sect. 3 we prove this to be false; we construct a polynomial transformation of cut-free deep inference proofs to ones whose inference rules are not only bounded in depth but "shallow", in the sense that sequent calculus rules are shallow.

The result is possible because deep inference systems benefit over sequent systems not only in the depth of their inference steps, but also in the top-down symmetry they exhibit. A CoS derivation is a sequence of formulae in which the main connective may change many times, and so the system admits a notion of duality of inference rules. In contrast, sequent calculi have a strict tree structure with the implicit connective between branches being conjunction. For example consider the following rules from deep inference:

$$c{\uparrow}\frac{A}{A \wedge A} \qquad\qquad m\frac{(A \wedge B) \vee (C \wedge D)}{[A \vee C] \wedge [B \vee D]}$$

$$\text{cocontraction} \qquad\qquad\qquad \text{medial}$$

The first rule is an example of duality in deep inference systems: it is the dual rule for contraction. However neither rule can be fully captured by a sequent calculus; looking at the rules bottom-up, if the conjuncts in the conclusions are separate branches in a sequent calculus proof, the two branches would need to collapse into a single branch in order to obtain the premiss, which is not permitted. However this flexibility alone, it turns out, admits enough top-down symmetry to enjoy the same proof complexity as deep inference systems, and in Conclusion 5.1 we present a sequent-like system that exemplifies this.

In the literature there is generally a distinction made between systems containing cocontraction and ones that do not, as it is conjectured that cocontraction allows for an exponential speedup in size of proofs [3]. In this paper we consider only systems containing cocontraction and show that bounded-depth systems can polynomially simulate full deep inference. The analogous problem for systems without cocontraction remains open, although in Conclusion 5.2 we conjecture that an analogous result does not hold. Work in this area is ongoing, and may provide new directions for the wider problem of the effect of cocontraction on proof complexity in general (see Conclusion 5.3).

2   Preliminaries

Here we give only a brief account of the open deduction formalism and its usual proof systems for propositional logic, but a more comprehensive introduction can be found in [8].

Definition 1 (Formulae and Contexts). *The language of open deduction is a propositional language consisting of units* t, f, *countably many atoms which we denote* a, b, c, d, *possibly with subscripts and superscripts, two binary connectives* $\wedge$ *and* $\vee$ *and an involution* $a \mapsto \bar{a}$, *defined only on the set of atoms, representing negation, all with their usual classical interpretations.*

Formulae are built freely in the usual way and we use A, B, C, D *as metavariables ranging over formulae of the language. We extend negation to all formulae by identifying* $\bar{A}$ *with the negation normal form of* A. *For clarity we use parentheses for conjunctions and brackets for disjunction, and we sometimes omit external parentheses/brackets of a formula, and internal ones under associativity. For example the following are all formulae:*

$$a \wedge [\bar{b} \vee c] \qquad t \wedge d \qquad \overline{f \vee (a \wedge \bar{b})} \equiv t \wedge [\bar{a} \vee b]$$

Definition 2 (Derivations). *All formulae are derivations, and we define, for a formula* A, *its premiss and conclusion* $(pr(A), cn(A)$ *resp.) as* A. *If* Φ, Ψ *are derivations then* $\Phi \star \Psi$ *is a derivation for* $\star \in \{\wedge, \vee\}$, *with* $pr(\Phi \star \Psi) \equiv pr(\Phi) \star pr(\Psi)$ *and* $cn(\Phi \star \Psi) \equiv cn(\Phi) \star cn(\Psi)$. $\rho \dfrac{\Phi}{\Psi}$ *is a derivation just if* $\rho \dfrac{cn(\Phi)}{pr(\Psi)}$ *is an inference step associated with some rule* ρ, *and has premiss* $pr(\Phi)$ *and conclusion* $cn(\Psi)$. *Inference rules can operate anywhere in a formula, not just on the main connective. If* $pr(\Phi) \equiv t$ *then we call* Φ *a proof.*

Rebracketing rules   *Unit* rules

$$= \frac{A \lor B}{B \lor A} \qquad = \frac{[A \lor B] \lor C}{A \lor [B \lor C]} \qquad u_1\uparrow \frac{A}{A \land t} \qquad u_2\uparrow \frac{A \land t}{A} \qquad u_3\uparrow \frac{f}{f \land f} \qquad u_4\uparrow \frac{f \land f}{f}$$

$$= \frac{A \land B}{B \land A} \qquad = \frac{(A \land B) \land C}{A \land (B \land C)} \qquad u_1\downarrow \frac{A \lor f}{A} \qquad u_2\downarrow \frac{A}{A \lor f} \qquad u_3\downarrow \frac{t \lor t}{t} \qquad u_4\downarrow \frac{t}{t \lor t}$$

$\qquad$ *commutativity* $\qquad$ *associativity*

Fig. 1. Inference rules for equality

For a derivation Φ its size, $|\Phi|$, *is the number of unit and atom occurrences in it and its* length, $l(\Phi)$, *is the number of inference steps appearing in it.*

Definition 3 (Contexts). *A* context *is a formula with one hole appearing in place of a subformula, e.g. $a \land \{ \ \}$, $b \lor (a \land \{ \ \}) \lor f$, and is denoted by $\xi\{ \ \}$. The hole can be filled with any formula or derivation; we denote a context $\xi\{ \ \}$ filled with a derivation Φ by $\xi\{\Phi\}$.*

Definition 4 (Systems). *A* system *is a set of inference rules, and if all inference rules appearing in a derivation (resp. proof) Φ belong to a system $\mathcal{S}$ then we say Φ is a $\mathcal{S}$-derivation (resp. $\mathcal{S}$-proof). If Φ is a $\mathcal{S}$-derivation with premiss A and conclusion B we write $\Phi \| \mathcal{S} \begin{smallmatrix} A \\ B \end{smallmatrix}$. If $A \equiv t$, i.e. Φ is a proof, then we write $\begin{smallmatrix} \Phi \| \mathcal{S} \\ B \end{smallmatrix}$.*

Definition 5 (Sequential and Synchronal Forms). *We define two important forms of a derivation. The first is* sequential form, *where the derivation is just a sequence of formulae, and so also a CoS derivation. The second is* synchronal form, *where every inference step operates as shallow as possible, i.e. every inference step is just an instance of the inference rule itself with formulae substituted in for the metavariables. For every derivation both forms exist; synchronal form is unique while sequential form, in general, is not, and there is at most only a quadratic difference in the size of the two forms [4]. For example we present a derivation in synchronal and two sequential forms:*

$$\frac{A}{C} \land \frac{B}{D} \qquad \frac{\dfrac{A \land B}{A \land D}}{C \land D} \qquad \frac{\dfrac{A \land B}{C \land B}}{C \land D}$$

Note 6 (Equality Rules). We define the equality inference rules on formulae in Fig. 1. For the sake of clearer analysis of proof complexity and depth we consider them as real inference rules inducing actual inference steps (like in [9]), rather than a set of equations governing the sameness of formulae. When we introduce our notion of depth, and bounded-depth systems, the same restrictions we impose

Structural rules   *Logical* rules

$$\mathsf{KSg^+} \left\{ \begin{array}{c} \\ \\ \end{array} \right.$$

$$\mathsf{c\uparrow} \frac{A}{A \wedge A} \qquad \mathsf{m} \frac{(A \wedge B) \vee (C \wedge D)}{[A \vee C] \wedge [B \vee D]}$$

$$\textit{cocontraction} \qquad \textit{medial}$$

$$\mathsf{i\downarrow} \frac{\mathsf{t}}{A \vee \bar{A}} \qquad \mathsf{w\downarrow} \frac{\mathsf{f}}{A} \qquad \mathsf{c\downarrow} \frac{A \vee A}{A} \qquad \mathsf{s} \frac{A \wedge [B \vee C]}{(A \wedge B) \vee C} \left. \begin{array}{c} \\ \\ \end{array} \right\} \mathsf{KSg}$$

$$\begin{array}{cccc} \textit{interaction} & \textit{weakening} & \textit{contraction} & \textit{switch} \\ \textit{or identity} & & & \end{array}$$

Fig. 2. Systems KSg and KSg$^+$

on the other inference rules also apply to the equality rules, so there is no doubt that the inference rules we apply really do have bounded depth.

When defining proof systems in this section, we implicitly assume that all the equality inference rules are also in that system. However we distinguish between the *rebracketing* rules and the *unit* rules in notation as we usually consider them separately. We in fact make little use of the unit rules and include them only as convention. In Sect. 4 we show that units and the unit rules can be dropped with no major effect on proof complexity.

Definition 7. *We define* KSg $= \{\mathsf{i\downarrow}, \mathsf{w\downarrow}, \mathsf{c\downarrow}, \mathsf{s}\}$, *and* KSg$^+$ $=$ KSg $\cup \{\mathsf{c\uparrow}, \mathsf{m}\}$ *and these rules are defined in Fig. 2. As usual, both these systems also contain all equality inference rules. These systems are sound and complete [1].*

Definition 8 (Complexity). *We say that a system $\mathcal{S}$ p-simulates a system $\mathcal{T}$ if there is a polynomial p such that for every $\mathcal{T}$-proof Ψ there is a $\mathcal{S}$-proof Φ with the same conclusion such that $|\Phi| \leq p(|\Psi|)$. If the condition also holds for all derivations, preserving premises as well as conclusions, then we say that $\mathcal{S}$ strongly p-simulates $\mathcal{T}$. When two systems p-simulate (resp. strongly p-simulate) each other, we say they are p-equivalent (resp. strongly p-equivalent).*

Definition 9 (Depth). *For a formula A its depth, $d(A)$, is the maximum number of alternations of $\wedge$ and $\vee$ in its formula tree. The depth of a hole (resp. subformula) in a context, $d(\{\ \}, \xi\{\ \})$, is the number of alternations in the path to the hole (resp. subformula) in the context's formula tree. In a sequential derivation the depth of an inference step is the depth of the hole of the largest context common to both its premiss and conclusion. The depth of an inference step is invariant among its various sequential forms and so we extend uniquely this notion for all derivations. When calculating depth we adopt the convention that every formula or context has an outer $\wedge$. For example:*

$$d(a \vee (b \wedge c)) = d(\{\ \}, a \vee (b \wedge \{\ \})) = 2 \qquad d(a \wedge (b \wedge (c \wedge d))) = 0$$

Notation 10. *For a system S we write k-S to denote the system whose derivations are just S-derivations where all inference steps have depth less than or
equal to k. We call k-S a k-depth system. For an inference step ρ, we often
indicate its depth in parentheses on the right, e.g. $\rho(3) \dfrac{A}{B}$ indicates that $d(\rho) = 3$,
and we write $S \cup \{\rho(k)\}$ to denote the system whose derivations are just $S \cup \{\rho\}$-
derivations with all ρ steps having depth k. For a context $\xi\{\ \}$, the depth of its
hole may be indicated as a superscript, e.g. $\xi^2\{\ \}$ for a context with a hole at
depth 2.*

3   The Depth-Change Trick

In this section we present our main result, that bounded-depth KSg^+ strongly p-
simulates any cut-free deep inference system. The result also holds for $\mathsf{KSg} \cup \{\mathsf{c}\!\uparrow\}$,
and the problem remains open for systems without cocontraction.

Throughout this section we present derivations in sequential form, i.e. CoS
derivations, both for clarity and to establish complexity results directly comparable to existing ones. Derivations are often presented with long sequences of
commutativity and associativity steps, and sometimes brackets (resp. paranthe-
ses) are omitted in large disjunctions (resp. conjunctions). From the point of
view of complexity this shortens proofs by at most cubic degree and so preserves
p-simulation. A proof of the following lemma can be found in [3]:

Lemma 11. *Every rebracketing $\Phi \|_{\{=\}} \dfrac{A}{B}$ can be achieved with quadratic length,
i.e. there exists $\Psi \|_{\{=\}} \dfrac{A}{B'}$ such that $l(\Psi) = O(B^2)$, and so $|\Psi| = O(B^3)$.*

In this section we work in KSg^+, the system of all the usual "analytic" rules for
propositional logic. The medial rule is, in fact, derivable from the other rules
and so does not have a major effect the complexity of the system:

$$
\mathsf{c}\!\downarrow \cfrac{4 \cdot \mathsf{w}\!\downarrow \cfrac{4 \cdot \mathsf{u}_2\!\downarrow \cfrac{(A \wedge B) \vee (C \wedge D)}{([A \vee \mathsf{f}] \wedge [B \vee \mathsf{f}]) \vee ([A \vee \mathsf{f}] \wedge [B \vee \mathsf{f}])}}{([A \vee C] \wedge [B \vee D]) \vee ([A \vee C] \wedge [B \vee D])}}{[A \vee C] \wedge [B \vee D]}
$$

In particular the main result presented here, that bounded-depth KSg^+ strongly
p-simulates unbounded-depth KSg^+, also holds for $\mathsf{KSg} \cup \{\mathsf{c}\!\uparrow\}$, i.e. without medial. However since the derivation of medial contains depth 3 rule applications
(the weakening steps), the result would only hold for systems of depth greater
than or equal to 3, which is somewhat less clean than the result for KSg^+.

Definition 12. *Observe the following derivations in* 1-KSg$^+$ *:*

$$\text{c}\!\uparrow\!(1)\frac{A \vee (B \wedge C)}{\dfrac{(A \wedge A) \vee (B \wedge C)}{[A \vee B] \wedge [A \vee C]}}\text{m}(0)$$

$$\text{m}(0)\frac{(A \wedge B) \vee (A \wedge C)}{\dfrac{[A \vee A] \wedge [B \vee C]}{A \wedge [B \vee C]}}\text{c}\!\downarrow\!(0)$$

$$=(0)\frac{[A \vee B] \wedge [A \vee C]}{\dfrac{[A \vee B] \wedge [C \vee A]}{\dfrac{A \vee (B \wedge C) \vee A}{\dfrac{A \vee A \vee (B \wedge C)}{A \vee (B \wedge C)}}}}\begin{array}{l}\\ \text{s}(1),\text{s}(0)\\ \\ =(1)\\ \\ \text{c}\!\downarrow\!(1)\end{array}$$

$$\text{c}\!\uparrow\!(0)\frac{A \wedge [B \vee C]}{\dfrac{A \wedge A \wedge [B \vee C]}{\dfrac{A \wedge [B \vee C] \wedge A}{\dfrac{(A \wedge B) \vee (C \wedge A)}{(A \wedge B) \vee (A \wedge C)}}}}\begin{array}{l}\\ =(0)\\ \\ 2 \cdot \text{s}(0)\\ \\ =(1)\end{array}$$

From these we define four macro-rules, collectively known as the distributivity laws, which should be understood as abbreviations for the above derivations:

$$\text{d}_2\!\uparrow\frac{A \vee (B \wedge C)}{[A \vee B] \wedge [A \vee C]} \qquad \text{d}_2\!\downarrow\frac{(A \wedge B) \vee (A \wedge C)}{A \wedge [B \vee C]}$$

$$\text{d}_1\!\downarrow\frac{[A \vee B] \wedge [A \vee C]}{A \vee (B \wedge C)} \qquad \text{d}_1\!\uparrow\frac{A \wedge [B \vee C]}{(A \wedge B) \vee (A \wedge C)}$$

Like switch and medial, these rules can increase or decrease the depth of a formula. However, unlike switch and medial, all the above rules are invertible, indeed rules in the same column are inverse to each other, and rules in the same row are dual to each other. This invertibility allows us to "unfold" formulae at will, bringing subformulae out to whatever depth we wish, and then pushing them back down again. For example the following transformation decreases the depth of an inference step by 1, where D is a formula at depth 2 containing its premiss and ξ^2 is the context of D:

$$\rho(k+1)\frac{\xi^2\{D\}}{\xi^2\{D'\}} \qquad \rightsquigarrow \qquad \rho':\ \rho(k)\frac{\begin{array}{c}\xi^2\{D\}\\ \Big\|\{=(k)\}\\ \text{d}_2\!\uparrow\dfrac{A \wedge [B \vee (C \wedge D)]}{A \wedge [B \vee C] \wedge [B \vee D]}\\ \text{d}_1\!\downarrow\dfrac{}{A \wedge [B \vee C] \wedge [B \vee D']}\\ \dfrac{}{A \wedge [B \vee (C \wedge D')]}\end{array}}{\begin{array}{c}\\ \Big\|\{=(k)\}\\ \xi^2\{D'\}\end{array}} \tag{1}$$

The transformation is local and so preserves derivability. We extend this trick to show that a 1-depth system strongly p-simulates unbounded depth systems.

$$
\rho(2r)\,\frac{\xi^{2r}\{D\}}{\xi^{2r}\{D'\}} \quad \rightsquigarrow \quad \rho' :
\begin{array}{c}
\xi^{2r}\{D\} \\
\Psi_1^{-1} \Big\| \{=(1)\} \\
\mathsf{d}_2\!\uparrow \dfrac{A \wedge \left[B_1 \vee \left(C_1 \wedge \xi_1^{2(r-1)}\{D\}\right)\right]}{A \wedge \left([B_1 \vee C_1] \wedge \left[B_1 \vee \xi_1^{2(r-1)}\{D\}\right]\right)} \\
\Psi_2^{-1} \Big\| \{=(1)\} \\
\vdots \\
\Psi_r^{-1} \Big\| \{=(1)\} \\
\mathsf{d}_2\!\uparrow \dfrac{A \wedge [B_1 \vee C_1] \wedge \cdots \wedge [B_r \vee (C_r \wedge D)]}{\rho(1)\,\dfrac{A \wedge [B_1 \vee C_1] \wedge \cdots \wedge ([B_r \vee C_r] \wedge [B_r \vee D])}{\mathsf{d}_1\!\downarrow \dfrac{A \wedge [B_1 \vee C_1] \wedge \cdots \wedge ([B_r \vee C_r] \wedge [B_r \vee D'])}{A \wedge [B_1 \vee C_1] \wedge \cdots \wedge [B_r \vee (C_r \wedge D')]}}} \\
\Psi_r \Big\| \{=(1)\} \\
\vdots \\
\Psi_3 \Big\| \{=(1)\} \\
\mathsf{d}_1\!\downarrow \dfrac{(A \wedge [B_1 \vee C_1]) \wedge \left([B_2 \vee C_2] \wedge \left[B_2 \vee \xi_2^{2(r-2)}\{D'\}\right]\right)}{(A \wedge [B_1 \vee C_1]) \wedge \left[B_2 \vee \left(C_2 \wedge \xi_2^{2(r-2)}\{D'\}\right)\right]} \\
\Psi_2 \Big\| \{=(1)\} \\
\mathsf{d}_1\!\downarrow \dfrac{A \wedge \left([B_1 \vee C_1] \wedge \left[B_1 \vee \xi_1^{2(r-1)}\{D'\}\right]\right)}{A \wedge \left[B_1 \vee \left(C_1 \wedge \xi_1^{2(r-1)}\{D'\}\right)\right]} \\
\Psi_1 \Big\| \{=(1)\} \\
\xi^{2r}\{D'\}
\end{array}
$$

Fig. 3. Full depth-decreasing transformation of an inference step

Theorem 13 (The Depth-Change Trick). 1-KSg^+ *strongly p-simulates* KSg^+.

Proof. Suppose ρ is an inference rule with depth $2r \geq 2$ [1]. Let D be its premiss, D' its conclusion and ξ its context. Let $\xi_i\{D\}$ be the smallest subformula of $\xi\{D\}$ at depth $2i$ containing D, so that $d(\xi_i\{\ \}) = 2(r-i)$. In Fig. 3 we define a transformation of ρ to a derivation ρ' that has the same premiss and conclusion but contains only at most depth 1 inference steps.
When $d(\rho) \leq 1$ we define $\rho' = \rho$, with ρ construed as a length 1 derivation. We can now extend the transformation to whole derivations as follows:

[1] If $d(\rho)$ is odd then the derivation is the same, but in the middle D would now appear in a disjunction, still at depth 1.

$$\rho \frac{A \wedge [B \vee [C \vee D]]}{A \wedge [B \vee [C \vee D']]} \quad \leadsto \quad \rho' : \quad \begin{array}{c} = \cfrac{A \wedge [B \vee [C \vee D]]}{A \wedge [[B \vee C] \vee D]} \\[2pt] \rho \cfrac{}{A \wedge [[B \vee C] \vee D']} \\[2pt] = \cfrac{}{A \wedge [B \vee [C \vee D']]} \end{array}$$

$$\rho \frac{A \wedge [B \vee (C \wedge D)]}{A \wedge [B \vee (C \wedge D')]} \quad \leadsto \quad \rho' : \quad \begin{array}{c} \mathsf{d_2 {\uparrow}} \cfrac{A \wedge [B \vee (C \wedge D')]}{A \wedge ([B \vee C] \wedge [B \vee D'])} \\[2pt] = \cfrac{}{(A \wedge [B \vee C]) \wedge [B \vee D']} \\[2pt] \rho \cfrac{}{(A \wedge [B \vee C]) \wedge [B \vee D]} \\[2pt] = \cfrac{}{A \wedge ([B \vee C] \wedge [B \vee D])} \\[2pt] \mathsf{d_1 {\downarrow}} \cfrac{}{A \wedge [B \vee (C \wedge D)]} \end{array}$$

Fig. 4. Interweaving rebracketing and distributivity steps

$$\Phi : \quad \begin{array}{c} A_0 \\ \rho_1 \overline{} \\ \vdots \\ \rho_n \overline{} \\ A_n \end{array} \quad \leadsto \quad \Phi' : \quad \begin{array}{c} A_0 \\ \rho_1' \overline{\overline{}} \\ \vdots \\ \rho_n' \overline{\overline{}} \\ A_n \end{array}$$

The depth of a formula is less than or equal to its size so we have $r_i \leq |A_i|$, where $2r_i$ is the depth of ρ_i. Each Ψ_k is a rebracketing step which has cubic complexity in the size of its conclusion, by Lemma 11, and the conclusions of Ψ_k have size at most $k \cdot |A_i|$. From this we calculate $|\rho_i'| \leq 2 \cdot \sum_{k=1}^{r} |\Psi_k| \leq \sum_{k=1}^{r} (k \cdot |A_i|)^3 \leq |A_i|^3 \sum_{k=1}^{r} k^3 = O(|A_i|^3 \cdot r^4) = O(|A_i|^7)$, and so $|\Phi'| = O(|\Phi|^7)$.   □

Note 14 (The Complexity of the Depth-Change Trick). The upper bound of the polynomial degree of inefficiency estimated above, 7, can be improved upon vastly, for example by interweaving the rebracketing and distributivity steps.

Consider the transformation of an inference rule in Fig. 4. When $d(\rho) \leq 1$ we define $\rho' = \rho$, with ρ construed as a length 1 derivation. If the size of the conclusion is n, then the transformation only needs to be applied at most $n - 1$ times (i.e. the number of connectives) to guarantee that ρ applies at depth less than or equal to 1. Each application of the transformation at most adds n then multiplies by 6, and so applying it $n - 1$ times gives $|\rho'| \leq \sum_{i=1}^{n-1} 6 \cdot i \cdot n = O(n^3)$. So the depth-change trick can be achieved with at most a cubic loss in efficiency. In comparison, *local* systems in CoS, ones that operate only on atoms, suffer a quadratic loss in efficiency, as shown in [3].

4   Reducing Non-determinism

Having shown that bounded-depth systems have similar size proofs as deep inference, we can now construct systems that have far less non-determinism than those in deep inference: at each stage of a proof there are fewer choices available.

Axiom   Structural rules   Logical rules

$$\mathsf{K\dot{S}g^+}\left\{\begin{array}{l}\\ \mathsf{i\downarrow}\,\dfrac{}{A\vee\bar{A}}\quad\mathsf{i\downarrow}\,\dfrac{A}{A\wedge[B\vee\bar{B}]}\quad\mathsf{w\downarrow}\,\dfrac{A}{A\vee B}\quad\mathsf{c\downarrow}\,\dfrac{A\vee A}{A}\quad\mathsf{s}\,\dfrac{A\wedge[B\vee C]}{(A\wedge B)\vee C}\\ \\ \qquad\qquad identity\qquad\quad weakening\qquad contraction\qquad\quad switch\end{array}\right.$$

$$\mathsf{c\uparrow}\,\dfrac{A}{A\wedge A}\qquad\mathsf{m}\,\dfrac{(A\wedge B)\vee(C\wedge D)}{[A\vee C]\wedge[B\vee D]}$$

cocontraction   medial

Fig. 5. Unit-free systems $\mathsf{K\dot{S}g}$ and $\mathsf{K\dot{S}g^+}$

In this section we restrict our bounded-depth system to further reduce this non-determinism. Proofs and derivations are given in synchronal form for convenience and we introduce a new measure, known as the *height* of a derivation, for inductions. We give only proof sketches of theorems for the sake of brevity.

Definition 15 (Height of a Derivation). *The height of a proof/derivation is defined inductively as follows:*

$$\begin{aligned}h(a) &= 0\\ h(\Phi\wedge\Psi) &= \max(h(\Phi),h(\Psi)) \qquad h\left(\dfrac{\Phi}{\Psi}\right)=1+h(\Phi)+h(\Psi)\\ h(\Phi\vee\Psi) &= \max(h(\Phi),h(\Psi))\end{aligned}$$

Remark 16. The height of a derivation is not invariant among its various forms. Height is equal to length for sequential derivations but this is not, in general, true for derivations in synchronal form. For example, the three forms of a derivation given in Definition 5 have heights 1, 2, 2 respectively.

Units and unit rules, it turns out, do not play a major role in proof complexity; in most circumstances we can polynomially transform a proof with units and unit rules to one without. The system we present in Fig. 5 is similar to the unit-free system appearing in [10]. From the point of view of proof search, the advantage of this is clear: fewer rules and no constants means less non-determinism.

Definition 17 (Unit-Free Systems). *The language of unit-free open deduction is just the language of open deduction with all units removed. Unit-free derivations are derivations containing no units (and so no instances of the unit rules), and a unit-free proof is a unit-free derivation with empty premiss. With inference rules defined as in Fig. 5 define* $\mathsf{K\dot{S}g} = \{\mathsf{i\downarrow},\mathsf{w\downarrow},\mathsf{c\downarrow},\mathsf{s}\}$ *and* $\mathsf{K\dot{S}g^+} = \{\mathsf{i\downarrow},\mathsf{w\downarrow},\mathsf{c\downarrow},\mathsf{c\uparrow},\mathsf{s},\mathsf{m}\}$ *respectively, along with all rebracketing rules but not the unit rules.*

The special cases when a proof-with-units cannot be transformed to a unit-free proof is when the conclusion "reduces", in some sense, to just a unit. Otherwise we reduce the conclusion to some unique unit-free formula and construct a proof of that. This reduction is captured by the following equivalence relation:

Definition 18 (Unitary Equivalence on Formulae). *We define unitary equivalence,* $\cong$, *on formulae by closing the following equations by reflexivity, symmetry, transitivity and by applying context closure.*

$$A \vee f \cong A \cong f \vee A$$
$$A \wedge t \cong A \cong t \wedge A \qquad \text{Context Closure:}$$
$$A \vee t \cong t \cong t \vee A$$
$$A \wedge f \cong f \cong f \wedge A \qquad \textit{if } A \cong B \textit{ then } \xi\{A\} \cong \xi\{B\}$$

Remark 19. $\cong$ is an equivalence relation on formulae, and each formula's equivalence class contains either t, f or a unique unit-free formula, which we call its *reduction*. The reduction of a formula can be calculated in polynomial time [3].

Theorem 20 (Dropping Units). *A* KSg^+-*proof whose conclusion reduces to a unit-free formula A can be polynomially transformed to a unit-free proof of A.*

Proof. Replace instances of units and unit rules with the appropriate unit-free rules and formulae. The exceptional cases are when t appears in a disjunction or f appears in a conjunction in the conclusion. For example:

$$\left({}_{\mathsf{w}\downarrow} \frac{\overset{\mathbb{T}}{A \wedge B}}{A \wedge [B \vee t]} \right) \qquad \left({}_{\mathsf{s}} \frac{{}_{\mathsf{u}_2\downarrow} \dfrac{\overset{\mathbb{T}}{A \wedge B}}{[A \vee f] \wedge B}}{A \vee (B \wedge f)} \right)$$

In both examples the conclusion reduces to A from premiss $A \wedge B$, which is an instance of *coweakening* (see [3]). We show the admissibility of coweakening by transforming the proof of $A \wedge B$ to a proof, of equal length, of a formula that reduces to A as follows: replace each atom of B in the conclusion with t, then mimic the proof of $A \wedge B$ upwards. Identity steps affected by this substitution are replaced by weakening to give a valid proof.   □

Corollary 21. 1-$\dot{\mathsf{KSg}}^+$ *p-simulates* KSg^+ *over unit-free formulae.*

Proof. The proof of the depth-change trick (Theorem 13) makes no use of units and so can be replicated for the unit-free system in the obvious manner.   □

Henceforth rules and systems are assumed to be unit-free if not already specified, implicitly containing the rebracketing rules but not the unit rules.

In what follows we drop the structural rules contraction, identity and weakening from the system; again, this provides a clear advantage from the point of view of proof search. It is known that these rules can be dropped in both sequent and deep inference systems and dropping these rules for bounded-depth systems does not have a major effect on proof complexity.

Before we can drop the structural rules, we must replace switch and medial with distributivity rules $\mathsf{d}_1\downarrow$ and $\mathsf{d}_2\downarrow$. Whether these rules are better or worse for proof search is debatable: on one hand they can blow up a formula exponentially large, while the former rules are linear, but on the other hand, since they

$$\mathsf{d_1{\downarrow}}\,\frac{\mathsf{w{\downarrow}}\,\dfrac{A}{A \vee C} \wedge [B \vee C]}{(A \wedge B) \vee C}$$

$$switch(0)$$

$$\mathsf{d_2{\downarrow}}\,\frac{\mathsf{d_2{\downarrow}}\,\dfrac{\mathsf{w{\downarrow}}\,\dfrac{A \wedge B}{(A \wedge B) \vee (A \wedge D)} \vee \mathsf{w{\downarrow}}\,\dfrac{C \wedge D}{(C \wedge B) \vee (C \wedge D)}}{A \wedge [B \vee D]} \quad C \wedge [B \vee D]}{[A \vee C] \wedge [B \vee D]}$$

$$medial(0,1)$$

$$\mathsf{d_2{\downarrow}}\,\frac{\mathsf{d_2{\downarrow}}\,\dfrac{\mathsf{w{\downarrow}}\,\dfrac{A \wedge [B \vee C]}{(A \wedge [B \vee C]) \vee (D \wedge [B \vee C])} \vee \mathsf{w{\downarrow}}\,\dfrac{\mathsf{d_2{\downarrow}}\,\dfrac{D}{(A \wedge D) \vee \mathsf{c{\uparrow}}\,\dfrac{D}{D \wedge D}}}{[A \vee D] \wedge D}}{[A \vee D] \wedge [B \vee C]}}{\mathsf{d_1{\downarrow}}\,\dfrac{\mathsf{w{\downarrow}}\,\dfrac{A \vee D}{A \vee C \vee D} \wedge [B \vee C \vee D]}{(A \wedge B) \vee C \vee D}}$$

$$switch(1)$$

Fig. 6. Derivations of switch and medial in 1-$\{\mathsf{i{\downarrow}}, \mathsf{w{\downarrow}}, \mathsf{c{\downarrow}}, \mathsf{c{\uparrow}}, \mathsf{d_1{\downarrow}}, \mathsf{d_2{\downarrow}}\}$

are invertible, there is no need to check the validity of the inference, which is beneficial from the point of view of automated deduction. In actuality the two sets of rules are easily derivable from each other in the presence of contraction and cocontraction, and so the first point is irrelevant.

Theorem 22. 1-$\{\mathsf{i{\downarrow}}, \mathsf{w{\downarrow}}, \mathsf{c{\downarrow}}, \mathsf{c{\uparrow}}, \mathsf{d_1{\downarrow}}, \mathsf{d_2{\downarrow}}\}$ *p-simulates* KSg^+.

Proof. See Fig. 6 for derivations of switch and medial in the former system.   □

Corollary 23. $\mathsf{d_1{\uparrow}}(0), \mathsf{d_2{\uparrow}}(0)$ *are derivable in* 1-$\{\mathsf{w{\downarrow}}, \mathsf{c{\uparrow}}, \mathsf{d_1{\downarrow}}, \mathsf{d_2{\downarrow}}\}$.

Proof. Immediate from Definition 12 and derivations in Fig. 6.   □

Remark 24. Since we can derive the inverse distributivity rules without identity or contraction, we can also use the depth-change trick after absorbing these rules.

Lemma 25. $\mathsf{c{\downarrow}}(2)$ *is derivable in* 2-$\{\mathsf{w{\downarrow}}, \mathsf{c{\uparrow}}, \mathsf{d_1{\downarrow}}, \mathsf{d_2{\downarrow}}\}$.

Proof. See Fig. 7.   □

Theorem 26 (Dropping Contraction). 1-$\{\mathsf{i{\downarrow}}, \mathsf{w{\downarrow}}, \mathsf{c{\uparrow}}, \mathsf{d_1{\downarrow}}, \mathsf{d_2{\downarrow}}\}$ *p-simulates* KSg^+.

Proof. Call the former system 1-$\mathcal{S}$ for convenience. We work in 2-$(\mathcal{S} \cup \{\mathsf{c{\downarrow}}\})$, which contains 1-$(\mathcal{S} \cup \{\mathsf{c{\downarrow}}\})$ and so p-simulates KSg by Theorem 22, and observe that every sound instance of contraction can either be pushed to depth 2 using distributivity or otherwise trivially eliminated. By Lemma 25 it follows that 2-$\mathcal{S}$ p-simulates KSg^+. Finally 1-$\mathcal{S}$ p-simulates 2-$\mathcal{S}$ by Remark 24.   □

$$
=
\left[
\frac{
\left[
\cfrac{
\dfrac{B}{B\wedge B}\,c\!\uparrow \;\vee\;
\left(
\cfrac{
C\wedge\;
\cfrac{
\cfrac{
\cfrac{
\cfrac{\dfrac{D\vee D}{[D\vee D]\wedge[D\vee D]}\,c\!\uparrow}{D\vee(D\wedge D)}\,d_1\!\downarrow
}{
\cfrac{[D\vee(D\wedge D)]\wedge[D\vee(D\wedge D)]}{(D\wedge D)\vee(D\wedge D)}\,c\!\uparrow
}\,d_1\!\downarrow
}{
\cfrac{D}{D\wedge D}\,c\!\uparrow \;\wedge\;[D\vee D]
}\,d_2\!\downarrow
}{(D\wedge D)\vee(D\wedge C)}\,w\!\downarrow
\right)
}{
\cfrac{C\wedge D}{B\vee(C\wedge B)\vee(C\wedge D)}\,w\!\downarrow \;\wedge\;
\cfrac{
\cfrac{[D\vee C]\wedge[D\vee D]}{D}\,d_1\!\downarrow
}{D\vee(C\wedge B)}\,w\!\downarrow \;\vee\;(C\wedge D)
}\,d_2\!\downarrow
}{(B\wedge D)\vee(C\wedge B)\vee(C\wedge D)}\,d_1\!\downarrow
\right]
}{
\cfrac{
\cfrac{(B\wedge B)\vee(B\wedge D)}{B\wedge[B\vee D]}\,d_2\!\downarrow \;\vee\;
\cfrac{(C\wedge B)\vee(C\wedge D)}{C\wedge[B\vee D]}\,d_2\!\downarrow
}{
\cfrac{[B\vee C]\wedge[B\vee D]}{B\vee(C\wedge D)}\,d_1\!\downarrow
}\,d_2\!\downarrow
}
\right]
$$

Fig. 7. Derivation of $c\!\downarrow(2)$ in $2\text{-}\{w\!\downarrow, c\!\uparrow, d_1\!\downarrow, d_2\!\downarrow\}$

Identity can be dropped since all instances can be pushed to the top of a proof and incorporated within an axiom. Weakening, on the other hand plays an essential role in the depth-change trick and dropping identity, but can nonetheless be proved from scratch. The following lemma is proved in [1]:

Lemma 27. *A $\mathsf{K\dot{S}g^{+}}$-derivation can be polynomially transformed into one where all identity steps appear at the top and have depth 0.*

Definition 28. Generalized identity *is the axiom* $\mathsf{id}\,\dfrac{}{\bigwedge_{i} B_i \vee A_i \vee \bar{A}_i}$.

Theorem 29 (Dropping Identity). $1\text{-}\{\mathsf{id}, w\!\downarrow, c\!\uparrow, d_1\!\downarrow, d_2\!\downarrow\}$ *p-simulates* $\mathsf{KSg^{+}}$.

Proof. Identity is not used in the depth-change trick so just drop identity first, by Lemma 27, then apply the depth-change trick (Theorem 13). □

Theorem 30 (Dropping Weakening). $1\text{-}\{\mathsf{id}, c\!\uparrow, d_1\!\downarrow, d_2\!\downarrow\}$ *p-simulates* $\mathsf{KSg^{+}}$.

Proof. We notice that any sound instance of weakening in a proof can be transformed to depth 1 instances, of the same height, using distributivity. Then observe that any depth 1 instance of weakening in a proof can always be "moved" up above another rule, possibly reducing depth and using distributivity if necessary, thereby reducing the height of its application. The theorem follows by induction on the height of an instance of weakening. □

$$\mathsf{c_2} \frac{\Gamma}{\Gamma \quad \Gamma} \qquad \vee_2 \frac{\Gamma, A \vee B}{\Gamma, A, B} \qquad \wedge_2 \frac{\Gamma, A \wedge B, C \wedge D}{\Gamma, A, C \quad \Gamma, B, D}$$

$$\mathsf{id} \frac{}{A, \bar{A}} \qquad \mathsf{w} \frac{\Gamma}{\Gamma, A} \qquad \mathsf{c_1} \frac{\Gamma, A, A}{\Gamma, A} \qquad \vee_1 \frac{\Gamma, A, B}{\Gamma, A \vee B} \qquad \wedge_1 \frac{\Gamma, A \quad B, \Delta}{\Gamma, A \wedge B, \Delta}$$

$$\qquad identity \qquad weakening \qquad contraction \qquad disjunction \qquad conjunction$$

Fig. 8. System cut-free $\mathsf{GS1p^+}$

5   Conclusions

In this paper we showed that cut-free bounded-depth systems containing cocontraction can polynomially simulate their unbounded-depth counterparts, and have discussed their complexity. We argued the favorability of such systems for proof-search and further improved the situation by showing the admissibility of units, unit rules and certain structural rules with at most polynomial increase in proof size. Now we present some directions in which research in this area may continue, and for which the results presented here may be beneficial.

5.1   Applications to Sequent Calculi

Sequent calculi can essentially be considered depth 1 systems, since the relation between branches is conjunction and the comma is interpreted as disjunction. It is therefore possible to embed our systems into a sequent-like system, augmented slightly to give it top-down symmetry. We present an example of such a system in Fig. 8, based on the one-sided calculus called $\mathsf{GS1p}$ in [11], although less non-deterministic systems can be designed by making use of the results in Sect. 4. While this system is less deterministic than standard sequent calculi it is still a vast improvement to the non-determinism present in unbounded deep inference.

5.2   Bounded-Depth Systems Not Containing Cocontraction

While we have proved that bounded-depth $\mathsf{KSg} \cup \{\mathsf{c{\uparrow}}\}$ polynomially simulates unbounded-depth $\mathsf{KSg} \cup \{\mathsf{c{\uparrow}}\}$, it remains open whether a similar result can be obtained for KSg. We think that this is unlikely as the depth-change trick is reliant on cocontraction to compress proofs. It is simple to observe that the inverse distributivity rules, $\mathsf{d_1{\uparrow}}$ and $\mathsf{d_2{\uparrow}}$, cannot be derived in a system not containing cocontraction. We make the following conjecture:

Conjecture 31. No bounded-depth KSg system polynomially simulates KSg.

If the conjecture is true, then it would be interesting to see how the efficiency of bounded-depth systems without cocontraction change as the bound on depth is increased. One might intuitively expect a hierarchy of systems, each unable to p-simulate its successor, however it is also possible that all bounded-depth systems are p-equivalent but still not p-equivalent to the unbounded depth system.

5.3   The Effect of Cocontraction on Proof Complexity

It is currently an open problem as to whether KSg can p-simulate KSg $\cup$ {c↑} but this is thought unlikely to be the case [3]. It is believed that cocontraction compresses proofs by sometimes an exponential factor and this is supported by observational evidence, as well as research in "atomic flows" [7].

An answer to the previous question, on bounded-depth KSg, is probably easier, but may shed some light on this situation.

Acknowledgement. The author thanks Alessio Guglielmi for reading the manuscript thoroughly and making several suggestions including, significantly, that the depth-change trick could be extended to simulate systems of unbounded depth.

References

1. Brünnler, K.: Deep Inference and Symmetry in Classical Proofs. Logos Verlag, Berlin (2004), http://www.iam.unibe.ch/~kai/Papers/phd.pdf
2. Brünnler, K.: Deep inference and its normal form of derivations. In: Beckmann, A., Berger, U., Löwe, B., Tucker, J.V. (eds.) CIE 2006. LNCS, vol. 3988, pp. 65–74. Springer, Heidelberg (2006), http://www.iam.unibe.ch/~kai/Papers/n.pdf
3. Bruscoli, P., Guglielmi, A.: On the proof complexity of deep inference. ACM Transactions on Computational Logic 10(2), article 14, 1–34 (2009), http://cs.bath.ac.uk/ag/p/PrComplDI.pdf
4. Bruscoli, P., Guglielmi, A., Gundersen, T., Parigot, M.: Quasipolynomial normalisation in deep inference via atomic flows and threshold formulae (2009), http://cs.bath.ac.uk/ag/p/QuasiPolNormDI.pdf (submitted)
5. Clote, P., Kranakis, E.: Boolean Functions and Computation Models. Springer, Heidelberg (2002)
6. Cook, S.A., Reckhow, R.A.: The relative efficiency of propositional proof systems. Journal of Symbolic Logic 44(1), 36–50 (1979)
7. Guglielmi, A., Gundersen, T.: Normalisation control in deep inference via atomic flows. Logical Methods in Computer Science 4(1:9), 1–36 (2008), http://www.lmcs-online.org/ojs/viewarticle.php?id=341
8. Guglielmi, A., Gundersen, T., Parigot, M.: A proof calculus which reduces syntactic bureaucracy. In: Lynch, C. (ed.) RTA 2010. Leibniz International Proceedings in Informatics (LIPIcs), vol. 6, pp. 135–150. Schloss Dagstuhl–Leibniz-Zentrum für Informatik (2010), http://drops.dagstuhl.de/opus/volltexte/2010/2649
9. Straßburger, L.: From deep inference to proof nets. In: Bruscoli, P., Lamarche, F., Stewart, C. (eds.) Structures and Deduction. pp. 2–18. Technische Universität Dresden, iCALP Workshop (2005) ISSN 1430-211X, http://www.lix.polytechnique.fr/~lutz/papers/deepnet-SD05.pdf
10. Straßburger, L.: Extension without cut (2009), http://www.lix.polytechnique.fr/~lutz/papers/psppp.pdf (submitted)
11. Troelstra, A., Schwichtenberg, H.: Basic Proof Theory. Cambridge Tracts in Theoretical Computer Science, vol. 43. Cambridge University Press, Cambridge (1996)

The Modal μ-Calculus Caught Off Guard

Oliver Friedmann[1] and Martin Lange[2]

[1] Dept. of Computer Science, University of Munich, Germany
[2] Dept. of Elect. Eng. and Computer Science, University of Kassel, Germany

Abstract. The modal μ-calculus extends basic modal logic with second-order quantification in terms of arbitrarily nested fixpoint operators. Its satisfiability problem is EXPTIME-complete. Decision procedures for the modal μ-calculus are not easy to obtain though since the arbitrary nesting of fixpoint constructs requires some combinatorial arguments for showing the well-foundedness of least fixpoint unfoldings. The tableau-based decision procedures so far also make assumptions on the unfoldings of fixpoint formulas, e.g. explicitly require formulas to be in guarded normal form. In this paper we present a tableau calculus for deciding satisfiability of arbitrary, i.e. not necessarily guarded μ-calculus formulas. The novel contribution is a new unfolding rule for greatest fixpoint formulas which shows how to handle unguardedness without an explicit transformation into guarded form, thus avoiding a (seemingly) exponential blow-up in formula size. We prove soundness and completeness of the calculus, and discuss its advantages over existing approaches.

1 Introduction

The modal μ-calculus $\mathcal{L}_\mu$ as introduced by Kozen [12] is a fundamental modal fixpoint logic. It is expressively equivalent to the bisimulation-invariant fragment of monadic second-order logic [10] and can therefore express all bisimulation-invariant properties of Kripke structures that can be defined using finite automata or any other machinery with at most regular expressive power. Consequently, there are embeddings of temporal logics like CTL and CTL* into $\mathcal{L}_\mu$ [5,3], as well as of dynamic logics like PDL [12], even when extended with certain extras [7].

Decidability of $\mathcal{L}_\mu$ can be established [13] by observing that its semantics can be expressed in monadic second-order logic which is known to be decidable due to Rabin's famous result from 1969 [18]. This, however, only gives a non-elementary upper complexity bound. The easy embedding of PDL yields a lower bound of deterministic exponential time, also known by the time of $\mathcal{L}_\mu$'s invention [8].

Closing this gap has taken some time and effort. Emerson and Streett showed decidability in deterministic triple exponential time [20]. Their procedure reduces the satisfiability problem to the problem of testing a finite tree automaton for emptiness. This finite tree automaton is obtained as the product of two automata: the first, called *local* automaton, accepts all locally-consistent Hintikka-tree structures for the input formula. A second automaton, called *global* automaton, is needed which checks for well-foundedness of the unfolding relation for least

K. Brünnler and G. Metcalfe (Eds.): TABLEAUX 2011, LNAI 6793, pp. 149–163, 2011.

fixpoint constructs. The product of these two accepts exactly the Hintikka tree models of the original formula which is sufficient for deciding satisfiability. Later, Emerson and Jutla have improved the involved automata-theoretic constructions to obtain EXPTIME-completeness of this problem [6].

There are also tableau-based decision procedure for (fragments) of $\mathcal{L}_\mu$. Kozen gave a tableau calculus in the introductory paper but could only prove soundness and completeness for the so-called aconjunctive fragment [12]. This has been extended by Walukiewicz to the so-called weak aconjunctive fragment [22] in the context of finding a complete axiom system for $\mathcal{L}_\mu$. The differences between tableau-based satisfiability checking and a proof system for validity are, however, merely a matter of taste in this setting. The property of being aconjunctive implies that any least fixpoint construct can only regenerate in a foreseeable way through a sequence of Hintikka sets which eliminates a large part of the difficulty in deciding well-foundedness of the unfolding relation. Bradfield and Stirling wrote *"it is an open question whether the tableau technique can be made to work directly for all formulae"* [2]. A tableau calculus which also works for non-aconjunctive formulas has recently been presented by Jungteerapanich [11].

These tableau-based decision procedures still impose a restriction on the syntax of formulas. They only work for formulas in guarded form which intuitively ensures that every infinite sequence of Hintikka sets corresponds to an infinite sequence of states in a Kripke model. Guardedness synchronizes all subformulas in a tableau node via the usual rule for modalities. When applying rules to unguarded formulas in an arbitrary order, it is possible to leave infinite unfoldings of least fixpoint formulas undetected by continuously unfolding a greatest fixpoint construct.

It is known that every formula can be transformed into an equivalent guarded one. Such constructions are presented in several places in the literature, either without an explicit analysis of the incurring blow-up which is easily seen to be exponential [1,22], or stating that the blow-up is polynomial, for instance quadratic [15] or even just linear [14]. While the latter two seem to be correct, their analyzes are both flawed. This is also indicated by the fact that both constructions are actually the same but are said to be linear once and quadratic the other time. Still, both analyzes do not handle multiple occurrences of variables correctly, and there are unguarded formulas which are transformed into exponentially larger ones by these constructions, e.g. $\mu X_1 \ldots \mu X_n.X_1 \vee \ldots \vee X_n \vee \langle a \rangle (X_1 \wedge \ldots \wedge X_n)$. This is even true for the stronger measurement of size as number of subformulas. Thus, all transformations into guarded form known until now are exponential, and we strongly doubt the existence of a polynomial translation.

In this paper we present a tableau-based decision procedure for the full $\mathcal{L}_\mu$ in unrestricted form. The requirement for guardedness is eliminated using a special unfolding rule for greatest fixpoint formulas. Intuitively, unfolding of greatest fixpoint constructs leads to two subgoals: one containing this unfolding, the other one not containing it. We prove soundness and completeness of this calculus and show how to obtain a decision procedure from it. This uses some automata-theoretic machinery similar to the use of the global automata in the approaches of Emerson et al.

The paper provides the following benefits: it presents a novel approach of dealing with unguarded fixpoint formulas inside a tableau calculus. This may be applicable to other logics with similar syntactic facets (like nested Kleene stars in PDL for instance). With the required pre-transformation into guarded form, Jungteerapanich's tableaux only lead to a nondeterministic double exponential time algorithm. The decision procedure derived from the tableaux presented here runs in deterministic single exponential time. This even marginally beats the worst-case runtime of the automata-theoretic procedure. Finally, the tableaux presented here are used in what seems to be the first attempt at implementing a decision procedure for $\mathcal{L}_\mu$, realized in the tool MLSOLVER [9].

The paper is organised as follows. Sect. 2 recalls $\mathcal{L}_\mu$ and necessary technicalities. Sect. 3 presents the tableaux calculus. The proofs of soundness and completeness of these tableaux are tedious and require the usual combinatorial arguments seen in other correctness proofs for $\mathcal{L}_\mu$. Therefore they are deferred to an appendix. Sect. 4 shows how to obtain a complexity-theoretically optimal decision procedure for $\mathcal{L}_\mu$ from these tableaux.

2   The Modal μ-Calculus

Transition Systems. A *labeled transition system* (LTS) over a set of *action names* Σ and a set of *atomic propositions* $\mathcal{P}$ is a tuple $\mathcal{T} = (S, \rightarrow, \ell)$ where S is a set of *states*, $\rightarrow \,\subseteq S \times \Sigma \times S$ defines a set of *transitions* between states that are labeled with action names, and $\ell : S \rightarrow 2^{\mathcal{P}}$ labels each state with a set of atomic propositions that are true in this state.

Syntax. Let Σ and $\mathcal{P}$ be as above and $\mathcal{V}$ be a set of variables. Formulas of the modal μ-calculus $\mathcal{L}_\mu$ in positive normal form are given as follows.

$$\varphi \quad ::= \quad q \mid \overline{q} \mid X \mid \varphi \vee \varphi \mid \varphi \wedge \varphi \mid \langle a \rangle \varphi \mid [a]\varphi \mid \mu X.\varphi \mid \nu X.\varphi$$

where $X \in \mathcal{V}$, $q \in \mathcal{P}$, and $a \in \Sigma$.

The operators μ and ν act as *binders* for the variables in a formula. A *free occurrence* of a variable X is therefore one that does not occur under the scope of such a binder. We assume all formulas φ to be *well-named* in the sense that each variable is bound at most once. We will write σ for either μ or ν.

We write $\varphi[\psi/X]$ to denote the formula that results from φ by replacing every free occurrence of the variable X in it with the formula ψ.

Fischer-Ladner Closure. The Fischer-Ladner closure of a formula φ is the least set $Cl(\varphi)$ that contains φ and satisfies the following.

  − If $\psi_1 \wedge \psi_2 \in Cl(\varphi)$ or $\psi_1 \vee \psi_2 \in Cl(\varphi)$ then $\psi_1, \psi_2 \in Cl(\varphi)$.
  − If $\langle a \rangle \psi \in Cl(\varphi)$ or $[a]\psi \in Cl(\varphi)$ then $\psi \in Cl(\varphi)$.
  − If $\sigma X.\psi \in Cl(\varphi)$ then $\psi[\sigma X.\psi/X] \in Cl(\varphi)$.

It is a standard exercise to show that $|Cl(\varphi)|$ is linear in the syntactic length of φ. We therefore define $|\varphi| := |Cl(\varphi)|$.

Fixpoint Nestings. Let φ be fixed and take two fixpoint formulas $\sigma X.\psi, \sigma' Y.\psi' \in Cl(\varphi)$. The latter *depends on* the former if this X occurs freely inside of ψ'. Let $\succ_\varphi$ be the reflexive-transitive closure of this dependency order. The *alternation depth* of φ, $ad(\varphi)$, is the maximal length of a $\succeq_\varphi$-chain s.t. adjacent formulas in this chain are of different fixpoint type μ or ν.

Semantics. Formulas of $\mathcal{L}_\mu$ are interpreted in states s of an LTS $\mathcal{T} = (S, \rightarrow, \ell)$ which we assume fixed for the moment. Let $\rho : \mathcal{V} \rightarrow 2^S$ be an environment used to interpret free variables. We write $\rho[X \mapsto T]$ to denote the environment which maps X to T and behaves like ρ on all other arguments. The semantics is given as a function mapping a formula to the set of states that it is true in w.r.t. the environment.

$$
\begin{aligned}
\llbracket q \rrbracket_\rho &= \{s \in S \mid q \in \ell(s)\} \\
\llbracket \bar{q} \rrbracket_\rho &= \{s \in S \mid q \notin \ell(s)\} \\
\llbracket X \rrbracket_\rho &= \rho(X) \\
\llbracket \varphi \vee \psi \rrbracket_\rho &= \llbracket \varphi \rrbracket_\rho \cup \llbracket \psi \rrbracket_\rho \\
\llbracket \varphi \wedge \psi \rrbracket_\rho &= \llbracket \varphi \rrbracket_\rho \cap \llbracket \psi \rrbracket_\rho \\
\llbracket \langle a \rangle \varphi \rrbracket_\rho &= \{s \in S \mid \exists t \in \llbracket \varphi \rrbracket_\rho \text{ with } s \xrightarrow{a} t\} \\
\llbracket [a]\varphi \rrbracket_\rho &= \{s \in S \mid \forall t \in \mathcal{S} : \text{ if } s \xrightarrow{a} t \text{ then } t \in \llbracket \varphi \rrbracket_\rho\} \\
\llbracket \mu X.\varphi \rrbracket_\rho &= \bigcap \{T \subseteq S \mid \llbracket \varphi \rrbracket_{\rho[X \mapsto T]} \subseteq T\} \\
\llbracket \nu X.\varphi \rrbracket_\rho &= \bigcup \{T \subseteq S \mid T \subseteq \llbracket \varphi \rrbracket_{\rho[X \mapsto T]}\}
\end{aligned}
$$

Two formulas φ and ψ are equivalent, written $\varphi \equiv \psi$, iff for all LTS and all environments ρ we have $\llbracket \varphi \rrbracket_\rho = \llbracket \psi \rrbracket_\rho$. We may also write $s \models_\rho \varphi$ instead of $s \in \llbracket \varphi \rrbracket_\rho$.

Guarded Form. A formula φ is *guarded w.r.t. a variable* X iff every occurrence of X that is bound by some $\sigma X.\psi$ is in the scope of a modal operator $\langle a \rangle$ or $[a]$ within ψ. A formula φ is *guarded* iff φ is guarded w.r.t. every bound variable.

Proposition 1 ([1,22,14,15]). *For every* $\varphi \in \mathcal{L}_\mu$ *there is a guarded* φ' *s.t.* $\varphi' \equiv \varphi$, $|\varphi'| = 2^{\mathcal{O}(|\varphi|)}$, *and* $ad(\varphi') = ad(\varphi)$.

We remark that guarded transformation can increase the number of μ-bound variables in a formula, even exponentially. This measure is used at the end of Sect. 4 in a comparison of different decision procedures.

3   Tableaux for the Modal μ-Calculus

We fix a formula ϑ and present a calculus of infinite tableaux for this particular ϑ. A *pre-tableau* for ϑ is a possibly infinite but finitely-branching tree in which nodes are labeled with subsets of $Sub(\vartheta)$, the set of subformulas of ϑ. The root is labeled with the singleton set containing ϑ, and successors in the tree are being built using the rules in Fig. 1.

$$\text{(Or)}\ \frac{\varphi_0 \vee \varphi_1, \Phi}{\varphi_i, \Phi} \qquad \text{(And)}\ \frac{\varphi_0 \wedge \varphi_1, \Phi}{\varphi_0, \varphi_1, \Phi} \qquad \text{(FP}_\mu)\ \frac{\mu X.\varphi, \Phi}{\varphi[\mu X.\varphi/X], \Phi}$$

$$\text{(FP}_\nu^U)\ \frac{\nu X.\varphi, \Phi}{\Phi \qquad \varphi[\nu X.\varphi/X], \Phi} \qquad\qquad \text{(FP}_\nu^G)\ \frac{\nu X.\varphi, \Phi}{\varphi[\nu X.\varphi/X], \Phi}\ X \text{ guarded in } \varphi$$

$$\text{(Mod)}\ \frac{\langle a_1\rangle\varphi_1, \ldots, \langle a_n\rangle\varphi_n, [b_1]\psi_1, \ldots, [b_m]\psi_m, q_1, \ldots, q_k, \overline{p_1}, \ldots, \overline{p_h}}{\varphi_1, \{\psi_i \mid a_1 = b_i\} \quad \varphi_2, \{\psi_i \mid a_2 = b_i\} \quad \cdots \quad \varphi_n, \{\psi_i \mid a_m = b_i\}}\ \forall i, j.q_i \neq p_j$$

Fig. 1. The tableaux rules for $\mathcal{L}_\mu$ satisfiability

The rules for the boolean connectives are straight-forward, and the modal rule (Mod) is also the usual one. Least fixpoint variables are handled using simple unfolding with rule (FP$_\mu$). The handling of greatest fixpoints is different, though. Rule (FP$_\nu^U$) creates two subgoals, one containing the usual unfolding of the fixpoint formula, the other one consisting of the current side formulas only. This rule can be applied to unfold any greatest fixpoint formula. On the other hand, rule (FP$_\nu^G$) is the usual unfolding rule which can only be applied to formulas in which the bound variable is guarded.

A formula ϑ induces the *connection* relation $\rightsquigarrow \subseteq 2^{Sub(\vartheta)} \times Sub(\vartheta) \times 2^{Sub(\vartheta)} \times Sub(\vartheta)$ defined as follows. We have $\Phi, \varphi \rightsquigarrow \Psi, \psi$ iff there is an instance of a rule of Fig. 1 s.t.

- $\varphi \in \Phi$, $\psi \in \Psi$, and
- Φ is the conclusion (on top), Ψ is one of the premises (below), and
- either φ is not principal in this rule application and $\psi = \varphi$, or φ is a principal formula in Φ and ψ is a replacement of φ.

For example, in rule (And), $\varphi_0 \wedge \varphi_1$ is connected to both φ_0 and φ_1. In rule (Mod), $\Box\psi_j$ is connected to ψ_j in any premiss, literals are not connected to anything, and $\Diamond\varphi_i$ is only connected to φ_i in the i-th premiss; etc.

A *thread* in an infinite pre-tableaux branch $\Phi_0, \Phi_1, \Phi_2, \ldots$ is an infinite sequence $\varphi_0, \varphi_1, \varphi_2, \ldots$ s.t. $\Phi_i, \varphi_i \rightsquigarrow \Phi_{i+1}, \varphi_{i+1}$ for every $i \in \mathbb{N}$. It is called *active* if the thread's formulas are principal infinitely often.

Note that only the unfolding rules (FP$_\mu$) and (FP$_\nu^U$) do not decrease the size of a principal formula. Hence, each active thread must contain infinitely many formulas of the form $\sigma X.\psi$. A thread is called μ-thread if the greatest (w.r.t. $\succeq_\vartheta$) formula occurring in it is of the form $\mu X.\varphi$. If it is of the form $\nu X.\varphi$ then the thread is a ν-thread. The variable X is called *thread variable*. The following is not hard to see.

Lemma 1. *Every infinite branch in pre-tableau contains at least one active thread and every active thread is either of type μ or ν.*

A *tableau* for ϑ is a pre-tableau s.t. every finite branch ends in a node labeled with $\Box$-formulas and consistent literals only, and every infinite branch does not have an active μ-thread.

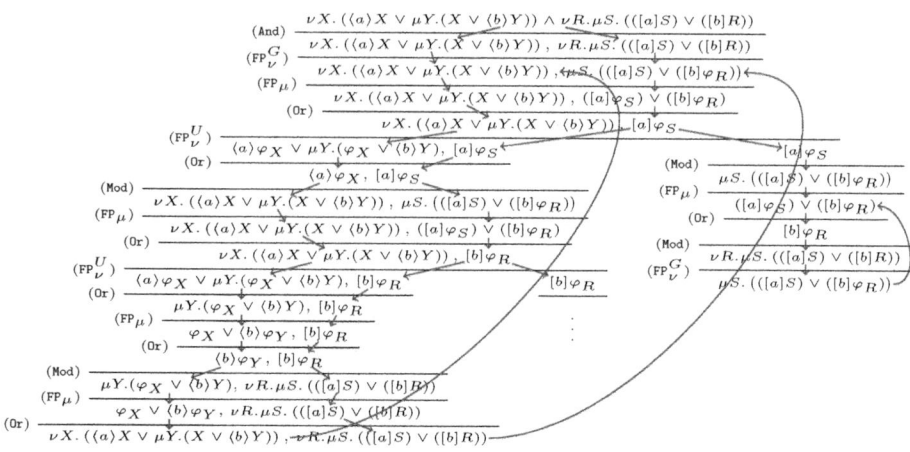

Fig. 2. A tableau for $\nu X.\,(\langle a\rangle X \vee \mu Y.(X \vee \langle b\rangle Y)) \wedge \nu R.\mu S.\,(([a]S) \vee ([b]R))$.

Example 1. Consider $\varphi = \nu X.\,(\langle a\rangle X \vee \mu Y.(X \vee \langle b\rangle Y)) \wedge \nu R.\mu S.\,(([a]S) \vee ([b]R))$ which states that every path consists of a- and b-labelings, every path has infinitely many b's, and that there exists a path with infinitely many a's. This formula is obviously satisfiable.

See Fig. 2 for a tableau witnessing the satisfiability of φ. We write φ_F as an abbreviation for the fixpoint bodies, i.e. $\varphi_S = ([a]S) \vee ([b]R)$, etc.; the tableau has only infinite branches, and every thread is a ν-thread. All threads are marked by the arrow notation.

At this point, we only state correctness of the tableau calculus. The proofs of soundness and completeness are technical using some combinatorial machinery – as is usual for $\mathcal{L}_\mu$ – but do not necessarily provide new insights into the theory of this logic. Therefore they are deferred to an appendix.

Theorem 1. *Let $\vartheta \in \mathcal{L}_\mu$. Then ϑ is satisfiable iff there is a tableau for ϑ.*

We conclude this section with a remark on the handling of greatest fixpoint formulas. Many formulas used in applications are naturally guarded. Since the tableau calculus is sound and complete for the entire $\mathcal{L}_\mu$, it can be used for guarded formulas as well. However, handling guarded greatest fixpoint operators with rule (FP_ν^U) may introduce unnecessary subgoals. Rule $(FP_\nu^G$ can therefore be regarded as an optimization. However, it is not a priori clear whether it is advisable to use this optimization. It clearly reduces the number of immediate subgoals in a tableau but these subgoals may be present somewhere else anyway in which case it only reduces the number of connections between subgoals. Neither decreases the asymptotic complexity of the calculus.

4   A Decision Procedure Based on Tableaux

A natural question is: can the tableaux of the previous section be used to decide satisfiability for $\mathcal{L}_\mu$? In this section we will show that the answer is positive and compare the resulting procedure with existing ones. The procedure works as follows. We first show that pre-tableau branches without μ-threads can be recognized by a deterministic parity automaton (DPA). The pre-tableaux nodes can be annotated with states of this DPA resulting in a graph equipped with a parity condition. There are two kinds of branching in this graph: existential branching corresponding to choices with rule (OR), and universal branching corresponding to choices between different subgoals. This graph is finite and forms a parity game [16]. The question whether or not a tableau exists for an input formula reduces to the problem of solving this game.

4.1   Automata-Theoretic Machinery

Again, we fix a formula ϑ. It induces an alphabet Σ_ϑ representing transitions from a goal to a subgoal in a rule application. These symbolic alphabet letter should determine a subgoal of a given goal uniquely and succinctly. Clearly this can be done by naming the principal formula, possibly its replacement, as well as the number of the subgoal of which there can at most be $|\vartheta|$ many. It is clearly possible to realize this in an alphabet Σ_ϑ of size $\mathcal{O}(|\vartheta|^3)$.

With an infinite branch $\rho = \Phi_0, \Phi_1, \ldots$ of a pre-tableau for ϑ we associate a word $w_\rho \in \Sigma_\vartheta^\omega$ in the natural way: the i-th letter of w_ρ is the symbol representing the application of the rule between Φ_i and Φ_{i+1}. Let $BadBranch(\vartheta)$ be the set of all words representing an infinite branch in a pre-tableau for ϑ which contains an active μ-thread, i.e. the set of all branches which may not occur in a tableau.

A nondeterministic parity automaton (NPA) is a tuple $\mathcal{A} = (Q, \Sigma, q_0, \delta, \Omega)$ where Q is a finite set of states, Σ is the underlying alphabet, $q_0 \in Q$ is a designated starting state, $\delta \subseteq Q \times \Sigma \times Q$ is the transition relation as usual, and $\Omega : Q \to \mathbb{N}$ is the priority function. A run $\rho = q_0, q_1, \ldots$ on an infinite word $w \in \Sigma^\omega$ is defined as usual. It is accepting if the highest priority occurring infinitely often in $\Omega(q_0), \Omega(q_1), \ldots$ is even. Let $|\mathcal{A}|$ denote the size of $\mathcal{A}$, measured as its number of states. Its index, $idx(\mathcal{A})$, is the number of distinct priorities assigned to its states. An NPA as above is deterministic (DPA) if $\delta : Q \times \Sigma \to Q$ in effect. A nondeterministic Büchi automaton (NBA) is an NPA as above with $\Omega : Q \to 1, 2$.

Lemma 2. *There is an NPA $\mathcal{B}'_\vartheta$ over Σ_ϑ s.t. $|\mathcal{B}'_\vartheta| \leq 2 \cdot |\vartheta|$, $idx(\mathcal{B}'_\vartheta) \leq ad(\vartheta) + 2$, and $L(\mathcal{B}'_\vartheta) = BadBranch(\vartheta)$.*

Proof. The NPA simply guesses threads by tracing single formulas from $Cl(\vartheta)$ in its state set. Upon reading an input letter it knows whether the next rule application transforms the currently traced subformula or whether it remains the same on that thread. In order to distinguish inactive threads from active threads, the NBA utilizes a bit to indicate that the focussed thread has been unfolded in the last transition. A parity condition that reflects the alternation depth of each formula inside $Cl(\vartheta)$ can then be used in order to recognise $BadBranch(\vartheta)$.   □

It is a standard exercise in automata theory to show that every NPA can equivalently be transformed into an NBA with a quadratic blow-up only.

Lemma 3. *There is an NBA $\mathcal{B}_\vartheta$ over Σ_ϑ s.t. $|\mathcal{B}_\vartheta| \leq 2 \cdot |\vartheta| \cdot (ad(\vartheta) + 2)$, and $L(\mathcal{B}_\vartheta) = BadBranch(\vartheta)$.*

As said above, the goal is to create a parity game as a product of all possible pre-tableau nodes with the states of a automaton recognizing branches that do *not* contain a μ-thread. Hence, complementation of the automaton $\mathcal{B}_\vartheta$ is needed. Moreover, this automaton needs to be deterministic to ensure that common prefixes of two different branches can be paired with a single run of the automaton.

Theorem 2 ([17]). *For every NBA $\mathcal{B}$ with n states there is a DPA $\mathcal{A}$ with $2^{\mathcal{O}(n \log n)}$ states and index $\mathcal{O}(n)$ s.t. $L(\mathcal{A}) = \overline{L(\mathcal{B})}$.*

Combining this theorem with Lemma 3 yields the following. Note that $ad(\vartheta) \leq |\vartheta|$, and that if $k \leq n$ then $\log(nk) \leq 2 \cdot \log n$.

Corollary 1. *Let $\vartheta \in \mathcal{L}_\mu$ with $n := |\vartheta|$ and $k := ad(\vartheta)$. There is a DPA $\mathcal{A}_\vartheta$ over Σ_ϑ s.t. the number of states in $\mathcal{A}_\vartheta$ is bounded by $2^{\mathcal{O}(n \cdot k \cdot \log n)}$, its index is $\mathcal{O}(n \cdot k)$, and $L(\mathcal{B}_\vartheta) = \overline{BadBranch(\vartheta)}$.*

4.2   Reduction to Parity Game Solving

The algorithmic solution to the satisfiability problem is provided by a reduction to parity game solving. A parity game is a tuple $G = (V, V_0, V_1, E, v_0, \Omega)$ s.t. (V, E) is a directed graph with total edge relation E and node set partitioned into V_0 and V_1, v_0 is a designated starting node, and $\Omega : V \to \mathbb{N}$ is a priority function. The game is played between two players 0 and 1 who push a token along the edges of a the graph starting in v_0. If the token is on a node in V_i then player i chooses a successor node. An infinite sequence of nodes created in this way is a ply and it is won by player i iff the highest priority seen infinitely often in this sequence is i modulo 2. A winning strategy is as usual a strategy for a player that lets them win every play regardless of the opponent's choices. We write $|G|$ for the number of nodes in the game G, and $idx(G)$ for its index, i.e. number of distinct priorities.

Proposition 2. *Let ϑ be a formula with $n := |\vartheta|$ and $k := ad(\vartheta)$. There is a parity game G_ϑ with $|G| \leq 2^{\mathcal{O}(n \cdot k \cdot \log n)}$ and $idx(G) \leq \mathcal{O}(n \cdot k)$, that is won by player 0 iff ϑ is satisfiable.*

Proof. Let $\mathcal{A}_\vartheta = (Q, \Sigma_\vartheta, q_0, \delta, \Omega)$. The nodes of the game G_ϑ are of the form $2^{Cl(\vartheta)} \times Q$; the designated node v_0 is $(\{\vartheta\}, q_0)$. A node $w = (\Psi, q')$ is a successor of $v = (\Phi, q)$ if a uniquely (for (Φ, q)) chosen rule is applied to Φ that yields Ψ as one of its premises, this rule is represented by $r \in \Sigma_\vartheta$ and $\delta(q, r) = q'$ where δ is the transition function of $\mathcal{A}_\vartheta$. The node ownership in the game is determined by these uniquely chosen rules: player 0 owns nodes in which rule (Or) is applied,

	AUT [6]	TAB [11]	GAME^G (here)	GAME (here)
unguardedness welcome	yes	no	no	yes
worst-case runtime	$2^{\mathcal{O}(n^2 m^2 \log n)}$	2NEXPTIME	$2^{2^{\mathcal{O}(n)}}$	$2^{\mathcal{O}(n^2 k^2 \log n)}$
small model property	$2^{\mathcal{O}(nm \log n)}$	$2^{2^{\mathcal{O}(n)}}$	$2^{2^{\mathcal{O}(n)}}$	$2^{\mathcal{O}(nk \log n)}$
branching-degree	n	$2^{\mathcal{O}(n)}$	$2^{\mathcal{O}(n)}$	n
implemented	no	no	yes [9]	yes [9]

Fig. 3. Comparison of different decision methods on formulas of size n and alternation depth k and number of least fixpoint variables m

while player 1 owns all the other nodes. Finally, the priority of a game node $(\varPhi, q)$ is simply $\varOmega(q)$.

It is not hard to see that winning strategies for player 0 exactly correspond to tableaux for ϑ. Hence, with Thm. 1, player 0 wins node v_0 iff ϑ is satisfiable. □

Proposition 3. *Satisfiability of a $\mathcal{L}_\mu$ formula ϑ with $n := |\vartheta|$ and $k := ad(\vartheta)$ can be decided in time $2^{\mathcal{O}(n^2 \cdot k^2 \cdot \log n)}$.*

Proof. Follows immediately from Prop. 2 with the fact that the asymptotically best known algorithms for solving parity games run in time $m^{\mathcal{O}(p)}$ where m is the number of nodes and p is the number of priorities in the game [19]. □

The subgame induced by a winning strategy for player 0 is in effect a model for ϑ. This immediately yields a small model property for $\mathcal{L}_\mu$.

Proposition 4. *Let $\vartheta \in \mathcal{L}_\mu$ with $n := |\vartheta|$ and $k := ad(\vartheta)$. If ϑ is satisfiable then it has a model of size $2^{\mathcal{O}(nk \cdot \log n)}$ and branching-degree at most n.*

4.3   Comparison

We compare the presented method (GAME) to existing methods, namely the automata-theoretic one by Emerson et al. (AUT) [21,6] and the purely tableau-based one by Jungteerapanich (TAB) [11]. Additionally we consider the method which works as described above but uses pre-transformation into guarded form and rule (FP$_\nu^G$) instead (GAME^G). The input formula is parameterized by its size n, its alternation-depth k, and the number of distinct μ-bound variables in it m. Note that we always have $k \leq m < n$.

The reasoning behind the run-time and small model property of method AUT are as follows. A formula ϑ of size n with m μ-bound variables can be translated into a Streett automaton of size $2^{\mathcal{O}(n \cdot m \cdot \log n)}$ and $\mathcal{O}(n \cdot m)$ acceptance pairs [21].[1] Emptiness of a Streett tree automaton with s states and p pairs can be decided in time $(s \cdot p)^{\mathcal{O}(p)}$ [6], hence the worst-case runtime of $2^{\mathcal{O}(n^2 \cdot m^2 \log n)}$ observing that $m < n$. This uses an equivalence-preserving reduction from Streett automata

---

[1] Emerson et al. claim that the global automaton used in their construction is of linear size n, but its description shows that it really is of size $n \cdot m$.

of that size to Rabin automata of size s^2 with p pairs [6]. Every Rabin tree automaton with e edges and p pairs accepts a tree that is finitely representable with $\mathcal{O}(e)$ nodes [4]. In this case, we have $e = \mathcal{O}(n \cdot m \cdot s^2)$ because a transition to a tuple of size j counts as j edges, and the branching-degrees of these automata are linear in the size of the original formula. Putting this all together, we obtain a small model property of $2^{\mathcal{O}(n \cdot m \cdot \log n)}$.

It is worth mentioning that conceptually, the method presented here is very close to the purely automata-theoretic method AUT. However, separating the local and global consistency checks into pre-tableau rules and automata-theoretic machinery for the thread structure in tableaux yields a cleaner presentation of the method's ingredients. The slight asymptotic speed-up using the exponent k instead of m where $k \leq m$ is owed to using the more modern concept of parity automata rather than Streett automata.

The main advantage of TAB is the fact that tableaux in that calculus are finite as opposed to the infinite ones used here. The price to pay for this seems to be the non-optimal complexity bound. It is not clear whether there is also a deterministic algorithm for that calculus and whether it can be made to work on unguarded formulas as well thus losing one exponential in worst-case runtime and small model property.

Finally, we remark on the lack of experimental data in this paper. Note that the only two decision procedures which can be compared empirically are GAME and GAME^G. However, since guarded transformation incurs an exponential blow-up, the results are pretty unspectacular: on guarded formulas there is no real difference between the two, and on unguarded formulas GAME^G is generally exponentially worse than GAME.

References

1. Banieqbal, B., Barringer, H.: Temporal logic with fixed points. In: Banieqbal, B., Pnueli, A., Barringer, H. (eds.) Temporal Logic in Specification. LNCS, vol. 398, pp. 62–73. Springer, Heidelberg (1989)
2. Bradfield, J., Stirling, C.: Modal logics and μ-calculi: an introduction. In: Bergstra, J., Ponse, A., Smolka, S. (eds.) Handbook of Process Algebra. Elsevier, Amsterdam (2001)
3. Dam, M.: CTL* and ECTL* as fragments of the modal μ-calculus. TCS 126(1), 77–96 (1994)
4. Emerson, E.A.: Automata, tableaux and temporal logics. In: Parikh, R. (ed.) Logic of Programs 1985. LNCS, vol. 193, pp. 79–87. Springer, Heidelberg (1985)
5. Emerson, E.A.: Temporal and modal logic. In: van Leeuwen, J. (ed.) Handbook of Theoretical Computer Science. Formal Models and Semantics, vol. B, ch. 16, pp. 996–1072. Elsevier and MIT Press, New York, USA (1990)
6. Emerson, E.A., Jutla, C.S.: The complexity of tree automata and logics of programs. SIAM Journal on Computing 29(1), 132–158 (2000)
7. Emerson, E.A., Lei, C.L.: Efficient model checking in fragments of the propositional μ-calculus. In: Symposion on Logic in Computer Science, pp. 267–278. IEEE, Washington, D.C. (1986)

8. Fischer, M.J., Ladner, R.E.: Propositional dynamic logic of regular programs. Journal of Computer and System Sciences 18(2), 194–211 (1979)
9. Friedmann, O., Lange, M.: A solver for modal fixpoint logics. In: Proc. 6th Workshop on Methods for Modalities, M4M-6. Elect. Notes in Theor. Comp. Sc., vol. 262, pp. 99–111 (2010)
10. Janin, D., Walukiewicz, I.: On the expressive completeness of the propositional μ-calculus with respect to monadic second order logic. In: Sassone, V., Montanari, U. (eds.) CONCUR 1996. LNCS, vol. 1119, pp. 263–277. Springer, Heidelberg (1996)
11. Jungteerapanich, N.: A tableau system for the modal μ-calculus. In: Giese, M., Waaler, A. (eds.) TABLEAUX 2009. LNCS, vol. 5607, pp. 220–234. Springer, Heidelberg (2009)
12. Kozen, D.: Results on the propositional μ-calculus. TCS 27, 333–354 (1983)
13. Kozen, D., Parikh, R.: A decision procedure for the propositional μ-calculus. In: Clarke, E., Kozen, D. (eds.) Logic of Programs 1983. LNCS, vol. 164, pp. 313–325. Springer, Heidelberg (1984)
14. Kupferman, O., Vardi, M.Y., Wolper, P.: An automata-theoretic approach to branching-time model checking. Journal of the ACM 47(2), 312–360 (2000)
15. Mateescu, R.: Local model-checking of modal mu-calculus on acyclic labeled transition systems. In: Katoen, J.-P., Stevens, P. (eds.) TACAS 2002. LNCS, vol. 2280, pp. 281–295. Springer, Heidelberg (2002)
16. McNaughton, R.: Infinite games played on finite graphs. Annals of Pure and Applied Logic 65(2), 149–184 (1993)
17. Piterman, N.: From nondeterministic Büchi and Streett automata to deterministic parity automata. In: Proc. 21st Symp.on Logic in Computer Science (LICS 2006), pp. 255–264. IEEE Computer Society, Los Alamitos (2006)
18. Rabin, M.O.: Decidability of second-order theories and automata on infinite trees. Trans.of Amer. Math.Soc. 141, 1–35 (1969)
19. Schewe, S.: Solving parity games in big steps. In: Arvind, V., Prasad, S. (eds.) FSTTCS 2007. LNCS, vol. 4855, pp. 449–460. Springer, Heidelberg (2007)
20. Streett, R.S., Emerson, E.A.: The propositional μ-calculus is elementary. In: Paredaens, J. (ed.) ICALP 1984. LNCS, vol. 172, pp. 465–472. Springer, Heidelberg (1984)
21. Streett, R.S., Emerson, E.A.: An automata theoretic decision procedure for the propositional μ-calculus. Information and Computation 81(3), 249–264 (1989)
22. Walukiewicz, I.: Completeness of Kozen's axiomatisation of the propositional μ-calculus. Inf. and Comput. 157(1–2), 142–182 (2000)

A   Correctness Proofs

A.1   Approximants and Signatures

We need *fixpoint approximants* in order to prove absence of any μ-threads in tableaux. Here we introduce them via annotations of fixpoint formulas with ordinal numbers. These annotated fixpoint formulas are interpreted in a way that is different to ordinary fixpoint formulas. Let $\mathcal{T} = (S, \rightarrow, \ell)$ be the underlying transition system.

$$[\![\mu^0 X.\psi]\!]_\rho := \emptyset \qquad\qquad [\![\nu^0 X.\psi]\!]_\rho := S$$

$$[\![\mu^{\alpha+1} X.\psi]\!]_\rho := [\![\psi]\!]_{\rho[X \mapsto [\![\mu^\alpha X.\psi]\!]_\rho]} \qquad [\![\nu^{\alpha+1} X.\psi]\!]_\rho := [\![\psi]\!]_{\rho[X \mapsto [\![\nu^\alpha X.\psi]\!]_\rho]}$$

$$[\![\mu^\lambda X.\psi]\!]_\rho := \bigcup_{\alpha<\lambda} [\![\mu^\alpha X.\psi]\!]_\rho \qquad [\![\nu^\lambda X.\psi]\!]_\rho := \bigcap_{\alpha<\lambda} [\![\nu^\alpha X.\psi]\!]_\rho$$

where α is an arbitrary ordinal and λ is a limit ordinal.

A *signature* is an annotation of a formulas fixpoint subformulas with ordinal numbers. We distinguish two types of signatures: a *μ-signature* annotates least fixpoint subformulas, a *ν-signature* annotates greatest fixpoint subformulas. We write φ^ζ to denote the annotation of fixpoint formulas of corresponding type in φ with the values in ζ. Remember that fixpoint subformulas of a formula ϑ are partially ordered by $\succeq$. This extends to a lexicographic and well-founded order of μ- or ν-signatures on ϑ which we will also call $\succeq$.

The following lemma summarizes well-known facts about signatures that will be used in the proofs later on.

Lemma 4. *Let s be a state in a transition system $\mathcal{T}$, $\varphi \in \mathcal{L}_\mu$.*

1. *$s \in [\![\varphi]\!]_\rho$ iff there is a μ-signature ζ s.t. $s \in [\![\varphi^\zeta]\!]_\rho$.*
2. *$s \notin [\![\varphi]\!]_\rho$ iff there is a ν-signature ζ s.t. $s \notin [\![\varphi^\zeta]\!]_\rho$.*
3. *Let φ' result from φ by replacing some $\mu X.\psi$ in it with its unfolding $\psi[\mu X.\psi/X]$. Suppose there is a μ-signature ζ s.t. $s \in [\![\varphi^\zeta]\!]_\rho$. Then there is a μ-signature ζ' with $\zeta \succneqq \zeta'$ and $s \in [\![\varphi'^{\zeta'}]\!]_\rho$.*
4. *Let φ' result from φ by replacing some $\nu X.\psi$ in it with its unfolding $\psi[\nu X.\psi/X]$. Suppose there is a ν-signature ζ s.t. $s \notin [\![\varphi^\zeta]\!]_\rho$. Then there is a ν-signature ζ' with $\zeta \succneqq \zeta'$ and $s \notin [\![\varphi'^{\zeta'}]\!]_\rho$.*

A.2   Soundness

We represent (pre-)tableaux as pointed directed acyclic graphs $(V, v_0, \prec, \mathcal{M})$ with V being the set of nodes, v_0 being the initial node, $\prec$ being the transition relation and $\mathcal{M}$ being a labeling function that maps each node $v \in V$ to the corresponding sequent.

Let $\mathcal{P} = (V, v_0, \prec, \mathcal{M})$ be a tableau for ϑ. A *ν-strategy for $\mathcal{P}$* is a partial map $\varrho : V \to V$ that is defined on every node v that is the conclusion of the application of the (FP_ν^U)-rule and fulfills for every such v that $v \prec \varrho(v)$.

A branch $v_0, v_1, \dots$ in $\mathcal{P}$ *conforms* with ϱ iff for every i with v_i being the conclusion of the application of the (FP_ν^U)-rule it holds that $\varrho(v_i) = v_{i+1}$. We say that a node $v \in V$ is *ϱ-reachable* iff v belongs to a ϱ-conforming branch. The set of ϱ-reachable nodes is denoted by V_ϱ. The pair $(\mathcal{P}, \varrho)$ is called *collapsible* if every ϱ-conforming branch in $\mathcal{P}$ is either finite or comprises infinitely many applications of the (Mod)-rule.

Let $(\mathcal{P}, \varrho)$ be collapsible. We define a *lift operation* $l_{(\mathcal{P},\varrho)} : V_\varrho \to V_\varrho$ that maps every node $v \in V_\varrho$ to v if v is a sink or the conclusion of the application of the (Mod)-rule and otherwise to $l_{(\mathcal{P},\varrho)}(w)$ where w is the uniquely defined ϱ-conforming successor of v. As $(\mathcal{P}, \varrho)$ is collapsible, $l_{(\mathcal{P},\varrho)}$ is indeed well-defined.

Every collapsible $(\mathcal{P}, \varrho)$ for a formula ϑ induces an generic interpretation $\mathcal{T}_{(\mathcal{P},\varrho)} = (V_\varrho, \to, l)$ with $l : v \mapsto \mathcal{M}(v) \cap \mathcal{P}$ and $v \xrightarrow{a} w$ for two nodes $v, w \in V_\varrho$ iff there is an $u \in V$ with $v \prec u$ connected via an a-label and $l_{(\mathcal{P},\varrho)}(u) = w$.

Next, we define an annotation that counts for every formula φ in a sequent, how often every ν-bound variable has been unfolded since the last occurrence of the modal rule. This will help us to define a generic ν-strategy that results in collapsible tableaux while ensuring that every potentially relevant unguarded ν-bound variable that occurs in a thread is unfolded at least once.

Let $\mathcal{P} = (V, v_0, \prec, \mathcal{M})$ be a tableau for ϑ. The ν-*variable annotation for* $\mathcal{P}$ is a function $\mathcal{A}_{\mathcal{P}}$ that maps every node $v \in V$ and every formula $\varphi \in \mathcal{M}(v)$ to a set of sets of ν-variables $\mathcal{A}_{\mathcal{P}}(v, \varphi)$.

We define the function inductively. For the initial v_0, $\mathcal{A}_{\mathcal{P}}(v_0, \vartheta) = \{\emptyset\}$. Let now $v, u \in V$ with $v \prec u$ and $\mathcal{A}_{\mathcal{P}}(v, *)$ be already defined. Then

- $\mathcal{A}_{\mathcal{P}}(u, \varphi) = \{\emptyset\}$ if $\mathcal{M}(v)$ is the conclusion of a (Mod)-application,
- $\mathcal{A}_{\mathcal{P}}(u, \varphi) = \{U \cup \{X\} \mid (U \setminus \{X\}) \in \mathcal{A}'_{\mathcal{P}}(u, \varphi)\}$ if $\varphi = \psi[\nu X.\psi/X]$ and $\nu X.\psi$ is principal in $\mathcal{M}(v)$, and
- $\mathcal{A}_{\mathcal{P}}(u, \varphi) = \mathcal{A}'_{\mathcal{P}}(u, \varphi)$ otherwise,

where $\mathcal{A}'_{\mathcal{P}}(u, \varphi) := \bigcup \{\mathcal{A}_{\mathcal{P}}(v, \psi) \mid (\mathcal{M}(v), \psi) \rightsquigarrow (\mathcal{M}(u), \varphi)\}$.

Next, we define a *canonic ν-strategy* $\varrho_{\mathcal{P}}$ for a tableau $\mathcal{P}$ as follows. Let v be a node in $\mathcal{P}$ s.t. $\mathcal{M}(v)$ is the conclusion of an application of the (FP_ν^U)-rule with $\nu X.\psi$ as principal formula and let u be the successor of v discarding the fixpoint body and w be the successor following the fixpoint body. Then $\varrho_{\mathcal{P}}(v) = w$ if there is an $U \in \mathcal{A}_{\mathcal{P}}(v, \nu X.\psi)$ with $X \notin U$ and $\varrho_{\mathcal{P}}(v) = u$ otherwise.

Lemma 5. *Let $\mathcal{P}$ be a tableau for φ. Then $(\mathcal{P}, \varrho_{\mathcal{P}})$ is collapsible.*

Proof. Assume that $(\mathcal{P}, \varrho_{\mathcal{P}})$ is not collapsible, hence there is an infinite $\varrho_{\mathcal{P}}$-conforming branch $v_0, v_1, \ldots$ in $\mathcal{P}$ that contains only finitely many applications of the (Mod)-rule. Let $i^* \geq 0$ s.t. $\mathcal{M}(v_i)$ is not the conclusion of the application of a (Mod)-rule for all $i \geq i^*$.

First observe the following fact. Let $i \geq i^*$ and $\varphi \in \mathcal{M}(v_i)$. Let $U \in \mathcal{A}_{\mathcal{P}}(v_i, \varphi)$. This implies that there is a (prefix of a) thread s going through φ in the node v_i s.t. between i^* and i, we have

- zero unfoldings for fixpoints $\nu X.\psi$ with $X \notin U$, and
- one unfolding for fixpoints $\nu X.\psi$ with $X \in U$.

Let now $t = \varphi_0, \varphi_1, \ldots$ be an active thread with thread variable X, existing due to Lemma 1. Due to the fact that $\mathcal{P}$ is a tableau, X must be of type ν.

Let $j_0, j_1, \ldots$ be an infinite sequence of ascending numbers with $j_0 \geq i^*$ s.t. $\varphi_{j_k} = \nu X.\psi$ is the principal formula in $\mathcal{M}(v_{j_k})$ for all k.

For every j_k, there is an $U \in \mathcal{A}_{\mathcal{P}}(v_{j_k}, \nu X.\psi)$ s.t. $X \notin U$ by the canonic ν-strategy. In other words, for every k there is a (prefix of a) thread s_k going through $\nu X.\psi$ in the node v_{j_k} s.t. between i^* and j_k, we have no more than one unfolding per ν-fixpoint.

Now note that by the pigeonhole principle (infinitely many s_k share the same prefixes and they need to split infinitely often), there are infinitely many s_k which are principal between i^* and j_k. By König's Lemma, this implies that there is an active thread s that has no more than one unfolding per ν-fixpoint.

Since s is clearly not a ν-fixpoint, it follows by Lemma 1 that s is a μ-fixpoint. But this is impossible with $\mathcal{P}$ being a tableau. $\qquad\square$

Due to the fact that $(\mathcal{P}, \varrho_\mathcal{P})$ is always collapsible, we can define the *canonic interpretation* $\mathcal{T}_\mathcal{P}$ as $\mathcal{T}_{(\mathcal{P}, \varrho_\mathcal{P})}$.

Theorem 3 (Soundness). *A formula ϑ is satisfiable if there is a tableau $\mathcal{P}$ for ϑ. Particularly, $\mathcal{T}_{(\mathcal{P}, \varrho_\mathcal{P})} \models \vartheta$.*

Proof. By contradiction assume that $\mathcal{T}_{(\mathcal{P}, \varrho_\mathcal{P})} \not\models \vartheta$. We extract a branch $v_0, v_1, \dots$ in $\mathcal{P}$, a sequence of formulas $\varphi_0, \varphi_1, \dots$ with $\varphi_i \in \mathcal{M}(v_i)$ for all i and a sequence of ν-signatures $\zeta_0 \succeq \zeta_1 \succeq \dots$ s.t. the following conditions hold for all i.

1. ζ_i is the least ν-signature s.t. $l_{(\mathcal{P}, \varrho_\mathcal{P})}(v_i) \not\models \varphi_i^{\zeta_i}$
2. $(\mathcal{M}(v_i), \varphi_i) \rightsquigarrow (\mathcal{M}(v_{i+1}), \varphi_{i+1})$
3. $\varphi_i = \nu X.*$ principal implies that $\zeta_i \not\succsim \zeta_{i+1}$

In the following construction of signatures, we will simply show that there are signatures fulfilling all properties disregarding being the least one. Then, we simply select the subsequent signature to be the least one fulfilling the first property. Note that this signature then also fulfills all the other properties.

For $i = 0$ let v_0 be the root of $\mathcal{P}$, $\varphi_0 := \vartheta$ and ζ_0 be the smallest ν-signature s.t. $l_{(\mathcal{P}, \varrho_\mathcal{P})}(v_0) \not\models \varphi_0^{\zeta_0}$ which exists due the Lemma 4.

For $i \rightsquigarrow i + 1$ we distinguish on the subsequent rule application. Note that is impossible that v_i ends in a sink. If the next rule to be applied is the (Mod)-rule, we distinguish on whether $\varphi_i = \langle a \rangle \varphi_{i+1}$ or $\varphi_i = [a]\varphi_{i+1}$ which are the only possible cases due to the construction of $\mathcal{T}_{(\mathcal{P}, \varrho_\mathcal{P})}$. If $\varphi_i = \langle a \rangle \varphi_{i+1}$ let v_{i+1} be the successor of v_i following φ_{i+1} and note that $l_{(\mathcal{P}, \varrho)}(v_{i+1}) \not\models \varphi_{i+1}^{\zeta_i}$ indeed holds. If $\varphi_i = [a]\varphi_{i+1}$, select $v_i \prec v_{i+1}$ s.t. $l_{(\mathcal{P}, \varrho)}(v_{i+1}) \not\models \varphi_{i+1}^{\zeta_i}$ holds.

Otherwise let v_{i+1} be the unique successor of v_i. Assume that φ_i is principal in the following rule application since otherwise simply set $\varphi_{i+1} := \varphi_i$. Otherwise, if $\varphi_i = \psi_0 \vee \psi_1$ let φ_{i+1} be the unique successor of φ_i and note that all conditions hold. If $\varphi_i = \psi_0 \wedge \psi_1$ let $j = 0, 1$ s.t. $l_{(\mathcal{P}, \varrho_\mathcal{P})}(v_{i+1}) \not\models \psi_j^{\zeta_i}$ and set $\varphi_{i+1} := \psi_j$.

If otherwise $\varphi_i = \sigma X.\psi$ let φ_{i+1} be the unique successor of φ_i and note that due to Lemma 4 there is a signature ζ'_{i+1} s.t. all conditions hold.

We finally need to show that it is impossible that $\varphi_i = \nu X.\psi$ for some ν-bound X whenever the respective (FP_ν^U)-rule application does not follow ψ. By contradiction assume that $\varphi_i = \nu X.\psi$ principal for some ν-bound X and there is no set $U \in \mathcal{A}_\mathcal{P}(v_i, \nu X.\psi)$ with $X \notin U$. By construction of $\mathcal{A}_\mathcal{P}$, this implies that there is some $j < i$ with $l_{(\mathcal{P}, \varrho_\mathcal{P})}(v_j) = l_{(\mathcal{P}, \varrho_\mathcal{P})}(v_i)$, $v_j = \nu X.\psi$ and $v_{j+1} = \psi[\nu X.\psi/X]$. By construction of the sequence of signatures, it follows that $\zeta_j \succeq \zeta_{j+1} \succeq \zeta_i$. But this cannot be the case with ζ_j and ζ_i both being the least ν-signature that falsifies X w.r.t. the same state.

As the modal rule is applied infinitely often in the extracted branch, $\varphi_0, \varphi_1, \dots$ is an active thread. Since $\mathcal{P}$ is a tableau, $\varphi_0, \varphi_1, \dots$ is a ν-thread.

Let X^* be the outermost variable in $\varphi_0, \varphi_1, \dots$ that is unfolded infinitely often. Let i^* be arbitrary s.t. there is no variable $Y > X^*$ with $\varphi_j = \sigma Y.*$ for any $j \geq i^*$. Consider the sequence of signatures $\zeta_{i^*} \succeq \zeta_{i^*+1} \succeq \dots$ and note that we have:

$$\zeta_i \not\succeq \zeta_{i+1} \text{ whenever } \varphi_i = \nu X^*.\psi \text{ and } \varphi_{i+1} = \psi[\nu X^*.\psi/X^*]$$

Therefore we have an infinitely descending sequence $\zeta_{i^*}, \zeta_{i^*+1}, \ldots$ which is impossible as ordinals are well-founded. $\qquad\square$

A.3 Completeness

Theorem 4 (Completeness). *There is a tableau for a fromula ϑ if ϑ is satisfiable.*

Proof. Let ϑ be a closed formula and $\mathcal{T} = (\mathcal{S}, \longrightarrow, \ell)$ be a transition system and $s_0 \in \mathcal{S}$ be a state s.t. $s_0 \models \vartheta$.

We inductively construct a state-labeled pre-tableau as follows. Starting with the labeled sequence $s_0 : \vartheta$, we apply the following rules in an arbitrary but eligible ordering systematically backwards.

$$(\text{Or}) \ \frac{s : \varphi_0 \vee \varphi_1, \Phi}{s : \varphi_i, \Phi} \ (*) \qquad\qquad (\text{And}) \ \frac{s : \varphi_0 \wedge \varphi_1, \Phi}{s : \varphi_0, \varphi_1, \Phi}$$

$$(\text{FP}_\mu) \ \frac{s : \mu X.\varphi, \Phi}{s : \varphi[\mu X.\varphi/X], \Phi} \qquad\qquad (\text{FP}_\nu^U) \ \frac{s : \nu X.\varphi, \Phi}{s : \Phi \qquad s : \varphi[\nu X.\varphi/X], \Phi}$$

$$(\text{Mod}) \ \frac{s : \langle a_1 \rangle \varphi_1, \ldots, \langle a_n \rangle \varphi_n, [b_1]\psi_1, \ldots, [b_m]\psi_m, q_1, \ldots, q_k, \overline{p_1}, \ldots, \overline{p_h}}{s_1{:}\varphi_1, \{\psi_i \mid a_1{=}b_i\} \quad s_2{:}\varphi_2, \{\psi_i \mid a_2{=}b_i\} \quad \ldots \quad s_m{:}\varphi_n, \{\psi_i \mid a_m{=}b_i\}} \ (**)$$

with the following side conditions:

- $(*)$: For every μ-signature ζ with $s \models (\varphi_0 \vee \varphi_1)^\zeta$ it holds that $s \models \varphi_i^\zeta$.
- $(**)$: $s \models (\langle a_1 \rangle \varphi_1, \ldots, \langle a_n \rangle \varphi_n, [b_1]\psi_1, \ldots, [b_m]\psi_m, q_1, \ldots, q_k, \overline{p_1}, \ldots, \overline{p_h})$ implies for every i that $s \longrightarrow^{a_i} s_i$ and $s_i \models (\varphi_i, \{\psi_j \mid a_i = b_j\})$. Additionally, for every μ-signature ζ and every i it holds that $s \models (\langle a \rangle \varphi_i)^\zeta$ implies $s_i \models \varphi_i^\zeta$.

Consider that this construction indeed yields pre-tableau with each state-labeled sequence $s : \Phi$ satisfying $s \models \Phi$ as well as all side conditions due to Lemma 4. Moreover note that every finite branch ends in a node labeled with $[*]$-formulas and consistent literals only.

By contradiction assume that the pre-tableau is not a tableau, hence there is a labeled branch $s_0 : \Phi_0, s_1 : \Phi_1, \ldots$ (with $\Phi_0 = \{\vartheta\}$) and a μ-thread $t = t_0, t_1, \ldots$ with $t_i \in \Phi_i$ for all i.

We argue as in the soundness proof that this is impossible. $\qquad\square$

A Conditional Constructive Logic for Access Control and Its Sequent Calculus

Valerio Genovese[1,*], Laura Giordano[2], Valentina Gliozzi[3], and Gian Luca Pozzato[3]

[1] University of Luxembourg and Università di Torino, Italy
valerio.genovese@uni.lu
[2] Dip. di Informatica, Università del Piemonte Orientale, Italy
laura@mfn.unipmn.it
[3] Dip. di Informatica, Università di Torino, Italy
{gliozzi,pozzato}@di.unito.it

Abstract. In this paper we study the applicability of constructive conditional logics as a general framework to define decision procedures in access control logics. To this purpose, we formalize the assertion A **says** ϕ, whose intended meaning is that *principal A says that* ϕ, as a conditional implication. We introduce $\mathsf{Cond}_{\mathsf{ACL}}$, which is a conservative extension of the logic *ICL* recently introduced by Garg and Abadi. We identify the conditional axioms needed to capture the basic properties of the "says" operator and to provide a proper definition of boolean principals. We provide a Kripke model semantics for the logic and we prove that the axiomatization is sound and complete with respect to the semantics. Moreover, we define a sound, complete, cut-free and terminating sequent calculus for $\mathsf{Cond}_{\mathsf{ACL}}$, which allows us to prove that the logic is decidable. We argue for the generality of our approach by presenting canonical properties of some further well known access control axioms. The identification of canonical properties provides the possibility to craft access control logics that adopt *any* combination of axioms for which canonical properties exist.

1 Introduction

Access control is concerned with the decision of accepting or denying a request from a *principal* (e.g., user, program) to do an operation on an object. In practice, an access control system is a product of several, often independent, distributed entities with different policies that interact in order to determine access to resources. In order to specify and reason about such systems, many formal frameworks have been proposed [2,5,15,18,19]. A common feature of most well-known approaches is the employment of constructive logics enriched with formulas of the form A **says** φ, intuitively meaning that the principal A *asserts* or *supports* φ to hold in the system. In [1] it is shown that an intuitionistic interpretation of the modality "says" allows to avoid unexpected conclusions that are derivable when **says** is given an axiomatization in classical logic.

In [11] an access control logic, ICL, is defined as an extension of intuitionistic propositional logic, in which the operator **says** is given a modal interpretation in the logic

---

* Valerio Genovese is supported by the National Research Fund, Luxembourg.

K. Brünnler and G. Metcalfe (Eds.): TABLEAUX 2011, LNAI 6793, pp. 164–179, 2011.
© Springer-Verlag Berlin Heidelberg 2011

S4. The treatment of the operator **says** as a modality can also be found in [6], which introduces a logical framework, FSL, based on multi-modal logic methodology.

Even if there is some agreement on looking at the **says** construct as a modal operator, the correspondence between its axiomatization and the semantic properties associated with axioms in the Kripke semantics is mainly unexplored. In fact, some of the axioms of access control logics are non-standard in modal literature. The identification of canonical properties for well-known axioms of access control logics permits to study them separately and naturally yields completeness for logics that adopt combinations of them. This methodology is significant if we want logic to be employed to compare different access control models, because different systems adopt different axioms depending on the specific application domain.

In this paper we show that conditional logics [21] can provide a general framework to define axiomatization, semantics and proof methods for access control logics. As a starting point, we concentrate on a specific combination of axioms, those of the logic Cond_{ACL}, which is a conservative extension of the logic *ICL* introduced in [11]. In Section 5 we will point out a few possible extra axioms, which are well known in the access control literature, and we provide semantic conditions for them.

Cond_{ACL} integrates access control logics with intuitionistic conditional logics. We formalize the **says** operator as a conditional normal modality so that A **says** ϕ is regarded as a conditional implication $A \Rightarrow \phi$, meaning that proposition ϕ holds in all the preferred worlds for the principal A. The generality of this approach allows a natural formalization of boolean principals [11], that is, principals which are formed by boolean combination of atomic principals.

From the access control point of view, the **says** operator satisfies some basic axioms of access control logics [11,10]. We define a sound and complete Kripke semantics for Cond_{ACL} as well as a sound, complete, cut-free labelled sequent calculus for it. We are also able to obtain a decision procedure and a complexity upper bound for Cond_{ACL}, namely that provability in Cond_{ACL} is decidable in PSPACE. This is in agreement with [11], which provides a PSPACE complexity result for the logic ICL.

The paper is structured as follows. In Section 2 we introduce the axiomatization and the semantics for the intuitionistic conditional logic Cond_{ACL} and we compare it with existing approaches. In Section 3 we show that the axiomatization is sound and complete with respect to the semantics. In Section 4 we define a cut-free sequent calculus for Cond_{ACL}, we prove its soundness, completeness and termination, and we provide a complexity upper bound. In Section 5 we provide semantic conditions for some further axioms of access control logics. Section 6 contains the conclusions and a discussion of related work.

2   The Logic Cond_{ACL}

In this section, we introduce the conditional intuitionistic logic Cond_{ACL} for access control by defining its axiomatization and Kripke semantics. The formulation of the "says" modality as a conditional operator allows boolean principals to be modelled in a natural way, since in a conditional formula A **says** ϕ, both A and ϕ are arbitrary formulas. For instance, we can write, $A \wedge B$ **says** ϕ to mean that principals A and B jointly say that ϕ, and $A \vee B$ **says** ϕ to mean that principals A and B independently say that ϕ. Indeed, conditional logics provide a natural generalization of multimodal logics to the case when modalities are labelled by arbitrary formulas.

2.1 Axiom System

We define the language $\mathcal{L}$ of the logic Cond_{ACL} . Let ATM be a set of atomic propositions. The formulas of $\mathcal{L}$ are defined inductively as follows: if $P \in ATM$, then $P \in \mathcal{L}$; $\bot \in \mathcal{L}$, where $\bot$ is a proposition which is always false; if A, φ, φ_1 and φ_2 are formulas of $\mathcal{L}$, then $\neg\varphi$, $\varphi_1 \wedge \varphi_2$, $\varphi_1 \vee \varphi_2$, $\varphi_1 \to \varphi_2$, and A **says** φ are formulas of $\mathcal{L}$.

The intended meaning of the formula A **says** φ, where A and φ are arbitrary formulas, is that *principal A says that φ*, namely, "the principal A asserts or supports φ" [11]. Although the principal A is an arbitrary formula, in order to stress the fact that a formula is playing the role of a principal, we will denote it by $A, B, C, \ldots$ while we will use greek letters for arbitrary formulas.

The axiomatization of Cond_{ACL} contains few basic axioms for access control logics [11,1], as well as additional axioms governing the behavior of boolean principals. Because we privilege the modularity of the approach, we are interested in considering each axiom separately. As a consequence, the resulting axiomatization might be redundant.

Basic Axioms. The *axiom system* of Cond_{ACL} contains the following axioms and inference rules, which are intended to capture the basic properties of the **says** operator.

(TAUT)	all tautologies of intuitionistic logic
(K)	A **says** $(\alpha \to \beta) \to (A$ **says** $\alpha \to A$ **says** $\beta)$
(UNIT)	$\alpha \to (A$ **says** $\alpha)$
(C)	A **says** $(A$ **says** $\alpha \to \alpha)$
(MP)	If $\vdash \alpha$ and $\vdash \alpha \to \beta$ then $\vdash \beta$
(RCEA)	If $\vdash A \leftrightarrow B$ then $\vdash (A$ **says** $\gamma) \leftrightarrow (B$ **says** $\gamma)$
(RCK)	If $\vdash \alpha \to \beta$ then $\vdash (A$ **says** $\alpha) \to (A$ **says** $\beta)$

We say that a formula α is a theorem of the logic, and write $\vdash \alpha$ if there is a derivation of α from the above axioms and rules. We say that α can be derived from a set of formulas Γ, and write $\Gamma \vdash \alpha$, if there are $\gamma_1, \ldots \gamma_n$ in Γ such that $\vdash \gamma_1 \wedge \ldots \wedge \gamma_n \to \alpha$. The rule (MP) is modus ponens. (RCK) and (RCEA) are standard inference rules for conditional logics. (RCK) plays the role of the rule of Necessitation (if $\vdash \phi$ then $\vdash \Box\phi$) in modal/multimodal logic. (RCEA) makes the formulas A **says** ϕ and B **says** ϕ equivalent when the principals A and B are equivalent. The axiom (K) belongs to the axiomatization of all normal modal logics and it is derivable in "normal" conditional logics. (UNIT) and (K) are the characterizing axioms of the logic ICL [11], while (C) has been included in the axiomatization of the logic DTL_0 in [10]. The choice of the above axiom is meaningful in the context of access control, in fact it can be proved that what can be derived in ICL can also be derived in Cond_{ACL} , i.e. $\vdash_{ICL} \varphi$ implies $\vdash \varphi$.

Axioms for boolean principals. The axioms introduced above do not enforce by themselves any intended property of boolean principals. In this subsection, we discuss the properties that are intended for boolean principals and we introduce axioms which capture such properties. Specifically, we focus on the intended meaning of conjunctions and disjunctions among principals.

Our interpretation of the statement $A \wedge B$ **says** ϕ is that *A and B jointly (combining their statements) say that* ϕ. It comes from the interpretation of the statement as a conditional implication: A and B (jointly) conditionally prove ϕ. Instead, our interpretation of the statement $A \vee B$ **says** ϕ is that *A and B disjointly (independently) say that* ϕ, which comes from the reading of the conditional formula as A and B (disjointly) conditionally prove ϕ. Concerning the statement $A \vee B$ **says** ϕ, we expect that if both A says ϕ and B says ϕ, then A and B disjointly (independently) say that ϕ. This property can be captured by the following axiom:

$$A \textbf{ says } \phi \wedge B \textbf{ says } \phi \rightarrow A \vee B \textbf{ says } \phi$$

which corresponds to the well known axiom (CA) of conditional logics [21]. Similarly, we can expect that the converse axiom

$$A \vee B \textbf{ says } \phi \rightarrow A \textbf{ says } \phi \wedge B \textbf{ says } \phi$$

holds. The two axioms together enforce the property that A and B disjointly say that ϕ if and only if A says that ϕ and B says that ϕ .

Concerning $A \wedge B$ **says** ϕ, we expect that A and B jointly say that ϕ when either A or B says that ϕ. This condition can be enforced by introducing the axiom

$$A \textbf{ says } \phi \rightarrow A \wedge B \textbf{ says } \phi$$

which, although is a controversial axiom of conditional logics, called monotonicity[1], is harmless in this intuitionistic setting. Also, we would like to have the property that if $A \wedge B$ **says** ϕ then, by combining the statements of A and B, ϕ can be concluded. This is not equivalent to saying that either A says ϕ or B says ϕ. Indeed, the axiom $(A \wedge B \textbf{ says } \phi) \rightarrow (A \textbf{ says } \phi) \vee (B \textbf{ says } \phi)$ is too strong and not wanted. In the following we show that the wanted property can be captured in a propositional axiomatization.

Although a principal is an arbitrary formula and it also includes negation and implication, no specific properties are intended for such formulas, and no specific axioms are introduced for them.

The axiomatization of $\mathsf{Cond}_{\mathrm{ACL}}$ includes (in addition) the following axioms:

(CA)	$A \textbf{ says } \phi \wedge B \textbf{ says } \phi \rightarrow A \vee B \textbf{ says } \phi$
(CA-conv)	$A \vee B \textbf{ says } \phi \rightarrow A \textbf{ says } \phi$
(Mon)	$A \textbf{ says } \phi \rightarrow A \wedge B \textbf{ says } \phi$
(DT)	$A \wedge B \textbf{ says } \phi \rightarrow (A \textbf{ says } (B \rightarrow \phi))$
(ID)	$A \textbf{ says } A$

The first three axioms are those introduced above. (DT) and (ID) are used together to enforce the property that if $A \wedge B$ **says** ϕ then, by combining the statements of A and B, ϕ can be concluded. The two axioms allow propositions representing principals to occur on the right of the **says** modality. The intended meaning of (DT) is that, if $A \wedge B$ **says** ϕ, then A says that ϕ holds in all B worlds (worlds visible to the principal B). The meaning of (ID) is that "A says that principal A is visible". We will come back to the intended meaning of these axioms when describing the semantic conditions associated with the axioms. Nonetheless, our axiomatization does account for arbitrary

---

[1] In general, conditional logics only allow weaker forms of monotonicity, encoded, for instance, by the axiom (CV) of Lewis' logic VC.

Boolean combinations of principals (as in [11]), as a principal A can be an arbitrary formula. As a difference, we do not force any specific interpretation for implication within principals, which instead in ICL^B [11] is used to capture the "speaks for" operator. Observe that, by the normality of the conditional **says** modality, the principal $A \wedge B$ is, for instance, equivalent to the principal $A \wedge B \wedge A$. This is an advantage of conditional logic over a multi-modal logic in which principals are simply regarded as labels of modalities.

Theorem 1. *The above axiomatization is consistent.*

Proof. Consistency immediately follows from the fact that, by replacing A **says** B with the intuitionistic implication $A \rightarrow B$, we obtain axioms which are derivable in intuitionistic logic. $\square$

Let us observe that the above interpretation of conjunction and disjunction between principals is different from the one given in the logic ICL^B [11], which actually adopts the opposite interpretation of $\wedge$ and $\vee$: in Garg and Abadi's logic ICL^B, $A \wedge B$ **says** ϕ is the same as A **says** $\phi \wedge B$ **says** ϕ, while $A \vee B$ **says** ϕ means that, by combining the statements of A and B, ϕ can be concluded. Due to this, the properties of the principal $A \wedge B$ in our logic are properties of the principal $A \vee B$ in their logic, and vice-versa, the properties of the principal $A \vee B$ in our logic are properties of the principal $A \wedge B$ in their logic. Observe that the axioms, (trust), (untrust) and (cuc') of the logic ICL^B are not derivable from our axiomatization. Also, the addition of the axiom (untrust) $\top$ **says** $\bot$ to our axiomatization would entail that for all principals A, A **says** $\bot$, which is an unwanted property.

2.2 Semantics

The semantics of the logic Cond_{ACL} is defined as follows.

Definition 1. *A Cond_{ACL} model has the form $\mathcal{M} = (S, \leq, \{R_A\}, h)$ where: $S \neq \emptyset$ is a set of items called worlds; $\leq$ is a preorder over S; R_A is a binary relation on S associated with the formula A; h is an evaluation function $ATM \longrightarrow Pow(S)$ that associates to each atomic proposition P the set of worlds in which P is true.*

We define the truth conditions of a formula $\phi \in \mathcal{L}$ with respect to a world $t \in S$ in a model $\mathcal{M}$, by the relation $\mathcal{M}, t \models \phi$, as follows. We use $[\|\phi\|]$ to denote $\{y \in S \mid \mathcal{M}, y \models \phi\}$.

1. *$\mathcal{M}, t \models P \in ATM$ iff, for all s such that $t \leq s$, $s \in h(P)$*
2. *$\mathcal{M}, t \models \varphi \wedge \psi$ iff $\mathcal{M}, t \models \varphi$ and $\mathcal{M}, t \models \psi$*
3. *$\mathcal{M}, t \models \varphi \vee \psi$ iff $\mathcal{M}, t \models \varphi$ or $\mathcal{M}, t \models \psi$*
4. *$\mathcal{M}, t \models \varphi \rightarrow \psi$ iff for all s such that $t \leq s$ (if $\mathcal{M}, s \models \varphi$ then $\mathcal{M}, s \models \psi$)*
5. *$\mathcal{M}, t \models \neg\varphi$ iff, for all s such that $t \leq s$, $\mathcal{M}, s \not\models \varphi$*
6. *$\mathcal{M}, t \not\models \bot$*
7. *$\mathcal{M}, t \models A$ **says** ψ iff, for all s such that $t R_A s$, $\mathcal{M}, s \models \psi$.*

We say that ϕ is valid in a model $\mathcal{M}$ if $\mathcal{M}, t \models \phi$ for all $t \in S$. We say that ϕ is valid tout court (and write $\models \phi$) if ϕ is valid in every model. We extend the notion of validity to a set of formulas Γ in the obvious way: for all t, $\mathcal{M}, t \models \Gamma$ if $\mathcal{M}, t \models \psi$ for all

$\psi \in \Gamma$. *Last, we say that* ϕ *is a* logical consequence *of* Γ *(and write* $\Gamma \models \phi$*) if, for all models* $\mathcal{M}$, *for all worlds* t, *if* $\mathcal{M}, t \models \Gamma$, *then* $\mathcal{M}, t \models \phi$.
The relations $\leq$ *and* R_A *must satisfy the following conditions:*

(S-Int) $\forall t, s, z \in S$, if $s \leq t$ and $t R_A z$ then $s R_A z$;

(S-UNIT) $\forall t, s \in S$, if $s R_A t$, then $s \leq t$;

(S-C) $\forall t, s, z \in S$, if $s R_A t$ and $t \leq z$, then $z R_A z$;

(S-CA) $R_{A \vee B}(t) = R_A(t) \cup R_B(t)$.

(S-Mon) $\forall t, s, z \in S$, if $s R_{A \wedge B} t$, then $s R_A t$ and $s R_B t$;

(S-DT) $\forall t, s, z \in S$, if $s R_A t$ and $t \leq z$, and $z \in [||B||]$, then $s R_{A \wedge B} z$;

(S-ID) $\forall t, s \in S$, if $s R_A t$, then $t \in [||A||]$;

(S-RCEA) if $[||A||] = [||B||]$, then $R_A = R_B$.

Condition (S-Int) enforces the property that when a formula A **says** ϕ is true in a world t, it is also true in all worlds reachable from s by the relation $\leq$ (i.e., in all worlds s such that $t \leq s$). All the other semantic conditions are those associated with the axioms of the logic, apart from condition (S-RCEA), which is the well-known condition for normality in conditional logics, claiming that the accessibility relation R_A is associated with the semantic interpretation of A. (S-CA) is the semantic condition for both axioms (CA) and its converse. Notice that, the fact that we represent the binary relation R_A as indexed by an *arbitrary* formula does not mean that the semantics for conditional logic is second-order. In fact, R_A represent a selection function (which is used in most formulations of conditional logic semantics), in which $s R_A t$ corresponds to $t \in f([||A||], s)$, where $[||A||]$ is a set of worlds. In this view, the semantic conditions above must be intended as first-order because they quantify over individuals (i.e. worlds) and subsets of the domain (indexes of the binary relation) identified by formulas of the language [2].

Note also that the semantic conditions for some of the axioms, as for instance (DT), slightly departs from the semantic condition usually given to these axioms in conditional logic. This is due to the fact that $\mathsf{Cond}_{\mathsf{ACL}}$ is an intuitionistic conditional logic and the implication occurring within axioms is intuitionistic implication.

Concerning the interpretation of boolean conditionals and, in particular, of the conjunction between principals, it can be proved that, from the semantic conditions (S-Mon), (S-ID) and (S-DT) it follows that:

$$R_{A \wedge B}(t) = R_A(t) \cap R_B(t).$$

By the presence of the axiom (C), it turns out that the semantic condition (S-DT) can be equivalently expressed as follows:

Proposition 1. *In the axiomatization of* $\mathsf{Cond}_{\mathsf{ACL}}$ *, the following are equivalent:*

1. $\forall t, s, z \in S$, *if* $s R_A t$ *and* $t \leq z$, *and* $z \in [||B||]$, *then* $s R_{A \wedge B} z$;

2. $\forall t, s \in S$, *if* $s R_A t$ *and* $t \in [||B||]$, *then* $s R_{A \wedge B} t$.

This allows the semantic condition (S-DT) to be equivalently expressed as follows:

---

[2] It is well known that the extension of first-order logic with quantification over a family of subsets of the domain does not add expressivity because it is equivalent to multi-sorted first-order logic (see [8] Section 4.4).

(S-DT) $\forall t, s \in S$, if $sR_A t$ and $t \in [|B|]$, then $sR_{A \wedge B} t$.

It is worth noticing that the notion of logical consequence defined above can be used to verify that a request ϕ of a principal A is compliant with a set of policies. Intuitively, given a set of formulas Γ representing policies, we say that A is compliant with Γ iff Γ, A **says** $\phi \models \phi$. For instance, if Γ contains the following formulas:

- $Admin_1$ **says** $(SuperUser\_user_1 \rightarrow write\_perm\_user_1)$
- $Admin_2$ **says** $SuperUser\_user_1$
- $((Admin_1 \wedge Admin_2)$ **says** $delete\_file_1) \rightarrow delete\_file_1$
- $Admin_1 \wedge Admin_2$ **says** $((write\_perm\_user_1 \wedge (user_1$ **says** $delete\_file_1)) \rightarrow delete\_file_1)$

we obtain that $\Gamma, user_1$ **says** $delete\_file_1 \models delete\_file_1$.

3 Soundness and Completeness

In this section we prove that the axiomatization of the logic $\mathsf{Cond}_{\mathrm{ACL}}$ given above is sound and complete with respect to the semantics of Definition 1. The completeness proof we present is based on the proof of completeness for the Kripke semantics of intuitionistic logic in [23] and extends it to deal with the modalities **says** in the language and, more precisely, with the interplay between the relation $\leq$ and the accessibility relations R_A associated with the modalities.

Definition 2 (Consistency). *Let Γ be a set of well formed formulas. Γ is consistent iff $\Gamma \nvdash \bot$. If Γ has an infinite number of formulas, we say that Γ is consistent iff there are no finite $\Gamma_0 \subset \Gamma$ such that $\Gamma_0 \vdash \bot$.*

Definition 3 (Saturation). *Let Γ be a set of well formed formulas, we say that Γ is saturated iff 1. Γ is consistent (Definition 2); 2. if $\Gamma \vdash \varphi$, then $\varphi \in \Gamma$; 3. if $\Gamma \vdash \varphi \vee \psi$, then $\Gamma \vdash \varphi$ or $\Gamma \vdash \psi$.*

Lemma 1 (Saturated Extensions). *Let Γ be a set of well formed formulas. Suppose $\Gamma \nvdash \varphi$, then there is a saturated set Γ^* such that $\Gamma^* \nvdash \varphi$.*

Definition 4 (Canonical model construction). *Let Γ_0 be any saturated set of formulas. Then we define $\mathbf{M} = (S, \leq, \{R_A\}, h)$ such that: S is the set of all saturated $\Gamma \supseteq \Gamma_0$; $\Gamma_1 \leq \Gamma_2$ iff $\Gamma_1 \subseteq \Gamma_2$; $\Gamma_1 R_A \Gamma_2$ iff $\{\alpha \mid A$ **says** $\alpha \in \Gamma_1\} \subseteq \Gamma_2$; for all $P \in ATM, h(P) = \{\Gamma \in S \mid P \in \Gamma\}$.*

We can prove the following Lemmas:

Lemma 2. *For all $\Gamma \in S$ and each formula $\varphi \in \mathcal{L}$, we have that $\mathbf{M}, \Gamma \models \varphi$ iff $\varphi \in \Gamma$.*

Lemma 3. *Let $\mathbf{M}$ be the canonical model as defined in Definition 4. $\mathbf{M}$ satisfies the conditions (S-Int), (S-UNIT), (S-C), (S-CA), (S-Mon), (S-DT), (S-ID), and (S-RCEA).*

By the above lemmas, we can conclude tha the axiomatization of the logic $\mathsf{Cond}_{\mathrm{ACL}}$ given in Section 2.1 is complete with respect to the semantics in Definition 1:

Theorem 2 (Soundness and Completeness). *Given a formula* $\varphi \in \mathcal{L}$, $\models \varphi$ *iff* $\vdash \varphi$.

Proof. Soundness is straightforward. Concerning the completeness, for a contradiction, suppose $\nvdash \varphi$. Then by Lemma 1 there is a saturated extension Γ^* such that $\Gamma^* \nvdash \varphi$, hence $\varphi \notin \Gamma^*$. By Definition 4 and Lemmas 2 and 3, we conclude that there is a (canonical) model $\mathbf{M} = (S, \leq, \{R_A\}, h)$, with $\Gamma^* \in S$, such that $\mathbf{M}, \Gamma^* \nvDash \varphi$. It follows that φ is not logically valid, i.e. $\nvDash \varphi$. $\square$

4   A Sequent Calculus for Cond$_{\mathsf{ACL}}$

In this section we present a cut-free sequent calculus for Cond$_{\mathsf{ACL}}$. Our calculus is called $\mathcal{S}\mathrm{Cond}_{\mathsf{ACL}}$ and it makes use of labels to represent possible worlds, following the line of SeqS, a sequent calculus for standard conditional logics introduced in [22]. We also show that we can control the application of some crucial rules of $\mathcal{S}\mathrm{Cond}_{\mathsf{ACL}}$, obtaining a terminating calculus $\widehat{\mathcal{S}\mathrm{Cond}_{\mathsf{ACL}}}$. This calculus describes a decision procedure for Cond$_{\mathsf{ACL}}$, and allows us to conclude that provability is decidable in $O(n^2 log n)$ space.

In addiction to the language $\mathcal{L}$ of the logic Cond$_{\mathsf{ACL}}$, we consider a denumerable alphabet of labels $\mathcal{A}$, whose elements are denoted by $x, y, z, \ldots$. Moreover, in order to obtain a terminating calculus, we define the set $\mathcal{L}_{\mathbf{P}} \subseteq \mathcal{L}$ of principals involved in the computation. Given a set of policies Γ, a request φ of compliance of a principal A (i.e. we want to verify whether Γ, A **says** $\varphi \models \varphi$), we assume that the set $\mathcal{L}_{\mathbf{P}}$ contains at least A and all principals B such that, for some ϕ, B **says** ϕ appears in Γ.

The calculus $\mathcal{S}\mathrm{Cond}_{\mathsf{ACL}}$ manipulates three types of labelled formulas: 1. *world formulas*, denoted by $x : \alpha$, where $x \in \mathcal{A}$ and $\alpha \in \mathcal{L}$, used to represent that the formula α holds in a world x; 2. *transition formulas*, denoted by $x \xrightarrow{A} y$, representing that $xR_A y$; 3. *order formulas* of the form $y \geq x$ representing the preorder relation $\leq$. A *sequent* is a pair $\langle \Gamma, \Delta \rangle$, usually denoted with $\Gamma \Rightarrow \Delta$, where Γ and Δ are multisets of labelled formulas. The intuitive meaning of a sequent $\Gamma \Rightarrow \Delta$ is: every model that satisfies all labelled formulas of Γ in the respective worlds (specified by the labels) satisfies at least one of the labelled formulas of Δ (in those worlds). This is made precise by the notion of *validity* of a sequent given in the next definition:

Definition 5 (Sequent validity). *Given a model* $\mathcal{M} = (S, \leq, \{R_A\}, h)$ *for* $\mathcal{L}$, *and a label alphabet* $\mathcal{A}$, *we consider a mapping* $I : \mathcal{A} \rightarrow S$. *Let F be a labelled formula, we define* $\mathcal{M} \models_I F$ *as follows:* • $\mathcal{M} \models_I x : \alpha$ *iff* $\mathcal{M}, I(x) \models \alpha$; • $\mathcal{M} \models_I x \xrightarrow{A} y$ *iff* $I(x)R_A I(y)$; • $\mathcal{M} \models_I y \geq x$ *iff* $I(x) \leq I(y)$. *We say that* $\Gamma \Rightarrow \Delta$ *is* valid in $\mathcal{M}$ *if, for every mapping* $I : \mathcal{A} \rightarrow S$, *if* $\mathcal{M} \models_I F$ *for every* $F \in \Gamma$, *then* $\mathcal{M} \models_I G$ *for some* $G \in \Delta$. *We say that* $\Gamma \Rightarrow \Delta$ *is* valid in Cond$_{\mathsf{ACL}}$ *if it is valid in every* $\mathcal{M}$.

In Figure 1 we present the rules of the calculus $\mathcal{S}\mathrm{Cond}_{\mathsf{ACL}}$ for Cond$_{\mathsf{ACL}}$. As usual, we say that a sequent $\Gamma \Rightarrow \Delta$ is *derivable* in $\mathcal{S}\mathrm{Cond}_{\mathsf{ACL}}$ if it admits a *derivation*. A derivation is a tree whose nodes are sequents. A branch is a sequence of nodes $\Gamma_1 \Rightarrow \Delta_1, \Gamma_2 \Rightarrow \Delta_2, \ldots, \Gamma_n \Rightarrow \Delta_n, \ldots$ Each node $\Gamma_i \Rightarrow \Delta_i$ is obtained from its immediate successor $\Gamma_{i-1} \Rightarrow \Delta_{i-1}$ by applying *backward* a rule of $\mathcal{S}\mathrm{Cond}_{\mathsf{ACL}}$, having $\Gamma_{i-1} \Rightarrow \Delta_{i-1}$ as the conclusion and $\Gamma_i \Rightarrow \Delta_i$ as one of its premises. A branch is closed if one

$$(AX)\ \Gamma, F \Rightarrow \Delta, F \qquad\qquad (AX_\perp)\ \Gamma, x:\perp \Rightarrow \Delta \qquad (AX_\geq)\ \Gamma \Rightarrow \Delta, x\geq x \qquad \dfrac{\Gamma, x:P \Rightarrow \Delta, y\geq x \quad \Gamma, x:P, y:P \Rightarrow \Delta}{\Gamma, x:P \Rightarrow \Delta}\,(ATM)$$
$$F \text{ either } x:P, P\in ATM \text{ or } y\geq x \qquad\qquad\qquad\qquad\qquad\qquad\qquad\qquad\qquad\qquad\qquad\qquad P\in ATM$$

$$\dfrac{\Gamma, y\geq x \Rightarrow \Delta, y:\alpha \quad \Gamma, y\geq x \Rightarrow \Delta, y:\beta}{\Gamma \Rightarrow \Delta, x:\alpha\wedge\beta}\,(\wedge R) \qquad \dfrac{\Gamma, x:\alpha\wedge\beta \Rightarrow \Delta, y\geq x \quad \Gamma, x:\alpha\wedge\beta, y:\alpha, y:\beta \Rightarrow \Delta}{\Gamma, x:\alpha\wedge\beta \Rightarrow \Delta}\,(\wedge L)$$
$$y \text{ new}$$

$$\dfrac{\Gamma, y\geq x, y:\alpha \Rightarrow \Delta, y:\beta}{\Gamma \Rightarrow \Delta, x:\alpha\to\beta}\,(\to R) \qquad \dfrac{\Gamma, x:\alpha\to\beta \Rightarrow \Delta, y\geq x \quad \Gamma, x:\alpha\to\beta \Rightarrow \Delta, y:\alpha \quad \Gamma, x:\alpha\to\beta, y:\beta \Rightarrow \Delta}{\Gamma, x:\alpha\to\beta \Rightarrow \Delta}\,(\to L)$$
$$y \text{ new}$$

$$\dfrac{\Gamma, y\geq x, y:\alpha \xrightarrow{A} z \Rightarrow \Delta, z:\alpha}{\Gamma \Rightarrow \Delta, x:A\text{ says }\alpha}\,(\text{says }R) \qquad \dfrac{\Gamma, x:A\text{ says }\alpha \Rightarrow \Delta, y\geq x \quad \Gamma, x:A\text{ says }\alpha \Rightarrow \Delta, y\xrightarrow{A} z \quad \Gamma, x:A\text{ says }\alpha, z:\alpha \Rightarrow \Delta}{\Gamma, x:A\text{ says }\alpha \Rightarrow \Delta}\,(\text{says }L)$$
$$y \text{ and } z \text{ new}$$

$$\dfrac{u:A \Rightarrow u:B \quad u:B \Rightarrow u:A}{\Gamma, x\xrightarrow{A} y \Rightarrow \Delta, x\xrightarrow{B} y}\,(EQ) \qquad \dfrac{\Gamma, z\geq x, z\geq y, y\geq x \Rightarrow \Delta}{\Gamma, z\geq y, y\geq x \Rightarrow \Delta}\,(TR) \qquad \dfrac{\Gamma, y\geq x, x\xrightarrow{A} y \Rightarrow \Delta}{\Gamma, x\xrightarrow{A} y \Rightarrow \Delta}\,(Unit) \qquad \dfrac{\Gamma, x\xrightarrow{A} y, y:A \Rightarrow \Delta}{\Gamma, x\xrightarrow{A} y \Rightarrow \Delta}\,(ID)$$
$$u \text{ new}$$

$$\dfrac{\Gamma, z\geq y, x\xrightarrow{A} y, y\xrightarrow{A} z \Rightarrow \Delta}{\Gamma, z\geq y, x\xrightarrow{A} y \Rightarrow \Delta}\,(C) \qquad \dfrac{\Gamma, x\xrightarrow{A\vee B} y, x\xrightarrow{A} y \Rightarrow \Delta \quad \Gamma, x\xrightarrow{A\vee B} y, y\xrightarrow{B} y \Rightarrow \Delta}{\Gamma, x\xrightarrow{A\vee B} y \Rightarrow \Delta}\,(CA) \qquad \dfrac{\Gamma, x\xrightarrow{A\vee B} y, x\xrightarrow{A} y \Rightarrow \Delta}{\Gamma, x\xrightarrow{A} y \Rightarrow \Delta}\,(CA-conv)$$
$$A\vee B \in \mathcal{L}_P$$

$$\dfrac{\Gamma, x\xrightarrow{A} y \Rightarrow \Delta, y:B \quad \Gamma, x\xrightarrow{A} y, x\xrightarrow{A\wedge B} y \Rightarrow \Delta}{\Gamma, x\xrightarrow{A} y \Rightarrow \Delta}\,(DT) \qquad\qquad \dfrac{\Gamma, x\xrightarrow{A\wedge B} y, x\xrightarrow{A} y, y\xrightarrow{B} y \Rightarrow \Delta}{\Gamma, x\xrightarrow{A\wedge B} y \Rightarrow \Delta}\,(MON)$$
$$A\wedge B \in \mathcal{L}_P$$

Fig. 1. The sequent calculus $\mathcal{S}_{\text{Cond}_{\text{ACL}}}$. Rules for $\neg$ and $\vee$ are omitted to save space.

$$\dfrac{\dfrac{\overline{\ldots, z\geq x \Rightarrow z:\alpha, z\geq x}\,(AX) \quad \overline{\ldots, x:\alpha, z:\alpha \Rightarrow z:\alpha}\,(AX)}{\dfrac{z\geq x, z\geq y, y\geq x, x\geq u, x:\alpha, y\xrightarrow{A} z \Rightarrow z:\alpha}{\dfrac{z\geq y, y\geq x, x\geq u, x:\alpha, y\xrightarrow{A} z \Rightarrow z:\alpha}{\dfrac{y\geq x, x\geq u, x:\alpha, y\xrightarrow{A} z \Rightarrow z:\alpha}{\dfrac{x\geq u, x:\alpha \Rightarrow x:A\text{ says }\alpha}{\Rightarrow u:\alpha\to(A\text{ says }\alpha)}\,(\to R)}\,(\text{says }R)}\,(Unit)}\,(TR)}\,(ATM)}$$

Fig. 2. A derivation in $\mathcal{S}_{\text{Cond}_{\text{ACL}}}$ for (UNIT)

of its nodes is an instance of axioms, namely (AX), $(AX_\geq)$, and $(AX_\perp)$, otherwise it is open. We say that a tree is closed if all its branches are closed. A sequent $\Gamma \Rightarrow \Delta$ has a derivation in $\mathcal{S}_{\text{Cond}_{\text{ACL}}}$ if there is a closed tree having $\Gamma \Rightarrow \Delta$ as a root.

The rule (EQ) is used in order to support the rule (RCEA): if a sequent $\Gamma, x \xrightarrow{A} y \Rightarrow \Delta, x \xrightarrow{B} y$ has to be proved, then the calculus $\mathcal{S}_{\text{Cond}_{\text{ACL}}}$ checks whether A and B are equivalent, i.e. $A \leftrightarrow B$. To this aim, the (EQ) rule introduces a branch in the backward derivation, trying to find a proof for both sequents $u : A \Rightarrow u : B$ and $u : B \Rightarrow u : A$. The restrictions on the rules $(\vee R)$, $(\wedge R)$, $(\neg R)$, $(\to R)$, $(\text{says }R)$, and (EQ) are necessary to preserve the soundness of the calculus. As an example, in Figure 2 we show a derivation in $\mathcal{S}_{\text{Cond}_{\text{ACL}}}$ of an instance of the axiom (UNIT). In order to show that the formula $\alpha \to (A \text{ says } \alpha)$ is valid, we build a derivation in $\mathcal{S}_{\text{Cond}_{\text{ACL}}}$ for the sequent $\Rightarrow u : \alpha \to (A \text{ says } \alpha)$.

The calculus $\mathcal{S}_{\text{Cond}_{\text{ACL}}}$ is sound and complete with respect to the semantics:

Theorem 3 (Soundness and Completeness of $\mathcal{S}_{\text{Cond}_{\text{ACL}}}$). *A sequent $\Gamma \Rightarrow \Delta$ is valid in the sense of Definition 5 if and only if $\Gamma \Rightarrow \Delta$ is derivable.*

Proof. (**Soundness**). By induction on the height of the derivation of $\Gamma \Rightarrow \Delta$. We only present the inductive step for the case in which the derivation of $\Gamma', x \xrightarrow{A} y \Rightarrow \Delta$ ends by an application of $(Unit)$: by inductive hypothesis, the premise $\Gamma', x \xrightarrow{A} y, y \geq x \Rightarrow \Delta$ is a valid sequent. By absurd, the conclusion is not, i.e. there is a model $\mathcal{M}$ and a function I such that $\mathcal{M} \models_I F$ for every $F \in \Gamma'$, $\mathcal{M} \models_I x \xrightarrow{A} y$ (i.e., $I(x)R_A I(y)$), whereas $\mathcal{M} \not\models_I G$ for any $G \in \Delta$. By (S-UNIT) in Definition 1, we have that, since $I(x)R_A I(y)$, also $I(x) \leq I(y)$, then $\mathcal{M} \models_I y \geq x$, against the validity of the premise.

(**Completeness**). It is an easy consequence of the admissibility of *cut* and of some basic standard structural properties (height-preserving admissibility of weakening and invertibility of the rules). The proof of the admissibility of (cut) is inspired by the work of Negri [20] and is omitted due to space limitations. We have to prove that the axioms are derivable and that the set of derivable formulas is closed under (MP), (RCEA), and (RCK). In Figure 2 we have shown a derivation of the axiom (UNIT). Derivations for (TAUT), (K), (C), (CA), (CA-conv), (Mon), (DT), and (ID) are omitted for lack of space. For (MP), suppose we have a derivation for $(i) \Rightarrow x : \alpha$ and $(ii) \Rightarrow x : \alpha \to \beta$. Since weakening is admissible, we have that also $(i') \Rightarrow x : \alpha, x : \beta$ and $(ii') x : \alpha \Rightarrow x : \alpha \to \beta, x : \beta$ have a derivation in $\mathcal{S}_{\text{Cond}_{\text{ACL}}}$. Since (cut) is admissible, we can conclude that $\Rightarrow x : \beta$ is derivable as follows:

$$
\cfrac{
(i') \Rightarrow x : \alpha, x : \beta
\qquad
\cfrac{
(ii')x : \alpha \Rightarrow x : \alpha \to \beta, x : \beta
\qquad
\cfrac{
\cfrac{
\cfrac{
x : \alpha \to \beta, x : \alpha \Rightarrow x : \beta, x \geq x
}{
x : \alpha \to \beta, x : \alpha \Rightarrow x : \beta, x : \alpha
}
\quad
x : \alpha \to \beta, x : \alpha, x : \beta \Rightarrow x : \beta
}{
x : \alpha \to \beta, x : \alpha \Rightarrow x : \beta
} (\to L)
}{
x : \alpha \Rightarrow x : \beta
} (cut)
}{
\Rightarrow x : \beta
} (cut)
$$

For (RCEA), we proceed as follows. As usual, $\vdash A \leftrightarrow B$ is a shorthand for $\vdash A \to B$ and $\vdash B \to A$. Suppose we have a derivation for $\Rightarrow u : A \to B$ and for $\Rightarrow u : B \to A$. We have shown that we have derivations for $u : A \Rightarrow u : B$ and $u : B \Rightarrow u : A$. The following derivation shows that also $\Rightarrow u : (A \textbf{ says } \gamma) \to (B \textbf{ says } \gamma)$ is derivable in $\mathcal{S}_{\text{Cond}_{\text{ACL}}}$ (the other half is symmetric):

$$
\cfrac{
\cfrac{
\cfrac{
\cfrac{u : A \Rightarrow u : B \qquad u : B \Rightarrow u : A}{\ldots, y \geq x \Rightarrow y \geq x, \ldots \quad \ldots, y \xrightarrow{B} z \Rightarrow y \xrightarrow{A} z, \ldots} (EQ) \quad \ldots, z : \gamma \Rightarrow z : \gamma, \ldots
}{
y \geq x, x \geq u, x : A \textbf{ says } \gamma, y \xrightarrow{B} z \Rightarrow z : \gamma
} (\textbf{says } L)
}{
x \geq u, x : A \textbf{ says } \gamma \Rightarrow x : B \textbf{ says } \gamma
} (\textbf{says } R)
}{
\Rightarrow u : (A \textbf{ says } \gamma) \to (B \textbf{ says } \gamma)
} (\to R)
$$

For (RCK), suppose there is a derivation for $\Rightarrow y : \alpha \to \beta$. Since $(\to R)$ is invertible, we have also a derivation of $(I) z \geq y, z : \alpha \Rightarrow z : \beta$ and, by weakening, of $(I') z \geq y, y \geq x, y \xrightarrow{A} z, x \geq u, x : A \textbf{ says } \alpha, z : \alpha \Rightarrow z : \beta$, from which we conclude:

$$\cfrac{\cfrac{\ldots, y \geq x \Rightarrow y \geq x \ldots \qquad (I')\, z \geq y, y \geq x, y \xrightarrow{A} z, x \geq u, x : A \textbf{ says } \alpha, z : \alpha \Rightarrow z : \beta}{\cfrac{\ldots, y \xrightarrow{A} z \Rightarrow y \xrightarrow{A} z, \ldots \qquad y \geq x, y \xrightarrow{A} z, x \geq u, x : A \textbf{ says } \alpha, z : \alpha \Rightarrow z : \beta}{\cfrac{y \geq x, y \xrightarrow{A} z, x \geq u, x : A \textbf{ says } \alpha \Rightarrow z : \beta}{\cfrac{x \geq u, x : A \textbf{ says } \alpha \Rightarrow x : A \textbf{ says } \beta}{\Rightarrow u : (A \textbf{ says } \alpha) \rightarrow (A \textbf{ says } \beta)}\,(\rightarrow R)}\,(\textbf{ says } R)}\,(\textbf{ says } L)}}\,(Unit)$$

$\square$

Completeness of $\mathcal{S}_{\mathsf{Cond}_{\mathsf{ACL}}}$ with respect to $\mathsf{Cond}_{\mathsf{ACL}}$ models of Definition 1 immediately follows from the completeness of the axiomatization of $\mathsf{Cond}_{\mathsf{ACL}}$ with respect to the semantics, shown in Theorem 2. We have that a formula $\varphi \in \mathcal{L}$ is valid if and only if the sequent $\Rightarrow u : \varphi$ has a derivation in $\mathcal{S}_{\mathsf{Cond}_{\mathsf{ACL}}}$.

4.1   Termination and Complexity of $\mathcal{S}_{\mathsf{Cond}_{\mathsf{ACL}}}$

In general, cut-freeness alone does not ensure the termination of proof search in a sequent calculus; the presence of labels and of rules such as ($\textbf{says } L$), ($\rightarrow L$), ($Unit$), (ID), ..., which increase the complexity of the sequent in a backward proof search, are potential causes of a non-terminating proof search. However, we can prove that the above mentioned "critical" rules can be applied in a controlled way, and then that the rules of $\mathcal{S}_{\mathsf{Cond}_{\mathsf{ACL}}}$ introduce only a finite number of labels. These facts allow us to describe a decision procedure $\widehat{\mathcal{S}_{\mathsf{Cond}_{\mathsf{ACL}}}}$ for the logic $\mathsf{Cond}_{\mathsf{ACL}}$, and to give an explicit complexity bound for it. First of all, we need the following lemmas:

Lemma 4. *If a sequent* $\Gamma \Rightarrow \Delta, y \geq x$ *is derivable in* $\mathcal{S}_{\mathsf{Cond}_{\mathsf{ACL}}}$, *then either* $\Gamma \Rightarrow \Delta$ *is derivable or* $y \geq x \in \Gamma$ *or* $y = x$.

Lemma 5. *If a sequent* $\Gamma \Rightarrow \Delta, y \xrightarrow{A} z$ *is derivable in* $\mathcal{S}_{\mathsf{Cond}_{\mathsf{ACL}}}$, *then either* $\Gamma \Rightarrow \Delta$ *is derivable or* $y \xrightarrow{A'} z \in \Gamma$.

The following facts allow to obtain a terminating calculus from $\mathcal{S}_{\mathsf{Cond}_{\mathsf{ACL}}}$:

• The rules of $\mathcal{S}_{\mathsf{Cond}_{\mathsf{ACL}}}$ introduce only a finite number of labels in a backward proof search: labels are only introduced by the rules $(\otimes R)$, where $\otimes$ stands for $\{\neg, \rightarrow, \wedge, \vee\}$, by formulas occurring negatively in the initial sequent, which are finite.

• It is useless to apply the rules (TR), $(Unit)$, (ID), (C), (CA), $(CA - conv)$, (DT), and (MON) more than once on the same principal formula. As an example, let us consider the rule $(Unit)$: we can restrict its application to $\Gamma, x \xrightarrow{A} y \Rightarrow \Delta$ only to the case in which the rule has not been previously applied to $x \xrightarrow{A} y$ in that branch, i.e. if $y \geq x \notin \Gamma$. Similarly for the other rules.

• A backward application of $(CA - conv)$ introduces $A \vee B$ in the premise, where $A \vee B$ is a principal belonging to $\mathcal{L}_{\mathbf{P}}$. The same for (DT), introducing $A \wedge B$. Since $\mathcal{L}_{\mathbf{P}}$ is finite, these rules will be applied a finite number of times in the same branch.

• Each of the rules $(\otimes L)$, applied to a sequent $\Gamma, x : \phi \Rightarrow \Delta$, leads to a premise of the form $\Gamma, x : \phi \Rightarrow \Delta, y \geq x$, and can thus be reapplied without any control. However, it is useless to apply $(\otimes L)$ on the same formula $x : \phi$ more than once in each branch in a backward proof search, introducing the same formula $y \geq x$ in the leftmost premise. Moreover, by Lemma 4 we can restrict the choice of the order formula $y \geq x$ to introduce in a way such that either $y \geq x \in \Gamma$ or $y = x$: this is explained by the fact that no rule of $\mathcal{S}_{Cond_{ACL}}$ have a formula $y \geq x$ in the right-hand side of a sequent as a principal formula. Therefore, the only way to prove it in a backward search is either by (AX), i.e. by a sequent also having $y \geq x$ in its left-hand side (then, we can choose among $y \geq x$ already in Γ) or by $(AX_\geq)$, thus choosing $y = x$. The same for (ATM).

This is not enough to ensure termination. Indeed, a sequence of applications of $(\otimes L)$, $(\otimes R)$ and (TR) might lead to the generation of infinite labels in a branch. As an example, consider the sequent $x : (P \rightarrow Q) \rightarrow R \Rightarrow$, to which $(\rightarrow L)$ can be applied by using x itself, obtaining $x : (P \rightarrow Q) \rightarrow R \Rightarrow x : P \rightarrow Q$ in the premise in the middle. We can then apply $(\rightarrow R)$, obtaining $y \geq x, x : (P \rightarrow Q) \rightarrow R, y : P \Rightarrow y : Q$, where y is a new label. y can then be used to apply $(\rightarrow L)$, leading to a premise $y \geq x, x : (P \rightarrow Q) \rightarrow R, y : P \Rightarrow y : Q, y : P \rightarrow Q$, to which a further application of $(\rightarrow R)$ introduces a new label z in the premise $z \geq y, y \geq x, x : (P \rightarrow Q) \rightarrow R, y : P, z : P \Rightarrow y : Q, z : Q$. An application of (TR) introduces $z \geq x$ in the left-hand side of the sequent, then $(\rightarrow L)$ can be applied to $x : (P \rightarrow Q) \rightarrow R$ by using z, obtaining the sequent $z \geq x, z \geq y, y \geq x, x : (P \rightarrow Q) \rightarrow R, y : P, z : P \Rightarrow y : Q, z : Q, z : P \rightarrow Q$, to which $(\rightarrow R)$ can be further applied to introduce a new label $z' \geq z$, then $z' \geq x$ by (TR) and so on. Termination is ensured by the following side condition on the application of the rules $(\otimes L)$. Given a sequent $\Gamma \Rightarrow \Delta$ and two labels x and y such that $y \geq x \in \Gamma$, we define the distance $d(y, x)$ between the two labels as: $d(x, x) = 0$ and $d(y, x) = n$ if n is the length of the *longest* sequence of *order formulas* in Γ "connecting" the two labels, i.e. $y \geq z_1, z_1 \geq z_2, \ldots, z_{n-1} \geq x \in \Gamma$. Given a derivation starting with $\Rightarrow x_0 : \phi$, let τ be the heigth of the parse tree of ϕ. We can show that we can restrict the application of a rule $(\otimes L)$ to $x : \alpha \otimes \beta$ to the case in which the label y used in the premise(s) is such that $d(y, x) \leq \tau$, that is to say it is useless to apply the rule by using a label whose distance with x is higher than the height of the parse tree of the initial formula.

• Similarly to the previous point, it is useless to apply (**says** L) on the same formula $x : A$ **says** α more than once in each branch, introducing (backward) the same formulas $y \geq x$ and $y \xrightarrow{A} z$ in the leftmost and in the inner premises, respectively. Moreover, by Lemma 5, the choice of the transition $y \xrightarrow{A} z$ to be used is restricted to formulas such that, for some formula A', there exists $y \xrightarrow{A'} z \in \Gamma$. Intuitively, this follows from the fact that a transition formula on the right-hand side of a sequent can only be proved by an application of (EQ). Moreover, since (EQ) only involves transition formulas, the premise introducing $y \xrightarrow{A} z$ can be reduced to $y \xrightarrow{A'} z \Rightarrow y \xrightarrow{A} z$.

The resulting terminating calculus $\widehat{\mathcal{S}_{Cond_{ACL}}}$ is shown in Figure 3. $\widehat{\mathcal{S}_{Cond_{ACL}}}$ is equivalent to $\mathcal{S}_{Cond_{ACL}}$, i.e. $\Gamma \Rightarrow \Delta$ in $\mathcal{S}_{Cond_{ACL}}$ if and only if $\Gamma \Rightarrow \Delta$ in $\widehat{\mathcal{S}_{Cond_{ACL}}}$. This itself gives the decidability of $Cond_{ACL}$.

Theorem 4. *The sequent calculus $\widehat{\mathcal{S}_{Cond_{ACL}}}$ ensures a terminating proof search, and the logic* $Cond_{ACL}$ *is decidable.*

(AX) $\Gamma, x : P \Rightarrow \Delta, x : P$
if $P \in ATM$

$(AX_\perp)$ $\Gamma, x : \perp \Rightarrow \Delta$

$\dfrac{\Gamma, x : P, y : P \Rightarrow \Delta}{\Gamma, x : P \Rightarrow \Delta}\ (ATM)$
if $y : P \notin \Gamma$ and $y \geq x \in \Gamma$
$P \in ATM$

$\dfrac{\Gamma, x : \alpha \to \beta \Rightarrow \Delta, y : \alpha \quad \Gamma, x : \alpha \to \beta, y : \beta \Rightarrow \Delta}{\Gamma, x : \alpha \to \beta \Rightarrow \Delta}\ (\to L)$
if $y \geq x \in \Gamma$ and $d(y, x) \leq r$
or $x = y$

$\dfrac{\Gamma, y \geq x, y : \alpha \Rightarrow \Delta, y : \beta}{\Gamma \Rightarrow \Delta, x : \alpha \to \beta}\ (\to R)$
y new

$\dfrac{y \xrightarrow{A'} z \Rightarrow y \xrightarrow{A} z \quad \Gamma, x : A \textbf{ says } \alpha, z : \alpha \Rightarrow \Delta}{\Gamma, x : A \textbf{ says } \alpha \Rightarrow \Delta}\ (\textbf{says } L)$
if $y \geq x \in \Gamma$ or $x = y$
$y \xrightarrow{A'} z \in \Gamma$

$\dfrac{\Gamma, y \geq x, y \xrightarrow{A} z \Rightarrow \Delta, z : \alpha}{\Gamma \Rightarrow \Delta, x : A \textbf{ says } \alpha}\ (\textbf{says } R)$
y and z new

$\dfrac{u : A \Rightarrow u : B \quad u : B \Rightarrow u : A}{\Gamma, x \xrightarrow{A} y \Rightarrow \Delta, x \xrightarrow{B} y}\ (EQ)$
u new

$\dfrac{\Gamma, z \geq x, z \geq y, y \geq x \Rightarrow \Delta}{\Gamma, z \geq y, y \geq x \Rightarrow \Delta}\ (TR)$
if $z \geq x \notin \Gamma$

$\dfrac{\Gamma, y \geq x, x \xrightarrow{A} y \Rightarrow \Delta}{\Gamma, x \xrightarrow{A} y \Rightarrow \Delta}\ (Unit)$
if $y \geq x \notin \Gamma$

$\dfrac{\Gamma, x \xrightarrow{A} y, y : A \Rightarrow \Delta}{\Gamma, x \xrightarrow{A} y \Rightarrow \Delta}\ (ID)$
if $y : A \notin \Gamma$

$\dfrac{\Gamma, z \geq y, x \xrightarrow{A} y, z \xrightarrow{A} z \Rightarrow \Delta}{\Gamma, z \geq y, x \xrightarrow{A} y \Rightarrow \Delta}\ (C)$
if $z \xrightarrow{A} z \notin \Gamma$

$\dfrac{\Gamma, x \xrightarrow{A \vee B} y, x \xrightarrow{A} y \Rightarrow \Delta \quad \Gamma, x \xrightarrow{A \vee B} y, x \xrightarrow{B} y \Rightarrow \Delta}{\Gamma, x \xrightarrow{A \vee B} y \Rightarrow \Delta}\ (CA)$
if $\{x \xrightarrow{A} y, x \xrightarrow{B} y\} \cap \Gamma = \emptyset$

$\dfrac{\Gamma, x \xrightarrow{A \vee B} y, x \xrightarrow{A} y \Rightarrow \Delta}{\Gamma, x \xrightarrow{A} y \Rightarrow \Delta}\ (CA - conv)$
if $x \xrightarrow{A \vee B} y \notin \Gamma$
$A \vee B \in \mathcal{L}_P$

$\dfrac{\Gamma, x \xrightarrow{A} y \Rightarrow \Delta, y : B \quad \Gamma, x \xrightarrow{A} y, x \xrightarrow{A \wedge B} y \Rightarrow \Delta}{\Gamma, x \xrightarrow{A} y \Rightarrow \Delta}\ (DT)$
if $x \xrightarrow{A \wedge B} y \notin \Gamma$
$A \wedge B \in \mathcal{L}_P$

$\dfrac{\Gamma, x \xrightarrow{A \wedge B} y, x \xrightarrow{A} y, x \xrightarrow{B} y \Rightarrow \Delta}{\Gamma, x \xrightarrow{A \wedge B} y \Rightarrow \Delta}\ (MON)$
if $\{x \xrightarrow{A} y, x \xrightarrow{B} y\} \not\subseteq \Gamma$

Fig. 3. The terminating calculus $\widehat{\mathcal{S}_{\mathsf{Cond}_{ACL}}}$. To save space, we omit the rules for $\wedge$. (AX) is restricted to atomic formulas. $(AX_\geq)$ is no needed due to the reformulation of the other rules.

Proof. Given a formula ϕ, just observe that there is only a finite number of derivations of the sequent $\Rightarrow x_0 : \phi$, as both the length of a proof and the number of labelled formulas which may occur in it is finite. $\quad\square$

We can give an explicit space complexity bound for Cond_{ACL}. As usual, a proof may have an exponential size because of the branching introduced by the rules. However we can obtain a much sharper space complexity bound since we do not need to store the whole proof, but only a sequent at a time plus additional information to carry on the proof search; this standard technique is similar to the one adopted in [16,22].

Theorem 5. *Provability in* Cond_{ACL} *is decidable in* $O(n^2 \log n)$ *space.*

5   Other Axioms

This work can be considered as a first step towards providing a general framework for the definition of axiomatization, semantics and proof methods for access control logics by the application of constructive conditional logics. While here we have considered the logic Cond_{ACL}, other axioms have been proposed in the literature and different access control logics have been defined through their combination. Among the most relevant axioms we mention the following ones:

(C4) $(A \textbf{ says } (A \textbf{ says } \alpha)) \to (A \textbf{ says } \alpha)$
(I) $(A \textbf{ says } \alpha) \to (B \textbf{ says } A \textbf{ says } \alpha)$
(Speaks For) $(A \Rightarrow B) \to ((A \textbf{ says } \alpha) \to (B \textbf{ says } \alpha))$
(Handoff) $(A \textbf{ says } (B \Rightarrow A)) \to (B \Rightarrow A)$

(C4) belongs to the original axiomatization of the logic ICL defined in [11], where it replaces the axiom (C). In [13] it has been shown that the semantical property corresponding to (C4) is the following:

(S-C4) $\forall t, s \in S$, if $s R_A t$, then $\exists z \in S$ such that $s R_A z$ and $z R_A t$

(I) is introduced in the axiomatization of the logic Binder [7], which extends the logic ABLP [3,17] in order to express the so called *authorization policies*. Notice that this is a weaker version of (Unit). The corresponding semantical property is:

(S-I) $\quad \forall t, s, u \in S$, if $t R_B s$ and $s R_A u$, then $t R_A u$

The connective $\Rightarrow$ occurring in (Speaks For) and (Handoff) is a well known connective introduced in the logic ABLP [3,17] to reason about transfer of authority from one principal to another. $A \Rightarrow B$ (A speaks for B) means that if A says α, then also B says α for any α. The axioms (Speaks for) and (Handoff) relate the connective $\Rightarrow$ with the **says** modality. The semantic conditions for the axioms (Speaks For) and (Handoff) have been studied in [14]. Our next step will be to extend our conditional framework in order to capture these axioms, so to provide automated deduction tools for the above mentioned logics including them.

6 Related Work and Conclusions

Related Work. The formal study of properties of access control logics is a recent research trend. As reported in [12], constructive logics are well suited for reasoning about authorization, because constructive proofs preserve the justification of statements during reasoning and, therefore, information about accountability is not lost. Classical logics, instead, allows proofs that discard evidence.

Abadi in [1] presents a formal study about connections between many possible axiomatizations of the says, as well as higher-level policy constructs such as delegation (speaks-for) and control. Abadi provides a strong argument to use constructivism in logic for access control, in fact he shows that from a well-known axiom like Unit in a classical logic we can deduce K says $\varphi \rightarrow (\varphi \vee K$ says $\psi)$. The axiom above is called *Escalation* and it represents a rather degenerate interpretation of says, i.e., if a principal says φ then, either φ is permitted or the principal says *anything*. On the contrary, if we interpret the says within an intuitionistic logic we can avoid Escalation.

Although several authorization logics employ the says modality, a limited amount of work has been done to study the formal logical properties of says, speaks-for and other constructs.

Garg and Abadi [11] translate existing access control logics into S4 by relying on a slight simplification of Gödel's translation from intuitionistic logic to S4, and extending it to formulas of the form A says φ.

Garg [10] adopts an ad-hoc version of constructive S4 called DTL_0 and embeds existing approaches into it. Constructive S4 has been chosen because of its intuitionistic Kripke semantics which DTL_0 extends by adding *views* [10], i.e., a mapping from worlds to sets of principals.

Boella et al. [6] define a logical framework called FSL (Fibred Security Language), based on fibring semantics [9] by looking at says as a (fibred) modal operator.

It has to be observed that, adopting a fixed semantics like S4 does not permit to study the correspondence between axioms of access control logics and Kripke structures. Suppose we look at says as a principal indexed modality $\Box_K$, if we rely on S4 we would have as an axiom $\Box_K \varphi \to \varphi$, which means: *everything* that K says is permitted. To overcome this problem, both in [10,11], Kripke semantics is sweetened with the addition of *views* which relativize the reasoning to a subset of worlds. Although this approach provides sound and complete semantics for a certain combination of axioms (those included in ICL), it breaks the useful bound between modality axioms and relations of Kripke structures.

Conclusions. We defined an intuitionistic conditional logic for Access Control called Cond_{ACL}. The major contribution of our conditional approach w.r.t. works in [10,11] is the identification of canonical properties for axioms of the logic (in particular Unit and C), i.e., first-order conditions on Kripke structures that are *necessary* and *sufficient* for the corresponding axiom to hold. [6,13,14] identify canonical properties for other access control axioms (e.g., C4, speaks-for, hand-off).

We believe that this methodology has several advantages. First, conditional logics allow a natural formalization of the **says** modality including the specification of boolean principals as arbitrary formulas. In spite of this generality, we have shown that provability in Cond_{ACL} is decidable in $O(n^2 log n)$ space, in agreement with the results given in [11] for the logic ICL. Second, the identification of canonical properties for access control axioms provides a natural deconstruction of access control logics. By deconstruction we mean the possibility to craft access control logics that adopt *any* combination of axioms for which canonical properties exist. For instance, not all access control systems adopt Unit as an axiom [18,4,15], but the translation in [11] does not provide an embedding in S4 for a logic without Unit. In general, the approach in [11] does not provide a methodology to deconstruct access control logics. In our approach, instead, we can formalize a logic and a calculus without Unit which is still sound and complete, by dropping the semantic condition (S-UNIT) and the corresponding rule (*Unit*) in the calculus.

We believe that choosing axioms for access control logics depends on the needs of security practitioners. By looking at **says** as a conditional modality, we can offer a formal framework to study the axioms of access control via canonical properties on the semantics, and to build calculi to carry out automated deduction. Of course, for each combination of axioms, the decidability and the complexity of the resulting logic as well as the termination of the calculus have to be determined. To this concern, we have followed the approach proposed in [22] for standard normal conditional logics, which we have extended here to deal with an intuitionistic logic as well as with specific access control axioms.

For the time being, Cond_{ACL} only includes few widely accepted axioms of access control logics but it can be extended in order to cope with richer axioms, as well as with the well known notion of "speaks for". This is what we plan to do in future work.

References

1. Abadi, M.: Variations in Access Control Logic. In: van der Meyden, R., van der Torre, L. (eds.) DEON 2008. LNCS (LNAI), vol. 5076, pp. 96–109. Springer, Heidelberg (2008)
2. Abadi, M., Burrows, M., Lampson, B.W., Plotkin, G.D.: A calculus for access control in distributed systems. In: Feigenbaum, J. (ed.) CRYPTO 1991. LNCS, vol. 576, pp. 1–23. Springer, Heidelberg (1992)

3. Abadi, M., Burrows, M., Lampson, B.W., Plotkin, G.D.: A calculus for access control in distributed systems. ACM Trans. on Progr. Languages and Systems 15(4), 706–734 (1993)
4. Becker, M.Y., Fournet, C., Gordon, A.D.: Design and semantics of a decentralized authorization language. In: IEEE Comp. Security Foundations Symp (CSF), pp. 3–15 (2007)
5. Bertolissi, C., Fernández, M., Barker, S.: Dynamic event-based access control as term rewriting. In: Barker, S., Gail-Joon, A. (eds.) DBSec 2007. LNCS, vol. 4602, pp. 96–109. Springer, Heidelberg (2007)
6. Boella, G., Gabbay, D., Genovese, V., van der Torre, L.: Fibred security language. Studia Logica 92(3), 395–436 (2009)
7. DeTreville, J.: Binder, a logic-based security language. In: IEEE Symposium on Security and Privacy, pp. 105–113 (2002)
8. Enderton, H.B.: A Mathematical Introduction to Logic, 2nd edn. Academic Press, New York (2000)
9. Gabbay, D.M.: Fibring Logics. Oxford University Press, Oxford (1999)
10. Garg, D.: Principal centric reasoning in constructive authorization logic. In: IMLA (2008)
11. Garg, D., Abadi, M.: A modal deconstruction of access control logics. In: Amadio, R.M. (ed.) FOSSACS 2008. LNCS, vol. 4962, pp. 216–230. Springer, Heidelberg (2008)
12. Garg, D., Pfenning, F.: Non-interference in constructive authorization logic. In: CSFW-19, pp. 283–296 (2006)
13. Genovese, V., Giordano, L., Gliozzi, V., Pozzato, G.L.: A constructive conditional logic for access control: a preliminary report. In: Proc. of ECAI 2010. Frontiers in Artificial Intelligence and Applications, vol. 215, pp. 1073–1074. IOS Press, Amsterdam (2010) (short paper)
14. Genovese, V., Rispoli, D., Gabbay, D.M., van der Torre, L.: Modal Access Control Logic: Axiomatization, Semantics and FOL Theorem Proving. In: Proc. of STAIRS 2010. Frontiers in Artificial Intelligence and Applications, vol. 222, pp. 114–126. IOS Press, Amsterdam (2010)
15. Gurevich, Y., Roy, A.: Operational semantics for DKAL: Application and analysis. In: Fischer-Hübner, S., Lambrinoudakis, C., Pernul, G. (eds.) TrustBus 2009. LNCS, vol. 5695, pp. 149–158. Springer, Heidelberg (2009)
16. Hudelmaier, J.: An $\mathcal{O}$(n log n)-space decision procedure for intuitionistic propositional logic. Journal of Logic and Computation 3(1), 63–75 (1993)
17. Lampson, B.W., Abadi, M., Burrows, M., Wobber, E.: Authentication in distributed systems: Theory and practice. ACM Trans. on Computer Systems 10(4), 265–310 (1992)
18. Lesniewski-Laas, C., Ford, B., Strauss, J., Morris, R., Kaashoek, M.F.: Alpaca: extensible authorization for distributed services. In: Proc. of ACM CCS 2007, pp. 432–444 (2007)
19. Li, N., Grosof, B.N., Feigenbaum, J.: Delegation logic: A logic-based approach to distributed authorization. ACM Trans. Inf. Syst. Secur. 6(1), 128–171 (2003)
20. Negri, S.: Proof analysis in modal logic. J. of Philosophical Logic 34, 507–544 (2005)
21. Nute, D.: Topics in Conditional Logic. Reidel, Dordrecht (1980)
22. Olivetti, N., Pozzato, G.L., Schwind, C.B.: A Sequent Calculus and a Theorem Prover for Standard Conditional Logics. ACM Transactions on Computational Logics 8(4) (2007)
23. Troelstra, A.S., van Dalen, D.: Constructivism in Mathematics: An Introduction (1988)

A Tableau Calculus for a Nonmonotonic Extension of $\mathcal{EL}^{\perp}$

Laura Giordano[1], Valentina Gliozzi[2], Nicola Olivetti[3], and Gian Luca Pozzato[2]

[1] Dip. di Informatica, U. Piemonte O., Alessandria, Italy
`laura@mfn.unipmn.it`
[2] Dip. Informatica, Univ. di Torino, Italy
`{gliozzi,pozzato}@di.unito.it`
[3] LSIS-UMR CNRS 6168, Marseille, France
`nicola.olivetti@univ-cezanne.fr`

Abstract. We introduce a tableau calculus for a nonmonotonic extension of low complexity Description Logic $\mathcal{EL}^{\perp}$ that can be used to reason about typicality and defeasible properties. The calculus deals with Left Local knowledge bases in the logic $\mathcal{EL}^{\perp}\mathbf{T}_{min}$ recently introduced in [8] . The calculus performs a two-phase computation to check whether a query is minimally entailed from the initial knowledge base. It is sound, complete and terminating. Furthermore, it is a decision procedure for Left Local $\mathcal{EL}^{\perp}\mathbf{T}_{min}$ knowledge bases, whose complexity matches the known results for the logic, namely that entailment is in Π_2^p.

1   Introduction

Nonmonotonic extensions of Description Logics (DLs) have been actively investigated since the early 90s, [14,4,2,3,7,11,10,9,6]. The reason is that DLs are used to represent classes and their properties, so that a nonmonotonic mechanism is wished to express defeasible inheritance of prototypical properties. A simple but powerful nonmonotonic extension of DL is proposed in [11,10,9]: in this approach "typical" or "normal" properties can be directly specified by means of a "typicality" operator $\mathbf{T}$ enriching the underlying DL; the typicality operator $\mathbf{T}$ is essentially characterised by the core properties of nonmonotonic reasoning axiomatized by *preferential logic* [12]. In $\mathcal{ALC} + \mathbf{T}$ [11], one can consistently express defeasible inclusions and exceptions such as: typical students do not pay taxes, but working students do typically pay taxes, but working student having children normally do not: $\mathbf{T}(Student) \sqsubseteq \neg TaxPayer$; $\mathbf{T}(Student \sqcap Worker) \sqsubseteq TaxPayer$; $\mathbf{T}(Student \sqcap Worker \sqcap \exists HasChild.\top) \sqsubseteq \neg TaxPayer$. Although the operator $\mathbf{T}$ is nonmonotonic in itself, the logics $\mathcal{ALC} + \mathbf{T}$ and $\mathcal{EL}^{+\perp}\mathbf{T}$ [10] are monotonic. As a consequence, unless a knowledge base (KB) contains explicit assumptions about typicality of individuals (e.g. that john is a typical student), there is no way of inferring defeasible properties of them (e.g. that john does not pay taxes). In [9], a non monotonic extension of $\mathcal{ALC} + \mathbf{T}$ based on a minimal models semantics is proposed. The resulting logic, called $\mathcal{ALC} + \mathbf{T}_{min}$, supports typicality assumptions; as an example, for a TBox specified by the inclusions above, in $\mathcal{ALC} + \mathbf{T}_{min}$ the following inference holds: TBox $\cup \{Student(john)\} \models_{\mathcal{ALC}+\mathbf{T}_{min}} \neg TaxPayer(john)$.

K. Brünnler and G. Metcalfe (Eds.): TABLEAUX 2011, LNAI 6793, pp. 180–195, 2011.

Similarly to other nonmonotonic DLs, adding the typicality operator with its minimal models semantics to a standard DL, such as $\mathcal{ALC}$, leads to a very high complexity (namely query entailment in the resulting logic is in CO-NEXP^{NP} [9]). This fact has motivated the study of nonmonotonic extensions of low complexity DLs [3] such as $\mathcal{EL}^\perp$ of the $\mathcal{EL}$ family [1] which are nonetheless well-suited for encoding large KBs. In the same vein, we consider here the extension of the low complexity logic $\mathcal{EL}^\perp$ with the typicality operator based on the minimal models semantics introduced in [9]. But the restriction to $\mathcal{EL}^\perp$ does not suffice: as recently shown, deciding entailment in the resulting logic $\mathcal{EL}^\perp\mathbf{T}_{min}$ is unfortunately ExpTime-hard [8]. This result is analogous to the one for *circumscribed* $\mathcal{EL}^\perp$ KBs [3]. However, it has been shown in [8] that the complexity drops to Π_2^p for the fragment of *Left Local* $\mathcal{EL}^\perp\mathbf{T}_{min}$ KBs. Similar fragments have been previously studied for *circumscribed* $\mathcal{EL}^\perp$ KBs [3] obtaining the same complexity. To the best of our knowledge, however, no deduction calculi for these fragments with circumscription are known at present.

In this paper, we concentrate on the *Left Local* fragment of $\mathcal{EL}^\perp\mathbf{T}_{min}$. This fragment is determined by restricting the extistential quantification on concepts appearing on the *left* side of a concept inclusion: only existentially quantified concepts of the form $\exists R.\top$ are allowed. For this fragment, we propose a tableau calculus for deciding minimal entailment in Π_2^p. It is a two-phase calculus: in the first phase, candidate models (complete open branches) falsifying the given query are generated, in the second phase the minimality of candidate models is checked by means of an auxiliary tableau construction. The latter tries to build a model which is "more preferred" than the candidate one: if it fails (being closed) the candidate model is minimal, otherwise it is not. Both tableaux constructions comprise some non-standard rules for existential quantification in order to constrain the domain (and its size) of the model being constructed. The second phase makes use in addition of special closure conditions to prevent the generation of non-preferred models. It comes as a surprise that the modification of the existential rule is sufficient to match the optimal complexity, so that the calculus provide in itself a constructive proof of the upper bound of this fragment (obtained in [8] by a non-constructive semantical argument).

2 The Typicality Operator T, the Logic $\mathcal{EL}^\perp\mathbf{T}_{min}$ and its Left Local Fragment

Before describing $\mathcal{EL}^\perp\mathbf{T}_{min}$, let us briefly recall the underlying monotonic logic $\mathcal{EL}^{+\perp}\mathbf{T}$ [10], obtained by adding to $\mathcal{EL}^\perp$ the typicality operator $\mathbf{T}$. The intuitive idea is that $\mathbf{T}(C)$ selects the *typical* instances of a concept C. In $\mathcal{EL}^{+\perp}\mathbf{T}$ we can therefore distinguish between the properties that hold for all instances of concept C ($C \sqsubseteq D$), and those that only hold for the normal or typical instances of C ($\mathbf{T}(C) \sqsubseteq D$).

Formally, the $\mathcal{EL}^{+\perp}\mathbf{T}$ language is defined as follows.

Definition 1. *We consider an alphabet of concept names* $\mathcal{C}$, *of role names* $\mathcal{R}$, *and of individuals* $\mathcal{O}$. *Given* $A \in \mathcal{C}$ *and* $R \in \mathcal{R}$, *we define*

$$C := A \mid \top \mid \perp \mid C \sqcap C \qquad C_R := C \mid C_R \sqcap C_R \mid \exists R.C \qquad C_L := C_R \mid \mathbf{T}(C)$$

A KB is a pair (TBox, ABox). TBox contains a finite set of general concept inclusions (or subsumptions) $C_L \sqsubseteq C_R$. ABox contains assertions of the form $C_L(a)$ and $R(a, b)$, where $a, b \in \mathcal{O}$.

The semantics of $\mathcal{EL}^{+^\perp} \mathbf{T}$ [10] is defined by enriching ordinary models of $\mathcal{EL}^\perp$ by a *preference relation* $<$ on the domain, whose intuitive meaning is to compare the "typicality" of individuals: $x < y$, means that x is more typical than y. Typical members of a concept C, that is members of $\mathbf{T}(C)$, are the members x of C that are minimal with respect to this preference relation.

Definition 2 (Semantics of T). *A model $\mathcal{M}$ is any structure $\langle \Delta, <, I \rangle$ where Δ is the domain; $<$ is an irreflexive and transitive relation over Δ that satisfies the following Smoothness Condition: for all $S \subseteq \Delta$, for all $x \in S$, either $x \in Min_<(S)$ or $\exists y \in Min_<(S)$ such that $y < x$, where $Min_<(S) = \{u : u \in S$ and $\nexists z \in S$ s.t. $z < u\}$. Furthermore, $<$ is multilinear: if $u < z$ and $v < z$, then either $u = v$ or $u < v$ or $v < u$. I is the extension function that maps each concept C to $C^I \subseteq \Delta$, and each role r to $r^I \subseteq \Delta^I \times \Delta^I$. For concepts of $\mathcal{EL}^\perp$, C^I is defined in the usual way. For the $\mathbf{T}$ operator: $(\mathbf{T}(C))^I = Min_<(C^I)$.*

Definition 3 (Model satisfying a Knowledge Base). *Given a model $\mathcal{M}$, I can be extended so that it assigns to each individual a of $\mathcal{O}$ a distinct element a^I of the domain Δ. $\mathcal{M}$ satisfies a KB (TBox,ABox), if it satisfies both its TBox and its ABox, where:*

- *$\mathcal{M}$ satisfies an inclusion $C \sqsubseteq D$ if $C^I \subseteq D^I$. $\mathcal{M}$ satisfies TBox if it satisfies all its inclusions.*
- *$\mathcal{M}$ satisfies $C(a)$ if $a^I \in C^I$ and aRb if $(a^I, b^I) \in R^I$. $\mathcal{M}$ satisfies ABox if it satisfies all its formulas.*

The operator $\mathbf{T}$ [11] is characterized by a set of postulates that are essentially a reformulation of KLM [12] axioms of *preferential logic* $\mathbf{P}$. $\mathbf{T}$ has therefore all the "core" properties of nonmonotonic reasoning as it is axiomatised by $\mathbf{P}$. The semantics of the typicality operator can be specified by modal logic. The interpretation of $\mathbf{T}$ can be split into two parts: for any x of the domain Δ, $x \in (\mathbf{T}(C))^I$ just in case (i) $x \in C^I$, and (ii) there is no $y \in C^I$ such that $y < x$. Condition (ii) can be represented by means of an additional modality $\square$, whose semantics is given by the preference relation $<$ interpreted as an accessibility relation. Observe that by the Smoothness Condition, $\square$ has the properties of Gödel-Löb modal logic of provability G. The interpretation of $\square$ in $\mathcal{M}$ is as follows:

$$(\square C)^I = \{x \in \Delta \mid \text{for every } y \in \Delta, \text{ if } y < x \text{ then } y \in C^I\}$$

We immediately get that $x \in (\mathbf{T}(C))^I$ iff $x \in (C \sqcap \square \neg C)^I$. From now on, we consider $\mathbf{T}(C)$ as an abbreviation for $C \sqcap \square \neg C$.

The main limit of $\mathcal{EL}^{+^\perp} \mathbf{T}$ is that it is *monotonic*. Even if the typicality operator $\mathbf{T}$ itself is nonmonotonic (i.e. $\mathbf{T}(C) \sqsubseteq E$ does not imply $\mathbf{T}(C \sqcap D) \sqsubseteq E$), the logic $\mathcal{EL}^{+^\perp} \mathbf{T}$ is monotonic: what is inferred from KB can still be inferred from any KB' with KB $\subseteq$ KB'. In order to perform nonmonotonic inferences, as done in [9], we strengthen the semantics of $\mathcal{EL}^{+^\perp} \mathbf{T}$ by restricting entailment to a class of minimal (or preferred) models. We call the new logic $\mathcal{EL}^\perp\mathbf{T}_{min}$. Intuitively, the idea is to restrict our consideration to models that *minimize the non typical instances of a concept.*

Given a KB, we consider a finite set $\mathcal{L}_\mathbf{T}$ of concepts: these are the concepts whose non typical instances we want to minimize. We assume that the set $\mathcal{L}_\mathbf{T}$ contains at least all concepts C such that $\mathbf{T}(C)$ occurs in the KB or in the query F, where a *query* F is either an assertion $C(a)$ or an inclusion relation $C \sqsubseteq D$. As we have just said, $x \in C^I$ is typical if $x \in (\Box\neg C)^I$. Minimizing the non typical instances of C therefore means to minimize the objects not satisfying $\Box\neg C$ for $C \in \mathcal{L}_\mathbf{T}$. Hence, for a given model $\mathcal{M} = \langle \Delta, <, I \rangle$, we define:

$$\mathcal{M}_{\mathcal{L}_\mathbf{T}}^{\Box^-} = \{(x, \neg\Box\neg C) \mid x \notin (\Box\neg C)^I, \text{ with } x \in \Delta, C \in \mathcal{L}_\mathbf{T}\}.$$

Definition 4 (Preferred and minimal models). *Given a model* $\mathcal{M} = \langle \Delta <, I \rangle$ *of a knowledge base KB, and a model* $\mathcal{M}' = \langle \Delta', <', I' \rangle$ *of KB, we say that* $\mathcal{M}$ *is preferred to* $\mathcal{M}'$ *with respect to* $\mathcal{L}_\mathbf{T}$, *and we write* $\mathcal{M} <_{\mathcal{L}_\mathbf{T}} \mathcal{M}'$, *if (i)* $\Delta = \Delta'$, *(ii)* $\mathcal{M}_{\mathcal{L}_\mathbf{T}}^{\Box^-} \subset \mathcal{M}'_{\mathcal{L}_\mathbf{T}}^{\Box^-}$, *(iii)* $a^I = a^{I'}$ *for all* $a \in \mathcal{O}$. $\mathcal{M}$ *is a* minimal model *for KB (with respect to* $\mathcal{L}_\mathbf{T}$) *if it is a model of KB and there is no other model* $\mathcal{M}'$ *of KB such that* $\mathcal{M}' <_{\mathcal{L}_\mathbf{T}} \mathcal{M}$.

Definition 5 (Minimal Entailment in $\mathcal{EL}^\perp\mathbf{T}_{min}$). *A query F is minimally entailed in* $\mathcal{EL}^\perp\mathbf{T}_{min}$ *by KB with respect to* $\mathcal{L}_\mathbf{T}$ *if F is satisfied in all models of KB that are minimal with respect to* $\mathcal{L}_\mathbf{T}$. *We write* $KB \models_{\mathcal{EL}^\perp\mathbf{T}_{min}} F$.

Example 1. The KB of the Introduction can be reformulated as follows in $\mathcal{EL}^{+\perp}\mathbf{T}$: *TaxPayer $\sqcap$ NotTaxPayer $\sqsubseteq \perp$; Parent $\sqsubseteq \exists HasChild.\top$; $\exists HasChild.\top \sqsubseteq$ Parent;* $\mathbf{T}(Student) \sqsubseteq NotTaxPayer$; $\mathbf{T}(Student \sqcap Worker) \sqsubseteq TaxPayer$; $\mathbf{T}(Student \sqcap Worker \sqcap Parent) \sqsubseteq NotTaxPayer$. *Let* $\mathcal{L}_\mathbf{T} = \{Student, Student \sqcap Worker, Student \sqcap Worker \sqcap Parent\}$. *Then* $TBox \cup \{Student(john)\} \models_{\mathcal{EL}^\perp\mathbf{T}_{min}} NotTaxPayer(john)$, *since* $john^I \in (Student\sqcap\Box\neg Student)^I$ *for all minimal models* $\mathcal{M} = \langle \Delta <, I \rangle$ *of the KB. In contrast, by the nonmonotonic character of minimal entailment, TBox* $\cup \{Student(john), Worker(john)\} \models_{\mathcal{EL}^\perp\mathbf{T}_{min}} TaxPayer(john)$. *Last, notice that TBox* $\cup \{\exists HasChild.(Student \sqcap Worker)(jack)\} \models_{\mathcal{EL}^\perp\mathbf{T}_{min}}$ $\exists HasChild.TaxPayer (jack)$. *The latter shows that minimal consequence applies to implict individuals as well, without any ad-hoc mechanism.*

In [8] (Theorem 3.1), it has been proven that entailment in $\mathcal{EL}^\perp\mathbf{T}_{min}$ is ExpTime hard. In order to lower the complexity of minimal entailment in $\mathcal{EL}^\perp\mathbf{T}_{min}$, we consider a syntactic restriction on the KB called Left Local KBs. This restriction is similar to the one introduced in [3] for circumscribed $\mathcal{EL}^\perp$ KBs.

Definition 6 (Left Local knowledge base). *A Left Local KB only contains subsumptions* $C_L^{LL} \sqsubseteq C_R$, *where C and C_R are as in Definition 1 and:*

$$C_L^{LL} := C \mid C_L^{LL} \sqcap C_L^{LL} \mid \exists R.\top \mid \mathbf{T}(C)$$

There is no restriction on the ABox.

Observe that the KB in the Example 1 is Left Local, as no concept of the form $\exists R.C$ with $C \neq \top$ occurs on the left hand side of inclusions.

In [8] (Theorem 3.12), it has been proven that the problem of deciding whether KB $\models_{\mathcal{EL}^\perp \mathbf{T}_{min}} F$ is in Π_2^p. In this paper, we focus our attention to Left Local KBs.

3   The Tableau Calculus for Left Local $\mathcal{EL}^\perp \mathbf{T}_{min}$

In this section we present a tableau calculus $\mathcal{TAB}_{min}^{\mathcal{EL}^\perp \mathbf{T}}$ for deciding whether a query F is minimally entailed from a Left Local knowledge base in the logic $\mathcal{EL}^\perp \mathbf{T}_{min}$.

The calculus $\mathcal{TAB}_{min}^{\mathcal{EL}^\perp \mathbf{T}}$ performs a two-phase computation in order to check whether a query F is minimally entailed from the initial KB. In the first phase, a tableau calculus, called $\mathcal{TAB}_{PH1}^{\mathcal{EL}^\perp \mathbf{T}}$, simply verifies whether KB $\cup \{\neg F\}$ is satisfiable in an $\mathcal{EL}^\perp \mathbf{T}$ model, building candidate models. In the second phase another tableau calculus, called $\mathcal{TAB}_{PH2}^{\mathcal{EL}^\perp \mathbf{T}}$, checks whether the candidate models found in the first phase are *minimal* models of KB, i.e. for each open branch of the first phase, $\mathcal{TAB}_{PH2}^{\mathcal{EL}^\perp \mathbf{T}}$ tries to build a model of KB which is preferred to the candidate model w.r.t. Definition 4. The whole procedure $\mathcal{TAB}_{min}^{\mathcal{EL}^\perp \mathbf{T}}$ is formally defined at the end of this section (Definition 12).

As usual, $\mathcal{TAB}_{min}^{\mathcal{EL}^\perp \mathbf{T}}$ tries to build an open branch representing a minimal model satisfying KB $\cup \{\neg F\}$. The negation of a query $\neg F$ is defined as follows:

Definition 7 (Negation of a query). *Given a query F, we define its negation $\neg F$:*

  – *if $F \equiv C(a)$, then $\neg F \equiv (\neg C)(a)$*
  – *if $F \equiv C \sqsubseteq D$, then $\neg F \equiv (C \sqcap \neg D)(x)$, where x does not occur in KB.*

Notice that we introduce the connective $\neg$ in a very "localized" way. This is very different from introducing the negation all over the knowledge base, and indeed it does not imply that we jump out of the language of $\mathcal{EL}^\perp \mathbf{T}_{min}$.

$\mathcal{TAB}_{min}^{\mathcal{EL}^\perp \mathbf{T}}$ makes use of labels, which are denoted with $x, y, z, \ldots$. Labels represent either a variable or an individual of the ABox, that is to say an element of $\mathcal{O} \cup \mathcal{V}$. These labels occur in *constraints* (or *labelled* formulas), that can have the form $x \xrightarrow{R} y$ or $x : C$, where x, y are labels, R is a role and C is either a concept or the negation of a concept of $\mathcal{EL}^\perp \mathbf{T}_{min}$ or has the form $\Box \neg D$ or $\neg \Box \neg D$, where D is a concept.

Let us now analyze the two components of $\mathcal{TAB}_{min}^{\mathcal{EL}^\perp \mathbf{T}}$, starting with $\mathcal{TAB}_{PH1}^{\mathcal{EL}^\perp \mathbf{T}}$.

3.1   First Phase: The Tableaux Calculus $\mathcal{TAB}_{PH1}^{\mathcal{EL}^\perp \mathbf{T}}$

A tableau of $\mathcal{TAB}_{PH1}^{\mathcal{EL}^\perp \mathbf{T}}$ is a tree whose nodes are tuples $\langle S \mid U \mid W \rangle$. S is a set of constraints, whereas U contains formulas of the form $C \sqsubseteq D^L$, representing subsumption relations $C \sqsubseteq D$ of the TBox. L is a list of labels, used in order to ensure the termination of the tableau calculus. W is a set of labels x_C used in order to build a "small" model, matching the results of the Small Model Theorem in [8]. A branch is a sequence of nodes $\langle S_1 \mid U_1 \mid W_1 \rangle, \langle S_2 \mid U_2 \mid W_2 \rangle, \ldots, \langle S_n \mid U_n \mid W_n \rangle \ldots$, where each node $\langle S_i \mid U_i \mid W_i \rangle$ is obtained from its immediate predecessor $\langle S_{i-1} \mid U_{i-1} \mid W_{i-1} \rangle$ by applying a rule of $\mathcal{TAB}_{PH1}^{\mathcal{EL}^\perp \mathbf{T}}$, having $\langle S_{i-1} \mid U_{i-1} \mid W_{i-1} \rangle$ as the premise and $\langle S_i \mid U_i \mid W_i \rangle$ as one of its conclusions. A branch is closed if one of its nodes is an instance of a (Clash) axiom, otherwise it is open. A tableau is closed if all its branches are closed.

The calculus $\mathcal{TAB}_{PH1}^{\mathcal{EL}^\perp \mathbf{T}}$ is significantly different in two respects from the calculus $\mathcal{ALC} + \mathbf{T}_{min}$ presented in [9]. First, the rule $(\exists^+)$ is split in the following two rules:

$$\frac{\langle S, u : \exists R.C \mid U \mid W \rangle}{\langle S, u \xrightarrow{R} x_C, x_C : C \mid U \mid W \cup \{x_C\} \rangle \quad \langle S, u \xrightarrow{R} y_1, y_1 : C \mid U \mid W \rangle \cdots \langle S, u \xrightarrow{R} y_m, y_m : C \mid U \mid W \rangle} (\exists^+)_1$$
$$\text{if } x_C \notin W \text{ and } y_1, \ldots, y_m \text{ are all the labels occurring in } S$$

$$\frac{\langle S, u : \exists R.C \mid U \mid W \rangle}{\langle S, u \xrightarrow{R} x_C \mid U \mid W \rangle \quad \langle S, u \xrightarrow{R} y_1, y_1 : C \mid U \mid W \rangle \cdots \langle S, u \xrightarrow{R} y_m, y_m : C \mid U \mid W \rangle} (\exists^+)_2$$
$$\text{if } x_C \in W \text{ and } y_1, \ldots, y_m \text{ are all the labels occurring in } S$$

When the rule $(\exists^+)_1$ is applied to a formula $u : \exists R.C$, it introduces a new label x_C only when the set W does not already contain x_C. Otherwise, since x_C has been already introduced in that branch, $u \xrightarrow{R} x_C$ is added to the conclusion of the rule rather than introducing a new label. As a consequence, in a given branch, $(\exists^+)_1$ only introduces a new label x_C for each concept C occurring in the initial KB in some $\exists R.C$, and no blocking machinery is needed to ensure termination. As it will become clear in the proof of Theorem 1, this is possible since we are considering Left Local KBs, which have small models; in these models all existentials $\exists R.C$ occurring in KB are made true by reusing a single witness x_C (Theorem 3.12 in [8]). Notice also that the rules $(\exists^+)_1$ and $(\exists^+)_2$ introduce a branching on the choice of the label used to realize the existential restriction $u : \exists R.C$: just the leftmost conclusion of $(\exists^+)_1$ introduces a new label (as mentioned, the x_C such that $x_C : C$ and $u \xrightarrow{R} x_C$ are added to the branch); in all the other branches, each one of the other labels y_i occurring in S may be chosen.

Second, in order to build multilinear models of Definition 2, the calculus adopts a strengthened version of the rule $(\Box^-)$ used in $\mathcal{TAB}_{min}^{\mathcal{ALC}+\mathbf{T}}$ [9]. We write $\overline{S}$ as an abbreviation for $S, u : \neg\Box\neg C_1, \ldots, u : \neg\Box\neg C_n$. Moreover, we define $S_{u \to y}^M = \{y : \neg D, y : \Box\neg D \mid u : \Box\neg D \in S\}$ and, for $k = 1, 2, \ldots, n$, we define $\overline{S}_{u \to y}^{\Box^{-k}} = \{y : \neg\Box\neg C_j \sqcup C_j \mid u : \neg\Box\neg C_j \in \overline{S} \wedge j \neq k\}$. The strengthened rule $(\Box^-)$ is as follows:

$$\frac{\langle S, u : \neg\Box\neg C_1, \neg\Box\neg C_2, \ldots, u : \neg\Box\neg C_n \mid U \mid W \rangle}{\langle S, x : C_k, x : \Box\neg C_k, S_{u \to x}^M, \overline{S}_{u \to x}^{\Box^{-k}} \mid U \mid W \rangle} (\Box^-)$$
$$\langle S, y_1 : C_k, y_1 : \Box\neg C_k, S_{u \to y_1}^M, \overline{S}_{u \to y_1}^{\Box^{-k}} \mid U \mid W \rangle \cdots \langle S, y_m : C_k, y_m : \Box\neg C_k, S_{u \to y_m}^M, \overline{S}_{u \to y_m}^{\Box^{-k}} \mid U \mid W \rangle$$

for all $k = 1, 2, \ldots, n$, where $y_1, \ldots, y_m$ are all the labels occurring in S and x is new.

Rule $(\Box^-)$ contains: - n branches, one for each $u : \neg\Box\neg C_k$ in $\overline{S}$; in each branch a *new* typical C_k individual x is introduced (i.e. $x : C_k$ and $x : \Box\neg C_k$ are added), and for all other $u : \neg\Box\neg C_j$, either $x : C_j$ holds or the formula $x : \neg\Box\neg C_j$ is recorded; - other $n \times m$ branches, where m is the number of labels occurring in S, one for each label y_i and for each $u : \neg\Box\neg C_k$ in $\overline{S}$; in these branches, a given y_i is chosen as a typical instance of C_k, that is to say $y_i : C_k$ and $y_i : \Box\neg C_k$ are added, and for all other

$u : \neg\Box\neg C_j$, either $y_i : C_j$ holds or the formula $y_i : \neg\Box\neg C_j$ is recorded. As shown in the proof of Theorem 1, this rule is sound with respect to multilinear models. The advantage of this rule over the $(\Box^-)$ rule in the calculus $\mathcal{TAB}_{min}^{ALC+\mathbf{T}}$ is that all the negated box formulas labelled by u are treated in one step, introducing only a new label x in (some of) the conclusions.

Notice that in order to keep $\overline{S}$ readable, we have used $\sqcup$. This is the reason why our calculi contain the rule for $\sqcup$, even if this constructor does not belong to $\mathcal{EL}^{\perp}\mathbf{T}_{min}$.

In order to check the satisfiability of a KB, we build its *corresponding constraint system* $\langle S \mid U \mid \emptyset \rangle$, and we check its satisfiability.

Definition 8 (Corresponding constraint system). *Given a knowledge base* KB=*(TBox,ABox), we define its* corresponding constraint system $\langle S \mid U \mid \emptyset \rangle$ *as follows:*

- $S = \{a : C \mid C(a) \in ABox\} \cup \{a \xrightarrow{R} b \mid R(a,b) \in ABox\}$
- $U = \{C \sqsubseteq D^{\emptyset} \mid C \sqsubseteq D \in TBox\}$

Definition 9 (Model satisfying a constraint system). *Let* $\mathcal{M} = \langle \Delta, I, < \rangle$ *be a model as defined in Definition 2. We define a function* α *which assigns to each variable of* $\mathcal{V}$ *an element of* Δ, *and assigns every individual* $a \in \mathcal{O}$ *to* $a^I \in \Delta$. $\mathcal{M}$ *satisfies a constraint* F *under* α, *written* $\mathcal{M} \models_{\alpha} F$, *as follows:*

- $\mathcal{M} \models_{\alpha} x : C$ *iff* $\alpha(x) \in C^I$
- $\mathcal{M} \models_{\alpha} x \xrightarrow{R} y$ *iff* $(\alpha(x), \alpha(y)) \in R^I$

A constraint system $\langle S \mid U \mid W \rangle$ *is satisfiable if there is a model* $\mathcal{M}$ *and a function* α *such that* $\mathcal{M}$ *satisfies every constraint in* S *under* α *and that, for all* $C \sqsubseteq D^L \in U$ *and for all* $x \in \Delta$, *we have that if* $x \in C^I$ *then* $x \in D^I$.

Proposition 1. *Given a KB=(TBox,ABox), it is satisfiable if and only if its corresponding constraint system* $\langle S \mid U \mid \emptyset \rangle$ *is satisfiable.*

To verify the satisfiability of KB $\cup \{\neg F\}$, we use $\mathcal{TAB}_{PH1}^{\mathcal{EL}^{\perp}\mathbf{T}}$ to check the satisfiability of the constraint system $\langle S \mid U \mid \emptyset \rangle$ obtained by adding the constraint corresponding to $\neg F$ to S', where $\langle S' \mid U \mid \emptyset \rangle$ is the corresponding constraint system of KB. To this purpose, the rules of the calculus $\mathcal{TAB}_{PH1}^{\mathcal{EL}^{\perp}\mathbf{T}}$ are applied until either a contradiction is generated (Clash) or a model satisfying $\langle S \mid U \mid \emptyset \rangle$ can be obtained from the resulting constraint system.

Given a node $\langle S \mid U \mid W \rangle$, for each subsumption $C \sqsubseteq D^L \in U$ and for each label x that appears in the tableau, we add to S the constraint $x : \neg C \sqcup D$: we refer to this mechanism as *unfolding*. As mentioned above, each formula $C \sqsubseteq D$ is equipped with a list L of labels in which it has been unfolded in the current branch. This is needed to avoid multiple unfolding of the same subsumption by using the same label, generating infinite branches.

Before introducing the rules of $\mathcal{TAB}_{PH1}^{\mathcal{EL}^{\perp}\mathbf{T}}$ we need some more definitions. First, as in [5], we define an ordering relation $\prec$ to keep track of the temporal ordering of insertion of labels in the tableau, that is to say if y is introduced in the tableau, then $x \prec$

$$\langle S, x : C, x : \neg C \mid U \mid W\rangle \ (\text{Clash}) \qquad\qquad \langle S, x : \neg\top \mid U \mid W\rangle \ (\text{Clash})_{\neg\top} \qquad\qquad \langle S, x : \perp \mid U \mid W\rangle \ (\text{Clash})_{\perp}$$

$$\frac{\langle S, x : C \sqcap D \mid U \mid W\rangle}{\langle S, x : C, x : D \mid U \mid W\rangle}(\sqcap^+) \qquad \frac{\langle S, x : \neg(C \sqcap D) \mid U \mid W\rangle}{\langle S, x : \neg C \mid U \mid W\rangle \ \langle S, x : \neg D \mid U \mid W\rangle}(\sqcap^-) \qquad \frac{\langle S, x : C \sqcup D \mid U \mid W\rangle}{\langle S, x : C \mid U \mid W\rangle \ \langle S, x : D \mid U \mid W\rangle}(\sqcup^+)$$

$$\frac{\langle S, x : \mathbf{T}(C) \mid U \mid W\rangle}{\langle S, x : C, x : \square\neg C \mid U \mid W\rangle}(\mathbf{T}^+) \qquad \frac{\langle S, x : \neg\mathbf{T}(C) \mid U \mid W\rangle}{\langle S, x : \neg C \mid U \mid W\rangle \ \langle S, x : \neg\square\neg C \mid U \mid W\rangle}(\mathbf{T}^-) \qquad \frac{\langle S \mid U, C \sqsubseteq D^L \mid W\rangle}{\langle S, x : \neg C \sqcup D \mid U, C \sqsubseteq D^{L,x} \mid W\rangle}(\text{Unfold})$$
$$\text{if } x \text{ occurs in } S \text{ and } x \notin L$$

$$\frac{\langle S, u : \exists R.C \mid U \mid W\rangle}{\langle S, u \xrightarrow{R} x_C, x_C : C \mid U \mid W \cup \{x_C\}\rangle \quad \langle S, u \xrightarrow{R} y_1, y_1 : C \mid U \mid W\rangle \cdots \langle S, u \xrightarrow{R} y_m, y_m : C \mid U \mid W\rangle}(\exists^+)_1$$
$$\text{if } x_C \notin W \text{ and } y_1, \ldots, y_m \text{ are all the labels occurring in } S$$

$$\frac{\langle S, u : \exists R.C \mid U \mid W\rangle}{\langle S, u \xrightarrow{R} x_C \mid U \mid W\rangle \quad \langle S, u \xrightarrow{R} y_1, y_1 : C \mid U \mid W\rangle \cdots \langle S, u \xrightarrow{R} y_m, y_m : C \mid U \mid W\rangle}(\exists^+)_2$$
$$\text{if } x_C \in W \text{ and } y_1, \ldots, y_m \text{ are all the labels occurring in } S$$

$$\frac{\langle S, x : \neg\exists R.C, x \xrightarrow{R} y \mid U \mid W\rangle}{\langle S, x : \neg\exists R.C, x \xrightarrow{R} y, y : \neg C \mid U \mid W\rangle}(\exists^-) \qquad \frac{\langle S \mid U \mid W\rangle}{\langle S, x : \neg\square\neg C \mid U \mid W\rangle \ \langle S, x : \square\neg C \mid U \mid W\rangle}(\text{cut})$$
$$\text{if } y : \neg C \notin S \qquad\qquad \text{if } x : \neg\square\neg C \notin S \text{ and } x : \square\neg C \notin S$$
$$x \text{ occurs in } S \qquad C \in \mathcal{L}_{\mathbf{T}}$$

$$\frac{\langle S, u : \neg\square\neg C_1, \neg\square\neg C_2, \ldots, u : \neg\square\neg C_n \mid U \mid W\rangle}{\langle S, x : C_k, x : \square\neg C_k, S^M_{u\to x}, \overline{S}^{\square^{-k}}_{u\to x} \mid U \mid W\rangle}(\square^-)$$
$$\langle S, y_1 : C_k, y_1 : \square\neg C_k, S^M_{u\to y_1}, \overline{S}^{\square^{-k}}_{u\to y_1} \mid U \mid W\rangle \cdots \langle S, y_m : C_k, y_m : \square\neg C_k, S^M_{u\to y_m}, \overline{S}^{\square^{-k}}_{u\to y_m} \mid U \mid W\rangle$$
$$x \text{ new}$$
$$\text{if } y_1, \ldots, y_m \text{ are all the labels occurring in } S, y_1 \neq u, \ldots, y_m \neq u$$
$$k = 1, 2, \ldots, n$$

Fig. 1. The calculus $\mathcal{TAB}^{\mathcal{EL}^{\perp}\mathbf{T}}_{PH1}$

y for all labels x that are already in the tableau. Furthermore, if x is the label occurring in the query F, then $x \prec y$ for all y occurring in the constraint system corresponding to the initial KB. Moreover, we define the satisfiability of a branch of a tableau:

Definition 10 (Satisfiability of a branch). *A branch* **B** *of a tableau of* $\mathcal{TAB}^{\mathcal{EL}^{\perp}\mathbf{T}}_{PH1}$ *is satisfiable by a model* $\mathcal{M}$ *if there is a mapping* α *from the labels in* **B** *to the domain of* $\mathcal{M}$ *such that for all constraint systems* $\langle S \mid U \mid W\rangle$ *on* **B**, $\mathcal{M}$ *satisfies under* α *(see Definition 9) every constraint in* S *and, for all* $C \sqsubseteq D^L \in U$ *and for all* x *occurring in* S, *we have that if* $\alpha(x) \in C^I$ *then* $\alpha(x) \in D^I$.

The rules of $\mathcal{TAB}^{\mathcal{EL}^{\perp}\mathbf{T}}_{PH1}$ are presented in Figure 1. Rules $(\exists^+_1)$ and $(\square^-)$ are called *dynamic* since they can introduce a new variable in their conclusions. The other rules are called *static*. We do not need any extra rule for the positive occurrences of the $\square$ operator, since these are taken into account by the computation of $S^M_{x\to y}$ of $(\square^-)$. The (cut) rule ensures that, given any concept $C \in \mathcal{L}_{\mathbf{T}}$, an open branch built by $\mathcal{TAB}^{\mathcal{EL}^{\perp}\mathbf{T}}_{PH1}$ contains either $x : \square\neg C$ or $x : \neg\square\neg C$ for each label x: this is needed in order to allow $\mathcal{TAB}^{\mathcal{EL}^{\perp}\mathbf{T}}_{PH2}$ to check the minimality of the model corresponding to the open branch.

The rules of $\mathcal{TAB}^{\mathcal{EL}^\perp\mathbf{T}}_{PH1}$ are applied with the following *standard strategy*: 1. apply a rule to a label x only if no rule is applicable to a label y such that $y \prec x$; 2. apply dynamic rules only if no static rule is applicable. The calculus so obtained is sound and complete with respect to the semantics in Definition 9.

Fact 1. *The only negated existential formulas that can occur in the tableau are (i) either general existential formulas $x : \neg\exists R.C$ that derive from the negation of the query; (ii) or $y : \neg\exists R.\top$, that can occur at any point of the branch and that derive from (Unfold) applied to a subsumption $\exists R.\top \sqsubseteq D$.*

Theorem 1 (Soundness of $\mathcal{TAB}^{\mathcal{EL}^\perp\mathbf{T}}_{PH1}$). *If $KB \not\models_{\mathcal{EL}^\perp\mathbf{T}_{min}} F$, then the tableau for the constraint system corresponding to $KB \cup \{\neg F\}$ contains an open branch, which is satisfiable (via an injective assignment from labels to domain elements) in a minimal model of KB.*

Proof. (Sketch) If $KB \not\models_{\mathcal{EL}^\perp\mathbf{T}_{min}} F$, then there is a minimal model of KB that satisfies $\neg F$. By Definition 3, each individual occurring in KB is assigned to a different domain element (unique name assumption). It can be shown that this also holds for the constraint system corresponding to KB, which is therefore satisfiable by a minimal model of KB via an injective mapping from labels to domain elements. We show that each rule of $\mathcal{TAB}^{\mathcal{EL}^\perp\mathbf{T}}_{PH1}$ preserves satisfiability by an injective mapping in a minimal model of KB. From this, we conclude that the branch is open, since no instance of the clash axioms would be satisfiable by an injective mapping in a minimal model of KB.

As an example of how we show that rules preserve satisfiability in a minimal model through an injective mapping, we consider here rules $(\exists^+)_1$, $(\exists^+)_2$, and $(\Box^-)$.

For $(\exists^+)_1$, assume there is a minimal model $\mathcal{M} = \langle \Delta, I, < \rangle$ of KB that satisfies the branch obtained before the application of the rule and premise of the rule (under an injective assignment α). In this model, $\alpha(u) \in (\exists R.C)^I$, i.e. there is $z \in \Delta$ with $(\alpha(u), z) \in R^I$ and $z \in C^I$. If the branch contains a label y_i such that $\alpha(y_i) = z$, then the consequence of the rule in which $u \xrightarrow{R} y_i, y_i : C$ appear is satisfiable by the same model under the same assignment. Otherwise, consider the branch containing $u \xrightarrow{R} x_C, x_C : C$. x_C is new, hence we can extend α so that $\alpha(x_C) = z$. α so extended is obviously still injective, and $\mathcal{M}$ satisfies this branch.

For $(\exists^+)_2$ the reasoning is a bit more tricky. Suppose the portion of the branch already obtained and the premise of the rule, $\langle S, u : \exists R.C \mid U \mid W \rangle$, are satisfiable by a minimal model $\mathcal{M}$ of KB under an assignment α. In $\mathcal{M}$, $(\alpha(u), z) \in R^I$ and $z \in C^I$, for some z. We reason by cases. (A) If the branch contains a label y_i such that $\alpha(y_i) = z$, then the consequence of the rule in which $u \xrightarrow{R} y_i, y_i : C$ appear is satisfiable by the same model under the same assignment. (B) Otherwise, we show that the conclusion containing $u \xrightarrow{R} x_C$ is satisfiable by a minimal model $\mathcal{M}'$ of KB, that also satisfies the previous portion of the branch. We distinguish two cases. (i) In the branch there is no occurrence of $\neg\exists R.D$ (for any D), then $\mathcal{M}'$ is obtained from $\mathcal{M}$ by simply adding $(\alpha(u), \alpha(x_C))$ to R^I. α has not been modified and therefore remains injective. Furthermore, since this addition does not modify the valuation function, and by this fact it does not modify the boxed formulas holding in the model, $\mathcal{M}'$ is still a minimal model of KB. Furthermore, $\mathcal{M}'$ satisfies the same branch formulas as $\mathcal{M}$, as well as

$\langle S, u : \exists R.C \mid U \mid W \rangle$. (ii) In the branch there is an occurrence of $u : \neg\exists R.D$. Then by Fact 1, this is the only negated formula different from $\exists R.C$ occurring in the branch, and hence u is the starting label. Since $\mathcal{M}$ satisfies $u : \exists R.C$ under α, $(\alpha(u), z) \in R^I$, and $z \in C^I$. Consider now α', equal to α, apart from the fact that $\alpha'(x_C) = z$. α' is still injective. Indeed, the branch does not contain a label y_i such that $\alpha(y_i) = z$, otherwise we would be in case (A). It can be verified that $\mathcal{M}$ satisfies $\langle S, u : \exists R.C \mid U \mid W \rangle$, as well as the previous branch formulas, under α'. Indeed, by the strategy, the only formula labelled by x_C at the moment in which we apply $(\exists^+)_2$ is $x_C : C$ (we start considering x_C only after having applied all the rules to u, which is the starting label), and this is satisfied in $\mathcal{M}'$ under α'. All the other constraints that do not involve x_C remain satisfied even in α' that coincides with α on all other labels.

For $(\square^-)$, we prove that if a node $\langle S, u : \neg\square\neg C_1, \ldots, u : \neg\square\neg C_n \mid U \mid W \rangle$ is satisfiable in a minimal multi-linear model $\mathcal{M} = \langle W, <, V \rangle$ under a certain injective α then also one of the conclusions of the rule, namely $\langle S, x : C_k, x : \square\neg C_k, S^M_{u \to x}, \overline{S}^{\square^{-k}}_{u \to x} \mid U \mid W \rangle$ where x is a new label, is satisfiable in the same minimal model, under an extension of α. Let $\alpha(u) = u^I$, where $u^I \in \Delta$. There are $z_1 < u^I, \ldots, z_n < u^I$, such that $z_i \in Min_<(C_i)$, thus $z_i \in (C_i \sqcap \square\neg C_i)^I$, for $i = 1, 2, \ldots, n$. Since $\mathcal{M}$ is a multi-linear model, the z_i, $i = 1, 2, \ldots, n$, whenever distinct, are totally ordered: we have that $z_i < u^I$, so that they must belong to the same component. Let z_k be the maximum of z_i ($1 \leq i \leq n$), i.e. for each z_i, $i = 1, 2, \ldots, n$, we have either (i) $z_i = z_k$ or (ii) $z_i < z_k$. In case (i), we have that $z_k \in C_i^I$. In case (ii) we have that $z_k \in (\neg\square\neg C_i)^I$. We have shown that for each $i \neq k$, $z_k \in C_i^I$ or $z_k \in (\neg\square\neg C_i)^I$. If there is a label y on the branch such that $\alpha(y) = z_k$, then the conclusion $\langle S, y : C_k, y : \square\neg C_k, S^M_{u \to y}, \overline{S}^{\square^{-k}}_{u \to x} \mid U \mid W \rangle$ is satisfiable under an assignment α, which is injective. Indeed, we have that $\mathcal{M} \models_\alpha S^M_{u \to y}$ and $\mathcal{M} \models_\alpha \overline{S}^{\square^{-k}}_{u \to y}$. Otherwise, since x does not occur in S, we extend α in a way such that $\alpha(x) = z_k$, and the conclusion $\langle S, x : C_k, x : \square\neg C_k, S^M_{u \to x}, \overline{S}^{\square^{-k}}_{u \to x} \mid U \mid W \rangle$ is satisfiable under the injective assignment α. ∎

We can furthermore prove completeness of $\mathcal{TAB}^{\mathcal{EL}^\perp \mathbf{T}}_{PH1}$. The proof is quite straightforward and is omitted due to space limitations.

Theorem 2 (Completeness of $\mathcal{TAB}^{\mathcal{EL}^\perp \mathbf{T}}_{PH1}$). *Given a constraint system $\langle S \mid U \mid W \rangle$, if it is unsatisfiable, then it has a closed tableau in $\mathcal{TAB}^{\mathcal{EL}^\perp \mathbf{T}}_{PH1}$.*

Let us conclude this section by analyzing termination and complexity of $\mathcal{TAB}^{\mathcal{EL}^\perp \mathbf{T}}_{PH1}$. In general, non-termination in labelled tableau calculi can be caused by two different reasons: 1. some rules copy their principal formula in the conclusion(s), and can thus be reapplied over the same formula without any control; 2. dynamic rules may generate infinitely-many labels, creating infinite branches. As mentioned above, differently from the calculus for $\mathcal{ALC} + \mathbf{T}_{min}$ in [11,9], the calculus $\mathcal{TAB}^{\mathcal{EL}^\perp \mathbf{T}}_{PH1}$ ensures termination *without* adopting the standard blocking machinery.

Concerning the first source of non-termination (point 1), the only rules copying their principal formulas in their conclusions are $(\exists^-)$ and (Unfold). However, the side conditions on the application of such rules avoid multiple applications on the same formula.

Concerning the second source of non-termination (point 2), we can prove that only finitely-many labels are introduced on a branch. Intuitively, the $(\exists^+)_1$ rule introduces at most one new label x_C for each concept C belonging to the initial node. Moreover, thanks to the properties of $\square$, no other additional machinery is required to ensure termination. Indeed, it can be shown that the interplay between rules $(\mathbf{T}^-)$ and $(\square^-)$ does not generate branches containing infinitely-many labels. Intuitively, the application of $(\square^-)$ to $x : \neg\square\neg C, x : \neg\square\neg C_1, \ldots, x : \neg\square\neg C_k$ adds $y : \square\neg C$ to the conclusion, so that $(\mathbf{T}^-)$ can no longer consistently introduce $y : \neg\square\neg C$. It is also worth noticing that the (cut) rule does not affect termination, since it is applied only to the finitely many formulas belonging to $\mathcal{L}_{\mathbf{T}}$.

Theorem 3 (Termination of $\mathcal{TAB}_{PH1}^{\mathcal{EL}^\perp \mathbf{T}}$). *Let $\langle S \mid U \mid \emptyset \rangle$ be the corresponding constraint system of a KB. Any tableau generated by $\mathcal{TAB}_{PH1}^{\mathcal{EL}^\perp \mathbf{T}}$ for $\langle S \mid U \mid \emptyset \rangle$ is finite.*

Let us conclude this section by estimating the complexity of $\mathcal{TAB}_{PH1}^{\mathcal{EL}^\perp \mathbf{T}}$. Let n be the size of the initial KB, i.e. the length of the string representing KB, and let $\langle S \mid U \mid \emptyset \rangle$ its corresponding constraint system. We assume that the size of F and $\mathcal{L}_{\mathbf{T}}$ is $O(n)$.

Theorem 4 (Complexity of Phase 1). *Given a KB and a query F, the problem of checking whether KB $\cup \{\neg F\}$ is satisfiable is in NP.*

Proof. (Sketch) The calculus builds a tableau for $\langle S \mid U \mid \emptyset \rangle$ whose branches's size is $O(n)$. This immediately follows from the fact the dynamic rules $(\exists^+)_1$ and $(\square^-)$ generate at most $O(n)$ labels in a branch. Indeed, the rule $(\exists^+)_1$ introduces a new label x_C for each concept C occurring in KB, then at most $O(n)$ labels. Concerning $(\square^-)$, consider a branch generated by its application to a constraint system $\langle S, u : \neg\square\neg C_1 \ldots, u : \neg\square\neg C_n \mid U \mid W \rangle$. In the worst case, a new label x_1 is introduced. Suppose also that the branch under consideration is the one containing $x_1 : C_1$ and $x_1 : \square\neg C_1$. The $(\square^-)$ rule can then be applied to formulas $u : \neg\square\neg C_k$, introducing also a further new label x_2. However, by the presence of $x_1 : \square\neg C_1$, the rule $(\square^-)$ can no longer consistently introduce $x_2 : \neg\square\neg C_1$, since $x_2 : \square\neg C_1 \in S_{x_1 \to x_2}^M$. Therefore, $(\square^-)$ is applied to $\neg\square\neg C_1 \ldots \neg\square\neg C_n$ in u. This application generates (at most) one new world x_1 that labels (at most) $n - 1$ negated boxed formulas. A further application of $(\square^-)$ to $\neg\square\neg C_1 \ldots \neg\square\neg C_{n-1}$ in x_1 generates (at most) one new world x_2 that labels (at most) $n - 2$ negated boxed formulas, and so on. Overall, at most $O(n)$ new labels are introduced by $(\square^-)$ in each branch. For each of these labels, static rules apply at most $O(n)$ times: (Unfold) is applied at most $O(n)$ times for each $C \sqsubseteq D \in U$, one for each label introduced in the branch. The rule (cut) is also applied at most $O(n)$ times for each label, since $\mathcal{L}_{\mathbf{T}}$ contains at most $O(n)$ formulas. As the number of different concepts in KB is at most $O(n)$, in all steps involving the application of boolean rules, there are at most $O(n)$ applications of these rules. Therefore, the length of the tableau branch built by the strategy is $O(n^2)$. Finally, we observe that all the nodes of the tableau contain a number of formulas which is polynomial in n, therefore to test that a node is an instance of a (Clash) axiom has at most complexity polynomial in n. ∎

Notice that the above strategy is able to build branches of polynomial length thanks to the presence of the rule (cut). Indeed, the key point is that, when the rule $(\square^-)$ building

$\langle S, x : C, x : \neg C \mid U \mid K \rangle$ (Clash) $\langle S, x : \neg\top \mid U \mid K \rangle$ (Clash)$_{\neg\top}$ $\langle S, x : \bot \mid U \mid K \rangle$ (Clash)$_\bot$

$\langle S \mid U \mid \emptyset \rangle$ (Clash)$_\emptyset$ $\langle S, x : \neg\Box\neg C \mid U \mid K \rangle$ (Clash)$_{\Box -}$
 if $x : \neg\Box\neg C \notin K$

$$\frac{\langle S \mid U, C \sqsubseteq D^L \mid K \rangle}{\langle S, x : \neg C \sqcup D \mid U, C \sqsubseteq D^{L,x} \mid K \rangle} \text{(Unfold)}$$
$$x \in \mathcal{D}(\mathbf{B}) \text{ and } x \notin L$$

$$\frac{\langle S, x : C \sqcap D \mid U \mid K \rangle}{\langle S, x : C, x : D \mid U \mid K \rangle} (\sqcap^+) \qquad \frac{\langle S, x : \neg(C \sqcap D) \mid U \mid K \rangle}{\langle S, x : \neg C \mid U \mid K \rangle \quad \langle S, x : \neg D \mid U \mid K \rangle} (\sqcap^-) \qquad \frac{\langle S, x : \mathbf{T}(C) \mid U \mid K \rangle}{\langle S, x : C, x : \Box\neg C \mid U \mid K \rangle} (\mathbf{T}^+)$$

$$\frac{\langle S, x : \neg\mathbf{T}(C) \mid U \mid K \rangle}{\langle S, x : \neg C \mid U \mid K \rangle \quad \langle S, x : \neg\Box\neg C \mid U \mid K \rangle} (\mathbf{T}^-) \qquad \frac{\langle S \mid U \mid K \rangle}{\langle S, x : \Box\neg C \mid U \mid K \rangle \quad \langle S, x : \neg\Box\neg C \mid U \mid K \rangle} (cut)$$
$$ \text{if } x : \neg\Box\neg C \notin S \text{ and } x : \Box\neg C \notin S$$
$$ x \in \mathcal{D}(\mathbf{B}) \quad C \in \mathcal{L}_\mathbf{T}$$

$$\frac{\langle S, u : \exists R.C \mid U \mid K \rangle}{\langle S, u \xrightarrow{R} y_1, y_1 : C \mid U \mid K \rangle \ \cdots \ \langle S, u \xrightarrow{R} y_m, y_m : C \mid U \mid K \rangle} (\exists^+)$$
$$\text{if } \mathcal{D}(\mathbf{B}) = \{y_1, \ldots, y_m\}$$

$$\frac{\langle S, u : \neg\Box\neg C_1, \ldots, u : \neg\Box\neg C_n \mid U \mid K, u : \neg\Box\neg C_1, \ldots, u : \neg\Box\neg C_n \rangle}{\langle S, y_1 : C_k, y_1 : \Box\neg C_k, S^M_{u \to y_1}, \overline{S}^{\Box^{-k}}_{u \to y_1} \mid U \mid K \rangle \ \cdots \ \langle S, y_m : C_k, y_m : \Box\neg C_k, S^M_{u \to y_m}, \overline{S}^{\Box^{-k}}_{u \to y_m} \mid U \mid K \rangle} (\Box^-)$$
$$\text{if } \mathcal{D}(\mathbf{B}) = \{y_1, \ldots, y_m\} \text{ and } y_1 \neq u, \ldots, y_m \neq u$$

Fig. 2. The calculus $\mathcal{TAB}^{\mathcal{EL}^\perp \mathbf{T}}_{PH2}$. To save space, we omit the rule $(\sqcup^+)$.

multilinear models is applied to a given label u, *all negated boxed formulas* $u : \neg\Box\neg C_k$ belong to current set of formulas. It could be the case that, after an application of $(\Box^-)$ by using u, the same label u is used in one of the conclusions of another application of $(\Box^-)$, say to some x_i. Therefore, the application of static rules could introduce $u : \neg\Box\neg C$, and a further application of $(\Box^-)$ could be needed. However, since (cut) is a static rule, and since $C \in \mathcal{L}_\mathbf{T}$ because $\neg\Box\neg C$ has been generated by unfolding some $\mathbf{T}(C) \sqsubseteq D$ in the TBox, either $u : \neg\Box\neg C$ or $u : \Box\neg C$ have already been introduced in the branch *before* the second application of $(\Box^-)$, which is a dynamic rule.

3.2 The Tableaux Calculus $\mathcal{TAB}^{\mathcal{EL}^\perp \mathbf{T}}_{PH2}$

Let us now introduce the calculus $\mathcal{TAB}^{\mathcal{EL}^\perp \mathbf{T}}_{PH2}$ which, for each open branch $\mathbf{B}$ built by $\mathcal{TAB}^{\mathcal{EL}^\perp \mathbf{T}}_{PH1}$, verifies whether it represents a minimal model of the KB.

Definition 11. *Given an open branch $\mathbf{B}$ of a tableau built from $\mathcal{TAB}^{\mathcal{EL}^\perp \mathbf{T}}_{PH1}$, we define:*

- $\mathcal{D}(\mathbf{B})$ *as the set of labels occurring on $\mathbf{B}$;*
- $\mathbf{B}^{\Box^-} = \{x : \neg\Box\neg C \mid x : \neg\Box\neg C \text{ occurs in } \mathbf{B}\}$.

A tableau of $\mathcal{TAB}^{\mathcal{EL}^\perp \mathbf{T}}_{PH2}$ is a tree whose nodes are tuples of the form $\langle S \mid U \mid K \rangle$, where S and U are defined as in a constraint system, whereas K contains formulas of the form $x : \neg\Box\neg C$, with $C \in \mathcal{L}_\mathbf{T}$. The basic idea of $\mathcal{TAB}^{\mathcal{EL}^\perp \mathbf{T}}_{PH2}$ is as follows. Given an open branch $\mathbf{B}$ built by $\mathcal{TAB}^{\mathcal{EL}^\perp \mathbf{T}}_{PH1}$ and corresponding to a model $\mathcal{M}^\mathbf{B}$ of

KB $\cup \{\neg F\}$, $\mathcal{TAB}_{PH2}^{\mathcal{EL}^\perp \mathbf{T}}$ checks whether $\mathcal{M}^\mathbf{B}$ is a minimal model of KB by trying to build a model of KB which is preferred to $\mathcal{M}^\mathbf{B}$. To this purpose, it keeps track (in K) of the negated box used in $\mathbf{B}$ ($\mathbf{B}^{\Box^-}$) in order to check whether it is possible to build a model of KB containing less negated box formulas. The tableau built by $\mathcal{TAB}_{PH2}^{\mathcal{EL}^\perp \mathbf{T}}$ closes if it is not possible to build a model smaller than $\mathcal{M}^\mathbf{B}$, it remains open otherwise. Since by Definition 4 two models can be compared only if they have the same domain, $\mathcal{TAB}_{PH2}^{\mathcal{EL}^\perp \mathbf{T}}$ tries to build an open branch containing all the labels appearing on $\mathbf{B}$, i.e. those in $\mathcal{D}(\mathbf{B})$. To this aim, the dynamic rules use labels in $\mathcal{D}(\mathbf{B})$ instead of introducing new ones in their conclusions. The rules of $\mathcal{TAB}_{PH2}^{\mathcal{EL}^\perp \mathbf{T}}$ are shown in Fig. 2.

More in detail, the rule $(\exists^+)$ is applied to a constraint system containing a formula $x : \exists R.C$; it introduces $x \xrightarrow{R} y$ and $y : C$ where $y \in \mathcal{D}(\mathbf{B})$, instead of y being a new label. The choice of the label y introduces a branching in the tableau construction. The rule (Unfold) is applied to *all the labels of* $\mathcal{D}(\mathbf{B})$ (and not only to those appearing in the branch). The rule $(\Box^-)$ is applied to a node $\langle S, u : \neg\Box\neg C_1, \ldots, u : \neg\Box\neg C_n \mid U \mid K\rangle$, when $\{u : \neg\Box\neg C_1, \ldots, u : \neg\Box\neg C_n\} \subseteq K$, i.e. when the negated box formulas $u : \neg\Box\neg C_i$ also belong to the open branch $\mathbf{B}$. Even in this case, the rule introduces a branch on the choice of the individual $y_i \in \mathcal{D}(\mathbf{B})$ to be used in the conclusion. In case a tableau node has the form $\langle S, x : \neg\Box\neg C \mid U \mid K\rangle$, and $x : \neg\Box\neg C \notin K$, then $\mathcal{TAB}_{PH2}^{\mathcal{EL}^\perp \mathbf{T}}$ detects a clash, called (Clash)$_{\Box^-}$: this corresponds to the situation where $x : \neg\Box\neg C$ does not belong to $\mathbf{B}$, while the model corresponding to the branch being built contains $x : \neg\Box\neg C$, and hence is *not* preferred to the model represented by $\mathbf{B}$.

The calculus $\mathcal{TAB}_{PH2}^{\mathcal{EL}^\perp \mathbf{T}}$ also contains the clash condition (Clash)$_\emptyset$. Since each application of $(\Box^-)$ removes the negated box formulas $x : \neg\Box\neg C_i$ from the set K, when K is empty all the negated boxed formulas occurring in $\mathbf{B}$ also belong to the current branch. In this case, the model built by $\mathcal{TAB}_{PH2}^{\mathcal{EL}^\perp \mathbf{T}}$ satisfies the same set of $x : \neg\Box\neg C_i$ (for all individuals) as $\mathbf{B}$ and, thus, it is not preferred to the one represented by $\mathbf{B}$.

Let us now analyze soundness and completeness of $\mathcal{TAB}_{PH2}^{\mathcal{EL}^\perp \mathbf{T}}$. First, given a branch $\mathbf{B}$, we associate with $\mathbf{B}$ a relation $<$ defined as follows: $y < u$ if y is the label chosen in the conclusion of the application of the rule $(\Box^-)$ to $u : \neg\Box\neg C$. We define a canonical model $\mathcal{M}^B$ for $\mathbf{B}$ as follows: $\mathcal{M}^B = \langle \Delta_B, <', I\rangle$ where: - $\Delta_B = \{x : x$ is a label appearing in $\mathbf{B}\}$; - $<'$ is the transitive closure of relation $<$ associated with $\mathbf{B}$; - I is an interpretation function such that for all atomic concepts A, $A^I = \{x$ such that $x : A$ occurs in $\mathbf{B}\}$. I is then extended to all concepts C in the standard way, according to the semantics of the operators. For role names R, $R^I = \{(x,y) : x \xrightarrow{R} y$ occurs in $\mathbf{B}\}$.

Lemma 1. *If a branch* $\mathbf{B}$ *is satisfiable by an injective mapping in a minimal model of KB, then the canonical model* $\mathcal{M}^B$ *for* $\mathbf{B}$ *is a minimal model of KB satisfying* $\mathbf{B}$.

Theorem 5 (Soundness and completeness of $\mathcal{TAB}_{PH2}^{\mathcal{EL}^\perp \mathbf{T}}$). *Given a KB and a query* F, *let* $\langle S' \mid U \mid \emptyset\rangle$ *be the corresponding constraint system of KB, and* $\langle S \mid U \mid \emptyset\rangle$ *the corresponding constraint system of KB* $\cup \{\neg F\}$. *An open branch* $\mathbf{B}$ *built by* $\mathcal{TAB}_{PH1}^{\mathcal{EL}^\perp \mathbf{T}}$ *for* $\langle S \mid U \mid \emptyset\rangle$ *is satisfiable by an injective mapping in a minimal model of KB iff the tableau in* $\mathcal{TAB}_{PH2}^{\mathcal{EL}^\perp \mathbf{T}}$ *for* $\langle S' \mid U \mid \mathbf{B}^{\Box^-}\rangle$ *is closed.*

Proof. In order to show the soundness (if direction), we show that if the tableau in $\mathcal{TAB}_{PH2}^{\mathcal{EL}^\perp\mathbf{T}}$ for $\langle S' \mid U \mid \mathbf{B}^{\square^-} \rangle$ is closed, then $\mathcal{M}^B$ (which by Theorem 2 is a model of **B**) is a minimal model of KB that satisfies **B** (hence **B** is satisfiable by an injective mapping in a minimal model of KB). We show the contrapositive, that if $\mathcal{M}^{\mathbf{B}}$ was not minimal (i.e. if there was a model $\mathcal{M}$ of KB with same domain as $\mathcal{M}^{\mathbf{B}}$ but with $\mathcal{M}^{\square^-} \subset \mathcal{M}^{B^{\square^-}}$) then there would be an open branch in $\mathcal{TAB}_{PH2}^{\mathcal{EL}^\perp\mathbf{T}}$ by showing that: (i)$\langle S' \mid U \mid \mathbf{B}^{\square^-} \rangle$ would be satisfiable in $\mathcal{M}$, (ii) each rule of the calculus preserves the satisfiability in $\mathcal{M}$, and (iii) that no clash condition is satisfiable in such a model.

We now consider the completeness (only if direction). By hypothesis **B** is satisfiable by an injective mapping in a minimal model for KB. By Lemma 1, $\mathcal{M}^B$ is a minimal model of KB satisfying **B**. We want to show that the tableau in $\mathcal{TAB}_{PH2}^{\mathcal{EL}^\perp\mathbf{T}}$ for $\langle S' \mid U \mid \mathbf{B}^{\square^-} \rangle$ is closed. For a contradiction, suppose that the tableau was open, with an open branch **B'**. It can be easily shown that the canonical model for **B'**, $\mathcal{M}^{B'}$, is still a model of KB which is preferred to $\mathcal{M}^B$. Indeed, the domain of $\mathcal{M}^B$ coincides with that of $\mathcal{M}^{B'}$ (which is $\mathcal{D}(\mathbf{B})$). Clearly, $\mathcal{M}_{\mathcal{L}_\mathbf{T}}^{B'^{\square^-}} \subset \mathcal{M}_{\mathcal{L}_\mathbf{T}}^{B^{\square^-}}$, since $\mathbf{B'}^{\square^-} \subset \mathbf{B}^{\square^-}$, otherwise by (Clash)$_\emptyset$ **B'** would be closed, and by (cut) for all $C \in \mathcal{L}_\mathbf{T}$, for all labels x, either $x : \square\neg C \in$ **B'** or $x : \neg\square\neg C \in$ **B'** . Hence, $\mathcal{M}^{B'}$ would be preferred to $\mathcal{M}^B$, against the minimality of $\mathcal{M}^B$. This contradiction forces us to conclude that there cannot be an open **B'** in $\mathcal{TAB}_{PH2}^{\mathcal{EL}^\perp\mathbf{T}}$, and that the tableau must be closed. ∎

$\mathcal{TAB}_{PH2}^{\mathcal{EL}^\perp\mathbf{T}}$ always terminates. Termination is ensured by the fact that dynamic rules make use of labels belonging to $\mathcal{D}(\mathbf{B})$, which is finite, rather than introducing "new" labels in the tableau.

Theorem 6 (Termination of $\mathcal{TAB}_{PH2}^{\mathcal{EL}^\perp\mathbf{T}}$). *Let $\langle S' \mid U \mid \mathbf{B}^{\square^-} \rangle$ be a constraint system starting from an open branch **B** built by $\mathcal{TAB}_{PH1}^{\mathcal{EL}^\perp\mathbf{T}}$, then any tableau generated by $\mathcal{TAB}_{PH2}^{\mathcal{EL}^\perp\mathbf{T}}$ is finite.*

It is possible to show that the problem of verifying that a branch **B** represents a minimal model for KB in $\mathcal{TAB}_{PH2}^{\mathcal{EL}^\perp\mathbf{T}}$ is in NP in the size of **B**.

The overall procedure $\mathcal{TAB}_{min}^{\mathcal{ALC}+\mathbf{T}}$ is defined as follows:

Definition 12. *Let KB be a knowledge base whose corresponding constraint system is $\langle S \mid U \mid \emptyset \rangle$. Let F be a query and let S' be the set of constraints obtained by adding to S the constraint corresponding to $\neg F$. The calculus $\mathcal{TAB}_{min}^{\mathcal{EL}^\perp\mathbf{T}}$ checks whether a query F is minimally entailed from a KB by means of the following procedure:* (phase 1) *the calculus $\mathcal{TAB}_{PH1}^{\mathcal{EL}^\perp\mathbf{T}}$ is applied to $\langle S' \mid U \mid \emptyset \rangle$; if, for each branch **B** built by $\mathcal{TAB}_{PH1}^{\mathcal{EL}^\perp\mathbf{T}}$, either (i) **B** is closed or (ii)* (phase 2) *the tableau built by the calculus $\mathcal{TAB}_{PH2}^{\mathcal{EL}^\perp\mathbf{T}}$ for $\langle S \mid U \mid \mathbf{B}^{\square^-} \rangle$ is open, then KB $\models_{min}^{\mathcal{L}_\mathbf{T}} F$, otherwise KB $\not\models_{min}^{\mathcal{L}_\mathbf{T}} F$.*

Theorem 7 (Soundness and completeness of $\mathcal{TAB}_{min}^{\mathcal{EL}^\perp\mathbf{T}}$). *$\mathcal{TAB}_{min}^{\mathcal{EL}^\perp\mathbf{T}}$ is a sound and complete decision procedure for verifying if KB $\models_{min}^{\mathcal{L}_\mathbf{T}} F$.*

Proof. (Soundness) If KB $\not\models_{min}^{\mathcal{L}_\mathbf{T}} F$, and KB $\cup \{\neg F\}$ is satisfiable by a minimal model of KB, then by Theorem 1, $\mathcal{TAB}_{PH1}^{\mathcal{EL}^\perp\mathbf{T}}$ generates an open branch, which is satisfiable (via an injective assignment from labels to domain elements) in a minimal model of KB. By Theorem 5 for this branch the tableau in $\mathcal{TAB}^{\mathcal{EL}^{\perp}\mathbf{T}}_{PH2}$ is closed. In this case, (i) and (ii) in Definition 12 do not hold, and the procedure correctly says that KB $\not\models^{\mathcal{L}_{\mathbf{T}}}_{min} F$.

(Completeness) Let KB $\models^{\mathcal{L}_{\mathbf{T}}}_{min} F$. For contraposition, let **B** be an open branch (if any) generated by $\mathcal{TAB}^{\mathcal{EL}^{\perp}\mathbf{T}}_{PH1}$. If this branch were satisfiable by an injective mapping in a minimal model of KB, then by Proposition 1, also KB $\cup \{\neg F\}$ would be, against the hypothesis that KB $\models^{\mathcal{L}_{\mathbf{T}}}_{min} F$. Hence, **B** is not satisfiable by an injective mapping in a minimal model of KB, and by Theorem 5 the tableau in $\mathcal{TAB}^{\mathcal{EL}^{\perp}\mathbf{T}}_{PH2}$ for $\langle S' \mid U \mid \mathbf{B}^{\square^-}\rangle$ is open. ∎

We can also prove that the complexity of $\mathcal{TAB}^{\mathcal{EL}^{\perp}\mathbf{T}}_{min}$ matches the known results for minimal entailment in Left Local $\mathcal{EL}^{\perp}\mathbf{T}_{min}$:

Theorem 8 (Complexity of $\mathcal{TAB}^{\mathcal{EL}^{\perp}\mathbf{T}}_{min}$). *The problem of deciding whether* KB $\models^{\mathcal{L}_{\mathbf{T}}}_{min}$ *F by means of $\mathcal{TAB}^{\mathcal{EL}^{\perp}\mathbf{T}}_{min}$ is in Π^p_2.*

Proof. We first consider the complementary problem: KB $\not\models^{\mathcal{L}_{\mathbf{T}}}_{min} F$. This problem can be solved according to the procedure in Definition 12: by nondeterministically generating an open branch of polynomial length in the size of KB in $\mathcal{TAB}^{\mathcal{EL}^{\perp}\mathbf{T}}_{PH1}$ (a model $\mathcal{M}^{\mathbf{B}}$ of KB $\cup \{\neg F\}$), and then by calling an NP oracle which verifies that $\mathcal{M}^{\mathbf{B}}$ is a minimal model of KB. In fact, the verification that $\mathcal{M}^{\mathbf{B}}$ is not a minimal model of the KB can be done by an NP algorithm which nondeterministically generates a branch in $\mathcal{TAB}^{\mathcal{EL}^{\perp}\mathbf{T}}_{PH2}$ of polynomial size in the size of $\mathcal{M}^{\mathbf{B}}$ (and of KB), representing a model $\mathcal{M}^{\mathbf{B}'}$ of KB preferred to $\mathcal{M}^{\mathbf{B}}$. Hence, the problem of verifying that KB $\not\models^{\mathcal{L}_{\mathbf{T}}}_{min} F$ is in NP^{NP}, i.e. in Σ^p_2, and the problem of deciding whether KB $\models^{\mathcal{L}_{\mathbf{T}}}_{min} F$ is in CO-NP^{NP}, i.e. in Π^p_2. ∎

4   Conclusions

In this work we have provided a two-phase tableau calculus $\mathcal{TAB}^{\mathcal{EL}^{\perp}\mathbf{T}}_{min}$ for checking minimal entailment in a nonmonotonic extension of the Left Local fragment of the logic $\mathcal{EL}^{\perp}\mathbf{T}_{min}$, a family of low complexity DLs $\mathcal{EL}^{\perp}$. The proposed calculus matches the known complexity results for such DL, namely that entailment is in Π^p_2 [8]. Of course, many optimizations are possible and we intend to study them in future work.

As mentioned in the Introduction, several nonmonotonic extensions of DLs have been proposed in the literature [14,4,2,3,7,11,10,9,6] and we refer to [11] for a survey. Concerning nonmonotonic extensions of low complexity DLs, the complexity of *circumscribed* fragments of the $\mathcal{EL}^{\perp}$ and DL-lite families have been studied in [3]. The contribution of this paper is to provide a calculus for the Left Local fragment of $\mathcal{EL}^{\perp}$ under minimal entailment. We expect that our tableau calculus can also be adapted to deal with the DL-lite$_c\mathbf{T}$ fragment, for which a Π^p_2 upper bound has been proved in [8]. Recently, a fragment of $\mathcal{EL}^{\perp}$ for which the complexity of circumscribed KBs is polynomial has been identified in [13]. In future work, we shall investigate complexity of minimal entailment and proof methods for such a fragment extended with **T**.

Acknowledgements. This work has been partially supported by the Project "MIUR PRIN08 LoDeN: Logiche Descrittive Nonmonotone: Complessitá e implementazioni".

References

1. Baader, F., Brandt, S., Lutz, C.: Pushing the $\mathcal{EL}$ envelope. In: IJCAI, pp. 364–369 (2005)
2. Baader, F., Hollunder, B.: Priorities on defaults with prerequisites, and their application in treating specificity in terminological default logic. J. of Automated Reasoning (JAR) 15(1), 41–68 (1995)
3. Bonatti, P., Faella, M., Sauro, L.: Defeasible inclusions in low-complexity dls: Preliminary notes. In: IJCAI, pp. 696–701 (2009)
4. Bonatti, P.A., Lutz, C., Wolter, F.: Description logics with circumscription. In: KR, pp. 400–410 (2006)
5. Buchheit, M., Donini, F.M., Schaerf, A.: Decidable reasoning in terminological knowledge representation systems. J. Artif. Int. Research (JAIR) 1, 109–138 (1993)
6. Casini, G., Straccia, U.: Rational closure for defeasible description logics. In: Janhunen, T., Niemelä, I. (eds.) JELIA 2010. LNCS, vol. 6341, pp. 77–90. Springer, Heidelberg (2010)
7. Donini, F.M., Nardi, D., Rosati, R.: Description logics of minimal knowledge and negation as failure. ACM Trans. Comput. Log. 3(2), 177–225 (2002)
8. Giordano, L., Gliozzi, V., Olivetti, N., Pozzato, G.L.: Reasoning about typicality in low complexity DLs: the logics $\mathcal{EL}^\perp T\mathbf{T}_{min}$ and DL-lite$_c T\mathbf{T}_{min}$. To appear in IJCAI (2011)
9. Giordano, L., Gliozzi, V., Olivetti, N., Pozzato, G.L.: Reasoning about typicality in preferential description logics. In: Hölldobler, S., Lutz, C., Wansing, H. (eds.) JELIA 2008. LNCS (LNAI), vol. 5293, pp. 192–205. Springer, Heidelberg (2008)
10. Giordano, L., Gliozzi, V., Olivetti, N., Pozzato, G.L.: Prototypical reasoning with low complexity description logics: Preliminary results. In: Erdem, E., Lin, F., Schaub, T. (eds.) LP-NMR 2009. LNCS, vol. 5753, pp. 430–436. Springer, Heidelberg (2009)
11. Giordano, L., Gliozzi, V., Olivetti, N., Pozzato, G.L.: $\mathcal{ALC}+T\mathbf{T}_{min}$: a preferential extension of description logics. Fundamenta Informaticae 96, 1–32 (2009)
12. Kraus, S., Lehmann, D., Magidor, M.: Nonmonotonic reasoning, preferential models and cumulative logics. Artificial Intelligence 44(1-2), 167–207 (1990)
13. Bonatti, P.A., Faella, M., Sauro, L.: $\mathcal{EL}$ with default attributes and overriding. In: Patel-Schneider, P.F., Pan, Y., Hitzler, P., Mika, P., Zhang, L., Pan, J.Z., Horrocks, I., Glimm, B. (eds.) ISWC 2010, Part I. LNCS, vol. 6496, pp. 64–79. Springer, Heidelberg (2010)
14. Straccia, U.: Default inheritance reasoning in hybrid kl-one-style logics. In: IJCAI, pp. 676–681 (1993)

Correctness and Worst-Case Optimality of Pratt-Style Decision Procedures for Modal and Hybrid Logics

Mark Kaminski[1], Thomas Schneider[2], and Gert Smolka[1]

[1] Saarland University, Germany
{kaminski,smolka}@ps.uni-saarland.de
[2] University of Bremen, Germany
tschneider@informatik.uni-bremen.de

Abstract. We extend Pratt's worst-case optimal decision procedure for PDL to a richer logic with nominals, difference modalities, and inverse actions. We prove correctness and worst-case optimality. Our correctness proof is based on syntactic models called demos. The main theorem states that a formula is satisfiable if and only if it is contained in a demo. From this theorem the correctness of the decision procedure is easily obtained. Our development is modular and we extend it stepwise from modal logic with eventualities to the full logic.

1   Introduction

Propositional dynamic logic (PDL) is an expressive extension of modal logic designed for reasoning about properties of programs and goes back to Fischer and Ladner [9]. Its satisfiability problem is ExpTime-complete [24], and the first worst-case optimal decision procedure was given in [25]. Nominals are the basic feature of hybrid logic, which extends modal logic and goes back to Arthur Prior [26]. Nominals denote single states in models, allowing to express properties that are not expressible in standard modal logic, such as irreflexivity. The difference modality D says that a property holds in some state different from the current state, and was first described in [28]. It can be simulated using nominals and the global modality E via a satisfiability-preserving translation [11]. Nominals can be expressed using $\overline{D}$, the dual of D.

We consider combinations of PDL with nominals, difference modalities and converse actions, and we are interested in worst-case optimal decision procedures for such combinations. Let $\mathsf{HPDL}_{\overline{D}}$ denote the logic that combines all these features. Its computational complexity is known: the satisfiability problem is ExpTime-complete. The lower bound follows from that for PDL by Fischer and Ladner [10]. The upper bound is due to [5, 1] via a chain of reductions that consecutively replaces D with E, removes E and converse, and ends in PDL.

The bounded model property of PDL [10]—every satisfiable formula s is satisfiable in a model of size exponential in $|s|$—yields a straightforward guess-and-check decision procedure, whose determinization requires doubly exponential time. Pratt devised a worst-case optimal decision procedure for PDL in [25],

K. Brünnler and G. Metcalfe (Eds.): TABLEAUX 2011, LNAI 6793, pp. 196–210, 2011.

based on Hintikka structures as a nonstandard notion of a model. These consist of Hintikka sets—consistent, downward saturated theories—and syntactic links. The search for a model is performed using tree-shaped tableaux of potentially infinite size. Using the classical filtration argument from [10] underlying the bounded model theorem (BMT), the possibly infinite tableau is filtered into a graph-shaped tableau of at most exponential size, and a straightforward procedure for searching a subgraph that represents a satisfying model is applied. In [24], Pratt describes a much leaner worst-case optimal procedure that, again, starts from all Hintikka subsets of the given formula's closure and then deletes those that contain unsatisfied diamonds. The resulting substructure contains a satisfying model if one exists. We call this type of procedure Pratt-style and its two stages construct and prune. Pratt's procedure is described in [16, 22, 17, 3], where [3] uses a stricter notion of Hintikka sets and excludes tests.

A practical problem with Pratt-style procedures is that the initial construct stage is "best-case exponential", although certainly not every Hintikka set plays a role in a satisfying model. This problem is reduced in decision procedures based on (non-branching) tableaux, such as Pratt's procedure in [25]. They make construct more goal-directed by restricting the creation of new nodes—representatives of Hintikka sets—to those that reduce formulas in nodes already present. Such tableau-based procedures exist for different modal-like logics and are often optimized further by interleaving construct and prune [12, 14].

Decision procedures based on branching tableau systems [27, 18, 6, 4, 21] enjoy wide regard in automated reasoning with modal and description logics.They typically run in worst-case non-deterministic doubly exponential time, but highly optimized systems work well in practice [15, 30]. However, there are exponential-time algorithms based on branching tableaux for description logics [7, 12].

Automata-theoretic decision procedures exploit some form of tree-model property of the logic in question, transfer a given formula into an automaton of typically exponential size, and thus reduce satisfiability to the emptiness problem of the automata model corresponding to the logic. This approach is applied to expressive modal logics extending PDL [31, 29]. However, in general, the complexity is "best-case exponential" again.

This paper presents a modular approach to obtaining lean proofs of the BMT and the correctness of worst-case optimal Pratt-style decision procedures for the above mentioned extensions of PDL. These decision procedures will be able to handle hybrid operators in an additional deterministic guess stage. We use the notion of a demo—a syntactic representation of a satisfying model in terms of Hintikka sets. With this notion, we tailor the proofs of the BMT for said logics to the expressive features involved. We will analyze the conceptual, technical and computational costs required for incorporating each of those features, as well as their combinability. The strengths of the modular approach are the following.

- We refactor the standard proofs leading to the the BMT such that standard induction over term lengths suffices.
- The explicit use of demos makes the BMT proofs transparent and reusable for the correctness of the decision procedure.

- The addition of the above named expressive features is modular: different features can be added independently by combining the techniques needed for every single feature.
- To our knowledge, this is the first explicit and simple worst-case optimal decision procedure for a logic that combines PDL and hybrid operators.

The paper is organized as follows. We will introduce hybrid PDL, introduce demos for test-free PDL and discuss their relevant properties, present the decision procedure, discuss extentions of the language separately, and relate this approach to those in the literature.

2   Preliminaries: Hybrid PDL

Let PRED and ACT be countably infinite sets, whose elements are called *predicates* and *actions*, respectively. Let NOM $\subseteq$ PRED be the set of all *nominals*. We assume formulas to be in negation normal form (NNF), i.e., negation is allowed to occur only directly in front of predicates. We also assume programs to be in converse normal form (CNF), i.e., the converse operator is allowed to occur only directly after actions. Formulas s and programs α of $\mathsf{HPDL}_\mathsf{D}^-$ are defined by mutual recursion as follows, where $p \in$ PRED and $a \in$ ACT.

$$s ::= p \mid \neg p \mid s \wedge s \mid s \vee s \mid \langle \alpha \rangle s \mid [\alpha]s \mid \mathsf{D}s \mid \overline{\mathsf{D}}s \qquad \alpha ::= a \mid a^- \mid \alpha\beta \mid \alpha{+}\beta \mid \alpha^* \mid s$$

We denote predicates by $p, q, \ldots$, nominals by $x, y, \ldots$, formulas by $s, t, \ldots$, actions by $a, b, \ldots$ and programs by $\alpha, \beta, \ldots$ The operator D is called the difference modality, and $\overline{\mathsf{D}}$ is its dual. If we want to denote the fragment of $\mathsf{HPDL}_\mathsf{D}^-$ without converse, nominals, and/or difference modalities, we leave out the superscript "$-$", the leading H and/or the subscript D.

Choosing to adapt NNF and CNF is not crucial for our approach to work. It merely simplifies technical details and is no computational obstacle: any formula can be transformed into an equivalent formula in NNF and CNF in linear time.

In order to capture tests as programs, and only for this purpose, we use Tait negation: $\sim s$ denotes the NNF of $\neg s$, with the obvious consequence $\sim\sim s = s$. We further use the notation $|s|$ to denote the size of a formula, which is defined as usual, with the only exception being $|\neg p| = |p|$. This ensures that $|\sim s| = |s|$.

We recall the standard operations on binary relations R, S over a set X.

$$R^0 = \{(x, x) \mid x \in X\} \qquad R^n = R \circ R^{n-1} \; (n \geqslant 1) \qquad R^* = \bigcup_{n \geqslant 0} R^n$$
$$R^- = \{(x, y) \mid (y, x) \in R\}$$
$$R \circ S = \{(x, z) \mid \exists y \in X : (x, y) \in R \text{ and } (y, z) \in S\}$$

As usual, the semantics of $\mathsf{HPDL}_\mathsf{D}^-$ is defined in terms of Kripke models. A *model* $\mathfrak{M}$ consists of

- a nonempty set $|\mathfrak{M}|$ of states,
- a *transition relation* $\xrightarrow{a}_{\mathfrak{M}} \subseteq |\mathfrak{M}| \times |\mathfrak{M}|$ for every $a \in$ ACT,

− a set $\mathfrak{M}p \subseteq |\mathfrak{M}|$ for every $p \in \text{PRED}$,   where $|\mathfrak{M}x| = 1$ for every $x \in \text{NOM}$.

The transition relations for complex programs and the *satisfaction relation* between models, states and formulas $(\mathfrak{M}, w \models s)$ are defined via mutual induction.

$$\xrightarrow{\alpha\beta}_{\mathfrak{M}} = \xrightarrow{\alpha}_{\mathfrak{M}} \circ \xrightarrow{\beta}_{\mathfrak{M}} \qquad \xrightarrow{a^-}_{\mathfrak{M}} = \xrightarrow{a}_{\mathfrak{M}}{}^- \qquad \xrightarrow{\alpha^*}_{\mathfrak{M}} = \xrightarrow{\alpha}_{\mathfrak{M}}{}^*$$

$$\xrightarrow{\alpha+\beta}_{\mathfrak{M}} = \xrightarrow{\alpha}_{\mathfrak{M}} \cup \xrightarrow{\beta}_{\mathfrak{M}} \qquad \xrightarrow{s}_{\mathfrak{M}} = \{(w,w) \mid \mathfrak{M}, w \models s\}$$

$$\mathfrak{M}, w \models p \iff w \in \mathfrak{M}p \quad \text{for } p \in \text{PRED}$$
$$\mathfrak{M}, w \models \neg p \iff w \notin \mathfrak{M}p \quad \text{for } p \in \text{PRED}$$
$$\mathfrak{M}, w \models s \wedge t \iff \mathfrak{M}, w \models s \text{ and } \mathfrak{M}, w \models t$$
$$\mathfrak{M}, w \models \langle \alpha \rangle s \iff \mathfrak{M}, v \models s \text{ for some } v \in |\mathfrak{M}| \text{ with } w \xrightarrow{\alpha}_{\mathfrak{M}} v$$
$$\mathfrak{M}, w \models \mathsf{D}s \iff \mathfrak{M}, v \models s \text{ for some } v \neq w$$

The satisfaction relation for the remaining operators can be obtained from the equivalences $s \vee t \equiv \neg(\neg s \wedge \neg t)$, $[\alpha]s \equiv \neg\langle\alpha\rangle\neg s$, and $\overline{\mathsf{D}}s \equiv \neg\mathsf{D}\neg s$.

We extend the notion of satisfaction to sets A of formulas in the obvious way: $\mathfrak{M}, w \models A$ if $\mathfrak{M}, w \models s$ for all $s \in A$.

A *literal* is a formula of the form p, $\neg p$, $\langle a \rangle s$, $[a]s$, $\langle a^- \rangle s$, $[a^-]s$, $\mathsf{D}s$ or $\overline{\mathsf{D}}s$, where $p \in \text{PRED}$, $a \in \text{ACT}$, and s is an arbitrary formula.

A *Hintikka set is a partial description of a possible state.* It contains formulas satisfied by that state. A system of Hintikka sets then represents a satisfying model, and our goal is to show that every satisfiable formula is contained in a Hintikka set that is part of a finite such system. More precisely, a *Hintikka set* is a nonempty set H that satisfies the following properties.

For every $p \in \text{PRED}$: $\{p, \neg p\} \not\subseteq H$ $\langle\alpha\beta\rangle s \in H \implies \langle\alpha\rangle\langle\beta\rangle s \in H$

$s \wedge t \in H \implies s \in H$ and $t \in H$ $[\alpha\beta]s \in H \implies [\alpha][\beta]s \in H$

$s \vee t \in H \implies s \in H$ or $t \in H$ $\langle\alpha+\beta\rangle s \in H \implies \langle\alpha\rangle s \in H$ or $\langle\beta\rangle s \in H$

$\langle t \rangle s \in H \implies t \in H$ and $s \in H$ $[\alpha+\beta]s \in H \implies [\alpha]s \in H$ and $[\beta]s \in H$

$[t]s \in H \implies \sim t \in H$ or $s \in H$ $\langle\alpha^*\rangle s \in H \implies \langle\alpha\rangle\langle\alpha^*\rangle s \in H$ or $s \in H$

    $[\alpha^*]s \in H \implies [\alpha][\alpha^*]s \in H$ and $s \in H$

A *Hintikka system* $\mathcal{S}$ is a finite, nonempty set of Hintikka sets. We say that a formula s is *contained in* $\mathcal{S}$ if it is contained in some $H \in \mathcal{S}$.

In order to restrict the choice of possible elements of a Hintikka set, we assume a finite, nonempty *formula universe* $\mathcal{F}$, which is modelled on the Fischer-Ladner closure [10] of a given formula s. $\mathcal{F}$ consists of formulas in NNF and satisfies the following closure properties.

$s \in \mathcal{F}$ and t is a subformula of $s \implies t \in \mathcal{F}$

$\langle\alpha\beta\rangle s \in \mathcal{F} \implies \langle\alpha\rangle\langle\beta\rangle s \in \mathcal{F}$

$[\alpha\beta]s \in \mathcal{F} \implies [\alpha][\beta]s \in \mathcal{F}$ $\langle\alpha^*\rangle s \in \mathcal{F} \implies \langle\alpha\rangle\langle\alpha^*\rangle s \in \mathcal{F}$

$\langle\alpha+\beta\rangle s \in \mathcal{F} \implies \langle\alpha\rangle s,\ \langle\beta\rangle s \in \mathcal{F}$ $[\alpha^*]s \in \mathcal{F} \implies [\alpha][\alpha^*]s \in \mathcal{F}$

$[\alpha+\beta]s \in \mathcal{F} \implies [\alpha]s,\ [\beta]s \in \mathcal{F}$ $[t]s \in \mathcal{F} \implies \sim t \in \mathcal{F}$

This is a slight variation of the definitions in the literature [9, 22, 17]. Still, we can use the following original result.

Lemma 1 ([9]). *For every formula s, one can compute a finite formula universe $\mathcal{F}$ such that $s \in \mathcal{F}$ and the cardinality of $\mathcal{F}$ is linear in the size of s.*

3   Demos as a Syntactic Representation of Models

From now on, all formulas, Hintikka sets and systems range over a given $\mathcal{F}$.

We aim at the following criterion for syntactically *demonstrating* that a given formula s is satisfiable: s is satisfiable if and only if s occurs in a Hintikka system $\mathcal{S}$ that sufficiently describes a model. We call such a system a demo. A maximal demo corresponds to the result of any of the elimination procedures for Hintikka systems described in [25, 17, 3]. The notion of a demo derives from that of an evident subset of a Pratt-style graph tableau in [20]. Making the demo notion explicit will allow for factoring the bounded model theorem into lemmas that use simpler inductions. The main lemmas, demo existence and satisfaction lemmas will almost immediately imply correctness of the decision procedure.

In this section, we introduce the notion of a demo and study it in depth. In order to keep the presentation simple, we begin with test-free PDL and will add nominals, difference modalities, tests and converse separately in Sections 5–8. This will allow us to to isolate the conceptual, technical, and computational cost of adding those features.

Definition 2. Let $\mathcal{S}$ be a Hintikka system. The *transition relation* $\xrightarrow{\alpha}_{\mathcal{S}} \subseteq \mathcal{S} \times \mathcal{S}$ is defined as follows.

$$\xrightarrow{a}_{\mathcal{S}} = \left\{ (H, H') \mid \forall s : ([a]s \in H \Rightarrow s \in H') \right\}$$

$$\xrightarrow{\alpha\beta}_{\mathcal{S}} = \xrightarrow{\alpha}_{\mathcal{S}} \circ \xrightarrow{\beta}_{\mathcal{S}} \qquad \xrightarrow{\alpha+\beta}_{\mathcal{S}} = \xrightarrow{\alpha}_{\mathcal{S}} \cup \xrightarrow{\beta}_{\mathcal{S}} \qquad \xrightarrow{\alpha^*}_{\mathcal{S}} = \xrightarrow{\alpha}_{\mathcal{S}}^*$$

Proposition 3. *Let $\mathcal{S} \subseteq \mathcal{S}'$ be Hintikka systems. Then $\xrightarrow{\alpha}_{\mathcal{S}} \subseteq \xrightarrow{\alpha}_{\mathcal{S}'}$.*

Definition 4. A Hintikka system $\mathcal{D}$ is a *demo* if the following is satisfied.

(D$\diamondsuit$) If $\langle\alpha\rangle s \in H \in \mathcal{D}$, then there is some $H' \in \mathcal{D}$ with $H \xrightarrow{\alpha}_{\mathcal{D}} H'$ and $s \in H'$.

It suffices to require (D$\diamondsuit$) only for programs α that are actions or iterations β^*. The remaining cases would then follow via the definition of Hintikka sets. For clarity of the presentation, however, we do not make this restriction.

Example 5. The figure below shows a demo that consists of three Hintikka sets: $\{\langle a^*\rangle p, \langle a\rangle\langle a^*\rangle p, [a]\neg p\}$, $\{\langle a^*\rangle p, \langle a\rangle\langle a^*\rangle p, \neg p\}$ and $\{p\}$. Sets related by $\xrightarrow{a}$ are connected with an arrow. Arrows for $\xrightarrow{a^*}$ are implicit.

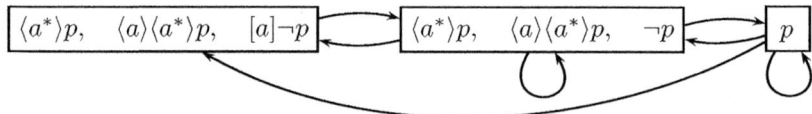

The following fact is obvious from the formulation of Demo Condition (D$\diamondsuit$): demos are closed under union, and therefore there is a unique maximal demo for $\mathcal{F}$. This will be important for the correctness of the decision procedure.

In order to establish that demos represent exactly models modulo $\mathcal{F}$, we show that (a) every model induces a demo in the natural way, and (b) every demo has a model that satisfies all of the demo's members. We start with (a).

Given a model $\mathfrak{M}$ and a state $w \in |\mathfrak{M}|$, let $H_{\mathfrak{M},w} = \{s \in \mathcal{F} \mid \mathfrak{M}, w \models s\}$ be the Hintikka set induced by w in $\mathfrak{M}$. The following proposition is obvious.

Proposition 6. $H_{\mathfrak{M},w}$ *is a Hintikka set.*

From now on, we write H_w instead of $H_{\mathfrak{M},w}$ if no confusion can arise. We now consider the system of all Hintikka sets induced by $\mathfrak{M}$, i.e., $\mathcal{S}_{\mathfrak{M}} = \{H_w \mid w \in |\mathfrak{M}|\}$. In order to establish that $\mathcal{S}_{\mathfrak{M}}$ is a demo, we need the following lemma, which is proven via straightforward induction on the size of α in [19].

Lemma 7. *Let $\mathfrak{M}$ be a model and $v, w \in |\mathfrak{M}|$. If $v \xrightarrow{\alpha}_{\mathfrak{M}} w$, then $H_v \xrightarrow{\alpha}_{\mathcal{S}_{\mathfrak{M}}} H_w$.*

Lemma 8. $\mathcal{S}_{\mathfrak{M}}$ *is a demo.*

Proof. Let $\langle \alpha \rangle s \in H_w \in \mathcal{S}_{\mathfrak{M}}$. Then $\mathfrak{M}, w \models \langle \alpha \rangle s$, that is, there is some $v \in |\mathfrak{M}|$ such that $w \xrightarrow{\alpha}_{\mathfrak{M}} v$ and $\mathfrak{M}, v \models s$. Due to Lemma 7 and the definition of H_v, we obtain $H_w \xrightarrow{\alpha}_{\mathcal{S}_{\mathfrak{M}}} H_v$ and $s \in H_v$.

Lemma 9 (Demo existence). *For every satisfiable formula $s \in \mathcal{F}$, there is a demo $\mathcal{D}$ over $\mathcal{F}$ that contains s.*

Proof. Let $\mathfrak{M}, w \models s$. Take $\mathcal{D} = \mathcal{S}_{\mathfrak{M}}$, which contains H_w with $s \in H_w$.

As for the direction (b) above, we start by making some general statements about Hintikka systems. The first such statement is that $\mathcal{S}$, together with the transition relations $\xrightarrow{a}_{\mathcal{S}}$, induces a model $\mathfrak{M}_{\mathcal{S}}$ as follows.

Definition 10. Let $\mathcal{S}$ be a Hintikka system. $\mathfrak{M}_{\mathcal{S}}$ is the model defined by $|\mathfrak{M}_{\mathcal{S}}| = \mathcal{S}$, $\xrightarrow{a}_{\mathfrak{M}_{\mathcal{S}}} = \xrightarrow{a}_{\mathcal{S}}$, $\mathfrak{M}_{\mathcal{S}} p = \{H \in \mathcal{S} \mid p \in H\}$.

In general, $\mathfrak{M}_{\mathcal{S}}$ does not need to satisfy the Hintikka sets in $\mathcal{S}$. However, under additional conditions categorized under the notion of a demo, there is a direct correspondence between Hintikka systems and models. The following two lemmas are proven via straightforward induction on the size of α in [19].

Lemma 11. *Let $\mathcal{S}$ be a Hintikka system and α a program. Then $\xrightarrow{\alpha}_{\mathcal{S}} \subseteq \xrightarrow{\alpha}_{\mathfrak{M}_{\mathcal{S}}}$.*

Lemma 12. *Let $\mathcal{S}$ be a Hintikka system with $H, H' \in \mathcal{S}$ and $[\alpha]s \in H \xrightarrow{\alpha}_{\mathfrak{M}_{\mathcal{S}}} H'$. Then $s \in H'$.*

Lemma 13 (Demo satisfaction). *If $\mathcal{D}$ is a demo then, for all $H \in \mathcal{D}$: $\mathfrak{M}_{\mathcal{D}}, H \models H$.*

The proof is via induction on the size of the formulas in H, see [19]. The following central insight about demos follows directly from Lemmas 9, 13.

Theorem 14. *A formula s is satisfiable if and only if s is contained in a demo.*

Lemmas 9 and 13 also imply the Bounded Model Theorem for test-free PDL, which has been established in [10] for PDL: every satisfiable formula s is satisfiable in a finite model of size exponential in $|s|$.

4   The Decision Procedure

We use Pratt's approach of constructing the set of all Hintikka sets and pruning it to the greatest demo. The correctness of this procedure will immediately follow from the fact that pruning respects demos: every single pruning action does not remove any Hintikka set that is part of a demo contained in the system before the pruning action. This argument exploits the existence of a maximal demo, which is not guaranteed in the presence of nominals or $\overline{D}$.

We define a relation between Hintikka systems that represents a single pruning action: let $\mathcal{S} \xrightarrow{p} \mathcal{S}'$ if $\mathcal{S}'$ can be obtained from $\mathcal{S}$ by deleting some $H \in \mathcal{S}$ that violates the Demo Condition (D$\Diamond$), i.e., for some $\langle \alpha \rangle s \in H \in \mathcal{S}$, there is no $H' \in \mathcal{S}$ such that $H \xrightarrow{\alpha}_{\mathcal{S}} H'$ and $s \in H'$. We further define $\mathcal{S} \xrightarrow{p}{\rightsquigarrow} \mathcal{S}'$ to hold if $\mathcal{S} \xrightarrow{p}{}^* \mathcal{S}'$ and $\mathcal{S}' \xrightarrow{p} \mathcal{S}''$ for no $\mathcal{S}''$.

The following proposition is immediate because (1) every pruning action removes only Hintikka sets that violate the demo condition, and (2) when no more pruning can be done, all Hintikka sets in $\mathcal{S}'$ satisfy the demo condition.

Proposition 15. *1. If $\mathcal{S} \xrightarrow{p} \mathcal{S}'$ and $\mathcal{D}$ is a demo with $\mathcal{D} \subseteq \mathcal{S}$, then $\mathcal{D} \subseteq \mathcal{S}'$.*
2. If $\mathcal{S} \xrightarrow{p}{\rightsquigarrow} \mathcal{S}' \neq \emptyset$, then $\mathcal{S}'$ is a demo.

Theorem 16. *If $\mathcal{S} \xrightarrow{p}{\rightsquigarrow} \mathcal{S}'$ and $\mathcal{S}$ contains a demo, then $\mathcal{S}'$ is the greatest demo contained in $\mathcal{S}$.*

Proof. Due to Prop. 15 $\mathcal{S}'$ contains all demos contained in $\mathcal{S}$, including the greatest such demo. Due to $\mathcal{S}'$ is a demo itself, hence it is contained in the greatest demo contained in $\mathcal{S}$. Both inclusions together yield the equality.   □

The following method decides satisfiability of a given formula s by pruning the system of all Hintikka sets and checking whether s is contained in the resulting demo.

Decision method for PDL-satisfiability

Input: formula s

  1. Compute the formula universe $\mathcal{F}$ for s.
  2. $\mathcal{H} = \{H \mid H \text{ is a Hintikka set with } H \subseteq \mathcal{F}\}$
  3. Compute $\mathcal{D}$ with $\mathcal{H} \xrightarrow{p}{\rightsquigarrow} \mathcal{D}$.
  4. s is satisfiable iff $s \in H$ for some $H \in \mathcal{D}$.

The above decision method is a notational variant of Pratt's [24] decision procedure. By making the notion of a demo explicit. We can conclude correctness directly from Theorem 16, while the correctness proofs in [22, 17] use complex inductive arguments quite similar to the proofs of the filtration theorem. Steps 1 and 2 correspond to Stage `construct`, and Step 3 to `prune`. The transition relations $\xrightarrow{\alpha}_{\mathcal{S}}$ are not computed upfront. Instead, whenever the decision procedure needs to decide for a pair of Hintikka sets whether they are in some $\xrightarrow{\alpha}_{\mathcal{S}}$, it does so via the inductive definition of $\xrightarrow{\alpha}_{\mathcal{S}}$, in time polynomial in $|\alpha|$ multiplied by the sizes of the Hintikka sets.

We now convince ourselves that the above method is worst-case optimal, i.e., that it runs in time exponential in $|s|$, looking at each step in turn.

1. Due to Lemma 1, the cardinality of $\mathcal{F}$ is linear in $|s|$. Furthermore, if $\mathcal{F}$ is taken to be the smallest formula universe that contains s, then $\mathcal{F}$ can be computed in time polynomial in $|s|$ by following the closure properties.

2. In order to compute $\mathcal{H}$, one can create all exponentially many subsets of $\mathcal{F}$ and remove those that are not Hintikka sets. Checking the Hintikka set properties of any such H requires time at most polynomial in the cardinality of H, which in turn is linear in $|s|$. In preparation for the following step, all transition relations $\xrightarrow{\alpha}_{\mathcal{S}}$ over $\mathcal{H}$ can be precomputed and reused for every $\mathcal{S}$ during the pruning phase. For every α, determining $\xrightarrow{\alpha}_{\mathcal{S}}$ takes time quadratic in the cardinality of $\mathcal{H}$.

3. Since the number of Hintikka sets decreases with every single pruning action, there can be at most exponentially many pruning actions. Each of them can be performed in time exponential in $|s|$: traverse through all Hintikka sets H in the remaining system $\mathcal{S}$ and all formulas $\langle\alpha\rangle s \in H$, and check whether some $H' \in \mathcal{S}$ exists with $H \xrightarrow{\alpha}_{\mathcal{S}} H'$.

4. Traversing through all Hintikka sets left and through their contents to search for s is clearly in exponential time as well.

For practical purposes, creating all Hintikka sets in the first place is highly inefficient. We have discussed possible optimizations in Section 1.

5   Nominals

Extending the demo notion with nominals is rather straightforward. We need to introduce the notion of nominal coherence: a Hintikka system $\mathcal{H}$ is *nominally coherent* if every nominal $x \in \mathcal{F}$ occurs in exactly one $H \in \mathcal{S}$. Now the definition of a demo (Def. 4) and of $\mathfrak{M}_{\mathcal{S}}$, as well as the assumptions of Lemma 11 have to be extended by the requirement (DN) that $\mathcal{D}$ and $\mathcal{S}$ be nominally coherent.[1]

Demos for PDL with nominals are no longer closed under union, but this will not affect the proofs of Section 3. We only need to extend the proof of Lemma

---

[1] While it would suffice for the proofs in this section to require that every nominal $x \in \mathcal{F}$ occurs in *at most* one $H \in \mathcal{S}$, this would not be enough in the presence of difference modalities. Otherwise, $\{\{x, \neg y, Dx\}\}$ would be a nominally coherent demo although its only member is unsatisfiable.

8 by saying that $S_{\mathfrak{M}}$ satisfies (DN): if $x \in \mathcal{F}$, then x denotes a unique state $w_x \in |\mathfrak{M}|$. Therefore, x is contained in the unique induced Hintikka set H_{w_x}.

So far, the addition of nominals has been at no extra conceptual or technical cost. When it comes to pruning, however, we can no longer remove arbitrary Hintikka sets that "violate the demo conditions". For example, if the same nominal x is contained in two Hintikka sets H, H' of the system S and we remove H, then further pruning actions carried out to restore (D$\diamond$) could lead to H' being deleted as well. More generally, since there may not need to be a unique maximal demo, Theorem 16 does not hold. However, it can be reestablished using an additional assumption here and in the preceding proposition.

Proposition 17. *Let S be nominally coherent. Then the following hold.*

1. *If S contains a demo, then it contains a unique maximal demo.*
2. *If $S \xrightarrow{p} S'$ and $D \subseteq S$ is a demo, then $D \subseteq S'$ and S' is nominally coherent.*
3. *If $S \overset{p}{\rightsquigarrow} S'$ and S' is nominally coherent, then S' is a demo.*

Proof. We call a Hintikka set that contains a nominal a *nominal set*.

1. Let D_1, D_2 be two demos contained in S. Then, due to S, D_1, D_2 being nominally coherent, both D_i contain all nominal sets in S. Therefore and because (D$\diamond$) is robust under union, we have that $D_1 \cup D_2 \subseteq S$.
2. Every pruning action removes only Hintikka sets that violate (D$\diamond$); hence no Hintikka set from D is removed. Because S is nominally coherent and D contains all nominal sets in S, S' is nominally coherent too.
3. Since S' is nominally coherent, it cannot be empty. Because no more pruning can be done, all Hintikka sets in S' satisfy (D$\diamond$) as well. $\square$

Theorem 18. *If $S \overset{p}{\rightsquigarrow} S'$ with S and S' being nominally coherent, then S' is the unique maximal demo contained in S.*

Proof. The unique maximal demo contained in S exists because of Proposition 17 (1);we call it D. Due to (3),S' is a demo contained in S and therefore contained in D. Due to 2,S' contains all demos contained in S, including D. Both inclusions together yield the equality. $\square$

The decision method from Section 4 can now be extended by inserting a **guess** stage between Steps 2 and 3 that guesses a maximal nominally coherent subsystem of the system $\mathcal{H}$ of all Hintikka sets, which contains one maximal demo. As explained above, the transition relations $\xrightarrow{\alpha}_S$ do not need to be computed upfront. The nondeterministic procedure is given below.

Decision method for HPDL-satisfiability

Input: formula s

1. Compute the formula universe $\mathcal{F}$ for s.
2. $\mathcal{H} = \{H \mid H \text{ is a Hintikka set with } H \subseteq \mathcal{F}\}$
3. Guess a maximal nominally coherent subset $\mathcal{H}'$ of $\mathcal{H}$.
4. Compute D with $\mathcal{H}' \overset{p}{\rightsquigarrow} D$.
5. Return "satisfiable" iff D is nominally coherent and $s \in H$ for some $H \in D$.

We now show that this method has a determinization that runs in exponential time. Let $x_1, \ldots, x_n$ be the linearly many nominals in $\mathcal{F}$. For x_1, Step 3 can guess a Hintikka set in $\mathcal{H}$ that contains x_1 and remove all other Hintikka sets that contain x_1. This action can be iterated for all other x_i. Should no Hintikka set be left that contains x_i, then Step 3 rejects straightaway. Otherwise the reduced Hintikka system after the n-th iteration is a maximal nominally coherent subset of $\mathcal{H}$. Steps 4 and 5 are then applied deterministically to that subset.

We consider the set of computation paths of this nondeterministic algorithm. Every path contains n guesses of an element from a subset of $\mathcal{H}$—from a set exponential in $|s|$. Each such exponential guess can be implemented as a sequence of polynomially many binary guesses, inducing a binary tree of polynomial depth. Since n is linear in $|s|$, the binary tree induced by the sequence of all n exponential guesses is still of polynomial depth. In every leaf of this tree, a deterministic exponential time computation takes place. Hence, the tree has only exponentially many nodes and can be searched deterministically in exponential time.

To summarize, adding nominals requires no significant computational costs as long as only worst-case complexity is concerned. Our decision method remains correct if Step 2 is replaced by the creation of a closed tableau completed via rules extending those in [20]. However, both versions of our method are impractical because **prune** is repeated a number of times that is linear in the size of $\mathcal{H}$ or the completed tableau. It would be more practical to interleave **guess** with **construct**, but it is currently not clear how to realize this.

6   Difference Modalities

To deal with the difference operators, several changes to the conceptual, technical and computational part are necessary.

Since $\mathsf{D}s$ and $\overline{\mathsf{D}}s$ do not say anything about the current state, it is not the notion of a Hintikka set that needs extending, but the notion of a demo. We add the following conditions to Def. 4.

(DD) If $\mathsf{D}s \in H \in \mathcal{D}$, then there is some $H' \in \mathcal{D}$ such that $H' \neq H$ and $s \in H'$.
(D$\overline{\mathsf{D}}$) If $\overline{\mathsf{D}}s \in H \in \mathcal{D}$, then, for all $H' \in \mathcal{D}$ such that $H' \neq H$, we have $s \in H'$.

Because of Condition (D$\overline{\mathsf{D}}$) alone, demos for PDL extended by $\overline{\mathsf{D}}$ are not closed under union. This is not surprising because $\overline{\mathsf{D}}$ can be used to express that a given predicate behaves as a nominal: $p \wedge \overline{\mathsf{D}}\neg p$. We will therefore have to adapt the decision procedure to the presence of $\overline{\mathsf{D}}$ at the end of this section. In contrast, adding only D to PDL does not make closure under unions invalid.

However, the proof of Lemma 8 does not go through for the D case without further assumptions. Consider, for example, $\mathcal{F} = \{p, \mathsf{D}p\}$ and the model $\mathfrak{M}$ with $|\mathfrak{M}| = \{v, w\}$ and $\mathfrak{M}p = \{v, w\}$. Then $\mathfrak{M}, v \models \mathsf{D}p$ and $\mathsf{D}p \in H_v$. Since $H_v = H_w$, the system $\mathcal{S}_{\mathfrak{M}}$ consists of only H_v and (DD) is violated.

To solve this problem, we assume an injective function that assigns to every literal $\mathsf{D}s \in \mathcal{F}$ a nominal $x_{\mathsf{D}s} \in \mathcal{F}$ that is isolated, i.e., which occurs in no other formula in $\mathcal{F}$. Intuitively, $x_{\mathsf{D}s}$ is supposed to denote a state that satisfies s, provided that such a state exists. If it does, all states that are different from the one denoted by $x_{\mathsf{D}s}$ satisfy $\mathsf{D}s$. As we will see below, this implies that, whenever a state w satisfies $\mathsf{D}s$, then there is a state v that satisfies s with $H_v \neq H_w$.

It remains to ensure that the $x_{\mathsf{D}s}$ denote the correct states in $\mathfrak{M}$. We call a model $\mathfrak{M}$ *nice* for $\mathcal{F}$ if, for all $\mathsf{D}s \in \mathcal{F}$ such that s is satisfiable in $\mathfrak{M}$, the conjunction $s \wedge x_{\mathsf{D}s}$ is satisfiable in $\mathfrak{M}$ too. Since we require that the $x_{\mathsf{D}s}$ are isolated, we do not restrict generality by assuming that satisfying models are nice. Lemma 8 is now reformulated as follows.

Lemma 19. *If $\mathfrak{M}$ is nice for $\mathcal{F}$, then $\mathcal{S}_{\mathfrak{M}}$ is a demo.*

Proof. (D$\diamond$) and (DN) are shown as in the proof of Lemma 8.

(DD) Let $\mathsf{D}s \in H_w \in \mathcal{S}_{\mathfrak{M}}$. Then there is some $v \neq w$ with $\mathfrak{M}, v \models s$. In case $\mathfrak{M}, w \models x_{\mathsf{D}s}$, we conclude that $x_{\mathsf{D}s} \in H_w$ and $x_{\mathsf{D}s} \notin H_v$. Therefore, $H_v \neq H_w$. Otherwise, since $\mathfrak{M}$ is nice, we can assume w.l.o.g. that v is precisely the state with $\mathfrak{M}, v \models x_{\mathsf{D}s} \wedge s$. This implies $H_v \neq H_w$, too. In both cases, we have $s \in H_v$ from $\mathfrak{M}, v \models s$.

(D$\overline{\mathsf{D}}$) Let $\overline{\mathsf{D}}s \in H_w \in \mathcal{S}_{\mathfrak{M}}$, and let $H' \in \mathcal{S}_{\mathfrak{M}}$ with $H' \neq H_w$. Hence $H' = H_v$ for some $v \neq w$. From $\mathfrak{M}, w \models \overline{\mathsf{D}}s$, we conclude $\mathfrak{M}, v \models s$, i.e., $s \in H_v$.   □

We further need to incorporate the assumptions of models being nice into Lemma 9 and its proof (see [19]).

Lemma 20 (Demo existence for HPDL$_\mathsf{D}$). *For every satisfiable formula $s \in \mathcal{F}$, there is a demo $\mathcal{D}$ over $\mathcal{F}$ that contains s.*

Extending the proof of Lemma 13 is straightforward if we add two cases.

$s = \mathsf{D}t$. If $\mathsf{D}t \in H \in \mathcal{D}$, then Demo Condition (DD) requires the existence of an $H' \in \mathcal{D}$ with $H' \neq H$ and $t \in H'$. The induction hypothesis yields $\mathfrak{M}_{\mathcal{D}}, H' \models t$ and, therefore, $\mathfrak{M}_{\mathcal{D}}, H \models \mathsf{D}t$.

$s = \overline{\mathsf{D}}t$. Analogous to the previous case, using Demo Condition (D$\overline{\mathsf{D}}$).

We conclude that the conceptual cost of adding the existential difference modality is significant, while the technical additions are straightforward once a suitable definition of the auxiliary nominals is in place. The universal difference operator has not caused any difficulties so far, but it will lose its harmlessness when it comes to the decision procedure.

First, we need to incorporate D into the definition of pruning, which is now defined as follows: let $\mathcal{S} \xrightarrow{p} \mathcal{S}'$ if $\mathcal{S}'$ can be obtained from $\mathcal{S}$ by deleting some $H \in \mathcal{S}$ that violates (D$\diamond$) or (DD), i.e., one of the following two cases occurs:

1. For some $\langle\alpha\rangle s \in H \in \mathcal{S}$, there is no $H' \in \mathcal{S}$ such that $H \xrightarrow{\alpha}_{\mathcal{S}} H'$ and $s \in H'$.
2. For some $\mathsf{D}s \in H \in \mathcal{S}$, there is no $H' \in \mathcal{S}$ such that $H' \neq H$ and $s \in H'$.

Since we have lost the existence of a greatest demo not only because of the auxiliary nominals, but also due to the presence of $\overline{\mathsf{D}}$, we will have to revisit the assumptions of Proposition 17 and Theorem 18. It suffices to add the requirement that $\mathcal{S}$ satisfies (D$\overline{\text{D}}$) to both assumptions and observe that all subsets of $\mathcal{S}$ then satisfy (D$\overline{\text{D}}$). The proofs then go through unchanged.

Therefore, the decision method from the previous section can be reused if we reformulate Step 3 as follows:

Guess a maximal subset $\mathcal{H}'$ of $\mathcal{H}$ that is nominally coherent and satisfies (D$\overline{\text{D}}$).

Since $\mathcal{H}'$ needs to be pruned to a demo (candidate) $\mathcal{D}$, we ensure (D$\overline{\text{D}}$) by distinguishing three cases for every formula $\overline{\text{D}}s \in \mathcal{F}$ about its occurrence in a maximal demo $\mathcal{D} \subseteq \mathcal{H}$.

($\overline{\text{D}}1$) $\overline{\text{D}}s$ is not contained in $\mathcal{D}$. We can therefore discard all Hintikka sets in $\mathcal{H}$ that contain $\overline{\text{D}}s$ because they cannot occur in $\mathcal{H}'$. This ensures that neither $\mathcal{H}$ nor $\mathcal{H}'$ violates (D$\overline{\text{D}}$) with $\overline{\text{D}}s$.

($\overline{\text{D}}2$) All Hintikka sets in $\mathcal{D}$ contain s. Then, for the same reason as above, it is safe to discard all Hintikka sets in $\mathcal{H}$, ensuring that neither $\mathcal{H}$ nor $\mathcal{H}'$ violates (D$\overline{\text{D}}$) with $\overline{\text{D}}s$.

($\overline{\text{D}}3$) $\mathcal{D}$ contains Hintikka sets H, H' with $\overline{\text{D}}s \in H$ and $s \in H'$. If $s \in H$, we are in Case ($\overline{\text{D}}2$) due to (D$\overline{\text{D}}$). Hence $s \notin H$, and therefore $\overline{\text{D}}s$ is in no Hintikka set other than H. In this case, it is safe to choose one H containing $\overline{\text{D}}s$ and not s to remain in $\mathcal{H}$ and $\mathcal{H}'$, and all other Hintikka sets that contain $\overline{\text{D}}s$ or not s can be discarded.

It therefore suffices to add another linear number of guessing actions out of an exponential supply to the guessing phase, and the previous arguments about the determinization in exponential time still apply.

While the addition of D causes significant conceptual overhead, the extension of the decision method with $\overline{\text{D}}$ within the given time bounds is non-trivial.

7   Tests

We redefine the transition relation for tests: $\xrightarrow{s}_{\mathcal{S}} = \{(H, H) \mid s \in H \in \mathcal{S}\}$.

In order to prove that the Hintikka system $\mathcal{S}_{\mathfrak{M}}$ induced by a model is a demo, it suffices to add one straightforward case to the proof of Lemma 7.

$\alpha = t$. If $v \xrightarrow{t}_{\mathfrak{M}} w$, then $v = w$ and $\mathfrak{M}, v \models t$. Then we also have that $H_v = H_w$ and $t \in H_v$. Hence, $H_v \xrightarrow{t}_{\mathcal{S}_{\mathfrak{M}}} H_w$.

For the other direction—every demo is satisfied by its induced model—the missing cases in Lemmas 11 and 12 require additional assumptions, which are added in the following. The proofs need to be redone only for the cases of tests, see [19].

Lemma 21. *Let $\mathcal{S}$ be a Hintikka system and α a program such that, for all tests t in α and all $H \in \mathcal{S}$, $t \in H$ implies $\mathfrak{M}_{\mathcal{S}}, H \models t$. Then $\xrightarrow{\alpha}_{\mathcal{S}} \subseteq \xrightarrow{\alpha}_{\mathfrak{M}_{\mathcal{S}}}$.*

Lemma 22. *Let $\mathcal{S}$ be a Hintikka system with $H, H' \in \mathcal{S}$ satisfying*

- $[\alpha]s \in H \xrightarrow{\alpha}_{\mathfrak{M}_{\mathcal{S}}} H'$,   and
- For all tests t in α and $H \in \mathcal{S}$: if $\sim t \in H$, then $\mathfrak{M}_{\mathcal{S}}, H \models \sim t$.

Then $s \in H'$.

The formulation of the decision procedure is unaffected by the addition of tests. The only difference in detail is that $\xrightarrow{t}_{\mathcal{H}}$ needs to be computed by cycling through all the exponentially many $H \in \mathcal{H}$ and their linear-size contents.

The surprising consequence is that, even in the presence of tests, a complicated induction order can be avoided in the proofs leading to the demo theorem, provided that the theorem is sufficiently factored out into lemmas.

8   Converse Actions

The extension with converse actions is straightforward: in Definition 2, we need to replace the case for $\xrightarrow{a}_{\mathcal{S}}$ with

$$\xrightarrow{a}_{\mathcal{S}} = \Big\{(H, H') \mid \forall s : \big([a]s \in H \Rightarrow s \in H'\big) \text{ and } \big([a^-]s \in H' \Rightarrow s \in H\big)\Big\},$$

and add the case $\xrightarrow{a^-}_{\mathcal{S}} = \xrightarrow{a}_{\mathcal{S}}^-$, where $\xrightarrow{a}_{\mathcal{S}}^-$ denotes the inverse of $\xrightarrow{a}_{\mathcal{S}}$. All proofs of Sections 3 and 4 go through after a straightforward converse case has been added for Lemmas 7, 11, and 12; details are given in [19].

We conclude that adding converse is conceptually, technically and computationally easy in our setting. This is different for tableau-based decision procedures, where converse operators cause significant technical difficulties [2, 14].

9   Related Work

We have given a Pratt-style worst-case optimal decision procedure for test-free PDL and step-wise extended it to capture nominals, difference modalities, tests and converse. The correctness of this method is based on transparent proofs of the bounded model theorem (BMT). We now discuss how our approach relates to known approaches of this type.

The basis for our approach is Pratt's work [24], where he sketches a decision method that adds pruning to Fischer and Ladner's method [10], without a formal correctness proof. This is probably the most straightforward way of obtaining the exponential-time upper bound. We have extended Pratt's method with hybrid operators and converse.

Variations of Pratt's straightforward approach are given in the literature [16, 22, 17, 3]. In order to establish the BMT, the authors of [16, 22, 17] use either simultaneous induction over formulas and programs, or a non-standard induction over an order on formulas with and without flags. The correctness of the decision procedure is not immediate, and requires to partially repeat the course of the proof of the BMT. The procedure in [3, Section 6.8] requires Hintikka sets to be upwards saturated, and its proofs use a simpler induction scheme. However, that approach does not include tests. In contrast to [16, 22, 17], our technique factorizes the BMT in a way that every lemma can be proven using a single induction over the subterm relation. The demo notion and its properties can be directly used to conclude the correctness of the decision procedure.

In [23], the authors state that HPDL^- has the same deterministic upper bound as PDL without giving an explicit decision procedure. The work in [5, 1] establishes a chain of polynomial-time satisfiability-preserving translations $\mathsf{HPDL}_\mathsf{D}^- \to \mathsf{HPDL}_\mathsf{E}^- \to \mathsf{HPDL}^- \to \mathsf{PDL}^- \to \mathsf{PDL}$, again without an explicit decision procedure.

In contrast to the work in [25, 12, 14, 20], our approach does not build a tableau in Stage `construct`, and therefore the edges of the transition relation do not need to be an explicit part of our Hintikka systems. The approach in [20] uses the notion of a clause instead of a Hintikka set and a support relation between clauses and formulas. The support closures of clauses—i.e., their supported sets of formulas—are exactly the Hintikka sets. Without the need for computational optimizations, Hintikka sets are sufficient for our approach and more convenient. While the decision procedure in [20] runs in NExpTime for nominals, we show how to obtain an ExpTime procedure, answering the question from [20] whether a demo can be found efficiently w.r.t. the size of the tableau.

In [14], a more practical worst-case optimal decision method for PDL^- is given and implemented. In contrast, we have acknowledged above that our procedure is not implementable, and this is not the purpose of this paper. We have examined how Pratt's most simple optimal procedure scales to more expressive features and, in our point of view, this serves the understanding of this type of procedure rather than its implementation.

Syntactic descriptions of models related to demos can be found in [8]. Their Hintikka structures for CTL are richer: they contain the transition relation explicitly and may contain several copies of a Hintikka set.

For future work, it would be interesting to examine whether our approach can be extended to the hybrid μ-calculus and whether graded modalities can be incorporated. On the more practical side, a natural next step is to study how to transfer our approach into a decision procedure that interleaves building a (graph) tableau and pruning in the presence of hybrid operators.

Acknowledgments. We thank the anonymous reviewers for helpful comments.

References

[1] Areces, C., Blackburn, P., Marx, M.: The computational complexity of hybrid temporal logics. L. J. IGPL 8(5), 653–679 (2000)

[2] Baader, F., Sattler, U.: Tableau algorithms for description logics. In: Dyckhoff, R. (ed.) TABLEAUX 2000. LNCS, vol. 1847, pp. 1–18. Springer, Heidelberg (2000)

[3] Blackburn, P., de Rijke, M., Venema, Y.: Modal Logic. CUP (2001)

[4] Bolander, T., Blackburn, P.: Termination for hybrid tableaus. J. Log. Comput. 17(3), 517–554 (2007)

[5] De Giacomo, G.: Decidability of class-based knowledge representation formalisms. Ph.D. thesis, Università degli Studi di Roma "La Sapienza" (1995)

[6] De Giacomo, G., Massacci, F.: Combining deduction and model checking into tableaux and algorithms for converse-PDL. Inf. Comput. 162(1-2), 117–137 (2000)

[7] Donini, F.M., Massacci, F.: EXPtime tableaux for $\mathcal{ALC}$. AI 124(1), 87–138 (2000)

[8] Emerson, E.A., Halpern, J.Y.: Decision procedures and expressiveness in the temporal logic of branching time. J. Comput. System Sci. 30(1), 1–24 (1985)

[9] Fischer, M.J., Ladner, R.E.: Propositional modal logic of programs. In: Proc. STOC, pp. 286–294. ACM, New York (1977)

[10] Fischer, M.J., Ladner, R.E.: Propositional dynamic logic of regular programs. J. Comput. System Sci., 194–211 (1979)

[11] Gargov, G., Goranko, V.: Modal logic with names. J. Philos. L. 22, 607–636 (1993)

[12] Goré, R., Widmann, F.: An optimal on-the-fly tableau-based decision procedure for PDL-satisfiability. In: Schmidt, R.A. (ed.) CADE-22. LNCS, vol. 5663, pp. 437–452. Springer, Heidelberg (2009)

[13] Goré, R.P., Nguyen, L.A.: EXPTIME tableaux with global caching for description logics with transitive roles, inverse roles and role hierarchies. In: Olivetti, N. (ed.) TABLEAUX 2007. LNCS (LNAI), vol. 4548, pp. 133–148. Springer, Heidelberg (2007)

[14] Goré, R., Widmann, F.: Optimal and cut-free tableaux for propositional dynamic logic with converse. In: Giesl, J., Hähnle, R. (eds.) IJCAR 2010. LNCS, vol. 6173, pp. 225–239. Springer, Heidelberg (2010)

[15] Haarslev, V., Möller, R.: RACER system description. In: Goré, R.P., Leitsch, A., Nipkow, T. (eds.) IJCAR 2001. LNCS (LNAI), vol. 2083, pp. 701–705. Springer, Heidelberg (2001)

[16] Harel, D.: Dynamic logic. In: Gabbay, D., Guenthner, F. (eds.) Handbook of Philosophical Logic, vol. II, pp. 497–604. Reidel, Dordrechtz (1984)

[17] Harel, D., Kozen, D., Tiuryn, J.: Dynamic Logic. The MIT Press, Cambridge (2000)

[18] Hollunder, B., Nutt, W., Schmidt-Schauß, M.: Subsumption algorithms for concept description languages. In: Proc. ECAI, pp. 348–353 (1990)

[19] Kaminski, M., Schneider, T., Smolka, G.: Correctness and worst-case optimality of Pratt-style decision procedures for modal and hybrid logics. Technical report, Saarland University (2011), http://tinyurl.com/hpdldc

[20] Kaminski, M., Smolka, G.: Clausal graph tableaux for hybrid logic with eventualities and difference. In: Fermüller, C.G., Voronkov, A. (eds.) LPAR-17. LNCS, vol. 6397, pp. 417–431. Springer, Heidelberg (2010)

[21] Kaminski, M., Smolka, G.: Terminating tableaux for hybrid logic with eventualities. In: Giesl, J., Hähnle, R. (eds.) IJCAR 2010. LNCS, vol. 6173, pp. 240–254. Springer, Heidelberg (2010)

[22] Kozen, D., Tiuryn, J.: Logics of programs. In: Handbook of Theoretical Computer Science. Formal Models and Sematics, vol. B, pp. 789–840. Elsevier, Amsterdam (1990)

[23] Passy, S., Tinchev, T.: An essay in combinatory dynamic logic. Inf. Comput. 93(2), 263–332 (1991)

[24] Pratt, V.R.: Models of program logics. In: Proc. FOCS, pp. 115–122 (1979)

[25] Pratt, V.R.: A near-optimal method for reasoning about action. J. Comput. System Sci. 20(2), 231–254 (1980)

[26] Prior, A.: Past, Present and Future. OUP, England (1967)

[27] Schmidt-Schauß, M., Smolka, G.: Attributive concept descriptions with compliments. AI 48(1), 1–26 (1991)

[28] Segerberg, K.: A note on the logic of elsewhere. Theoria 46(2-3), 183–187 (1980)

[29] Streett, R.S., Emerson, E.A.: An automata theoretic decision procedure for the propositional μ-calculus. Inform. and Control 81, 249–264 (1989)

[30] Tsarkov, D., Horrocks, I., Patel-Schneider, P.F.: Optimizing terminological reasoning for expressive description logics. J. Autom. Reas. 39(3), 277–316 (2007)

[31] Vardi, M.Y., Wolper, P.: Automata-theoretic techniques for modal logics of programs. J. Comput. System Sci. 32, 183–221 (1986)

Cut Elimination for Shallow Modal Logics[*]

Björn Lellmann and Dirk Pattinson

Department of Computing, Imperial College London, UK

Abstract. Motivated by the fact that nearly all conditional logics are axiomatised by so-called shallow axioms (axioms with modal nesting depth ≤ 1) we investigate sequent calculi and cut elimination for modal logics of this type. We first provide a generic translation of shallow axioms to (one-sided, unlabelled) sequent rules. The resulting system is complete if we admit pseudo-analytic cut, i.e. cuts on modalised propositional combinations of subformulas, leading to a generic (but sub-optimal) decision procedure. In a next step, we show that, for finite sets of axioms, only a small number of cuts is needed between any two applications of modal rules. More precisely, completeness still holds if we restrict to cuts that form a tree of logarithmic height between any two modal rules. In other words, we obtain a small (PSPACE-computable) representation of an extended rule set for which cut elimination holds. In particular, this entails PSPACE decidability of the underlying logic if contraction is also admissible. This leads to (tight) PSPACE bounds for various conditional logics.

1 Introduction

Cut elimination is without doubt a central theme in proof theory. Not only do cut-free sequent systems provide for reasonably simple syntactical proofs of results like interpolation, they also pave the way for decision procedures via backwards proof search. While there are a variety of methods to construct a cut-free sequent system for specific logics (and at least as many different sequent calculi), the general approach is to come up with a sequent system tailored to the logic at hand, and then show cut elimination for this particular system. While this approach works very well for specific logics, a good deal of ingenuity is required to construct the actual system. Since this method consumes both a lot of time and effort, this raises the question whether there is a generic method to construct cut-free calculi, and in particular, whether we can delegate the task of constructing these systems. Our motivation for investigating this question mainly stems from automated proof search and questions of complexity, where the shape and structure of the rules of a cut-free system are not important, as long as we can recognise rule instances fast enough. Our ultimate aim in this somewhat radical endeavour is to synthesise algorithms that recognise instances of a cut-free sequent system, given an axiomatisation of the logic under consideration.

This paper reports on our first results on this programme in the context of modal logic: we study the question to what extent we can convert a Hilbert-style axiomatisation of a general, not necessarily normal modal logic into a cut-free sequent system such

---

[*] Supported by EPSRC-Project EP/H016317/1.

K. Brünnler and G. Metcalfe (Eds.): TABLEAUX 2011, LNAI 6793, pp. 211–225, 2011.

that rule instances are decidable in a moderate complexity class. Our point of departure is the class of logics that can be axiomatised by *shallow axioms*, i.e. axioms of modal nesting depth ≤ 1. These logics are known to be decidable by semantic arguments via coalgebraic semantics [10] and the finite model property, and (reassuringly) exclude modal logics that are known to be undecidable [6]. Indeed, one of the questions is to what extent the decidability of these logics can be reflected purely syntactically.

The motivating examples in this endeavour are the systems of conditional logics. While there is a plethora of systems [7], nearly all of these are axiomatised by shallow axioms. Recent activity in this area has led to methods for constructing (labelled) sequent systems for some of these systems [8], and to generic cut elimination proofs for unlabelled systems given by a set of rules [11]. We extend the latter approach by a generic method to construct rules of an unlabelled sequent system from a set of shallow axioms. For the system obtained in this way we show two main results, namely completeness and decidability of the system, where the cut rule is replaced by the pseudo-analytic cut rule (a variant of the analytic cut rule), and full cut elimination for the system extended by a tractable set of rules. The latter result breathes the spirit of our radical approach driven by proof search. The crucial fact is that the extended rule set is generically constructed and has a small (polysize) representation. We also show that admissibility of the contraction rule in the extended system implies a PSPACE decidability result for the corresponding logic. While this still leaves the question whether generic positive results concerning admissibility of contraction hold, we apply our method successfully to various conditional logics.

Related work. Criteria for cut elimination are discussed for instance in [12] for a wide class of logics, but not touching upon the automatic construction of rules or calculi that admit cut elimination. Cut elimination for canonical calculi (where each sequent rule only allows the introduction of one logical connective) are discussed in [1]. This approach in general is unsuitable for modal calculi, since these typically introduce more than one connective at a time. Algorithmic aspects of cut elimination are investigated in [2] but with a focus on deciding whether a calculus enjoys this property, in contrast to the main aspect of this paper which aims to construct a calculus that enjoys cut elimination algorithmically. The present paper is a continuation of work reported in [11] that gives criteria and a semi-algorithmic method to obtain calculi admitting cut elimination, and our focus here is to obtain these calculi purely algorithmically.

2   Preliminaries and Notation

Throughout the paper, we consider a *modal similarity type* Λ consisting of modal operators with arities and a denumerable set V of propositional variables. Given Λ, the set of Λ-*formulas* is given by the grammar

$$\mathcal{F}(\Lambda) \ni \phi, \psi ::= p \mid \neg\phi \mid \phi \wedge \psi \mid \heartsuit(\phi_1, \ldots, \phi_n)$$

where $p \in V$ and $\heartsuit \in \Lambda$ is n-ary. We employ a classical reading of the propositional part of the language and use the standard abbreviations for other propositional connectives. The *modal rank* of a formula is given inductively by $\mathrm{rk}(p) = 0$, $\mathrm{rk}(\neg\phi) = \mathrm{rk}(\phi)$,

$\mathrm{rk}\,(\phi_1 \wedge \phi_2) = \max_{i=1,2} \mathrm{rk}\,(\phi_i)$ and $\mathrm{rk}\,(\heartsuit(\phi_1, \ldots, \phi_n)) = 1 + \max_{1 \leq i \leq n} \mathrm{rk}\,(\phi_i)$. If $\sigma : V \to \mathcal{F}(\Lambda)$ is a substitution, we write $\phi\sigma$ for the result of replacing every occurrence of p in ϕ by $\sigma(p)$ and $[\phi/p]$ is the substitution defined by $[\phi/p](q) = \phi$ if $p = q$ and $[\phi/p](q) = q$ otherwise. We denote the propositional variables that occur in a formula ϕ by $\mathrm{Var}(\phi)$. If $S \subseteq \mathcal{F}(\Lambda)$ is a set of formulas, we write $\Lambda(S)$ for the set $\{\heartsuit(\phi_1, \ldots, \phi_n) \mid \heartsuit \in \Lambda\ n\text{-ary}, \phi_1, \ldots, \phi_n \in S\}$ of formulas that arise by applying precisely one modality $\heartsuit \in \Lambda$ to formulas in S, and $\neg S$ is the set $\{\neg\phi \mid \phi \in S\}$ of negations of formulas in S. Similarly, $\mathrm{Prop}(S)$ is the set of propositional combinations of formulas in S. A *clause* over S is a finite disjunction $l_1 \vee \cdots \vee l_n$ of literals $l_i \in S \cup \neg S$ $(i = 1, \ldots, l)$. If $l \in S \cup \neg S$, then $\sim l$ is the *normalised negation* of l, given by $\sim l = \neg l$ if $l \in S$ and $\sim l = l'$ if $l = \neg l' \in \neg S$. Two formulas $\phi, \psi \in \mathcal{F}(\Lambda)$ are *propositionally equivalent* if $\phi \leftrightarrow \psi$ is a substitution instance of a propositional tautology. To make contraction explicit, we take a Λ-*sequent* to be a finite multiset of Λ-formulas. If $S \subseteq \mathcal{F}(\Lambda)$ is a set of formulas, we write $\mathcal{S}(S)$ for the set of sequents containing only elements in S and $\mathcal{S}(\Lambda)$ for $\mathcal{S}(\mathcal{F}(\Lambda))$. The number of elements of $\Gamma \in \mathcal{S}(\Lambda)$ counting multiplicities is written as $\|\Gamma\|$. We employ usual notation and identify a formula $\phi \in \mathcal{F}(\Lambda)$ with the singleton sequent ϕ and write Γ, Δ for the (multiset) union of sequents $\Gamma, \Delta \in \mathcal{S}(\Lambda)$. If Γ is a Λ-sequent, $\mathrm{Supp}\,(\Gamma)$ denotes the *support* of Γ, i.e. the set of Λ-formulas that occur in Γ with positive multiplicity. Substitution extends to sequents pointwise (preserving multiplicity), that is, $\Gamma\sigma = \phi_1\sigma, \ldots, \phi_n\sigma$ if $\Gamma = \phi_1, \ldots, \phi_n$. A sequent $\Gamma \in \mathcal{S}(\Lambda)$ is *propositionally equivalent* to a formula $\phi \in \mathcal{F}(\Lambda)$ if $\bigvee \Gamma \leftrightarrow \phi$ is a propositional tautology. A set $\{\Gamma_1, \ldots, \Gamma_n\}$ of sequents is a *conjunctive normal form* (cnf) of a formula $\phi \in \mathcal{F}(\Lambda)$ if ϕ and $(\bigvee \Gamma_1) \wedge \cdots \wedge (\bigvee \Gamma_n)$ are propositionally equivalent. If $\phi, \psi \in \mathcal{F}(\Lambda)$, we use the shorthand $\phi = \psi$ to denote the set of sequents containing $\neg\phi, \psi$ and $\phi, \neg\psi$. This convention is extended to chains of equations $\phi_1 = \cdots = \phi_n$ in the obvious way.

3   From Hilbert Systems to Sequent Systems

Our starting point in this paper is a modal logic axiomatised by shallow axioms (axioms with modal rank ≤ 1) in a Hilbert system that we convert to a set of sequent rules, taking special care of propositional formulas occurring in the scope of a modality.

Definition 1. A *shallow axiom* over a similarity type Λ is a formula $\phi \in \mathcal{F}(\Lambda)$ with $\mathrm{rk}\,(\phi) \leq 1$. A *shallow clause* is of the form $c = c_p \vee c_d$ where c_p is a clause over V and c_d is a clause over $\Lambda(\mathrm{Prop}(V))$. A *decomposition* of a shallow clause c is a triple (c_p, c_d, σ) where c_p, c_d are clauses as above with $\mathrm{Var}(c_d) \cap \mathrm{Var}(c_p) = \emptyset$, and $\sigma : V \to \mathrm{Prop}(V)$ is a substitution with $c = c_p \vee c_d\sigma$.

Insisting that a modal logic is axiomatised purely in terms of shallow axioms clearly excludes a large variety of logics (the most basic example is the modal logic K extended with the transitivity axiom $\Box p \to \Box\Box p$). On the other hand, nearly all conditional logics studied in the literature are axiomatised using shallow axioms [7]. Technically, the restriction to (finitely many) shallow axioms implies that all logics under consideration are in fact decidable, a property that fails for logics that are axiomatised by more general classes of axioms [6].

Example 2.   1. Over the similarity type $\Lambda = \{\Box\}$, the axioms defining the modal logic (K), i.e. $\Box p \wedge \Box q \to \Box(p \wedge q)$ and $\Box\top$ as well as the reflexivity axiom $\Box p \to p$ are shallow. Transitivity $\Box\Box p \to \Box p$ fails to be shallow.

2. The syntax of many conditional logics is given by the similarity type $\Lambda = \{>\}$ where $>$ is a binary operator that we write in infix notation. All of the axioms

(CM)	$(p > (q \wedge r)) \to (p > q)$	(CC)	$(p > q) \wedge (p > r) \to (p > (q \wedge r))$
(CS)	$(p \wedge q) \to (p > q)$	(CA)	$(p > r) \wedge (q > r) \to ((p \vee q) > r)$
(MP)	$(p > q) \to (p \to q)$	(CMon)	$(p > q) \wedge (p > r) \to ((p \wedge q) > r)$
(ID)	$(p > p)$	(CV)	$(p > q) \wedge \neg(p > \neg r) \to ((p \wedge r) > q)$

that define e.g. the conditional systems $B = \{\mathrm{CM}, \mathrm{CC}, \mathrm{CA}, \mathrm{CMon}, \mathrm{ID}\}$, $\mathrm{SS} = B \cup \{\mathrm{CS}, \mathrm{MP}\}$, and $\mathrm{V} = B \cup \{\mathrm{CV}\}$ are shallow [7].

We define modal Hilbert systems in the standard way by closing under modus ponens, uniform substitution and the modal congruence rule. This allows us e.g. to derive the necessitation rule $p/\Box p$ for $\Box$ from the axiom $\Box\top$.

Definition 3. Suppose $\mathcal{A} \subseteq \mathcal{F}(\Lambda)$. The predicate $\mathcal{HA} \vdash$ is the least subset of formulas containing $\mathcal{A}$ and all propositional tautologies that is closed under uniform substitution ($\mathcal{HA} \vdash \phi\sigma$ if $\mathcal{HA} \vdash \phi$), modus ponens ($\mathcal{HA} \vdash \psi$ if $\mathcal{HA} \vdash \phi \to \psi$ and $\mathcal{HA} \vdash \phi$) and congruence ($\mathcal{HA} \vdash \heartsuit(\phi_1, \ldots, \phi_n) \leftrightarrow \heartsuit(\psi_1, \ldots, \psi_n)$ if $\mathcal{HA} \vdash \phi_i \leftrightarrow \psi_i$ for all $i = 1, \ldots, n$).

Given a set of shallow axioms, we now construct an equivalent sequent system that extends propositional logic with *shallow rules*. As we are working in a generic setup, it is more convenient to have negation as an explicit logical operator rather than dealing with formulas in negation normal form as the latter would require that the similarity type Λ is closed under formal duals. Consequently our analysis is based on the system G consisting of all rule instances

$$\frac{}{\Gamma, p, \neg p} \qquad \frac{}{\Gamma, \neg\bot} \qquad \frac{\Gamma, \neg\phi, \neg\psi}{\Gamma, \neg(\phi \wedge \psi)} \qquad \frac{\Gamma, \phi \quad \Gamma, \psi}{\Gamma, \phi \wedge \psi} \qquad \frac{\Gamma, \phi}{\Gamma, \neg\neg\phi}$$

where $p \in V$ is a propositional variable, $\phi, \psi \in \mathcal{F}(\Lambda)$ are formulas and $\Gamma \in \mathcal{S}(\Lambda)$ is a sequent. Here, Γ is the *context* and a formula that appears in the conclusion but not the context is called *principal*. The system G is complete for classical propositional logic [14]. Extensions of G with weakening, cut, context-sensitive cut and contraction

$$(\mathsf{W})\frac{\Gamma}{\Gamma, \phi} \qquad (\mathsf{Cut})\frac{\Gamma, \phi \quad \Delta, \neg\phi}{\Gamma, \Delta} \qquad (\mathsf{Cut_{cs}})\frac{\Gamma, \phi \quad \Gamma, \neg\phi}{\Gamma} \qquad (\mathsf{Con})\frac{\Gamma, \phi, \phi}{\Gamma, \phi}$$

are denoted by suffixing with the respective rule names so that e.g. GWCon is the system G extended with weakening and contraction. We write $\Omega \vdash_{\mathsf{G}} \Delta$ if Δ can be derived in G from premises in Ω and we use the same notation for extensions of G with a subset of $\{\mathsf{W}, \mathsf{Con}, \mathsf{Cut}, \mathsf{Cut_{cs}}\}$. A sequent Γ is a *propositional consequence* of sequents in Ω

if $\Omega \vdash_{\mathsf{GCutCon}} \Gamma$, this is also denoted by $\Omega \vdash_{\mathsf{PL}} \Gamma$. Shallow axioms are incorporated into these systems by converting them into sequent rules of a specific form:

Definition 4. A *shallow rule* is given by a triple $R = (\mathsf{Prem}_c(R), \mathsf{Prem}_n(R), \Sigma)$ consisting of a finite set $\mathsf{Prem}_c(R) = \{\Gamma_1, \ldots, \Gamma_l\} \subseteq \mathcal{S}(V \cup \neg V)$ of *contextual premises*, a finite set $\mathsf{Prem}_n(R) = \{\Delta_1, \ldots, \Delta_m\} \subseteq \mathcal{S}(V \cup \neg V)$ of *non-contextual premises* and a sequent $\Sigma \in \mathcal{S}(\Lambda(V) \cup \neg \Lambda(V))$ of *principal formulas* where all variables that occur in Σ are pairwise distinct. If $\sigma : V \to \mathcal{F}(\Lambda)$ is a substitution and $\Gamma \in \mathcal{S}(\Lambda)$ is a sequent (the *context*), then

$$(R\sigma) \frac{\Gamma, \Gamma_1\sigma, \Sigma\sigma \quad \ldots \quad \Gamma, \Gamma_l\sigma, \Sigma\sigma \quad \Delta_1\sigma \quad \ldots \quad \Delta_m\sigma}{\Gamma, \Sigma\sigma}$$

is an *instance* of R. If no confusion between contextual and non-contextual premises can arise, we write a shallow rule given by the above data in the more suggestive form

$$(R) \frac{\Gamma_1, \Gamma, \Sigma \ldots \Gamma_l, \Gamma, \Sigma \quad \Delta_1 \ldots \Delta_m}{\Gamma, \Sigma}.$$

The *principal formulas* of a shallow rule R (or rule instance $R\sigma$) of the form above are the (substituted) elements of Σ, written as $\mathsf{PF}(R)$ (resp. $\mathsf{PF}(R\sigma)$). We write $\mathsf{Prem}(R)$ (resp. $\mathsf{Prem}(R\sigma)$) for the set of (substituted) premises of R, and $\mathsf{Concl}(R\sigma)$ for the conclusion of $(R\sigma)$. We identify shallow rules modulo injective renaming of variables.

The requirement that the variables in the principal formulas are pairwise distinct poses no restriction, since we may introduce fresh variables and new premises stating equivalences. The separation between contextual and non-contextual premises is important for two reasons: first, when passing from rules to instances, the contextual premises not only copy the context from premise to conclusion, but also the principal formulas. This is important for admissibility of contraction, as it allows to propagate a contraction between principal formulas and context. *Mutatis mutandis*, it is precisely this mechanism that allows to show admissibility of contraction in a sequent calculus for the modal logic T, i.e. K extended with the rule $\Gamma, \neg\phi, \neg\Box\phi / \Gamma, \neg\Box\phi$. Second, contextual premises receive special treatment in proof search, as the premise is a superset of the conclusion.

Example 5. Over the similarity types introduced in Section 2, we can form the following shallow rules, which we present in the suggestive notation of Definition 4.

1. Over $\Lambda = \{\Box\}$, both $(\mathcal{R}_{\mathrm{K}}) \frac{\neg p, \neg q, r \quad \neg r, p \quad \neg r, q}{\Gamma, \neg\Box p, \neg\Box q, \Box r}$ and $(\mathcal{R}_{\mathrm{T}}) \frac{\Gamma, \neg p, \neg\Box p}{\Gamma, \neg\Box p}$ are shallow. Here the premises in $\mathcal{R}_K$ are non-contextual whereas the premise in $\mathcal{R}_T$ is contextual.

2. Over $\Lambda = \{>\}$, both $(\mathcal{R}_{\mathrm{CC}}) \frac{p_1 = p_2 = p_3 \quad \neg q, \neg r, s \quad \neg s, q \quad \neg s, r}{\Gamma, \neg(p_1 > q), \neg(p_2 > r), (p_3 > s)}$ and $(\mathcal{R}_{\mathrm{CS}}) \frac{\Gamma, p \quad \Gamma, q}{\Gamma, (p > q)}$ are shallow.

Every set $\mathcal{R}$ of shallow rules induces a sequent calculus by augmenting instances of rules in $\mathcal{R}$ with the modal congruence rule and propositional reasoning.

Definition 6. Suppose $\mathcal{R}$ is a set of shallow rules. The predicate $\mathsf{G}\mathcal{R} \vdash$ is the least set of sequents closed under the propositional rules of G, instances of shallow rules in $\mathcal{R}$, and instances of the modal congruence rules

$$\frac{\neg\phi_1, \psi_1 \quad \neg\psi_1, \phi_1 \quad \ldots \quad \neg\phi_n, \psi_n \quad \neg\psi_n, \phi_n}{\Gamma, \neg\heartsuit(\phi_1, \ldots, \phi_n), \heartsuit(\psi_1, \ldots, \psi_n)}$$

where $\Gamma \in \mathcal{S}(\Lambda)$, $\heartsuit \in \Lambda$ is n-ary and $\phi_1, \ldots, \phi_n \in \mathcal{F}(\Lambda)$. Use of additional rules is indicated by suffixing so that e.g. $\mathsf{GRWCut_{cs}} \vdash$ denotes derivability in GR extended with weakening and context-sensitive cut.

We employ the usual definitions of a proof (a tree constructed from proof rules), the depth of a proof (the height of this tree) and (depth-preserving) admissibility of proof rules [14]. Often, a statement holds for extensions of GR with several principles. We indicate this using square brackets. For example, a statement involving $\mathsf{GR[WCon]}$ holds for an extension of GR with a (possibly empty) subset of $\{\mathsf{W}, \mathsf{Con}\}$.

Lemma 7 (Admissibility of weakening and inversion). *Suppose $\mathcal{R}$ is a set of shallow rules over a similarity type Λ. Then the weakening rule* (W) *and the rules*

$$\frac{\Gamma, \phi \wedge \psi}{\Gamma, \phi} \qquad \frac{\Gamma, \phi \wedge \psi}{\Gamma, \psi} \qquad \frac{\Gamma, \neg(\phi \wedge \psi)}{\Gamma, \neg\phi, \neg\psi} \qquad \frac{\Gamma, \neg\neg\phi}{\Gamma, \phi}$$

are depth-preserving admissible in $\mathsf{GR[CutCut_{cs}WCon]}$.

Our next goal is to convert shallow axioms into shallow rules and confirm that (for now, with help of cut and contraction) this does not change the notion of derivability.

Definition 8. Suppose that c is a shallow clause with decomposition (c_p, c_d, σ) where $\mathsf{Var}(c_d) = \{q_1, \ldots, q_n\}$ and $c_p = l_1 \vee \cdots \vee l_m$. If furthermore

- the sequents $\Delta_1, \ldots, \Delta_k$ are a cnf of $\bigwedge_{i=1}^{n}(q_i \leftrightarrow \sigma(q_i))$
- the sequent $\Sigma \subseteq \Lambda(V) \cup \neg\Lambda(V)$ is propositionally equivalent to c_d

then the shallow rule

$$\frac{\Gamma, \sim l_1 \quad \cdots \quad \Gamma, \sim l_m \quad \Delta_1 \quad \cdots \quad \Delta_k}{\Gamma, \Sigma}$$

is called a *rule form* of c. A *rule form* of a shallow axiom ϕ is a set $R = \{r_1, \ldots, r_k\}$ of shallow rules where each r_i is a rule form of a shallow clause c_i such that $\bigwedge_{i=1}^{n} c_i$ and ϕ are propositionally equivalent. Finally, a rule form of a set $\mathcal{A} = \{\phi_1, \ldots, \phi_n\}$ of shallow axioms is a set $\mathcal{R} = \mathcal{R}_1 \cup \cdots \cup \mathcal{R}_n$ where each $\mathcal{R}_i$ is a rule form of ϕ_i.

In other words, a rule form of a shallow axiom ϕ is constructed by first converting ϕ into conjunctive normal form, obtaining shallow clauses $c_1, \ldots, c_n$. For each shallow clause, we obtain a rule by replacing propositional formulas ϕ_i that occur as arguments of modal operators by new variables q_i and then add the clauses of a conjunctive normal form of $q_i \leftrightarrow \phi_i$ to the premises. The operation of adding a context amounts to considering a shallow clause $c = c_p \vee c_m$ as an implication $\neg c_m \rightarrow c_p$ that induces a rule $c_p \rightarrow \phi/\neg c_m \rightarrow \phi$ which is then interpreted as a sequent rule.

Example 9. The rules $\mathcal{R}_K$, $\mathcal{R}_T$, $\mathcal{R}_{CC}$ and $\mathcal{R}_{CS}$ presented in Example 5 are rule forms of the homonymous axioms introduced in Example 2.

As a first sanity check, we confirm that the Hilbert calculus given by a set of shallow axioms is equivalent to the sequent calculus given by their rule forms, at least as long as we admit cut and contraction in the latter.

Proposition 10. *Suppose that $\mathcal{A}$ is a set of shallow axioms and $\mathcal{R}$ is a rule form of $\mathcal{A}$.*

1. GRCutCon $\vdash \phi$ for every $\phi \in \mathcal{A}$.

2. $\mathcal{HA} \vdash \bigvee \Gamma_0$ whenever $\mathcal{HA} \vdash \bigvee \Gamma_i$ (all $1 \leq i \leq n$) and $\Gamma_1 \ldots \Gamma_n / \Gamma_0$ is an instance of a shallow rule in $\mathcal{R}$.

In the presence of cut and contraction, equivalence of both systems is then immediate:

Corollary 11. *Suppose that $\mathcal{A}$ is a set of shallow axioms and $\mathcal{R}$ is a rule form of $\mathcal{A}$. Then $\mathcal{HA} \vdash \bigvee \Gamma$ whenever GRCutCon $\vdash \Gamma$, for all sequents $\Gamma \in \mathcal{S}(\Lambda)$.*

Clearly, our goal is the elimination of both cut and contraction where the latter can (at least in the first instance) be handled on the basis of rule forms.

Definition 12. A set $\mathcal{R}$ of shallow rules is *contraction closed*, if, for every rule instance $(R\sigma)$ with $\mathsf{Concl}\,(R\sigma) = \Gamma, \phi, \phi$ there exists an instance $(S\tau)$ with $\mathsf{Concl}\,(S\tau) = \Gamma, \phi$ such that $\mathsf{Prem}_c\,(R\sigma) \vdash_{\mathsf{GWCon}} \Delta$ for all $\Delta \in \mathsf{Prem}_c\,(S\tau)$, and $\mathsf{Prem}_n\,(R\sigma) \vdash_{\mathsf{GWCon}} \Pi$ for all $\Pi \in \mathsf{Prem}_n\,(S\tau)$.

This definition allows us to propagate contraction over the application of modal rules. Combined with an induction on the depth of the derivation this yields:

Proposition 13. *Suppose that $\mathcal{R}$ is contraction closed. Then $\mathsf{GR}[\mathsf{Cut}_{cs}] \vdash \Gamma$ iff $\mathsf{GRCon}[\mathsf{Cut}_{cs}] \vdash \Gamma$ for all sequents $\Gamma \in \mathcal{S}(\Lambda)$. Moreover, the proof in $\mathsf{GR}[\mathsf{Cut}_{cs}]$ has at most the same height, uses the same number of (instances of) shallow rules and the same cut formulas.*

4   Cut-Closure and Pseudo-Analytic Cut

We now set out to establish the first main result of this paper, and show that the cut rule can be restricted to *pseudo-analytic* cut, i.e. cuts on formulas that arise by applying a modal operator to a propositional combination of subformulas of the conclusion of the cut rule, which leads to a generic decidability result for logics axiomatised with shallow rules. To achieve this, we first normalise shallow rules so that only variables occurring in the conclusion are allowed in the premise. This way backwards proof search does not introduce new variables. In a second step, we close a normalised rule set under cuts between rule conclusions, and observe that this closure process can be simulated with pseudo-analytic cut. We first analyse the process of eliminating unnecessary variables.

Definition 14. A set $\mathcal{R}$ of shallow rules is *normalised* if in each rule in $\mathcal{R}$ all variables occurring in the premises also occur in the conclusion.

Superfluous variables in the premises of rules are eliminated as follows.

Definition 15 (p-elimination). Let S be a set of sequents and $p \in V$ a propositional variable. The *p-elimination* of S, written S_p is defined by

$$S_p = \{\Gamma \ominus p, \Delta \ominus \neg p \in N \mid \Gamma, p \in S \text{ and } \Delta, \neg p \in S\} \cup \{\Delta \in S \cap N \mid \{p, \neg p\} \cap \Delta = \emptyset\}$$

where $\Gamma \ominus \phi$ denotes the sequent Γ with all occurrences of ϕ removed (in the multiset sense) and $N = \{\Gamma \in \mathcal{S}(\Lambda) \mid \Gamma \cap \neg \Gamma = \emptyset\}$ is the set of non-axiomatic sequents over Λ. If $\boldsymbol{p} = (p_1, \ldots, p_n)$ is a finite sequence of variables, we write $S_{\boldsymbol{p}} = (\ldots (S_{p_1}) \ldots)_{p_n}$.

In other words, S_p contains all results of multicutting elements of S on p that are not trivially derivable. The next lemma shows that S_p is propositionally equivalent to S.

Lemma 16. *Suppose $S \subseteq \mathcal{S}(\Lambda(V))$ is a finite set of sequents over $\Lambda(V)$ and $p \in V$. Then all $\Delta \in S_p$ are derivable from S in GCutCon with cuts only on p. Moreover, there exists a formula $\phi = \phi(S, p)$ such that $\Gamma[\phi/p]$ is derivable from S_p in G for each $\Gamma \in S$. The formula ϕ can be chosen as a conjunction of disjunctions of sequents in S_p.*

Rules with unnecessary variables in the premises can therefore be normalised by successively eliminating these variables.

Example 17. If S contains the sequents $p = t$ and $q \wedge r = s$, then S_r consists of $p = t$ and $\neg s, q$. We may therefore replace the rule form of the axiom $(\text{CM})(p > (q \wedge r)) \to (p > q)$ on the left

$$\frac{p = t \quad \neg q, \neg r, s \quad \neg s, r \quad \neg s, q}{\Gamma, \neg(p > s), (t > q)} \qquad \mathcal{R}_{\text{CM}} \frac{p = t \quad \neg s, q}{\Gamma, \neg(p > s), (t > q)}$$

with its r-eliminated version (shown on the right).

Lemma 16 allows us to replace shallow rules with their normalised version, and we will assume from now on that all shallow rules are normalised. We now construct a cut-closed set cc $(\mathcal{R})$ from a set $\mathcal{R}$ of shallow rules: we consider two shallow rules together with an application of cut to their conclusions as a rule in its own right, but eliminate all variables that occur in the premises, but not in the conclusion, of (new) rules that arise in this way. This process then takes the following form:

Definition 18. Let $R_1, R_2 \in \mathcal{R}$ be given by $(\Omega_c, \Omega_n, \Gamma)$ and $(\Upsilon_c, \Upsilon_n, \Delta)$, respectively and suppose that σ, τ are renamings such that $\Gamma\sigma = \Gamma', M$ and $\Delta\tau = \Delta', \neg M$. Then cut$(R_1\sigma, R_2\tau, M)$ is the shallow rule given by $((\Upsilon_c \cup \Upsilon_n \cup \Omega_c \cup \Omega_n)_p, (\Upsilon_n \cup \Omega_n)_p, \Gamma', \Delta')$ if $M = \heartsuit p$ for $\boldsymbol{p} = (p_1, \ldots, p_n)$.

This definition ensures that the new (non-) contextual premises arise from the old (non-contextual) premises by removing variables that no longer occur in the conclusion.

Example 19. For the rules $(R_{\text{CC}}) = \frac{p_1 = p_2 = p \quad \neg q_1, \neg q_2, q \quad \neg q, q_1 \quad \neg q, q_2}{\Gamma, \neg(p_1 > q_1), \neg(p_2 > q_2), (p > q)}$ and $(R_{\text{CM}}) = \frac{p = r \quad \neg q, s}{\Gamma, \neg(p > q), (r > s)}$ from $\mathcal{R}_{(CM)}$ we obtain the rule

$$(\text{CC}_\text{m}) = \text{cut}(R_{\text{CC}}, R_{\text{CM}}, (p > q)) = \frac{p_1 = p_2 = r \quad \neg q_1, \neg q_2, s}{\Gamma, \neg(p_1 > q_1), \neg(p_2 > q_2), (r > s)} \,.$$

The *cut closure* of a rule set is then constructed by adding more and more (normalised) cuts until the set is saturated. Formally we have:

Definition 20. Let $\mathcal{R}$ be a set of shallow rules. The *cut closure of $\mathcal{R}$* is the $\subseteq$-minimal set cc $(\mathcal{R})$ with $\mathcal{R} \subseteq$ cc $(\mathcal{R})$, such that for every $R_1, R_2 \in$ cc $(\mathcal{R})$ and renamings σ, τ with Concl $(R_1\sigma) = \Gamma, M$ and Concl $(R_2\tau) = \Delta, \neg M$ we have cut$(R_1\sigma, R_2\tau, M) \in$ cc $(\mathcal{R})$.

Not surprisingly, cut is admissible over the cut closure of a rule set.

Proposition 21. $G\mathcal{R}\mathsf{CutCon} \vdash \Gamma$ *iff* $\mathsf{G}\,cc\,(\mathcal{R})\,\mathsf{Con} \vdash \Gamma$ *for all sequents* Γ.

In general, we may restrict cuts to formulas that arise as $\phi = \phi(p, S)$ in Lemma 16, i.e. conjunctions of disjunctions, which allows the following restriction on the cut rule:

Definition 22. A *pseudo-analytic cut* is a cut $\dfrac{\Gamma, \varphi \quad \Delta, \neg\varphi}{\Gamma, \Delta}$, where $\varphi = \heartsuit(\psi_1, \ldots, \psi_n)$, and for $1 \leq i \leq n$ each ψ_i is a conjunction of disjunctions of formulas occurring possibly negated under a modal operator in Γ, Δ. For a set S of sequence rules define $S\mathsf{Cut}_{\mathsf{pa}}$ to be the set S together with the cut rule restricted to pseudo-analytic cuts.

Corollary 23. $G\mathcal{R}\mathsf{CutCon} \vdash \Gamma$ *iff* $G\mathcal{R}\mathsf{Cut}_{\mathsf{pa}}\mathsf{Con} \vdash \Gamma$ *for all sequents* Γ.

Distributivity allows us to restrict to a single layer of conjunctions and disjunctions.

Lemma 24. *If* $G\mathcal{R}\mathsf{Cut}_{\mathsf{pa}}\mathsf{Con} \vdash \Gamma$ *for a set* $\mathcal{R}$ *of shallow rules and a sequent* Γ, *then* $G\mathcal{R}\mathsf{CutCon} \vdash \Gamma$ *with cuts only on modalised conjunctions of disjunctions of possibly negated subformulas of* Γ.

As pseudo-analytic cuts suffice, for a conclusion of a cut rule there are only finitely many possible cut formulas. In order to get a generic decidability result, we need to assume that the rule set is tractable in the following sense.

Definition 25 (from [13]). A set $\mathcal{R}$ of shallow rules is PSPACE-*tractable*, if there are multivalued functions f taking sequents to sets of encodings of instances of rules in $\mathcal{R}$, and g, taking encodings of rule instances to sets of sequents, such that for all sequents Γ, Δ and encodings $\ulcorner R\sigma \urcorner$ of a rule instance we have $\ulcorner R\sigma \urcorner \in f(\Gamma) \iff$ $\mathsf{Concl}\,(R\sigma) = \Gamma$ and $\Delta \in g(\ulcorner R\sigma \urcorner) \iff \Delta \in \mathsf{Prem}\,(R\sigma)$, and whose graphs are decidable in space polynomial in the length of the first argument.

We assume that sequents are encoded as lists of formulas. Note that the length of the encoding of a sequent is at least the number of formulas in the sequent.

Theorem 26. *Let* $\mathcal{R}$ *be a* PSPACE-*tractable and contraction closed set of shallow rules. Then the derivability problem for* $G\mathcal{R}\mathsf{ConCut}$ *is in* 3EXPTIME.

Example 27. This theorem induces a uniform decidability proof (albeit with a suboptimal complexity bound) for all logics axiomatised by finitely many shallow axioms, e.g. for the conditional logics B, SS and V of Example 2.

5   Cut Elimination Using Small Representations

In the previous section, we have constructed the cut-closure of a given set of shallow rules, and we have argued that a sequent calculus using this set enjoys cut elimination. However, the construction of the cut closure does not yield a concrete representation of a cut-closed rule set. The main result of this section establishes that the rules constituting a cut-closed set can always be represented in space polynomial in the rule conclusion. In particular, we demonstrate that instances of cut-closed rule sets can be decided in PSPACE. This entails that the corresponding derivability problem is decidable in polynomial space. Technically, we show that rules of a cut-closed rule set are represented by proof trees whose inner nodes are applications of cut, and we give explicit bounds on the size of these trees, which yield polynomial representability.

Definition 28. A shallow rule $R_1 = (\Omega_c, \Omega_n, \Sigma)$ *subsumes* a shallow rule $R_2 = (\Xi_c, \Xi_n, \Pi)$, if there is a renaming σ with $\Sigma\sigma = \Pi$ such that $\Xi_c \cup \Xi_n \vdash_{\mathsf{PL}} \Delta\sigma$ for every $\Delta \in \Omega_c$, and $\Xi_n \vdash_{\mathsf{PL}} \Upsilon\sigma$ for every $\Upsilon \in \Omega_n$. Two shallow rules are *equivalent* if they mutually subsume each other.

While the pseudo-analytic cut yields decidability, there is room for improvement in complexity by considering polynomial-size representations of $\mathrm{cc}\,(\mathcal{R})$.

Definition 29. Let $\mathcal{R}$ be a set of shallow rules. An $\mathcal{R}$-*cut tree* with conclusion Γ and leafs $(R_i\sigma)$ (where $1 \leq i \leq n$, $R_i \in \mathcal{R}$ and $\sigma_i : V \to V$ is a renaming) is a proof of Γ from the conclusions of the $(R_i\sigma)$ using only cuts on principal formulas of the $R_i\sigma$. The number of nodes in a cut tree is denoted by $\mathrm{size}\,(\mathcal{D})$, its height by $\mathrm{depth}\,(\mathcal{D})$.

In the above definition, we emphasise that *only* applications of cut are allowed in a cut tree, and the cut formulas have to be principal formulas of the rules at the leafs.

Example 30. The following is a KT-cut-tree for the sequent $u, \neg\Box p, \neg\Box q, \neg\Box r$:

$$
\cfrac{
\cfrac{\neg p, \neg q, s \quad \neg s, p \quad \neg s, q}{\neg\Box p, \neg\Box q, \Box s}\,(\mathcal{R}_{\mathrm{K}})
\qquad
\cfrac{
\cfrac{\neg s, \neg r, t \quad \neg t, s \quad \neg t, r}{\neg\Box s, \neg\Box r, \Box t}\,(\mathcal{R}_{\mathrm{K}})
\qquad
\cfrac{u, \neg t}{u, \neg\Box t}\,(\mathcal{R}_{\mathrm{T}})
}{u, \neg\Box s, \neg\Box r}
}{u, \neg\Box p, \neg\Box q, \neg\Box r}
$$

Clearly, the cuts introduced in a cut tree may introduce new variables that are present in the premises of the $R_i\sigma$, but not in the conclusion Γ. We eliminate these as before.

Definition 31. Let $\mathcal{R}$ be a set of shallow rules, and $\mathcal{D}$ an $\mathcal{R}$-cut-tree. The shallow rule $r(\mathcal{D})$ *represented by* $\mathcal{D}$ is the leaf of $\mathcal{D}$ if $\mathrm{depth}\,(\mathcal{D}) = 0$. If $\mathrm{depth}\,(\mathcal{D}) > 0$, then $\mathcal{D}$ is of the form $\frac{\mathcal{D}_1 \quad \mathcal{D}_2}{\Gamma}$, where Γ arises from the conclusions of $\mathcal{D}_1$ and $\mathcal{D}_2$ by a cut on M. In this case, $r(\mathcal{D}) = \mathrm{cut}(r(\mathcal{D}_1), r(\mathcal{D}_2), M)$ where $r(\mathcal{D}_1)$ and $r(\mathcal{D}_2)$ are the rules represented by $\mathcal{D}_1$ and $\mathcal{D}_2$.

Equivalence of cut trees and cut closure is clear from the definitions:

Lemma 32. *A shallow rule lies in* $\mathrm{cc}\,(\mathcal{R})$ *iff it is represented by an* $\mathcal{R}$-*cut tree.*

Application of Lemma 16 shows that cut trees differing only in the order of the cuts represent basically the same rule instance, a fact that we record here for later use.

Lemma 33. *Let* $\mathcal{R}$ *be a set of shallow rules. Let* Γ *be a sequent and let* $\mathcal{D}_1, \mathcal{D}_2$ *be* $\mathcal{R}$-*cut-trees with conclusion* Γ *and leafs* $R_1\sigma_1, \ldots, R_n\sigma_n$. *Then the rules represented by* $\mathcal{D}_1$ *and* $\mathcal{D}_2$ *are equivalent.*

The main difficulty that we have to overcome in order to obtain small representations of cut-closed rules lies in the fact that the number of literals in either premise of an application of cut may both increase and decrease as we move up a cut tree. This non-monotonic behaviour disappears if we only consider cuts involving sequents consisting of at least three elements. This suffices for our purpose, since we can absorb cuts involving smaller sequents into the rule set at very little extra cost.

Definition 34. A shallow rule is *small* if it has at most two principal formulas. A set $\mathcal{R}$ of shallow rules is *2-cut closed* if for every two rules $R_1, R_2 \in \mathcal{R}$ with conclusions Σ_1 and Σ_2, such that R_1 or R_2 is small, and any two renamings $\sigma_1, \sigma_2 : V \to V$ for which $\Sigma_1\sigma_1 = \Gamma, M$ and $\Sigma_2\sigma_2 = \Delta, \neg M$ there exists a rule $R \in \mathcal{R}$ that subsumes $\text{cut}(R_1\sigma_1, R_2\sigma_2, M)$. The *2-cut closure* $2\text{cc}(\mathcal{R})$ of a set $\mathcal{R}$ of shallow rules is the $\subseteq$-minimal, 2-cut closed set of shallow rules containing $\mathcal{R}$.

Example 35. The rule set CK containing $(\mathcal{R}_{\text{CM}})$, $(\mathcal{R}_{\text{CC}})$ and (CC_{m}) is 2-cut closed, but not cut closed.

Passing from a finite set of shallow rules to its 2-cut closure is a preprocessing step that adds finitely many missing rules. Crucially, computing a 2-cut closure is independent of the size of any sequent to which proof search is applied and therefore adds a constant time overhead. The most important ramification of 2-cut closure is the existence of small representations of elements in the cut closure of a given set of shallow rules. We approach this result by means of a sequence of lemmas, the first one establishing that we may always assume that leafs of a cut tree are labelled with 'large' rules.

Lemma 36. *Let $\mathcal{R}$ be a 2-cut closed set of shallow rules, and let $\mathcal{D}$ be an $\mathcal{R}$-cut-tree with conclusion Γ and leafs $R_1, \sigma_1, \ldots, R_n\sigma_n$. Then there exists an $\mathcal{R}$-cut-tree $\mathcal{D}'$ with conclusion Γ and leafs $R'_1\sigma'_1, \ldots, R'_k, \sigma'_k$ such that*

1. *if $\|\Gamma\| \leq 2$ then $\mathcal{D}'$ has depth 0 (and therefore consists of a single leaf $R'_1\sigma'$ only)*
2. *if $\|\Gamma\| > 2$ then $R'_i\sigma'$ have at least 3 principal formulas each*
3. *size$(\mathcal{D}') \leq$ size$(\mathcal{D})$ and the rules represented by $\mathcal{D}$ and $\mathcal{D}'$ are equivalent.*

Since cuts between sequents of length at least three increase the length of the sequent, the size of the cut-tree is bounded in terms of the conclusion of the represented rules.

Corollary 37. *Let $\mathcal{R}$ be a 2-cut closed set of shallow rules, and let Γ be a sequent with $\|\Gamma\| \geq 3$. Then every rule in $\text{cc}(\mathcal{R})$ with conclusion Γ is represented by an $\mathcal{R}$-cut tree of size $\leq 2\|\Gamma\| - 5$.*

A bound on the depth of a cut tree is obtained from the following adaption of the 2-3-Lemma of [5]. Here for a tree $\mathcal{T}$ and a node x in $\mathcal{T}$ the subtree of $\mathcal{T}$ generated by x is denoted by $\mathcal{T}_x$, and the number of nodes in $\mathcal{T}$ by $|\mathcal{T}|$.

Lemma 38. *Let $k \in \mathbb{N}$ and $\mathcal{T}$ be a tree, such that $k+1 < |\mathcal{T}|$ and each node has at most k children. Then there is a node x in $\mathcal{T}$, such that $\left\lceil \frac{1}{k+2} \cdot |\mathcal{T}| \right\rceil \leq |\mathcal{T}_x| \leq \left\lfloor \frac{k+1}{k+2} \cdot |\mathcal{T}| \right\rfloor$.*

Lemma 39. *Let $\mathcal{R}$ be a 2-cut closed set of shallow rules where the every rule has at most k principal formulas, and let Γ be a sequent with $\|\Gamma\| \geq 3$. Then every instance of a rule in $\text{cc}(\mathcal{R})$ with conclusion Γ can be represented by an $\mathcal{R}$-cut-tree of size at most $2\|\Gamma\| - 5$ and depth at most $c_k \cdot \log_2 \|\Gamma\| + k$ for $c_k = (\log_2 \frac{k+2}{k+1})^{-1}$.*

Crucially, his bound ensures a small size of the cut-tree and the premises of the represented rule. This provides us with a tractable representation of the cut closure of $\mathcal{R}$.

Definition 40. Let $\mathcal{R}$ be a set of shallow rules with at most k principal formulas each. The *rule set generated by* $\mathcal{R}$ is the set $\mathcal{R}^*$ of rules represented by 2cc $(\mathcal{R})$-cut-trees with conclusion Γ and depth at most $c_k \cdot \log_2 \|\Gamma\| + k$.

Theorem 41. *Let $\mathcal{R}$ be a finite set of shallow rules. Then $\mathcal{R}^*$ is* PSPACE-*tractable and cut elimination holds in* G$\mathcal{R}$Con, *i.e.* G$\mathcal{R}$CutCon $\vdash \Gamma$ *iff* G$\mathcal{R}^*$Con $\vdash \Gamma$.

6   Proof Search in G$\mathcal{R}^*$

In the previous section, we have seen that cut can be eliminated by passing from a given rule set to its cut closure. The polynomial representability of the latter does not yet guarantee that proof search can be accomplished in polynomial space, as instances of shallow rules propagate the conclusion to contextual premises. In this section, we introduce histories (in the spirit of [4]) that avoid infinite branches during proof search.

Definition 42. Let $\mathcal{R}$ be a set of shallow rules. An $\mathcal{R}$-*history* is a multiset h with $\text{Supp}(h) \subseteq \{(R, \sigma) \mid R \in \mathcal{R}, \ \sigma : \text{Var}(R) \to \mathcal{F}(\Lambda)\}$ consisting of rule/substitution pairs. A *sequent with history* is a pair (h, Γ), written as $h \mid \Gamma$ where h is a $\mathcal{R}$-history. We write $h, (R, \sigma)$ for the (multiset) union of h and $\{(R, \sigma)\}$.

The notion of $\mathcal{R}$-histories extends to equivalence classes of rules modulo injective renamings in the obvious way. Histories are used to prevent shallow rules from being applied repeatedly to the same formulas in the system $G\mathcal{R}_2$ introduced next. The system $G\mathcal{R}_1$ is an intermediate system, which only keeps track of the rules.

Definition 43. Let $\mathcal{R}$ be a set of shallow rules. The system $G\mathcal{R}_1$ consists of the propositional rules extended with history

$$\frac{}{h \mid \Gamma, p, \neg p} \quad \frac{}{h \mid \Gamma, \neg\bot} \quad \frac{h \mid \Gamma, \neg\phi, \neg\psi}{h \mid \Gamma, \neg(\phi \wedge \psi)} \quad \frac{h \mid \Gamma, \phi \quad h \mid \Gamma, \psi}{h \mid \Gamma, \phi \wedge \psi} \quad \frac{h \mid \Gamma, \phi}{h \mid \Gamma, \neg\neg\phi}$$

and all instances-with-history

$$(R\sigma) \ \frac{h, (R, \sigma) \mid \Gamma, \Gamma_1\sigma, \Sigma\sigma \quad \ldots \quad h, (R, \sigma) \mid \Gamma, \Gamma_n\sigma, \Sigma\sigma \quad \emptyset \mid \Delta_1\sigma \quad \ldots \quad \emptyset \mid \Delta_k\sigma}{h \mid \Gamma, \Sigma\sigma}$$

of shallow rules $R \in \mathcal{R}$ with contextual premises $\Gamma_1, \ldots, \Gamma_n$, non-contextual premises $\Delta_1, \ldots, \Delta_k$ and principal formulas Σ. In $G\mathcal{R}_2$, instances-with-history above are subject to the side condition $(R, \sigma) \notin h$.

Since propositional rules do not interfere with histories, it is easy to see that admissibility of weakening, contraction and inversion carries over to $G\mathcal{R}_1$.

Lemma 44 (Admissibility of Weakening and inversion). *For every $\varphi, \psi \in \mathcal{F}(\Lambda)$, sequent Σ, and $\mathcal{R}$-history h the rule instances*

$$\frac{h \mid \Sigma, \neg\neg\varphi}{h \mid \Sigma, \varphi} \quad \frac{h \mid \Sigma, \neg(\varphi \wedge \psi)}{h \mid \Sigma, \neg\varphi, \neg\psi} \quad \frac{h \mid \Sigma, (\varphi \wedge \psi)}{h \mid \Sigma, \varphi} \quad \frac{h \mid \Sigma, (\varphi \wedge \psi)}{h \mid \Sigma, \psi} \quad \frac{h \mid \Gamma}{h, (R, \sigma) \mid \Gamma, \Delta}$$

are depth-preserving admissible in $G\mathcal{R}_1$. Moreover, the number of instances of shallow rules in the proof is preserved.

Lemma 45 (Admissibility of Contraction). *Let $\mathcal{R}$ be a contraction closed set of shallow rules. Then all instances of*

$$\frac{h,(R,\sigma)\mid \Gamma}{h\mid \Gamma} \qquad \frac{h\mid \Gamma,\phi,\phi}{h\mid \Gamma,\phi}$$

are admissible in $G\mathcal{R}_1$ preserving the number of shallow rules in a proof.

This gives the equivalence of $G\mathcal{R}\mathrm{Con}$ and $G\mathcal{R}_1$.

Lemma 46. *Let $\mathcal{R}$ be a set of shallow rules and Γ a sequent.*

1. $G\mathcal{R}_1 \vdash \emptyset \mid \Gamma$ *iff there is a history h such that $G\mathcal{R}_1 \vdash h \mid \Gamma$.*
2. *if $\mathcal{R}$ is contraction closed, then $G\mathcal{R}\mathrm{Con} \vdash \Gamma$ iff $G\mathcal{R}_1 \vdash \emptyset \mid \Gamma$.*

In fact, subsequent applications of a shallow rule to the same formulas in a branch of a proof in $G\mathcal{R}_1$ can be eliminated. This gives us equivalence with $G\mathcal{R}_2$.

Lemma 47. *Let $\mathcal{R}$ be a set of shallow rules and Γ a sequent. If $G\mathcal{R}_1 \vdash h \mid \Gamma$, then $G\mathcal{R}_2 \vdash h \mid \Gamma$. Moreover, there exists a proof of $h \mid \Gamma$ in $G\mathcal{R}_2$ where every contextual premise of an application of a shallow rule contains a formula not in the conclusion.*

The fact that contextual premises of applications of shallow rules are bigger than the conclusion ensures that the search space in backwards proof search for $G\mathcal{R}_2$ is of depth polynomial in the number of subformulas of the root sequent. Summing up we get:

Theorem 48. *Let $\mathcal{R}$ be a contraction closed set of shallow rules.*

1. *For every sequent Γ we have $G\mathcal{R}\mathrm{Con} \vdash \Gamma$ iff $G\mathcal{R}_2 \vdash \emptyset \mid \Gamma$.*
2. *For PSPACE-tractable $\mathcal{R}$, derivability in $G\mathcal{R}_2$ is in PSPACE.*

Together with the results of the previous section this gives the following main theorem:

Theorem 49. *Let $\mathcal{A}$ be a finite set of shallow axioms and $\mathcal{R}$ be a 2-cut-closed rule form of $\mathcal{A}$. If $\mathcal{R}^*$ is contraction closed, then derivability in $\mathcal{H}\mathcal{A}$ is in PSPACE.*

Clearly the requirement of $\mathcal{R}^*$ being contraction closed presents a gaping hole in our treatment so far. However, we can establish this property for several examples.

7   Applications: Exemplary Complexity Bounds

Using the machinery of the previous sections, proving PSPACE-bounds for shallow logics boils down to proving admissibility of contraction in the rule set generated by the rules corresponding to the axioms. In Example 35 we have seen that the set

$$CK = \left\{ \begin{array}{cc} \dfrac{p_1 = p_2 = p \quad q_1 \wedge q_2 = q}{\Gamma, \neg(p_1 > q_1), \neg(p_2 > q_2), (p > q)}, & \dfrac{p = r \quad \neg q, s}{\Gamma, \neg(p > q), (r > s)}, \\[2ex] \multicolumn{2}{c}{\dfrac{p_1 = p_2 = p \quad \neg q_1, \neg q_2, q}{\Gamma, \neg(p_1 > q_1), \neg(p_2 > q_2), (p > q)}} \end{array} \right\}$$

is 2-cut closed. It is clear that it is also contraction closed. This also holds for CK^*:

Lemma 50. *The set CK^* is contraction closed.*

As another example consider the axiom $CEM = (p > q) \vee (p > \neg q)$ of conditional excluded middle. Turning this into a rule yields

$$(CEM) \frac{p_1 = p_2 \quad \neg q_1, \neg q_2 \quad q_1, q_2}{\Gamma, (p_1 > q_1), (p_2 > q_2)} .$$

Let $CKCEM := 2\mathrm{cc}\,(CK \cup \{CEM\})$. A little computation shows

Lemma 51. *The set $CKCEM^*$ is closed under contraction.*

In order to add more axioms to CK and $CKCEM$ we need to reconcile the definitions of cut and contraction closed rule sets. This can be done by restricting the rule format.

Definition 52. A shallow rule has *complete premises*, if every variable occurring in a principal formula occurs in every premise.

By soundness of the rules of PL and reasoning about propositional valuations it can be seen that for these rules the two definitions are compatible:

Lemma 53. *Let A be a finite set of variables, and let $\Gamma_1, \ldots, \Gamma_n, \Gamma$ be sequents over $A \cup \neg A$ with every variable occurring in every sequent. Then $\{\Gamma_1, \ldots, \Gamma_n\} \vdash_{\mathsf{PL}} \Gamma$ iff $\{\Gamma_1, \ldots, \Gamma_n\} \vdash_{\mathsf{GWCon}} \Gamma$.*

This allows us to add rules with at most one principal formula to a rule set without destroying contraction closure.

Theorem 54. *Let $\mathcal{R}$ be a finite set of shallow rules with complete premises, and let R be a shallow rule with complete premises and one principal formula. If $\mathcal{R}^*$ is contraction closed, then there is a PSPACE-tractable set $\mathcal{Q}$ of shallow rules, such that for every sequent Γ we have $\mathsf{G}(\mathcal{R} \cup \{R\})\mathsf{CutCon} \vdash \Gamma$ iff $\mathsf{G}\mathcal{Q} \vdash \Gamma$.*

As a special case, this means that we may add shallow rules with one literal in the conclusion to the sets CK and $CKCEM$, and still retain the PSPACE bound.

Theorem 55. *Let $\mathcal{A} \subseteq \{\mathrm{CEM}, \mathrm{ID}, \mathrm{MP}, \mathrm{CS}\}$. Then the logic $CK + \mathcal{A}$ is in PSPACE.*

This reproves the PSPACE upper bounds for these logics found in [9], [8], and [11].

8   Conclusion

In this paper we have reported our first successes in synthetically constructing sequent calculi that admit cut elimination. We have converted shallow modal axioms into sequent rules so that the resulting system together with the cut and contraction rules is sound and complete with respect to the Hilbert-system. It was also shown to stay complete, if the cuts are restricted to pseudo-analytic cuts. This led to a generic decidability result and a 3EXPTIME upper bound for logics axiomatised by a PSPACE-tractable set of shallow axioms. Since in particular all finite sets of axioms are PSPACE-tractable, logics axiomatised by a finite set of shallow axioms are decidable in 3EXPTIME. The method then was extended to generically construct PSPACE-tractable sets of rules from finite sets of shallow axioms in such a way, that the resulting sequent system eliminates the cut rule. If the so constructed rule set is closed under the contraction rule, then the logic axiomatised by the corresponding axioms is decidable in polynomial space.

Our success is clearly partial in that we do not yet know under which conditions closure under contraction can also be obtained. This is the subject of future work, possibly borrowing from the theory of vector addition systems [3] to control the multiplicities of formulas. For now, contraction closure needs to be established by hand, and doing so, we have applied our method to various systems in conditional logics. This led to new proofs of PSPACE upper bounds for these systems.

References

1. Avron, A., Lev, I.: Canonical propositional gentzen-type systems. In: Goré, R.P., Leitsch, A., Nipkow, T. (eds.) IJCAR 2001. LNCS, vol. 2083, pp. 529–544. Springer, Heidelberg (2001)
2. Ciabattoni, A., Leitsch, A.: Towards an algorithmic construction of cut-elimination procedures. Math. Struct. in Comp. Sci. 18(1), 81–105 (2008)
3. Esparza, J., Nielsen, M.: Decidability issues for petri nets - a survey. Bulletin of the EATCS 52, 244–262 (1994)
4. Heuerding, A., Seyfried, M., Zimmermann, H.: Efficient loop-check for backward proof search in some non-classical propositional logics. In: Miglioli, P., Moscato, U., Ornaghi, M., Mundici, D. (eds.) TABLEAUX 1996. LNCS, vol. 1071, pp. 210–225. Springer, Heidelberg (1996)
5. Lewis II, P.M., Stearns, R.E., Hartmanis, J.: Memory bounds for recognition of context-free and context-sensitive languages. In: FOCS, pp. 191–202 (1965)
6. Kurucz, Á., Németi, I., Sain, I., Simon, A.: Decidable and undecidable logics with a binary modality. J. of Log., Lang. and Inf. 4(3), 191–206 (1995)
7. Nute, D., Cross, C.B.: Conditional logic. In: Gabbay, D.M., Guenthner, F. (eds.) Handbook of Philosophical Logic, vol. 4, pp. 1–98. Kluwer, Dordrecht (2001)
8. Olivetti, N., Pozzato, G.L., Schwind, C.B.: A sequent calculus and a theorem prover for standard conditional logics. ACM Trans. Comput. Logic 8(4), 22/1–22/51 (2007)
9. Olivetti, N., Schwind, C.B.: A calculus and complexity bound for minimal conditional logic. In: ICTCS, pp. 384–404 (2001)
10. Pattinson, D., Schröder, L.: Beyond rank 1: Algebraic semantics and finite models for coalgebraic logics. In: Amadio, R. (ed.) FOSSACS 2008. LNCS, vol. 4962, pp. 66–80. Springer, Heidelberg (2008)
11. Pattinson, D., Schröder, L.: Generic modal cut elimination applied to conditional logics. In: Giese, M., Waaler, A. (eds.) TABLEAUX 2009. LNCS, vol. 5607, pp. 280–294. Springer, Heidelberg (2009)
12. Rasga, J.: Sufficient conditions for cut elimination with complexity analysis. Ann. Pure Appl.Logic 149, 81–99 (2007)
13. Schröder, L., Pattinson, D.: PSPACE bounds for rank-1 modal logics. ACM Trans. Comput. Logic (TOCL) 10(2), 13:1–13:33 (2009)
14. Troelstra, A.S., Schwichtenberg, H.: Basic Proof Theory, 2nd edn. Cambridge Tracts In Theoretical Computer Science, vol. 43. Cambridge University Press, Cambridge (2000)

A Non-clausal Connection Calculus

Jens Otten

Institut für Informatik, University of Potsdam
August-Bebel-Str. 89, 14482 Potsdam-Babelsberg, Germany
jeotten@cs.uni-potsdam.de

Abstract. A non-clausal connection calculus for classical first-order logic is presented that does not require the translation of input formulae into any clausal form. The definition of clauses is generalized, which may now also contain (sub-) matrices. Copying of appropriate (sub-)clauses in a dynamic way, i.e. during the actual proof search, is realized by a generalized extension rule. Thus, the calculus combines the advantage of a non-clausal proof search in tableau calculi with the more efficient goal-oriented proof search of clausal connection calculi. Soundness, completeness, and (relative) complexity results are presented as well as some optimization techniques.

1 Introduction

Connection calculi are a well-known basis to automate formal reasoning in classical first-order logic. Among these calculi are the connection method [3,4], the connection tableau calculus [9] and the model elimination calculus [10]. The main idea of connection calculi is to connect two atomic formulae P and $\neg P$ with the same predicate symbol but different polarity. The set $\{P, \neg P\}$ is called a *connection* and corresponds to a closed branch in the tableau framework [6] or an axiom in the sequent calculus [5]. As the proof search is guided by connections it is more goal-oriented compared to the proof search in sequent calculi or (standard) analytic tableau calculi.

The *clausal* connection calculus works for first-order formulae in disjunctive normal form or *clausal form*. Formulae that are not in this form have to be translated into clausal form. The standard transformation translates a first-order formula F into clausal form by applying the distributivity laws. In the worst case the size of the resulting formula grows exponentially with respect to the size of the original formula F. This increases the search space significantly when searching for a proof of F in the connection calculus.

A *structure-preserving* translation into clausal form, e.g. [14], introduces definitions for subformulae. Tests show that even such an optimized translation introduces a significant overhead for the proof search [12] as additional formulae are introduced. Both clausal form translations modify the structure of the original formula, making it more difficult to translate a found proof back into a more human-oriented form, e.g. [5]. For some logics, e.g. intuitionistic logic, these translations do *not* preserve logical validity.

A *non-clausal* connection calculus that works directly on the structure of the original formula does not have these disadvantages. There already exist a few descriptions of non-clausal connection calculi [1,4,7,8]. But the cores of these calculi do not add any copies of quantified subformulae to the original formulae, i.e. they are only complete for ground formulae. To deal with first-order logic, e.g., copies of subformulae need

K. Brünnler and G. Metcalfe (Eds.): TABLEAUX 2011, LNAI 6793, pp. 226–241, 2011.

to be added iteratively [8]. But this introduces a large amount of redundancy as copies of subformulae that are not required for a proof are still used during the proof search. Implementations of this approach, e.g. [16], show a rather modest performance. For a more effective non-clausal proof search, clauses have to be added carefully and dynamically during the proof search, in a way similar to the approach used for copying clauses in clausal connection calculi. To this end, the existing clausal connection calculus has to be generalized and its rules have to be carefully extended.

The rest of the paper is structured as follows. In Section 2 the standard clausal connection calculus is presented. Section 3 introduces the main ideas of a non-clausal proof search before the actual non-clausal calculus is described in Section 4. Section 5 contains correctness, completeness and complexity results. Some optimizations and extensions are presented in Section 6, before Section 7 concludes with a short summary.

2   The Clausal Connection Calculus

The reader is assumed to be familiar with the language of classical first-order logic, see, e.g., [4]. In this paper the letters P, Q, R are used to denote predicate symbols, f to denote function symbols, a, b, c to denote constants and x to denote variables. Terms are denoted by t and are built from functions, constants and variables. *Atomic formulae*, denoted by A, are built from predicate symbols and terms. The connectives $\neg, \wedge, \vee, \Rightarrow$ denote negation, conjunction, disjunction and implication, respectively. A *(first-order) formula*, denoted by F, G, H, consists of atomic formulae, the connectives and the existential and universal quantifiers, denoted by $\forall$ and $\exists$, respectively. A *literal*, denoted by L, has the form A or $\neg A$. The complement $\overline{L}$ of a literal L is A if L is of the form $\neg A$, and $\neg A$ otherwise. A *clause*, denoted by C, is of the form $L_1 \wedge \ldots \wedge L_n$ where L_i is a literal. A formula in *disjunctive normal form* or *clausal form* has the form $\exists x_1 \ldots \exists x_n (C_1 \vee \ldots \vee C_n)$ where each C_i is a clause. For classical logic every formula F can be translated into a validity-preserving formula F' in clausal form. A clause can be written as a set of literals $\{L_1, \ldots, L_n\}$. A formula in clausal form can be written as a set of clauses $\{C_1, \ldots, C_n\}$ and is called a *matrix*, denoted by M. In the graphical representation of a matrix, its clauses are arranged horizontally, while the literals of each clause are arranged vertically. A *polarity* is used to represent negation in a matrix, i.e. literals of the form A and $\neg A$ are represented by A^0 and A^1, respectively.

Example 1 (Matrix in Clausal Form). Let F_1 be the formula
$(\forall x((\neg P(x) \vee Q(f(x))) \Rightarrow (Q(x) \wedge (Q(a) \Rightarrow R(b)) \wedge \neg R(x))) \wedge Q(f(b))) \Rightarrow P(a)$.

The matrix M_1 of the formula F_1 is

$$\{ \{P^0(a)\}, \{P^1(x), Q^1(x)\}, \{P^1(x), Q^0(a), R^1(b)\}, \{P^1(x), R^0(x)\},$$
$$\{Q^0(f(x)), Q^1(x)\}, \{Q^0(f(x)), Q^0(a), R^1(b)\}, \{Q^0(f(x)), R^0(x)\}, \{Q^1(f(b))\} \} .$$

The graphical representation of M_1 (with some variables renamed) is shown in Figure 1.

A *connection* is a set of the form $\{A^0, A^1\}$. A *path* through $M = \{C_1, \ldots, C_n\}$ is a set of literals that contains one literal from each clause $C_i \in M$, i.e. $\cup_{i=1}^n \{L_i'\}$ with $L_i' \in C_i$. A *term substitution* σ is a mapping from the set of variables to the set of terms.

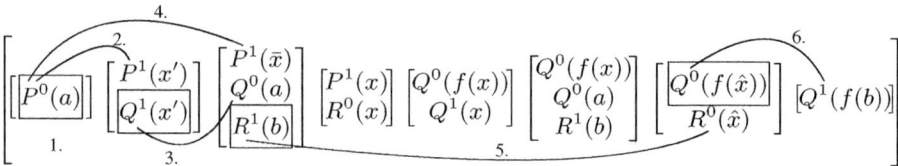

Fig. 1. Proof search in the connection calculus using the graphical matrix representation

In $\sigma(L)$ all variables of the literal L are substituted according to their mapping in σ. $A[x\backslash t]$ denotes the formula in which all free occurrences of x in A are replaced by t.

Example 2 (Connection, Path, Term Substitution). Consider the matrix M_1 of Example 1. $\{P^0(a), P^1(x)\}$ and $\{R^0(x), R^1(b)\}$ are connections, $\{P^0(a), P^1(x), Q^0(f(x)), R^0(x), Q^1(f(b))\}$ is a path through M_1, and $\sigma(x) = a$ is a term substitution.

The matrix characterization [4] of validity is the underlying basis of the connection calculus and used for the proof in Section 5.1. The notion of *multiplicity* is used to encode the number of clause copies used in a connection proof. It is a function $\mu : \mathcal{C} \to \mathbb{N}$, where $\mathcal{C}$ is the set of clauses in M, that assigns each clause in M a natural number specifying how many copies of this clause are considered in a proof. In the *copy of a clause* C all variables in C are replaced by new variables. M^μ is the matrix that includes these clause copies. A connection $\{L_1, L_2\}$ with $\sigma(L_1) = \sigma(\overline{L_2})$ is called σ-*complementary*.

Theorem 1 (Matrix Characterization). *A matrix M is classically valid iff there exist a multiplicity μ, a term substitution σ and a set of connections $\mathcal{S}$, such that every path through M^μ contains a σ-complementary connection $\{L_1, L_2\} \in \mathcal{S}$.*

See [4] for a proof of Theorem 1. The connection calculus uses a *connection-driven* search strategy in order to calculate an appropriate set of connections $\mathcal{S}$. Proof search in the connection calculus starts by selecting a start clause. Afterwards connections are successively identified in order to make sure that all paths through the matrix contain a σ-complementary connection for some term substitution σ. This process is guided by an *active path*, a subset of a path through M.

Example 3 (Proof Search in the Clausal Connection Calculus). Consider the matrix M_1 of Example 1. The six steps required for a proof in the connection calculus for M_1, using the graphical matrix representation, are depicted in Figure 1. The literals of each connection are connected with a line. The literals of the active path are boxed. In the *start* step the first clause $\{P^0(a)\}$ is selected as start clause (step 1). While the *extension* step connects to a literal in a copy of a clause (steps 2, 3, 5 and 6), the *reduction* step connects to a literal of the active path (step 4). x', $\bar{x}$ and $\hat{x}$ are fresh variables. With the term substitution $\sigma(x') = a$, $\sigma(\bar{x}) = a$ and $\sigma(\hat{x}) = b$ all paths through the matrix M_1 contain a σ-complementary connection from the set $\{\{P^0(a), P^1(x')\}, \{Q^1(x'), Q^0(a)\}, \{P^1(\bar{x}), P^0(a)\}, \{R^1(b), R^0(\hat{x})\}, \{Q^0(f(\hat{x})), Q^1(f(b))\}\}$. Therefore, M_1 and F_1 are valid.

The proof search is now specified more precisely by a formal calculus [4,12,13].

Axiom (A)	$\dfrac{}{\{\}, M, Path}$
Start (S)	$\dfrac{C_2, M, \{\}}{\varepsilon, M, \varepsilon}$ and C_2 is copy of $C_1 \in M$
Reduction (R)	$\dfrac{C, M, Path \cup \{L_2\}}{C \cup \{L_1\}, M, Path \cup \{L_2\}}$ with $\sigma(L_1) = \sigma(\overline{L_2})$
Extension (E)	$\dfrac{C_2 \setminus \{L_2\}, M, Path \cup \{L_1\} \quad C, M, Path}{C \cup \{L_1\}, M, Path}$ and C_2 is a copy of $C_1 \in M$ and $L_2 \in C_2$ with $\sigma(L_1) = \sigma(\overline{L_2})$

Fig. 2. The clausal connection calculus

Definition 1 (Clausal Connection Calculus). *The axiom and the rules of the* clausal connection calculus *are given in Figure 2. The words of the calculus are tuples of the form "$C, M, Path$", where M is a matrix, C and $Path$ are sets of literals or ε. C is called the* subgoal clause *and $Path$ is called the* active path. *C_1 and C_2 are clauses, σ is a term substitution, and $\{L_1, L_2\}$ is a σ-complementary connection. The substitution σ is global (or rigid), i.e. it is applied to the whole derivation.*

An application of the start, reduction or extension rule is called a *start, reduction,* or *extension step*, respectively. A derivation for $C, M, Path$ with the term substitution σ, in which all leaves are axioms, is called a *clausal connection proof* for $C, M, Path$. A *clausal connection proof* for the matrix M is a clausal connection proof for $\varepsilon, M, \varepsilon$.

Theorem 2 (Correctness and Completeness). *A matrix M is valid in classical logic iff there is a clausal connection proof for M.*

The proof is based on the matrix characterization and can be found in [4]. Proof search in the clausal connection calculus is carried out by applying the rules of the calculus in an analytic way, i.e. from bottom to top. During the proof search backtracking might be required, i.e. alternative rules need to be considered if the chosen rule does not lead to a proof. Alternative applications of rules occur whenever more than one rule or more than one instance of a rule can be applied, e.g. when choosing the clause C_1 in the start and extension rule or the literal L_2 in the reduction and extension rule. No backtracking is required when choosing the literal L_1 in the reduction or extension rule as all literals in C are considered in subsequent proof steps anyway. The term substitution σ is calculated, step by step, by one of the well-known algorithms for term unification, e.g. [15], whenever a reduction or extension rule is applied.

Example 4 (Clausal Connection Calculus). Consider the matrix M_1 of Example 1. A derivation for M_1 in the clausal connection calculus with $\sigma(x') = a$, $\sigma(\bar{x}) = a$ and $\sigma(\hat{x}) = b$ is given in Figure 3 (some parentheses are omitted). Since all leaves are axioms it represents a clausal connection proof and therefore M_1 and F_1 are valid.

3 Non-clausal Proof Search

In this section the definitions of matrices and paths are generalized and the main ideas of the non-clausal connection calculus are illustrated with an introductory example.

$$\cfrac{\cfrac{\overline{\{\}, M_1, \{P^0a, Q^1x', R^1b, Q^0f\hat{x}\}}\ A \quad \overline{\{\}, M_1, \{P^0a, Q^1x', R^1b\}}\ A}{\{Q^0f\hat{x}\}, M_1, \{P^0a, Q^1x', R^1b\}}\ E}{\cfrac{\cfrac{\{R^1b\}, M_1, \{P^0a, Q^1x'\}}{\{P^1\bar{x}, R^1b\}, M_1, \{P^0a, Q^1x'\}}\ R \quad \overline{\{\}, M_1, \{P^0a\}}\ A}{\cfrac{\{Q^1x'\}, M_1, \{P^0a\}}{\cfrac{\{P^0a\}, M_1, \{\}}{\varepsilon, M_1, \varepsilon}\ S}\ E}}$$

$$\cfrac{\overline{\{\}, M_1, \{P^0a, Q^1x'\}}\ A}{}\ E$$

$$\cfrac{\overline{\{\}, M_1, \{\}}\ A}{}\ E$$

Fig. 3. A proof in the clausal connection calculus

Table 1. Matrix of a formula F^p

type	F^p	$M(F^p)$	type	F^p	$M(F^p)$
atomic	A^0	$\{\{A^0\}\}$	β	$(G \wedge H)^0$	$\{\{M(G^0), M(H^0)\}\}$
	A^1	$\{\{A^1\}\}$		$(G \vee H)^1$	$\{\{M(G^1), M(H^1)\}\}$
α	$(\neg G)^0$	$M(G^1)$		$(G \Rightarrow H)^1$	$\{\{M(G^0), M(H^1)\}\}$
	$(\neg G)^1$	$M(G^0)$	γ	$(\forall x G)^1$	$M(G[x \backslash x^*]^1)$
	$(G \wedge H)^1$	$\{\{M(G^1)\}, \{M(H^1)\}\}$		$(\exists x G)^0$	$M(G[x \backslash x^*]^0)$
	$(G \vee H)^0$	$\{\{M(G^0)\}, \{M(H^0)\}\}$	δ	$(\forall x G)^0$	$M(G[x \backslash t^*]^0)$
	$(G \Rightarrow H)^0$	$\{\{M(G^1)\}, \{M(H^0)\}\}$		$(\exists x G)^1$	$M(G[x \backslash t^*]^1)$

3.1 Non-clausal Matrices

First of all, the definition of matrices is generalized to arbitrary first-order formulae.

Definition 2 (Matrix). *A (non-clausal) matrix is a set of clauses, in which a* clause *is a set of literals and matrices. Let F be a formula and p be a polarity. The* matrix *of F^p, denoted by $M(F^p)$, is defined inductively according to Table 1. The* matrix *of F is the matrix $M(F^0)$. x^* is a new variable, t^* is the Skolem term $f^*(x_1, \ldots, x_n)$ in which f^* is a new function symbol and $x_1, \ldots, x_n$ are the free variables in $\forall x G$ or $\exists x G$.*

In the *graphical representation* of a matrix, its clauses are arranged horizontally, while the literals and (sub-)matrices of each clause are arranged vertically. A matrix M can be simplified by replacing matrices and clauses of the form $\{\{X_1, ..., X_n\}\}$ within M by $X_1, ..., X_n$. Whereas the definition of paths needs to be generalized to non-clausal matrices, all other concepts used for clausal matrices, e.g. the definitions of connections and term substitutions and the matrix characterization, remain unchanged.

Definition 3 (Path). *A path through a matrix M (or a clause C) is inductively defined as follows. The (only) path through a literal L is $\{L\}$. If $p_1, \ldots, p_n$ are paths through the clauses $C_1, \ldots, C_n$, respectively, then $p_1 \cup \ldots \cup p_n$ is a path through the matrix $M = \{C_1, \ldots, C_n\}$. If $p_1, \ldots, p_n$ are paths through the matrices/literals $M_1, \ldots, M_n$, respectively, then $p_1, \ldots, p_n$ are also paths through the clause $C = \{M_1, \ldots, M_n\}$.*

Example 5 (Matrix, Path). Consider the formula F_1 of Example 1. The simplified (non-clausal) matrix M_1^* of F_1 is $\{\{P^0(a)\}, \{\{\{P^1(x)\}, \{Q^0(f(x))\}\}, \{\{Q^1(x)\}, \{Q^0(a),$

$$\left[\begin{array}{c}\left[P^0(a)\right]\end{array}\left[\begin{array}{c}[\ [P^1(x)]\ [Q^0(f(x))]\ ]\\ [Q^1(x)]\begin{bmatrix}Q^0(a)\\R^1(b)\end{bmatrix}[R^0(x)]\end{array}\right]\left[Q^1(f(b))\right]\right]$$

Fig. 4. Graphical representation of M_1^*

$R^1(b)\}, \{R^0(x)\}\}\}, \{Q^1(f(b))\}\}$. Its graphical representation is shown in Figure 4. $\{P^0(a), Q^1(x), Q^0(a), R^0(x), Q^1(f(b))\}$ is one of the three paths through M_1^*.

3.2 An Introductory Example

In order to carry out proof search for non-clausal matrices the rules of the clausal connection calculus need to be adapted. The following example illustrates the main ideas.

Example 6 (Proof Search Using Non-clausal Matrices). Consider the first-order formula F_1 of Example 1 and its graphical matrix representation in Figure 4. The non-clausal connection proof is depicted in Figure 5. Again, the proof search is guided by an active path, whose literals are boxed. Literals of connections are connected with a line. In the first step the start clause $\{P^0(a)\}$ is selected. The second proof step is an extension step and connects $P^0(a)$ with $P^1(x')$ applying the substitution $\sigma(x') = a$. Variables of the clause used for the extension step are always renamed. Next, all remaining paths through the second matrix of the second clause have to be investigated. To this end, the next extension step connects $Q^1(x')$ with $Q^0(a)$ of the clause $\{Q^0(a), R^1(b)\}$. Now, all paths containing the literals $P^0(a)$, $Q^1(x')$, and $R^1(b)$ still need to be investigated. The fourth proof step connects $R^1(b)$ with $R^0(\hat{x})$ contained in a copy of the second clause, as a connection to $R^0(x')$ with $\sigma(x') = a$ is not possible. The clauses in the copied clause occurring next to $R^0(\hat{x})$, i.e. $\{Q^1(\hat{x})\}$ and $\{Q^0(a), R^1(b)\}$, are deleted, as all paths through these two clauses contain the σ-complementary connection $\{R^1(b), R^0(\hat{x})\}$ with $\sigma(\hat{x}) = b$ as well. The fifth and last (extension) step connects $Q^0(f(\hat{x}))$ with $Q^1(f(b))$. This concludes the proof and every path through the shown matrix contains a σ-complementary connection. Hence, F_1 is valid. The proof uses only four connections compared to five connections required in the clausal connection proof.

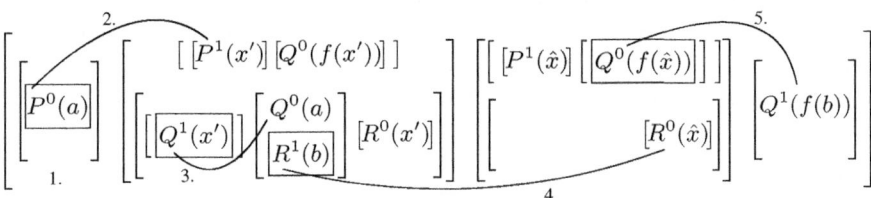

Fig. 5. Proof search in the *non-clausal* connection calculus using the graphical representation

The study of the previous example suggests the following. The axiom as well as the start and reduction rules are the same for the clausal and the non-clausal calculus. The extension rule connects a literal L_1 of the subgoal clause to a literal L_2 occurring in a copy C_2 of an *extension clause* C_1. $\{L_1, L_2\}$ need to be σ-complementary for some σ and L_1 is added to the active path. Either C_1 contains a literal of the active path (fourth step in Example 6); or there is a path that contains the active path and L_2, and if C_1 has a *parent clause*, it contains a literal of the active path (third step). All literals of the new subgoal clause of C_2 that occur besides L_2, i.e. in a common path with L_2, are deleted from the new subgoal clause (fourth step). Finally, if a subgoal clause contains a matrix M, the proof search continues with a clause $C \in M$ (third step). Alternative clauses $C' \in M$ have to be considered on backtracking.

4   The Non-clausal Connection Calculus

This section introduces basic concepts and the formal non-clausal connection calculus.

4.1   Basic Concepts

The term α-related is used to express the fact that a clause occurs besides a literal in a matrix. Furthermore, the definitions of free variables and clause copies have to be generalized to cover non-clausal matrices.

Definition 4 (α-Related Clause). *Let C be a clause in a matrix M and L be a literal in M. C is α-related to L, iff M contains (or is equal to) a matrix $\{C_1, \ldots, C_n\}$ such that $C = C_i$ or C_i contains C, and C_j contains L for some $1 \le i, j \le n$ with $i \ne j$. C is α-related to a set of literals $\mathcal{L}$, iff C is α-related to all literals $L \in \mathcal{L}$.*

Definition 5 (Free Variables). *Let M be a matrix and C be a clause in M. The* free variables *of C are all variables that do only occur in C and (possibly) in literals L such that C is α-related to L.*

In the non-clausal calculus copies of clauses could be simply added to the matrix. As this would widen the search space, clauses are replaced by their copies instead.

Definition 6 (Copy of Clause). *Let M be a matrix and C be a clause in M. In the* copy *of the clause C, all free variables in C are replaced by new variables. $M[C_1 \backslash C_2]$ denotes the matrix M, in which the clause C_1 is replaced by the clause C_2.*

As explained in Section 3.2 an appropriate clause C_1 has to be used when the extension rule is applied. Either C_1 has to contain an element of the active path, then it was already used before, or C_1 needs to be α-related to all literals of the active path and it has to contain all subgoals that still need to be investigated. This is the case if C_1 has no parent clause or its parent clause contains a literal of the active path. The parent clause of a clause C is the smallest clause that contains C.

Definition 7 (Parent Clause). *Let M be a matrix and C be a clause in M. The clause $C' = \{M_1, \ldots, M_n\}$ in M is called the* parent clause *of C iff $C \in M_i$ for some $1 \le i \le n$.*

Definition 8 (Extension Clause). *Let M be a matrix and $Path$ be a set of literals. Then the clause C in M is an* extension clause *of M with respect to $Path$, iff either C contains a literal of $Path$, or C is α-related to all literals of $Path$ occurring in M and if C has a parent clause, it contains a literal of $Path$.*

In the extension rule of the clausal connection calculus (see Section 2) the new subgoal clause is $C_2 \setminus \{L_2\}$. In the non-clausal connection calculus the extension clause C_2 might contain clauses that are α-related to L_2 and do not need to be considered for the new subgoal clause. Hence, these clauses can be deleted from the subgoal clause. The resulting clause is called the β-clause of C_2 with respect to L_2.

Definition 9 (β-Clause). *Let $C = \{M_1, \ldots, M_n\}$ be a clause and L be a literal in C. The β-clause of C with respect to L, denoted by β-clause$_L(C)$, is inductively defined:*

$$\beta\text{-clause}_L(C) := \begin{cases} C \setminus \{L\} & \text{if } L \in C, \\ \{M_1, \ldots, M_{i-1}, \{C^\beta\}, M_{i+1}, \ldots, M_n\} & \text{otherwise,} \end{cases}$$

where $C' \in M_i$ contains L and $C^\beta := \beta$-clause$_L(C')$.

4.2   The Calculus

The non-clausal connection calculus has the same axiom, start rule, and reduction rule as the clausal connection calculus. The extension rule is slightly modified and a decomposition rule is added that splits subgoal clauses into their subclauses.

Definition 10 (Non-Clausal Connection Calculus). *The axiom and the rules of the non-clausal connection calculus are given in Figure 6. The words of the calculus are tuples "$C, M, Path$", where M is a matrix, C is a clause or ε and $Path$ is a set of literals or ε. C is a called the* subgoal clause. *C_1, C_2, and C_3 are clauses, σ is a term substitution, and $\{L_1, L_2\}$ is a σ-complementary connection. The substitution σ is rigid, i.e. it is applied to the whole derivation.*

An application of the start, reduction, extension or decomposition rule is called *start, reduction, extension,* or *decomposition step,* respectively. Observe that the non-clausal calculus reduces to the clausal calculus for matrices that are in clausal form.

Definition 11 (Non-Clausal Connection Proof). *Let M be a matrix, C be a clause, and $Path$ be a set of literals. A derivation for $C, M, Path$ with the term substitution σ in the non-clausal connection calculus, in which all leaves are axioms, is called a* (non-clausal) connection proof *for $C, M, Path$. A (non-clausal) connection proof for M is a non-clausal connection proof for $\varepsilon, M, \varepsilon$.*

Proof search in the non-clausal connection calculus is carried out in the same way as in the clausal connection calculus (see Section 2), i.e. the rules of the calculus are applied in an analytic way. Additional backtracking might be required when choosing the clause C_1 in the decomposition rule. No backtracking is required when choosing the matrix M_1 in the decomposition rule as all matrices (and literals) in C are considered in subsequent proof steps anyway. The term substitution σ is calculated by one of the well-known algorithms for term unification, e.g. [15].

$$\textit{Axiom (A)} \qquad \frac{}{\{\},M,Path}$$

$$\textit{Start (S)} \qquad \frac{C_2,M,\{\}}{\varepsilon,\ M,\ \varepsilon} \quad \text{and } C_2 \text{ is copy of } C_1{\in}M$$

$$\textit{Reduction (R)} \qquad \frac{C,M,Path{\cup}\{L_2\}}{C{\cup}\{L_1\},M,Path{\cup}\{L_2\}} \quad \text{with } \sigma(L_1){=}\sigma(\overline{L_2})$$

$$\textit{Extension (E)} \qquad \frac{C_3,M[C_1\backslash C_2],Path{\cup}\{L_1\} \qquad C,M,Path}{C{\cup}\{L_1\},M,Path}$$

and $C_3{:=}\beta\text{-}clause_{L_2}(C_2)$, C_2 is copy of C_1, C_1 is an extension clause of M wrt. $Path \cup \{L_1\}$, C_2 contains L_2 with $\sigma(L_1) = \sigma(\overline{L_2})$

$$\textit{Decomposition (D)} \qquad \frac{C \cup C_1,M,Path}{C{\cup}\{M_1\},M,Path} \quad \text{with } C_1{\in}M_1$$

Fig. 6. The non-clausal connection calculus

Example 7 (Non-Clausal Connection Calculus). Consider the matrix M_1^* of Example 5. A derivation for M_1^* in the non-clausal connection calculus with $\sigma(x') = a$, $\sigma(\hat{x}) = b$, $M' = \{\{P^0(a)\}, \{\{\{P^1(x')\}, \{Q^0(f(x'))\}\}, \{\{Q^1(x')\}, \{Q^0(a), R^1(b)\}, \{R^0(x')\}\}\}, \{Q^1(f(b))\}\}$ and $\hat{M}{=}\{\{P^0(a)\}, \{\{\{P^1(\hat{x})\}, \{Q^0(f(\hat{x}))\}\}, \{\{Q^1(\hat{x})\}, \{Q^0(a), R^1(b)\}, \{R^0(\hat{x})\}\}\}, \{Q^1(f(b))\}\}$ is given in Figure 5. Since all leaves are axioms it represents a (non-clausal) connection proof and, therefore, M_1^* and F_1 are valid. This proof corresponds to the graphical proof representation given in Figure 1.

5 Correctness, Completeness and Complexity

In this section it is shown that the non-clausal connection calculus is sound and complete. Furthermore, its complexity is compared to the clausal connection calculus.

5.1 Correctness

Definition 12 (Superset Path through Clause). *Let p be a set of literals. p is a* superset path through C, *denoted by $C{\sqsubseteq}p$, iff there is path p' through $\{C\}$ with $p' \subseteq p$.*

$$\frac{\dfrac{}{\{\},\hat{M},\{P^0a,Q^1x',R^1b,Q^0f\hat{x}\}}\,A \qquad \dfrac{}{\{\},\hat{M},\{P^0a,Q^1x',R^1b\}}\,A}{\{Q^0f\hat{x}\},\hat{M},\{P^0a,Q^1x',R^1b\}}\,E$$

$$\frac{\{Q^0f\hat{x}\},\hat{M},\{P^0a,Q^1x',R^1b\}}{\{\{\{P^1\hat{x}\},\{Q^0f\hat{x}\}\}\},\hat{M},\{P^0a,Q^1x',R^1b\}}\,D$$

$$\frac{\{\{\{P^1\hat{x}\},\{Q^0f\hat{x}\}\}\},\hat{M},\{P^0a,Q^1x',R^1b\} \qquad \dfrac{}{\{\},M',\{P^0a,Q^1x'\}}\,A}{\{R^1b\},M',\{P^0a,Q^1x'\}}\,E$$

$$\frac{\{R^1b\},M',\{P^0a,Q^1x'\} \qquad \dfrac{}{\{\},M',\{P^0a\}}\,A}{\{Q^1x'\},M',\{P^0a\}}\,E$$

$$\frac{\{Q^1x'\},M',\{P^0a\}}{\{\{\{Q^1x'\},\{Q^0a,R^1b\},\{R^0x'\}\}\},M',\{P^0a\}}\,D$$

$$\frac{\{\{\{Q^1x'\},\{Q^0a,R^1b\},\{R^0x'\}\}\},M',\{P^0a\} \qquad \dfrac{}{\{\},M_1^*,\{\}}\,A}{\{P^0a\},M_1^*,\{\}}\,E$$

$$\frac{\{P^0a\},M_1^*,\{\}}{\varepsilon,M_1^*,\varepsilon}\,S$$

Fig. 7. A proof in the non-clausal connection calculus

Lemma 1 (Correctness of the Non-Start Rules). *If there is a connection proof for*
$C, M, Path$ *with the term substitution* σ, *then there is a multiplicity* μ *such that every*
path p through M^μ with $Path \subseteq p$ and $C \sqsubseteq p$ contains a σ-complementary connection.

Proof. The proof is by structural induction on the construction of connection proofs.
Induction hypothesis (IH): If $Proof$ is a connection proof for $C, M, Path$ with σ, then
there is a μ such that every path p through M^μ with $Path \subseteq p$ and $C \sqsubseteq p$ contains a
σ-complementary connection.

1. Axiom: Let $\overline{\{\}, M, Path}$ be a connection proof. Let $\mu \equiv 1$ and $\sigma(x) = x$ for all
x. Then $\{\} \sqsubseteq p$ holds for no path p through M^μ. Thus, *IH* follows.

2. Reduction: Let $\dfrac{Proof}{C, M, Path \cup \{L_2\}}$ be a connection proof for $C, M, Path \cup \{L_2\}$
for some σ. According to *IH* there is a μ such that every p through M^μ with
$Path \cup \{L_2\} \subseteq p$ and $C \sqsubseteq p$ contains a σ-complementary connection. Then the deriva-
tion $\dfrac{\dfrac{Proof}{C, M, Path \cup \{L_2\}}}{C \cup \{L_1\}, M, Path \cup \{L_2\}} R$ with $\tau(\sigma(L_1)) = \tau(\sigma(\overline{L_2}))$ for some term substitution
τ is a connection proof for $C \cup \{L_1\}, M, Path \cup \{L_2\}$. Let $\mu' := \mu$ and $\sigma' := \tau \circ \sigma$.
Every path p' through $M^{\mu'}$ with $Path \cup \{L_2\} \subseteq p'$ and $C \cup \{L_1\} \sqsubseteq p'$ contains a σ'-
complementary connection as well, since $\sigma'(L_1) = \sigma'(\overline{L_2})$.

3. Extension: Let $\dfrac{Proof_1}{C_3, M[C_1 \backslash C_2], Path \cup \{L_1\}}$ and $\dfrac{Proof_2}{C, M, Path}$ be connection proofs for
$C_3, M[C_1 \backslash C_2], Path \cup \{L_1\}$ and $C, M, Path$, respectively, for some σ, with $C_3 := \beta$-
$clause_{L_2}(C_2)$, C_2 is a copy of C_1, C_1 is an extension clause of M wrt. $Path \cup \{L_1\}$,
and C_2 contains the literal L_2 with $\tau(\sigma(L_1)) = \tau(\sigma(\overline{L_2}))$ for some substitution τ.
According to *IH* there is a μ_1 such that every path p through $(M[C_1 \backslash C2])^{\mu_1}$ with
$Path \cup \{L_1\} \subseteq p$ and $C_3 \sqsubseteq p$ contains a σ-complementary connection, and there is a μ_2
such that every p through M^{μ_2} with $Path \subseteq p$ and $C \sqsubseteq p$ contains a σ-complementary
connection. Then $\dfrac{\dfrac{Proof_1}{C_3, M[C_1 \backslash C_2], Path \cup \{L_1\}} \quad \dfrac{Proof_2}{C, M, Path}}{C \cup \{L_1\}, M, Path} E$ is a connection proof for
$C \cup \{L_1\}, M, Path$. This last extension step is illustrated below. It has to be shown
that there is a multiplicity μ' and a substitution σ' such that every path p' through $M^{\mu'}$
with $Path \subseteq p'$ and $C \cup \{L_1\} \sqsubseteq p'$ contains a σ'-complementary connection. Let M' be
the matrix M in which the (sub-)matrix $\{\ldots, C_1, \ldots\}$ that contains C_1 is replaced by
the matrix $\{\ldots, C_1, C_2, \ldots\}$, i.e. the clause C_2 is added to M as shown below.

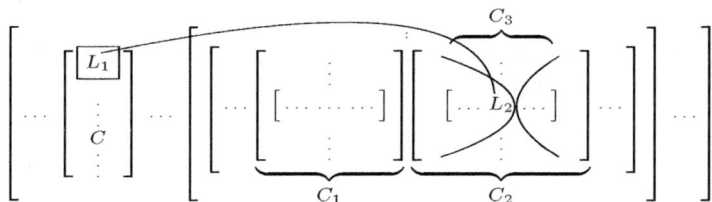

According to Def. 8 the following cases for the extension clause C_1 need to be considered:

1. If the extension clause C_1 contains a literal of $Path$, then every path p' through M'
   with $Path \cup \{L_1\} \subseteq p'$ is a superset path through C_2 as well, i.e. $C_2 \sqsubseteq p'$.

2. Otherwise, C_1 is α-related to all literals in $Path \cup \{L_1\}$ occurring in M'.

  (a) If C_1 has no parent clause, then for every p' through M' $C_1 \sqsubseteq p'$ holds. Then for every p' through M' with $Path \cup \{L_1\} \subseteq p'$ it is $C_1 \sqsubseteq p'$ and hence $C_2 \sqsubseteq p'$.

  (b) Otherwise, the parent clause of C_1 contains an element of $Path \cup \{L_1\}$. As C_1 is α-related to $Path \cup \{L_1\}$, there is a $\hat{C}$ containing a literal of $Path \cup \{L_1\}$ with $C_1, \hat{C} \in \hat{M}$. Therefore, for every p' through M' with $Path \cup \{L_1\} \subseteq p'$ it is $C_1 \sqsubseteq p'$ and thus $C_2 \sqsubseteq p'$.

C_3 is the β-clause of C_2 with respect to L_2, i.e. L_2 and all clauses that are α-related to L_2 are deleted from C_2. According to Def. 9 the only element deleted from a *clause* is the literal L_2. Therefore, for all p' through M' with $Path \cup \{L_1\} \subseteq p'$ it is $C_3 \sqsubseteq p'$ or $\{L_2\} \sqsubseteq p'$. The same holds if copies of clauses are added to M'. Let μ' be the multiplicity where all copies according to μ_1 and μ_2 as well as the clause copy C_2 are considered. Let $\sigma' := \tau \circ \sigma$. Then $C_3 \sqsubseteq p'$ or $L_2 \in p'$ holds for every p' through $M^{\mu'}$ with $Path \cup \{L_1\} \subseteq p'$. As there is a proof for $C_3, M[C_1 \backslash C_2], Path \cup \{L_1\}$ with σ, every p through $(M[C_1 \backslash C_2])^{\mu_1}$, and hence through $M^{\mu'}$, with $Path \cup \{L_1\} \subseteq p$ and $C_3 \sqsubseteq p$ contains a σ-complementary, and hence a σ'-complementary connection. Furthermore, every p' with $Path \cup \{L_1\} \subseteq p'$ that includes L_2 contains a σ'-complementary connection as $\sigma'(L_1) = \sigma'(\overline{L_2})$. Therefore, every p' through $M^{\mu'}$ with $Path \cup \{L_1\} \subseteq p'$ contains a σ'-complementary connection. Then every p' through $M^{\mu'}$, with $Path \subseteq p'$ and $\{L_1\} \sqsubseteq p'$ contains a σ'-complementary connection. As there is a proof for $C, M, Path$ with σ, every p through M^{μ_2}, and thus through $M^{\mu'}$, with $Path \subseteq p$ and $C \sqsubseteq p$ contains a σ-complementary, and hence a σ'-complementary, connection. Then every p' through $M^{\mu'}$, with $Path \subseteq p'$ and $C \cup \{L_1\} \sqsubseteq p'$ contains a σ'-complementary connection.

4. Decomposition: Let $\dfrac{Proof}{C \cup C_1, M, Path}$ be a connection proof for $C \cup C_1, M, Path$ for some σ. According to *IH* there is a μ such that every p through M^{μ} with $Path \subseteq p$ and $C \cup C_1 \sqsubseteq p$ contains a σ-complementary connection. Then $\dfrac{\dfrac{Proof}{C \cup C_1, M, Path}}{C \cup \{M_1\}, M, Path} D$ with $C_1 \in M_1$ is a connection proof for $C \cup \{M_1\}, M, Path$. Let $\mu' := \mu$ and $\sigma' := \sigma$. Every p' through $M^{\mu'}$ with $Path \subseteq p'$ and $C \cup \{M_1\} \sqsubseteq p'$ contains a σ'-complementary connection as well, since $C_1 \in M_1$ and thus for all p' the following holds: if $C \cup \{M_1\} \sqsubseteq p'$ then $C \cup C_1 \sqsubseteq p'$.   □

Theorem 3 (Correctness of the Non-Clausal Connection Calculus). *A formula F is valid in classical logic, if there is a non-clausal connection proof for its matrix M.*

Proof. Let M be the matrix of F. If there is a non-clausal connection proof for $\varepsilon, M, \varepsilon$, it has the form $\dfrac{\vdots}{\dfrac{C_2, M, \{\}}{\varepsilon, M, \varepsilon}} S$ in which the clause C_2 is a copy of $C_1 \in M$. There has to be a proof for $C_2, M, \{\}$ for some σ. According to Lemma 1 there is a μ such that every path p through M^{μ} with $\{\} \subseteq p$ and $C_2 \sqsubseteq p$ contains a σ-complementary connection. As $\{\} \subseteq p$ and $C_2 \sqsubseteq p$ hold for all p through M^{μ}, every path through M^{μ} contains a σ-complementary connection. According to Theorem 1 the formula F is valid.   □

5.2   Completeness

Definition 13 (Vertical Path Through Clause). *Let X be a matrix, clause, or literal. A vertical path p through X, denoted by $p\|X$, is a set of literals of X and inductively defined as follows: $\{L\}\|L$ for literal L; $p\|M$ for matrix M where $p\|C$ for some $C \in M$; $p\|C$ for clause $C \neq \{\}$ where $p = \bigcup_{M_i \in C} p_i$ and $p_i\|M_i$; $\{\}\|C$ for clause $C = \{\}$.*

Lemma 2 (Clauses and Vertical Paths). *Let M be the (non-clausal) matrix of a first-order formula F and M' be the matrix of the standard translation of F into clausal form (see Example 1). Then for every clause $C' \in M'$ there is an "original" clause $C \in M$ with $C'\|C$. If there is a connection proof for $C', M, Path$, then there is also a connection proof for $C, M, Path$. This also holds if the clauses $D' := C' \setminus \{L\}$ and $D := \beta\text{-clause}_L(C)$ are used, for some literal L, instead of C' and C, respectively.*

Proof. The existence of a clause $C \in M$ for every $C' \in M'$ with $C'\|C$ follows from Def. 2 and Def. 13. $C, M, Path$ can be derived from $C', M, Path$ by several decomposition steps. In D the literal L and all clauses that are α-related to L, i.e. that do not contain literals of D', are deleted from C. Therefore, it is $D'\|D$ and $D, M, Path$ can be derived from $D', M, Path$ as well.   □

Lemma 3 (Completeness of the Non-Start Rules). *Let M be the matrix of a first-order formula F and M' be the matrix of the standard translation of F into clausal form. If there is a clausal connection proof for $C, M', Path$ with the term substitution σ, then there exists a non-clausal connection proof for $C, M, Path$ with σ.*

Proof. The idea is to translate a clausal connection proof for M' into a non-clausal connection proof for M. The proof is by structural induction on the construction of a clausal connection proof. *Induction hypothesis*: If there is a clausal connection proof for $C, M', Path$ with the term substitution σ, then there exists a non-clausal connection proof for $C, M, Path$ with the substitution σ. For the *induction start* the (only) axiom of the calculus is considered. For the *induction step* reduction and extension rules are considered. The axiom and reduction rule are essentially identical for the clausal and non-clausal calculus. For the extension rule Lemma 2 has to be applied. The details of the (straightforward) proof are left to the interested reader.   □

Theorem 4 (Completeness of the Non-Clausal Connection Calculus). *If a formula F is valid in classical logic, there is a non-clausal connection proof for its matrix M.*

Proof. Let F be a valid formula, M be the non-clausal matrix of F and M' its matrix in clausal form. According to Theorem 2 there exists a clausal connection proof for M' and for $\varepsilon, M', \varepsilon$. Let C_2', M', ε be the premise of the start step in which C_2' is a copy of $C_1' \in M'$. According to Lemma 3 there is a non-clausal proof for C_2', M, ε. Let C_1 be the original clause of C_1' in M. According to Lemma 2 there is a non-clausal proof for C_2, M, ε where C_2 is a copy of C_1. Thus, there is a proof for $\varepsilon, M, \varepsilon$ and for M.   □

5.3   Complexity

Definition 14   (Size of Connection Proof). *The* size *of a (clausal or non-clausal) connection proof is the number of proof steps in the connection proof.*

Theorem 5   (Linear Simulation of Clausal Calculus). *Let M be the matrix of a formula F and M' be the matrix of the standard translation of F into clausal form. Furthermore, let n be the size of a clausal connection proof for M' and m be the size of its largest subgoal clause. Then there is a non-clausal proof for M with size $\mathcal{O}(m \cdot n)$.*

Proof. The same technique used for the proof of Lemma 3 can be used to translate a clausal proof for M' into a non-clausal proof for M. Reduction steps can be directly translated without any modifications. Every start or extension step is translated into one start or extension step and a number of decomposition steps in the non-clausal proof, respectively. The number of decomposition steps is limited by twice the size of the subgoal clause in the clausal proof.   □

Theorem 6   (No Polynomial Simulation of Non-Clausal Calculus). *Let M be the matrix of a formula F and M' be the matrix of the standard translation of F into clausal form. There is a class of formulae for which there is no clausal proof for M' with size $\mathcal{O}(n^k)$ for a fixed $k \in I\!N$, where n is the size of a non-clausal proof for M.*

Proof. Consider the (valid) formula class $((\forall x_1 P_1 x_1) \Rightarrow P_1 c_1)) \wedge \ldots \wedge ((\forall x_m P_m x_m) \Rightarrow P_m c_m))$ for some $m \in I\!N$ and the graphical representation of its matrix M shown below. The non-clausal connection proof for M with the term substitution $\sigma(x_i) = c_i$, for $1 \le i \le m$, has the following (simplified) graphical matrix representation

$$
\left[\; \left[\begin{array}{c} [\, [\overbrace{P_1^1 x_1}] \; [P_1^0 c_1]\,] \\ \vdots \\ [\, [\underbrace{P_m^1 x_m}] \; [P_m^0 c_m]\,] \end{array} \right] \; \right]
$$

and consists of one start step, m decomposition steps, and m extension steps. Therefore, the size of the non-clausal connection proof is $n = 2m + 1$. The clausal matrix M' has the form $\{\{P_1^1 x_1, \ldots, P_m^1 x_m\}, \{P_1^1 x_1, \ldots, P_m^0 c_m\}, \ldots, \{P_1^0 c_1, \ldots, P_m^0 c_m\}, \{P_1^0 c_1, \ldots, P_m^0 c_m\}\}$ and consists of $m \cdot 2^m$ literals. In a clausal proof for M' every clause of M' has to be considered, i.e. every literal of M' has to be an element of at least one connection. Therefore, $m \cdot 2^{m-1}$ is the minimal number of connections and the minimal size of every clausal connection proof for M'. Hence, there is no clausal connection proof for M' with size $\mathcal{O}(n^k)$ for some fixed $k \in I\!N$.

□

Theorem 6 holds for the structure-preserving translation into clausal form introduced in [12] as well. An example for an appropriate problem class is given in [2].

6   Optimizations and Extensions

In this section the connection calculus is further simplified. Some optimizations techniques and an extension of the calculus to some non-classical logics are described.

6.1   A Simplified Connection Calculus

If the matrices that are used in the non-clausal connection calculus are slightly modified, the start and reduction rule are subsumed by the decomposition and extension rule.

Definition 15 (Simplified Connection Calculus). *The* simplified connection calculus *consists only of the axiom, the extension rule and the decomposition rule of the non-clausal connection calculus (see Definition 10). It is shown in Figure 8.*

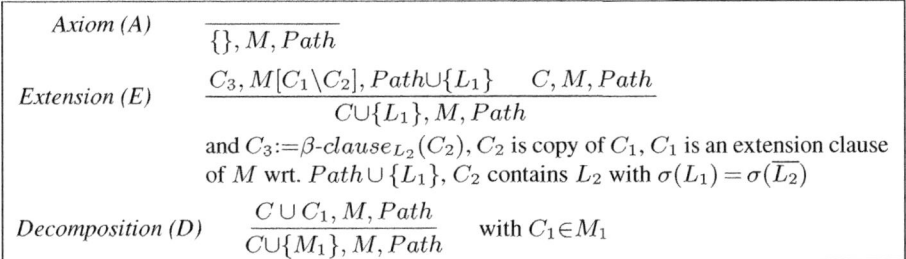

Axiom (A)	$\overline{\{\}, M, Path}$

Extension (E)
$$\frac{C_3, M[C_1 \backslash C_2], Path \cup \{L_1\} \quad C, M, Path}{C \cup \{L_1\}, M, Path}$$
and $C_3 := \beta\text{-}clause_{L_2}(C_2)$, C_2 is copy of C_1, C_1 is an extension clause of M wrt. $Path \cup \{L_1\}$, C_2 contains L_2 with $\sigma(L_1) = \sigma(\overline{L_2})$

Decomposition (D)
$$\frac{C \cup C_1, M, Path}{C \cup \{M_1\}, M, Path} \quad \text{with } C_1 \in M_1$$

Fig. 8. The simplified connection calculus

Theorem 7 (Correctness & Completeness of the Simplified Connection Calculus).
Let F be a first-order formula and M its matrix. Let M^* be the matrix M, in which all literals $L \in C$ with $|C| > 1$ in M are replaced by the matrix $\{\{L\}\}$. Then F is valid in classical logic iff there is a simplified connection proof for $\{M^*\}, M^*, \{\}$.

Proof. The start rule and the reduction rule are subsumed by the decomposition rule and the extensions rule, respectively. As the remaining rules of the calculus are not modified, the simplified connection calculus is correct and complete.   □

6.2   Optimizations

Positive Start Clause. As for the clausal connection calculus, the start clause of the non-clausal connection calculus can be restricted to positive clauses.

Definition 16 (Positive Clause). *A* clause C *is* a positive clause *iff there is a vertical path p through C, i.e. $C\|p$, that contains only literals with polarity 0.*

Lemma 4 (Positive Start Clause). *The non-clausal connection calculus remains correct and complete, if the clause C_1 of the start rule is restricted to positive clauses and all clauses in C_2 that are not positive are deleted from C_2.*

Proof. Correctness is preserved. Completeness follows from the fact that every connection proof for M has to use all literals (within connections) from a vertical path p through some clause $C \in M$ such that p contains only literals with polarity 0.   □

Regularity. Regularity is an effective technique for pruning the search space in clausal connection calculi [9]. It can be used for the non-clausal calculus as well.

Definition 17 (Regularity). *A connection proof is* regular *iff there are no two literals* L_1, L_2 *in the active path with* $\sigma(L_1) = \sigma(L_2)$.

The regularity condition is integrated into the calculus of Figure 6 by adding a restriction to the reduction and extension rule: $\forall L' \in C \cup \{L_1\} : \sigma(L') \notin \sigma(Path)$.

Lemma 5 (Regularity). *M is valid iff there is a regular connection proof for M.*

Proof. Regularity preserves correctness. Completeness follows from the fact that the clausal connection calculus with regularity is complete [9] and that it can be simulated by the non-clausal calculus with regularity (see Section 5.2).   □

Restricted Backtracking. Proof search in the (clausal and non-clausal) connection calculus is *not* confluent, i.e. it might end up in dead ends. To achieve completeness *backtracking* is required (see remarks in Section 2 and 4.2), i.e. alternative rules or rule instances need to be considered. The main idea of *restricted backtracking* [12] is to cut off any so-called *non-essential backtracking* that occurs after a literal is *solved*. Even though this strategy is incomplete, it is very effective [12]. It can be used straight away to prune the search space in the non-clausal connection calculus as well.

6.3   Non-classical Logics

The matrix characterization of classical validity (see Theorem 1) can be extended to some non-classical logics, such as modal and intuitionistic logic [18]. To this end a *prefix*, i.e. a string consisting of variables and constants, which essentially encodes the *Kripke world* semantics, is assigned to each literal. For a σ-complementary connection $\{L_1 : p_1, L_2 : p_2\}$ not only the terms of both literals need to unify under a term substitution σ, i.e. $\sigma(L_1) = \sigma(\overline{L_2})$, but also the corresponding prefixes p_1 and p_2 are required to unify under a prefix substitution σ', i.e. $\sigma'(p_1) = \sigma'(p_2)$. Therefore, by adding prefixes to the presented non-clausal connection calculus, it can be used for some non-classical logics as well [8]. For the proof *search* an additional *prefix unification* algorithm [11,17] is required that unifies the prefixes of the literals in every connection.

7   Conclusion

A *formal* non-clausal connection calculus has been introduced that can be used for proof search in classical and some non-classical first-order logics. It does not require the translation of the input formula into any clausal form but preserves its structure. The calculus generalizes the clausal connection calculus by modifying the extension rule and adding a decomposition rule. Copying of clauses is done in a dynamic way and significant redundancy is removed by considering only β-clauses for new subgoal clauses. Thus, the calculus combines the advantages of a non-clausal proof search in tableau calculi [6] with the more goal-oriented search of clausal connection calculi [4].

In [7] a technique similar to β-clauses is used to prove completeness for non-clausal connection tableaux. But this technique is not used explicitly within the tableau calculus itself. Furthermore, only ground formulae are considered and a more general regularity condition is used, which is not restricted to literals of the active path.

This paper provides the formal basis for a planned *competitive* implementation of a non-clausal connection calculus in an elegant and compact style [12,13]. Future work includes the development of further *non-clausal* optimization techniques.

Acknowledgements. The author would like to thank Wolfgang Bibel for his helpful comments on a preliminary version of this paper.

References

1. Andrews, P.B.: Theorem Proving via General Matings. Journal of the ACM 28, 193–214 (1981)
2. Antonsen, R., Waaler, A.: Liberalized Variable Splitting. Journal of Automated Reasoning 38, 3–30 (2007)
3. Bibel, W.: Matings in Matrices. Communications of the ACM 26, 844–852 (1983)
4. Bibel, W.: Automated Theorem Proving. Vieweg, Wiesbaden (1987)
5. Gentzen, G.: Untersuchungen über das logische Schließen. Mathematische Zeitschrift 39, 176–210, 405–431 (1935)
6. Hähnle, R.: Tableaux and Related Methods. In: Robinson, A., Voronkov, A. (eds.) Handbook of Automated Reasoning, pp. 100–178. Elsevier, Amsterdam (2001)
7. Hähnle, R., Murray, N.V., Rosenthal, E.: Linearity and Regularity with Negation Normal Form. Theoretical Computer Science 328, 325–354 (2004)
8. Kreitz, C., Otten, J.: Connection-based Theorem Proving in Classical and Non-classical Logics. Journal of Universal Computer Science 5, 88–112 (1999)
9. Letz, R., Stenz, G.: Model Elimination and Connection Tableau Procedures. In: Robinson, A., Voronkov, A. (eds.) Handbook of Automated Reasoning, pp. 2015–2114. Elsevier, Amsterdam (2001)
10. Loveland, D.: Mechanical Theorem-Proving by Model Elimination. Journal of the ACM 15, 236–251 (1968)
11. Otten, J.: Clausal Connection-Based Theorem Proving in Intuitionistic First-Order Logic. In: Beckert, B. (ed.) TABLEAUX 2005. LNCS (LNAI), vol. 3702, pp. 245–261. Springer, Heidelberg (2005)
12. Otten, J.: Restricting Backtracking in Connection Calculi. AI Communications 23, 159–182 (2010)
13. Otten, J., Bibel, W.: leanCoP: Lean Connection-based Theorem Proving. Journal of Symbolic Computation 36, 139–161 (2003)
14. Plaisted, D., Greenbaum, S.: A Structure-preserving Clause Form Translation. Journal of Symbolic Computation 2, 293–304 (1986)
15. Robinson, A.: A Machine-oriented Logic Based on the Resolution Principle. Journal of the ACM 12, 23–41 (1965)
16. Schmitt, S., Lorigo, L., Kreitz, C., Nogin, A.: JProver: Integrating Connection-Based Theorem Proving into Interactive Proof Assistants. In: Goré, R., Leitsch, A., Nipkow, T. (eds.) IJCAR 2001. LNCS (LNAI), vol. 2083, pp. 421–426. Springer, Heidelberg (2001)
17. Waaler, A.: Connections in Nonclassical Logics. In: Robinson, A., Voronkov, A. (eds.) Handbook of Automated Reasoning, pp. 1487–1578. Elsevier, Amsterdam (2001)
18. Wallen, L.: Automated Deduction in Nonclassical Logics. MIT Press, Washington (1990)

MetTeL: A Tableau Prover with Logic-Independent Inference Engine*

Dmitry Tishkovsky, Renate A. Schmidt, and Mohammad Khodadadi

School of Computer Science, The University of Manchester
{dmitry,schmidt,khodadadi}@cs.man.ac.uk

Abstract. MetTeL is a generic tableau prover for various modal, intuitionistic, hybrid, description and metric logics. The core component of MetTeL is a logic-independent tableau inference engine. A novel feature is that users have the ability to flexibly specify the set of tableau rules to be used in derivations. Termination can be achieved via a generalisation of a standard loop checking mechanism or unrestricted blocking.

1 Introduction

MetTeL is a lightweight generic tableau prover implemented in Java. Its main purpose is to provide a tool for experimenting with tableau calculi for newly invented non-classical logics for which there are no known sound and complete decision procedures. The first versions of MetTeL were designed for deciding logics of metric and topology [4]. In 2005, when the implementation started, there were no known tableau calculi for these logics. To allow for the testing of different sets of tableau rules, much effort was invested in a generic, modular design of MetTeL. A natural hierarchy of Java classes was implemented so that tableau calculi could be implemented quickly and with little effort.

The extendable design led to quick implementations of tableau decision procedures for many other non-classical logics including, e.g., intuitionistic propositional logic, the expressive description logic $\mathcal{ALBO}$ [5], and the extension $\mathcal{ALBO}^{\mathsf{id}}$ with role identity. Most recently, we have extended MetTeL with a rule specification language giving users the facility to define the tableau rules to be used during the derivation. Skolem terms have replaced the use of nominals in the rules for expanding existential quantification formulae. MetTeL provides several novel engineering solutions. For enforcing termination it implements generic loop-checking mechanisms and is the first to implement the unrestricted blocking mechanism introduced in [5].

MetTeL decides the following logics: classical and intuitionistic propositional logic, hybrid logic HL(@,u) with the universal modality, the logic $\mathcal{MT}$ of metric and topology, and all sublogics of the description logic $\mathcal{ALBO}^{\mathsf{id}}$. At the moment, MetTeL is the only tableau prover that can decide logics of metric and topology and description logics with role negation [5]. Using the facility to specify

---

* The work is supported by research grant EP/H043748/1 of the UK EPSRC.

K. Brünnler and G. Metcalfe (Eds.): TABLEAUX 2011, LNAI 6793, pp. 242–247, 2011.
© Springer-Verlag Berlin Heidelberg 2011

tableau rules MᴇᴛTᴇʟ can be used as a prover for many other more expressive or even undecidable logics. MᴇᴛTᴇʟ has been compared on a class of metric and topology problems with the first-order resolution provers Sᴘᴀss and Vᴀᴍᴘɪʀᴇ, where it performed better [4].

Closely related to MᴇᴛTᴇʟ are the prover engineering platforms LoTREC [3] and the Tableau WorkBench [1]. These systems give users the possibility to program their own tableau prover for modal-type logics using meta-programming languages for building and manipulating formulae, and controlling the tableau derivation process. Being targeted at users and logicians with limited experience in constructing tableau derivations or building tableau provers, the objective of MᴇᴛTᴇʟ is slightly different. MᴇᴛTᴇʟ has been designed to have a simple and easy to use input language. Tableau rules are specified following the standard premises/conclusions notation found in the literature and are always interpreted as expansion rules. The specification language is therefore easy to learn and remember. Notable is that Skolem terms are used and that these can occur in both conclusion and premise positions of the same or different rules. E.g., the following rule is specifiable in MᴇᴛTᴇʟ: $@_{g(i)} \Diamond j$, $@_j p / @_{g(i)} p \mid @_i \Diamond h(p,i,j)$, $@_{h(p,i,j)} p$. The rule partly formalises the co-cover property in models for modal logic S4, where $g(i)$ denotes a Skolem term representing the co-cover of nominal i, and $h(p,i,j)$ represents a successor of i depending on nominal j and proposition p [2]. Another difference is that LoTREC and the Tableau WorkBench do not yet implement unrestricted blocking.

MᴇᴛTᴇʟ is available from `http://www.mettel-prover.org`.

2 Input Syntax

The language for specifying formulae is a many-sorted language with five sorts, namely, formulae, relational formulae (or roles), nominal terms including Skolem terms, attributes and rational parameters from metric logic. The available predefined connectives include negation `~`, conjunction `&`, disjunction `|`, logical equivalence `<->`, implication `->`, modal **box** and **dia** (synonyms: description logic **forall** and **exists**), the 'closer' operator `<<` of similarity logic, the `@` operator of hybrid logic, and the relational operators: inverse `-`, union `+`, intersection `&`, negation `~`, composition `;`, and reflexive-transitive closure `*`. The language also includes the propositional constants **FALSE** and **TRUE** and allows arbitrary names for relational constants. E.g., although relational identity **id** is not a predefined symbol it can be encoded in the rule specification language. Here are three examples of formulae specifiable in MᴇᴛTᴇʟ:

```
box box{~(~R | S)} FALSE
( @i dia{R} j & @j dia{R} k ) -> @i dia{R} k
exists{a<x;a<y} P -> exists{a<(x+y)} P
```

The first formula encodes role inclusion $R \sqsubseteq S$ in $\mathcal{ALBO}^{\text{id}}$. The second formula defines R as a transitive relation in hybrid logic. The last formula expresses the triangle property of metric relations (if there is a path to a property P consisting of two distances for an attribute a which are strictly less than x and y respectively, then there is an a-distance to P which is strictly less than $x + y$).

The tableau rule specification language is illustrated by these examples.

```
@i (P|Q) / { @i P } | { @i Q };
@i (~P & ~Q) / { @i ~P, @i ~Q };
@i ~(dia{R} P), @i dia{R} j / { @j ~P };
@i dia{R} P / { @f[i,R,P] P, @i dia{R} f[i,R,P] };
@i P, @i ~P / { FALSE };
```

The premises and conclusions are separated by **/** and each rule is terminated by **;**. The first rule is the or rule, defined as a branching rule which creates a splitting point adding **@i P** to the left branch and **@i Q** to the right branch. The other rules are non-branching rules. The second rule is an instance of the standard and rule. The third rule is the standard box rule rewritten in terms of the negated diamond. Note the use of the Skolem term **f[i,R,P]** in the next rule; it represents the created witness with dependence on **i,R,P**. Rules, like the last rule, with **FALSE** belonging to the conclusion are closure rules.

3   Implementation Details

All expressions over the five sorts are internally represented as extensions of the basic MettelExpression interface. For efficiency reasons, each kind of expression is represented as a separate JAVA class which is not parameterised by connectives. At runtime, the creation of expression objects is managed by means of a factory pattern implemented as MettelObjectFactory and ensures that each expression is represented by a single object. Each class implementing the interface MettelExpression is required to implement two methods: (i) a method for matching the current object with the expression object supplied as a parameter. This method returns the substitution which unifies the current expression with the parameter. (ii) The second method is the inverse of the first method, i.e., it returns an instance of the current expression with respect to a given substitution.

In order to allow user-defined rules, tableau rules are implemented by a single class called MettelGeneralTableauRule.

Every expression undergoes on-the-fly preprocessing during its creation in the appropriate factory object. The default implementation of the MettelObjectFactory interface automatically simplifies formulae, removing, e.g., multiple negations in subformulae and reformulating formulae in terms of a minimal and independent set of connectives. Since there is a direct dependence between the connectives and the specified rules, and all rules are created by a factory object, rules are automatically simplified as well.

Various implementations of the MettelPreprocessor interface are available to perform more complex preprocessing: E.g., MettelAtPreprocessor attaches $@_{n_0}$ to (unprefixed) formulae in the problem set, where n_0 is a fresh nominal. The MettelGodelPreprocessor translates intuitionistic formulae into modal logic S4.

Every node of the tableau is represented as a tableau state object comprising of a set of formulae associated with the node and methods for manipulating the formulae and realising rule applications.

Rule application is implemented as follows. Every rule is applied to a tableau state. A tuple of formulae from the set of active formulae associated with the tableau state is selected and the formulae in the tuple are matched with the premises of the chosen rule. Since matching is computationally expensive, it is performed only once for any given formula and a premise of a rule. This is achieved by maintaining sets of all the substitutions obtained from matching the selected formula with the rule premise. All the selected formulae are discarded from the set of active formulae associated with the rule. If the tuple of the selected formulae match the premises of the rule, the resulting substitution object is passed to the conclusions of the rule. The final result of a rule application is a set of branches which are sets of formulae obtained by applying the substitution to the conclusions of the rule.

Two blocking mechanisms for detecting 'loops' in derivations are implemented in MetTeL. The first blocking mechanism is a generalisation of anywhere equality loop checking used in some description logic systems. The main difference is that instead of requiring that all local rules are applied before rules that introduce new nominal terms, every rule keeps track of formulae that depend on a given nominal term. Once no more local rules are applicable to any pair of nominals the blocking test is performed for the nominals. If successful, an equality is added to the current tableau state for subsequent rewriting. The second available blocking mechanism is the unrestricted blocking mechanism [5]. This is realised through a branching rule which attempts to equate nominal terms by case analysis.

During the inference process nominal terms, including those introduced during existential quantifier expansion, are kept in a linear ordering that is compatible with the subterm ordering and the order in which they are introduced. As soon as equalities are added by the blocking mechanisms or a tableau rule, these are used to rewrite all expressions in the current branch. Larger nominal terms are always rewritten to nominal terms smaller under the ordering.

4   Using MetTeL

The binary version of MetTeL is distributed as a **jar**-file and requires Java Runtime Environment, Version 1.5.0 or later. MetTeL can be called from the command line as follows.

```
> java −jar mettel.jar [ −tbl <tabl−fname> ] [ −i <in−fname> ]
```

In which file the tableau calculus and the input problem are defined can be specified with the **−tbl** and **−i** options. The predefined calculi can be used via the options listed in Table 1. If the options are in conflict then the last one given has priority. The input problem can optionally be read from standard input.

Assuming the sample tableau rules from Section 2 are stored in the file **sampleTableau.t.mtl**, executing this command

```
> java −jar mettel.jar −tbl sampleTableau.t.mtl
  box{R}(Q&P) & dia{R}~Q
```

Table 1. Predefined tableau calculi

Option	Tableau calculus for
-bool	Classical propositional logic.
-hl	Hybrid logic HL(@) with relational union and composition (Default).
-hlu	Like -hl plus the universal modality.
-met	Metric logic without the 'closer' operator.
-topo	Metric logic with the topology operator but without the 'closer' operator [4].
-albo	$\mathcal{ALBO}$ with the unrestricted blocking rule mechanism [5].
-alboid	Like -albo plus identity

produces the output: **Unsatisfiable**. If the formula **box{R}(Q&P)&dia{R}P** had been typed at the terminal, the output would have been:

```
Satisfiable
MODEL:[(@{f(n0,R,P)}P), (@{n0}(exists{R}f(n0,R,P))), (@{f(n0,R,P
)}(~((~Q)|(~P)))), (@{n0}(~((exists{R}((~Q)|(~P)))|(~(exists{R}P
))))), (@{n0}(~(exists{R}((~Q)|(~P))))), (@{n0}(exists{R}P)), (@
{f(n0,R,P)}Q)]
Filtered model:[(@{f(n0,R,P)}P), (@{n0}(exists{R}f(n0,R,P))), (@
{f(n0,R,P)}Q)]
```

As can be seen in this example models are presented in long and compact format.

5   Concluding Remarks

Mettel is a new type of tableau prover where users have the option of either using one of several predefined tableau calculi or define their own set of tableau rules to be used for constructing derivations. In order to make it even easier for users to obtain an automated theorem prover designed for a specific logic we plan to implement the tableau calculus synthesis framework described in [6] and incorporate it into METTEL.

References

1. Abate, P., Goré, R.: The Tableaux Work Bench. In: Cialdea Mayer, M., Pirri, F. (eds.) TABLEAUX 2003. LNCS, vol. 2796, pp. 230–236. Springer, Heidelberg (2003)
2. Babenyshev, S., Rybakov, V., Schmidt, R.A., Tishkovsky, D.: A tableau method for checking rule admissibility in S4. Electron. Notes Theor. Comput. Sci. 262, 17–32 (2010)
3. Gasquet, O., Herzig, A., Longin, D., Sahade, M.: LoTREC: Logical tableaux research engineering companion. In: Beckert, B. (ed.) TABLEAUX 2005. LNCS (LNAI), vol. 3702, pp. 318–322. Springer, Heidelberg (2005)
4. Hustadt, U., Tishkovsky, D., Wolter, F., Zakharyaschev, M.: Automated reasoning about metric and topology (System description). In: Fisher, M., van der Hoek, W., Konev, B., Lisitsa, A. (eds.) JELIA 2006. LNCS (LNAI), vol. 4160, pp. 490–493. Springer, Heidelberg (2006)

5. Schmidt, R.A., Tishkovsky, D.: Using tableau to decide expressive description logics with role negation. In: Aberer, K., Choi, K.-S., Noy, N., Allemang, D., Lee, K.-I., Nixon, L.J.B., Golbeck, J., Mika, P., Maynard, D., Mizoguchi, R., Schreiber, G., Cudré-Mauroux, P. (eds.) ASWC 2007 and ISWC 2007. LNCS, vol. 4825, pp. 438–451. Springer, Heidelberg (2007)
6. Schmidt, R.A., Tishkovsky, D.: Automated synthesis of tableau calculi. In: Giese, M., Waaler, A. (eds.) TABLEAUX 2009. LNCS, vol. 5607, pp. 310–324. Springer, Heidelberg (2009)

A Hypersequent System for Gödel-Dummett Logic with Non-constant Domains

Alwen Tiu

College of Engineering and Computer Science
The Australian National University

Abstract. Gödel-Dummett logic is an extension of first-order intuitionistic logic with the linearity axiom $(A \supset B) \vee (B \supset A)$, and the so-called "quantifier shift" axiom $\forall x (A \vee B(x)) \supset A \vee \forall x B(x)$. Semantically, it can be characterised as a logic for linear Kripke frames with constant domains. Gödel-Dummett logic has a natural formalisation in hypersequent calculus. However, if one drops the quantifier shift axiom, which corresponds to the constant domain property, then the resulting logic has to date no known hypersequent formalisation. We consider an extension of hypersequent calculus in which eigenvariables in the hypersequents form an explicit part of the structures of the hypersequents. This extra structure allows one to formulate quantifier rules which are more refined. We give a formalisation of Gödel-Dummett logic without the assumption of constant domain in this extended hypersequent calculus. We prove cut elimination for this hypersequent system, and show that it is sound and complete with respect to its Hilbert axiomatic system.

1 Introduction

Gödel logics refer to a family of intermediate logics (i.e., logics between intuitionistic and classical logics) that can be characterised by the class of rooted linearly ordered Kripke models, or alternatively, as many-valued logics whose connectives are interpreted as functions over subsets of the real interval $[0, 1]$. Its conception dates back to the seminal work by Gödel on the (non-existence of) finite matrix characteristic for propositional intuitionistic logic [14]. Dummett [12] gives an axiomatisation of a (propositional) Gödel logic over an infinite set of truth values, by extending intuitionistic logic with the *linearity axiom* $(A \supset B) \vee (B \supset A)$. This logic is called **LC**, but also known as Gödel-Dummett logic. In the first-order case, Gödel logics (viewed as logics of linear Kripke frames) are usually formalised with the assumption of constant domain, i.e., it assumes the same domain of individuals for all worlds, which is captured via the *quantifier shift* axiom $(\forall x.A \vee B) \supset \forall x.(A \vee B)$, where x is not free in B.

Traditional cut-free sequent calculi for **LC** have been studied in several previous works [21,10,1,13]. Due to the linearity axiom, the formalisation of **LC** in traditional sequent calculi requires a non-standard form of introduction rule for implication, e.g., in Corsi's calculus [10], the introduction rule for $\supset$ involves a simultaneous introduction of several $\supset$-formulae (see Section 6). Avron proposed

K. Brünnler and G. Metcalfe (Eds.): TABLEAUX 2011, LNAI 6793, pp. 248–262, 2011.

another proof system for Gödel-Dummett logic in the framework of *hypersequent calculus* [3] (see also [5] for related work on Gödel logics in hypersequent calculi). A hypersequent is essentially a multiset of sequents. In Avron's notation, a hypersequent with n member sequents is written as $\Gamma_1 \Rightarrow C_1 \mid \cdots \mid \Gamma_n \Rightarrow C_n$. The structural connective $\mid$ here is interpreted as disjunction.

In contrast to Corsi's sequent calculus, the introduction rules for the hypersequent calculus for Gödel-Dummett logic are the standard ones. Linearity is captured, instead, using a structural rule, called the *communication* rule:

$$\frac{G \mid \Gamma, \Delta \Rightarrow C \quad G \mid \Gamma, \Delta \Rightarrow D}{G \mid \Gamma \Rightarrow C \mid \Delta \Rightarrow D} \; com$$

In the first-order case, a standard right-introduction rule for $\forall$ is

$$\frac{G \mid \Gamma \Rightarrow A(y)}{G \mid \Gamma \Rightarrow \forall x.A(x)} \; \forall r$$

where y is not free in the conclusion. Notice that in the premise of the rule, implicitly the scope of y is over the entire hypersequent. If the structural connective $\mid$ is interpreted as disjunction and eigenvariables are interpreted as universally quantified variables, the rule essentially encapsulates the quantifier shift axiom. It would seem therefore that in the traditional hypersequent calculus, one is forced to accept the quantifier shift axiom as part of the logic.

In this paper, we are interested in seeing whether there is a way to formalise intermediate logics in hypersequent calculus in which the quantifier shift axiom may not hold. We study a particular logic with this property, i.e., what is called *quantified* **LC** in [11] (we shall refer to it as **QLC** below) , which is an extension of the first-order intuitionistic logic with the linearity axiom (but without the quantifier shift axiom). In semantic terms, this logic is just a logic of linearly ordered frames with nested domains. A sequent calculus for this logic was first considered by Corsi [10], and later Avellone, et. al. [2], where, again as in the propositional case, there is a simultaneous introduction rule for *both* $\forall$ and $\supset$.

The key idea to the hypersequent formalisation of **QLC** here is to explicitly represent eigenvariables as part of the structure of a hypersequent and to use that extra structure to control the use of eigenvariables. The idea of explicit representation of eigenvariables in sequent calculus is not new and has been considered in the abstract logic programming literature, see e.g., [17]. An intuitionistic sequent in this case is a structure of the form $\Sigma; \Gamma \Rightarrow C$ where Σ here is a set of eigenvariables, called the *signature* of the sequent. The introduction rules for $\forall$ would then be of the forms:

$$\frac{\Sigma \vdash t : \text{term} \quad G \mid \Sigma; A(t), \Gamma \Rightarrow C}{G \mid \Sigma; \forall x.A(x), \Gamma \Rightarrow C} \; \forall l \qquad \frac{G \mid \Sigma, y; \Gamma \Rightarrow A(y)}{G \mid \Sigma; \Gamma \Rightarrow \forall x.A(x)} \; \forall r$$

Notice that in $\forall r$, the eigenvariable y is explicitly added to Σ (reading the rule upward). Notice also that in instantiating a universal quantifier on the left, one needs to be able to form the term t given the signature Σ. This is enforced by the judgment $\Sigma \vdash t :$ term in the premise. In the simplest case, it just means that the free variables of t need to be already in Σ. It is easy to see that the quantifier shift axiom may not be immediately provable using the above rules.

An immediate problem with the explicit representation of eigenvariables in hypersequents is that there seems to be no way to interpret rules in the hypersequent calculus as valid formulae in **QLC**. This complicates the proof of soundness of the hypersequent calculus via an encoding in the Hilbert system for **QLC** (see the discussion in Section 5). For example, if one were to interpret the signature Σ as universal quantifiers whose scope is over the sequent it is attached to, then the *com*-rule (see Section 3) turns out to be unsound for **QLC**. The solution attempted here is to interpret eigenvariables in a signature as an encoding of an *existence predicate*, that was first introduced in Scott's existence logic [19]. Intuitively, a sequent such as $x; A(x) \Rightarrow B(x)$ can be interpreted as the formula $E(x) \wedge A(x) \supset B(x)$, where E here is an existence predicate. Using this interpretation, however, we cannot directly prove soundness of our hypersequent system with respect to **QLC**, as **QLC** does not assume such an existence predicate. To overcome this problem, we use a result by Iemhoff [15] relating Gödel logics with non-constant domains with Gödel logics with constant domains extended with the existence predicate. Section 5 gives more details of this correspondence.

The remainder of this paper is structured as follows. Section 2 reviews the syntax and the semantics of Corsi's **QLC**. Section 3 presents a hypersequent calculus for **QLC**, called **HQLC**, and Section 4 shows how cut elimination can be proved for **HQLC**. The hypersequent system **HQLC** actually captures a richer logic than **QLC**, as it permits a richer term language than that allowed in **QLC**. What we aim to show here is that cut elimination still holds provided the term formation judgment ($\Sigma \vdash t :$ term) satisfies four abstract properties, so our cut elimination result applies to extensions of **QLC** with richer term structures. Section 5 shows that **HQLC**, restricted to a term language containing only constant symbols as in **QLC**, is sound and complete w.r.t. **QLC**. Section 6 discusses related work and some directions for future work.

2   Semantics and an Axiomatic System of Quantified LC

The language GD of first-order Gödel-Dummett logic with nested domain is as in first-order intuitionistic logic. We consider here the connectives $\bot$ ('false'), $\top$ ('true'), $\wedge$, $\vee$, $\supset$, $\exists$ and $\forall$. We assume some given constants, but do not assume any function symbols. First-order variables are ranged over by x, y and z; constants by a, b, c; and predicate symbols by p and q. Given a formula C, $FV(C)$ denotes the set of free variables in C. This notation generalizes straightforwardly to sets of formulas, e.g., if Γ is a (multi)set of formulas, then $FV(\Gamma)$ is the set of free variables in all the formulas in Γ.

A Kripke model $\mathcal{M}$ for GD is a quadruple $\langle W, R, D, I \rangle$ where

- W is a non-empty set of worlds;
- R is a binary relation on W;

- D is the domain function assigning each $w \in W$ a non-empty set D_w such that $D_v \subseteq D_w$ whenever vRw;
- I is an interpretation function such that for each $w \in W$, for each constant c, $I_w(c) \in D_w$, and for each n-ary predicate p, $I_w(p) \subseteq D_w^n$, such that $I_v(c) = I_w(c)$ and $I_v(p) \subseteq I_w(p)$ whenever vRw.

The forcing relation $\mathcal{M}, w \models A$ is defined as in the usual definition in first-order intuitionistic logic (see, e.g., [24]). Let **QLC** [11] be the axiomatic system extending Hilbert's system for first-order intuitionistic logic (see, e.g., [23]) with the linearity axiom $(A \supset B) \vee (B \supset A)$.

Theorem 1 ([11]). **QLC** *is sound and complete with respect to GD, for the class of Kripke models based on linearly ordered frames (reflexive, transitive, connected and antisymmetric) with nested domains.*

3   The Hypersequent System HQLC

Definition 2. *A* sequent *is a syntactic expression of the form* $\Sigma; \Gamma \Rightarrow C$ *where* Σ *is a set of eigenvariables,* Γ *is a multiset of formulae and* C *is a formula.* Σ *here is called the* signature *of the sequent. A* hypersequent *is a multiset of sequents. When writing hypersequents, we shall use the symbol* | *to separate individual sequents in the multiset. Thus, the following is a hypersequent with n members:* $\Sigma_1; \Gamma_1 \Rightarrow C_1 \mid \cdots \mid \Sigma_n; \Gamma_n \Rightarrow C_n$.

A *substitution* θ is a mapping from variables to terms such that the *domain* of θ, i.e., $\{x \mid \theta(x) \neq x\}$ is finite. We denote with $dom(\theta)$ the domain of θ, and with $ran(\theta)$ the *range* of θ, i.e., the set $\{\theta(x) \mid x \in dom(\theta)\}$. When we want to be explicit about the domain and range of a substitution, we enumerate them as a list of mappings, e.g, $[t_1/x_1, \ldots, t_n/x_n]$ denotes a substitution which maps x_i to t_i, with domains $\{x_1, \ldots, x_n\}$. A *renaming substitution* is a substitution which is an injective map between variables.

Substitutions are extended to mappings from terms to terms or formulae to formulae in the obvious way, taking care of avoiding capture of free variables in the range of substitutions. Given a multiset Γ and a substitution θ, $\Gamma\theta$ denotes the multiset resulting from applying θ to each element of Γ. The result of applying a substitution θ to a signature Σ is defined as follows:

$$\Sigma\theta = \bigcup \{FV(\theta(x)) \mid x \in \Sigma\}.$$

For example, if $\Sigma = \{x, y\}$ and $\theta = [a/x, y/z]$ then $\Sigma\theta = \{y\}$. The result of applying a substitution θ to a sequent $\Sigma; \Gamma \Rightarrow C$ is the sequent $\Sigma\theta; \Gamma\theta \Rightarrow C\theta$. Application of a substitution to a hypersequent is defined as applications of the substitution to its individual sequents.

We shall assume a given relation $\vdash$ between a signature Σ and a term t, capturing a notion of wellformedness of terms. We shall write $\Sigma \vdash t$: term to denote that the term t is wellformed under Σ. The judgment $\Sigma \vdash t$: term can

Cut and identity:

$$\overline{\Sigma; \Gamma, p(\vec{t}) \Rightarrow p(\vec{t}) \mid H} \; id \qquad \frac{\Sigma; \Gamma \Rightarrow B \mid H_1 \quad \Sigma; B, \Delta \Rightarrow C \mid H_2}{\Sigma; \Gamma, \Delta \Rightarrow C \mid H_1 \mid H_2} \; cut$$

Structural rule:

$$\frac{\Sigma_1, \Sigma_2; \Gamma, \Delta \Rightarrow B \mid \Sigma_2; \Delta \Rightarrow C \mid H \quad \Sigma_1; \Gamma \Rightarrow B \mid \Sigma_1, \Sigma_2; \Gamma, \Delta \Rightarrow C \mid H}{\Sigma_1; \Gamma \Rightarrow B \mid \Sigma_2; \Delta \Rightarrow C \mid H} \; com$$

Logical rules:

$$\overline{\Sigma; \bot, \Gamma \Rightarrow A \mid H} \; \bot l \qquad \overline{\Sigma; \Gamma \Rightarrow \top} \; \top r$$

$$\frac{\Sigma; \Gamma, A \supset B \Rightarrow A \mid \Sigma; \Gamma, A \supset B \Rightarrow C \mid H \quad \Sigma; \Gamma, A \supset B, B \Rightarrow C \mid H}{\Sigma; \Gamma, A \supset B \Rightarrow C \mid H} \; \supset l$$

$$\frac{\Sigma; \Gamma, A \Rightarrow B \mid H}{\Sigma; \Gamma \Rightarrow A \supset B \mid H} \; \supset r$$

$$\frac{\Sigma; \Gamma, A_1, A_2 \Rightarrow B \mid H}{\Sigma; \Gamma, A_1 \wedge A_2 \Rightarrow B \mid H} \; \wedge l \qquad \frac{\Sigma; \Gamma \Rightarrow A \mid H \quad \Sigma; \Gamma \Rightarrow B \mid H}{\Sigma; \Gamma \Rightarrow A \wedge B \mid H} \; \wedge r$$

$$\frac{\Sigma; \Gamma, A \Rightarrow C \mid H \quad \Sigma; \Gamma, B \Rightarrow C \mid H}{\Sigma; \Gamma, A \vee B \Rightarrow C \mid H} \; \vee l \qquad \frac{\Sigma; \Gamma \Rightarrow A_1 \mid \Sigma; \Gamma \Rightarrow A_2 \mid H}{\Sigma; \Gamma \Rightarrow A_1 \vee A_2 \mid H} \; \vee r$$

$$\frac{\Sigma \vdash t : \mathrm{term} \quad \Sigma; \Gamma, A[t/x], \forall x.A \Rightarrow B \mid H}{\Sigma; \Gamma, \forall x.A \Rightarrow B \mid H} \; \forall l \qquad \frac{\Sigma, y; \Gamma \Rightarrow A[y/x] \mid H}{\Sigma; \Gamma \Rightarrow \forall x.A \mid H} \; \forall r$$

$$\frac{\Sigma, y; \Gamma, A[y/x] \Rightarrow B \mid H}{\Sigma; \Gamma, \exists x.A \Rightarrow B \mid H} \; \exists l \qquad \frac{\Sigma \vdash t : \mathrm{term} \quad \Sigma; \Gamma \Rightarrow A[t/x] \mid \Sigma; \Gamma \Rightarrow \exists x.A \mid H}{\Sigma; \Gamma \Rightarrow \exists x.A \mid H} \; \exists r$$

Fig. 1. The hypersequent system **HQLC**. In the rules $\exists l$ and $\forall r$, the eigenvariable y is not free in the conclusion.

be seen as a typing judgment familiar from programming languages. It can also be thought as a formalisation of a form of *existence predicate* from existence logic [19] (see Section 5).

For the purpose of proving cut-elimination, the particular definition of the judgment $\vdash$ is not important, as long as it satisfies the following properties:

P1 If $\Sigma \vdash t : \mathrm{term}$ then $FV(t) \subseteq \Sigma$.
P2 If $\Sigma \vdash t : \mathrm{term}$ and $x \notin \Sigma$, then $\Sigma, x \vdash t : \mathrm{term}$.
P3 If $\Sigma \vdash t : \mathrm{term}$ and θ is a renaming substitution, then $\Sigma\theta \vdash t\theta : \mathrm{term}$.
P4 If $\Sigma, x \vdash t : \mathrm{term}$, where $x \notin \Sigma$, and $\Sigma \vdash s : \mathrm{term}$ then $\Sigma \vdash t[s/x] : \mathrm{term}$.

A consequence of **P1** is that $(\Sigma \vdash x : \text{term})$ implies $x \in \Sigma$. The converse does not hold in general, e.g., consider the case where $\vdash$ is the empty relation.

In the case of **QLC**, since we assume no function symbols, the term formation rule is very simple; $\Sigma \vdash t : \text{term}$ holds iff either t is a constant or it is a variable in Σ. It is obvious that **P1** – **P4** hold in this case. But in general, any term formation judgments that satisfy the above four properties can be incorporated in our proof system and cut elimination will still hold. For example, one can have a term language based on Church's simply typed λ-calculus, e.g., as in the (first-order/higher-order) intuitionistic systems in [17]. The term formation judgment in this case would be the usual typing judgment for simply typed λ-calculus.

The hypersequent system **HQLC** is given in Figure 1. Notice that unlike traditional hypersequent calculi for Gödel-Dummett logic, **HQLC** does not have external weakening or external contraction rules. Both contraction and weakening are absorbed into logical rules. But as we shall see in Section 4, weakening and contraction are admissible in **HQLC**. Admissibility of contraction allows one to simplify slightly the Gentzen style cut elimination for **HQLC** (see Section 4). The $\lor r$ rule is non-standard, but is needed to absorb contraction. If one ignores the signature part of the hypersequents and the term formation judgments, the inference rules of **HQLC** are pretty standard for a hypersequent calculus.

Given a formula A, we say that A *is provable in* **HQLC** if the sequent $FV(A); . \Rightarrow A$ is derivable in **HQLC**.

4   Cut Elimination for HQLC

The cut elimination proof presented here is a variant of a Gentzen style cut elimination procedure for Gödel-Dummett logic [3,5]. But we note that it is also possible to extend the Schütte-Tait style of cut elimination in [4,9] to **HQLC**. We use a different form of multicut (see Section 4.3) to simplify slightly the main argument in cut elimination, but the proof is otherwise a fairly standard Gentzen style cut elimination proof. Before we proceed to the main cut elimination proof, we first establish some properties of derivations and rules in **HQLC**. Some proofs are omitted here, but they can be found in an extended version of this paper.

In a derivation of a hypersequent, one may encounter eigenvariables which are not free in the root hypersequent; we call these internal eigenvariables of the derivation. The names of those eigenvariables are unimportant, so long as they are chosen to be sufficiently fresh, in the context of the rules in which they are introduced. It is easy to prove by induction on the length of derivation and the fact that $\vdash$ is closed under renaming (property **P3**) that given a derivation of a hypersequent, there is an isomorphic derivation of the same hypersequent which differs only in the choice of naming of the internal eigenvariables. In the following proofs, we shall assume implicitly such a renaming is carried out during an inductive step so as to avoid name clash. Given a derivation Π, we denote with $|\Pi|$ its length.

4.1   Signature Weakening and Substitution

Lemma 3 (Signature weakening). *Let Π be a derivation of the hypersequent $\Sigma; \Gamma \Rightarrow \Delta \mid H$. Then for every variable x, there is a derivation Π' of $\Sigma, x; \Gamma \Rightarrow \Delta \mid H$ such that $|\Pi'| = |\Pi|$.*

Proof. By simple induction on $|\Pi|$ and property **P2**.   □

Definition 4. *A substitution $[t/x]$ is said to* respect *a sequent $\Sigma; \Gamma \Rightarrow C$ if $x \in \Sigma \cup FV(\Gamma, C)$ implies $\Sigma \setminus \{x\} \vdash t : \text{term}$. It is said to* respect *a hypersequent H if it respects every sequent in H.*

Lemma 5 (Substitution.). *Let Π be a derivation of a hypersequent H and let $[t/x]$ be a substitution respecting H. Then there exists a derivation Π' of $H[t/x]$ such that $|\Pi'| = |\Pi|$.*

Proof. By induction on Π. The only non-trivial cases are when Π ends with $\forall l$ or $\exists r$. We show the former here, the latter can be dealt with analogously. So suppose Π is as shown below (we assume w.l.o.g. y is not free in H):

$$\frac{\Sigma \vdash s : \text{term} \quad \overset{\Pi_1}{\Sigma; \Gamma, A[s/y] \Rightarrow B \mid H'}}{\Sigma; \Gamma, \forall y.A \Rightarrow B \mid H'} \; \forall l$$

Then Π' is the derivation below

$$\frac{\Sigma' \vdash s[t/x] : \text{term} \quad \overset{\Pi'_1}{\Sigma'; \Gamma[t/x], A[t/x][s[t/x]/y] \Rightarrow B[t/x] \mid H'[t/x]}}{\Sigma'; \Gamma[t/x], \forall y.A[t/x] \Rightarrow B[t/x] \mid H'[t/x]} \; \forall l$$

where $\Sigma' = \Sigma[t/x]$ and Π'_1 is obtained from the induction hypothesis. Note that as y is not free in t, we have $A[t/x][s[t/x]/y] = A[s[t/x]/y][t/x]$, so the induction hypothesis is indeed applicable to Π_1.

We still need to make sure that Π' is indeed a well-formed derivation, i.e., that the judgment $(\Sigma' \vdash s[t/x] : \text{term})$ is valid. There are two subcases to consider. The first is when $x \in \Sigma$, i.e., $\Sigma = \Sigma' \cup \{x\}$. The fact that $\Sigma \vdash s[t/x] : \text{term}$ holds follows from property **P4** of the relation $\vdash$.

Otherwise, $x \notin \Sigma$. In this case we have $\Sigma' = \Sigma$ and $\Sigma \vdash s : \text{term}$. The latter, together with **P1**, implies that $x \notin FV(s)$, and therefore $s[t/x] = s$ and $\Sigma' \vdash s[t/x] : \text{term}$ holds.   □

4.2   Invertible and Admissible Rules

A rule ρ is said to be *strictly invertible* if for every instance of ρ, whenever its conclusion is cut-free derivable, then there is a cut-free derivation with the same or smaller length of for each of its premises. We say that ρ is *invertible* if it satisfies the same condition, except for the proviso on the length of derivations.

Lemma 6. *Suppose Π is a derivation of $\Sigma; \Gamma \Rightarrow C \mid H$. Then for any A, there exists a derivation Π' of $\Sigma; A, \Gamma \Rightarrow C \mid H$ such that $|\Pi| = |\Pi'|$.*

Lemma 7. *The rules* $\wedge l$, $\wedge r$, $\vee l$, $\supset r$, $\exists l$ *and* $\forall r$ *are strictly invertible.*

Proof. Straightforward by induction on the length of derivation. In the cases of $\exists l$ and $\forall r$, we need Lemma 3, and in the case of $\supset r$, we need Lemma 6.   □

Lemma 8. *The rule* $\vee r$ *is invertible.*

A rule ρ is said to be *admissible* if whenever all its premises are cut-free derivable, then its conclusion is also cut-free derivable, without using ρ. It is said to be *height-conserving admissible* if given the derivations of its premises, one can derive the conclusion with less or the same length as the maximum length of its premise derivations. Using the invertibility of rules in Lemma 7 and Lemma 8, it can be proved that the following structural rules are admissible:

$$\frac{\Sigma; \Gamma \Rightarrow B \mid H}{\Sigma; A, \Gamma \Rightarrow B \mid H} \; wl \qquad \frac{\Sigma; A, A, \Gamma \Rightarrow B \mid H}{\Sigma, A, \Gamma \Rightarrow B \mid H} \; cl \qquad \frac{H}{H \mid G} \; ew \qquad \frac{H \mid H}{H} \; ec$$

Lemma 9. *The rules* wl *and* cl *are height-conserving admissible.*

Lemma 10. *The rules* ew *and* ec *are admissible.*

4.3   Cut Elimination

We first generalise the cut rule to the following *multicut*

$$\frac{\Sigma_1; \Delta_1 \Rightarrow A \mid H_1 \qquad \cdots \qquad \Sigma_n; \Delta_n \Rightarrow A \mid H_n \qquad G}{\Sigma_1; \Delta_1, \Gamma_1 \Rightarrow B_1 \mid \cdots \mid \Sigma_n; \Delta_n, \Gamma_n \Rightarrow B_n \mid H_1 \mid \cdots \mid H_n \mid H} \; mc$$

where G is the hypersequent $\Sigma_1; A, \Gamma_1 \Rightarrow B_1 \mid \cdots \mid \Sigma_n; A, \Gamma_n \Rightarrow B_n \mid H$. The formula A is called the *cut formula* of the mc rule. The premise $\Sigma_i; \Delta_i \Rightarrow A \mid H_i$ is called a *minor premise* of the mc rule. The premise G is called the *major premise*. Notice that each minor premise pairs with only one sequent in the major premise, unlike Avron's extended multicut [3] where the minor premise can pair with more than one sequent in the major premise.

A version of multicut similar to mc was proposed by Slaney [20] and was later used by McDowell and Miller in a cut-elimination proof for an intuitionistic logic [16]. In permutation of mc over (implicit) contraction in logical rules in the major premise, there will be no need to contract the hypersequents in the corresponding minor premise as is typical in Gentzen's multicuts, but one would instead duplicate the derivation of the minor premise (see the cut elimination proof below for more details). The use of mc allows one to simplify slightly the structure of the main arguments in the cut elimination proof (i.e., permutation of mc rule over other rules). In the cut elimination proof in [5], which uses Avron's multicuts [3], one needs to prove a lemma concerning cut-free admissibility of certain generalised $\exists l$ and $\vee r$ rules, e.g.,

$$\frac{H \mid \Gamma_1, A(a) \Rightarrow C_1 \mid \cdots \mid \Gamma_n, A(a) \Rightarrow C_n}{H \mid \Gamma_1, \exists x.A(x) \Rightarrow C_1 \mid \cdots \mid \Gamma_n, \exists x.A(x) \Rightarrow C_n} \exists l^*$$

where a is not free in the conclusion. The need to prove admissibility of this rule (and a similar version for $\vee l$) does not arise in here, due to the admissibility of (both internal and external) contraction and the mc rule.

The *cut rank* of an instance of an mc rule, with minor premise derivations $\Pi_1, \ldots, \Pi_n$, major premise derivation Π, and cut formula A, is the triple

$$\langle |A|, |\Pi|, \{|\Pi_1|, \ldots, |\Pi_n|\} \rangle$$

of the size of the cut formulae, the length of the major premise derivation, and the multiset of lengths of the minor premise derivations. Cut ranks are ordered lexicographically, where the last component of the triple is ordered according to multiset ordering. It can be shown that this order is wellfounded.

Theorem 11. *Cut elimination holds for* **HQLC.**

Proof. Suppose we have a derivation Ξ ending with an mc, with minor premise derivations $\Pi_1, \ldots, \Pi_n$ and major premise derivation Π, and the cut formula A. We assume w.l.o.g. that all Π_i and Π are cut free. Cut elimination is proved by induction on the cut rank, by removing the topmost cuts in succession.

We show that, we can reduce the mc rule to one with a smaller cut rank. In the reduction of mc, the last rule applied to the major premise derivation will determine which of the minor premises is selected for reduction. Note that since the order of the sequents in the major premise and the order of the minor premises in mc do not affect the cut rank, w.l.o.g., we assume that the derivation Π ends with a rule affecting $\Sigma_1; A, \Gamma_1 \Rightarrow C_1$, and/or $\Sigma_2; A, \Gamma_2 \Rightarrow C_2$ (if it ends with a com rule). So, in the case analysis on the possible reductions we shall only look at the first and/or the second minor premises.

If Π ends with any rule affecting only H, then the mc rule can be easily permuted up over the rule, and it is eliminable by the induction hypothesis.

Otherwise, Π must end with a rule affecting one (or two, in case of com) of the sequents used in the cut rule. Without loss of generality, assume it is either the first and/or the second sequent. There are several cases to consider. We show a case involving the $\exists$ quantifier to illustrate the use of the substitution lemma.

Suppose Π_1 ends with $\exists r$ and Π ends with $\exists l$, both with the cut formula as the principal formula, i.e., they are of the following forms, respectively:

$$\frac{\Sigma_1 \vdash t : \text{term} \quad \overset{\Pi'_1}{\Sigma_1; \Delta_1 \Rightarrow A'(t) \mid \Sigma_1; \Delta_1 \Rightarrow \exists x.A'(x) \mid H_1}}{\Sigma_1; \Delta_1 \Rightarrow \exists x.A'(x) \mid H_1} \exists r$$

$$\frac{\overset{\Psi}{\Sigma_1, x; A'(x), \Gamma_1 \Rightarrow B_1 \mid \cdots}}{\Sigma_1; \exists x.A'(x), \Gamma_1 \Rightarrow B_1 \mid \cdots} \exists l$$

Let Ξ_1 be

$$\frac{\begin{array}{cccc} \Pi_2 & \cdots & \Pi_n & \Psi[t/x] \\ \Sigma_2; \Delta_2 \Rightarrow A \mid H_2 & & \Sigma_n; \Delta_n \Rightarrow A \mid H_2 & \Sigma_1; A'(t), \Gamma_1 \Rightarrow B_1 \mid \cdots \end{array}}{\Sigma_1; A'(t), \Gamma_1 \Rightarrow B_1 \mid \Sigma_2; \Delta_2, \Gamma_2 \Rightarrow B_1 \mid \cdots \mid \Sigma_n; \Delta_n, \Gamma_n \Rightarrow B_n \mid \cdots} \; mc$$

where $\Psi[t/x]$ is the result of substituting x by t in Ψ (see Lemma 5). Let Ξ_2 be

$$\frac{\begin{array}{ccccc} & \Pi_1' & & & \\ \Sigma_1; \Delta_1 \Rightarrow A'(t) \mid \Sigma_1; \Delta_1 \Rightarrow A \mid H_1 & \Pi_2 & \cdots & \Pi_n & \Pi \\ & & \cdots & & \cdots & \cdots \end{array}}{\Sigma_1; \Delta_1 \Rightarrow A'(t) \mid \Sigma_1; \Delta_1, \Gamma_1 \Rightarrow B_1 \mid \cdots} \; mc$$

Then Ξ reduces to the derivation:

$$\frac{\dfrac{\overset{\Xi_1}{\Sigma_1; \Delta_1 \Rightarrow A'(t) \mid \Sigma_1; \Delta_1, \Gamma_1 \Rightarrow B_1 \mid \cdots} \quad \overset{\Xi_2}{\Sigma_1; A'(t), \Gamma_1 \Rightarrow B_1 \mid \cdots}}{\Sigma_1; \Delta_1, \Gamma_1 \Rightarrow B_1 \mid \Sigma_1; \Delta_1, \Gamma_1 \Rightarrow B_1 \mid \cdots} \; mc}{\Sigma_1; \Delta_1, \Gamma_1 \Rightarrow B_1 \mid \cdots \mid \Sigma_n; \Delta_n, \Gamma_n \Rightarrow B_n \mid \cdots} \; ec$$

where the double lines indicate multiple applications of the rule ec (which is cut-free admissible by Lemma 10). It is clear that the cut ranks in the reduct of Ξ are smaller than the cut rank of Ξ so by the induction hypothesis, all the cuts in the reduct can be eliminated. □

5   Soundness and Completeness of HQLC

One way of proving soundnesss of **HQLC** would be to interpret hypersequents as formulae, and show that the formula schemes corresponding to inference rules can be proved in the Hilbert system **QLC**. Unfortunately, there does not seem to be an easy way to interpret hypersequent rules as valid formulae in **QLC**. The main problem is in the interpretation of eigenvariables in hypersequents, in particular, their intended scopes within the hypersequents. If a variable, say x, appears in the signatures of two different sequents in a hypersequent, then there is a question of what should be the scope of that variable. There are two possible encodings: one in which the signature in a sequent is seen as implicitly universally quantified over the sequent, and the other in which the scope of signatures is over the entire hypersequent. Consider for example the following hypersequent:

$$x, y; A(x, y) \Rightarrow B(x, y) \mid x, z; C(x, z) \Rightarrow D(x, z).$$

The standard encoding of hypersequents without signatures is to interpret $\Rightarrow$ as implication and $\mid$ as disjunction. If we interpret signatures as having local scopes over the individual sequents, then the above hypersequent would be encoded as

$$(\forall x \forall y.(A(x, y) \supset B(x, y)) \vee (\forall x \forall z.(C(x, z) \supset D(x, z)).$$

If we interpret signatures as having global scopes, then the two occurrences of x in the signatures will be identified as a single universal quantifier:

$$\forall x \forall y \forall z.(A(x,y) \supset B(x,y)) \vee (C(x,z) \supset D(x,z)).$$

Under the second interpretation, the $\forall r$ rule is obviously invalid in **QLC** as its validity would entail the quantifier shift axiom. Under the first interpretation, the *com*-rule would be unsound. To see why, consider the hypersequent:

$$x; p(x) \Rightarrow q(x) \mid x; q(x) \Rightarrow p(x).$$

This hypersequent is provable in **HQLC**. But if we follow the first interpretation, then it would entail that $(\forall x.p(x) \supset q(x)) \vee (\forall x.q(x) \supset p(x))$ is valid in **QLC**, which is wrong, as it is not valid even classically. It might be possible to reformulate the *com*-rule to avoid this problem, but it is at present not clear how this could be done.

The approach followed in this paper is to interpret the rules of **HQLC** in a Gödel-Dummett logic extended with an existence predicate [15]. The existence predicate was introduced by Scott [19] in an extension to intuitionistic logic, and has recently been formalised in sequent calculus [6]. We first extend the language of intuitionistic logic with a unary predicate E representing the existence predicate. The semantics of the extended logic is as in intuitionistic logic, but with the interpretation of the existence predicate satisfying: $I_w(c) \in I_w(E)$ for every $w \in W$ and every constant symbol c in **QLC**.

Let GD^c be the standard Gödel-Dummett logic with constant domain, and let GD^{ce} be GD^c extended with the existence predicate. The key to the soundness proof is a result by Iemhoff [15] which relates GD and GD^{ce}. This is achieved via a function $\lceil . \rceil$ encoding an intuitionistic formula without the existence predicate into one with the existence predicate, satisfying:

- $\lceil p(\vec{t}) \rceil = p(\vec{t})$, for any predicate symbol p,
- $\lceil . \rceil$ commutes with all propositional connectives,
- $\lceil \exists x.A \rceil = \exists x.E(x) \wedge \lceil A \rceil$, and
- $\lceil \forall x.A \rceil = \forall x.E(x) \supset \lceil A \rceil$.

The following is a corollary of a result by Iemhoff (see Lemma 4.3 in [15]).

Theorem 12. *A closed formula A is valid in GD iff $\lceil A \rceil$ is valid in GD^{ce}.*

The soundness proof below uses the following interpretation of sequents and hypersequents. Given a multiset $\Gamma = \{A_1, \ldots, A_n\}$, we denote with $\lceil \Gamma \rceil$ the formula $\lceil A_1 \rceil \wedge \cdots \wedge \lceil A_n \rceil$. Given a set of eigenvariable $\Sigma = \{x_1, \ldots, x_n\}$, we write $E(\Sigma)$ to denote the formula $E(x_1) \wedge \cdots \wedge E(x_n)$. Let τ_s be a function from sequents to formulaes such that

$$\tau_s(\Sigma; \Gamma \Rightarrow C) = E(\Sigma) \wedge \lceil \Gamma \rceil \supset \lceil C \rceil.$$

The function τ_h mapping a hypersequent to a formula is defined as:

$$\tau_h(S_1 \mid \cdots \mid S_n) = \forall \vec{x}. \bigvee_i \tau_s(S_i)$$

where $\vec{x}$ is the list of all variables in the hypersequent and each S_i is a sequent. We shall overload the symbol τ_h to denote the translation function for the term formation judgment, which is defined as follows (where $\Sigma = \{\vec{x}\}$):

$$\tau_h(\Sigma \vdash t : \text{term}) = \forall \vec{x}.E(\Sigma) \supset E(t).$$

For the remainder of this section, we shall assume that the term formulation judgment $\vdash$ is defined as follows:

$$\frac{x \in \Sigma}{\Sigma \vdash x : \text{term}} \qquad \frac{}{\Sigma \vdash c : \text{term}} \ c \text{ is a constant}$$

Since the domains are assumed to be always non-empty, we assume that there is at least one constant symbol. It is easy to show that properties **P1** – **P4** hold for this definition of $\vdash$. Additionally, we also have the following lemma.

Lemma 13. *For any term t, $\Sigma \vdash t$: term, provided that $FV(t) \subseteq \Sigma$.*

Lemma 14. *If H is provable in **HQLC** then $\tau_h(H)$ is valid in GD^{ce}.*

Proof. Given a rule ρ with premises $H_1, \ldots, H_n$ and conclusion H, we show that if $\tau_h(H_1), \ldots, \tau_h(H_n)$ are valid in GD^{ce} then $\tau_h(H_{n+1})$ is valid in GD^{ce}. It is not difficult to verify that (e.g., using the hypersequent system in [5])

$$\tau_h(H_1) \wedge \cdots \wedge \tau_h(H_n) \supset \tau_h(H_{n+1})$$

is a tautology in GD^c, hence it is also valid in GD^{ce}. Therefore a cut-free derivation in **HQLC** can be simulated by a chain of modus ponens using the tautologies encoding its rule instances, with two assumptions: the encodings of the identity rule and the term formation judgment. The former is obviously valid, so we show the latter. That is, $\tau_h(\Sigma \vdash t : \text{term})$ is valid in GD^{ce}, whenever $\Sigma \vdash t : \text{term}$ holds. This is straightforward from the definition of $\vdash$. □

Theorem 15. *If A is provable in **HQLC** then A is provable in **QLC**.*

Proof. We first show that for every *closed* formula A, if A is provable in **HQLC** then A is provable in **QLC**. By Lemma 14, $\tau_h(FV(A); . \Rightarrow A)$ is valid in GD^{ce}. Since A is closed, $FV(A) = \emptyset$, therefore $\tau_h(FV(A); . \Rightarrow A) = \lceil A \rceil$. Then, by Theorem 12, A is valid in GD, and by Theorem 1, A is provable in **QLC**.

Now, if A is not closed, i.e., $FV(A) \neq \emptyset$, then we have that $\forall \vec{x}.A$, where $\{\vec{x}\} = FV(A)$, is also provable in **HQLC**, hence by the above result, $\forall \vec{x}.A$ is provable in **QLC**. To show that A is also provable in **QLC**, we do a detour through Corsi's sequent calculus for **QLC** [10], where it is easily shown that $\forall \vec{x}.A$ is provable iff A is provable in the sequent calculus. □

Theorem 16. *If A is provable in **QLC** then A is provable in **HQLC**.*

Proof. We first show that whenever A is provable in **QLC** then the sequent $\Sigma; . \Rightarrow A$ is derivable in **HQLC** for some $\Sigma \supseteq FV(A)$. This is done by induction on the length of derivation in **QLC**.

It is enough to show that every instance of the axioms of **QLC** and its inference rules, modus ponens and the quantifier introduction (i.e., generalisation), are derivable in **HQLC**. The generalisation rule is trivially derivable. To derive modus ponens, in addition to using cut, we need Lemma 3 and Lemma 7 (invertibility of $\supset$). The linearity axiom is easily derived using the *com*-rule. The non-trivial part is the derivations of the following axioms that involve quantifiers:

$$(Ax1) \quad \forall x.A \supset A[t/x] \qquad (Ax2) \quad A[t/x] \supset \exists x.A$$

We show here a derivation of (any instance of) $(Ax1)$; the other is similar. In this case, we let Σ be the set of all free variables in $(Ax1)$. Then we have:

$$\cfrac{\cfrac{\Sigma \vdash t : \text{term} \quad \cfrac{}{\Sigma; \forall x.A, A[t/x] \Rightarrow A[t/x]}\ id}{\Sigma; \forall x.A \Rightarrow A[t/x]}\ \forall l}{\Sigma; .\ \Rightarrow \forall x.A \supset A[t/x]}\ \supset r$$

Note that the judgment $\Sigma \vdash t : \text{term}$ is valid, by Lemma 13.

Now, we need to show that A is provable in **HQLC**, i.e., that the sequent $FV(A); .\ \Rightarrow A$ is derivable. By the above result, we have a derivation Π of the sequent $\Sigma; .\ \Rightarrow A$ for some $\Sigma \supseteq FV(A)$. Note that Σ may contain more variables than $FV(A)$. But since we assume that the domains are non-empty, we have at least one constant, say c, in the language. Let $\vec{y}$ be the variables in $\Sigma \setminus FV(A)$. Then by applying the substitution lemma (Lemma 5), i.e., substituting all $\vec{y}$ with c, to Π, we get a derivation of $FV(A); .\ \Rightarrow A$.   □

The derivation of $\forall x.A \supset A[t/x]$ in the completeness proof above relies on the underlying assumption that all closed terms denote existing objects (see Lemma 13). A similar completeness result is shown in [6], where Gentzen's LJ is shown to be equivalent to a specific existence logic called **LJE**$(\Sigma_{\mathcal{L}})$. The intuitionistic fragment of **HQLC** can be seen as the equivalent of **LJE**$(\Sigma_{\mathcal{L}})$.

6   Related and Future Work

A cut-free sequent calculus for **QLC** was first introduced by Corsi in [10]. Avellone, et. al., gave a tableau calculus for the same logic [2], and showed how their tableau calculus can also be converted into a cut-free sequent calculus. Both sequent calculi are multiple-conclusion calculi and use a simultaneous introduction rule for $\supset$ and $\forall$:

$$\cfrac{\Gamma, A_1 \Rightarrow B_1, \Delta_1 \quad \cdots \quad \Gamma, A_m \Rightarrow B_m, \Delta_m \quad \Gamma \Rightarrow C_1(a), \Lambda_1 \quad \cdots \quad \Gamma \Rightarrow C_n(a), \Lambda_n}{\Gamma \Rightarrow \Delta}$$

where $\Delta = \{A_1 \supset B_1, , \cdots, A_m \supset B_m, \forall x.C_1(x), \cdots, \forall x.C_n(x)\}$, $\Delta_i = \Delta \setminus \{A_i \supset B_i\}$ and $\Lambda_i = \Delta \setminus \{\forall x.C_i(x)\}$.

The idea of giving quantifiers an explicit structural component in sequents has been considered in a number of previous work. Wansing [25] studies substructural quantifiers in modal logic, in which the Barcan formula may or may not hold, using the display calculus framework. The treatment of quantifiers as structural connectives has also been explored in the calculus of structures, e.g., [7,22], and in nested sequent calculi [8].

As should be clear from the soundness proof in Section 5, the existence predicate is implicit in our notion of hypersequents. One could also consider an approach where the existence predicate is an explicit part of the language of hypersequents and extends the methods in [6] to prove cut elimination. In this setting, the term formation judgment would be encoded as a set of axioms governing the derivability of the existence predicate, and a form of cut elimination can be proved following [6], showing that cuts can be restricted to a simple form where the cut formula contains only the existence predicate.

We note that although we prove soundness w.r.t. a logic without function symbols, the soundness proof shown here can be generalised straightforwardly to logics with function symbols.

From a proof theoretic perspective, the solution proposed here is not entirely satisfactory, due to the lack of a clear formula-interpretation of hypersequents, hence the inability to get a direct encoding of **HQLC** into the Hilbert axiomatic system **QLC**. It would seem more natural to treat the signature in a sequent as *binders*, along the line of the framework proposed in [8]. This would entail a move from hypersequent to a sort of nested hypersequent (or perhaps a variant of tree-hypersequent [18]) and deep-inference rules. Our reliance on the semantic correspondence in Theorem 12 means that the current approach is difficult to generalize to other logics where the existence predicate is not so well understood.

References

1. Avellone, A., Ferrari, M., Miglioli, P.: Duplication-free tableau calculi and related cut-free sequent calculi for the interpolable propositional intermediate logics. In: Logic Journal of the IGPL, vol. 7(4), pp. 447–480 (1999)
2. Avellone, A., Ferrari, M., Miglioli, P., Moscato, U.: A tableau calculus for Dummett predicate logic. In: *Proc. of the Eleventh Brazilian Conference on Mathematical Logic 1996.* Contemporary Mathematics, vol. 235, pp. 135–150. American Mathematical Society, Providence (1999)
3. Avron, A.: Hypersequents, logical consequence and intermediate logics for concurrency. Ann. Math. Artif. Intell. 4, 225–248 (1991)
4. Baaz, M., Ciabattoni, A.: A schütte-tait style cut-elimination proof for first-order gödel logic. In: Egly, U., Fermüller, C. (eds.) TABLEAUX 2002. LNCS (LNAI), vol. 2381, pp. 24–37. Springer, Heidelberg (2002)
5. Baaz, M., Ciabattoni, A., Fermüller, C.G.: Hypersequent calculi for Gödel logics - a survey. J. Log. Comput. 13(6), 835–861 (2003)
6. Baaz, M., Iemhoff, R.: Gentzen calculi for the existence predicate. Studia Logica 82(1), 7–23 (2006)
7. Brünnler, K.: Cut elimination inside a deep inference system for classical predicate logic. Studia Logica 82(1), 51–71 (2006)
8. Brünnler, K.: How to universally close the existential rule. In: Fermüller, C.G., Voronkov, A. (eds.) LPAR-17. LNCS, vol. 6397, pp. 172–186. Springer, Heidelberg (2010)

9. Ciabattoni, A.: A proof-theoretical investigation of global intuitionistic (fuzzy) logic. Arch. Math. Log. 44(4), 435–457 (2005)
10. Corsi, G.: A cut-free calculus for Dummett's LC quantified. Zeitschr. f. math. Logik und Grundlagen d. Math. 35, 289–301 (1989)
11. Corsi, G.: Completeness theorem for Dummett's LC quantified and some of its extensions. Studia Logica 51(2), 317–336 (1992)
12. Dummett, M.: A propositional calculus with denumerable matrix. J. Symbolic Logic 24(2), 97–106 (1959)
13. Dyckhoff, R.: A deterministic terminating sequent calculus for Gödel-Dummett logic. Logic Journal of the IGPL 7(3), 319–326 (1999)
14. Gödel, K.: On the intuitionistic propositional calculus. In: Feferman, S., Dawson Jr, S.W., Kleene, S.C., Moore, G.H., Solovay, R.M., van Heijenoort, J. (eds.) Collected Works, vol. 1. Oxford University Press, Oxford (1986)
15. Iemhoff, R.: A note on linear Kripke models. J. Log. Comput. 15(4), 489–506 (2005)
16. McDowell, R., Miller, D.: Cut-elimination for a logic with definitions and induction. Theor. Comput. Sci. 232(1-2), 91–119 (2000)
17. Miller, D.: A logic programming language with lambda-abstraction, function variables, and simple unification. J. Log. Comput. 1(4), 497–536 (1991)
18. Poggiolesi, F.: The tree-hypersequent method for modal propositional logic. Trends in Logic: Towards Mathematical Philsophy, 9–30 (2009)
19. Scott, D.: Identity and existence in intuitionistic logic. In: Fourman, M., Mulvey, C., Scott, D. (eds.) Applications of Sheaves. Lecture Notes in Mathematics, vol. 753, pp. 660–696. Springer, Berlin (1979)
20. Slaney, J.K.: Solution to a problem of Ono and Komori. Journal of Philosophical Logic 18, 103–111 (1989)
21. Sonobe, O.: A Gentzen-type formulation of some intermediate propositional logics. J. Tsuda College 7, 7–14 (1975)
22. Tiu, A.: A local system for intuitionistic logic. In: Hermann, M., Voronkov, A. (eds.) LPAR 2006. LNCS (LNAI), vol. 4246, pp. 242–256. Springer, Heidelberg (2006)
23. Troelstra, A., Schwichtenberg, H.: Basic Proof Theory. Cambridge University Press, Cambridge (1996)
24. van Dalen, D.: Logic and Structure. Springer, Heidelberg (2004)
25. Wansing, H.: Displaying Modal Logic. Kluwer Academic Publishers, Boston (1998)

MaLeCoP
Machine Learning Connection Prover

Josef Urban[1,*], Jiří Vyskočil[2,**], and Petr Štěpánek[3,***]

[1] Radboud University Nijmegen, The Netherlands
[2] Czech Technical University
[3] Charles University, Czech Republic

Abstract. Probabilistic guidance based on learned knowledge is added to the connection tableau calculus and implemented on top of the lean-CoP theorem prover, linking it to an external advisor system. In the typical mathematical setting of solving many problems in a large complex theory, learning from successful solutions is then used for guiding theorem proving attempts in the spirit of the MaLARea system. While in MaLARea learning-based axiom selection is done outside unmodified theorem provers, in MaLeCoP the learning-based selection is done inside the prover, and the interaction between learning of knowledge and its application can be much finer. This brings interesting possibilities for further construction and training of self-learning AI mathematical experts on large mathematical libraries, some of which are discussed. The initial implementation is evaluated on the MPTP Challenge large theory benchmark.

1   Introduction

This paper describes addition of machine learning and probabilistic guidance to connection tableau calculus, and the initial implementation in the leanCoP system using an interface to an external advice system. The paper is organized as follows:[1] Section 1 describes the recent developments in large-theory automated reasoning and motivation for the research described here. Section 2 describes the machine learning (data-driven) paradigm and its use in guiding automated reasoning. Section 3 shortly summarizes the existing leanCoP theorem prover based on connection tableaux. Section 4 explains the general architecture for combining external machine learning guidance with a tableau prover. Section 5 describes our experimental implementation. Section 6 describes some experiments done with the initial implementation. Section 7 concludes and discusses future work and extensions.

---

* Supported by The Netherlands Organization for Scientific Research (NWO) grants *Learning2Reason* and *MathWiki*.
** Supported by the Czech institutional grant MSM 6840770038.
*** Supported by the Grant Agency of Charles University, grant 9828/2009.
[1] We would like to thank the anonymous referees for helping to significantly improve the presentation of this work.

K. Brünnler and G. Metcalfe (Eds.): TABLEAUX 2011, LNAI 6793, pp. 263–277, 2011.
© Springer-Verlag Berlin Heidelberg 2011

1.1   Large-Theory Automated Reasoning

In the recent years, increasing amount of mathematics and knowledge in general is being expressed formally, in computer-understandable and computer-processable form. Large formal libraries of re-usable knowledge are built with interactive proof assistants, like Mizar, Isabelle, Coq, and HOL (Light). For example, the large Mizar Mathematical Library (MML) contains now (February 2011) over 1100 formal articles from various fields, covering substantial part of undergraduate mathematics. At the same time, the use of the formal approach is also increasing in non-mathematical fields, for example in software and hardware verification and in common-sense reasoning about real-world knowledge. This again leads to growth of formal knowledge bases in these fields.

Large formal theories are a recent challenge for the field of automated reasoning. The ability of ATP systems to reason inside large theories has started to improve after 2005, when first-order ATP translations of the particular formalisms used e.g. by Mizar [16], Isabelle [5], SUMO, and Cyc started to appear, and large theory benchmarks and competitions like MPTP Challenge and CASC LTB were introduced. The automated reasoning techniques developed so far for large theories can be broadly divided into two categories:

1. Techniques based purely on heuristic symbolic analysis of formulas available in problems.
2. Techniques taking into account also previous proofs.

The SInE preprocessor by Kryštof Hoder [4,17] seems to be so far the most successful heuristic in the first category. In domains like common-sense reasoning that typically lack large number of previous nontrivial and verified proofs and lemmas, and mostly consist of hierarchic definitions, such heuristics can sometimes even provide complete strategies for these domains.[2] MaLARea [18] is an example of a system from the second category. It is strong in hard mathematical domains, where the knowledge bases contain much less definitions than nontrivial lemmas and theorems, and previous verified proofs can be used for learning proof guidance. This approach is described in the next section, giving motivation for the work described in this paper.

2   Machine Learning in Large Theory ATP

The data-driven [12] approaches to constructing algorithms have been recently successful in AI domains like web search, consumer choice prediction, autonomous vehicle control, and chess. In contrast to purely theory-driven approaches, when whole algorithms are constructed explicitly by humans, the data-driven approaches rely on deriving substantial parts of algorithms from large amounts of data. In the ATP domain, the use of machine learning started to be explored by the Munich

---

[2] For example, a Prolog-based premise selection preprocessor was used by Vampire in the CYC category of the 2008 CASC LTB competition to solve all problems.

group [3]. The E prover [11] by Stephan Schulz contains several hooks where algorithms can be optimized based on machine learning. The most advanced technique there being probably matching of abstracted previous proof traces for guiding the inference (given clause loop) process. Simpler techniques like optimization of strategy selection or scheduling are used not only by E prover, but also, e.g., by the Vampire system [10]. In 2007 the Machine Learner for Automated Reasoning (MaLARea [18]) started to be developed, triggered by the translation of the Mizar library to first-order ATP format and the need to provide efficient reasoning over the ca 50000 theorems and definitions in it. We explain here the basic idea of learning from proofs, which is in several modified forms used also in MaLeCoP.

The basic idea of the machine learning approach is to learn an association from features (in the machine learning terminology) of the conjectures (or even of the whole problems when speaking generally) to proving methods that are successful when the features are present. In MaLARea, this general setting is instantiated in the following way: The features characterizing a conjecture are the symbols appearing in them, and the proving method is an ordering of all the axioms according to their expected relevance to proving the conjecture. One might think of this as the particular set of symbols determining a particular sublanguage (and thus also a subtheory) of a large theory, and the corresponding ordering of all the available axioms as, e.g., a frequency of their usage in a book written about that particular subtheory. Once a sufficient body of proofs is known, a machine learning system (SNoW [2] is used by MaLARea in naive Bayes mode) is trained on them, linking conjecture symbols with the axioms that were useful for proving the conjectures. For learning and evaluation in SNoW, all symbols and axiom names are disjointly translated to integers. The integers corresponding to symbols are the input features, and those corresponding to axioms are the output features of the learning process.

MaLARea can work with arbitrary ATP backends (E and SPASS by default), however, the communication between learning and the ATP systems is high-level: The learned relevance is used to try to solve problems with varied limited numbers of the most relevant axioms. Successful runs provide additional data for learning (useful for solving related problems), while unsuccessful runs can yield countermodels, which can be in MaLARea re-used for semantic pre-selection and as additional input features for learning.

An advantage of the high-level approach is that it gives a generic inductive (learning)/deductive (ATP) metasystem to which any ATP can be easily plugged as a blackbox. Its disadvantage is that it does not attempt to use the learned knowledge for guiding the ATP search process once the axioms are selected. Hence the logical next step described in this paper: We try to suggest how to use the learned knowledge for guiding proof search *inside* a theorem prover. We choose the leanCoP theorem prover for the experiments, both because of its simplicity and easiness of modification, and for a number of interesting properties described below that make it suitable for interaction with learning. The next section summarizes leanCoP.

3   leanCoP: Lean Connection-Based Theorem Prover

3.1   Why leanCoP

leanCoP is an economically written connection-based theorem prover. The main theorem prover can be written on a couple of lines in Prolog, while its performance is surprisingly good, especially when goal-directness is important. The reasons for choosing leanCoP for our experiments can be summarized in the following points:

- leanCoP already has good performance on the MPTP Challenge benchmark [7]. This guarantees sufficient amount of proofs to learn from.
- The implementation is simple, high-level, and Prolog-based, making it easy to experiment with. Our experience with modifying C-written ATPs (even very nicely written like the E prover as in [15]) is that it always involves a lot of low-level implementation work.
- The tableau calculus seems to be quite suitable for the kind of additions that we want to experiment with. It has a transparent notion of proof state (branch that needs to be closed, open goals) to which advising operations can be applied. This contrasts with resolution ATPs that have just several large piles of clauses describing the proof state.
- The integration of learning and ranking and its use can be very tight, allowing implementation of techniques similar to just-in-time compilation. This means keeping track of frequent requests – especially in the many-problems/large-theory setting – and providing (possibly asynchronous) advice for them.
- We hope that the simple Prolog setting should allow easy additional experiments. This could include simple addition of other kinds of external advisors (e.g. for computer algebra), experiments with online learning from closed branches, and experiments with probabilistic finding of decision procedures (expressed just as sets of Prolog clauses), with the possibility of Prolog techniques for program transformation of the found algorithms.

3.2   The Basic leanCoP Procedure and its Parametrization

For further understanding, it is good to summarize the main features of lean-CoP [6,8]. leanCoP is an automated theorem prover for classical first-order logic with equality. It uses an optimized structure-preserving transformation into clausal form (DNF, see also below), to which connected tableau search (with iterative deepening to guarantee completeness) is then applied. The reduction rule of the connection calculus is applied before the extension rule, and open branches are selected in a depth-first way. Additional inference rules and strategies are regularity, lemmata, and restricted backtracking. leanCoP has several parameters influencing its work [8][3], which can also be used for defining various strategies and scheduling over them:

- if the option *def* is used, new definitions are introduced systematically during the clausification to shorten the resulting clause set

---

[3] This description is also relevant for leanCoP 2.1.

- if the option *nodef* is used, no new definitions are introduced in clausification
- if none of the options *def, nodef* is used, and the formula has the form $X \rightarrow Y$, then X is processed as in the *nodef* case, while Y as in the *def* case
- if option *reo(N)* is used, the set of clauses is shuffled using N as a parameter
- if option *cut* is used, there is no backtracking after successfully closed branches
- if option *scut* is used, backtracking is restricted for alternative start clauses
- if option *conj* is used, a special literal is added to the conjecture clauses in order to mark them as the only possible start clauses.

4   The General Architecture

As mentioned in the introduction, our goal is to experiment with smart (external) proof search guidance used inside theorem provers' internal mechanisms, not just outside them for premise pruning as MaLARea does. Our goal is an AI architecture that is closer to human thinking in that it does not blindly try every deductive possibility, but chooses the best course of action based on its knowledge of the world and previous experiences. The architecture should be able to learn both from successes and from mistakes, and update its decision mechanisms when such new knowledge is available. We also want our architecture to be not just a theoretical toy, but a system that actually proves theorems, and does that (at least often) more efficiently than the unguided systems thanks to the smart guidance. This set of requirements seems to be quite an ambitious program, below we explain our general approach, problems encountered, and the initial implementation.

4.1   The Concerns

The particular task that we initially consider is advising clause selection in the extension steps of the tableau proving process. The obvious intuition that this is the core source of possible speedups (once smart guidance is provided) is demonstrated below in the Evaluation section.

Several concerns like speed, generality, and extendability influence the general design. Measurements show that leanCoP can do an order of several hundred thousands basic inferences (extension steps) per minute on recent hardware.[4] In large mathematical theories, typically thousands of different symbols appear, and thousands of theorems are available for proving. If a smart (external) mechanism for formula/clause selection in such large theories took a minute for its recommendation, and we were using the mechanism for each inference, the inference speed would drop from hundreds of thousands to one per minute. With sufficiently "complicated AI" implementations of the external advice such (and much higher) times are conceivable. Even worse, one can still argue that it might be the right thing to do when solving hard problems, because the raw inference

---

[4] All measurements are done on the server of the Foundations group at Radboud University Nijmegen (RU), which is eight-core Intel Xeon E5520 2.27GHz with 8GB RAM and 8MB CPU cache.

speed matters very little when we traverse superexponential search space. Obviously, doing experimental research in such setting would be very costly. That's why we want to have reasonable speed of the guiding mechanism for experiments, and possibly use it only in the most critical choices.

Several options can be considered for implementing the guidance mechanism:

1. Using a raw external learning/advising system like SNoW in MaLARea, via socket communication with the theorem proving process.
2. Implementing the learning/advising system directly as a part of the prover.
3. Compiling/linking an external system directly with the theorem prover's binary (to avoid communication overhead).
4. Using an interface layer (directly in the prover or as a separate tool) that talks to the external tools, organizes their work, and talks to the prover.
5. Combinations of above.

Generality and extendability requirements tell us to avoid the second option, at least in the experimental phase, because we want to be able to easily plug in different external advice systems. For example, the SNoW system itself provides several learning mechanisms (winnow, perceptron, naive bayes) and a number of options to them. Kernel-based learning has been also recently experimented with in the context of premise selection [14], improving the guidance precision. The general design suggested below and instantiated in our prototype[5] uses the fourth option from the above list.

4.2   The Design

The general design that we propose is as follows (see also Figure 1): The theorem prover (P) should have a sufficiently fast communication channel to a general advisor (A) that accepts queries (proof state descriptions) and training data (characterization of the proof state[6] together with solutions[7] and failures) from the prover, processes them, and replies to the prover (advising, e.g., which clauses to choose). The advisor A also talks to external system(s) (E). A translates the queries and information produced by P to the formalism used by a particular E, and translates E's guidance back to the formalism used by P. At suitable time, A also hands over the (suitably transformed) training data to E, so that E can update its knowledge of the world on which its advice is based. A is free to spawn/query as many instances/versions of Es as necessary, and A is responsible for managing the guidance provided by them. Particular instances of Es that we have in mind are learning systems, however we believe that the tableau setting is also suitable for linking of SMT solvers, computer algebra systems, and all kinds of other AI systems, probably in a more straightforward way than for the resolution-based systems [13,9].

---

[5] http://mws.cs.ru.nl/~urban/malecop/
[6] Instantiated, e.g., as the set of literals/symbols on the current branch.
[7] Instantiated, e.g., as the description of clauses used at particular proof states.

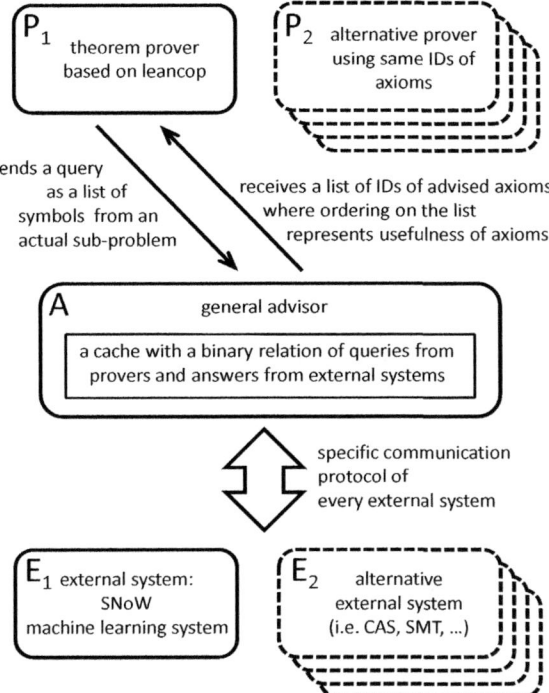

Fig. 1. The General Architecture

5 MaLeCoP: Machine Learning Connection Prover

The above general ideas have been initially implemented by using a modified version of leanCoP as P, the SNoW machine learner/advisor as E, and writing a general managing library in Perl for A. These components and their linking are explained below.

5.1 The Theorem Prover

The theorem prover we choose is leanCoP (version 2.1), however a number of modifications have to be made so that it fits into the general architecture. Here we mention some of them.

Consistent Clausification. The original leanCoP interleaves various clausification strategies with the tableau search. This means that sometimes significant changes can be done by changing the clausification (see, e.g., the options *def, nodef, reo* in Section 3). Changing the clausification however means that different skolem symbols and new definitions are produced, and clauses have different names and shapes. Additionally, the original leanCoP works in a one-problem-at-a-time setting, always inventing new names for skolem symbols and new definitions for each problem, despite the fact that the formulas/clauses are shared among many problems. This would not work in our setting, because the guidance is trained on symbol names and clause names. In other words, it is necessary to change leanCoP in such a way so that its various settings always work with the same clause normal form, and so that the new symbols are introduced consistently (with the same name) in all problems that share a particular formula. This is done by splitting the work of leanCoP on a large number of problems into two phases:

1. Common clausification done for all problems together, with consistent introduction of new symbols.
2. The separate tableau search, starting already with the clausified problem.

The 252 large MPTP Challenge problems contain 1485 unique formulas with a lot of repetition across the problems (this is the large consistent theory aspect), yielding 102331 (nonunique) formulas in all 252 problems all together. These 1485 formulas are consistently clausified in the first phase to 6969 unique clauses, appearing all together 396927 times in the jointly clausified problems, and containing 2171 unique symbols. This level of consistency and sharing on the symbol and clause level should ensure good transfer of knowledge during the learning and advice phases. As a byproduct of the clausification we also produce a mapping of clauses to symbols contained in them, a mapping of clauses to hashes of all terms contained in them, and a listing of all symbol names and clause names. These are later used by the general advisor (A) and external system(s) E.[8]

Strategies for Guidance. While we try to make the access to the advice as fast as possible (by caching in the advisor, etc.), it turns out that on average it takes about 0.2 second to the SNoW system to produce advice. This is certainly a bottleneck we need to work on, on the other hand, evaluation of a Bayes net on nearly 7000 targets, and their sorting according to the activation weight might really justify these times. In that case further work on faster external systems will be needed. As it is now, one external advice costs an order of one thousand leanCoP inferences. That is why we need to define strategies trading in a reasonable way the external advice for internal inferencing. The current set of strategies is as follows:

1. `original_leancop`: This mode works exactly as the original core leanCoP prover, however using the consistent clausification (affecting some options) as described above.
2. `naive`: From all the literals on the current branch symbols are extracted, and sent to the advisor. The advisor replies with an ordered list of recommended clauses for the current inference. If none of these clauses succeeds, the conjecture clauses are tried. This mode can obviously be incomplete if

---

[8] The term hashes are not used yet for learning/advice, and we also do not provide semantic (model) features as in MaLARea SG1 [18].

the advice is bad and a non-conjecture clause is needed. It is also demands advice for every inference, making it currently very slow.

3. `naive_and_complete`: As `naive`, but if no advised clause succeeds, all remaining clauses from the problem are tried in their original order in the problem. This makes this strategy complete, yet still very slow.

4. `full_caching_and_complete`: Produces same results as `naive_and_complete`, however it applies internal caching in Prolog to cut down the number of slow external queries. For every external query the advised clauses are cached in the advised order in a new clause database, and if the query is repeated this clause database is used instead of asking the external advisor again. This obviously increases the memory consumption of the Prolog process.

5. `smart_caching_and_complete`: Works in the same way as `naive_and_complete`, using a similar method as `full_caching_and_complete`. However new clauses databases are created only for the advised clauses (not for all clauses as in `full_caching_and_complete`). If the new database is not successful, then the original leanCoP database is used.

6. `smart_caching`: Works as `smart_caching_and_complete`, however it caches only the advised clauses. The original clause database is never used, making this strategy incomplete.

7. `original_leancop_with_first_advice`: At the start of the proof search one query is made to the advisor sending all conjecture symbols. A new Prolog database is created containing the advised clauses in the advised order, followed by the rest of the clauses in the original order. This database is then used in the rest of proof search without further queries to the advisor. This is obviously very fast and complete, but the use of external advice is very limited.

8. `leancop_ala_malarea`: As `original_leancop_with_first_advice`, however only the advised clauses and conjecture clauses are asserted into the new database. This results in an incomplete search limited in the same way as in MaLARea.

9. `limited_smart_with_first_advice(Depth)`: This uses `smart_caching` until the Depth in tableau is reached, then it proceeds as `original_leancop_with_first_advice`. The first stages thus cause incompleteness. External queries are limited to Depth, which allows us to be flexible with trading speed for precision.

10. `limited_smart_and_complete_with_first_advice(Depth)`: Uses `smart_caching_and_complete` until Depth, then again `original_leancop_with_first_advice`.

11. `scalable_with_first_advice(Limit,Mode_After_Limit)`: This is a metastrategy. Its basis is `original_leancop_with_first_advice`. If the clause search does not succeed for Limit-th clause (in the original database) of a particular literal (extension step), the strategy `Mode_After_Limit` is used for the next clause search. This again is used to limit the uses of the (typically expensive) `Mode_After_Limit` strategy to "justified cases", when the original proof search seems to be bad.

12. `scalable_with_first_advice(Limit,Query_Limit,Mode_After_Limit)`:
    This is an extension of the previous metastrategy. When the Limit-th clause
    search fails, the branching factor is computed (by counting all clauses to which
    a connection can be made at the point). If it is greater than Query_Limit, the
    strategy `Mode_After_Limit` is used. Otherwise the original database
    (`original_leancop_with_first_advice`) is used. This strategy provides even
    finer language for limiting the number of external queries to the most impor-
    tant branchings.

Learning and Other Options. The basic learning in MaLARea is used to
associate conjecture symbols with premises used in the conjecture's proof.[9] This
learning mode corresponds well to the `original_leancop_with_first_advice`
strategy above, and various metastrategies re-using it. For learning clause selection on branches we can further use another information supplied by the
prover: successful clause choices done for particular paths in the proof. If the
`MACHINE_LEARNING_OF_SUBTREES` option is set, the prover generates for each
proved subtree a list of symbols present on the current path (input features for
learning), together with the successfully used clause (output feature for learning). However, the notion of "success" is relative: a success in a subtree does
not imply a success in the whole proof. That is why we only collect this information from successful proofs, after re-running them just with the necessary
clauses. This should avoid learning from any "pseudo successes". The information extracted from subtrees also contains the cost (again in terms of inference
numbers) of finishing the subtree. We do not use this information yet in learning,
however we plan to use learning on this data for gradually overcoming the most
costly bad clause choices. This could be used to attack hard unsolved problems,
by interleaving the learning to avoid such traps with re-newed proof attempts.

    The original options *cut, scut, comp(L), reo(N), conj* work (after possible re-
implementation) also in the modified leanCoP, i.e., it still makes sense to pass
them to the clausal prover. Options *def, nodef* however have to be fixed during
the clausification stage, and cannot be changed later.

5.2   The General Advisor and the External System

The general advisor is a simple layer of functions written in Perl providing communication with leanCoP via a TCP socket, and talking to SNoW either via a
TCP socket or via a UNIX FIFO (named pipe). The advisor takes queries in the
forms of symbol lists from the prover, and translates the symbols into the numeric
representation used by SNoW, feeding it to SNoW afterward and translating the
SNoW output (again a series of numbers) back into the clause names. The ordered list of clause names is then handed over to leanCoP. The advisor starts by
loading the symbol and clause tables produced by the clausification phase. The
library obviously also implements management of the training examples produced by the proof runs, it manages the prover runs and the external system's

---

[9] In machine learning terminology, the conjecture symbols are the input features, and
   the premises are the output features (targets).

training and querying. In addition to that, the advisor also implements a simple fast cache of queries (just a Perl hash) which considerably speeds up the external advice on previously seen queries. While the SNoW system averages to about five answered queries per second, the advisor cache can answer more than one thousand queries per second, which makes it comparable to the lean-CoP inference speed. Thus a sufficiently big pre-computed cache (typically from many problems) speeds up proof attempts relying on external advice considerably. The cache size for the experiments described below – which issued ca hundred thousand queries to SNoW in total – is about 500MB, which is quite manageable.

As already mentioned SNoW is used as the external learning/advice system, to which the prover talks via the advisor. The biggest concern is its raw speed in the advice mode. The overall SNoW CPU time used for about 120 thousand queries is seven hours. Future work could include experiments with using several SNoW instances using just a limited number of targets relevant for each problem, and improvement of SNoW's speed when evaluating a large number of targets.

6 Evaluation

6.1 Dataset

The evaluation is done on the MPTP Challenge[10] data (specifically on its harder – Chainy – division), and does not use the CASC LTB[11] data. This (together with our machine learning systems not competing in recent CASCs) has recently raised questions. The explanation follows.

The MPTP Challenge is a benchmark specifically created to allow comparison of learning and non-learning ATP approaches. While still reasonably small for experiments, it seems to provide sufficient amount of data for testing the data-driven approaches to ATP. Although the MPTP Challenge design (by the first author) was borrowed by the first CASC LTB in 2008, the main motivation, i.e., providing suitable benchmark for both learning and non-learning ATP methods, has been practically abandoned by CASC LTB in 2009. The number of problems in CASC LTB (and specifically hard problems solvable only by learning) and the learning options have been reduced, and the original "AI" competition mechanism was largely changed back towards the old-style one-problem-at-a-time CASC rules. In short, machine learning makes little sense when done only on a few examples, which is what CASC LTB currently allows. To help to remedy this, in addition to the MPTP Challenge, several mathematical large-theory benchmarks have been recently defined in [17] and used for ATP evaluation in real mathematical setting.

6.2 Results in Proof Shortening

The first test conducted is evaluation of the learning's ability to guide the search for proofs in problems that were already solved. This is a sanity check telling us

---

[10] http://www.tptp.org/MPTPChallenge/

[11] The CADE ATP System Competition Large Theory Batch division.

Table 1. Comparison of number of inferences for the 73 problems solved by original leanCoP, and by leanCoP using guidance trained on the 73 solutions

problem	orig. inferences	guided inferences	problem	orig. inferences	guided inferences
t69_enumset1	676	177	t12_xboole_1	314	291
t13_finset_1	397	99	t17_xboole_1	263	81
t15_finset_1	16	26	t19_xboole_1	1533	757
l82_funct_1	748	1106	t1_xboole_1	305	225
t35_funct_1	813	148	t26_xboole_1	55723	18209
t70_funct_1	1631	669	t28_xboole_1	320	327
t8_funct_1	388	664	t2_xboole_1	22	16
t7_mcart_1	15863	39	t36_xboole_1	477	113
t10_ordinal1	42729	645	t37_xboole_1	27	63
t12_pre_topc	29	26	t39_xboole_1	12452	68164
t116_relat_1	6751	162	t3_xboole_1	35	78
t117_relat_1	14191	2588	t45_xboole_1	3434	520
t118_relat_1	516	293	t48_xboole_1	108205	3863
t119_relat_1	32721	1431	t60_xboole_1	131	96
t144_relat_1	117908	1577	t63_xboole_1	2733	479
t146_relat_1	33580	1370	t7_xboole_1	211	89
t167_relat_1	156202	1629	t83_xboole_1	1885	326
t20_relat_1	1359	405	t8_xboole_1	4018	2612
t30_relat_1	754	583	t44_yellow_0	1533	989
t56_relat_1	3793	181	t6_yellow_0	3605	138
t60_relat_1	6251	148	l1_zfmisc_1	22281	233
t64_relat_1	43674	1491	l23_zfmisc_1	230	126
t88_relat_1	10285	1749	l25_zfmisc_1	4495	799
t90_relat_1	27169	875	l28_zfmisc_1	59233	6095
t99_relat_1	478	124	l50_zfmisc_1	3182	200
t16_relset_1	1931	130	t106_zfmisc_1	92	131
l3_subset_1	12295	5052	t10_zfmisc_1	2055	2115
t50_subset_1	46702	2071	t119_zfmisc_1	16954	199
t54_subset_1	1064	217	t1_zfmisc_1	13471	843
l1_wellord1	29925	4580	t37_zfmisc_1	46	63
l29_wellord1	1059	180	t39_zfmisc_1	45	116
t20_wellord1	60844	1821	t46_zfmisc_1	17	26
t32_wellord1	35573	3607	t65_zfmisc_1	23503	1966
t7_wellord2	107	63	t6_zfmisc_1	1650	112
t3_xboole_0	696	609	t8_zfmisc_1	71884	1321
t4_xboole_0	47	150	t92_zfmisc_1	19	26
l32_xboole_1	19088	589			
Averages:	15678	2042	Avrg. ratio:	19.80	

how much is the overall architecture working as expected. We want to know if it provides the right advice on the problems that it has already seen and been trained on.

The evaluation is done as follows. The original leanCoP (the `original_leancop` strategy, see 5.1) is run with 20s timelimit on the 252 large problems from the MPTP Challenge, solving 73 of them. The guidance system is then trained on the 73 proofs, together with 630 path/clause choices corresponding to the proofs,[12] 703

---

[12] See the option `MACHINE_LEARNING_OF_SUBTREES` described in 5.1.

training examples in total. Then we try to solve the 73 problems again, this time using the trained guidance in the `limited_smart_with_first_advice`(4) mode (see above for detailed description). Again, 20s timelimit (excluding the guidance) is used, and all 73 problems are solved with the guidance. For comparison of the proof search we use the number of extension steps done by leanCoP. This seems to be a suitable metric which abstracts from the communication overhead and the overhead for running the guidance system(s). The following Table 1 shows the results of this comparison. The guidance helps in this case to shorten the proof search on average by a factor of 20, and in some cases (t167_relat_1) by nearly a factor of 100. This seems to be sufficiently convincing as a sanity check for the guidance architecture. Several other strategies were evaluated in this mode too, however we do not show their results here for lack of space.

6.3 Solving New Problems

The main test of any learning system is its ability to generalize over the provided data, and give good advice for new queries. This is measured by attempting to solve the remaining MPTP Challenge problems by using the guidance system trained on the 73 problems solved by original leanCoP. We do not (yet) iterate the learning as in MaLARea, and just evaluate the performance and behavior of the overall architecture with various settings using the initially trained guidance.

As mentioned above, some settings now require a lot of CPU time from the trained advisor, so we only evaluate seven interesting advanced strategies that make the experiments feasible in a couple of hours. The seven strategies (numbered as follows) solve all together 15 problems unsolved in the first run (each

Table 2. Comparison of number of inferences for the 15 problems solved all together by the seven strategies (empty entries were not solved within the time limit)

problem	1	2	3	4	5	6	7
t26_finset_1						4033	
t72_funct_1	1310						
t143_relat_1		28458	59302				61660
t166_relat_1		17586			4067	5263	
t65_relat_1					79756	36217	
t43_subset_1		82610					
t16_wellord1					37148		
t18_wellord1			3517	2689			2524
t33_xboole_1	3659	16456				16902	17925
t40_xboole_1		16488			15702		28404
t30_yellow_0	24277						
l2_zfmisc_1							85086
l3_zfmisc_1							79786
l4_zfmisc_1		17074			9584	14299	30273
t9_zfmisc_1			80684				77532

again uses the 20s timelimit, excluding the guidance time). The comparison of
the successes and inference numbers are shown in Table 2.

1. leancop_ala_malarea
2. limited_smart_with_first_advice(3)
3. scalable_with_first_advice(40,limited_smart_and_complete_with_first_
   advice(3))
4. scalable_with_first_advice(3,20,original_leancop)
5. limited_smart_with_first_advice(4)
6. scalable_with_first_advice(3,20,limited_smart_with_first_advice(5))
7. limited_smart_and_complete_with_first_advice(3)

7   Discussion, Future Work

A number of future directions are already discussed above. The slow external advice is currently a clear bottleneck, necessitating further tuning of strategies that
can use the advice only in critical places. Combination of complete and incomplete strategies is an interesting topic for research, and when looking at Table 2,
there does not seem to be any clear choice. Learning has been so far done only
on symbols extracted from the clauses, while in MaLARea the term structure
and (counter) models are used too. This is probably a straightforward addition,
which will however again raise the number of features used by SNoW, possibly
making SNoW even slower. We have so far not run the full inductive/deductive
loop as in MaLARea, which will be enriched by the training data extracted from
successful subtrees. An interesting addition is also gradual learning of important
choices from unsuccessful proof attempts, which could lead to quite intelligently
behaving proving systems. Another option is learning of sequences of clauses
that lead to success for particular classes of inputs. Such sequences are sufficient
for defining algorithms in Prolog, and if it is possible to detect terminating behavior, they could be called decision procedures. A nice feature of such futuristic
scenarios is that the input classes together with the algorithms defined for them
could be tested for theoremhood, just by adding them as new conjectures to the
whole large theory we work in. Such data-driven methods might produce a large
number of heuristics that are easier to acquire automatically on a large number
of problems than both the existing manual research in finding of suitable simplification orderings for small domains, and research in manual crafting of decision
procedures for particular classes of problems and adding them to ATPs.

A probably much simpler (but less "AI") way how to add decision procedures
in our setting is just by querying external computer algebra systems and other
solvers for the literals on the current path. As mentioned above, the tableau
setting seems to be quite suitable for such extensions, and probably more suitable
than the resolution setting. Quite surprisingly, it seems that this is the first time
a tableau system is being linked to external advice mechanisms.

References

1. Armando, A., Baumgartner, P., Dowek, G. (eds.): IJCAR 2008. LNCS (LNAI), vol. 5195. Springer, Heidelberg (2008)
2. Carlson, A., Cumby, C., Rosen, J., Roth, D.: SNoW User's Guide. Technical Report UIUC-DCS-R-99-210, University of Illinois at Urbana-Champaign (1999)
3. Denzinger, J., Fuchs, M., Goller, C., Schulz, S.: Learning from Previous Proof Experience. Technical Report AR99-4, Institut für Informatik, Technische Universität München (1999)
4. Hoder, K., Voronkov, A.: Sine qua non for large theory reasoning. In: CADE 11 (2011) (To appear)
5. Meng, J., Paulson, L.C.: Translating higher-order clauses to first-order clauses. J. Autom. Reasoning 40(1), 35–60 (2008)
6. Otten, J., Bibel, W.: leanCoP: Lean Connection-Based Theorem Proving. Journal of Symbolic Computation 36(1-2), 139–161 (2003)
7. Otten, J.: leanCoP 2.0 and ileanCoP 1.2: High performance lean theorem proving in classical and intuitionistic logic (system descriptions). In: Armando, A., et al. (eds.) [1], pp. 283–291
8. Otten, J.: Restricting backtracking in connection calculi. AI Commun. 23(2-3), 159–182 (2010)
9. Prevosto, V., Waldmann, U.: SPASS+T. In: Sutcliffe, G., Schmidt, R., Schulz, S. (eds.) ESCoR 2006. CEUR, vol. 192, pp. 18–33 (2006)
10. Riazanov, A., Voronkov, A.: The Design and Implementation of Vampire. AI Communications 15(2-3), 91–110 (2002)
11. Schulz, S.: E: A Brainiac Theorem Prover. AI Communications 15(2-3), 111–126 (2002)
12. Shawe-Taylor, J., Cristianini, N.: Kernel Methods for Pattern Analysis. Cambridge University Press, Cambridge (2004)
13. Suda, M., Sutcliffe, G., Wischnewski, P., Lamotte-Schubert, M., de Melo, G.: External Sources of Axioms in Automated Theorem Proving. In: Mertsching, B., Hund, M., Aziz, Z. (eds.) KI 2009. LNCS, vol. 5803, pp. 281–288. Springer, Heidelberg (2009)
14. Tsivtsivadze, E., Urban, J., Geuvers, H., Heskes, T.: Semantic graph kernels for automated reasoning. In: SDM 2011 (to appear, 2011)
15. Urban, J.: MoMM - fast interreduction and retrieval in large libraries of formalized mathematics. International Journal on Artificial Intelligence Tools 15(1), 109–130 (2006)
16. Urban, J.: MPTP 0.2: Design, implementation, and initial experiments. J. Autom. Reasoning 37(1-2), 21–43 (2006)
17. Urban, J., Hoder, K., Voronkov, A.: Evaluation of automated theorem proving on the Mizar Mathematical Library. In: ICMS, pp. 155–166 (2010)
18. Urban, J., Sutcliffe, G., Pudlák, P., Vyskočil, J.: MaLARea SG1- machine learner for automated reasoning with semantic guidance. In: Armando, et al. (eds.) [1], pp. 441–456

Author Index